THE CHANGING FAMILY
INTERNATIONAL PERSPECTIVES ON
THE FAMILY AND FAMILY LAW

Edited by
JOHN EEKELAAR and THANDABANTU NHLAPO

With an Introduction by
JUSTICE ALBIE SACHS

Hart Publishing
Oxford
UK

Distributed in the United States by
Northwestern University Press
625 Colfax
Evanston
Illinois
60208–4210 USA

Distributed in Australia and New Zealand by
Federation Press Pty Ltd
PO Box 45
Annandale, NSW 2038
Australia

Distributed in Netherlands, Belgium and Luxembourg by
Intersentia, Churchillaan 108
B2900 Schoten
Antwerpen
Belgium

Published by South Africa by
Juta & Co Pty
Mercury Crescent
Hillstar Industrial Township
Wetton 7780
Republic of South Africa

Hart publishing is a specialist legal publisher based in Oxford, England.
To order further copies of this book or to request a list of other publications please write to:

Hart Publishing, 19 Whitehouse Road, Oxford, OX1 4PA
Telephone: +44 (0)1865 434459 Fax: +44 (0)1865 794882
email: hartpub@janep.demon.co.uk

British Library Cataloguing in Publication Data
Data Available

ISBN 1-901362-99-X (paper)

Typeset in 10pt Ehrhardt
by Hope Services (Abingdon) Ltd
Printed in Great Britain on acid-free paper
by Biddles Ltd, Guildford and King's Lynn.

Contents

Introductory Overview: Family Forms and Family Norms

JOHN EEKELAAR and THANDABANTU NHLAPO

The theme of the Ninth World Conference of the International Society of Family Law, held in Durban, South Africa, in July 1997, from which this book was created, was: Changing Family Forms: African Themes and World Issues. In fact, much of the material dwelt on changing family norms, in particular, the changes brought about, or capable of being brought about, by human rights norms found in constitutional documents or international instruments. This immediately raises the question of the relationship between form and norm. At one level, can we say that two families which appear to be structurally similar (each comprising, say, married parents with two children) but where one operates under norms of strict patriarchal legal authority over both wife and children and the other under norms of legal equality between the parents and extensive autonomy rights for the children share the same family form? If we think they do, because they both follow the nuclear structural model, then we would need to say that the married and the unmarried two-parent family have the same form, for they are distinguished only by the legal norms regulating them. This is a perfectly defensible position, and indeed it can be powerfully contended that the form of the family is dictated by the inner structure of its social dynamics rather than by external ideological constructions. On the other hand, the growth of the unmarried two-parent family is commonly given nowadays as an example of the emergence of a new "family form", posing challenges for official versions of what family life should be. We do not therefore think that it is possible to separate form and norm in any simple way, and this will become even clearer as we explore our materials more deeply.

Changes in family form might seem clearer when we consider one-parent families, reconstituted two-parent families and families constituted by artificial reproduction from an external genetic source, in all of which cases a child or children have a genetic parent outside the household. The evidence is clear that these types of families have greatly increased throughout the world over the past quarter century. But once again the extent to which these are significant new forms is related to normative issues. For example, if a parent who was living outside the household in which the child was living were to be treated as non-existent, then the one-parent family would be little different from the "standard" nuclear married model where one parent had died, and stepfamilies and families constituted by artificial reproductive means with external genetic material would be little different from the standard two-parent model. What makes these forms problematic as family forms (leaving aside economic issues associated with single parenthood) is the role of the "outside" parent. Is he or she really a member of the family at all? Is family membership just a question of blood relationship? Can it be acquired by playing a social role? The answers to these questions must refer to norms: do the individuals involved perceive they have rights and duties towards each other? To what extent are these perceptions reflected in the state's law?

Such issues form the subject matter, either implicitly or explicitly, of many of the contributions to this volume (especially in Parts One and Five). But the inter-action between norm and form arises in another way, suggested by the last sentence of the preceding paragraph. It concerns the relationship between the state's law and social behaviour. If more people are living together unmarried, or if more children have a genetic parent living outside their household, normative questions cannot be avoided. How should the state respond? Should it attempt to privilege certain types of behaviour over others? Should the law find ways of satisfying the normative expectations of people, and the needs of children, even if this requires departure from idealised normative models? Innovative judicial responses to unmarried cohabitation, including the "marriage by affidavit" in Kenya, have shown the inventiveness of legal officers on this issue throughout the world. But a much greater challenge has been posed by same-sex unions. Toleration of homosexual activity is now more widespread (but hardly universal), but movement beyond toleration to recognition and even approval has led to confrontation with deep-seated institutional ideologies about the nature of marriage and familial obligations. These issues, and the potential effect of the new set of norms deriving from human rights law (in particular, the explicit reference to sexual orientation as an unacceptable basis for discrimination in the South African Constitution) are also explored (especially in Parts Two, Three and Four). However, many chapters also testify to similar conflicts between deeply embedded patriarchal ideologies and "humanitarian" or "egalitarian" norms.

These relationships between form and norm, between social behaviour (which carries with it its own normative grammar) and institutional norm-systems constitute a recurring motif in the material in this book. But there is a further subtext to this relationship which is not perhaps best captured by the phrase: Changing Family Forms (though it is related to it). This is the extent to which there is, or should be, increasing recognition within nation states of a variety of traditional family forms. Here the emphasis is not so much on changes in familial behaviour but on the behaviour of dominant social groups, including, for these purposes, the international community. Of course some countries have always accepted the existence of a variety of personal laws, and even the colonial experience usually allowed for the co-existence of different family law systems. But it did so in a variety of ways (minimally in South Africa) and through institutions which were either ignorant of local customs or which accepted partial accounts of them. The post-colonial experience has generated a retrieval of these traditions, but with this have come problems of identification of the true character of the traditions and their compatibility with imported human rights norms. The problems are those generally associated with legal pluralism or multi-culturalism, and these receive special attention in Part Three.

In his account of the debates leading to the finalisation of the clauses relating to the family in the Polish Constitution of 1994, Kurczewski refers to a view which was put forward of the family as a natural form antecedent to the state, to which the state should be subservient. The opposing view sees the family as cast in the image of the state, or, at least, of the dominant social group in a political order, and under the control of the law to do the state's bidding. There is no lack of evidence of changing political ideologies being translated into family law. Russia and Japan, described in Part One, are particularly striking examples, but the phenomenon is pervasive. The state (to a large degree) sets the norms which control family life and which, as we have observed above, can also be said to determine the forms which are treated as being familial. But it would surely be wrong to conclude that families are nothing other than constructs of state norms. After all, the persistence of traditional family forms despite non-recognition, or skewed recognition, by colonial authorities testifies to the gulf that can exist between familial behaviour and state law. There is much evidence in this volume of disjunctures between "recognised" customary law and customary law as practised. This does not mean that form and norm are separate; rather that in some situations there can exist a set of norms governing family behaviour which are independent from, or only tenuously connected with, state norms. States can either ignore these social norms, or foster them by incorporating them into state law. Another tactic could be that the state deliberately refrains from regulation in the expectation that family members honour these social norms. As western welfare states contract, this policy is becoming increasingly evident. This might be described as the state indirectly achieving its policies through reliance on family networks. It shows that there is some evidence for the view of the family as having a "life" independent of the state, with the capacity, through its own norm-system, of defining its own parameters. After all, if a group of people treat each other as if they are "family" (that is, as if they owe one another special responsibilities merely by reason of their relationships) then that may be all that is needed for a definition of family relationships.

But the extent to which the state should recognise, or even protect, such relationships can be highly contestable. Relationships of these kinds can be a deep expression of the cultural inheritance of a particular group. Cultures clash with other cultures, and undergo their own internal tensions. Africa, and South Africa in particular, has experienced these events as deeply as anywhere, perhaps more so. It is for this reason that the project of the South African constitution to contain and resolve these clashes and tensions within the framework of law is of such significance. Thus a number of chapters deal with specific features of that constitution, sometimes comparing it with other constitutional traditions (for example, the United States), and the volume concludes with an account of an approach currently being suggested for South Africa which attempts to achieve those objectives. It is an approach which will be enriched by the international experiences revealed throughout this volume, but which, in turn, has potential to have influence upon the global community.

The ferment into which late twentieth-century family law has been thrown by the striking socio-economic changes since the end of the second world war, aggravated by the political consequences of de-colonisation and, more immediately, the retreat of communism and the growing dominance of human rights norms, is vividly revealed in these contributions. South Africa has perhaps become symbolic of these processes and it is fitting that the South African experience should provide the backdrop against which discussion of these worldwide issues is here presented.

Introduction

JUSTICE ALBIE SACHS

I am going to begin at the beginning. And in the beginning was Lucy. Everybody reading this—if the scientists are right—is descended from Lucy; who was not the first person on earth, but our common ancestor. All the others, her sisters and brothers did not leave descendants that created the human population. And I mention this because Lucy was an African. She lived, as Miriam Makeba would have said, in a native village not far from Johannesburg.[1] And I am saying this because in a few years time they might discover that in fact we are all descended from somebody who lived in Alaska or Tasmania, and while the going is good, we claim her. The one great progenitor of humanity whose seed is found in the genes of us all was an African. And as far as family law is concerned, we in South Africa have it all. We have every kind of family: extended families, nuclear families, one-parent families, same-sex families, and in relation to each one of these there are controversy, difficulty and cases coming before the courts or due to come before the courts. This is the result of ancient history and recent history. I am not proposing to go through the few hundred thousand years ever since Lucy, but one can say that family law in South Africa or the problems of family law are the product of the way our subcontinent was peopled, the way we were colonised, the way the colonists were subsequently colonised, the way we were separated and the way we came together again. Our families are suffused with history, as family law is suffused with history, culture, belief and personality. For researchers it's a paradise, for judges a purgatory.

In October 1996 the Constitutional Court of South Africa declared the Constitution of South Africa to be unconstitutional. That is another first that we claim and the context was the two-phase process of constitution making, in terms of which the original negotiators acknowledged that a final constitution could only be made by a democratic assembly but insisted that that assembly function within the framework not only of certain procedures with a two-thirds majority but also of certain principles agreed to in advance.

This was a confidence-building guarantee that majority rule in constitution making would not mean eliminating the interests and concerns of all the disparate communities in South Africa. Principle number 2 said—and I am paraphrasing roughly—that the final text of the Constitution had to enshrine and protect all

---

[1] There is some dispute whether the eldest known human was Lucy from further north, or Ms Ples from near Johannesburg. Present wisdom, however, is that we are all descended from ancient Africans.

fundamental rights universally recognised. One of the complaints about the final text was that there was no express recognition of a right to establish a family and to live a family life. We as a Court were confronted with a problem: was this a violation of principle 2? By not containing an express statement in constitutional language in the Bill of Rights to the effect that everybody has the right to marry freely the person of his/her choice, and to found a family, did the constitution makers fail to meet the requirements of principle 2? We struck down the constitutional text on a number of grounds, including failure properly to entrench the Bill of Rights. Yet we did not hold that the failure to include an express clause in the Constitution protecting the right to found a family or to enjoy family life, was a failure to enshrine universally accepted fundamental rights and freedoms. Basically our reasons were as follows: we accepted that a number of international instruments existed which made it very clear that the right to live in a family context was coupled with freedom of choice in establishing a family, and that these principles were universally accepted. But were they universally accepted as the kinds of rights that needed to be constitutionalised? Copyright is universally accepted but very few constitutions contain an intellectual property clause as such: there are some that do. Laws in relation to contract, delict, tort are universally accepted; commercial law is universally accepted; but they are not constitutionalised. We did a study of constitutions throughout the world and came up with interesting results. Many constitutions contain clauses expressly defending the family and a right to create a family, and there are enormous variations within that, but many constitutions do not. Germany has a clause, Austria does not; Pakistan has, India does not; China has, Taiwan and Singapore do not. There is no automatic correspondence even with national origin or history. It is an option that constitution makers have. And the reason we felt that so many countries do not constitutionalise the family and family law is that the very nature of the family, particularly in multicultural and multifaith societies, is so diverse that it is best to leave the fundamental rights and liberties in relation to family life to the basic principles of freedom, security and choice. Then, through legislation, the development of precedent in the courts, social custom and practice, the different forms of family life will manifest themselves and be appropriately protected.

The minute you constitutionalise the family, the courts are obliged to establish a prototype of what is meant by the family, and families take on such diverse forms in South Africa that this could impose a straitjacket on future development. At the same time the freedom to choose your partner is clearly defended in the Bill of Rights. The essential content of living in a family would be protected under the many clauses of privacy, dignity, and liberty that are enshrined in our constitution. There are other indirect supports, such as strong principles relating to the rights of children. And then there is a special format permitting (not requiring but permitting, depending on choice, legislative choice, community choice), different systems of personal law. So thus far, there is no vacuum or non-existence of the importance of the family, but neither is it prescribed in constitutional terms; what is universally accepted is that countries can put in express provisions relating to family law or they need not do so, and we took a middle road, that is, indirect protection of the families without prescribing any particular format.

How are we going to approach what inevitably is a tension between firm, express principles of equality which run right through our constitution from the preamble to the end, and the diversity of our country; the multiplicity of faiths, belief systems, modes of constituting and dissolving families? How are going to reconcile the two? I am going to step back from that problem, as it would be inappropriate for me as somebody who might be professionally involved in future, to lay down any principles in advance. I hide behind the fact that as a judge I am becoming accustomed to saying that I have to hear argument first before I pronounce on any difficult subject. But I am going to suggest a number of tensions which can be resolved in one of two ways and all of which have a, shall we say, contextual surrounding, environmental influence on this central issue. What is going to matter is acknowledging the tension and how to deal with it rather than suppressing it.

The first relates to the question of universality and particularism. Our country is in the process of formally adhering to a large number of international instruments which project themselves as being universal and many deal directly with the question of the family and family law. And yet we are a country of enormous diversity. Is it possible to reconcile the two? Does one have to make a choice between universal principles on the one hand, and local, historical, cultural, philosophical, personality-based particularities on the other? Or does one dissolve the universal and opt for a multiplicity of particular systems, all rooted in history, culture and tradition? Well, I do not think that we are faced with an either/or choice. I would resolve or approach the resolution of this tension (and there is a tension, it's a real tension), with the following two thoughts in mind.

First, we have to distinguish between globalisation and universalism. Globalisation presupposes that you have an idea or technique or thing, a means that starts in one part of the globe and then spreads to encompass the whole of the globe. It does not change its character; it simply spreads itself to envelope everybody and everything. That is globalisation. Universalism is just the opposite . Universalism starts everywhere where people are, with their practices and their ways, and finds that wherever people are, however they live, however they associate, there are certain commonalities, shared experiences and similar ways of seeing and doing things. Then you distil from the variety of human experience these commonalities, and they are universal. It is a complete opposite of globalisation. I would not say there is no interaction between the two, but the essential underlying concept is the opposite. And so if we envisage the process of deriving certain fundamental principles of family law and family life which might be enshrined in international instruments, which become points of reference for constitutional courts and other courts throughout the world, it is not because we are saying we want to prove we are civilised, that we can match up to the best thinking in this part of the globe or that part of the globe or this county or that country. We are saying, based on our own experiences, on our own suffering, disruption, idealism, hope and coming together in South Africa, that we feel that there are certain things we all have in common that form the foundation of our new constitutional order; that provide the lifeblood of the system of values under which we want to live.

I came across this universalism in a rather poignant and sad sense working, and doing research on family law, in Mozambique during the period of exile. I took a plane from Maputo up to Pemba in the North and then a car on a tarred road and then a four-wheel truck deep, deep, deep into the bush to a little village that had no radio, that had as its only contact this four-wheel-drive truck coming once a month, or once every two months. We discovered that the family law problems of people living in that small village were exactly the same as problems you would get in Cape Town or in London—of persons living together who were destroying each other; they just cannot get on as society expects them to, and there is a certain inertia, trapped, but they are just not making it any more. What is the court going to do about it, what is going to happen to the children, what is going to happen to the house? And the house might have been a reed hut but it was the home, it was the place where the people lived. There was a public sentiment about who associates with whom, what you are in the community depended very much on whom you were living with. I could not help thinking afterwards when Charles and Diana had their highly publicised misfortunes, they were no different from the misfortunes of a family struggling in Capo Delgado in northern Mozambique. I coined the sad phrase: the universality of matrimonial misery.

There are these commonalities, positive ones, hopeful ones, idealistic ones, negative ones, sad ones, but always coping. That is what the law is doing, the law is coping; it is not creating, it is coping with, handling, creating frameworks for, minimising the loss and damage of interpersonal relationships. All may be affected in different ways by different cultures, expressed in different languages, different procedural forms but in essence I would say it is the same processes that are involved. So we distinguish between globalisation and universalism in the way that I have just mentioned.

Secondly, the value of pluralism is a universally accepted value in itself. Diversity, the right to choose how to associate with others, the right to conscience, belief, preference, taste, lifestyle; these are universally accepted as values. So there is a commonality in the acceptance of pluralism and if we can allow that pluralism then to seep into our concepts of the universal, the tension remains but it is not inherently antagonistic or conflictual.

That brings me to my second dilemma, the tension between uniformity and pluralism, which is central to our preoccupations in South Africa. We have fought and fought and fought for the right to be citizens of one country, just to be South Africans, to have an undifferentiated legal personality, just to be human beings with dignity; and not to be Europeans or Non-Europeans or Bantu or Whites or

Zulus or whatever, just to be human beings. We needed a common platform of citizenship, of uniformity, of equality in that sense, non-discrimination, non-differentiation. But we have also fought for the right to be different, to express ourselves in different ways, to speak different languages, to organise our family lives in different ways. In the past, difference was imposed. The whole Bantustan Apartheid policy was based upon the state telling people how to live, where to live, how to be educated, whom to associate with. It was an imposed difference.

The way one reconciles the two to my mind is to say that the right to be the same (a uniform platform of rights) is the foundation, not the enemy, of the right to be different. If difference is related to inequality then difference becomes an instrument of domination and subordination and marginalisation and exclusion. But if difference is simply difference, on the basis of a common platform of equality, then they are not antagonistic, they are not enemies. So my right to vote, my right to participate in political life, my right to be a litigant, my right to enter into contracts, my right to be educated, my right to receive medical treatment, my right to housing, these things do not depend upon who my ancestors were, what my language is or my gender. I am a citizen, I am a South African and I have these rights. But my use of language, my lifestyle, my preferences, whom I want to marry; these are rights to be different, and these are things that are constitutionally protected. Until very recently in terms of the marriage law, the Christian marriage was the prototype marriage. When people mention the Hyde case, those in the Anglo-Saxon jurisprudential tradition will know what I am speaking about. One person, one woman for life became the point of reference for judging the validity of any marriage. This was not the right to be different. In fact it was on this very issue that M. K. Ghandi led one of the first passive resistance campaigns in South Africa. Thousands of men and women of Indian origin, Muslim and Hindu, broke the law deliberately, were caught and jailed because they insisted that their marriages should be treated on an equal basis with Christian marriages. Wives were not concubines, and children were not illegitimate; they were simply living in terms of a different religious, cultural framework that the law ought to recognise. It is quite clear that that kind of discrimination is completely incompatible with our new constitutional order. But there are many ways in which difference can be accommodated and one is not forced into a situation where you have either a totally dualistic or pluralistic legal system with completely different court structures and principles and values for people married in different ways, or else a completely uniform system. The art of the game is to find all the in-between possibilities, the reconciliation and balances that acknowledge the tensions.

One way of reconciling the huge cultural differences is to say that people can organise their affairs according to their religious principles, according to their belief systems in their own way. Catholics can marry in the church where the sacrament is binding on them in terms of the religious law, but as far as the state is concerned they are not bound by the religious law. The problem in South Africa is that the equivalent of Catholic marriages, Muslim marriages and Hindu marriages had no recognition at all. They had no validity, they were outside the pale. Now they must come into the pale but what will the implications be? To what extent will the Sharia apply as far as the state courts are concerned? That's something we leave open at the moment. The fact is that as far as the essential dignity and equal respect for the institutions of Islam are concerned, there has to be full equality with other religions. As far as the detailed application of the rules is concerned, there is a great variety of possibilities, but each country has to find the right kind of a way. Even in a country as unified as the United Kingdom— I think it is separating out a little bit these days—there is some tolerance, some recognition of what are called minority religions and their law. It is not very much but there is something: it is not completely excluded.

Another major dilemma is the tension between abstracting legal issues and concretising or contextualising them. I might say as a judge I find this possibly my greatest difficulty. To deal with a legal problem and to find an answer you have to isolate it, reduce the number of variables, to pose a problematic in a conceptual form. But the reality of life, particularly of family life, is ongoing, it is dynamic and it is not very susceptible to that abstraction. The advantage of abstraction is predictability. You have rules, you have principles, which you apply to situations as long as they fit more or less, and you end up with predictability. The disadvantage is you get injustice, it is unreal, artificial. Also, you are frequently compelled to establish, when you have competing principles, a hierarchy of principles in a rather formalistic way. Which comes first: personal freedom? property rights? cultural rights? and then you say one trumps the other which trumps the other again, and that too creates enormous problems in cases of conflict. One should be looking at the intensity of the value in relation to the particular circumstance, rather than whether that value trumps another value. Again I would think that the courts are moving more and more in the direction of proportionally balanced relationships rather than choice, with winner taking all.

If you look at the concrete context in which an issue arises, you are looking at the real lives of real people. And when it comes to family law jurisprudence and to equality jurisprudence, and the connections between the two, this concreteness is absolutely vital. A formalistic, technicist approach to equality in relation to family law can in fact perpetuate enormous injustice, whereas a contextualised approach that looks to the dignity and the real lives of the people concerned provides often completely different and much fairer consequences. It poses a heavier burden on the judges because you have to weigh up a whole lot of factors in each case, in each set of circumstances. It also presupposes that over time values and the lives of people change so that the same rule has to be reinterpreted in the light of new developments. It is not something totally new for jurisprudence, but it is something that is perhaps underestimated.

The next tension to which I draw attention is between insiders and outsiders. There are the people who make the law, who determine what the values are and who apply the law, and the people who are the subjects of the law. You have to have specialists, professionals, a certain continuity, a certain coherence and consistency; you have to have that. But at the same there is something almost inherently unfair and unjust in allowing people who are right outside the situations that they are adjudicating upon, whose lifestyles, experiences backgrounds and thoughts are totally abstracted and different from the situations they are dealing with, to be the ones who are determining the fates of those who appear before them. Again, you cannot solve the problem by denying it or by completely democratising the judicial process and leading to a kind of anarchistic spontaneity, because you can get immense injustices when local power takes over and there is no rule of law and no consistency. But I think the answer, especially in the family law context, is to involve people from the community as much as possible and the individuals concerned as much as possible in the resolution of disputes. Instead of lawyerising and professionalising everything in terms of abstract notions of rights, duties, responsibilities, it should be a much more participatory and involving process. Instead of the debate being, do we want a rights-based court system or a welfare-based court system, I think we should have a community-based family court system that is imbued with rights and rights principles. We have great possibilities in this country because that is our tradition, we have a great tradition of popular participation in resolving what are called social disputes and problems. The community gets involved in the old way but we need the new values and the new principles to be the guiding ones.

The public, private tension—public law, private law: in earlier times family law was public law. If you go to Vienna and visit the wonderful art museum of one of the queens of the eighteenth century, you will see beautiful pictures from Spain and the Netherlands, and that is because of the family alliances and the dynasties and the arrangements. Constitutional law was very much family law, and that is why Henry VIII's sex-life became a public issue, not just to sell newspapers but because it affected the future of the country. Certainly in South Africa until fairly recently, and in some parts of the country even now, family law is public law, it has public dimensions and consequences. Yet the processes of industrialisation, of creating a state separate from the dynastic, feudal arrangements of the past, the concept of one-person one-vote, personal autonomy, production outside the home or the field, have separated family law from public law. The family homestead ceases to be the centre of production, the family as such ceases to be the centre of one's rights and duties. For a long time the head of the family, the male patriarch, represented the family in public life in relation to other families and that was really what public life was all about. That patriarchy continued even into the era of democracy, but we are moving away from that now. Yet the argument in favour of a private domain so that the rigid rules of the old society do not apply automatically (so that there is freedom of choice, that there is autonomy) suddenly becomes a trap. The privacy of the home permits gross violations of fundamental rights, impervious in practice and sometimes in law to legal intervention from the state because one is dealing with a domestic situation and not a public situation.

What a dilemma there is here. We know the state used to send its police at night to raid homes looking for passes, looking for liquor, looking for people who were working—not unemployed—who were working illegally without permission. There was no respect for privacy, for domesticity, for an inviolable place where people could go and rest and dream and make love and read and act out the interior fantasy life that people need so much for themselves. That did not exist. So we cannot attack privacy as being a negative notion in itself. We acknowledge the two sides of privacy. If the state tortures it is regarded as one of the most gross, and it is one of the most gross, violations of fundamental human rights. But if the same actions take place systematically representing domination and subordination to terrorise people in the confines of the home it is not seen as torture, it is seen simply as a violation of the ordinary criminal law. International standards do not apply and again the public-private separation just does not meet the reality of people's lives.

Finally, in terms of these dilemmas, the tension between rights and relationships. Rights are seen as defensible areas against state intrusion, spheres of autonomy that can be invoked in a tribunal, in a court. I find increasingly the concept of rights in relation to family law incongruous. If rights are understood as that little bit of space and it is my space, whether in relation to property or in relation to a person, they just do not correspond to and describe what is going on. We are dealing with relationships. It is not "keep off the rest of the world, it's my relationship with my spouse, my parent, my child" that is involved. And these relationships are constantly in flux in a way that rights based on a property concept or defensible space just are not. They have their own internal dynamic and momentum. They involve interdependence; they have no meaning outside of other persons. So what the court is concerned with is not so much defending a right as protecting a relationship and managing it and mediating it and dealing with all the different parties to that relationship. And I would suspect that that has great implications for the future conceptualising and application of family law. What worries me about the rights concept is that family law is reduced very much to questions of property; where rights concepts fit in easily I say to myself: what profiteth a woman that she gains half or three-quarters of her husband's estate, and she loses her own soul? We globalise, commercialise, marketise relationships because they correspond to questions of rights, we put a money value on rights, and I think that often undermines rather than supports the rights. I am not saying this to weaken the importance for dignity of having a home and income. But the starting off point should be the dignity, the involvement, the rights of the person in the fullest global sense, the right to happiness and self-fullfilment and not just the right to get ahead or the right to survive.

I think in South Africa we have great opportunities and great dangers. I do not know myself how this mix is going to work out. In colonial and apartheid times there was an awful, unholy alliance between the patriarchs of colonial society and the patriarchs of traditional society who got together and formalised the law which rigidly placed the man as the head of household. Despite all the changes in African family life, despite the fact that millions of African women were heading households, were leading independent careers, were getting their own property, they were treated as minors. That was a solidified and perverted representation of traditional African law. We might have something similar happening in future, with a new opportunistic, bureaucratic élite manipulating the legal system in order to entrench advantage for themselves, and that might be the worst of both the old and the new. Or we might have the best of both, we might have the dynamism, the capacity for development that is so powerful in African society as we see in our country, the capacity to overcome enormous problems and difficulties. We might achieve the triumph of the values, as we put it, of Ubuntu, of respect for everybody else, of great sensitivity to the fact that we live in a community. I am a person because I acknowledge that you are a person.

The values of process, of hearing everybody, of dialogue, of involving everybody are deeply rooted in African cultural tradition. Our court logo in the Constitutional Court is a tree with people underneath, taken from the site of traditional African dispute resolution. What could be more open than that? Under a tree everybody walking past could join in. If these traditions are brought together with the best traditions of the common law and legislation and all the international inputs in our law under the overall umbrella of the Constitution then we might have a rich, vigorous, fair, just family law that really serves as a model for other countries, and not only in Africa.

Much depends on dialogue, and that there is a close relation between dialogue and dignity. You cannot prescribe the answers, you cannot say in a textbook way that this problem has to be solved in the following manner. You pose the dilemmas, you bring everybody together, you try out different things, you see how they work and you listen. The most important aspect of dignity is to respect the voices of everybody who might be affected by a particular law or principle or program. And so with dialogue and dignity, dignity and dialogue, I think we can make remarkable progress in this country, continuing the progress that we have already made.

PART ONE

The Changing Face of Family Law in the Context of Social and Ideological Change

This Part examines the way the content of family law has, to varying degrees and in different countries, mirrored changes that have occurred in the political and social structures of those countries and in their political ideologies. Rothenbacher (Chapter 1) gives details of changes in the structures of western European families. Ipaye (Chapter 2) illustrates the social context of similar changes in Nigeria, pointing out in particular the way in which changing economic conditions in a colonial and post-colonial setting have affected family life. She emphasises that discriminatory family and inheritance laws have persisted, depriving women of the opportunity to acquire a sound economic base. Willekens, Khazova, Matsushima, Cho and O'Halloran (Chapters 3, 4, 5, 6 and 7) provide accounts of how substantive family law has altered over time in western Europe, Japan, Korea and the island of Ireland in the context of socio-political developments in those regions. Agell and Hinz (Chapters 8 and 9) provide an opportunity to compare the relationship between legal reform and social acceptance in Sweden and Namibia respectively, each case raising the issue of how far it is possible or desirable for legal norms to attempt to guide social behaviour. Finally, Bainham (Chapter 10) concludes Part One with an exploration of the relationship between the language of family law and changes in social norms and behaviour.

1

Social Change in Europe and its Impact on Family Structures

FRANZ ROTHENBACHER

The transition of European societies from pre-modern times into modernity, a process that started around 1800 with the different revolutions (political revolution: French and American; industrial revolution (liberal economic principles), institutional revolution (change of juridical and legal framework conditions such as civil rights, principle of equality), has not yet come to an end. This could be the main thesis of this contribution ("unfinished modernity"). This process, which includes several partial processes, is usually labelled modernisation. Why, therefore, do these processes that led to modernity continue? One of the main arguments for ongoing modernisation is the supposition that societies never stand still; instead, they are characterised by permanent dynamics which are set off by innovations and spread by means of diffusion processes. Once a diffusion process is finished, the next one is already in the stage of "birth", growth and spreading. Examples for processes of "unfinished modernity" are the models of long-term social transitions which have characterised the last 200 years: the demographic transition, the epidemiological transition, the shifts in economic sectors, changes in the occupational structure and in the educational sectors. Consequences of these transitions are growth processes, and this is only an alternative way of looking at these transitional processes. Thus, the demographic transition causes population growth, the epidemiological transition leads to a growth in life expectancy, the transition of the economic sectors leads to a growth in the production of goods and of productivity, the transition of the educational sectors leads to a growth in human capital and educational status and therefore, in turn, indirectly to an increase in the production of goods and the application of rational scientific principles. These transitional processes—and these growth processes as well—come to an end once natural boundaries are reached, as for example in the field of mortality reduction or of child mortality, both having—at least up to now—natural barriers. The length of life of human beings is so far *naturally* limited. More and more people attain a high and very high age, but so far there is no evidence that the absolute life span has been prolonged due to medical progress. In the same way, in the extreme case, child mortality can be reduced to nil. Since natural limits exist, growth processes (and growth rates), such as population growth, growth of life expectancy, growth of industrial production after a phase of accelerated growth, will decline again. Not only in the domains of physique, duration of life, number of offspring to be fed, are there natural limits, but also in the fields of satisfaction of human needs. Thus, the law of diminishing returns explains the rapid spreading of a consumption good and the subsequent saturation, followed by a saturation with a benefit that becomes negative. After surpassing a certain optimal limit goods lose their highly valued incentive and become valueless. A new phase of societal development sets in after a new balance has been reached, i.e. once the long-term transition processes have been halted and new processes of change have started. This is for instance the case in Sweden, where, after a long-term decline in birth rates, the birth rate started to rise again. Similar new processes can be detected in their early stages in other fields, too.

The ideal typical processes of societal development into modernity are designed in such a way that they are valid independently of space and time and therefore are, in principle, applicable to all countries of the world. It could therefore be conceivable that all countries at different time points pass through the same stages, as they are postulated by the model. This model, however, is only imaginable in a world where individual countries and whole continents remain without influence from one other. Thus it cannot be assumed that all countries will move through the same stages, just because they are related in one way or another. Communication channels and, as a consequence, diffusion processes are different; there are insuperable barriers for some of them, innovations can be kept secret or be monopolised. Furthermore, there are developmental differences and *path dependencies* (North 1981, 1990), defining the starting level and evolution of similar processes. Thus, it becomes understandable why in Europe industrialisation processes, and therefore also processes of social and political mobilisation, have differed from country to country. It can even be said that a certain group of countries, the Mediterranean countries, skipped the stage of "industrial society" and developed directly from an agrarian society into a service society. It can be assumed that within Europe, and this is even more valid on a global level, there is a "contemporaneity of the non-contemporaneous", not allowing for homogeneity in the short term. Homogeneity of macro-conditions could not be attained through "natural" processes, but only through active political intervention, and mainly through the establishment of institutions.

II LONG-TERM AND SHORT-TERM SOCIAL CHANGES: MODERNISATION,
GROWTH, DIFFERENTIATION, DIFFUSION, SUBSTITUTION

On the macro-level of the society as a whole (or of social change of the society as a whole) there exist important processes with a long-term influence on household and family structures. Households and families have above all been influenced by long-term processes that started in the nineteenth century and have thus shaped the social structures of European societies during the last 150 years. These processes include the demographic and epidemiological transition, the sectorial changes in the economy and changes in the occupational system, the consecutive waves of educational expansion, and the long-term expansion of the welfare state.

Apart from these long-term "big" structural changes there are ongoing processes of minor historical deepness or influence, such as the Second Demographic Transition, the improvement of housing supply, the tertiary education, to mention only a few. These processes are not as all-embracing as the long-term changes, are of shorter duration and involve only segments of the population.

1 First and second demographic transition, epidemiological transition

One of the central long-term processes is the "demographic transition". This model is based on the assumption that a pre-industrial population equilibrium and a post-industrial population balance existed (or exists). The demographic transition starts with the decline of the high pre-industrial mortality rate; fertility, with a time lag, reacts with a decline. Mortality and fertility decline until a new state of balance is reached, with mortality as well as fertility now being on a low level. The result of this process is a strong population growth which reaches its maximum at the new supposed equilibrium level. In principle, this model describes very well the demographic developments until the 1960s. However, against the expectations of this model, a new equilibrium of the population processes on a new low level did not materialise. On the contrary, the reproduction rate of the population fell to a below-replacement level (Commission des Communautés Européennes 1992; Chesnais 1992; Coleman 1996a, 1996b; Marchetti/Meyer/Ausubel 1996). In order to explain this phenomenon, the thesis of a "Second Demographic Transition" was introduced. This hypothesis attempts to explain this second birth decline since about 1965 in all developed countries (van de Kaa 1987; Cliquet 1991, 1993a, 1993b; Höhn 1997; European Commission 1995; Grundy 1996). Several factors are made responsible for this "renewed" birth decline below the level of population replacement. Special importance is assigned to the technical possibilities of fertility control that are in standard use now and require an express positive decision for a child. Other explanatory factors for below-replacement fertility are considered to be the general social changes and their demographic consequences such as the postponement of age of marriage and first birth and, consequently, the compression of the procreative phase of women. This compression of the procreative phase to some few years is not least influenced by the professional orientation of women and the problems of reconciling work and childbirth.

The below-replacement level of the population in association with the *epi-*

demiological transition (Omran 1971, 1983) has two important consequences for the socio-demographic structure of the population: on the one hand, the life expectancy continues to grow not only because infectious diseases have been reduced during the last 100 years, but also because substantial efforts have meanwhile been made regarding the treatment of degenerative diseases and, especially, in the field of accident mortality. If this progress in mortality reduction continues, a further increase of the number of elderly in absolute as well as in relative terms will occur. This will influence the age structure of European populations significantly and affect more or less the whole social structure and social relations. The formal or informal social care systems will be forced to adapt to these changes.

2 Sectorial change of the economy (deagrarisation, industrialisation, tertiarisation), change of the occupational structure, urbanisation

One of the central processes influencing the development of household and family structures is the long-term development of the occupational structure. According to the model of occupational change, the agrarian society with predominantly agricultural employment is succeeded by the industrial society, where industrial employment becomes the main productive activity; in this phase, employment in agriculture is already declining and tertiary employment is rising. The industrial society is succeeded by the service society, where employment in the service sector makes up the largest part of labour. In this phase, the primary sector has already declined and accounts for a very small proportion of the economy; the industrial sector is already in a process of decline, too. According to writers such as Colin Clark, Jean Fourastié and Daniel Bell, the future will belong to the service society, where education and knowledge—that is, human capital—play the most important role. The large service sector is as heterogeneous as the industrial sector was. Public services play an important role due to the expansion of the welfare state. Different new concepts such as "information society", "knowledge society", etc., change this principal distinction only to a very small degree, because they also constitute services.

Parallel to changes in the occupational system, the process of urbanisation occurs, because deagrarisation and industrialisation inevitably entail migration from the country to the towns. An urban society develops, in the sense that the majority of the population lives in densely populated regions. Tertiarisation does not change urban structures significantly, but in regions where the information society is already well-developed, the depopulation of inner city regions can be observed as well as a growing population density in the suburban regions. Megalopolises such as Paris are meanwhile facing a process of deurbanisation which could become stronger due to the new technological possibilities of the information society as, for instance, networking.

The long-term change of the occupational structure exerts a fundamental

influence on changes in household and family structures. For agrarian populations, the extended family was the model and social norm, which, however, could
often not be realised in daily life due to high adult mortality, and therefore low
life expectancy; it thus had the effect that, in reality, nuclear families were and
still are the dominant family type. Furthermore, the family structure varied a
great deal with the social stratum, whereby the formation of extended families
correlated highly with the wealth of the peasant family, while labourers usually
formed nuclear families. The decline of the agrarian population in the aggregate
reduced the proportion of extended families and brought with it the quantitative
dominance of the nuclear family. This is the prototype of the urban family, which
could not become an extended family due to restricted urban living conditions.
The conditions of urban life promote the formation of small nuclear families as
opposed to other family types.

The differences regarding the economic development within Europe may illustrate the relationship between sectorial structure and family structure. A cross-
sectional analysis shows that a strong relationship between the size of the agrarian
sector and the frequency of extended families exists: thus, the extended family is
still relatively common in the Mediterranean countries of Greece, Portugal and
Spain, but also in Ireland, and these countries still have a rather high proportion
of agrarian employment (Rothenbacher 1995a, 1995b).

3 Change in the employment system: reduction in working hours, rise in female employment

In those countries which have moved far along the path towards the service society, changes within the employment system become visible which are associated
with the sectorial change of the economy. The tertiarisation of employment in
the public as well as in the private sector promotes the creation of female workplaces. While in the industrial sector male work dominates and therefore declines
because the whole sector declines, the expansion of the service sector favours
female employment. Thus, the majority of workplaces created in the European
Union since the 1980s are workplaces for women (European Commission 1996a).
Regarding public sector employment, one can even speak of a "feminisation" in
some countries (the Nordic countries), as 50 to 70 per cent of all workplaces are
occupied by women.

Another structural change in the employment system that is associated with
tertiarisation is the increase in part-time jobs, which again nearly completely concerns women. The job growth of the last decade can to a high degree or overwhelmingly be explained with the increase in part-time work. In general, a
flexibilisation of work contracts as well as of arrangements regarding working
hours can be observed. The structuring of the work process allows for a growing separation of work and physical presence.

Of special importance for changes in the employment system is, furthermore, the long-term reduction of working hours, especially lifetime working hours. In addition, the structuring of working hours is changing if one looks at it from a life course perspective. The first entry into an employment contract increasingly occurs later in life, often only at the end of the third life decade; in addition, the retreat from working life often occurs before the legal retirement age has been reached (Véron 1988; Hoem/Hoem 1989; Ausubel/Grübler 1996; European Commission 1996a).

The rising labour market participation of women and especially of mothers has substantial implications for the division of household work. In principle, there is a tendency toward a change in the conception of gender roles. Men as well as women accept paid female employment outside the home; however, concerning the family no principal changes in role definitions have taken place. As before, women are responsible for household tasks, whether they participate in the labour market or not, and men continue to concentrate mainly on instrumental household tasks. Nevertheless, an essential new trend can be observed that started in the 1960s: for women, the hours spent on household tasks have declined, and the participation of men in household tasks has increased (United Kingdom and USA) (Gershuny/Robinson 1988). Although many women only have part-time jobs, the double work load of women is obvious. The greater demand on women in terms of time if they work outside the home as compared to men underlines this fact.[1]

4 Educational expansion: aggregate growth, decline in gender inequality, but persisting socio-economic inequalities

The educational expansion also is a long-term process and is associated with the introduction of legal minimum standards through educational reforms. The nineteenth century already saw the breakthrough of literacy and of compulsory education. Within Europe, especially in Southern Europe (e.g. Portugal), the literacy of women has not been achieved to date. In the more developed countries of Europe, ongoing standard increases and upgrading of educational participation in the educational system can be observed. Thus, educational participation on the primary level has been declining for years in favour of a growing educational participation in the secondary educational sector and especially in the tertiary educational sector. The permanent upgrading of educational aspirations and the requirements of investments in human capital lead to a slow but continuous decline of participation in primary education.

The increase in educational participation and the levelling out of gender differences regarding school attendance in combination with the growing attendance at secondary schools extend the time span individuals spend within the school

---

[1] According to the German time-budget survey of 1990–91 women in paid employment have a higher total work load than women who are housewives or than their employed husbands (Fiebiger 1995).

system. This process is especially significant for young women, whose participation rate in the third educational sector in some European countries is already higher than that of young men. The fact that young women remain for a long time within the educational system and the growing opportunity costs for not being in paid employment are among the central factors leading to a higher age at first marriage and at first birth since the mid-1960s (Hoem 1986; Blossfeld/Huinink 1989; Müller/Haun 1993).

5 Value change: secularisation and decline in familism

One of the central trends embedded in the comprehensive process of modernisation is the process of secularisation. This process mainly includes the societal long-term process of a decline in the importance of religion, a reduction of religiousness and a general change regarding norms, values and attitudes. According to some authors, secularisation includes a rise in individualism as opposed to altruism. For others, an increase in the desire of people for self-fulfilment is the central trend. For Ronald Inglehart (1990) it is the rise of post-materialist as opposed to materialist values. "Postmaterialists are suspicious of technological innovation, criticise production processes that damage the environment and the endless acquisition of luxury goods, and put the emphasis on meaningful personal relationships, spontaneity, and self-reliance" (van de Kaa 1987: 7). The thesis of an increase in post-materialism is supported by the empirical result revealing that from the 1970s onwards the index of postmaterialism has risen from the oldest cohorts to the youngest cohorts. Different attitude and opinion surveys in several countries (as e.g. the Netherlands) show that attitudes towards sexual issues, marriage and living together have generally become more liberal since the 1960s, liberal in the sense of a lower "rigidity" of social norms and a higher permissiveness and tolerance in public attitudes.

It is only the other side of the same coin when Popenoe (1988: 212–14) stresses the decline of familism as a cultural value. Popenoe analyses this trend for Sweden. Familism to him is a trait of a society that places great importance on the family as an institution, and where the family remains one of the central institutions in the social structure. Such a society can be labelled familistic. The central historical trend seen by the author is a decline in familism which in his opinion has progressed most in Sweden. Nevertheless, this trend can principally be observed in all advanced industrialised countries of Europe, although to a varying degree. The Mediterranean countries are still considered to be familistic to the highest degree. Familism and individualism are supposed to co-vary in opposite direction: individualism substitutes familism as a cultural value in advanced societies.

One of the central explanations for this shift within the value system is associated with the idea that an increase in material security due to economic wealth and the extension of the welfare state replace the family as a unit of social security.

This shift in familial functions is accompanied by a change in the value system of the people. The dependency of the individual on the family is reduced in favour of an impersonal and legally guaranteed relationship with the state as the supplier of material and social security. It must be assumed that individualism and the decline of familism will be highest where the state intervenes most and directly into people's lives through public employment, public social benefits, etc.

6 Welfare state expansion and individualisation

The expansion of the welfare state in Europe is one of the central processes of the last 100 years. The development of households and families is in a close and interdependent relationship with this phenomenon. The development of the European welfare states had as its consequence the declining importance of primary social security systems such as households and families: this is the nucleus of the thesis of the loss of the function or the differentiation of the family. The more comprehensive social security systems became, the more they replaced family functions, thus weakening the role of the family as a safety net. Universal social security systems have therefore been essential prerequisites for processes of "individualisation" and of "pluralisation" of private life courses, family forms and household formations. The welfare state has not only made the development of new family forms easier, but has also contributed to the decline and disappearance of traditional family forms. Thus, the introduction of state pension systems was one factor constituting a precondition for the spreading of new family forms where the older generation lives alone in the form of couples and where later on, the widow is on her own forming a one-person household. In a society without pension systems, as still existed around 1850 in Europe, an extended family or a three-generation household—if only for some years—would have been formed regularly, if one disregards the few cases where the old widows would have been cared for by poor relief (public assistance). Pension insurance, together with the enlargement of the health system and the general increase in wealth, has not only increased life expectancy, but also enabled parents—after their children having left the parental home—to enter a new phase of life, without being materially dependent on the children's generation (Popenoe 1988; Alber 1989; Zapf et al. 1987; Gauthier 1996; European Commission 1996b, 1997).

III THE MICROLEVEL OF HOUSEHOLDS AND FAMILIES

In contrast to the macro-social structural changes treated above, this section deals with the micro-level of households and families. Families and households are the smallest social units in a society, if an individualistic approach is rejected. Macro-social changes are conceived as the framework and causal factors for changes in household and family. Here, households and families are rather seen as adaptive social units in contrast to innovative and active ones ("external approach": see Hoffmann-Nowotny 1996; Kaufmann 1995). According to the external approach, impulses for change can come from technological innovations, from a change in the productive system or from changes in the legal system. Several theoretical approaches try to explain family change: (1) economic theories take the primacy of technology and economic rationality for granted. Accordingly, social changes are caused by technological innovations which modify the economic system and, in the end, exert essential influence on the family structure and the legal system. (2) A more sociological tradition of theory emphasises ideological factors of culture or ideas and hypothesises that values and behavioural patterns change and therefore influence changes in the family structure. (3) A third line of theory hypothesises that there are autonomous changes in the legal system leading to social and familial change. The economic approach, however, postulates that the legal system only plays a reactive role. (4) Fourth, the approach of functional differentiation (Durkheim, Parsons, Smelser) postulates that with the differentiation of society in the general process of modernisation a dedifferentiation and, consequently, homogenisation of households occurred. Since institutions in traditional societies were less differentiated, households were subject to a much stronger functional differentiation. The dedifferentiation of the households led to a homogenisation of the household structure. In the 1960s a counter-process, leading to a new pluralisation of household and family structures started, showing new tendencies towards a further dissolution of the family. "Double scissors" (*"doppelte Schere"*, Gerhard Mackenroth) can thus be observed, where the older patterns disappear and new patterns or processes of substitution emerge (Schwarz 1983, 1988; Roussel 1986, 1992; Keilmann 1988; Boh 1989; Council of Europe 1990; Kiernan/Wicks 1990; Kuijsten/Oskamp 1991; Bégeot/Smith/Pearce 1993; Federkeil/Strohmeier 1993; Rothenbacher 1995a, 1996a, 1997a, 1997b; Haskey 1996; Kuijsten 1996; Höpflinger 1997; Commaille/de Singly 1996; INED 1996; Millar/Warman 1996).

1 From the extended to the nuclear family: nuclearisation until the 1960s

Here the question arises what is actually meant by *"traditional family"*. Essential characteristics of this family type are marriage as the starting point of a family, a high valuation and monopoly of marriage and family (e.g. in electoral law), exclusivity of marriage in the sense that not everyone can marry, i.e. there are high celibacy rates; no birth limitation, since high mortality reduces fertility; marriage is principally seen as a lifelong institution, but is not in reality, as the mortality rate is high for both sexes; the impossibility of planning one's life course and life expectancy due to "natural checks" (Thomas Malthus); a low life expectancy, i.e. one or both partners usually dies after her or his sixtieth year of life at the latest; the instability of family relationships due to the high mortality rate, leading to a high remarriage rate and many stepfamilies. Imperfect families come into being, where both natural parents died and the children had no natural but only social and legal parents. The necessity to take both parental roles (*"Rollenergänzungszwang"*, Michael Mitterauer) due to remarriage was very high. The traditional family was thus characterised by a very high level of insecurity through the inability to control environmental influences and social conditions.

The *modern family* as the ideal typical contrast is on the other hand characterised by the fact that its living conditions can be planned to a large extent, by a high degree of social security and of safety regarding physical life-threatening conditions. The general increase in "security" has encouraged notions of being able to plan and to calculate one's life, and even the claim to a certain length of life. The social security especially of women, but also of men, amplified trends towards individualisation (Zapf *et al.* 1987), opened up possibilities for living a solitary life, and destroyed the idea of the indissolubility of marriage. An increase in affluence makes possible the concepts of "enjoyment of life", of "nonrenunciation", which in turn have repercussions on the family.

From large households to small families: decline in household and family size

One of the most obvious processes of change in household and family structures is the development towards the small modern family. The traditional household was a large household and often included household members who did not belong to the family (such as servants, boarders and lodgers) or relatives (lateral relatives or grandparents, i.e. it was an extended household) and, finally, several children. The households and families of today are rather small, because household members who do not belong to the nuclear family have disappeared as a social category; the lateral relatives and the third generation live outside the household. Furthermore, the number of children born to a family has decreased. On an average, households and families have become much smaller. The proportion of small households has grown significantly, whereas the proportion of larger households has declined substantially. A further decline has occurred due to an increase in the number of childless couples, which did not exist to this extent in the past, and as a result of a rise in the number and proportion of lone-parent families, which on average have fewer children than married couples.

The decline in family household size was additionally strongly influenced by the disappearance of the non-family members from the households, such households having been rather numerous in history, for instance in Germany amounting to one quarter of all households in 1910 (in German towns as Frankfurt and Berlin the proportion of households with non-family members was much higher than the national average and exceeded partly 60 per cent). Households with non-family members in the process of modernisation of the last century died out slowly, in Germany already by 1970 becoming nearly non-existent.

The third and most important source of decline in family household size was the long-term reduction in fertility, a process described by the model of the demographic transition.

The decline of the size of households in general due to the disappearance of non-family members and the fertility decline had the effect of convergence of family size according to socio-economic status, at least in Germany. Thus, mean household size of employed household heads declined and converged strongly, the structure remaining stable. Thus the self-employed (peasants) still have larger households than workers (industry) and employees (white-collar). While there was a convergence of household size for employed household heads, the mean household size of heads without profession (pensioners) diverged strongly. This is explained by demographic and socio-economic developments in the segment of the pensioners.

Looking only at averages hides other important developments which have occurred on the household level. The decline in mean household size is largely caused by the decline of bigger households as can be seen for households with five and more persons. While in 1900 the proportion of those households varied from one third to two thirds, in the 1990s the respective proportions have gone down to 5–30 per cent. There is a convergence in the long run but a group of European countries (Ireland, Spain, Portugal, and Eastern European countries like Poland, Romania and Yugoslavia) with a still high share of large households remains.

Households with four persons show a more complicated pattern within Europe. For all countries there was an increase in the proportion of households with four persons until the 1960s and 1970s, but then the developments took different directions and a rather clear cleavage emerged between the group of countries with a strong birth decline and high individualisation (Nordic countries, England and Wales, Switzerland) and the other group of countries (Southern and Eastern Europe). In the former group the proportion declined, while in the latter group it increased. With respect to households with four persons there can be seen within of Europe a growing divergence from the 1960s onwards. This divergent development for 20–30 years has as a consequence a phase displacement of a similar time span because the group of countries lagging behind now also shows stagnating or declining shares of four-person households.

The situation is very similar for households with three persons. For those households, the same developmental pattern of growing divergence and phase displacement can be detected. Thus, households with five and more persons have been declining for a century, while households with three and four members increased first and declined later. Households with one and two members show a constant increase since the last century. The relations between countries are remarkably stable in these processes; only for one-person households are there signs of a divergence.

Therefore, at the level of households we can observe very different processes. We observe first a clear *nuclearisation* of family households in the sense that the nuclear family became the dominant family type through the disappearance of non-family members, the decline of the extended family and the universalisation of marriage. But on the other side of the coin we have the opposite trend of *individualisation* and *pluralisation*. Indicators for these countervailing processes can be seen in the increase in persons living single and of households consisting of only two persons, but also in the decline of the population living in nuclear families. In addition, also at the level of households there can be seen what has been called the *polarisation* of private living arrangements into a family sector and a non-family sector. The non-family sector would be households with one or two members, which are rising, and the family-sector would be represented by households with three and four members, i.e. with one or two children in the family. Families with three and more children in the family—in other words households with five and more persons—are declining so strongly and have such a low incidence in Europe, that they could be labelled a third sector of private living arrangements. Polarisation is most advanced in the Nordic countries and the countries of the continent, while in Southern and Eastern Europe polarisation does not yet exist (see also Gaspard 1985).

Substitution of the extended family

The extended family as the model of the traditional family system, even though it was not dominant in empirical reality due to high mortality and low life expectancy in nineteenth-century Europe, represented a substantial proportion of all families; however, the lack of statistics does not allow for exact figures. The extended family dominated in large regions with an agrarian population, but was not as widespread in the strata of landless labourers. The transition from the agrarian to the industrial and, finally, to the post-industrial society in combination with urbanisation reduced the proportion of extended families to only a few percentage points. A cross-sectional perspective within Europe reveals that the extended family is nowadays most common in those countries where the proportion of the agrarian population is still high, such as Greece, Portugal, Ireland and Spain. It can therefore be assumed that extended families can mainly be found in agricultural households, a thesis that is supported by the finding that in the advanced industrialised countries of central Europe the share of extended families in agriculture is highest. A rather strong bivariate relationship between employment in the agricultural sector and the proportion of extended families can be found (Rothenbacher 1996a). The remaining extended families have, in addition, changed in structure: the extension of the family through lateral relatives such as (unmarried) brothers and sisters of the parental generation has been reduced significantly due to the general decline in births; the importance of the extension through the grandparent generation, on the other hand, has grown in relative terms. The decrease in the number of extended families in Europe (as compared to other world regions, e.g. Japan) has been made possible due to the pension systems and social care services which have reduced old age poverty dramatically and enabled the elderly to live alone.

Dominance of the nuclear family

Long-term changes in Europe and the transition to modernity have made the nuclear family the dominant family form. But this is only a quantitative process of a real increase in importance, because the nuclear family existed in the social reality of the traditional family system, especially in the lower strata. Contrary to that, the hypothesis is put forward that a principal change occurred, namely that the normative and behavioural family model shifted from the "extended family" to the "nuclear family". Today, there is no longer a normative obligation for children to care for their parents, and most children reject such an obligation. The nuclear family as a model with the focus on marriage has established itself slowly during the last 150 years. The model of the nuclear family essentially still exerts its normative power, although this model is often no longer in concordance with reality in view of the large number of childless couples. But childlessness is often unwanted and a side-effect of family planning as the normal behaviour, where the conception of a child becomes a deliberate decision. The opposite was the case in times when family planning did not exist or was very unsystematic. The nuclear family is thus still the dominant family form and reached its peak in the 1960s with the universalisation of marriage and the baby boom in those years. Since that time there have been signs of an erosion of the model of the nuclear family: indicators for this are phenomena such as planned childlessness, unmarried cohabitation and successive monogamy.

2 Towards the post-nuclear family: the spreading of new family forms

In European societies, the formation and increase in importance of new family forms can be observed and is paralleled by the decline or substitution of traditional family forms. By "new" family forms or forms of private living arrangements we mean especially persons living alone, lone parents, and persons cohabiting unmarried. Furthermore, families reconstituted after divorce are also to be subsumed under the heading "new" family types. Strictly speaking, all those family forms are not "new" family types; they already existed in the first half of this century or even earlier in European history. Thus, cohabitation as a form of living together of unmarried adults existed earlier (concubinage), although it was not as common as it is today. The same holds true for lone parents, who were rather frequent in the second half of the nineteenth century due to the high illegitimacy rate. Reconstituted families, too, are not at all a new phenomenon; it is only their major cause—i.e. divorce—that has become increasingly important ever since the middle of the nineteenth century, whereas in the past mortality was the main reason for family disruption and reconstitution.

Even though these new family forms have spread and their social importance has increased, the dominant family type of the nuclear family has undergone major structural changes. The nuclear family continues to be the normative ideal, although in social reality the personal relationship between partners has become more fragile, and a system of "successive monogamy" has come into being in the last decades.

Nuclear families: dynamics of formation and dissolution

Family formation has changed since the 1960s. In the 1990s, the birth of children in the life course of women occurred at a very late stage and the age at first birth has increased since the 1960s. This also applies to the increase in age at first marriage. The postponement of family formation is a result of an increase in educational participation of women and rising opportunity costs for not working, making early family formation directly after school difficult; thus family formation is often postponed until the late twenties or rendered completely impossible (Schwarz 1989). Another phenomenon related to higher educational participation, but also to youth unemployment, is the later age at which adolescents leave the parental home (Hullen 1995; Festy 1994). The period of family formation is increasingly being compressed into a few years in a woman's life; the natural fertility period of women of more than thirty years (15–45) is therefore less and less used for reproduction (Sardon 1986; Munoz-Perez 1986).

Family growth in the proper sense of the word has become a rare phenomenon because, as a rule, only one or two children are born to a family. While still four fifths of all children are born to married couple families in nearly all European countries and about 20 per cent to lone parents, there is within the 'non-family sector' a growing importance of childlessness for women, be it voluntary or involuntary childlessness. The cohorts of women of the 1940s show proportions of childless which vary between 10 and 15 per cent. Until the cohorts of the 1950s the proportion of childless women increased considerably and varies between 15 and 20 per cent of all women (Dorbritz/Schwarz 1996: 240; Höpflinger 1991: 81). The long-term fertility decline also changed "childhood". Children became a scarce "commodity", although in history they had been a "commodity" that was available in abundance. The reduction of the number of children has changed the experience of childhood in such a way that childhood as a group experience has more or less disappeared and that children have often taken a monopoly position in the world of adults. The "peer group" has been reduced significantly, as well as the number of lateral relatives (Munoz-Perez 1987; Craig 1992; Hantrais 1992; Schwarz 1995; Festy 1994).

Family dissolution due to death has become very rare as a result of the long-term process of "epidemiological transition". On the other hand, family dissolution due to divorce and separation has become the most important factor. Data on separation during premarital cohabitation on the European level do not exist, but it can be assumed that premarital cohabitation is very unstable. Divorces— in a long-term perspective—have risen logistically (i.e. started slowly, accelerated, then slowed as they reached their peak), and reached the upper limit in those countries that have the highest divorce rates. Due to different starting conditions and phase-displaced developments in the "divorce explosion" we can find a divergence of divorce intensity in European countries (Haskey 1992; Sardon 1986).

The increase in divorces is associated with the new phenomenon of *family reconstitution* after divorce or separation. While the formation of new non-marital partnerships after separation cannot be described statistically due to a lack of studies, evidence on family reconstitution after divorce is available. Whereas the absolute number of second and third marriages has been increasing in the last decades, the remarriage rate[2] of divorced men and women has tended to decline since World War II. This means that in the 1960s, when divorce rates were low, people normally remarried. By contrast, the most recent pattern shows high divorce rates and low remarriage rates. All this indicates that a behavioural change has taken place as well as a normative change in such a way that after divorce there is either no possibility to remarry or that divorced people enter a cohabiting union without marriage (Höpflinger 1997; Rothenbacher 1996a, 1997b).

Non-standard family forms

Cohabitation without marriage

As Kathleen Kiernan (1993, 1996) has shown, there can be found three groups of countries within Europe: those where unmarried cohabitation is well established, those where it is emerging as a significant form of behaviour and those where it does not exist yet. All in all there is a strong North–South divide in this field. In the Nordic countries cohabitation has become an alternative to marriage; in the continental countries, where marriage has still privileged status in law, cohabitation is mostly pre-marriage and post-divorce cohabitation. In Southern European countries cohabitation probably only exists in some social milieux. In Iceland where the pattern of unmarried cohabitation has reached the highest diffusion even under the Nordic countries, (in 1993) more than 50 per cent of all children are born in consensual unions. Twenty years earlier, in 1973, this proportion was only about 10 per cent. Children born in marital unions have declined from 70 per cent of all in the early 1970s to roughly 40 per cent in 1993. Interestingly, the proportion of children neither born to married nor cohabiting couples decreased from 20 per cent in the early 1970s to about 10 per cent in the 1990s.

One indicator for the institutionalisation of marriage in the sense of privileging marriage as a form of familial living is the number of births out of wedlock. The proportion of non-marital births compared to all births is highest when differences between marriage and cohabitation have been levelled out to a large

---

[2] The remarriage rate of divorced men and women is defined as marriages of divorced men/women to 1,000 divorced men/women.

extent, when there are no disadvantages for the mother or especially for the father if they do not marry (Haskey 1995; Henkens/Meijer/Siegers 1993; Kiernan 1993; Kiernan/Estaugh 1993; Lillard/Brien/Waite 1995; Niemeyer 1994; Prioux 1995; Rothenbacher 1996a; Ditch *et al.* 1996).

In Germany, as in most continental countries of Europe where marriage is still highly privileged as compared to consensual unions, only a few children are born to cohabiting couples although with slightly rising proportions. In general, in the group of countries which is made up of Austria, Germany, the Netherlands and Switzerland, only Austria shows a traditionally high out-of-wedlock birth rate. But in all those countries consensual unions are not legally institutionalised on a level comparable to legal marriage.

In the "Latin" group of countries, made up of Belgium, France, Italy, Spain and Portugal, births out of wedlock are rising only in France and Belgium, but only in France is there some institutionalisation of unmarried cohabitation. In Italy, Spain and Greece there does not exist a pattern of unmarried cohabitation while in Portugal unmarried cohabitation has a long tradition and legal marriage is now preferred.

In the Eastern European countries of Poland, former Czechoslovakia and Hungary unmarried cohabitation and out-of-wedlock births had very different features until 1990. While in Hungary out-of-wedlock births increased again since the 1960s, in Poland and former Czechoslovakia there were no signs of a pattern of unmarried cohabitation until 1990. This result fits very well into the picture of enduring universal marriage, low age at first marriage and high marriage frequency in those countries.

Lone parents

The number of "incomplete families" or, in modern terminology, "lone parents" has steeply increased since the 1960s in all European countries. It is impossible to find one singular main cause for this increase; there are several factors responsible for this growth trend. Divorce is, for instance, an important cause, but not the most important one in every country. While in the United Kingdom, for instance, the never-married lone mother plays an important role due to frequent teenage pregnancies, in Southern European countries with few divorces and early marriages the father's (or mother's) death during the child's socialisation still plays the most important role. In yet other countries of the continent all three factors—never-married mothers, father's death and divorce—are of importance. The decrease in teenage pregnancies in the United Kingdom and the increase in divorces all over Europe have meanwhile led to the fact that divorce increasingly becomes the major cause for the formation of lone parenthood.

It has to be remembered that in all European countries the overwhelming majority of lone parents are women, with men accounting only for about 10 per cent of lone parents. Furthermore, the number of children born to lone parents is on average smaller than for "complete" nuclear families (Deven/Cliquet 1986; OECD 1990; Bradshaw *et al.* 1996; European Commission 1995; EUROSTAT

1994, 1995, 1996). There are only few countries where the share of lone parents exceeds 20 per cent of all families with children. But there is a rising tendency in Europe towards lone parenthood, not only for lone mothers, but in the same way for lone fathers. In no European country do lone fathers make up more than 5 per cent of all families with children. Future rates of increase in lone parenthood will eventually diminish when the number of divorces where children are involved declines further. This is the case for Germany (both West and East), where the percentage of divorced couples with minor children declined from 63.7 per cent in 1970 (West) to 49.2 per cent in 1992 (West). The number of minor children per 100 divorced couples was 113 in 1970 and 74 in 1992 (Schwarz 1995: 284). As more and more couples remain childless and the mean number of children per couple (and the fertility rate) is further declining, the increase in lone parents must cease in the near future. This is supported by the development of the divorce rate which in some countries reveals tendencies of a slower increase or even of a slight decline.

Reconstituted families

Only few statistical data on reconstituted families are available. However, their number has increased. One "proxy" indicator for reconstituted families could be the remarriage rate of divorced or widowed persons. In the most advanced industrialised countries, the remarriage rates of divorced persons were high after World War II due to the high proportion of divorces. Remarriage rates have fallen steadily during the last decades; they are higher for men than for women. The remarriage rate for widowed people has on the other hand declined steadily due to the high life expectancy. The decline in the remarriage rates after divorce, although divorce rates have strongly increased, is partly associated with the general decrease in marriage propensity. Another factor could be the open or hidden cohabitation after divorce in order to avoid disadvantages regarding social benefits. A third factor is the numerical imbalance of the sexes the older the divorcees are, because in higher age groups the high mortality of men is a crucial factor. It greatly restricts the chances of women to marry.

It can be assumed that this trend of declining remarriage occurs in all European countries. But there are significant differences between European countries concerning remarriage intensity. The number of marriages and remarriage frequency are in an inverse relationship to one another: the higher the divorce rate is, the lower is the remarriage rate. Thus, the remarriage rate in the Nordic countries, for instance, is the lowest one in Europe; it is highest in the Southern European countries of Portugal, Greece and Italy, but not in Spain. Therefore a high divorce rate and a low remarriage rate seem to be good indicators of the fundamental weakening of the institutions marriage and family and of still existing rigid marriage norms.

One important consequence of these developments is the creation of stepparenthood. A differentiation between 'married couple stepfamilies' and 'cohabiting couple stepfamilies' can be made. In Great Britain, in 1991–2 (General

Household Survey Data combined) 5.0 per cent of all families (head aged 16–59) with dependent children were married couple stepfamilies. Cohabiting couple stepfamilies amounted to 2.3 per cent of all families with dependent children (Haskey 1996: 14). In a compilation of information from different European countries, Höpflinger (1997: 121) shows that in no European country with data available does the proportion of children living in stepfamilies exceed 10 per cent of all children in families. The highest figures reported are 8 per cent for Germany (West) in 1980 and 9 per cent for Great Britain in 1985. There are signs of a rising tendency in the proportion of children living in stepfamilies over time.

Living alone as option and constraint

Demographic and social developments during the last 150 years have led to a strong increase in the number of single persons, a development that is caused by three factors. The divergence of the differential life expectancies of the sexes favouring women led to a strong increase in the number of widows, who usually remain as the last "rest of the family" after the death of their husbands and generally live alone. The second factor is divorced persons, mainly women, who remain alone after divorce if they have no children or if the children have left the household. The third factor is those young adults, in this case especially young men, who, after leaving the parental home, live "as singles" for a longer time period. This time period of "singleness" has increased considerably during the last two decades due to the growing participation in tertiary education and the higher age at first marriage. The increase in one-person households can therefore mainly be ascribed to the lower and upper sections of the age pyramid while the middle age groups overwhelmingly still live in family units (Roussel 1983; Kaufmann 1993; Bartiaux 1991). For Belgium and Finland the one-person households have been disaggregated by age, sex and marital status. In Belgium in 1990 28 per cent of all private households have been one-person households. In Finland the proportion was yet higher with 32 per cent. Therefore those two countries belong to the group of countries where individualisation has grown strongly. The question now is where does this strong increase in persons living alone originate? In the following calculation, percentages are related to all one-person households. Concerning men, it can be seen, that the strongest increases in men living alone from 1961 to 1981 are for single men aged 20–29. This corresponds to the falling age at marriage since the 1960s, young men increasingly living alone instead of marrying. With the rise of divorces the proportion of married-separated men living alone is rising for the younger age groups of 20–34 years. But the most remarkable increase has been of divorced men in the age-groups from 29–59. The proportion of widowed men has been declining in these two decades. Similar patterns emerge for Belgian women, but the trends are more moderate. There is also an increase over time in the phase of post-adolescence for single women; there is furthermore an increase in married-separated women in the 20–34 age bracket, and an increase in divorced women living alone similar to that among men. For widowed women no essential change occurred during this period.

In Finland, with a higher proportion of one-person households related to the total number of private households, trends for men towards individualisation are stronger. In relative terms, many more single men in their twenties live alone in Finland as compared to Belgium, and the same is true for divorced men. Interestingly, the proportion of married-separated men living single has declined between 1980–90. The structural difference between men and women in these distributions appears also in the case of Finland. The proportion of single women in their twenties did not rise any more between 1980 and 1990. Only for married-separated women is a rise in the proportion living single reported. But compared with Belgian women, the individualisation of Finnish women has progressed much further, especially for the single and divorced women.

The increase in one-person households therefore comes from three sides: from the adolescents (20–29), the divorced and the widowed. Strong increases can be detected for adolescents of both sexes and the divorced. But it is important to note that living alone is much more important for male adolescents and divorced men. Thus, if a family breaks up, men very often live alone, and women care for the children if there have been children born to the marriage. Given the low remarriage rates, especially in the Nordic countries in general and Finland especially, post-marital cohabitation will be the most probable solution after divorce. The increase of people living alone as adolescents is due to higher educational participation and the higher female labour force participation.

IV "THE CONTEMPORANEITY OF THE NONCONTEMPORANEOUS":
VARIATIONS IN EUROPE

Here variations in Europe are discussed at the macro- and micro-level, since they are thematically linked together. Variations of household and family structures within Europe depend on a plurality of different factors; one factor alone cannot explain them. On a purely empirical level within Europe the "contemporaneity of the noncontemporaneous" concerning household and family structures can be postulated. Historically older household and family forms coexist with historically younger household and family forms. This is the thesis of structural developmental differences. This thesis does not postulate "unconditionally" that all societies follow an identical developmental path and therefore move through the same stages of household and family development; instead, it maintains that certain household and family forms are determined by certain socio-economic structures (developmental differences: agrarian society, industrial society, service society). The result of such developmental differences are chronological phase displacements of similar developments, which become clearly evident if the chronologically most advanced countries are compared with the average and the countries lagging behind. The picture becomes much more complicated due to the phenomenon that on a different level of development new processes and behavioural patterns emerge, which are spreading intrasocietally and intersocietally. But since there is a social stratification within the European countries, the pace of these diffusion processes is different, thus resulting in the typical diffusion pattern of an initially growing divergence and increasing convergence afterwards.

1 "Stable territorial structures"

Eastern Europe and Western Europe: persistence of differences

One of the persisting structural differences within Europe is the difference between Eastern and Western Europe. This structural difference is long-term by nature and is astonishingly persistent. The structural difference between Eastern and Western Europe can mainly be observed in the field of marriage behaviour, as John Hajnal (1965) has demonstrated: in Eastern Europe marriages take place early and are universal; in Western Europe, on the other hand, marriages occur late, and many persons remain in celibacy. In Eastern Europe, by means of empirical indicators a low age at marriage, a high marriage rate and a high proportion of persons married can be found. In Western Europe the opposite is the case. On the other hand, processes of family dissolution do not differ fundamentally from those found in Western Europe and partly have divergent trends. Although Eastern Europe can be clearly separated from Western Europe concerning family formation, there is no clear-cut dividing line in the field of household and family structures. In Eastern Europe, too, the nuclear family has become the modal family type and "new" family forms such as lone parents are increasing just as they are in Western Europe. Cohabiting couples are not as frequent in Eastern Europe as in Northwest Europe, which is obviously caused by housing shortage, too. In Eastern Europe, with the exception of still very strongly agrarian societies such as Romania, Albania and Bulgaria (to mention only a few), extended families are the minority, too. On the other hand, family households are still rather large, because fertility is still high in some parts of Eastern and Southeast Europe. Albania and Kosovo not only belong to the most backward countries and regions of Europe, but also to those with the highest fertility rate in Europe as a whole, a rate that even exceeds the fertility rates of Ireland and Sweden, the countries with the highest fertility rates in Western Europe. The number of one-person households is low in Eastern European countries, because this household type strongly depends on economic wealth, good housing supply and high pensions, and all these factors are non-existent in Eastern Europe (Todorova 1993; Rothenbacher 1996b; Macura 1996; Link 1987; Haskey 1992; Council of Europe 1996; Chesnais 1992; Burguière *et al.* 1996; Anonymous 1996).

It can be expected that the Eastern European countries will move in the same direction as the countries of Western Europe have done, but it is disputable if there will be a convergence of household and family structures in the foreseeable future for several reasons. First, developments proceed faster in the West. A convergence of the East with the West is only possible if the economic catch-up process in the East happens faster than in the West. As this has not happened so far, the countries of Eastern Europe are now falling further and further behind. A convergence will probably only be attained if the demographic developments in Western Europe reach their upper limits, as e.g. in the case of divorces, and if Eastern European countries catch up. But since the internal dynamic of a country always creates new patterns, the result will more likely be stronger phase displacements regarding the development of household and family structures. A convergence of household and family structures between Eastern and Western Europe will probably not be attained in the near future.

The "*demographic crisis*" of the Eastern European transition countries has so far not altered the principal structural differences between Western and Eastern Europe in terms of demographic behaviour. The "*demographic revolution*" affected all key demographic variables: the birth rate, the marriage rate and the divorce rate declined substantially shortly after 1990. There are signs of a recovery and normalisation, but there is no evidence that births, marriages and divorces are "catching up". One important effect of the demographic crisis is the ongoing natural and also absolute population decline in Eastern European countries (Macura 1996; Chesnais 1997; Willekens/Scherbov 1995).

Centre and periphery

Centre and periphery are short formulae for the notion that an economic and power centre exists in Europe which influences the periphery. Within Europe there exists a clear territorial pattern of economic as well as power centres and peripheries. According to this theory, the structure of the centre defines the structure of the periphery. This approach is one of the main competitors of approaches which postulate a general "modernisation" or a convergence of economic development within Europe. This theory thus tries to explain diversity within Europe in socio-economic and socio-cultural terms. The association with the "family" is constituted by the fact that the family as an institution and different family characteristics partly depend on the socio-economic structure of a country. Thus, as long as centre-periphery relationships within Europe exist, there will probably also be differences regarding the importance of the family as an institution (Rokkan 1980; Sapelli 1995).

2 Dynamic processes

Socio-economic differences in development

Structural developmental differences between European countries are mainly a result of the different economic levels of those countries. All European countries are in a process of economic structural change that began at different points in time and proceeds at a different pace. The sectorial structure of the active population for instance determines family structures to a high degree. Thus, the extended family still exists in those countries where the agricultural sector is still strong.

It should be noted that this does not mean that an *evolutionary theory* is being advocated, postulating that the nuclear family evolved from the extended family. On the contrary, the coexistence of different family forms in different historical periods can be observed. But this does not mean that dominant family forms at one point in time could not be replaced by new family forms. The quantitative development of family forms is subject to historical change, and it is imaginable that certain household and family forms will die out, as was the case with households with servants or the "large" households.

On the contrary, it can be assumed that different household and family forms coexist within individual countries as well as within Europe. This contemporaneity of different family forms leads in principle to very complicated patterns of familial development within Europe, especially if one looks at processes on the regional level. It is on the level of regions where processes can be observed that take the opposite direction to those on national level.

Diffusion: pioneers and laggards

The diffusion theory maintains that international differences are the result of differences of pace regarding adaptation to innovations. This adaptation itself depends on many different factors; thus one innovation is adopted in one country, but does not fit into the cultural pattern of another country. The different pace at which this adaptation to innovations occurs is one of the main reasons for diverging developments in an international perspective. While in one country innovations are adopted fast, other countries may adapt slowly. Therefore patterns of pioneering countries and countries lagging behind emerge.

Phase displacements

Phase displacements are partly consequences of developmental differences, partly consequences of diffusion processes happening at a different speed. Phase displacements in demographic structures and in household and family structures within Europe are mainly to be found between Northern and Southern Europe, where time differences regarding the socio-demographic and the socio-economic development amount to several decades. This can be demonstrated with demographic indicators such as the marriage rate or the fertility rate, but also with indicators of the household and family structure. A comparison of Sweden as the most advanced country regarding "family change" with Spain or Portugal as countries lagging behind concerning their development of family structures may illustrate such phase displacements. The causes for such developments may have their roots in the political and economic history of these countries, their being isolated and cut off from international influences (dictatorships in Spain and Portugal), trying to preserve the traditional family structure and thus retarding the development not only of the family but also of the whole society.

V CONCLUSION

This contribution has dealt with the hypothetical influence of important social changes on household and family structures in Europe. Important social changes have been divided into long-term and short-term changes. Long-term social changes are those that are associated with the process of modernisation, which started about 200 years ago in Europe, following the collapse of the old political and economic order, and which have until today essentially determined our social and economic structure. Here modernisation is thought of as processes of growth and differentiation, as changes in the employment structure, as educational expansion, as the increasing inclusion of men, women and children in educational and employment systems and the systems of social security.

The thesis put forward was that macro-social developments have meanwhile entered into a new stage in which a new pattern of population has evolved, which has replaced the older pattern of high fertility and high mortality. This new pattern is characterised by low fertility and low mortality. Thus for a short time period, a new equilibrium in demographic dynamics could be established. But very soon, a new imbalance of below-replacement reproduction of the population came into being, leading to the now manifest ageing population. It could therefore be argued that in present-day Europe, we live in an age that is facing challenges which are the opposite of those the generations living before 1850 were experiencing, the days of "pauperism", when populations were very young and families had to care for only a few elderly, but—on the other hand—for a much larger number of "surviving" children.

As regards households and families that played a much more important role earlier in history than today because they were the social and at the same time multifunctional basic units of society, opposite processes started if one looks at them from a long-term perspective. While on the macro-level the whole society differentiated itself due to permanent growth processes, the micro-level of households and families shows processes of *dedifferentiation*, i.e. the complexity of households has become less. Family sociology tries to describe this phenomenon as "loss of function", "shift of function", etc. This process of dedifferentiation happened in several phases or stages. The first stage was the expulsion of household members that did not belong to the family (such as servants, boarders, lodgers). The second stage was the decline of the extended family, meaning the exclusion of lateral relatives and of the grandparent generation. The universalisation of social security, the improvement of social protection, and growing state redistribution made another stage of dedifferentiation possible, namely the possibility of living alone, the formation of units of unmarried cohabitation and finally the reduction of the family to the parent–child relationship, mainly to the mother–child relationship. These new forms of family structure became visible due to a steep increase in these forms during the last few decades; social categories developed which would not have been able to live independently and autonomously earlier in history.

REFERENCES

ALBER, JENS 1989: *Der Sozialstaat in der Bundesrepublik 1950–1983* (Frankfurt/New York: Campus Verlag).

ANONYMOUS 1996: "The Demographic Situation in Europe", *Population Trends*, no. 85, 39–44.

AUSUBEL, JESSE H., ARNULF GRÜBLER 1996: "Working Less and Living Longer: Long-term Trends in Working Time and Time Budgets", *Technological Forecasting and Social Change* 50, 113–31.

BARTIAUX, FRANÇOISE 1991: "La composition des ménages des personnes âgées en Italie (1981)", *European Journal of Population* 7, 59–98.

BÉGEOT, FRANÇOIS, LANA SMITH, DAVID PEARCE 1993: "First Results from Western European Censuses", *Population Trends*, no. 74, 18–23.

BLOSSFELD, HANS-PETER, JOHANNES HUININK 1989: "Die Verbesserung der Bildungs- und Berufschancen von Frauen und ihr Einfluß auf den Prozeß der Familienbildung", *Zeitschrift für Bevölkerungswissenschaft* 15 (4), 383–404.

BOH, KATJA *et al.* (eds.) 1989: *Changing Patterns of European Family Life. A Comparative Analysis of 14 European Countries* (London and New York: Routledge).

BRADSHAW, JONATHAN *et al.* 1996: *Policy and Employment of Lone Parents in 20 Countries* (York: SPRU).

BURGUIÈRE, ANDRÉ, CHRISTIANE KLAPISCH-ZUBER, MARTINE SEGALEN, FRANÇOISE ZONABEND (eds.) 1996: *A History of the Family*. Volume Two: *The Impact of Modernity* (Cambridge: Polity Press).

CHESNAIS, JEAN-CLAUDE 1992: *The Demographic Transition* (Oxford: University Press).

—— 1997: "La récession démographique dans l'ex-URSS", *Population* 52 (1), 234–40.

CLIQUET, ROBERT 1991: *The Second Demographic Transition: Fact or Fiction?* (Strasbourg: Council of Europe (= Population Studies, no. 23)).

—— 1993a: "Introduction", in Robert Cliquet, *The Future of Europe's Population. A Scenario Approach* (Strasbourg: Council of Europe Press (= Population Studies, no. 26)), 11–21.

—— 1993b: *The Future of Europe's Population. A Scenario Approach* (Strasbourg: Council of Europe Press (= Population Studies, no. 26)).

COLEMAN, DAVID 1996a: "New Patterns and Trends in European Fertility: International and Sub-national Comparisons", in David Coleman, *Europe's Population in the 1990s* (Oxford: Oxford University Press), 1–61.

—— 1996b: *Europe's Population in the 1990s* (Oxford: Oxford University Press).

COMMAILLE, JACQUES, FRANÇOIS DE SINGLY (eds.) 1996: *La Question Familiale en Europe* (Paris: L'Harmattan).

COMMISSION DES COMMUNAUTÉS EUROPÉENNES 1992: *L'Europe Dans le Mouvement Démographique (Mandat du 21 juin 1989)* (Luxembourg: Office des Publications Officielles des Communautés européennes).

COUNCIL OF EUROPE 1990: "Household Structures in Europe", *Report of the Select Committee of Experts on Household Structures* (Strasbourg: Council of Europe (= Population Studies, no. 22)).

—— 1996: *Recent Demographic Developments in Europe* (Strasbourg: Council of Europe Press).

CRAIG, JOHN 1992: "Recent Fertility Trends in Europe", *Population Trends*, no. 68, 20–3.

DEVEN, FREDDY, ROBERT L. CLIQUET 1986: *One-Parent Families in Europe. Trends, Experiences, Implications* (The Hague: NIDI).

DITCH, JOHN, HELEN BARNES, JONATHAN BRADSHAW 1996: *European Observatory on National Family Policies. A Synthesis of National Family Policies 1995* (York: Social Policy Research Unit (SPRU)/Commission of the European Communities).

DORBRITZ, JÜRGEN, KARL SCHWARZ 1996: "Kinderlosigkeit in Deutschland—ein Massenphänomen? Analysen zu Erscheinungsformen und Ursachen", *Zeitschrift für Bevölkerungswissenschaft* 21 (3), 231–61.

EUROPEAN COMMISSION 1995: "The Demographic Situation in the European Union", *Report 1994* (Luxembourg: Office for Official Publications of the European Communities (GD V-COM(94)595)).

—— 1996a: *Employment in Europe 1996* (Luxembourg: Office for Official Publications of the European Communities).

—— 1996b: *Social Security in Europe 1995* (Luxembourg: Office for Official Publications of the European Communities).

—— 1997: *Modernization and Improvement of Social Protection in the European Union* (Communication of the Commission. Brussels: European Commission).

EUROSTAT 1994: "Households and families in the European Union", *Rapid reports. Population and Social Conditions* (Luxembourg (François Bégeot)).

—— 1995: *Demographic Statistics 1995* (Luxembourg: Office for Official Publications of the European Communities).

—— 1996: *Demographic Statistics 1996* (Luxembourg: Office for Official Publications of the European Communities).

FEDERKEIL, GERO, KLAUS PETER STROHMEIER 1993: *Familiale Lebensformen, Lebenslagen und Familienalltag im internationalen Vergleich. Ergebnisbericht über eine Untersuchung im Auftrag des Bundesministeriums für Familie und Senioren* (Bielefeld: Universität Bielefeld, Institut für Bevölkerungsforschung und Sozialpolitik).

FESTY, PATRICK 1994: "L'enfant dans la famille. Vingt ans de changement dans l'environnement familial des enfants", *Population* 49 (6), 1245–96.

FIEBIGER, HILDE 1995: "Zeitverwendung erwerbstätiger Ehepartner. Unterschiede zwischen den neuen Ländern und Berlin-Ost sowie dem früheren Bundesgebiet", *Wirtschaft und Statistik* no. 10, 770–6.

GASPARD, MICHEL 1985: "Les ménages français en l'an 2000", *Futuribles*, Dec. 1985, 41–65.

GAUTHIER, ANNE HÉLÈNE 1996: "The Measured and Unmeasured Effects of Welfare Benefits on Families: Implications for Europe's Demographic Trends", in David Coleman, *Europe's Population in the 1990s* (Oxford: Oxford University Press), 297–331.

GERSHUNY, JONATHAN, JOHN P. ROBINSON 1988: "Historical Changes in the Household Division of Labor", *Demography* 25 (4), 537–52.

GRUNDY, EMILY 1996: "Population ageing in Europe", in David Coleman, *Europe's Population in the 1990s* (Oxford: Oxford University Press), 267–96.

HAJNAL, JOHN 1965: "European Marriage Patterns in Perspective", in D. V. Glass, D. E. C. Eversley (eds.), *Population in History. Essays in Historical Demography* (London), 101–43.

HANTRAIS, LINDA 1992: "La fécondité en France et au Royaume-Uni: les effets possibles de la politique familiale", *Population* 47 (4), 987–1016.

HASKEY, JOHN 1992: "Patterns of Marriage, Divorce, and Cohabitation in the Different Countries of Europe", *Population Trends*, no. 69, 27–36.

—— 1995: "Trends in Marriage and Cohabitation: The Decline in Marriage and the Changing Pattern of Living in Partnerships", *Population Trends*, no. 80, 5–15.

—— 1996: "Population Review: (6) Families and Households in Great Britain", *Population Trends*, no. 85, 7–24.

HENKENS, KÈNE, LIANA MEIJER, JACQUES SIEGERS 1993: "The Labour Supply of Married and Cohabiting Women in the Netherlands, 1981–1989", *European Journal of Population* 9, 331–52.

HÖHN, CHARLOTTE 1997: "Bevölkerungsentwicklung und demographische Herausforderung", in Stefan Hradil, Stefan Immerfall (eds.), *Die westeuropäischen Gesellschaften im Vergleich* (Opladen: Leske + Budrich), 71–95.

HOEM, JAN M. 1986: "The Impact of Education on Modern Family-union Initiation", *European Journal of Population* 2, 113–33.

HOEM, BRITTA, JAN M. HOEM 1989: "The Impact of Women's Employment on Second and Third Births in modern Sweden", *Population Studies* 43, 47–67.

HOFFMANN-NOWOTNY, HANS-JOACHIM 1996: "Partnerschaft—Ehe—Familie. Ansichten und Einsichten", *Zeitschrift für Bevölkerungswissenschaft* 21 (2), 111–30.

HÖPFLINGER, FRANÇOIS 1991: "Neue Kinderlosigkeit—demographische Trends und gesellschaftliche Spekulationen", *Acta Demographica* (Heidelberg, Physica Verlag), 81–100.

—— 1997: "Haushalts- und Familienstrukturen im intereuropäischen Vergleich", in Stefan Hradil, Stefan Immerfall (eds.), *Die westeuropäischen Gesellschaften im Vergleich* (Opladen: Leske + Budrich), 97–138.

HULLEN, GERT 1995: "Der Auszug aus dem Elternhaus im Vergleich von West- und Ostdeutschland. Ergebnisse des Family and Fertility Surveys (FFS) 1992", *Zeitschrift für Bevölkerungswissenschaft* 20 (2), 141–58.

INGLEHART, RONALD 1990: *Culture Shift in Advanced Industrial Society* (Princeton, New Jersey: Princeton University Press).

INSTITUT NATIONAL D'ETUDES DÉMOGRAPHIQUES (INED) 1996: *Population. L'Etat des Connaissances. La France, L'Europe, Le Monde* (Paris: La Découverte).

KAUFMANN, FRANZ-XAVER 1995: "Die ökonomische und soziale Bedeutung der Familie", in Bundesministerium für Familie, Senioren, Frauen und Jugend (ed.), *Zukunft der Familie. Die Familie in Europa am Ausgang des 20. Jahrhunderts. 13./14. September*

1994. Dokumentation (Bonn: Bundesministerium für Familie, Senioren, Frauen und Jugend), 87–98.

KAUFMANN, JEAN-CLAUDE 1993: *Single People, Single Person Households, Isolation, Loneliness. A Status Report* (Brussels: European Commission, Directorate General V Employment, Industrial Relations and Social Affairs, October 1993 (V/7069/93)).

KEILMAN, NICO 1988: "Recent Trends in Family and Household Composition in Europe", *European Journal of Population* 3, 297–325.

KIERNAN, KATHLEEN 1993: "The Future of Partnership and Fertility", in Robert Cliquet, *The Future of Europe's Population. A Scenario Approach* (Strasbourg: Council of Europe Press (= Population Studies, no. 26)), 23–44.

—— 1996: "Partnership Behaviour in Europe: Recent Trends and Issues", in David Coleman, *Europe's Population in the 1990s* (Oxford: Oxford University Press), 62–91.

—— VALERIE ESTAUGH 1993: *Cohabitation. Extra-marital Childbearing and Social Policy* (London: Family Policy Studies Centre (FPSC) (= Occasional Paper 17)).

—— MALCOLM WICKS 1990: *Family Change and Future Policy* (London: Family Policy Studies Centre (FPSC)).

KUIJSTEN, ANTON C. 1996: "Changing Family Patterns in Europe: A Case of Divergence?" *European Journal of Population* 12, 115–43.

—— ANTON OSKAMP 1991: "Huishoudensontwikkeling in Europa, 1950–1990", *Bevolking en Gezin*, no. 2, 107–41.

LILLARD, LEE A., MICHAEL J. BRIEN, LINDA J. WAITE 1995: "Premarital Cohabitation and Subsequent Marital Dissolution: A Matter of Self-selection?" *Demography* 32 (3), 437–57.

LINK, KRZYSZTOF 1987: *Household Trends in Eastern Europe since World War II* (The Hague: N.I.D.I. (= Working Papers of the Netherlands Interuniversity Demographic Institute (N.I.D.I.), No. 71)).

MACURA, MIROSLAV 1996: "Fertility and Nuptiality Changes in Central and Eastern Europe, 1982–1993", *Statistical Journal of the United Nations ECE* 13, 41–63.

MARCHETTI, CESARE, PERRIN S. MEYER, JESSE H. AUSUBEL 1996: "Human Population Dynamics Revisited with the Logistic Model: How Much can be Modeled and Predicted?" *Technological Forecasting and Social Change* 52, 1–30.

MILLAR, JANE, ANDREA WARMAN (eds.) 1996: *Family Obligations in Europe* (London: Family Policy Studies Centre).

MÜLLER, WALTER, DIETMAR HAUN 1993: "Bildungsexpansion und Bildungsungleichheit", in Wolfgang Glatzer (ed.), *Einstellungen und Lebensbedingungen in Europa* (Frankfurt/New York: Campus Verlag), 225–67.

MUNOZ-PEREZ, FRANCISCO 1986: "Changements récents de la fécondité en Europe occidentale et nouveaux traits de la formation des familles", *Population* 41 (3), 447–62.

—— 1987: "Le déclin de la fécondité dans le sud de l'Europe", *Population* 42 (6), 911–42.

NIEMEYER, FRANK 1994: "Nichteheliche Lebensgemeinschaften und Ehepaare—Formen der Partnerschaft gestern und heute", *Wirtschaft und Statistik* no. 7, 504–17.

NORTH, DOUGLASS C. 1981: *Structure and Change in Economic Theory* (New York).

—— 1990: *Institutions, Institutional Change and Economic Performance* (Cambridge).

OECD 1990: *Lone-parent Families. The Economic Challenge* (Paris: Organization for Economic Co-operation and Development).

OMRAN, A. R. 1971: "The Epidemiologic Transition: A Theory of the Epidemiology of Population Change", *Millbank Memorial Fund Quarterly* 49, 509–38.

—— 1983: "The Epidemiologic Transition Theory. A Preliminary Update", *Journal of Tropical Pediatrics* 29, 305–16.

POPENOE, DAVID 1988: *Disturbing the Nest. Family Change and Decline in Modern Societies* (New York: Aldine de Gruyter).

PRIOUX, FRANCE 1995: "La fréquence de l'union libre en France", *Population* 50 (1), 828–44.

ROKKAN, STEIN 1980: "Eine Familie von Modellen für die vergleichende Geschichte Europas", *Zeitschrift für Soziologie* 9 (2), 118–28.

ROTHENBACHER, FRANZ 1995a: "Household and Family Trends in Europe: From Convergence to Divergence", *EURODATA Newsletter*, No. 1, Spring 1995, 3–9.

—— 1995b: "European Social Indicators", *EURODATA Newsletter*, No. 2, Autumn 1995, 21–3.

—— 1996a: "European Family Indicators", *EURODATA Newsletter*, No. 3, Spring 1995, 19–23.

—— 1996b: "Social Indicators for East European Transition Countries", *EURODATA Newsletter*, No. 4, Autumn 1996, 19–21.

—— 1997a: "Familienberichterstattung *in* und *für* Europa", in Heinz-Herbert Noll (ed.), *Sozialberichterstattung in Deutschland. Konzepte, Methoden und Ergebnisse für Lebensbereiche und Bevölkerungsgruppen* (Weinheim, München: Juventa Verlag) 93–123.

—— 1997b: *Historische Haushalts- und Familienstatistik von Deutschland 1815–1990* (Frankfurt/New York: Campus).

ROUSSEL, LOUIS 1983: "Les ménages d'une personne: l'évolution récente", *Population* 38 (6), 995–1015.

—— 1986: "Evolution récente de la structure des ménages dans quelques pays industriels", *Population* 41 (6), 913–34.

—— 1992: "La famille en Europe occidentale: divergences et convergences", *Population* 47 (1), 133–52.

SAPELLI, GIULIO 1995: *Southern Europe Since 1945. Tradition and Modernity in Portugal, Spain, Italy, Greece and Turkey* (London and New York: Longman).

SARDON, JEAN-PAUL 1986: "Évolution de la nuptialité et de la divortialité en Europe depuis la fin des années 1960", *Population* 41 (3), 463–82.

SCHWARZ, KARL 1983: "Les ménages en République Fédérale d'Allemagne 1961–1972–1981", *Population* 38 (3), 565–84.

—— 1988: "Household Trends in Europe after World War II", in Keilman, Nico *et al.* (eds.), *Modelling Household Formation and Dissolution* (Oxford: Oxford University Press), 67–83.

—— 1989: "Die Bildungsabschlüsse der Frauen und ihre Bedeutung für den Arbeitsmarkt, die Eheschließung und die Familienbildung", *Zeitschrift für Bevölkerungswissenschaft* 15 (4), 361–82.

—— 1995: "In welchen Familien wachsen die Kinder und Jugendlichen in Deutschland auf?" *Zeitschrift für Bevölkerungswissenschaft* 20 (3), 27192.

TODOROVA, MARIA N. 1993: *Balkan Family Structure and the European Pattern. Demographic Developments in Ottoman Bulgaria* (Washington, D.C.: The American University Press).

VAN DE KAA, DIRK J. 1987: "Europe's Second Demographic Transition", *Population Bulletin* 42 (1), 1–57.

VÉRON, JACQUES 1988: "Activité féminine et structures familiales. Quelle dépendance?" *Population* 43 (1), 103–20.

WILLEKENS, FRANS, SERGEI SCHERBOV 1995: "Demographic trends in Russia", in H. van den Brekel, F. Deven (eds.), *Population and Family in the Low Countries 1994. Selected Current Issues* (Dordrecht/Boston/London: Kluwer Academic Publishers), 177–230.

ZAPF, WOLFGANG *et al.* 1987: *Individualisierung und Sicherheit. Untersuchungen zur Lebens-qualität in der Bundesrepublik Deutschland* (München: Verlag C. H. Beck).

2

The Changing Pattern of Family Structure in Nigeria: Issues, Problems and Strategies for Family Support

OLUWATOYIN A. IPAYE

A. INTRODUCTION

The family structure in Nigeria has always been complex. Family law and practice today has however been muddied by, amongst other things, the fact that different marriage systems from different cultures are applicable in a single legal system. For instance, in Nigeria three different forms of marriage can be contracted, all with different and sometimes conflicting legal and social consequences. There is statutory marriage, which is a close approximation to the monogamous union described by Lord Penzance as "the voluntary union for life of one man and one woman to the exclusion of all others".[1] There is also customary law marriage which is essentially a union which reflects the cultural beliefs and ethos of the people. Finally, there is the Islamic type of marriage which reflects the influence of Arabic culture in the Northern states of Nigeria. As an example of the problems caused by this multiple marriage system, consider the position of a wife. Under the statutory marriage a man is allowed to marry one wife to the exclusion of all others[2] whereas under customary law a man could marry a limitless number and according to the tenets of the Maliki school of Islamic law accepted in Nigeria, a man may not marry more than four wives and is under an obligation to treat them equally.[3] Another example of the different consequences attaching to each form of marriage is in the area of widowhood law and practice. A statutory marriage widow in the Southwestern states of Nigeria is entitled to her husband's personal estate in its entirety and one third of his real

---

[1] *Hyde* v. *Hyde* (1886) LR 1 P & M 130 at 133.
[2] Marriage Act, Cap 218, 1990 LFN ss. 33, 40.
[3] Other features of the Islamic regime include the husband's right to divorce his wife by unilateral repudiation, the tacit approval of child marriage and the power of "Ijbar" by which the marriage guardian (a marriage celebrated without the appointment of a marriage guardian is void) compels his bride to marry another. All these features not only accord the wife an inferior status but denigrate women's rights.

estate,[4] whereas the general norm under customary law is that succession follows the blood and a customary law wife cannot in any circumstances inherit her husband's property, real or otherwise.

This chapter highlights the changes that have taken place in Nigerian family structure. It starts with a brief description of the traditional family structure which, as a result of a compendium of factors such as poverty, population displacements and monetisation of the economy, has undergone major upheavals as the traditional systems of family and kinship come under increasing pressure from social and economic factors. The government's response to these pressures will be evaluated. Some of its policies, while not targeted specifically at the family, have had a profound effect on its fortunes. The chapter is divided into three parts. The first contains a descriptive analysis of the traditional family structure and the emergent forms identifiable in contemporary Nigeria. Secondly, an overview of factors responsible for these changes will be proffered. This section will also examine some government policies and the new Family Support programme. Finally, we shall suggest strategies to buttress current policy and law in order the assure the survival of the Nigerian family in the twenty-first century.

B. THE TRADITIONAL PRE-COLONIAL FAMILY STRUCTURE

Before the advent of colonialism, the multitude of indigenous tribal systems gave the family social and legal recognition. The indigenous systems are culture-based and the marriage customs differed between each ethnic group. In the context of Nigerian customary laws and traditional society it is almost impossible to define the word "family" with any degree of precision.[5] It has been said that the dynamic nature of the family as a social institution and the tenacity of kinship has strongly influenced the definition. It is typically un-African to consider a "family" as consisting merely of a man, his wife and children. We have already referred to the fact that polygamy is the most widely accepted practice although nothing prevents a monogamous union under customary law. In southern Nigeria, research shows that customary marriages are contracted in a variety of ways.[6] The essential requirements are the obtaining of parental consents, the bride's consent and the payment and acceptance of bride price, followed by formal handing over of the bride to the groom's family.[7]

The institution of marriage and family structure cannot be divorced from the political economy of the times under consideration. Indeed, political demands and the management and exploitation of natural resources to a large extent dic-

---

[4] S. 49 of the Administration of Estates Law 1959 of the Western Region, applicable to the eight states carved out of the now defunct region.

[5] Lloyd says that for the Yorubas the term "may connote any group from the smallest nuclear family of man-wife-child to several thousand persons tracing descent from a common ancestor": Lloyd, *Yoruba Land Law*, 31–2.

[6] S. N. C. Obi, *Modern Family Law in Southern Nigeria* (Sweet & Maxwell, 1966), 160.

[7] Aguda (ed.), *Marriage Laws in Nigeria* (NIALS).

tated the family patterns that evolved. The exploitation of natural resources by the crude hoe and scythe technology demanded a large number of farmhands. This propelled tribes to adopt strategies that would assure a steady supply of farm workers. Fecundity thus became evidence not only of a man's virility and status but also secured a steady stream of workers. Within and even outside marriage the position, status, authority and power of women in Nigeria has always been inferior to that of men in many ways.[8] Research also reveals a host of customary practices which enforce the continued subjugation of women within society and within the family. For a very long time it was acceptable for a young woman to be married by her father without her consent.[9] It took judicial activism slowly to put an end to this customary practice. Even so, being in an economically disadvantaged position, an illiterate woman is frequently unable to protest the violation of her rights and is forced to accede to the dictates of those in authority over her. The polygamous setting of marriage also forces wives to compete amongst themselves for the time and attention of their husbands—which is not only exploitative and degrading but also exposes women to sexually transmitted diseases. Other customs include female circumcision, the justification for which is purportedly to control sexual pleasure and indirectly to force women to be faithful to their partner.[10] Apart from perpetuating different moral and sexual standards for men and women, various other arguments used to justify female genital mutilation include the enhancement of fertility, achievement of safe childbirth and notions of female hygiene.

Together with these practices is the principle of primogeniture as a rule of inheritance of real property. This further consolidates male dominance in all aspects of traditional society and governance. The principle refers to adherence to the notion that succession only follows the blood. Although there are pockets of ethnic communities where matrilineal succession occurs,[11] it is notorious that a wife and female children[12] cannot inherit or administer the husband's estate. In the words of Berkeley J in *Sogurno-Davis* v. *Sogurno*[13] "this is because in an intestacy under native law and custom the devolution of property follows the blood. Therefore a wife or widow not being of the blood has no claim to any share."

---

[8] Rhoda Howard, "Women's Rights in English-speaking sub-Saharan Africa" in Claude Welch (ed.), *Human Rights and Development in Africa* (1984), 60.

[9] The exercise of the Islamic power of Ijbar is a continuation of this practice.

[10] I. Okagbue, "Igbo Customary Law and the Rights of Women in the Family" in Ayua *et al.* (eds.), *Law, Justice and Nigerian Society* (1995, NIALS Commemorative series No. 1, 204) describing the types of circumcision performed on women as including radical circumcision, infibulation and clitoridectomy.

[11] This is confined to a few communities in Eastern Nigeria, the Andoni ethnic group and the Verre and Languda tribes of Northern Nigeria. See Meek, *Tribal Studies in Northern Nigeria*, 415–16.

[12] With the exception that female children share equally with male children amongst the Yoruba: see *Lopez* v. *Lopez* (1924) 5 NLR 43; *Sule* v. *Aji Segirii* (1937) 13 NLR 146; *Richardo* v. *Abal*, 7 NLR 58.

[13] (1929) 9 NLR 79 at 80.

The customary practices which circumscribe the wife's right to inherit her husband's property should also be viewed in the light of the fact that most customs (with the exception of the tribes in south west Nigeria) also disallow female children to inherit land. Thus access to ready-made wealth in the form of bequests and devises is out of their reach. A correlative practice is, of course, widow inheritance. The basis of this, it is said, is to ensure the continued survival and protection of the widow despite her husband's demise. She is considered a chattel which has been bought and paid for at marriage. Thus an untimely death of her husband notwithstanding, she belongs to the family. Usually the widow is given little choice so that, unless she has some financial independence she has to accede to a serial marriage with any of her husband's paternal relations, or else she has to leave the matrimonial home.[14]

This amply demonstrates the traditional family pattern of Nigeria. It should be noted that in Northern Nigeria, where Islamic law is firmly entrenched, family structure is not much different. According to religious tenets, the husband is allowed up to four wives at any given time. Not only is the wife expected to do more than her fair share for the family on the farm, in fields or on the rivers, but she is also solely in charge of managing the home; she is the primary carer of the children, she must attend to food preparation, cleaning and so on. Although there is a dearth of research on decision-making in the home, evidence suggests that the woman is voiceless and is expected to be totally submissive to her husband or father as the case may be.[15]

C. NEW TRENDS IN FAMILY STRUCTURE

The changes which have occurred in the traditional family structure have been phenomenal. Explosions in population, rural to urban movements of the populace, wage labour, industrialisation, education, contact with western civilisation have all impacted on the Nigerian family such that its classic traditional structure in its pure form is probably no longer recognisable.

1 Monogamy

The traditional family had always been polygamous. Typically each wife was entitled to be given her own separate house or rooms in which she lived with her children, domestic servants and dependant relatives, if any, free from interference from any other wife, subject only to the overall supervision and control of the "iyale" or first wife and of her husband.[16] Each woman with her children

---

[14] O. A. Ipaye, "Women and the Law: the Nigerian Experience" [1995] *JARL & P.* 60.

[15] J. Akande, "Giving Women a Voice: The Media Imperatives" 1996 British Council Eminent Persons Lecture.

[16] Ward, *Marriage among the Yoruba*, 38.

formed a residential unit which competed with the other residential units within the family for resources and the husband's patronage. It is our assertion that polygamy is a reflection of the dominant position of men in virtually all African communities.[17] Polygamy served as a useful tool in ensuring a steady supply of labour which was necessary for the exploitation of natural resources and labour-intensive agriculture. Polygamy also provided social prestige and political power and represented an egoistical display of a man's virility.[18]

Contact with the British imperial legal system saw the introduction of western-type laws into Nigeria, particularly with respect to family relations, divorce and succession. Thus in 1914 the Marriage Act introduced the concept of monogamy. This legislation, although in no way tampering with customary marriage law, provided an avenue by which the moral tone of contemporary society could be set. Essentially, the Marriage Act, which was of general application throughout Nigeria, laid down the procedure for contracting statutory marriage. Whilst not explicitly Christian, the fact that section 35 prohibits multiple marriage renders it akin to the Christian idea of marriage. A number of statutory offences are created for violations of its provisions and of course the Criminal Code Act provides for the offence of bigamy.[19]

There is a prevailing perception that a wife monogamously married under the statute is in a superior position to a wife married under customary or Islamic law. The reasons for this are multifarious and include the fact that an "Act wife" to a large extent does not need to compete for the patronage and attention of her husband. The law specifically prohibits him from marrying other women under any other system of law during the subsistence of the statutory marriage. In addition, in the event of divorce, other western-type legislation, especially the Matrimonial Causes Act, puts the wife in a much stronger position. The law considers her as an equal partner in the marriage. She is entitled to be heard before the dissolution and, on the basis of the judge's discretion, she is entitled to an equitable redistribution of the marital property.[20] She may also have the right to financial support in the form of a maintenance order on dissolution.[21] Finally, compared to a wife after a customary law dissolution, she is in a better position to obtain custody of the children, either jointly or solely.[22]

Although no statistics are available, it is apparent that with increased access to formal education and acceptance of western values, a growing number of women enter marriage via the statute or by conversion of a customary marriage into a

---

[17] Phillips, *Survey of African Marriage and Family Life* (New York, 1953).

[18] I. Okagbue, "Igbo Customary Law and the Rights of Women and the Family" in Ayau *et al.* (eds.), *Law, Justice and Society* (NIALS).

[19] Criminal Code Act, 77 LFN 1990, Cap. s. 370

[20] Matrimonial Causes Act, LFN Cap. 220, s. 72(1).

[21] Matrimonial Causes Act, LFN Cap. 220, s. 70.

[22] Matrimonial Causes Act, LFN Cap. 220, s. 71(1). See *Williams* v. *Williams* [1987] 2 NWLR (Part 54) 66; *Kalejaiye* v. *Kalejaiye* [1986] 2 QLRN 161; A. A. Owolabi, "Some Reflections" in Ajai and Ipaye (eds.), *Rights of Women and Children in Divorce* (FEF Publications, 1997).

statutory marriage by a subsequent ceremony under the Act.[23] However, customary rules on marriage are still firmly in place, being observed particularly among rural dwellers and the urban poor.

2 Options outside marriage: single-parenthood

Unlike in pre-colonial times, more women now have access to education[24] and consequently find employment in the formal sector of the economy.[25] This allows them some financial independence. The development of towns and cities improved transport and this broadened the area in which women can seek marriage partners. Modern women are much older when they marry than the traditional wife. They have usually spent more years in education, which translates into better jobs and higher income. Access to information through the media enables them to make informed choices. Whilst all these factors have culminated in an enhanced social position, there has also been increased prejudice against women. They are often called prostitutes ("asewo") when they show independence. This reaction is no doubt a reflection of the failure or inability of the hitherto dominant group to handle the emergent strength of the hitherto subservient group. There is certainly a suspicion that women intend to challenge the *status quo* and hence the superior position held by men in society.

Whilst no statistics are available to confirm this, it appears that there is an increasing number of female headed households, particularly in the urban areas. Female headed households, whilst not the norm, often arise as a result of divorce or separation, women having children without marrying and single women who do not have children but have relatives living, apparently dependently, with them. The social structures of urban areas facilitate these life styles.[26] The third scenario may not be found frequently in rural areas.

3 Urbanisation

Urbanisation has significantly affected family structures. The catalyst for urbanisation was European colonisation, which required administrative centralisation.

[23] Marriage Act LFN 1990 Cap. 218. But see cases where attempts at conversion fell short of the requisite procedures: *Chukuma* v. *Chukuma* [1996] 1 NWLR (Part 426) 543; *Anyaegbunam* v. *Anyaegbunam* [1973] 4 SC 121; *Obiekwe* v. *Obiekwe* [1963] 7 ENLR 121; *Akuwudike* v. *Akuwidike* [1963] 7 ENLR 5.

[24] See *Blueprint on Women's Education in Nigeria* (Women's Education Branch of the Federal Ministry of Education), 1989.

[25] Available gender-related figures of workers in the federal civil service reveal that a preponderance of women is found in the lower cadres of the service: see O.A. Ipaye "Women in Labour: Some Legal Issues", unpublished paper delivered at a National Conference on Women in the management of the Nigerian Economy, Lagos, Apr. 1995.

[26] According to the Nigerian Demographic and Health Survey, female-headed households constitute 18% of urban households and 13% of rural households: Akande *et al.* (eds.), *Women and Households in Nigeria* (W.LDCN 1996) 35.

Towns such as Lagos, Enugu, Jos and Port Harcourt were developed initially because of their proximity to mineral deposits.[27] As wage labour gained acceptance in Nigeria there was a marked population drift from the countryside to the towns. At one time much of the drift was circulatory. For example, migrants would come to the cities, work for two or three years, and then return to their families and reaffirm their position in their original social networks. On their return to the villages they improved property and paid much needed attention to the farms. Often money earned in the cities enabled them to marry additional wives and purchase luxuries. This money was quickly spent and the migrant would return to the city, to come back to the village after a while. This circulatory migration led to the transformation of the rural communities as modern cement buildings began to replace mud huts.

Women also became more active in the city-rural trade, bringing in commodities such as canned milk, sugar, plastics, shoes and clothing. The traditional rural pattern of residence was that all family members lived together; sons and grandsons lived in a common dwelling established by their ancestor, together with their wives, children and dependants. Thus marriages, funerals, disputes, care for the home, the sick and the aged and infirm were the concern of the whole group. The authority of the single head, whose consent was sought for any major decision, was recognised. This pattern fostered strong kinship ties and provided support for each family member common in traditional Africa. But as the men migrated to the cities, life became increasingly difficult for the women. They were left to manage the home, care for the children and look after the farm. This was a difficult role and many women began leaving the villages for the cities to join their husbands. But on arrival, the families' problems were usually compounded. Usually the husband could only find work as an unskilled labourer. The accommodation available for this class of migrants is notoriously inadequate. Social problems such as alcoholism, formation of youth gangs, street children and teenage pregnancy are often associated with the urban poor.[28] Urban migration of single women throws up a different set of problems. Such women frequently fall prey to delinquency, violent crimes, teenage pregnancy and prostitution.[29]

D. GOVERNMENT RESPONSES

In 1900 Nigeria had an estimated population of 15 million people. By 1991 the provisional census figures revealed that the population had soared to 88.5 million.[30] This population explosion has unfortunately not been matched by a credible performance in agricultural production, education, industrialisation or

---

[27] Little, *Urbanization as a Social Process: An African Case Study* (Routledge & Kegan Paul).

[28] J. Bruce, C. B. Lloyd and A. Leonard, *Families in Focus* (The Population Council, New York, 1995).

[29] B. Owasanoye, "The Development of Extra-Legal Services for the Family in Crisis" in Ahai and Ipaye (eds.), *Rights of Women and Children in Divorce* (F.E.F. Publication, 1997), 60.

[30] *Central Bank of Nigeria Annual Report 1991.*

social services, all of which are the parameters by which development is measured. The bane of the Nigerian economy appears to be a lack of purposive planning and a general inability to match production and resource management with the demands of an ever growing populace. The economy is plagued with fundamental problems. For example, agriculture, which was the mainstay of the economy until the 1970s, provided well over 70 per cent of the GDP. Now this has declined to less than 30 per cent. The continued and increased exploitation of oil and gas to the detriment of other sectors saw the gradual transformation of Nigeria from a predominantly agricultural to a mono-product economy largely dependent on oil for foreign exchange earnings and government revenue. The government strategy of import substitution has been much criticised. Nigerian manufacturing industries have been heavily dependent on foreign imports and hence there has been no self-sustained growth in the sector. With the decline of foreign exchange earnings which itself was a result of sluggish demand for crude oil and profligate government spending, it became difficult to procure raw materials, spare parts and other capital inputs for domestic production. This led to low production, under-utilization of factories and retrenchment.

1 SAP economic policy and the family

At the suggestion of and in close collaboration with the International Monetary Fund, the government embarked on the Structural Adjustment programme (SAP) in 1986. This programme was designed to re-structure the consumption and production patterns of the economy, eliminate price distortions and the heavy dependence on crude oil. Essentially, its main pillars were based on a development of a free market economy. Unfortunately the austerity measures of the policy led to widespread shortages and eventual retrenchment of many workers. It has been concluded that more than ten years after the introduction and vacillating implementation of these economic policies the gains are hardly visible and the losses quite obvious. There has been increased social and economic insecurity and a significant reduction in the standard of living of many Nigerians. Many children have been withdrawn from school and forced into the informal economy.[31] Women have had to abandon their traditional occupation of homemaking to find employment, but with little chance of success in the formal sector owing to their lack of skills and education. Many are found in the informal sector, particularly the distributive trade. Children are left alone for long, unsupervised periods. Whilst there are no statistics to relate the high levels of delinquency in the cities to economic circumstances of families, the parallels cannot be dismissed as mere coincidence.

---

[31] See Ayua and Okogbue (eds.), *Rights of the Child in Nigeria* (NIALS Research Series No. 2, 1996).

2 Development policies and the family: the DFRRI and Better Life Programmes

Apart from the economic measures of the SAP, a number of developmental policies were introduced, including the Directorate of Food, Roads and Rural Infrastructure (DFRRI) And the Better Life Programme (BLP) The former was intended to increase the tempo of rural development. To bring this about the Directorate had always encouraged the participation of the community. Thus, in 1990, 1,076 Community Development Associations were registered with the DFRRI. Community projects frequently involved the identification and establishment of viable cottage industries, particularly the processing of agricultural produce by mechanical means. This reaching out to the community has given a voice to women. They have been consulted and empowered by organising into co-operative units and taking advantage of agricultural credit facilities and improved technologies from the services of extension workers.

In 1983 a military coup ousted the constitutional government of Alhaji Shehu Shagari and government once again passed to military dictators. The idea of the Better Life for Rural Women Programme was conceived by the wife of the military Head of State, Maryam Babangida. The programme was formally launched in 1987. It set out to address the myriad problems of inaccessibility of the hinterland, the low level of development in the rural areas and the ever-increasing urban migration. For the first time Nigeria had a visible First Lady who assumed political power to oversee the programme towards which huge sums of money were committed. To give the programme legal backing, the Better Life Programme Decree was promulgated. It was planned to coincide with the opening up of the rural countryside by the DFRRI, reaching out specifically to rural women. A 1992 survey conducted by the Central Bank showed that the BLP recorded significant achievements in all its core programmes. Thus, for example, in the period under survey, the number of women's co-operatives had risen to 9,044 with membership levels of 379,416 and in the same period 2,318 cottage industries were established.[32] But in spite of these impressive achievements, the BLP was beset with fundamental problems, the most damaging of which was that there was no credible machinery to monitor the expenditure. Furthermore, the Head of State's wife served as National Chairperson, the wives of the 30 state governors as state chairpersons and the wives of the local council chairmen as the local chairpersons. Through these unconstitutional offices the unflattering perception grew that the major beneficiaries were the state and local government chairpersons.

Whilst the objective of the BLP was to empower rural women economically, it did nothing significant to address the problem of limited access to and

---

[32] Central Bank of Nigeria, *Annual Reports & Statement of Accounts*, year ending December 1992. Figures indicate that 173 weaving centres and 28 women multi-purpose centres were established by the end of 1992.

ownership of land. Whilst the Land Use Act[33] is gender neutral, its provisions are insensitive to the peculiar needs of women.[34] On the other hand, the customary land tenure system is discriminatory and in spite of constitutional provisions to the contrary, the customary law precepts on landholding are still firmly entrenched. Thus in most communities women, either as wives or children, have no right to inherit the land.[35] Nor do they own land. At best they have a usufructuary right.[36] Particularly women who have been married under the prevailing customs find that, on divorce or separation, they are turned out of the matrimonial home with only their personal belongings. They have no right to a beneficial share in the matrimonial property which they have worked hard to acquire together with their husbands.

The programme could also be criticised for having a weak base for the provision of agricultural extension, credit and marketing services because it lacked the skilled manpower to provide them. However, for the first time, women as a group in society had been the target of government development efforts and to this extent it was a commendable programme.

3 The Family Support Programme (FSP) and the Family Economic Advancement Programme (FEAP)

Nigeria's hope of a return to democracy was dashed by the annulment of the 1993 presidential elections on 12 June. After a brief interregnum, government was taken over by Major General Sanni Abacha, the present Head of State, whose wife, Maryam Abacha, is the initiator of these twin socio-economic programmes.

The FSP was introduced in 1994 as a programme which emphasises the role of the family as a basic social unit of society. It is designed to promote the socio-economic empowerment of the family as a catalyst for development. The FSP has been divided into three phases, the first of which involved the mobilisation of support for the programme, whilst the second phase concentrated on promoting child and maternal health. Although not many data are available to assess the success or otherwise of these two phases, the third phase, which was formally launched on 3 March 1997, appears to be better thought out. In the 1997 annual budget of the Federation, $50m (about N4 billion) was committed to the implementation of the FSP for the year. Shortly after the budget was announced, the

---

[33] Cap. 202 LFN 1990.

[34] See J. O. Akande, "Women's Legal Right to land and Settlement" in Akande *et al.* (eds.), *Women's Legal Rights* (WLDCN 1996) 31.

[35] Uzodike, "Women's Rights in Law and Practice: Property Rights" in Obilade (ed.), *Women in Law* (Southern Univ. L. Centre & Faculty of Law University of Lagos, 1993).

[36] See S. N. C. Obi (ed.), *Customary Law Manual of Imo and Anambra States* (Government Printers, Enugu, 1977); *Olok* v. *Giwa* (1939) 15 MLR 31; *Nzekwu* v. *Nzekwu* [1989] 2 NWLR (Part 104) 373. See also Y. Aboki, "Property Rights of the Customary and Islamic Law Spouse in Divorce: Issues, Problems and Proposals for Reform" in Ajai and Ipaye (eds.), *Rights of Women and Children in Divorce* (FEF Publication, 1997).

FSP metamorphosed into the FEAP. Parallel to this is the Family Support Trust Fund, established in 1995. It is expected that money will be received into the Fund from statutory allocations, as in the case of the N4 billion earmarked in the 1997 budget. Donations from international organisations, multinationals and private citizens would also be held by the Fund.[37] In May 1997 a blueprint for the FEAP was published proclaiming as its main objectives:

- provision of loans to people at ward level to set up cottage enterprises;
- training for ward-based business operations;
- encouraging the design and manufacture of appropriate machinery and equipment;
- creation of employment opportunities;
- improvement of living standards;
- encouragement of the formation of cooperative societies by producers;
- maximisation of the use of local resources through improved production, storage, preservation processing, recycling, packaging and marketing.

These objectives are no doubt laudable, but certainly not original. Indeed, they coincide with the declared objectives of the other programmes discussed above. Nevertheless, unlike the BLP, which had a narrow focus on rural women, the FEAP targets family units, including children. Unlike the DFFRI, which focused on providing basic infrastructures in the communities and did a successful job of making the hinterland accessible, the FEAP reaches out to families as the primary beneficiaries. It will have a Board, headed by the National Chairperson of the FSP (who will be the Head of State's wife[38]), a Technical Advisory Committee (TAC), a State Co-ordinating Committee (SCC), a Local Government Committee (LGC) and a Ward Co-ordinating Committee (WCC). A pyramid-like structure emerges. The WCC identifies the group applying for a loan or other support being indigenous to that ward, after which the application is passed to the LGC, which collates and assesses applications on which it makes recommendations for decision by the Board through the SCC. There is unfortunately no time frame within which these decisions are to be made, and it is rather unimaginative that the Board comprising busy Ministers will consider applications from a ward, so far removed. Similarly, where applications are favourably considered by the Board, the channel of communication back to the ultimate recipient is too long, and fraught with potential disasters on the way. It appears that the door has been left open not only for nepotism but political patronage and it is doubtful that an application will be considered with the speed and objectivity it deserves.

[37] The Fund is managed by a 25 member Board appointed by the Head of State. It is empowered to (amongst other things) (i) provide decent health care delivery; (ii) assist families to identify economically viable enterprises for income generation; (iii) assist rural families increase their agricultural productivity and (iv) enhance the capacity of parents to act as role models for their children, etc. See Decree No. 10, 1995.

[38] Who will also chair the Trust Fund and the FEAP Board. This has been criticised as concentrating too much power in one person.

The FEAP gives support by granting loans of not more than N550,000 per application per project, repayable within three years at an interest of 10 per cent. It appears that only groups registered with the FEAP will be eligible for the loan. This appears somewhat confusing because at one moment the FEAP claims to empower families by granting credit to finance approved projects and at another the loans seem to be available only to groups of families, or co-operative associations. The guidelines on loan applications appear complicated which may be daunting in a country with high illiteracy.

E. CONCLUSIONS

The aim of the government is to provide institutional support for families and community-based associations. It certainly is not to provide a social welfare system such as those familiar in western European countries. But in spite of their laudable objectives, there is much doubt whether these programmes will be effective in bringing about much needed change in the economic fortunes of women and, ultimately, of the family. One fundamental flaw is that they have not significantly enhanced the access of women to land and capital. The customary land tenure system in much of Nigeria entrenches the principle of primogeniture. In isolated pockets, such as amongst the Yorubas, women have a right to inherit land equally with their brothers, but, in spite of this, there is no evidence that women in the Yoruba-speaking tribes are significantly richer than others or hold a commensurate proportion of land in their own names as individual holdings. Various factors led to the decline of this group of women and to their loss of control over the most vital requirement for production, namely, land and capital, and thus they became increasingly economically powerless, although socially autonomous.[39] Even the few women who had rights to individual holdings had to exercise constant vigilance to prevent the appropriation of their titles by unscrupulous male kin.[40] The failure of women to acquire and protect individually-owned land had adverse consequences on their economic status so that from the onset of commercialisation and privatisation women controlled relatively little of a resource that was rapidly becoming both a major form of wealth and means to wealth. Rural women were in no better position. The land tenure system amongst the Yorubas was collective, or family-based.[41] Whilst a woman

---

[39] See Kristin Mann, "Women, Landed Property and the Accumulation of Wealth in Early Colonial Lagos" (1991) *Signs: Journal of Women in Culture and Society*, vol. 16, No. 4, 682. See also Sean Davison (ed.), *Agriculture, Women and Land: the African Experience* (Boulder, Colo., Westview, 1988).

[40] The records are replete with cases where women take court action to wrest property from male relatives and husbands: see *Domingo Auguste* v. *Bernadino F. Damazis* (1887) JNCC 87; *Mary Macaulay* v. *Buari Apala* (1894) JNCC 300–5; *Maria Iherissa* v. *Pedro Feliciano* (1897) JNCC 18; 350; *Voight & Co.* v. *Rokosi* (1887) JNCC 7; 100.

[41] T. O. Elias, *Nigerian Land Law and Custom* (London, Routledge and Kegan Paul, 1962); G. B. A. Coker, *Family Property amongst the Yorubas* (London, Sweet & Maxwell, 1958).

might have a right to use the land for farming, she was rarely allocated a portion outright. The management was usually in the hands of a male elder and, outside the Yoruba tribes, the female had no right to inherit her father's or her husband's real estate. The Land Use Act failed to address the inequitable access of women to land. Under this enactment, all urban land lies in the respective state governor, who has the power to grant rights of occupancy. It has been asserted that the delays and frustration encountered in securing certificates of occupancy is an impediment to the equitable distribution to and access by women of individual grants of land.

This chapter has demonstrated that great social and economic changes have affected women in Nigeria both positively and negatively. It is difficult to do more than draw very general conclusions. Things have definitely changed from the traditional peasant-style of family grouping to new forms of family groupings, relationships and power-play both within and outside the home. Nigerian women may be downtrodden but they are certainly not spiritless creatures. Very often they have had cause to rise up against perceived social and political injustice.[42] The militant attitude of women is clearly carried into the family arena such that within the traditional confines of childbearing and domestic chores they have always worked hard to ensure the survival of the family as a unit. Indeed, the major cry of the women is that men are lazy, dirty, brutal and adulterous and that they do not perform their roles adequately. In defence of men, it has been argued that this is a result of dislocations in their role, so that jobless men have drifted into a pattern of sporadic work, drunkenness and broken marriages. The woman, left on her own to support the family, works hard to eke out a meagre living cultivating farm lands and trading at the local market. In caring for her family she develops a toughness lacking in her male counterpart. [43] It is this emergence from docility which accounts for the presence of female-headed households and the feminisation of agriculture. Nonetheless, it has not translated into an economic springboard for women. Although women are now in control of farm produce, they do not necessary have a legal right to the lands. Labour has always been controlled by a hierarchical system headed by the male family head who dictates how labour is utilised. In the traditional system, the flow of resources has always been from husbands to wives and juniors to elders, thus effectively blocking the exercise of women's autonomy over the utilisation of labour. Women are unable to rise much above poverty levels. Without control over land and labour, and in a system of subsistence agriculture, output levels per unit are low.

It is certainly necessary to strike down gender-biased customs. Customary laws become norms by the fact that members of a community choose to be bound by them. The movement for change thus proceeds from attitudinal changes of the people themselves. Nevertheless, customary laws which are discriminatory are

---

[42] See Nina Mba, *Nigerian Women Mobilized* (Institute of International Studies, University of California, 1982).

[43] Little, *African Women in Towns* (Cambridge University Press, 1973).

unconstitutional and should be nullified as being in violation of both national and international standards of behaviour.[44]

The various governmental policies examined above have not meaningfully addressed the problems faced by families confronted especially by the economic recession which began in the early 1980s. For example, in 1989 the Federal Government proclaimed that women should be discouraged from having more than four children. This policy has been criticised for being timorous and unlikely to solve the population problem which largely stems from inadequate planning and insufficient provision of social and educational structures. Inadequate planning translates into the over-concentration of population in certain areas, putting pressure on resources and creating inner-city problems. Merely to declare that the women should have no more than four children, in a country where polygamy is the dominant marriage form, is inadequate. Only by actively encouraging small families, for example, by providing housing and education for families with a lower number of children and denying certain amenities to families with a larger number of children will the desired changes in population growth be achieved.

Moreover, we have identified that the many programmes are too politically weighted to be likely to succeed. The FEAP looks good on paper but, as we have seen, there is not sufficient decentralisation of power and the hierarchical command structure is intimidating. Finally, our view is that the rigorous pursuit and implementation of so-called third generation rights, to decent housing, nutritious food, good health care at an affordable price, to education and to earn a living in an environmentally friendly workplace and above all to freedom from all kinds of discrimination are the minimum demanded of any government, especially third world governments. In this kind of enabling environment, the prognosis is good for the survival of stable, happy families in which every member of society can reach his full potential.

[44] See s. 39 of the Nigerian Constitution 1979 and Art. 16 of the Convention on the Elimination of Discrimination against Women (CEDAW).

3

Long Term Developments in Family Law in Western Europe: an Explanation[1]

HARRY WILLEKENS

During the last decades, western family law has undergone dramatic changes. These changes, however, are nothing but the intensification and provisional culmination of a process having its roots in a much earlier development, i.e. the emergence of what some would call modernity, the driving force and centrepiece of which was, in my view, industrial capitalism. To understand the wave of family law reforms that, in recent decades, has swept over most of the industrialised world, it is therefore necessary to take a look at legal and social developments over a much longer range of time.

It is the purpose of this chapter to try to develop an explanation of the changes in family law in Western Europe (or to be more precise: Norway, Sweden, Denmark, the United Kingdom, the Netherlands, Belgium, France, Spain, Portugal, Italy, Switzerland, Austria and Germany) since approximately 1800.[2] Obviously, such an undertaking has to start with a presentation of the facts to be explained: a synthetic overview of legal developments, from which it will be gathered that the general direction of change is the same in all legal systems under review, but that there are substantial differences in both the pace and the extent of change. This is followed by an explanation of the *general* developmental tendencies, and by some indications of how the *differences* between legal systems might be explained.

[1] The research leading up to this text was partly made possible by a research fellowship at the Max Planck Institut für europäische Rechtsgeschichte at Frankfurt-am-Main in 1997, by a visiting professorship at the Mannheimer Zentrum für europäische Sozialforschung in 1995 and by the facilities this Zentrum has put at my disposal since then.

[2] This has of necessity to be an approximation. Some countries (Belgium, Norway, Germany, Italy) did not yet exist as independent states in 1800. In Switzerland and Spain parts of family law remained subject to regional variations until into the twentieth century. In writing this, it has not been possible to take into account the variations within these countries (to be). The only exception is made for Prussian law, which has been covered since the Allgemeine Landrecht entered into force (1794).

A. THE DEVELOPMENT OF FAMILY LAW IN WESTERN EUROPE OVER THE LAST
TWO HUNDRED YEARS: A DESCRIPTION

It might seem to be rash, to say the least, to try to synthesise developments in a
diversity of legal systems, in most cases stretching over a period of nearly two
centuries, in a few pages. If, however, one takes one's distance from differences
in concepts and systematics, and concentrates on the changes in the *substance* of
the basic rules, there emerges a fairly clear picture.[3] In their main characteristics,
the family law systems of Western Europe were quite similar at the eve of the
appearance of industrial capitalism. Changes in the different legal systems do not
take place simultaneously nor at the same pace, but when change occurs the
direction is always the same. A purely synchronic comparison or one restricted
to developments within, say, "recent years" or a certain decade, will easily miss
this point and will give the impression of the existence of fundamental differences, where a comparison over a more extended period of time would rather
point to mere time lags. This is not to say that the time lags are not in themselves significant, especially if the temporal gap is large, as in some respects it
will be seen to be between the Nordic countries and the rest of the West; nor is
it to imply that all legal systems under consideration are fated to develop towards
the same horizon.

I will now first give a description of the fundamental traits of family law at the
beginning of the chosen period, then explain what has changed. I will only differentiate between legal systems insofar as there is at least a semblance (and often
it will be no more than a semblance) of a fundamental difference between them.
Whenever such a semblance is found, it will have to be looked into whether the
differing arrangements are really different in their social consequences, or
whether they are functionally equivalent, i.e. are different techniques facilitating
the emergence of similar social consequences.[4]

1. Nineteenth (and early twentieth) century family law

Family law is concerned with the organisation of three types of relationships:
relations between cohabiting sexual partners, between parents and children,
between the members of the nuclear family and those of the more extended family. Nowadays, these three types of relations are, at least to a certain extent, regulated independently of each other: the status of a child cannot be simply inferred
from the legal relation between its parents. In the older family law the legal

---

[3] That it is possible to sketch such a picture is due to the existence of a well developed comparative and historical family law literature. See especially Dörner (1974); Glendon (1977, 1981, 1987,
1989); Goode (1992); Holthöfer (1987), *International Encyclopedia of Comparative Law* (1972–80);
Müller-Freienfels (1993); Phillips (1988); Rheinstein (1972).

[4] As to the notion of "functional equivalence" and its use in comparative law and legal sociology,
see: Zweigert and Kötz (1996: 33–5), and Scheiwe and Willekens (1997).

nature of a child's relation to parents and their extended families was inextricably tied to the institutionalisation of the relations between cohabiting sexual partners. *Legitimacy* was the focal point of family law, at the same time the status conferred upon children through their parents' marriage and one of the main *raisons d'être* for marriage.

Children entered into a family solely through their birth or conception within a marriage or, if they had been born out of wedlock, through their legitimation by the consecutive marriage of their natural parents. An apparent exception is to be found in Swedish law, where children also had full rights of inheritance and maintenance if their conception had been preceded or followed by a promise of marriage or had resulted from a rape (Dopffel (1986: 189–90)). Leaving aside the rape hypothesis, the exception is only apparent. At the time of this rule's inception (1734), Sweden was a predominantly agricultural society, and it remained so until at least the late nineteenth century. In Northwest European agricultural societies it was far from unusual for marriage to be preceded by intercourse between the formally betrothed and for procreative abilities thus to be tested (a question of importance in a system which does not allow for divorce); witness to this was the high proportion of children born so shortly after marriage that they must have been conceived before it (Seccombe (1992: 114–15)). From this point of view, according legitimacy to the children of the abandoned fiancée was not so much an exception to the tie between marriage and legitimacy as a guarantee that marriage promises would be kept—a guarantee that was complemented by a rule giving the fiancée abandoned after she had had intercourse with her betrothed the right to bear his name and the right to share in a community of property between them, without awarding the man the usual rights of a husband (*inter alia*, the guardianship over his wife and the right to administer her property) (Agell (1980: 19–21)). If the child's biological father did not marry his fiancée, the child would nevertheless have the rights of a legitimate child within his family, but he would not have the rights of a father and husband: a formidable incentive to go through with the marriage, and thus a confirmation of the logic of making legitimacy dependent on marriage.

Children who were not legitimate in the sense here described did not become full members of a family. The rules regarding them were quite variable among legal systems, but in all legal systems the status of children born out of wedlock was markedly inferior to the status of legitimate children. In the Romanic legal systems, they could enter into a legal relationship with both parents, but (with a few exceptions regarding the relation to the mother) only if recognised. Recognition and the establishment of a legal bond between parent and child were not possible if the child had been conceived in adultery or incest (see, e.g., Article 335 of the Code Napoléon); the establishment of paternity against the will of the man who had conceived the child was explicitly prohibited (Article 342 of the Code Napoléon). Some authors (foremost Zweigert and Kötz (1987)) make a lot of these prohibitions and interpret them as a sign of an exceptional hostility towards children born out of wedlock, which they claim to be typical for the

Romanic systems. It is true that these prohibitions were not to be found in other legal systems, but this is to be explained by the very restricted significance in these systems of paternity outside marriage. In general, until well into the second part of our century, they granted the child at most a restricted right to maintenance from the father and excluded all other kinds of legal relation with him,[5] whereas the rights of both child and father in Romanic systems, in the cases where paternity could be established and was established, were much more extended, always included inheritance rights (Articles 756–761 of the Code Napoléon) and in several cases paternal authority over the child. If one does not limit oneself to the comparison of singular rules, but looks at the whole set of rules regulating illegitimacy, the treatment of illegitimate children in Romanic and non-Romanic systems looks, roughly speaking, functionally equivalent. In all systems the law functioned so as to limit or exclude the claims of children born out of wedlock against their natural fathers, in the Romanic systems by letting the fathers themselves be the judges of whether they would enter into a legal relation with the children, in the Nordic, Germanic and common law systems by giving the children only minimal claims to maintenance or no rights at all. With some national exceptions (e.g., Prussia, Italy[6]), illegitimate children furthermore had no claims against the family of their parents.

If the parents' marriage was decisive for the status of the children, the institutional character of marriage had to be protected. It was protected, first, by the restriction of divorce, and, secondly, by drawing a sharp line between marriage and unmarried cohabitation.

Divorce was either impossible (Italy, Spain, Portugal, France from 1816 to 1884) or to be obtained only under quite restrictive conditions. These conditions related to the grounds for divorce (in most countries only fault divorce, mainly on the ground of adultery, was available), to procedural rules tending to make divorce proceedings much lengthier or burdensome than proceedings in other civil cases (e.g., the imposition of waiting periods and the existence of special rules of proof in the few Romanic legal systems allowing divorce (Articles 239–266 and 281–294 of the Code Napoléon), the necessity to obtain an Act of Parliament in England until 1857 (Phillips 1988 (227–40)), and to the extremely onerous consequences of some divorce forms (the Code Napoléon knew divorce by mutual consent, but it was to be obtained only at the price of the forfeiture of half of the spouses' property to the benefit of their children (Article 305 of the Code Napoléon)). Prussian law formed an exception to this strictness, by allow-

---

[5] E.g. in Sweden illegitimate children had no claims at all against their father until 1917 (Dopffel (1986: 189–92)) (though it should not be forgotten that, as a result of the broad notion of legitimacy in Sweden, Swedish children ran a smaller chance of being considered illegitimate than children in comparable situations in other countries), in Germany the BGB of 1896–1900 excluded them from their father's intestate inheritance and awarded them only maintenance until 16 in accordance with the status of the *mother* (Weber (1907: 560–2)), in England they had no claims at all until 1872, whereafter they could claim a modest maintenance payment until the age of 13 (Weber (1907: 368–9)).

[6] Holthöfer (1987: 171).

ing couples to divorce on the ground of incompatibility (§ 718a of the Allgemeines Landrecht (ALR)) or, if they had no children, by mutual consent (§ 716 ALR). Lest this would be attributed to an early liberalism, it should be pointed out that the relative ease with which divorce could be obtained was explicitly motivated by natalist concerns, it being assumed that incompatible partners would not procreate enough (Dörner (1974: 54–60)).[7]

Insofar as there were any special rules as to the economic consequences of divorce (apart from the rules regarding the division of the community of goods), these consequences weighed exclusively on the guilty party[8] (obviously with the exception of the rare cases in which divorce was not fault based). This might have given women an incentive to divorce, were it not that divorce in many cases was more difficult to obtain against a man than against a woman (thus, neither the Code Napoléon nor the common law recognised adultery as such as a sufficient ground for a divorce claim against the husband, but required an aggravated form of adultery[9]).

Cohabitation outside marriage was ignored by the law, insofar as no positive legal consequences (rights) were attached to it. In the Romanic legal systems contracts and gifts normally allowed between private parties were deemed to be contrary to public order and morals and therefore considered to be void if made between unmarried cohabitees; for the same reason, compensation by way of damages was refused to the surviving partner of someone who had died as a consequence of the tortious behaviour of a third party, in cases in which the payment of damages would have been awarded if there had been no sexual relationship between the cohabiting persons (Carbonnier (1962: 477–80); Hubeau (1985: 270–6 and 314–15)).

The marriage institution was a union of one man and one woman, the man, as husband and father, being the head of the union. Authority within the family and the representation of the family in relation with third parties were in the hands of the husband/father. The duty to maintain was unilateral, from husband to wife; the wife had a complementary duty to obey the husband and to co-operate with him. There were variations within this general picture: in the common law the wife's legal personality was supposed to be absorbed by the husband's (Bromley and Lowe (1987: 103–5)), in Romanic legal systems she retained her legal subjectivity but was denied legal capacity (cp. Articles 213–224 of the Code Napoléon), in Prussia and especially Austria she retained a measure of legal capacity (Weber (1907: 333–4 and 343–4)). The differences, which at the technical level look formidable, should not be exaggerated, however. The English husband's powers were not boundless: his authority to force his wife to obey him did not extend to the right to kill or seriously injure her and was, according to

---

[7] It is noteworthy that divorce by mutual consent and on the ground of incompatibility was not received in other parts of Germany, and that the BGB of 1896/1900 essentially returns to a nearly pure system of fault divorce (Dörner (1974); Phillips (1988: 431); Weber (1907P: 548–9)).

[8] See, e.g., Arts. 299–301 of the Code Napoléon.

[9] See Art. 230 of the Code Napoléon, and for English law: Phillips (1988: 237–8 and 420).

some legal opinions, restricted to cases where her behaviour endangered his property or honour (Bromley and Lowe (1987: 106)); and in equity she could hold
and dispose of the property given her "to her separate use" (Bromley and Lowe
(1987: 497)). The legal subjectivity so royally left to wives in Romanic legal systems, on the other hand, was of little avail to them, since their lack of legal capacity made it impossible for them to transact with third parties without the
husband's consent. Prussian wives did have the legal capacity to administer their
"*Vorbehaltsgut*", but whether they had such property was dependent on the marriage contract, and thus subject to their husband's consent. The most remarkable
exception to the subordinate position of wives was to be found in the Austrian
Allgemeine Bürgerliche Gesetzbuch (ABGB). According to the Austrian code,
the separation of goods was the rule, and everybody had the right to administer
his own property. The practical impact of this rule of autonomous administration was, however, heavily qualified by (i) the rule that the wife had to obey the
husband and execute his orders insofar as necessary for the order of the household (§ 32 ABGB), (ii) the (rebuttable) presumption that the wife had transmitted the right to administer and use her property to the husband (§ 1238 ABGB),
and (iii) the husband's unilateral right to have his wife declared legally incapable
because of the disorderly management of her property (§ 1241 ABGB). In all legal
systems denying legal capacity to wives there was the same pragmatical exception: married women engaging in independent commercial enterprise were, with
certain exceptions, treated as legally competent for matters relating to their commercial activity.

There were differences in the extent of *paternal authority* too: whereas paternal authority both in the Code Napoleon and the Prussian law extended well
beyond the age of majority[10] (among others, limiting the freedom of children to
choose their own spouses), such was not the case in English law. In appreciating
this, it should be borne in mind, however, that in English law, as opposed to the
continental law, inheritances could be disposed of at will by the *de cuius*, with the
consequence that it was possible to disinherit disobedient children. In a society
in which inheritance was the main foundation of social security, the threat thus
hanging over the children must have had an effect on behaviour comparable to
the more direct means of control available in continental law.

Apart from the structure of personal authority of the husband over the wife
and children and from the strict and severely sanctioned requirement of the *wife's
sexual fidelity* (see, e.g., Article 298 of the Code Napoléon), marriage was all about
property relations: a set of rules designed to bring the properties of two families
together, to manage this property, to protect the property originating in the
wife's family from being misused by the husband, and to transmit this property

---

[10] According to the Code Napoléon, the son needed his parents' consent to his marriage until he
was 25 (Art. 148); children of any age who wished to marry without their parents' consent had to go
through laborious and expensive formalities (Arts. 151–158). According to Prussian law, paternal
authority over sons continued until they had established a proper economic basis for their subsistence
(§§ 210 and 212a ALR). Paternal consent to marriage was obligatory *whatever the child's age*, though
a refusal of consent had to be motivated (§§ 45–69 ALR).

to legitimate children. Within this logic, only legitimate descendants were heirs, since they, as opposed to the spouses themselves, belonged to both families. Marital property systems in the nineteenth century extended over the whole range from complete community to separation of goods, but this diversity should not blind one to the realities of property arrangements: practically everywhere marital property relations could be organised contractually in ways deviating considerably from the general model. In fact, in community systems where the wife's contribution would, according to the general rule, be brought under the husband's management, practically no marriages involving large properties would be concluded without built-in contractual devices to restrict the husband's control over the wife's property. More generally, and though this was not propitious to a flexible use of capital, family properties would be organised in the form of trusts or *fideicommissa*, making it impossible for them to be alienated by the individual owner and thus protecting them against dissipation by individual heirs or sons-in-law. (For more information, see especially Rheinstein and Glendon (1980).)

2. Changes and reforms

The picture given in the foregoing section has undergone tremendous change. For the larger part of our period, this change has taken the form of a long and slow accumulation of case law shifting the meaning of legal rules until these rules came to say something quite different from what was originally intended. In most countries, at some time between the late 1950s and the late 1970s a wave of broader legal, mostly legislative reforms was initiated; the pace of change was stepped up enormously, and the world of difference one can observe between present day and nineteenth century family law is mostly a creation of these last decades. There are exceptions to this pattern, however: many reforms which in the rest of the West were to come only in the 1960s, 1970s or 1980s were introduced in the Scandinavian countries from 1915 onwards; and it should also be noted that Portugal had an unexpectedly liberal divorce law in 1910, which was not thereafter entirely discarded by the Salazar regime (Phillips (1988: 505–7, 541–3, 577)).

As a result of the reforms, the *nexus between the marriage institution and the status of the child* has, if not been radically severed, then at least become quite loose. From a practical point of view, this may be far from the most important outcome of the reform process; but from the point of view of the *structure* and *function* of family law it certainly is. If there was, until recently, anything which "marriage" as a social institution had in common if compared over all known cultures, it was that it conferred legitimacy (i.e., access to the resources of a kin group and/or a couple) upon the children (cf. Weber (1985/1922: 213)). If there was anything which made it meaningful for "family law" to be treated as a separate and relatively autonomous object of knowledge, it was the connection between, on the one hand, the regulation of the relations between sexual partners and, on the other hand, the legal conferment of status upon the child and the arrangements regarding its care and education. Abstracting from children, there is no conceivable reason why economic and sexual rights and duties should be tied together, as they used to be in marriage law (and in many legal systems, to a lesser extent than before, still are), nor, indeed, why there should be any *special* regulation of the relations between a cohabiting man and woman; the legal problems following from this cohabitation could, in the absence of children, perfectly well be covered by general property, contract and tort law, whatever gender the cohabitees belong to and whether they have sexual relations or not. Insofar as marriage loses its relevance for the claims and status of children (but we will see that in *no* legal system it has *entirely* lost this relevance), it could just as well stop existing as a separate institution.

Children conceived and born outside marriage have, with some exceptions, obtained the same rights as children born or conceived within marriage. The exceptions pertain to the *access* to inheritances (although in the meantime children born out of wedlock have the right to the same *share* as do the children of a marriage, they do not always have the right to take possession of the inheritance itself, but must sometimes be satisfied with a financial compensation—a distinction not without an edge if there is a family farm or firm; see, e.g., § 1934a German BGB) and to the father's relation to the child. In some legal systems parental authority is a prerogative of the unmarried mother, to be shared with the father only with her consent and to be transferred to him only in exceptional circumstances.[11]

The equalisation of the claims to maintenance and inheritance has, in most cases, taken several steps. The bulk of the reforms has taken place since the late 1960s,[12] and in some cases the reforms were partly the result of pressure due to states' condemnations by the European Human Rights Court.[13]

As a corollary to the equalisation of children's status, both the individual will and biological truth have gained importance in the establishment of parent–child relations (Heyvaert (1995)). As long as a child's legitimate status was dependent upon its parents' marriage and as long as the entry into marriage itself was subject to family control, it would have been illogical to allow a third party (the child's genitor) to intrude into the marriage and rob the child of its legitimate status, to allow the husband's extramarital children to have equal claims against him and his family or to allow individuals to adopt children who would then enter into the family of the adoptive parent. All those hypotheses would have bypassed

---

[11] See, e.g., §§ 1600d and 1705 German BGB, and, for England, the Family Law Reform Act 1987 and Children Act 1989.

[12] See, e.g., the Dutch law of 27 Oct. 1982 (Meijer (1989: 36–7)), the Belgian law of 31 Mar. 1987, *Belgisch Staatsblad*, 27 May 1987, the German law of 19 Aug. 1969, *Bundesgesetzblatt*, 1969, I, 1243, the Swedish law of 1969 (Bradley (1990b: 385)).

[13] The leading case: European Human Rights Court, *Marckx* case, 13 June 1979, *Revue Trimestrielle de Droit Familial*, 1979, 227, holding that it is a violation of Arts. 8 and 14 European Human Rights Convention to withhold rights granted to children from a marriage from children born out of wedlock.

the principle of the acquisition of legitimacy through marriage. If, on the other hand, the difference between being born within or without a marriage is slight anyway and all children tend to the same status, there are no compelling grounds any more to exclude the establishment of parent–child relations on the basis of biological truth or the individual will or behaviour. Hence, the facilitation of adoption and the extension of the rights of adopted children (especially as regards the rights to be maintained by and to inherit from relatives other than the adoptive parents);[14] the (still restricted) possibility for biological truth to prevail over the rule ascribing children to the mother's husband; and the accruing significance of the ascription of parental responsibilities and rights on grounds such as the *fact* of caring for the children, the *fact* of treating them as one's children, etc., rather than on the ground of having the right *status* (i.e., in the first place, the status of the mother's husband[15]).

The disconnection between marriage and the rights of the child finds its limits, however, in the simple fact that, to have equal rights against their father, children must first have a father. It is still the case in every legal system that a father is automatically acquired by the fact of the mother's being married at the time of birth or conception, whereas paternity outside marriage has to be established by an act of will on the father's side or by judicial proceedings.

Now *marriage* has lost the function of conferring legitimacy and controlling children's entry into the family, it is not surprising that it has (to some extent) been *deinstitutionalised*. Deinstitutionalisation follows from two developments.

First, *divorce* has become easily available. In this respect, however, both the extent of liberalisation and its pace show large differences between national systems. Whereas in the Nordic countries access to divorce was already facilitated and marital breakdown grounds for divorce were already introduced in the first third of this century (Glendon (1977: 223–4)), in Spain and Italy divorce was introduced only recently (in 1981 and 1970 respectively). As the Nordic countries in the 1970s and 1980s tended to turn getting a divorce into a formality based on the self-reported breakdown of the relation, most other countries introduced no-fault alternatives in systems until then mainly based on fault. Germany and the Netherlands opted for a pure no-fault system based on the irremediable breakdown of the relation, but in the German case this was qualified by a hardship clause and by bringing the fault criterion in again in the treatment of the consequences of divorce. In countries like Italy, Belgium or France getting a divorce through the courts can still take several years.

---

[14] E.g. in Germany the adoption of minors has the same legal consequences as other parent–child relations only since the 1976 adoption law (*Bundesgesetzblatt*, 1976, I, 1749), in England (with some exceptions) since the Adoption of Children Act 1949.
[15] This trend is exemplified by the English Children Act 1989, which conceptually separates parental responsibility, a matter of who has the care of the child, from legal parenthood and makes it possible for parental responsibility to be vested in non-parents, even in state authorities (see Eekelaar (1994: 83–9)).

If obtaining a divorce has become much easier, its economic consequences often amount to a perpetuation of marriage under another name, especially in countries like Belgium, Italy or France, where lifelong alimony payments are not unusual, or can, even if a clean break policy is pursued, be quite onerous or deterrent, e.g. in cases where rights over the marital home are not allocated according to the rules of property law, but, in the presence of children, are made dependent on need. Although in Sweden, where the deinstitutionalisation of marriage may have progressed the most, alimony is awarded only in exceptional circumstances, redistribution of rights in the marital home (surely for most people the most important asset) can be effected.

The privileged position of marriage has not only been undermined by the relaxation of divorce rules, but also by the disappearance of legal sanctions for *unmarried cohabitation* and by the extension of marital rights to relations between cohabitees. This extension has started rather early in social security law and housing law, and has, in some countries (e.g. Germany) not (yet) penetrated family law. To a modest extent, the use of legal techniques from property law and contract law has made it possible, in some other countries (e.g. England, France), to obtain more or less the same results with regard to the division of property upon household break-up as in family law. Several countries now have laws which make it impossible for one partner, whether married or cohabiting outside marriage, to dispose of his rights in the marital home without the consent of the other partner; and sometimes, especially when there are minor children in the household, the use of this dwelling can, regardless of property or lease title, for a very long time after the breakdown of the relationship be granted to the partner taking care of the children. In Swedish law, the practically most important economic consequence of marriage, the right in the marital home, has been extended to cohabitees; and there is equality between married people and cohabitees in the fields of welfare and tax law (Hakansson (1989); Müller-Freienfels (1993: 761–2)). It is true that in Sweden this convergence is not only a result of the institutionalisation of cohabitation, but just as much of the reduction of post-divorce claims and of the more general individualisation of rights in welfare and tax law; but it is not the less striking for that.

It should be noted that these developments, though undermining the central position of formal marriage, amount to a reinstitutionalisation of household relations. What has happened is, therefore, not so much that marriage has been simply deinstitutionalised by the recognition of an alternative life style, but rather that the boundaries of marriage as a (weakened) institution have been extended beyond the boundaries of the legal term "marriage".

At the same time marriage has undergone a process of deinstitutionalisation, radical change has overcome its internal *authority structure*. The rights and duties of husbands and wives have everywhere been equalised. Parental authority is now shared equally between the father and the mother; an exception to this is formed by the status of the unmarried father in some legal systems (*vide supra*). However, parental authority nowadays does not have the same meaning as paternal power had in the nineteenth century. The exercise of parental authority is subject to general standards formulated by the state. This exercise is controlled by state institutions, and parental authority or some of its attributes may be taken away from the parents if its exercise is judged to be abusive. In general, this control is quite marginal; it is more extensive in the Scandinavian states, and is there exercised by administrative authorities not subject to much judicial control.

Gender difference is still a condition for entry into marriage and for shared parenthood. In Denmark, Sweden, Norway and the Netherlands, however, under different forms laws have been introduced extending either the rights of spouses or the (not unconsiderable) rights of cohabitees to partners of the same gender.[16] Until now, the rights relating to parent–child relations have been specifically excluded from this institutionalisation of same gender relations, although, if newspaper reports are to be believed, this may change soon.

The principle of *monogamy* has been maintained, but surreptitiously polygamy has been introduced in many family law systems. This is obvious as far as serial polygamy is concerned: where the remarriage of the widowed and divorced is allowed, serial polygamy will ensue; but this is nothing special, and, with a few exceptions, common to all known societies. But, less obviously, simultaneous polygamy has been introduced. This follows from four developments. First, insofar as Western legal orders are confronted with the legal consequences of polygamous marriages entered into validly in legal systems which explicitly recognise polygamy, there is a tendency to accept (some of) these consequences, which in earlier times used to be considered to be contrary to public order. Secondly, the combination of remarriage with the (sometimes) lifelong subsistence of some of the economic rights and duties of a former marriage has the effect that one person can have simultaneous institutional relations with two or more partners. Thirdly, the institutionalisation of unmarried cohabitation does just as well produce situations in which the same person has institutional rights and duties *vis-à-vis* two partners (one the spouse, the other the cohabitee). Fourthly, the fact that it has now become possible for a man simultaneously to have children with a fully legal status with two or more different women, would in any other society be considered to be the surest sign of the legality of polygamy, it being the case that in all societies hitherto marriage was co-defined by its monopoly of legitimacy.

The foregoing developments have a lot to do with changes in the subject matter of family law. Marriage is not any longer in the first place an institution

---

[16] Denmark (1989; see Boele-Woelki and Tange (1989); Nielsen (1990)), Sweden (1995; see Saldeen (1995: 508)) and Norway (1993; see Lodrup (1995: 375)) all have laws on "registered partnership" granting the same rights to registered same gender partners as to spouses, with the exception of the rights pertaining to children and, in Sweden, of some special economic benefits provided to married women and widows. In Sweden, the Lag om homosexuella sambor of 18 June 1987 (*Svensk författ-tningssammling* (1987: 813)) had already extended cohabitees' rights to partners of the same gender, and this law is still applicable to same gender couples who have not had their relation registered. At the time of writing this chapter, the Dutch law on registered partnership had just entered into force.

for the management and transmission of the means of production, but it has become a *social security institution* mainly concerned with the management and distribution of income and of durable consumption goods. This can be illustrated by reference to: the already mentioned laws regarding rights to the marital home; rules concerning the use of individual rights during marriage; marital property systems; and inheritance law. In continental legal systems, rules abound to ensure that, during marriage, rights are not exercised in ways detrimental to family interests (e.g., limitations of the freedom to make gifts). Marital property systems, whether starting from the principle of community or separation of goods or from a combination of both, tend, using different legal techniques, to converge to solutions which leave the spouses a certain (but in the above mentioned sense restricted) freedom of using their property as long as marriage lasts, but to throw most property items into one pot, to be divided between husband and wife, upon the dissolution of marriage. This would obviously not do if marital property systems reflected the property interests of the larger families, but it is more or less adequate as a solution for a situation in which two individuals have collaborated and pooled their resources, and then decide to separate. In this kind of family set-up, inheritances too acquire new functions; they serve not so much as a mode of transmission of the means of production to the next generation, but rather as a prolongation of the social security community dissolved by the death of one of the partners.

3. Synthesis

Generally speaking, the history of family law in Western Europe over the last 200 years can thus be seen to be characterised by:

1. the breakdown of the distinction between legitimate and illegitimate children;
2. a considerable relaxation of the conditions for divorce; combined, however, with
3. the partial survival, in many cases, of the dissolved marriage as a result of the economic consequences of divorce;
4. a convergence, in most cases still quite modest, of marriage and unmarried (but partly institutionalised) cohabitation;
5. a fundamental shift from marriage as a set of rules for managing properties originating in two distinct families to marriage as a set of rules organising social security and material solidarity within the nuclear group;
6. a change in the patterns of legal authority in the family, by the equalisation of husband and wife (as partners and as parents) and the limitation of parental rights;
7. the recent emergence of exceptions to the principles of gender difference between the partners and of monogamy (exceptions which in the first case are still rare, in the second case more widespread but largely unnoticed).

Tendencies 1 and 2 point to a deinstitutionalisation of marriage, 3 and 4 to a measure of reinstitutionalisation. The institution upheld by 3 and 4 is, however, of a much weaker kind than traditional marriage used to be. It is a relationship into which women need not enter to safeguard their children from bastardy, to which entry is no longer controlled by the larger family (and, in the case of institutionalised unmarried cohabitation, is hardly controlled at all), and from which one can escape (at a price) even if the other party has consistently fulfilled her duties.

There are considerable national variations in the picture. The liberalisation of divorce conditions and procedures was early in the Scandinavian countries and, with the exception of Portugal, late in the Southern countries; and there is no convergence as yet, if one contrasts the ease with which it is nowadays possible to get a divorce in the Scandinavian countries, England and the Netherlands with the complications (and the still important place of fault divorce besides other divorce grounds) still to be encountered in Spain, Portugal, Italy, France and Belgium. If unmarried cohabitation, even of people married to a third party, is nowadays nowhere any longer considered to be an infringement of public order or morals, its positive recognition in family law (as opposed to welfare law) is, with the exception of the Scandinavian countries, still minimal. The extension of this recognition to same sex couples has been limited to the Scandinavian countries and the Netherlands. The equalisation of husband and wife has taken place in the Scandinavian countries much earlier than in other countries. The same holds for the implementation of state control on the exercise of parental rights; it is also the case that the restrictions on this exercise cut deeper in the Scandinavian countries than elsewhere.

These are still differences at a quite general level. If one looks at the facts in some more detail, many (seeming) anomalies, such as the 1910 liberalisation of divorce in Portugal, emerge. There is no general system to be found in an overview of these differences, but for one thing: *since the early twentieth century, the Nordic countries, more often than not led by Sweden, have been in the vanguard of reform.*

B. AN EXPLANATORY SCHEME

Several ways of explaining the developments synthesised here suggest themselves. Some try to explain them by reference to factors internal to the law. Thus, e.g., the equalisation of husband and wife and of children born within or outside wedlock can be seen as an outcome of the gradual realisation of the legal principle of equality of all before the law. A corollary of this kind of approach is that family laws should differ in accordance with the differences between legal families; differences should be especially pronounced between common law and civil law systems (e.g., Castles and Flood (1991)). Others tend to explain legal change by ideological change: the law has come to be reformed because people's ideas about the relationships between important values such as liberty and solidarity and their representations of how gender and parent–child relations should be ordered have undergone change (see, e.g., as to the explanation of Scandinavian progressiveness: Graversen (1990); Rheinstein (1972: chapter 6)). Rather than to argue here why I consider such "explanations" to be insufficient, I will present an alternative explanation and hope that it speaks for itself.[17]

My approach leans on an already quite old tradition, which tries to explain the order of the family by its social, mainly economic, functions (cp. Engels (1975/1884); Goody (1976, 1990); Heyvaert (1995); Kahn-Freund (1971)). The existence and long term development of *institutions* (sets of rules), as opposed to the occurrence of *events*, cannot be explained by the intentions of the involved agents alone. Rules do not exist and survive simply because some agent of law creation has taken a decision. They only survive (in the sense of being applied and having consequences, whether intended or not intended, in social life) because of the functions they have for their users. It is to these functions we must look if we want to understand why the law has developed as it has.

It should, however, be clear, that the law cannot be derived directly from social needs. For rules to be changed, a conscious pursuit of purposes by social actors in a position to influence the rule-making process is required. Such pursuit is costly and will therefore only be undertaken if existing rules are felt to have shortcomings justifying the presumed cost of changing them, and if there are no alternative and less costly courses of action available which could serve as a functional equivalent for changing the rules. Whether, how and when changes in social needs will lead to changes in the law, will be dependent on (i) the relevance of the law for behaviour, (ii) the means at the disposal of interested parties, (iii) the nature of the rule making process (e.g., whether this process is democratic or in the hands of a political or professional elite). As long as law has *some* relevance to behaviour, some point in time must be reached where the discrepancies between the law and social needs become so stressing that something has to happen. This "something" might conceivably be the suppression of the social needs or the emergence of a widespread disregard for the law, but it is highly likely that, in a democratic regime with a rule of law ideology, the law will be changed instead. The pace of developments will then be determined by the factors mentioned above.

The explanation runs as follows. In the predominantly agrarian societies of the beginning of our period land was, obviously, the main source of wealth and the foundation of social security. Economic units were mostly households, consisting of members of the nuclear or stem family together with servants and kinsmen staying as a transitory phase in their lives. The usual way to acquire land was by inheritance[18] from one's family. Thus, survival was determined by family soli-

---

[17] For a critique of the above mentioned approaches and a methodological defence of my own approach, see Willekens (1997: 73–80).

[18] "Inheritance" in the broad sense of the intergenerational transmission of property, i.e. including arrangements *inter vivos*.

darity. This was not only the case for children who inherited, but also for their parents (who, for their survival in old age, depended on children taking over the exploitation of the farm) and for the children who did not inherit the farm (they were dependent on family production because they lived in on the farm, because the money earned by selling the farm's products could buy them an entry into a non-agricultural career, or, in the case of daughters, for the dowry enabling them to marry).[19]

Family solidarity was not much less important for the rising bourgeoisie and industrial capitalists. Capital had to be brought together and held together at a time when investment credit was much less developed than it is now. Trustworthy business partners had to be found in remote places. The problems of trust and of financing enterprise could, at least partly, be solved by marriages between the children of (aspiring) capitalists (cf. Goody (1996)). An accumulation of such marriages led to the formation of networks tying diverse families to each other. In the capitalist world from before the rise of the great corporations these ties were of the utmost importance for the involved families' economic success. In this world, marriage was something quite different from the formalisation of a personal relationship. It was, in more than one sense, family business.

As a result of the further development of industrial capitalism, land lost its central position as the foundation of social security for more and more people. It was replaced by wage labour as the primary source of the means of existence. Wage labour is an individual mode of access to these means; even if labour power is partly a product of family work (by virtue of the worker as a child having been cared for and socialised in a family and possibly still being cared for by a spouse or cohabitee), it is possible for a wage worker to thrive as an isolated individual, especially since the risks of not being able to work or not to find a buyer for one's labour power are, in most developed capitalist societies, covered by a collectivised social security system. This is not to the same extent true for entrepreneurs, for although big business could function very well without family relations (it does not, but that is another story: see Scott (1979)), small enterprises are still, for the same reasons as but somewhat less than in the pioneer times of capitalism, dependent on family solidarity (see Goody (1996)). As a result of this development, the greater part of the population could now survive without family solidarity. In fact—always with the exception of the relatively small group of the owners of substantial means of production—there would seem to be only one barrier left to complete individualisation: the immaturity of the human infant, whose care to an extent binds at least one adult to him. This individual (usually the mother) is, because of this work of care, severely handicapped in the competition in a market economy; barring social security provisions which would fully substitute the state for the father (and which do not prevail anywhere), the fact that rearing children is hard work remains a good reason (at least for women) to found families.

---

[19] See, e.g., Burguière, Klapisch-Zuber, Segalen and Zonabend (1986: 59–91); Seccombe 1992, and many contributions in the *Journal of Family History*.

Keeping this simplified overview of socio-economic developments in mind, the *general tendencies* of change in family law become comprehensible.

A good starting point for our explanatory scheme are the changes in the *economic content* of marriage; most of the other changes will be seen to follow from these. In the nineteenth century marriage brought two properties together; the fate of these properties was often determined by prenuptial contract. They were to be managed by the husband, but securities were built in to safeguard the interests of the wife and her family. The economic rights and duties of the spouses *vis-à-vis* each other were restricted to, at the most, a maintenance duty for the husband and a duty to co-operate with him for the wife, and with respect to the first duty enforcement mechanisms were what one could call underdeveloped. There was no or only a restricted inheritance right for the surviving spouse. Nowadays, the economic claims of the spouses *vis-à-vis* each other have been multiplied. Whatever their property rights as individuals may be, their rights to use and dispose of their income, the marital home and durable household goods have become relation oriented and have, as a result, become heavily qualified as individual rights. Enforcement mechanisms have been introduced. The inheritance rights of the surviving spouse have been extended. This transformation of the economic duties between spouses is to be explained by a combination of a certain loss of function of the old family law for the owners of means of production; an increased importance of some form of relation-oriented family law for the many non-owners of means of production; and the extension of democracy. As pointed out above, capitalism has become partly defamilialised; stakes in the family of the owners of the means of production have diminished. At the same time a huge mass of proletarians (in the sense of people who have to earn their living by selling their labour power) has been created, who have attained a relatively high level of welfare. Proletarianisation in itself would have had no impact on family law, for those who have nothing to lose but their chains have nothing to gain from family law: economic rights and duties make sense only if there is a material substance to which they can apply. It is only because the larger part of those who live off their wage labour have become modestly well-off that a new family law has become functional. This new situation of the existence of a large "middle group" of people who do not substantially own means of production, but still possess quite valuable consumption goods, and whose property has been self-acquired instead of inherited, poses new questions *re* the intrafamilial distribution of income and consumption goods. This is obvious for the still common case of a gendered division of labour between husband and wife, wherein the wife, even if earning her own income, disproportionately bears the burden of child care and household work; but it is also the case for those instances in which the partners share these burdens equally and, to be able to do so, have agreed to curtail their opportunities in the market. In both cases, at least one partner has given up individual opportunities for securing her material existence with the purpose of taking care of the children (and, to some extent, of the other partner); this is, in an otherwise individualised society, only workable insofar as the nuclear family functions as a social security device which redistributes the income acquired by market participation.

It has regularly been pointed out that the provision of social security and diverse welfare rights by the state is a functional substitute for family solidarity and that it is therefore to be expected that the growth of welfare claims against the state would go hand in hand with a loss of functionality of family law and a deinstitutionalisation of marriage (e.g., Heyvaert (1979–1980); Glendon (1981)). According to the logic of this argument, the new family law centred on household solidarity might itself be a transitory phenomenon on the way to a situation in which family law would have lost most of its significance, its functions being taken over by the state. It has in the meantime become clear that there are limits to the extension of welfare rights, which does not impugn the argument, but raises doubts about the prediction of the withering away of family law. But one can also question the argument itself. First, those best protected by state financed social security law are those (mostly men) well integrated in the exchange economy; the ones who need family law protection the most are those (most of the time women, and of course children) who are not well integrated in this economy. Secondly, the state, insofar as it guarantees social security to all, only guarantees a minimum, sufficient to survive, but certainly not covering most social needs or allowing for full social integration; even if family law can offer more only in a minority of cases, it is a significant instrument of social security for the families of the well-off salaried, and an instrument for which there is no functional substitute. Although family law and the welfare state have the same basic function of guaranteeing social security, they are not simply functional alternatives, but to a considerable extent fulfil the said function for different groups.

If the above specifies the *economic conditions* for the creation of new economic rights and duties between the spouses, these conditions were not yet sufficient to ensure changes in family law. The extension of democracy was the *political condition* under which the new configuration of interests could give rise to a new family law; in the absence of a democracy in which these interests could find a representation, there would not have been much of an incentive to reform family law.[20] (It should be pointed out, however, that the necessity of making compromises, which is a daily fact of life in most democracies, may have slackened the pace of reform in some countries—a fact which might contribute to an explanation of the special position of Scandinavian law, since it appears that Scandinavian democracies are characterised by a greater degree of consensus and thus a lesser degree of having to work out contorted compromises than other European democracies (cf. Battail, Boyer and Fournier (1992)).).

---

[20] At least, this is true when comparing generalised democracy with concensus democracy. When comparing democracy with modern, totalitarian dictatorships, the question is more complicated: since such dictatorships are much less hindered by the need to take all interests and opinions into account than democracies, they have much more freedom *both* to refrain from responding to new social needs *and* to innovate beyond what the population would like.

Once one knows how and why the economic content of marriage has changed, other changes in family law become comprehensible. Any marriage system has to cope with the problem of the breakdown of relations. As long as husband and wife are tied to farm and land because there is no realistic alternative for survival, the divorce question does not arise: whether husband and wife like each other or not, voluntary separation is out of the question. But once economic alternatives arise, first with urbanisation, and then, exponentially, with the development of capitalism, or simply, in an agricultural context, because one's family is so rich that it could afford to take back an unhappily married daughter, it becomes unavoidable that marriage breakdowns occur and that pressures emerge to give an institutional form (in general: divorce) to the consequences of the breakdown. These pressures will be withstood as long as there are weighty interests to do so: as long as marriage was a way of bringing together land or capital or of forging political or business alliances, access to divorce could be expected to be highly restricted, because the fate of the marriage was not important for the spouses alone, but was of the highest economic importance to their families. The families exercised control over the access to marriage (and, since only marriage children were legitimate, thereby also over the access of children to families), undoubtedly to a large extent by economic pressure, but also with the support of family law rules extending paternal authority beyond the age of majority. It would have been illogical to leave it to the emotions of the spouses to decide whether a complex family alliance was allowed to survive or not. The only way of preventing catastrophes of the kind was to have a tight divorce law; the only functional alternative I can think of would have been an extension of paternal authority to the married and without age limits, but this alternative would at the same time have been inferior, because it would have contained no solution for the (until the early twentieth century quite frequent) case of a (relatively early) decease of the father and would have been a hindrance of married sons' management of their household economy, it would also be more difficult to maintain, because it would unavoidably have exacerbated the generation conflict. It is worth pointing out that the functional optimum did not lie in a simple prohibition of divorce under all circumstances, for there were always bound to be situations in which a marriage had become both unbearable to the spouses and deleterious to the interests of one or both of the families. The functional optimum was something like divorce under strict conditions, and it was in fact approached in most legal systems, even in those Southern countries where divorce *as such* was unknown, for there the nullity of marriage, in the canon law tradition construed quite broadly, could be used as a functional alternative to divorce.

With the defamilialisation of capitalism and the economic loss of importance of landed property, the interests weighing against an easy divorce became weaker. The relaxation of divorce law was still upheld for a time by the temporary generalisation of the model of marriage as a union of the husband-provider and the wife-housekeeper—a model which made the wife wholly dependent on the husband and thus implied a strong argument against easy divorce. Once this model itself had broken down, divorce was liberalised as far as conditions and procedures were concerned. That it was *not* liberalised as to its consequences (which nowadays often can weigh on both partners, as opposed to the earlier days of fault divorce, when at least the innocent ex-spouse was freed of all marital duties) is perfectly in tune with the new social security functions of marriage: there would be no social *security* if a *full* and rapid exit from the relationship were possible and each partner could simply take his assets with him.

The nearly completed tendency towards the deconstruction of the distinction between legitimate and illegitimate children can be explained within the same logic. As long as marriages were elements in family strategies and ways of planning the transmission of the means of production to the next generation(s), it would have been highly inconvenient to have these strategies countered by the claims of children from unplanned unions. Had these children, in many cases the result of a sexual relationship between a man from a wealthy family and a woman from a poor family, had equal rights, they would have been burdens to a family (and have disturbed its economic strategies) without this family getting anything out of the bargain. The whole point of controlling the entry into marriage and of restricting divorce would have been lost if the offspring of uncontrollable liaisons would have been allowed to lay claims to the family property. As the said family strategies became less and less important, the rights of children born out of wedlock could be extended.

What remains of the old distinction between legitimate and illegitimate children is mainly the benefit of the paternity rule: the children of a marriage have a father without having to prove anything, which is not necessarily the case for children born out of wedlock (albeit that even this distinction has been weakened by the facilitation of paternity contestations). This is less an archaic remnant still to be washed away by the tides of progress than a rule which survives in the interests of children: without it the position of children born from a marriage would be less secure, and the position of the other children no more secure than it is now.

As a result of the abolition of the penalties for adultery and of the introduction of no fault divorce the sexual duties of the spouses (fidelity, the duty to have sexual relations) tend to become sanctionless. This is concomitant with the breakdown of the distinction between legitimacy and illegitimacy: if all children have the same rights versus their natural parents, whatever the civil status of these may be, an important rationale for sanctioning adultery disappears.

If the main contemporary function of marriage is the social security of the nuclear group, then there is not much ground left to distinguish between marriage and cohabitation. What matters is the factual existence and functioning of the nuclear group, not its formal character. There are no compelling reasons to withhold legal consequences from the fact of cohabitation. There may be policy reasons, though, leading the state to differentiate between married and unmarried cohabitation, e.g. in those cases where a marriage and a cohabitation are in competition and where one might prefer to give priority to the partner and children to whom the first engagement was taken (just as one might prefer to privilege the present household formation over the former one). Insofar as the social security union is no longer necessarily supposed to go hand in hand with a specific division of labour by gender (as is suggested by the equalisation of all rights and duties of husbands and wives), there would seem to be no good reasons to institutionalise micro-level social security arrangements between people of the same gender either.

The main reforms of inheritance law exactly fit the foregoing scheme. This has already been made clear with regard to the status of children born out of wedlock. It also holds true for the extension of inheritance rights to the surviving spouse: since inheritances have lost their function as the foundation of existence for the next generation, they have become available as an element of social security for the widow; and since it has become unusual that the wife, upon marriage, is provided with a protected property of her own stemming from her family of origin, such as a dowry or trust, inheritance from the husband has become more of a necessity.

The changes in the structure of authority within marriage are a consequence, not so much of changes in the social function of marriage, but of changes in the economic position of women: insofar as women have their own, individual sources of income and enter the labour market as men do, it is hardly tenable to keep them subordinated within marriage; and, in fact, the logic of the market demands that they can make their own decisions and that the allocation of their labour power should not be subject to the husbands' arbitrary choices. It could be objected that this logic was already in place in the nineteenth century and at that time did not lead to the abolition of women's subordination. But this can easily be explained: proletarian husbands did not need the law to keep them from withholding their wives' labour power from the market, for the harsh dictates of economic need did not allow them this option anyway; and in all legal systems exceptions to the wife's legal incapacity were provided for so as to enable bourgeois wives to engage in trade.

Husbands' and wives' formal equality will still, in many cases, coexist with inegalitarian life arrangements and a division of labour by gender; but this does not make legal equality dysfunctional. On the contrary, the present combination of equal rights with elaborate solidarity duties allows for the accommodation of quite diverse life arrangements: it is obviously compatible with egalitarian relations, but also with a division of tasks in which the husband is the main provider and the wife the homemaker (or vice versa). The gender-neutral rules granting an autonomy to the spouses (such as the right to choose their own profession or to cash their own income) are meaningless for a spouse who is not in a position to exercise this autonomy (because, e.g., she does not have a job or an income) and therefore do not impede inegalitarian practices; and the gender neutral rules prescribing solidarity (such as the duty to contribute to household expenses) are perfectly applicable to all couples, whatever their division of labour. The considerable advantage of the gender neutrality of the rules is that, contrary to rules giving decision taking priority to one party, they are compatible with all the varied lifestyles which at present exist besides each other (gender neutral divisions of labour, households with a housewife or houseman, and all the intermediate forms) and with the different divisions of labour the same couple may go through in different phases of the lifecycle—although gender neutrality will obviously produce different effects in different divisions of labour.

If all the foregoing legal changes can be functionally explained by the emergence of a new family type, this might appear not to be the case for the tendency to recognise and institutionalise polygamy. For if legal claims can be made against the same person in more than one family unit, the social security of all family units involved might be threatened; and that surely is dysfunctional for the new family type. It is, however, an inevitable by-product of other tendencies: if divorce is easy, but the dissolved marriage still survives in some of its economic consequences, if unmarried cohabitation is increasingly institutionalised, and if one can simultaneously have legitimate children with a spouse and with a lover, then the situations in which marriage-like claims against the same person can be made by several partners and by children from different relations are bound to multiply.

All this, if true, still does not explain (i) why the bulk of the reforms, except in the Scandinavian countries, has come so late, and (ii) whence the national differences.

The explanation of (i) follows from the above scheme in a straightforward way. The changes in family law are not *simply* a consequence of the emergence of industrial capitalism, with its tendency to reduce people to individuals competing in the market; if it were that simple, family law should have been deinstitutionalised much earlier, more radically and in the first place in the countries where industrial capitalism knew its first triumphs, i.e. England and Belgium. The limits of deinstitutionalisation are to be found in the vulnerability of human children, who have to be cared for for a long time and who remain economically dependent for a still much longer time. As long as the burden this places on mothers is not fully socialised, the institutions of paternity and marriage (or institutionalised cohabitation) remain necessary. The apparent tardiness of legal change is to be explained by three factors inherent in the above scheme:

— the important role of family capital and family alliances in the development of capitalism in the nineteenth century, especially in the countries where capitalism knew an early development;
— the fact that proletarianisation in itself was not sufficient to exert pressure towards a new family law, but only became so when groups of wage workers attained welfare levels high enough for wives to give up wage work and for the households to acquire durable consumption goods. It was only after these conditions had been fulfilled (and in most instances they were to be fulfilled only after World War II), that a new family law, oriented towards income management and the use of consumption goods in the nuclear family, became functional;

— the emergence of the political conditions (in general, extended democracy as compared to census democracy) under which these interests would be translated into new legal rules.

National differences are far too manifold to try to tackle their explanation here, but some words at least must be said about Scandinavian peculiarism. How to explain the early timing and radicality with which reforms in Scandinavia have been pursued ? I will concentrate on Sweden, in many instances the forerunner in these developments.

In a sense, the explanation follows in a straightforward way from the above scheme. What is special about Sweden is not the nature of the reforms its family law has undergone—for all have evolved in the same direction—but the fact that these reforms have not been slowed down as they have been in more southern countries. An attempt at explanation should therefore in the first place look to the *absence* in Sweden of the causal elements at work in other cases.

First, the family has retained much less of a function in production relations in Sweden than in some other countries. Industrialisation and capitalism came comparatively late to Sweden, were from the beginning strongly supported and influenced by the state, and led swiftly to a high degree of capital concentration; the family had only a marginal role to play in this economic development and was therefore deprived of its function in production relations in a much more brusque way than in other countries (Battail, Boyer and Fournier (1992)).

Secondly, although Sweden has a very effective system of the enforcement of the economic duties of parents (Glendon (1987)), family law is a much less needed form of protection of women and children against the risks of the breakdown of the partner relationship in Sweden than in most other countries. There are two grounds for this. Swedish women are nearly all in employment and, even if their position in the labour market is worse than men and many only work part time, they enjoy some measure of financial independence. Furthermore, abandoned partners' and children's risks are partly covered by welfare provisions (Scheiwe (1998)). This last point can also explain the extent of state intervention in the exercise of parental rights in Sweden (see section 2): the more the state directly takes care of children, the more it will feel itself legitimised (and will be felt by people to be legitimised) to interfere in their upbringing.

Thirdly, political conditions in Sweden were more conducive to a rapid adaptation of the law to changes in social needs than in most other countries. If generalised democracy was a condition for the reform of family law, as claimed above, then at the same time reform in most Western European democracies was hampered by the necessity to work out contorted compromises with coalition partners or social forces. In Sweden, Social Democracy dominated political life for several decades, most of the time governing alone. Moreover, Swedish society has been characterised to an uncommon degree by consensus on issues such as gender equality and the collective provision of a decent level of welfare to all; no marked difference in family policies is noticeable even in periods during which

Social Democracy did not have a parliamentary majority. To a certain extent, the absence of deep ideological conflicts probably results from the incorporation of the Protestant Church in the state. Whereas the Catholic Church, being an international organisation with independent infrastructures and means of existence, is a (potentially) countervailing power in both dominantly Catholic and mixed countries, therefore a power with which the state has to compromise or struggle, the Protestant Church has no such function, and is therefore much less of an impediment to family law reform than the Catholic Church can be.

REFERENCES

AGELL, A. (1980), "The Swedish Legislation on Marriage and Cohabitation: A Journey without a Destination", *Scandinavian Studies in Law*, 9–48.

BATTAIL, J., BOYER, R., and FOURNIER, V. (1992), *Les sociétés scandinaves de la Réforme à nos jours* (Paris, PUF).

BERMAN, H. (1983), *Law and Revolution. The Formation of the Western Legal Tradition* (Cambridge, Mass., Harvard University Press).

BOELE-WOELKI, K., and TANGE, P. (1989), "De Deense wet inzake het geregistreerd partnerschap. Een voorbeeld voor Nederland ?", *NJB*, 1537–43.

BRADLEY, D. (1990a), "Perspectives on Sexual Equality in Sweden", *Modern Law Review*, 283–303.

—— (1990b), "Marriage, Family, Property and Inheritance in Swedish Law", *I.C.L.Q.*, 370–95.

BROMLEY, P. and LOWE, N. (1987), *Family Law* (London, Butterworths).

BURGUIERE, A., KLAPISCH-ZUBER, C., SEGALEN, M. and ZONABEND, F. (1986), *Histoire de la famille*, II, *Le choc des modernités* (Paris, Colin).

CARBONNIER, J. (1962), *Droit civil*, I, *Introduction à l' étude du droit et droit des personnes* (Paris, PUF).

DÖRNER, H. (1974), *Industrialisierung und Familienrecht. Die Auswirkungen des sozialen Wandels dargestellt an den Familienmodellen des ALR, BGB und des französischen Code civil* (Berlin, Duncker & Humblot).

DOPFFEL, P. (1986), "Entwicklung des Erbrechts in Schweden und Finnland", in W. Wagner (ed.), *Das schwedische Reichsgesetzbuch (Sveriges Rikes Lag) von 1734. Beiträge zur Entstehungs- und Entwicklungsgeschichte einer vollständigen Kodifikation* (Frankfurt-am-Main, Klostermann), 185–269.

EEKELAAR, J. (1994), "Parenthood, Social Engineering and Rights", in D. Morgan and G. Douglas (eds.), *Constituting Families: A Study in Governance* (Stuttgart, Steiner), 80–97.

ENGELS, F. (1975, originally 1884), "Der Ursprung der Familie, des Privateigenthums und des Staats", in K. Marx and F. Engels, *Werke*, XXI (East Berlin, Dietz), 25–172.

Glendon, M. (1977), *State, Law and Family: Family Law in Transition in the United States and Western Europe* (Amsterdam, North Holland Publishing Company).

—— (1981), *The New Family and the New Property* (Toronto, Butterworths).

—— (1987), *Abortion and Divorce in Western Law* (Cambridge, Mass., Harvard University Press).

Glendon, M. (1989), *The Transformation of Family Law. State, Law and Family in the United States and Western Europe* (Chicago, Ill., Chicago University Press).

GOODE, W. (1992), "World Changes in Divorce Patterns", in L. Weitzman and M. Maclean (eds.), *Economic Consequences of Divorce. The International Perspective* (Oxford, Clarendon), 11–49.

GOODY, J. (1976), "Inheritance, Property and Women: Some Comparative Considerations", in J. Goody, J. Thirsk and E. Thompson (eds.), *Family and Inheritance. Rural Society in Western Europe 1200–1800* (Cambridge, Cambridge University Press), 10–36.

—— (1983), *The Development of the Family and Marriage in Europe* (Cambridge, Cambridge University Press).

—— (1990), *The Oriental, the Ancient and the Primitive. Systems of Marriage and the Family in the Pre-Industrial Societies of Eurasia* (Cambridge, Cambridge University Press).

—— (1996), *The East in the West* (Cambridge, Cambridge University Press).

GRAVERSEN, J. (1990), "Family Law as a Reflection of Family Ideology", *Scandinavian Studies in Law* 69–91

HAKANSSON, G. (1989), "Die rechtliche Behandlung der nichtehelichen Lebensgemeinschaften in Schweden", in U. Blaurock (ed.), *Entwicklungen im Recht der Familie und der ausserehelichen Lebensgemeinschaften* (Frankfurt-am-Main), 9–20.

HEYVAERT, A. (1979–1980), "Het wezen van de instituten afstamming en huwelijk", *Rechtskundig Weekblad* 737–70.

—— (1995), *Het personen- en gezinsrecht ont(k)leed* (Gent, Mys & Breesch).

HOLTHÖFER, E. (1987), "Fortschritte in der Erbrechtsgesetzgebung seit der französischen Revolution", in H. Mohnhaupt (ed.), *Zur Geschichte des Familien- und Erbrechts. Politische Implikationen und Perspektiven* (Frankfurt am Main, Klostermann), 121–75.

HUBEAU, B. (1985), *Ongehuwd samenwonen. Relatiewerkelijkheid en de integratie van ongehuwd samenwonen in rechtssystemen* (Antwerp, Kluwer).

International Encyclopedia of Comparative Law, IV, *Persons and Family*, Chloros, A. (ed.) (Tübingen, Mohr), 1972–80.

KAHN-FREUND, O. (1971), "Matrimonial Property and Equality before the Law: Some Sceptical Reflections", *Human Rights Journal* 493–510.

LODRUP, P. (1995), "Family Law in Norway" in C. Hamilton and K. Standley (eds.), *Family Law in Europe* (London, Butterworths), 353–75.

MEIJER, W. (1989), "De ontwikkeling in het personen-, familie- en erfrecht", in E. Luijten and others, *146 jaar Burgerlijk Wetboek* (Deventer, Kluwer), 29–47.

MÜLLER-FREIENFELS, W. (1993), "Rechtsfolgen nichtehelicher Gemeinschaften und Eheschließungsrecht" in H. Lange, K. Nörr and H. Westermann (eds.), *Festschrift für Joachim Gernhuber zum 70. Geburtstag* (Tübingen, Mohr), 737–79.

NIELSEN, L. (1990), "Family Rights and the 'Registered Partnership' in Denmark", *International Journal of Law and the Family* 297–307.

PHILLIPS, R. (1988), *Putting Asunder. A History of Divorce in Western Society* (Cambridge, Cambridge University Press).

RHEINSTEIN, M. (1972), *Marriage Stability, Divorce and the Law* (Chicago, Ill., University of Chicago Press).

—— and GLENDON, M. (1980), "Interspousal Relations", ch. 4 of A. Chloros (ed.), *International Encyclopedia of Comparative Law*, IV, *Persons and Family* (Tübingen, Mohr).

SALDEEN, A., "Family Law in Sweden" in C. Hamilton and K. Standley (eds.), *Family Law in Europe* (London, Butterworths), 471–510.

SCHEIWE, K. (1998), *Rechtsmodelle der Kinderversorgung und soziale Ungleichheiten zwische Frauen und Männern in vier Ländern (Belgien, BRD, Schweden und Vereinigtes Königreich)* (Frankfurt-am-Main, Klostermann).

—— and WILLEKENS, H. (1997), "Het functionele equivalent in rechtsvergelijking en rechtssociologie. Een bespreking aan de hand van de relatie tussen gezinsrecht en sociale zekerheidsrecht" in H. Willekens (ed.), *Het gezinsrecht in de sociale wetenschappen* (Den Haag, VUGA), 139–59.

SCOTT, J. (1979), *Corporations, Classes and Capitalism* (London).

SECCOMBE, W. (1992), *A Millennium of Family Change. Feudalism to Capitalism in Northwestern Europe* (London, Verso).

—— (1993), *Weathering the Storm. Working-Class Families from the Industrial Revolution to the Fertility Decline* (London, Verso).

WEBER, MARIANNE (1907), *Ehefrau und Mutter in der Rechtsentwicklung* (Tübingen, Mohr).

WEBER, MAX (1985, originally 1922), *Wirtschaft und Gesellschaft. Grundriss der verstehenden Soziologie* (Tübingen, Mohr).

WILLEKENS, H. (1997), "Explaining Two Hundred Years of Family Law in Western Europe" in H. Willekens (ed.), *Het gezinsrecht in de sociale wetenschappen* (Den Haag, VUGA), 59–93.

ZWEIGERT, K. and KÖTZ, H. (1987), *Introduction to Comparative Law* (Oxford, Clarendon).

4

The New Codification of Russian Family Law

OLGA KHAZOVA

The new Family Code was adopted by the Russian Parliament in December 1995 and came into force on 1 March 1996. The main aim of the new Code was to bring Russian family law into line with the current situation in the country, which has been radically changed since Perestroyka began, with the new RF Constitution 1993, new Civil Code 1994–6 and also the UN Convention on the Rights of the Child.

The Family Code of 1995 is the fourth codification of Russian family law. The first three were related to the soviet period and were enacted in 1918, 1926 and 1969. All of them, despite their shortcomings, were quite progressive at the time, and it will be useful to give their brief history.

I

The first Russian Family Code 1918[1] was adopted a year after the Revolution of 1917 and fixed and developed the ideas that were stipulated first in two Decrees of the new government.[2] These laws transferred the acts of civil status from the jurisdiction of the Church to that of the State, denied legal force to religious marriages, and established that the only form of legal marriage was civil (secular) marriage. The conditions for marriage were significantly simplified and the majority of the obstacles to marriage were abolished. The divorce procedure became also much easier: if there was mutual consent between the spouses, they could be divorced in the state agencies for the registration of civil status, and if one of them did not consent to divorce, the other could apply to the court.

The Code did away with the subordinate status of women as wives and mothers in personal and property relations. Women were considered by law as equal to men. The Code preserved the matrimonial regime of separation of property, from the pre-revolutionary law. "Marriage," declared the 1918 Code, "does not

---

[1] The full title is RSFSR Code on Acts of Civil Status, Marriage, Family, and Guardianship.

[2] Decree of 18 Dec. 1917 "On Civil Marriage, Children, and Registration of Civil Status" and Decree of 19 December 1917 "On Divorce".

create community of property". This decision was explained, in the conditions of 1918, when the Code was adopted, by the desire to protect women's rights and to stress that women were independent and in no way subordinate to their husbands. This rule appeared to be unfair towards housewives who had neither property, nor their own earnings. But it reflected the ideas and morals of that time, according to which there could be no private property at all, and everybody, married women including, should work, and non-working women were considered "a bourgeois survival of the past". Another "survival of the past" was a marriage contract. Therefore, the 1918 Code's rule on separation of marital property was strictly imperative in character and did not permit marriage contracts. Since that time marriage contracts have been strictly forbidden for more than 75 years, until the new RF Civil Code was enacted in 1995.

One of the most important provisions of this first post-revolutionary legislation concerned the status of children: it gave full equality to children born out of a wedlock, thereby eliminating, at least theoretically, the very notion of illegitimacy from our law. The parents of a child were registered in the child's birth certificate by their joint application irrespective of their marital status.

Under the 1918 Code it was very difficult for a father of a child born out of a wedlock "to escape" recognition of his paternity. The child's mother was entitled to apply to the local department registering civil status, indicating the name and place of residence of a child's father. A man named in such an application could contest it within two weeks. If he did not, his paternity was considered to be acknowledged.

As a rule, it was very difficult to rebut paternity at that time. The courts looked at the things easily: if the relationships between an alleged father and a child's mother led a court to the conclusion that by "natural course of events" he could be a child's father, a court made a paternity decision. Moreover, if a court established that there were several persons who had sexual relations with a child's mother at the time of a child's conception, all of them had to be involved in the proceedings as defendants and take part in the child's maintenance.

This provision was explained by the great number of children in need at that time, including those born out of a wedlock, and the inability of the state to take care of all of them. Therefore the state tried to force parents, close relatives and even persons, who did not succeed in proving their "non-implication" in a child's birth, to maintain the child.

The Code abolished adoption. It was explained by the danger of exploitation of children's labour, especially in the country. Obviously, such a danger existed, but, taking into account the great number of children left without parental care because of the Revolution and continued war, it was difficult to choose a worse moment to abolish this institution.[3]

The need for revision of the laws issued directly after the Revolution arose few years later, and the work began in 1923. The new Family Code was adopted in

---

[3] Antokolskaja, M. V. *Semeinoe pravo* (M. 1996), 68.

1926.[4] The most important innovation was recognition of *de facto* marriages. No doubt, to a significant extent it was influenced by the ideas, rather fashionable and popular at that period, about "withering away" of the institution of marriage. Simultaneously divorce procedure was significantly simplified: the spouses could be divorced in state bodies of registration of civil status, and there were no court proceedings.

The second important innovation of the 1926 Code was the introduction of community of marital property. By that time the shortcomings of the separation regime had become evident and, to give a woman equal rights in the family there was a need to recognise the social value of her work in the home. That is why it was necessary to recognise the right of both spouses to the property acquired in marriage, regardless of who was the legal owner of the property or in whose name it was acquired.

The 1926 Code made few amendments to paternity proceedings. Though the 1926 Code abolished the rule permitting the court to impose the responsibility of child's maintenance on several defendants, and the courts had "to choose" one of them, on the whole it continued to be very easy for a woman to have a man registered as a child's father. The courts were even "instructed" to conclude paternity cases only with a finding of paternity with all the consequences thereof, on the basis that: "mother knows better", "there must be somebody who is a child's father" and so on.[5] The courts considered it necessary to recover maintenance payments at any price, being guided by the idea that it was more dangerous to leave a child without any money at all than to impose the duty to maintain the child on a wrong person. Theoretically, such a "registered father" could later institute court proceedings rebutting his paternity. But it goes without saying that it was very difficult for him to succeed.

The 1926 Code was not very successful, though formally it existed until 1968. In 1936 and 1944 it was amended by two of Stalin's Acts which left nothing of its democratic provisions. Being guided by the idea of a necessity "to strengthen the soviet family", in the first of them the legislator abolished abortions. The second, the "well-known" Edict of 8 July 1944, abolished all the *de facto* marriages, made divorce very difficult and put it under strict control of the courts. It abolished also the institution of establishing paternity outside legal marriage, and went to the opposite extreme, since it became impossible for a man to recognise his child born out of a wedlock and for an unmarried mother to institute paternity proceedings. Thus, the principle of equality of children born in- and out of a legal marriage acquired a new and highly peculiar appearance.

What was the reason for such a radical change? As was explained in all the legal writings of the soviet period, it was the desire to strengthen the soviet family and by the necessity to struggle against light-minded attitudes towards family duties, marriage and divorce. The law aimed to make marriage and

---

[4] The full title is RSFSR Code on Marriage, the Family and Guardianship.

[5] Genkin, D. M., Novitskii, I. B., Rabinovitch, N. V., *The History of Soviet Civil Law* (M. 1949), 452, 479.

family relations more definite and stable. This task became especially pressing, from legislator's point of view, during the war-period when many families were separated. However this "war-period" did not finished in 1945, but lasted for nearly 25 years, when the Edict was repealed in 1968.

The third codification of family law,[6] held in 1968–9, was a significant event in the development of our law as a whole. It changed the main provisions of the family law and eliminated the majority of the rules of Stalin's period. In particular, it made divorce easier and abolished all the rules preventing a person from establishing paternity. Nevertheless the majority of its rules remained strictly imperative in character and we can find few, if any, dispositive provisions. By the end of the century, after the Soviet Union collapsed and after the radical political, economic, and social changes that followed, the 1969 Code became obsolete and a new revision of the family law became necessary.

The new Russian Family Code 1995 consists of eight parts, containing 170 sections. This chapter can consider only the most important provisions.

II

The main characteristics of the Code of 1995 are the following. An attempt is made to enlarge citizens' rights in family relations and to increase the number of dispositive rules. The legislator tried to extend the limits of permissive options in the field of family law, reducing the number of imperative rules. It concerns different aspects of family relations: property relations between the spouses while the marriage lasts and after its dissolution, divorce procedure, to a certain extent even the rules on marriage, the types of families in which children without parental care can be placed, and matters of of private international law.

The retreat from imperative rules with regard to property and maintenance relations within the family and the opportunity to deviate from the order stipulated by law, the most important innovations of the new Code, reveals itself, first, in the introduction of the institution of the marriage contract[7] and, secondly, in enlargement of family members' rights to regulate their maintenance relations. The move to the market economy made it necessary to revise all the rules on property and financial relations in the family. One of the results of this revision is the introduction of a marriage contract.

The marriage contract, as stated in the Code, is "an agreement made between persons, about to be married, or between spouses, which defines their property rights and duties in marriage and (or) in case of its dissolution" (section 40). A marriage contract can be concluded either before registration of marriage or at any time after it. In spite of the fact that such a contract can be made before registration of marriage, it will nevertheless come into force only at the moment of

---

[6] RSFSR Code on Marriage and the Family.

[7] See also *The International Survey of Family Law 1994* (The Hague: Martinus Nijhoff, 1996), 395–6.

conclusion of the marriage. A marriage contract must be made in written form and notarised. In the marriage contract the spouses are allowed to deviate from the legal regime of common joint property. The spouses are now free to choose the community regime, a regime of shared community or a regime of full or partial separation of property. The object of a contract may be not only the existing property, but also property that will be acquired by the spouses in the future. The spouses can define in the marriage contract their maintenance obligations towards each other, the way each of them participates in the other spouse's income, every day family expenses and other numerous financial matters that may arise in real life situations.

However, a marriage contract cannot limit spouses legal capacity or the right of each of them to apply to a court to protect his/her interests, regulate personal relations between the spouses and their rights and duties towards their children. It cannot stipulate provisions that restrict the right of an incapacitated spouse to work and a spouse in need to receive maintenance from another spouse. Nor can it contain other terms that place one of the spouses in "an extremely unfavourable position or contradict the basis of family legislation" (section 42, page 3).

If we turn to maintenance problems, there are two points in the new Russian legislation that cannot pass unnoticed. First, the introduction of maintenance agreements (chapter 16) allows members of a family to decide all their maintenance requirements, including those connected with a child's support, in a way that suits them best. Second, and to my mind, much more important, is the significant enlargement of the rights of a court, when making a maintenance decision, and the spouses/parents' rights, when making their own private agreement, to use different forms of regulation of their financial affairs, including child maintenance. Under the old law, maintenance of a child usually took the form of periodic payments, the amount of which was strictly determined as a proportion of the parent's earnings.[8] In circumstances when the families' incomes differ more and more widely, it was necessary to give judges more discretion and the right to depart from these strict rules. It was also necessary to give parents more freedom to settle maintenance conflicts by agreement. Now the court is also entitled to order maintenance to be paid in the form of periodic payments for a fixed sum, or combine these two ways of maintenance payments together (sections 81, 83). The family members' powers are much wider in this connection: in a maintenance agreement they are allowed even to establish maintenance being paid in a form of a lump sum, to make a transfer of property, and to use any other way of payment with regard to which they have reached an agreement (section 104, page 2).

In connection with *divorce* the Code gave much more freedom to the spouses and simplified the divorce procedure if there is mutual consent. Putting aside details, there are two types of divorce proceedings under the Russian family law: administrative (in a state agency for registry of a civil status)—if there are no

---

[8] The form of fixed sum was generally reserved for cases strictly settled by law and was used rarely (s. 71 of the RSFSR Code 1969).

under-age children and both spouses agree to divorce, and court proceedings—
if there are minor children and/or one of the spouses does not consent to the
divorce. The most important innovations of the 1995 Reform concern divorce
proceedings in court. Its main goal was to make divorce easier for those spouses
who mutually agree to divorce, and to protect the rights and interests of dependent members of a family, primarily minor children of a divorcing couple.

If both spouses agree to divorce, it is no longer necessary for them to prove
that their further joint life and preservation of the family have become impossible, as was stipulated previously.[9] Now the court must just check whether both
spouses have agreed to divorce, and make a divorce decree without ascertaining
the reasons and trying to reconcile the spouses (section 23). If one of the spouses
does not consent to divorce, the divorce procedure remains the same. The court
dissolves the marriage if all the attempts at conciliation have failed and "the
future joint life of the spouses and preservation of the family are impossible"
(section 22).

At the same time, however, there are cases when the legislator considered it
necessary to put the matter under strict control of the court. First, courts are
given wide powers to deal with child-related consequences of divorce. Whether
there is mutual consent to divorce or not, the court, when making a divorce
decree, must raise economic and other child-related questions on its own motion
and make an appropriate order if there is no agreement on these matters between
spouses or if their agreement, in court's opinion, infringes the rights of their children (section 24). Thus, now, according to the new law, marriage cannot be dissolved until the problems of the child's maintenance and place of residence are
resolved. This provision seems to be a crucial point in protecting the child's
interests after his parents' divorce. Under the new law, it is not sufficient for the
court, as it was previously, only to ascertain formally during the hearing if "the
spouses have come to an agreement on custody and upbringing of the children".[10]
There were many cases when a spouse did not bring a child maintenance or custody suit simultaneously with a divorce petition. However, silence of the parents
did not always mean the absence of a conflict and the existence of an agreement.
If a court does not properly investigate questions connected with child's life after
divorce and solve at least those of them that concern his financial support, there
is a great risk that a child will be left without any maintenance at all, taking into
account that in the majority of cases it was and continues to be the mothers who
look after the children after divorce.

If we turn to the family law provisions in the context of Private International
Law, until recently Russian family law has been characterized by a "territorial
approach" to family relations with a "foreign element". We could find few choice
of law rules in family law. It meant that, as a general rule, it was Russian law that
was applied in matrimonial relationships.

---

[9] S. 33 of the Code 1969.
[10] Decree of the Plenum of the USSR Supreme Court 1980, point 13.—Bulletin Verkhovnogo
Suda SSSR (1981) No. 1.

The new Code significantly enlarged the possibility of the application of foreign law. Nearly each conflict rule contains "references" to the foreign law: of a spouse's, parent's or child's nationality or domicile, the law of both parties' place of residence, and others. The Code stipulates, particularly, that the conditions to marriage be determined in accordance with the law of the country of which the future spouses are citizens at the moment of marriage registration,[11] provided that the requirements of section 14 of the Family Code on marriage prohibitions are observed.[12] Wide application of foreign law, in all probability, will lead to full elimination of the so-called "limping" marriages from Russian family law (i.e. marriage recognized as valid in one country and as invalid in another) with all the consequences thereof.

III

The recent trend in the development of family law in other countries and ratification by Russia the UN Convention on the Rights of the Child made it necessary to pay more attention to children's needs, to ensure a primary consideration of children's best interests and to treat them in law as individuals. The provisions devoted to the rights of minor children appeared in Russian family legislation for the first time, and the new Family Code made an attempt "to take children's rights seriously" and to treat them as individuals and as subjects of law, and not just as objects of "parental authority".[13] For a long period of time a "one-sided view" of the protection of children dominated the law of the former USSR—the view of a child through the prism of his parents. The child's interests used to be protected in an indirect way, primarily by means of protecting his mother's interests. In such an exclusively paternalistic (or maternalistic) position there was practically no place for the child himself with his own rights and interests.

The new Code contains a special chapter devoted to the rights of minor children, aiming to ensure a child an independent position in the family and to respect his opinion (chapter 11). A child's legal position is determined first by his "best interests", and not by the interests of his parents, as it was before. All the provisions of the chapter are based on the UN Convention on the Rights of the Child, which entered into force in Russia in 1990. Following the Convention, the Code sets out the main rights of a child: the right to live and be brought up in the family; the right to know, as far as possible, his parents; the right to be cared for by his parents and to live with them (except in cases when it contradicts child's interests); the right to all-round development, his interests being

---

[11] Compare the corresponding provision of the previous RSFSR Code 1969 (s. 161, part 1): "Marriages between soviet and foreign citizens, as well as marriages between foreigners, are concluded on the RSFSR territory in accordance with soviet legislation".

[12] Under s. 14, it is prohibited to conclude marriage between persons one of whom is already legally married, between close relatives, between adopter and adoptee, and between persons one of whom has been recognised by a court as incapable because of the mental illness.

[13] *Semeinyi Kodeks RF s Kratkim Kommentariem* (Moscow, BEK, 1996), XXVVI.

ensured and his human dignity being respected; the right to personal contact with his parents and other relatives; the right to protect his rights and interests and to apply personally to appropriate administrative authorities and, after having attained 14 years, to a court of law; the right to freedom of expression and "to have a say" in all matters affecting him; the right to have his own property, to receive maintenance; and some others.

The Code[14] has reacted to the problems connected with family violence and with child abuse, stipulating that the ways of upbringing children must exclude neglect, cruel, rude and humiliating treatment, as well as insult and exploitation (section 65, page 10).

The duty to protect the rights and interests of children who do not have parental care is laid on local authorities (custody and guardianship agencies) (section 121). They should identify the neglected children, register them, and, depending on the particular circumstances, choose the form of their upbringing and place them in a family or special child care institution. Their duties include also the subsequent control over the circumstances of such children. The Code is based on the idea of priority of family upbringing and provides for different forms of placement of children left without families. The system of adoption is considered to be the best form of family upbringing for such children. To secure the children's rights more protection the Code introduced a court procedure for adoption. Though considered an effective remedy to prevent offences in the field of adoption, the new adoption rules, nevertheless, do not yet work properly, to a certain extent because of the shortcomings in the system of records of neglected children subject to adoption.[15]

The Code extends the possibilities of placing children who do not have parental care in families of different types. In particular, it introduces the institution of a foster family into Russian family law. In accordance with the Code, a foster family is a family which takes at least one neglected child under a contract with an agency, receiving custody and guardianship on "transfer of a child". The number of children in a foster family cannot exceed eight.[16] The rights and duties of foster parents are similar to those of custodians and guardians, but they are limited by a period specified in the contract Besides, the "work" of foster parents on upbringing of such children is to be paid.

IV

The Russian legislator faced many serious problems connected with development of new reproductive and testing technologies, and important innovations were introduced into the regulation of parentage and affiliation.

---

[14] In the Chapter "Rights and Duties of the Parents".

[15] *Itogi vmeste s Newsweek* (Moscow), 20 May 1997, 60 ff.

[16] *Statute on A Foster Family*, 2.—Polozhenije o Priemnoi Sem'e (Postanovlenije Pravitel'stva RF o Priemnoi Sem'e, July 17, 1996), *Sobranije Zakonodatel'stva RF*, 1996, No. 31, it. 3721.

Properly registered blood parentage as the ground for creation of legal relations between parents and children has been stipulated in Russian family law as
one of its fundamental principles since the Revolution 1917. In one form or
another this idea has been present in all the previous family codes. The Code of
1995 repeats that "the rights and duties of parents and children are based on
properly registered parentage" (section 4). The most important innovations introduced in this connection are determined by the development of medicine and
biology. In particular, they are connected with the new possibilities of positive
identification of paternity and maternity through the method of genetic finger-
prints (or "genome dactiloscopy", as it is called in Russia) and with the new
reproductive technologies.

If a child's parents are not married to each other and one of them refuses to
present joint application, paternity may be established in court proceedings. Until
recently compulsory establishment of paternity in court proceedings was considered to be possible only in definite situations strictly stipulated by law: residence
in a common household of the mother and the respondent before the child's
birth; or the mother's and respondent's common upbringing or maintenance of
the child; or reliable evidence confirming the respondent's acceptance of his
paternity.[17] If it was necessary, a court could require a special examination to be
made (medical or biological tests). However, under the previous law, no tests
irrespective of their results, even if "genome dactyloscopy" established the paternity of a particular person, could be considered by courts as sufficient evidence
of paternity. Shortcomings of these legal rules often led to obvious inconsistency,
and in practice there were many cases when, despite the fact that a defendant's
biological paternity had been proved by DNA testing, his legal paternity could
not be established in court proceedings, since there were no formal "grounds"
stipulated by law.

The Code of 1995 abolished all these formal grounds for paternity proceedings and set out that a court when considering a paternity case should take into
account any evidence that proves child's filiation to a particular person (section
49).[18] Thus, the court is not limited any longer by any specific circumstances. Of
course, the court cannot ignore those "social factors" which were previously
treated as "the grounds" for establishment of paternity. Nevertheless, under the
new law, the court is entitled to make a positive paternity decision, even if none
of those "grounds" exist, provided paternity is proved by genetic testing.

As regards medically assisted procreation, in 1990 for the first time Russian
family law (at that time—soviet family law) was supplemented with provisions
legitimating the birth of a child conceived by artificial insemination.[19] The new

---

[17] S. 48 of the Code 1969.

[18] It is one of those new provisions that met the strongest opposition when passing through the
Parliament.

[19] The USSR Law on Amendments to the USSR Legislation Concerning Women, Family, and
Childhood 1990 (22 May), Part I. – Vedomosti S'ezda Narodnykh Deputatov SSSR i Verkhovnogo
Soveta SSSR (1990) No. 23, it. 422.

Code develops these provisions, determining the status of a child born through different methods of artificial reproduction.

In section 51 of the Code (paragraph 4, part 1) it is stated that a married couple who consent to artificial procreation, are to be registered as the child's parents. Part 2 of the same paragraph concerns registration of parents of a child born to a surrogate mother. It provides that a couple who agree to the implantation of an embryo in another woman can be registered as the child's parents only if the surrogate mother gives her consent to such a registration. It means that, under Russian law, it is a surrogate mother who is regarded by law as the mother, and it is she who has the right to decide whether to keep the child or not.

v.

Finally, there are a few other positions in the new family law that are worth pointing out. All of them concern the contracting of marriage. Therefore I shall end with the questions we usually start with.

The first of them concerns age of marriage. Under the new Code (sections 12–13), as before, the statutory marriage age for both men and women is 18 (the age of civil majority), and authorised state bodies are entitled to reduce the age to sixteen, if there are circumstances justifying such a reduction. However, the legislator had to react to the phenomenon of teenage pregnancies. The Code does not provide for any lower limit. Discussion of this provision in Parliament was characterised by a stormy debate, and the final wording of a corresponding provision is a compromise between different opinions. It is evident that the legislator preferred not to be responsible for the final decision on this matter and to delegate the right to make it to the subjects of the Russian Federation.[20] It read as follows: "The order and conditions, when it is possible as an exception, taking into account special circumstances, to grant permission to marry for those who are under sixteen, can be stipulated in the legislation of RF regional subjects" (section 13, paragraph 2, part 2). RF subjects reacted immediately. Though strange as it may seem, it was not the South or Asian republics of the Russian Federation which were the first to adopt such a law, but the central regions,[21] including Moscow, where less than a year after enactment of the Code laws were passed permitting marriage from 14 if a bride is pregnant or if she has already given birth to a child.

Another innovation concerns the requirements for the formation of legal marriage itself. For the first time marriage can take place without any waiting period, i.e. at the day of presenting an application to a state agency for registry of a civil status (section 11, paragraph 1, part 3). Of course, this rule is intended to be exceptional and is to be used in cases when the "special circumstances" exist. The

[20] The list of RF subjects (republics, regions, autonomous regions, territories and towns) is set out in art. 65 of RF Constitution 1993.

[21] Tverskaja, Vologodskaja, Nizhegorodskaja regions.

Code designates three particular situations (though the list is not closed). They are: (1) pregnancy of a bride, (2) birth of a child and (3) threat to the life of one of the parties. It is evident that the third position has been provoked by the recent events in the South of Russia, the war in Chechnja, in particular. However, it also covers other situations when there is a danger to a person's life, for example, forthcoming departure on a dangerous expedition or undergoing a dangerous surgical operation.

One further provision of the new Code concerning formation of marriage which is noteworthy is the introduction of a medical examination of future spouses (section 15). The results of a medical examination constitute a medical confidence and can be made known to another party only with the examined party's consent. Under the Code, such a medical testing is voluntary. The idea of medical testing is not new. Such a procedure exists in many countries, and in some of them medical examination of the future spouses is compulsory. In Russia, however, introduction of a compulsory medical testing of all couples about to be married is absolutely impossible at present, since there are neither financial means, nor a properly developed network of medical hospitals and clinics; nor do people seem to be prepared to accept compulsory examination with a view to marriage.

The last paragraph of the above-mentioned section (paragraph 3) contains a provision which may seem at first sight to be rather disputable: "If one of the parties to be married concealed from the other party that he/she was suffering from a venereal disease or was infected with the AIDS virus, the latter is entitled to file for nullity of marriage". The provision does not infringe the person's "right to marry", nor does it prevent an AIDS infected person or person suffering from venereal disease from being married. The aim of this provision is to give certain protection to another party to a marriage (though, of course, it is rather weak) and to give the right to contest the validity of marriage to someone deceived concerning the other party's health at the time of marriage. It will not be easy to apply the provision in practice, and the Code contains no guidelines in this connection.

Finally, the legislator had to react to the problems connected with same-sex couples and their demands to legalize their unions. Russian family law has always been based on the idea that marriage is a union of a man and a woman, and this has always been an "implied" condition to marriage. Previously it was just one of the general principles of family law[22] and was regarded as inherent in the course of nature and as a reflection of natural conditions of formation and functioning of a family. Formally, the new Family Code introduced nothing new in this connection, but did in fact seriously strengthen the importance of this provision. Now it is stipulated not only as a general rule in section 1 (paragraph 3), that sets out the basic principles of the family legislation, but once again—as a condition to marriage in section 12 (paragraph 2): "To conclude marriage it is necessary to obtain mutual voluntary consent of a man and a woman to be married . . . ". Thus, the legislator's answer was definitely negative.

---

[22] S. 1 of the RSFSR Code 1969.

5

The Development of Japanese Family Law from 1898 to 1997 and its Relationship to Social and Political Change

YUKIKO MATSUSHIMA

A INTRODUCTION

Family law is deeply rooted in the consciousness of the people, their morals and religion, their culture and social values, as well as their politics. Yet it is true that family law is in fact fundamentally based on and confined by the social and economic structure of the day. As the world becomes borderless, lifestyles become more diverse, and so the provisions of family law should also be broadened to reflect a certain degree of universality.

Japanese family law can be said to have been created and developed through three major legal reforms. The first of these was the establishment of the Civil Code in 1898, at approximately the same time as the promulgation of the Meiji constitution. This was the birth of modern law, based on the paternalistic *Iye* system, an extended family institution.[1] The second was the family law reforms instituted in 1947 following the Second World War, and the enactment of Japan's present democratic constitution, which resulted in the abolition of the *Iye* system and the introduction of the principle of equality between men and women. The third major reform has been carried out in the period from 1990 to the present day, during which the progress in legal reform has reflected changing family circumstances, such as a falling birth-rate, an increase in the aged population, greater numbers of working women, and a decline in common values in Japanese society.

This chapter discusses the characteristics of family law, the political and social background in each period, and the conflict between law and social customs. In

---

[1] *Iye* was the vertically extended family system in which every family member was subject to the control of the head of the family and in which women were always subordinate to men. See for details Fujiko Isono, "The Evolution of Modern Family Law in Japan", *International Journal of Law and the Family* 2, 1988, 183–202.

other words, how did the family law in the Meiji Civil Code come into being and what was the primary aim of that law? What are the characteristics of the present family law system? And how have the present provisions, since their creation, ceased to reflect the current situation in Japan? This chapter will also look at whether the current round of revisions, designed to correct the disparity, actually responds to people's needs.

After five years of deliberation, the Law Commission (the Legislative Council of the Ministry of Justice) recently published a *Report on the Partial Reform of the Civil Code*. The second half of this chapter will concentrate on a discussion of the main points in the report. It will illustrate the changes and problems which Japanese families face as they approach the twenty-first century and examine how the proposed reforms attempt to combat these problems.

B FAMILY LAW IN THE MEIJI CIVIL CODE IN 1898

1 Background to the Creation of Family Law: Political and Social Factors

Japan first started laying down laws as a modern country during the Meiji Restoration (1853–1877), a time of great upheaval. Prior to the Meiji era was a political system that lasted for about two and a half centuries, the Tokugawa Shogunate. At the centre of this society was the "Bakufu", the central government, which had a feudalistic lord–vassal relationship with the local lords. This society was extremely hierarchical. Below the local lords, in the lower levels of society, were four distinct classes: warriors, farmers, handicraft workers, and merchants, who were ranked in that order by militarist Confucianism. In the middle of the seventeenth century, the Tokugawa Bakufu adopted a policy of isolating Japan from Western countries. In 1853, America demanded that Japan open its ports to trade. Acting in unison, the great powers of Europe pushed Japan and an unwilling Bakufu to sign a one-sided treaty of amity and commerce with the Five Great Powers, opening Japan to trade with the outside world. Eventually, in 1867, the Bakufu yielded its ruling authority to the Emperor Meiji, an event known as the Meiji Restoration or revolution.

On the domestic front, the new Meiji government devoted its energies to endowing Japan with national wealth and military strength, modelling many aspects of its society on the Western nations. Several Western systems were introduced, including political, economic, legal, educational, and military practices. In foreign affairs, the government worked to revise the unfair treaties. Thus Japan was firmly on the path to modernisation.

2 Structure and Characteristics of Meiji Family Law

The new codes established during the Meiji period were designed to make the country modernise, in order to reverse the negative impact of the disadvantageous treaties. The family law in the Civil Code alone was retained as a relic of the feudal family order that prevailed under the old warrior class society. The reason for this was that it was thought that the standards of the warrior class were more appropriate for the purpose of creating the centralisation of government and were more conducive to the nation's economic and military policies. Family law formed the fourth and fifth parts of the Civil Code and these provisions became law in 1898.

Meiji family law centred around the *Iye* system and its origins lay in the *Koseki* system which was a form of a family register.[2] People in the same *Koseki* were given the same surname. These groups became *Iye* under the *Iye* system in Meiji family law so the *Iye* system had a close relationship with *Koseki*. At the time, the Meiji government needed to assert some measure of control over the people, and the *Koseki* acted as a database for the implementation of such new policies as conscription, tax collection and education. After revisions in 1947, children of unmarried parents were included in the registration system to a greater extent. The *Koseki* system is still in use. Even today, the *Koseki* continues to perform the identification function for Japanese people and carries great legal and social significance. For example, to prove that a person has Japanese nationality that person must show that they have been entered on the *Koseki* register.

The *Iye* system may be defined as a family group in which the head of the family had authority over all other members of the family and the family line was maintained through single succession. Meiji family law was characterised by a focus on three points: (i) the *Iye* system; (ii) the authority of the head of the family; and (iii) the system of a sole legal heir to the head of the family.

(i) The Iye system

First, the *Iye* group perspective, based on the Confucian precepts of an order according to seniority and male predominance over women, was given legal status at the core of family law. All people would belong to an *Iye* which would be a permanent group. Belonging would be determined by the blood lineage on the father's side.

The *Iye* was unconnected to the household or the unit which actually lived together but was an ideological grouping of blood relations, recorded together in the *Koseki*. By keeping the same clan or family name, family integrity was

---

[2] *Koseki* is a registration system under which every family is registered with the government. Birth, marriage, divorce and death are recorded as is the relationship between each person. The Family Registration Law of 1871 unified all citizens with each unit for registration, classifying people into either head of the family or family members.

maintained. Further, the role of the head of the family was to perform the religious rites for the family's ancestors.

(ii) Authority of the head of the family

The head of the family had authority over the family members in the *Iye*. Specific powers given to this person included: the right to approve family members' marriage and adoption (Meiji Civil Code, Article 750); the right to specify the family residence (Meiji Civil Code, Article 749); and the right to expel any family member who opposed his order (Meiji Civil Code, Article 749, Clause 3).

(iii) System of a sole legal heir to the head of the family

As the economic basis to facilitate strong leadership by the head of the family, a system of single succession was established, in which all family property passed from the head of the family to his successor, who was normally the eldest son (Meiji Civil Code, Article 970). The predominance of the *Iye* over the individual impeded the freedom of the family members. Although the head of the family was given the status of a sole heir, at the same time he had the legal obligation to support all the family members.

The *Iye* system rested not only on the relationship between the head of the family and the rest of the family members, but also on the relationship between husband and wife, father and mother, and parent and child. In each case this involved a legal relationship whereby the former controlled the latter. The head of the family was, in principle, a man, and a husband was given the right to manage the property owned by his wife (Meiji Civil Code, Article 801). Only the father held parental authority over children (Meiji Civil Code, Article 877).

3 Political and Social Roles of Meiji Family Law

What were the political and social functions of Meiji family law?

Looking broadly at the social and political context, the *Iye* system of the Meiji Civil Code was particularly laden with special functions. First, the primary function of the *Iye* was political. The nature of the Meiji totalitarian state was to maintain and strengthen the rule of the pre-war Imperial system, with the family serving to reinforce this. The people's obligation to the Emperor was "loyalty" and children's obligation to their parents was "piety". Loyalty and piety became the basic tenets of education as the highest moral obligation of the people. A family traced its roots back to its original family through indirect lines, while the reigning Imperial family, which was an unbroken line of royal succession, was the head family, upon which all families depended. A so-called "family state theory" in which the state was a larger model of the family unit, thus came to the fore. As a result, the *Iye* system worked politically as an ideology.

Secondly, economically, the obligation of the head of the family to support family members absorbed workers when they became ill, lost their jobs, or retired in the cities, and in doing so reduced the welfare burden for companies and the state. This contributed to the rapid development of capitalism in Japan. In the short term, this was useful in stabilising society, but it stood in the way of development of social solidarity and slowed the development of the social security system.

Finally, the system in which the social relationships in most companies replicate those of the family has engendered the idea of an unconditional attachment, and led to the loss of independence of individual characters and awareness of individual rights.

Certainly, the political use of the *Iye* system was successful to a certain extent; during the time when most of the population was engaged in farming and home industries,[3] the system of a sole legal heir to the head of the family prevented the dispersal of family assets. Also, the duty of the head of the family to support his family members was helpful in stabilising society. However some of the problems with the system were that: the citizens were forced into blind obedience towards the autocratic Meiji government; women were not given the right to vote and girls were unable to receive higher education. Even if women married, they were treated as having no legal capacity. The *Iye* system resulted in inequities within the family, such as system-sanctioned discrimination against women by men and the beholding of children to their parents. Even so, few Japanese resisted the system because people were thoroughly inculcated by the education system with the ideas of loyalty and filial piety and of a woman as a good wife and a wise mother.

C FAMILY LAW IN THE REVISED CIVIL CODE IN 1947

1 Political and Social Background to the Revisions

Entering the twentieth century, the period after the First World War saw greater development of capitalism and continued industrialisation and urbanisation. During this time the nuclear family became more prevalent. In fact, around 1920, more than half the population were members of a nuclear family,[4] and there was

---

[3] In 1920, more than 50% of the workforce was engaged in the primary sector, mainly farming, and 20.5% were engaged in the secondary sector, mainly home industry. At that time only 23.7% were engaged in the tertiary sector. After that the number of people who were engaged in farming decreased (25% in 1965, 7% in 1990) and the number of people who were engaged in the tertiary sector increased (60% in 1990).

[4] According to the composition of families by National Census, the number of nuclear family households (including husband and wife, parents and children, and one parent children) was 54% in 1920, 62.6% in 1965, and 59.5% in 1990. The number of extended families decreased (39.9% in 1920, 29.2% in 1965, and 17.2% in 1990) and the number of "single-member households" increased (6.0% in 1920, 7.8% in 1965, and 23.1% in 1990).

a significant gap between *Iye* under the system and the actual family member household. After its defeat in the Second World War in 1945, Japan was forced to undertake democratic reforms, both politically and socially, as a result of the governing policies of the Allied Forces. The new Constitution, promulgated on 3 November 1946, was created with the aim of rebuilding Japan democratically. It expressly provided for the principles of equality under the law (Constitution, Article 14), the dignity of individuals and the equality of sexes in the family (Constitution, Article 24). At the same time, all laws in breach of the articles of the Constitution were rescinded. Thus, the *Iye* system which was built on a principle of inequality, was abolished.

2 The Revised Family Law

Most conservatives resisted the abolition of the *Iye* system, believing that it would invite social chaos, and result in the loss of positive Japanese customs and traditions.[5]

However, the Law Commission, led by Professor Sakae Wagatsuma and Professor Zennosuke Nakagawa, abolished the *Iye* system, and positioned the modern nuclear family, comprising husband and wife and dependent children, as the central unit for family life. In the Civil Code the fourth and fifth parts were completely revised in 1947, and took effect in 1948.

First, the provisions relating to the head of the family were removed. In the *Koseki* it became the principle to include the husband, wife and children under the same name as one unit (Family Registration Law, Article 6). Marriage is now based on the free agreement between two individuals (Constitution, Article 24). The provisions of the former laws (Meiji Civil Code, Articles 750 and 772), which required the consent of the parents and the head of the family for marriages, were nullified. The wife's legal incapacity was abolished. She now has equal rights with her husband to hold assets and manage them. The husband and wife are to support each other mutually and share the expenses of married life (Civil Code, Articles 752 and 760). Also divorce, in which the wife was formerly subjected to unfair treatment, was made free and equal for both husband and wife (Civil Code, Article 770). In the past, the wife was forced to take the family name of the husband. Under the new law, the couple can now choose the family name of either the husband or the wife (Civil Code, Article 750). Formerly a wife generally did not have the right of succession, now the surviving spouse always becomes the legal successor (Civil Code, Article 890). Even parental rights over children were changed to be exercised jointly by the father and mother. Also, the system of adoption was modified from one where the purpose of the adoption was primarily for continuing the family line, to one where the adoption is for the

---

[5] For details see Yozo Watanabe, *Kazoku to Ho* (Tokyo University Publishers, 1973), 42.

welfare of the child. In particular, when a minor is adopted, the approval of the Family Court is now necessary. The system of having a sole legal heir to the head of the family has been abolished, and a system of equal inheritance is now in place whereby all children receive an equal amount, irrespective of whether they are male or female (Civil Code, Article 887).[6] However, illegitimate children became entitled to half the inheritance of legitimate children (Civil Code, the proviso to Article 900(4)). While all children now have equal rights, they also share an equal obligation. For example, the duty to support elderly parents must be borne equally among all children.

3 Political and Social Impact of Revisions in the Family Law

A post-war recovery was achieved with miraculous results, but what of the Japanese family, the engine that drove the high economic growth? The basic family unit of industrial society was one where the husband was responsible for being part of the workforce and his wife cared for him and their children. A fixed division of roles for men and women of "men at work, women at home" was firmly in place. The husband engaged in work in the harsh competitive society, while the wife concentrated on domestic duties. In policy terms as well, favourable treatment of housewives was adopted. For example, there is a spousal tax exemption, so that even if the housewife pays no social insurance at all, there is a system in place under which she can receive her own old age pension and the pension of her husband upon his death. Along with this, the concept of the legal married family with the division of roles between husband and wife has become entrenched in people's minds as the ideal family. In the 1970s, more than 70 per cent of households nationwide were nuclear households, and the size of the average household declined sharply. Consequently the actual social fabric itself has engendered a shift from the traditional *Iye* family system.

D MOVES TOWARDS FURTHER REFORMS IN THE PRESENT FAMILY LAW

1 Social Background

The high economic growth since 1955 brought with it increased industrialisation and urbanisation. Particularly from the 1970s families changed markedly. First, while the population started to age at a rate that was unprecedented anywhere in

---

[6] Many disputes arose on the renunciation of succession, immediately after the revised Civil Code was enforced. There was confusion between the custom of single succession and the new law concerning joint succession. Nowadays, a subject of debate is whether the family member supporting elderly parents should receive a larger inheritance.

the world,[7] the birth-rate declined.[8] As a result of an increased divorce rate,[9] which created single parent (father or mother) families,[10] families are declining in size.[11] Also, the number of single (unmarried) households is increasing sharply.[12] Since 1975, society has seen a great increase in the number of women joining the labour force.[13] By 1991 the number of women whose only occupation was to be a housewife fell below 30 per cent of the adult women population. Some 70 per cent of women participate in the workforce in one form or another, and this trend has brought a change in the conventional perception of husbands and wives having a fixed division of roles. Family circumstances have become diverse and the nuclear family has ceased to be the only model for family law. Even the perception of what a family is has diversified.[14]

International human rights movements changing the present family law are under way. These movements began with the Universal Declaration of Human Rights of 1948 and the International Covenant on Civil and Political Rights of 1966. For women, remarkable development has been achieved. This has come about through such things as the International Women's Year, held every 10

[7] The United Nations defines that the country in which the percentage of the population over age 65 is more than 7% is an "ageing society", and the country in which the percentage of the population over age 65 is more than 14% is an "aged society". It took 150 years in France, 85 years in Sweden, and 45 years in England for the figure of 7% to double to 14%, but it took only 25 years in Japan which shows how rapidly our society became aged. According to the Change in Age Structure, the percentage of people aged 0–19 years decreased (40% in 1960, 26.4% in 1990, and it is expected to be 20.2% in 2025). The percentage of people aged 20–64 years did not change so much (54.2% in 1960, 61.6% in 1990, and it is expected to be 54.0% in 2025). The percentage of those aged 65 years or older increased (5.7% in 1960, 12% in 1990, and expected 25.8% in 2025). Japanese society is quickly becoming a "super aged society" in which one quarter of all the population is 65 years or older.

[8] The total special birth-rate, which means the average number of children one woman gives birth to in her life, is decreasing rapidly (4.32 in 1950, 1.46 in 1993, 1.43 in 1996).

[9] According to 1994 statistics by the Ministry of Health and Welfare, the number of divorces per 1,000 population increased from 0.93 in 1970, 1.28 in 1990, and 1.57 in 1994.

[10] The number of one-parent households is increasing. For example, the number of single mother households increased from 1.5 million in 1975 to 2.3 million in 1990, and the number of single father households increased from 0.2 million in 1975 to 0.4 million in 1990.

[11] The average number of family members per household continues to decrease (5.0 in 1953, 3.06 in 1990, 2.95 in 1995).

[12] The rate of single member households was 20.2% in 1992. The reason why the number of single member households has increased is due to the increase in both the number of single elderly people and the number of younger people who have married late in their lives or have not wanted to marry.

[13] The number of women working has been increasing since 1975. In the 1990s, about 40% of those in employment are female workers. However, according to their age, their labour power constructs an "M" curve (there are many young women working, this number decreases as women have children and rises again as middle aged women return to the workforce). Many female workers are engaged in part-time jobs (one out of three).

[14] The opinion of the younger generation toward families has been dramatically changing. According to some opinion polls, the number of people who support the idea that a marriage is a matter of individual free choice and not all people should marry, is higher in the younger generation (80% of those in their 20s and 30s, less than 50% of those aged 60 and over). They do not feel reluctant to divorce, and do not stick to keeping their family name or following in their father's profession. More than 70% do not support the idea of fixed roles for men and women, and seek their individual freedom and dignity even inside the family.

years since 1975, and the International Plans of Action that follow these years. Even in Japan, since 1975, a National Plan of Action to raise the status of women has made progress. A number of measures have been implemented as a consequence. Next, at the same time as signing the UN Convention on the Elimination of All Forms of Discrimination Against Women, Japan revised the Nationality Law eliminating the patrilineal bias under which only children with a Japanese father were eligible for Japanese nationality. A flexible system was introduced whereby both Japanese men and women could pass their citizenship to their children. Other legal revisions were made with the aim of equality. For example, revisions in the Family Registration Law and the enactment of the Equal Employment Opportunity Act.

There are now calls for further reforms in the present family law. First, the aim is to shift from a lip-service equality for men and women to a real equality. Secondly, a reform in the law is sought to correspond to different lifestyles, by widening the range of choice rather than through a uniform enforcement of the conventional notion of a family.

2 Contents of the Proposed Reforms to Family Law

Work on revising Japanese family law started in January 1991 under the auspices of the Law Commission, and was finalised in January 1996 in a consultation paper entitled *Report on the Partial Reform of the Civil Code*,[15] which had been preceded by a *Working Paper on the Reform of the Civil Code*[16] in 1994 and an *Interim Report*[17] in 1995. The points in the report give much stronger consideration to the individual and aim to achieve real equality between men and women within the family, so as to bridge the gap between actual society and the law in a way the present law is unable to do. Thus, the revisions reflect the changes necessary to accommodate changing society. However, there has been strong opposition from conservative Diet members. At the time of writing (July 1997), there had been no progress on enacting the reforms.

The *Report on the Partial Reform of the Civil Code* of 16 January 1996 has many facets, with the main suggestions for reform given below:

(1) to introduce the legal minimum age of marriage as 18 for both sexes (under the present law, a man and a woman are required to have attained the ages of 18 and 16 years, respectively);

(2) to shorten the period during which women are prohibited from remarrying to 100 days (under the present law the period is six months and there is no equivalent law for men);

---

[15] *Jurist*, No. 1084, Feb. 1996, 126–7.

[16] *Jurist*, No. 1050, Aug. 1994, 214–55. Regarding the details on the movement of the family law reform from 1991 to 1993, see: Yukiko Matsushima, "Japan: Reforming Family Law", *University of Louisville Journal of Family Law* 32 (2), 359–67 (1994), and Yukiko Matsushima, "Japan: Continuing Reform in Family Law", *University of Louisville Journal of Family Law*, 33 (2), 417–29 (1995).

[17] *Jurist*, No. 1077, Oct. 1995, 167–83.

(3) to introduce a system whereby the husband and wife can choose either the surname of the husband or of the wife, or to retain the names they used before marriage. However, when separate surnames are chosen, the children's surnames shall be a name chosen at the time of marriage, and, as a rule, shall be the same (under the present law, the couple must choose either the surname of the husband or the surname of the wife);

(4) to stipulate the basis for the distribution of matrimonial property after divorce. The proposed revisions introduce a new principle that if the contributions toward the acquired property of the husband and wife are roughly the same, the distribution will be on the basis of one half to each of the parties. (Under the present statutes there is no such principle although recent case law has allowed such a distribution);

(5) to include living separately for more than five years as one of the grounds for judicial divorce; and

(6) to make the legal entitlement to inheritance the same for legitimate and illegitimate children (under the present law, illegitimate children are entitled to half the inheritance of legitimate children).

3 Key Issues of Controversy

Under the current draft revision in family law, the most controversial issues are considered to be: (i) separate surnames; (ii) separation as one of the grounds for judicial divorce; and (iii) illegitimate children's inheritance. The main points of these three issues are described below:

(i) Separate surnames

According to a survey of current opinion conducted by the Prime Minister's office in June 1996 on the introduction of this new system for surnames, 39.8 per cent were against the introduction, and 32.5 per cent were in favour. Of those against, men outnumbered women, while many older people (in their 50s, 60s or older), irrespective of gender, were opposed. Among those in favour, there was a preponderance of women in their 30s, as well as many young people (in their 20s and 30s) of both sexes.[18]

Under the present law, a husband and wife must choose either of their two surnames (Civil Code, Article 750). In practice, the majority of married couples (98 per cent) choose to use the husband's surname.[19] However, as increasing numbers of women receive higher education[20] and maintain careers, many

[18] *Gekkan Seron Chosa* (Monthly Opinion Survey), Prime Minister's Office (ed.), Jan. 1997, 21–2.

[19] Regarding the male-oriented character of Japanese surnames, see Emiko Ochiai, "Kojin wo Tan-i tosuru Shakai to Oyakokankei no Sokeika", *Jurist*, No. 1059, Jan. 1995, 43.

[20] According to the statistics on education continuance rates compiled by the Ministry of Education, the percentage of students who went on to senior high school is about 95% for both male

women argue that this *de facto* imposition of the husband's surname places yet another obstacle to a woman's career and should be abolished.[21] At present, the courts are hearing several cases in which the use of a separate surname is sought.[22] Viewing separate surnames for the husband and wife in Japan as merely the selection of a surname conceals the reality. The fact that only 2 per cent of men choose the surname of the wife clearly reflects the power relationship between man and woman, and the status between individuals and families in Japanese society. The reason women take their husbands' surnames when they marry is not only because of the effects of the traditional awareness of the *Iye* system, which persists in everyday customs and human relations, but also because of women's financial dependence on their husbands. In other words, the surname for the married couple reflects the division of roles for the husband and wife, which is still strongly embedded in Japanese society. The rise in woman's university admission rates and employment since the 1980s could mean that most women do not want to be forced into the outdated housewife model, but want to build a husband–wife partnership, and to respect individual lifestyles. This is essentially the theory behind the use of separate surnames by husband and wife. The surname is a mark of independence.

A contrary theory has it that if the husband and wife take separate names, the feeling of family unity would be lost, perhaps inviting a breakdown of the family. This would, in turn, lead to instability in family relations and the social order. However, this theory appears somewhat unconvincing. Even in present society, where there is a system for husband and wife to share the same name, there were 222,650 divorces in 1997.[23] Divorces are not significantly more common in other countries, like China and Korea, where husbands and wives are allowed to take separate names, and love and trust between husband and wife cannot be said to be weak. In particular, the system may be thought of as a catalyst for a shift to an age when women's rights of self-determination is respected, and where consideration of the individual and equality between man and woman are actually achieved in the real sense.

(ii) Separation as one of the grounds for divorce

The present law gives five grounds for judicial divorce: adultery, malicious desertion, the other spouse's whereabouts being unknown for more than three years, permanent mental disease or another grave reason making it difficult to continue

and female students. In 1995, 47.6% of female students (40.7% of male students) continued on to universities and technical colleges.

[21] The people who support the system of separate surnames are not only progressive female workers, but also parents who have only one daughter. It is interesting that of the people who want to destroy the *Iye* system and those who want to make it survive, both support the same reform in the law on surnames but for different ideological reasons.

[22] For example, judgement of the Tokyo District Court of 19 Nov. 1993, *Hanrei Jiho*, No. 1486, 21–55.

[23] According to the Asahi Shimbun Weekly Aera (29 June 1998), the divorce rate per 1,000 population in 1997 was 1.78.

the marriage (Civil Code, Article 770). These reasons are based on the principle of irretrievable breakdown, but still retain elements of fault. Since the Supreme Court's judgement in 1987,[24] allowing a husband to divorce his "innocent" wife against her wishes, the tide of judicial and academic thinking has been to uphold divorce when a marriage has irretrievably broken down. In the report, a new ground for divorce based on the principle of irretrievable breakdown without an element of fault is proposed in the following terms: "Where husband and wife have not been living together for more than five years, they can divorce". However the court is given discretionary rights to refuse such requests. This discretion is exercised when it is recognised that the request is not made in good faith. For example, in cases where divorce would cause grave social or economic hardship to the other party or to their children, or in cases where the person requesting the divorce is grossly neglecting to co-operate with and assist dependants.

It is also generally undesirable to require one spouse to prove that the other is at fault, because this tends to lead to bitter court battles. However, under the system of "separate matrimonial property" for husband and wife in the present family law, the matrimonial property is mostly held under the husband's name; women who are housewives generally do not have assets to manage so there is a need to ensure a proper distribution of property and to allow for financial support for children. Consequently, a hardship clause has been attached to the proposed reforms. When considering the distribution of matrimonial property after divorce, when there are no clear differences in the contribution towards the acquirement of that property, an equal contribution is assumed. In other words, as a rule, one half entitlement for each party has been introduced in the report. It is to be hoped that this will prove effective. Since the mother assumes custody of the children in 70 per cent of cases of divorce, and since there are many cases of delinquency when it comes to payment of child maintenance,[25] the law needs to establish a sure method of collection.

(iii) Inheritance by illegitimate children

Under the present law, a child born to a legally married couple is legitimate and a child born to an unmarried couple is illegitimate. The proviso to Article 900(4) of the Civil Code provides that an illegitimate child is entitled to inherit only half the amount to which a legitimate child is entitled. In the reforms suggested in the report, an illegitimate child would become entitled to a share equal to that of a legitimate child.

---

[24] Judgment of the Supreme Court on 2 Sept. 1987, *Minshu*, Vol. 41, No. 6, 1423–44.

[25] According to the national survey on single mother family households carried out by the Ministry of Welfare in 1988, as many as 75.4% of the mothers have never received any payments from their ex-husband. Even among the remaining 24.6% of the single mothers, 14% of them were receiving steady payments, whereas 10.6% had received payments in the past but were receiving nothing now.

Discriminatory treatment of illegitimate children was originally established under the *Iye* system under the Meiji Civil Code. Even after the Second World War, to encourage and respect legal marriage and to protect family relationships based on lawful marriage, illegitimate children have inevitably been at a disadvantage. This discrimination particularly affects children whose father also has a wife and legitimate children (as opposed to the children of an unmarried couple). However, in the light of the spirit of Article 24(1) of the International Covenant on Civil and Political Rights, and Article 2(2) of the UN Convention on the Rights of the Child, it is clear that every child has equal rights, and should not be subjected to discrimination by birth. The provision in Japan's current Civil Code that discriminates against illegitimate children in terms of their inheritance entitlement is unconstitutional, and as such is the subject of severe debate. In ratifying the UN Convention on the Rights of the Child, the Japanese government stated that any reforms of the provision were unnecessary, but there are several cases at the High Court level in which the provision is declared to be unconstitutional.[26] However, a Supreme Court judgment on 5 July 1995 held that the provision was not unconstitutional.[27] The reasons given were that the principle of respecting legal marriage was reasonable legislation, and the decision as to what inheritance system to adopt was a question for the legislature. However, five judges were in the minority opinion and of the ten judges who thought the regulations constitutional, four suggested that the discrimination be abolished through legislation. This means that nine of the 15 judges were in favour of a reform in the Civil Code. Thus, even at the draft revision stage, there is a predisposition towards the abolition of regulations that discriminate against illegitimate children in terms of their inheritance entitlement.

In Japan, the rate of illegitimate births is extremely low compared with that of the West (at 1.2 per cent in Japan in 1995, compared to 50 per cent in Sweden in 1994; 35 per cent in France in 1993 and 25 per cent in the United States in 1988). The reason for this is thought to be the strong social discrimination and prejudice against illegitimate children and single mothers in Japan. If a woman becomes pregnant before marriage, in most cases either the father marries the woman and they become a model married family or, if that is not possible, the woman has an abortion. As far as the children are concerned, whether the parents are married or not is something totally beyond their control, and it is unfair to disadvantage them for actions for which they have no responsibility. If equality for illegitimate children could be achieved through reforms in the law, this would be a breakthrough in setting a new path for the establishment of individual rights in family law.

---

[26] Decision of the Tokyo High Court of 23 June 1993, *Hanrei Jiho*, No. 1465, 55–65; Judgment of the Tokyo High Court of 30 Nov. 1994, *Hanrei Jiho*, No. 1512, 3–10.
[27] Decision of the Supreme Court of 5 July 1995, *Hanrei Jiho*, No. 1540, 3–12; *Minshu*, Vol. 49, No. 7, 1789.

E CONCLUSIONS

This chapter has discussed family law in Japan since the Meiji era. The rough sketch provided here offers the following conclusions.

Japanese law is characterised by the way its reforms were inspired by foreign systems. The two fundamental stages in the evolution of our modern family law were both influenced by pressures from the West. First, in 1889, the promulgation of our first modern constitution was brought about by the end of the warrior society and by the opening up of our country to foreign trade for the first time after 250 years of a policy of isolation. As I have indicated, this was a direct result of political, as well as military, pressure from Western Europe and America. Secondly, fundamental changes in our legal system occurred in 1945 following our defeat in the Second World War, when we were forced to abandon our old feudalistic and discriminatory system of family law and adopt a new and much more egalitarian code. The change in family law was carried out concurrently with the enactment of an American-style constitution. These latter changes were direct results of the policies of the allied forces occupying Japan.

Secondly, Japanese family law, compared with the family law of Western countries, was very much influenced by political ideology. The development of family law in the West has been marked by a steady succession of amendments made when such basic issues as human rights and equality between men and women emerged. In Japan, however, family law was positioned in the national law as an important apparatus to embody the political ideology demanded by the government of the day. In other words, family law was used as a means to regulate human relations uniformly. A good example was the *Iye* system, which was placed at the core of family law in the Meiji era in order to ensure such Confucian standards as a hierarchy according to the superiority of man over woman. The *Iye*, an enclosed social unit, functioned as a useful apparatus to constitute a totalitarian nation and embody its legal policy. It is for this reason that the old provisions in the Meiji Civil Code were mainly based on the collectively controlled family relations in the warrior society, not on the family relations of civilian society in the Edo period. Therefore, the old provisions in the Meiji Civil Code were not based on the lifestyles of the majority of the people. Law and reality were kept widely apart. This gap grew as capitalism marched relentlessly onward after the end of the First World War and as democracy movements became active. It can be safely said that the post-war legal reforms, although very strongly influenced by foreign pressure, were based on a social background that had already formed and on the reality of people's lives. The people then willingly accepted those reforms.

Thirdly, we cannot ignore the progressiveness and flexibility of the present family law. The current family law is now 50 years old, almost as venerable as its Meiji era predecessor was when it was rescinded. During this period, only minor amendments have been made[28] but no fundamental ones. It is important

[28] For example, based on the revisions of the Civil Code of 1980, when the inheritance of the dependent is shared with that of the children, the spouse's portion is raised from one-third to

to consider why the present family law was able to continue without major reform despite tremendous social changes. One reason is the progressiveness inherent in the law. Japanese family law was completely reformed after the Second World War on the basis of the dignity of the individual and the equality of the sexes in family life. At the time of the reform, the law was considerably more advanced than the reality of the family life it governed.

Another reason for the success of the current system is the flexibility of the law. The present family law entrusts the settlement of family relations, including family disputes, to the parties concerned in reaching their own agreement. This recognises the autonomy of private life. For instance: the basis of marriage is the mutual consent of both sexes; the surname is to be decided after discussion by the couple in the marriage; parental authority over children is to be exercised jointly by father and mother; husband and wife are obliged to co-operate with and assist each other; the couple is to share the expenses of married life; and divorce by consent is possible. When the required discussion between the parties is impossible or the discussion fails to reach a mutually accepted agreement, the case is then transferred to the Family Court and settled there. This flexibility explains why the present family law has survived for 50 years without any major amendments, despite deep-seated changes in society. Introducing a legal system that gives autonomy to the individuals involved is necessary at a time of great change in a nation when there can be a gap between traditional customs and modern society. In one sense, the system stood for non-interference by the state, but one problem with this is that inequalities of power between the parties allowed room for customs and politics to intrude into the system. For example, in a divorce by agreement it is usually the wife who is in a weak bargaining position so she will have to make sacrifices in the divorce agreement.

The legislative intention of the present family law was very advanced at the time that it was enacted, but it gradually became too superficial and without substance. There has been unprecedented social change within Japan in the last 50 years. The latent inconsistencies in the system began to emerge as social change called for greater real equality between the sexes and greater dignity for individuals. Problems have manifested themselves in the form of a large number of family-related litigated cases. In particular, the improvement of the economic status of women, along with more educational opportunities for women and the advancement of women into the workforce, prompted the enactment of the Equal Employment Opportunity Act. However, inequality between the sexes undeniably continues to exist in practice. It is under these most complex circumstances that the issues of having a separate surname for the husband and wife and discrimination between legitimate and illegitimate children are now up for serious

one-half (Civil Code, Art. 900). The contributory component has become recognised for the heir, who has made a special contribution to the maintenance and increase of the inherited assets (Civil Code, Art. 904(2)). In 1987, a special system was set up for adopted children who have been cut off from their real parents (Civil Code, Arts. 817–2 to 817–11).

discussion, and that the courts are being called on to have a more positive involvement in the settlement of a divorce.

Fourthly, the function of the family itself is under re-examination. I believe that discussions for the fundamental reform of the present family law should cover deeper grounds than those individual points which have been the subject of the law reform discussion up to now. Japanese society must inevitably confront a gradual shift towards a borderless and multi-cultural society. The imminent issues of the lower birth-rate, a rapidly ageing society and various life styles of the young generation now demand the re-examination of the concepts of family and marriage. For instance, the future debate should focus more on such questions as whether a marriage should be legal or factual, or between people of the same or the opposite sex. The concept of marriage itself will inevitably change. As in Western nations, family units in Japan may be destined to break up into units other than the nuclear family. Fundamental reform of the present family law will be required in the twenty-first century in order to regulate the relationship among family members with individuals as the core. How should family-related laws and policies respond to these changes, given the circumstances? In the writer's opinion, the government is misguided in trying to strengthen the role of the family in caring for the aged as a substitute for social insurance, in balking at reforming the legal system, in holding aloft the established morality of the family, and in using the family as a tool for social stability.

In the modern world, which demands individual dignity and equality between the sexes through declarations of human rights and international treaties, such issues as how far and how positively Japanese family law and family policy should support the family and how little they should interfere in the autonomy of individual life, are serious questions indeed.

REFERENCES

Books

HOZUMI, NOBUSHIGE, *Kanshu to Horitsu* (Iwanami-shoten, 1929).
—— *Hoten-Ron*, 1890 (Meiji Bunka Zenzhu, vol. 13, Nihon-Hyoronsha, 1957 included).
HOZUMI, YATSUKA, "Minpo Idete Chuko Horobu", *Hogakushinpo*, No. 5, 1891.
UME, KENJIRO, *Minpo Kogi* (Dobunkan, 1901).
TOMII, MASAAKIRA, *Minpo Genron* (Yuhikaku, 1905).
HOZUMI, SHIGETO, *Shinzoku-Ho Taii* (Iwanami-shoten, 1925).
TANIGICHI, TOMOHEI, *Nihon Shinzoku-Ho* (Kobundo-shobo, 1935).
NAKAGAWA, ZENNOSUKE, *Mibun-Ho no Sosoku-teki Kadai* (Iwanami-shoten, 1941).
—— *Nihon Shinsoku-Ho* (Nihon-Hyoronsha, 1942).
KAINO, MICHITAKA, *Horitsu Shakai-gaku no Shomondai* (Nihon-Hyoronsha, 1948).
KAWASHIMA, TAKEYOSHI, *Nihon-Shakai no Kazoku-teki Kosei* (Nihon-Hyoronsha, 1950).
—— *Ideology to Shiteno Kazoku-Seido* (Iwanami-Shoten, 1957).
NAKAGAWA, ZENNOSUKE, *Shinzoku-Ho*, Vol. 1, Vol. 2 (Seirin-Shoin, 1958).

WAGATSUMA, SAKAE, *Shinzoku-Ho*, Horitsugaku-Zenshu Vol. 23 (Yuhikaku, 1961).
ARICHI, TOHRU, *Kazoku Seido Kenkyu Josetsu* (Horitsu-bunka-sha, 1966).
FUKUSHIMA, MASAO, *Nihon Shihon-Shugi to Iye-Seido* (Tokyo-Daigaku-Shuppankai, 1967).
WATANABE, YOZO, *Kazoku to Ho* (Tokyo-Daigaku-Shuppankai, 1973).
AOYAMA, MICHIO, *Nihon Kazoku Seido-ron* (Kyushu-Daigaku-Shuppankai, 1978).
TOSHITANI, NOBUYOSHI, *Nihon no Ho wo Kangaeru* (Tokyo-Daigaku-Shuppankai, 1985).
TAKAYANAGI, SHINZO, *Meiji Zenki Kazoku-Ho no Shinso* (Yuhikaku, 1987).
SHIMAZU, ICHIRO, *Tenkan-ki no Kazoku-Ho* (Nihon-Hyoronsha, 1991).
BAI, KOICHI, *Sengo-Kaikaku to Kazoku-Ho* (Nihon-Hyoronsha, 1992).
NINOMIYA, SHUHEI, *Kazoku-Ho Kaikaku wo Kangaeru* (Nihon-Hyoronsha, 1993).
ISHIKAWA, MINORU, NAKAGAWA, JUN, and YONEKURA, AKIRA (eds.), *Kazoku-Ho Kaisei eno Kadai* (Nihon-Kajo-Shuppan, 1993).

Research Papers

TONOOKA, SHIGEJURO (ed.), *Meiji Zenki Kazoku-Ho Shiryo*, Vol. 1–3 (Waseda-Daigaku, 1973).
HOMUDAIJIN-KANBO SHIHO-HOSEI CHOSABU supervised, *Nihon Kindai Rippo Shiryososho; Hoten Chosakai Minpo Giji Sokkiroku*, Vols. 5–7 (Shoji-Homu-Kenkyukai, 1984).

Author's articles (in English)

MATSUSHIMA, YUKIKO, "Japan: Reforming Family Law", 32 (2) *University of Lousville Journal of Family Law* (1994).
—— "Japan: Continuing Reform in Family Law", 33 (2) *University of Lousville Journal of Family Law* (1995).
—— "Controversy and Dilemmas: Japan Confronts the Convention", in Michael Freeman (ed.), *Children's Rights: A Comparative Perspective* (Dartmouth, UK, 1996).

6

The Relationship between Social Change and Family Law in Korea

MI-KYUNG CHO

A INTRODUCTION

Since 1960, which is the year that Korean Civil Code became effective, Korean society has gone through turbulent changes. Korea has witnessed its economic condition greatly improved, its political situation democratised, its cultural consciousness elevated, and its social structure changed, along with successful industrialisation.

The law has also been modified as a result of these social changes. However, reforms of family law could not be smoothly implemented, because of the friction between two sides involved: the conservatives, whose Confucian beliefs assert the idea of predominance of man over woman and father over children, and the progressives who peacefully pursue the idea of equality of the sexes. Though Korean family law has been effective since 1960, major amendments have been made only twice during this period, first in 1977 and second in 1990.

This chapter briefly reviews the important social changes and the recent reform of family law in 1990[1] (in force since 1 January 1991) which could be described both as moderating the patriarchal character of the family and as the legal response to social change.

The main contents of this reform are:

1. weakening the head of the family system,
2. establishing a claim to division of property on divorce,
3. amending parental authority,
4. establishing an access right, and
5. amending the law of succession.

Among these regulations, the claim of division of property on divorce has been the most frequently used and it will be examined in detail in section D. In conclusion this chapter stresses the necessity of a further reform and suggests a direction of the new reform of family law in Korea.

---

[1] Mi-Kyung Cho, "Korea: The 1990 Family Law Reform and the Improvement of the Status of Women", 33 (2) *University of Louisville Journal of Family Law* 431–44.

B SOCIAL CHANGE SINCE 1960

The most important change of the social structure since 1960 (since the Korean Civil Code has been effective) up to the present in Korean society is that the *per capita* GNP has increased by 127.5 times. It was $79 in 1960,[2] but in 1995[3] it became $10,076. We can see a dramatic increase over three decades: $253 in 1970,[4] $1,597 in 1980,[5] $5,883 in 1990.[6] This clearly means a better quality of life for Koreans. Another index is the number of cars registered: this also has increased by 325 times: there were only 30,751 cars in 1960,[7] compared to about 10,000,000 in 1997.[8]

Along with economic improvements, there are other important social changes: first, the population has almost doubled: from 25 million in 1960 to 45 million in 1995;[9] average life expectancy was 52.4 years in 1960, rising to 71.6 years in 1991;[10] gender ratio[11] of male to female was 100.7 : 100 in 1960, changing to 101.4 : 100 in 1995. If we only look at the babies born in 1994, the ratio[12] is 115.5 : 100, indicating a higher number of boys than that of girls. This is explained by a general social trend of not having many children, but wanting to have a boy rather than a girl as a second child. If this ratio continues to increase, in 2010 it is expected to reach 123 : 100 for people who want to marry, thereby resulting in shortage of brides-to-be.[13]

Secondly, the extended form of family has given way to the nuclear form of family; the average number of family members falling from six in 1960[14] to three in 1995.[15] If the number of people in one household is taken into consideration, we can see that the number of one to four-member households is increasing, while the number of five of more member households is decreasing.[16] This means that the disintegration process of traditional families is continuing.

Thirdly, the divorce rate has dramatically risen by more than 400 per cent: from one divorce for every 27 marriages in 1960,[17] to one in six marriages in

---

[2] *Footsteps of Korea: in Statistics* (National Statistical Office, Republic of Korea, 1995), at 315.
[3] *Statistics in Life* (National Statistical Office, Republic of Korea, 1996), at 9.
[4] *Footsteps of Korea: in statistics, supra*, at 315.
[5] *Statistics in Life, supra*, at 9.
[6] *Statistics in Life, supra*, at 9.
[7] *Footsteps of Korea: in Statistics, supra*, at 249.
[8] *The Chosun Ilbo* (a newspaper), 15 July 1997, at 1.
[9] *Footsteps of Korea: in Statistics, supra*, at 63; 1995 population was estimated.
[10] *Footsteps of Korea: in Statistics, supra*, at 16, 70, 71.
[11] *Footsteps of Korea: in Statistics, supra*, at 63.
[12] *Statistics in Life, supra*, at 94.
[13] *The Dong-A Ilbo* (a newspaper), 9 January 1997, at 1.
[14] 5.7 in 1960, *Footsteps of Korea: in Statistics, supra*, at 15.
[15] "Number of household members decreases to 3": *The Chosun Ilbo* (a newspaper), 18 January 1997 at 35; 3.3 in 1995, *Advance Report of 1995 Population and Housing Census* (National Statistical Office, Republic of Korea, 1996), at 174.
[16] *Advance Report of 1995 Population and Housing Census, supra*, at 174.
[17] *Judicial Statistics Yearbook* (Office of Court Administration, 1960), at 169.

1995.[18] As it is in other developed countries, the divorce rate is rising at an incredible speed. The ratio of divorce by judicial decree to divorce by agreement has increased: divorce by judicial decree only constituted 3 per cent of all divorces in 1960,[19] but increased to 20 per cent in 1995.[20] The increase in divorce over three decades is as follows: one divorce for every 23 marriages in 1970,[21] for every 17 marriages in 1980,[22] and for every eight marriages in 1990.[23]

Fourthly, the relationship between the head of the family and family members has become comparatively equal, due to the weakening of a traditional patriarchal family system which was strongly influenced by Chinese Confucianism. This is the result of the common spread of perspectives on liberty and equality, based on democratic ideology.

Finally equality of the sexes has been partially realised, compared to the situation in the past. Western civilisation has been absorbed to realise greater women's rights, actualising the equality of sexes to a degree. However, Korea still not only faces many social injustices, but also legal injustices on this issue.

C WEAKENING OF HEAD OF THE FAMILY SYSTEM

The Korean Civil Code[24] consists of five books following the German *pandect* system. Korean Family Law consists of two parts among them: Book IV "Relatives" and Book V "Succession". In Chapter 2 of the Book IV defines the "head of the family" system, which is the hallmark of the Korean patriarchal system. This system derives from the deeply rooted male superiority found in traditional Confucianism.

The family consists of a "head of the family" and "members" of that family. There can be only one head of a family, and he could be succeeded only by "a male person who is a lineal descendant of the inheritee".[25] If there is no son, then the daughter can become the head of the family, but she will lose the title once she gets married.[26] According to the Korean Civil Code, the relationship between the head of the family and family members is one of command and obedience. Traditional Confucianism demanded absolute obedience from women. The three basic principles of obedience for women instructed that a woman ought to obey her father in childhood, her husband in marriage and her son after her husband's death.

[18] One divorce for every 5.5 marriages in 1995: *Judicial Yearbook* (Office of Court Administration, 1996), at 1078–9.

[19] *Judicial Statistics Yearbook* (Office of Court Administration, 1960), at 169.

[20] 58,843 divorces by agreement (≠ 80%); 14,371 divorces by judicial decree (≠ 20%) in: *Judicial Yearbook* (Office of Court Administration, 1996), at 1079.

[21] *Judicial Statistics Yearbook* (Office of Court Administration, 1970), at 264.

[22] *Judicial Yearbook* (Office of Court Administration, 1981), at 665.

[23] *Judicial Yearbook* (Office of Court Administration, 1991), at 991.

[24] Effective 1 January 1960.

[25] Korean Civil Code (hereinafter "KCC") Art. 984, item 1.

[26] KCC Art. 980, item 3.

In 1960, when the regulation about the head of the family was made, the title of the head of the family was actually meaningful, with 5.7 members of a household on average. With this number decreasing to 3.3 in 1995, however, the title of the head of the family has become less significant. The average number of household members decreasing to three means that there are only two people for every head of the family to control, making one wonder if there really is a need for the concept "head of the family". There is even a growing number of one-member families, constituting 12.7 per cent of all families in 1995.[27]

Feminist and family law academics have long argued for the abolition of the head of the family system, because it conflicts with the principles of democracy and the equality of the sexes.[28] Because of the resistance of traditional followers of Confucianism, the 1990 reformers were unable to abolish completely the head of the family system. However, its patriarchal character was moderated considerably, even though its framework remains. In particular, the Prohibition of Waiver of Right of Succession of the Headship of the Family[29] was amended. This was undoubtedly the most important reform of the head of the family system. As a result, the "right of succession to the headship of the family may be waived".[30]

In the Family Law Reform of 1990, Chapter 8, *succession to the headship of the family* was removed from Book V "Succession" and relegated to Book IV "Relatives". This subtle reform takes the "head of the family" notion from the realm of property succession and places it among other regulations of familial relationships. In addition, the head of the family was stripped of many rights as well as duties. For example, the head of the family's duty to support family members was repealed.[31] Also, the head of the family may no longer designate the place of residence of family members.[32] Despite the significant weakening of the head of the family system brought about by 1990 reform, the deletion of the entire system is still under discussion.

D ESTABLISHMENT OF CLAIM OF DIVISION OF PROPERTY ON DIVORCE[33]

Following the establishment of a new *claim of division of property on divorce* section in the modified family law in 1990,[34] significant developments have been achieved toward the improvement of the legal status of Korean women.

---

[27] *Advance Report of 1995 Population and Housing Census, supra*, at 174.
[28] Korean Constitution, Arts. 11, 36.
[29] Old version, Art 991.
[30] KCC, Art. 991.
[31] Old version, Art. 797.
[32] Old version, Art 798.
[33] Mi-Kyung Cho, "Korea: The Claim of Division of Property on Divorce", *The International Survey of Family Law 1995* (The International Society of Family Law, 1997) at 321–33.
[34] KCC, Art. 839–2.

Since the provision of the claim of division of property on divorce was introduced by the reform in 1990, the financial status of women in Korea after divorce has improved. Now, innocent wives can claim not only damages for mental distress in addition to property damages,[35] but also division of property on divorce. More importantly, even when a wife is responsible for the divorce, she can make a claim for the division of property.[36]

Article 839–2 of the Korean Civil Code provides: "One of the parties who has been divorced . . . may claim a division of property against the other party; If . . . it is impossible to reach an agreement, the Family Court shall, upon request of the parties, determine the amount and method of division taking into consideration the amount of property realised by cooperation of both parties and other circumstances."

This provision has been the most frequently used of the amended regulations in 1990. Along with the increase in divorce, claims for division of property have increased resulting in the many Supreme Court decisions. This will now be considered in more detail.

1 Property which becomes the Object of the Claim of Division of Property

1. Property realised by co-operation of both parties

Property with respect to which a claim of division may be made is property realised by co-operation of both parties during marriage. It has already been stated that the phrase "co-operation of both parties" acknowledges that the division of roles within a family consists of occupational activities of one party and household activities of the other. Supreme Court decisions[37] in 1993 and in 1994 have recognised the importance of household activities by indicating that if the help of the wife has significantly contributed to acquisition and maintenance of real property, then that real property becomes the object of the claim of division of property.

"Property" refers to the monetary value of the property at the time of appraisal less existing debts. Supreme Court decisions[38] deal with what amounts to "debts" for this purpose. A debt incurred by one spouse with a third party during marriage is a personal debt and will not be taken into account in the liquidation except where it was incurred in relation to the acquisition of the matrimonial property.

---

[35] KCC, Art. 806, para. 1, *mutatis mutandis* of KCC, Art. 843.

[36] Judgment of 11 May 1993, 93 su 6 (Supreme Court) in Korea.

[37] Judgment of 11 May 1993, 93 su 6 (Supreme Court) in Korea; Judgment of 11 June 1993, 92 mu 1054 (Supreme Court) in Korea; Judgment of 25 Oct. 1994, 94 mu 734 (Supreme Court) in Korea; Judgment of 13 Dec. 1994, 94 mu 598 (Supreme Court) in Korea.

[38] Judgment of 25 May 1993, 92 mu 501 (Supreme Court) in Korea: Judgment of 11 Nov. 1994, 94 mu 963 (Supreme Court) in Korea; Judgment of 2 Dec. 1994, 94 mu 1072 (Supreme Court) in Korea.

2. Pension and retirement allowance

The property which becomes the object of the claim of division of property includes the rights to the pension or the retirement allowance, and special licences for practice in law or medicine acquired during marriage (the so-called "New Property").

A Supreme Court decision[39] in 1995 states that the retirement allowance is a deferment of the value of the labour provided during marriage. Consequently it becomes a part of the matrimonial property during marriage. When one of the spouses already has a retirement allowance from work, this can be the object of liquidation. Where the amount of the retirement allowance has not yet been confirmed, a Supreme Court decision[40] in 1995 states that where the working party has not yet retired, the prospective retirement allowance cannot be included in the property for liquidation only on the basis of the probability of receiving it, unless there are special circumstances such as confirmation of the retirement date and the amount of the retirement allowance. But the decision states that a future allowance can be a factor to be considered in determining the amount of the division of property falling within the expression "other circumstances" in the Korean Civil Code Article 839–2 paragraph 2.

Attention should be drawn to a lower court decision[41] which ordered the division of property, taking into account new property, namely the licence for medical practice acquired during marriage. In other words, the co-operation of the wife in obtaining the husband's licence for the practice of medicine during marriage was acknowledged and the future income of the husband was also considered. The court stated that all factors must be considered. In addition to tangible property, intangible property, such as the licence for medical practice obtained by the husband with the co-operation of the wife, should be taken into account as well as the need to maintain the future life of the wife who had not had a regular income since the marriage.

2 The Method of the Division of Property

1. Division by the agreement of both parties

When one party to divorce by agreement or divorce by judicial decree[42] claims a division of property as against the other party, the agreement of both parties takes first priority in settling disputes about division of the property. And any method of division by agreement is legally acceptable.

---

[39] Judgment of 28 Mar. 1995, 94 mu 1584 (Supreme Court) in Korea.
[40] Judgment of 23 May 1995, 94 mu 1713 (Supreme Court) in Korea.
[41] Judgment of 13 June 1991, 91 du 1220 (Family Court of Seoul) in Korea, *Bupulshimun*, *The (Korea) Law Times*, 17 June 1991, at 1.
[42] KCC, Art. 839–2, para. 1, *mutatis mutandis* of KCC, Art. 843.

2. Division by court

On divorce, where no agreement is reached between the two parties regarding the division of property, the family court intervenes in the dispute. Either party may make a claim for division of property to the Family Court within two years of the divorce.[43] Since the court determines the consolation money payable on divorce, division of property at the time of divorce is viewed as part of this process, and the court has power to decide the amount and method of the division of property, taking into account the amount of the property realised by the co-operation of the parties concerned and other circumstances. A Supreme Court decision[44] also states, regarding the property capable of division, that the court is not restricted to the property claimed but may include other property as a result of its own factual investigations.

3 The Amount of Division and the Method of Payment

1. The amount of division

The amount of the division of matrimonial property depends on the exercise of the court's discretion. Regarding the amount of division, there is a Supreme Court decision[45] which states in the case of the wife only engaged in household labour that it would be excessive in these circumstances to order the husband to transfer one half of his interest in the property to her. This would violate the principle of equality where the wife has not engaged in any significant economic activity. However, other decisions[46] by and large order a half and half division. The lower court cases[47] generally order "equal distribution" where both spouses are engaged in occupational activities. There are also cases[48] ordering a division of one third where the wife happens to be a full time housekeeper.

Further, in view of the fact that there is no maintenance system after divorce in Korea, where the amount of property realised by the co-operation of both parties is so small that one party cannot support herself while the other party is capable of making payments, the court takes other circumstances into consideration and can order division of more property than the equal distribution implied by liquidation. A Supreme Court decision[49] which implies an obligation to support, holds that the sum for division which a husband must pay to a wife may in some

---

[43] KCC, Art 839–2, para. 3.

[44] Judgment of 28 Mar. 1995, 94 mu 1584 (Supreme Court) in Korea.

[45] Judgment of 2 Dec. 1994, 94 mu 1072 (Supreme Court) in Korea.

[46] "a little less than ½": Judgment of 28 Mar. 1995, 94 mu 1584 (Supreme Court) in Korea; "an amount that exceeds ½ by a little": Judgment of 25 Aug. 1995, 94 mu 1515 (Supreme Court) in Korea.

[47] Judgment of 16 May 1991, 90 du 62624 (Family Court of Seoul) in Korea; Judgment of 5 June 1991, 90 du 48598 (Family Court of Seoul) in Korea; Judgment of 7 June 1991, 89 du 58308 (Family Court of Seoul) in Korea; Judgment of 24 July 1991, 91 du 13452 (Family Court of Seoul) in Korea.

[48] Judgment of 5 Sept. 1991, 90 du 63436 (Family Court of Seoul) in Korea.

[49] Judgment of 25 Aug. 1995, 94 mu 1515 (Supreme Court) in Korea.

circumstances exceed one half of the value of the property in the husband's name. In such a case, the court will consider the extent of the wife's contribution to the acquisition of the property, the ages of the parties and various other circumstances. There is a lower court decision[50] where the husband, a doctor, had been ordered to support the wife after divorce.

2. The method of payment

Payment of the divided amount can be performed by any method, such as division of the actual property concerned or monetary division. Regarding monetary division a Supreme Court decision[51] has held that the monetary equivalent of the value of the property may be ordered to be paid. A number of lower court cases[52] have ordered division of actual articles, but there are more cases[53] ordering monetary division.

Property acquired during marriage should be shared fairly between the parties. This new provision acknowledges that the housewife's household labour is economically valuable work, because the Family Court determines the amount of property allocated to each party, taking into account the amount of property realised through the co-operation of both parties during the marriage. However, Article 830 of the Korean Civil Code (Matrimonial Property: property acquired during marriage in his or her own name shall constitute his or her specific property) is still in force, and consequently (but contradictorily),[54] the market value of the housewife's household labour is not yet properly considered. Therefore, Article 830 of the Korean Civil Code should be amended.

E REFORM OF PARENTAL AUTHORITY AND RESPONSIBILITY FOR CARE AND EDUCATION OF CHILDREN

According to the Korean Civil Code, the rights of parents over children are divided into two: parental authority[55] and responsibility for care and education of children on divorce.[56] These rights were amended in 1990, to promote further the welfare of the child. Parental authority is regulated under the provisions about Parents and Children in Article 909 of the Korean Civil Code. Responsibility for care and education and the access right on divorce are stated

---

[50] Judgment of 13 June 1991, 91 de 1220 (Family Court of Seoul) in Korea.

[51] Judgment of 28 Mar. 1995, 94 mu 1584 (Supreme Court) in Korea.

[52] Judgment of 7 June 1991, 89 du 58308 (Family Court of Seoul) in Korea; Judgment of 3 Sept. 1991, 90 du 74856 (Family Court of Seoul) in Korea.

[53] Judgment of 8 Aug. 1991, 90 du 63238 (Family Court of Seoul) in Korea; Judgment of 12 Sept. 1991, 90 du 74375 (Family Court of Seoul) in Korea; Judgment of 19 Sept. 1991, 90 du 24912 (Family Court of Seoul) in Korea.

[54] KCC, Art. 839–2.

[55] KCC, Art. 909.

[56] KCC, Art. 837.

in the context of divorce, provided in Articles 837 (responsibility for care and education) and 837–2 (access right) of the Korean Civil Code. The following subsection will explain these in depth.

1 Reform of Parental Authority

Korean family law regulates the "parental authority" over a child. The clause is most properly translated from Korean as "parental authority", not as "care" or "custody". Parental authority is distinguished from the parental responsibility for care and education of his or her child. "The parental authority shall be exercised jointly by parents, when the parents are married".[57]

Before the reform, in another hang-over from the patriarchal family system, a divorced mother was not allowed parental authority over her child.[58] Even if the divorced mother had the responsibility of caring for and educating her children,[59] parental authority was given only to the father.[60] This provision was amended in 1990. Now when "parents are divorced, the person who is to exercise the parental authority, shall be determined by an agreement between the father and mother, and if it is impossible to reach an agreement, or they fail to reach an agreement, the Family Court shall determine it upon a request of the parties".[61] Therefore, now a divorced mother may exercise parental authority as part of a divorce by agreement or divorce by judicial decree.

2 Reform of Responsibility for Care and Education of Children on Divorce

Article 837 of the Civil Code, dealing with the scope of responsibility for care and education of children, was also amended by the recent reform of family law in 1990. The old version provided that "in a case where an agreement has not been made on matters concerning care and education of the children born of the parties, the father is responsible for the care and education of his children".[62] But the reformed provision of Article 837 of the Korean Civil Code provides: "The parties shall determine by agreement matters concerning the care and education of their children after divorce.[63] If an agreement . . . has not been made nor can be reached, the Family Court may, upon the application filed by the parties, decide the matters necessary for such care and education by taking into

---

[57] KCC, Art. 909, para. 2.
[58] Old version, Art. 909, para. 5.
[59] KCC, Art. 837.
[60] Old version, Art 909, para. 5.
[61] KCC, Art. 909, para. 4.
[62] Old version, Art. 837.
[63] KCC, Art. 837, para. 1.

consideration the age of their child or children, property status of the father and mother and any other circumstances thereof . . . "[64]

3 Establishment of an Access Right

Reform of the family law in 1990 has established the new access right which could be a right of the child. Article 837–2 of the Korean Civil Code provides: "A father or mother, who does not directly raise his or her child or children, shall have the right to interview and negotiate." Before the reform, the father was solely responsible for the children when an agreement had not been reached.[65] The mother had no right to interview and negotiate over her child. Despite the reform, however, it is still the norm that the father gains parental authority over the children after a divorce. This practice reflects the patriarchal character of the Korean family custom and the economic weakness of the divorced mother. Before the reform, the divorced mother was absolutely prohibited from meeting her child. This extreme measure no longer is the case.

F REFORM OF THE LAW OF SUCCESSION

The law of succession in Korea was also amended in 1990, improving the status of women in this aspect as well. Changes in the *legal portions* section[66] have proved to contribute considerably to the enhancement of the status of women.

Before the reform, Korean family law held: "If there exist two or ore successors in the same rank, they inherit in equal portions. However, if a successor to property succeeds concurrently to the head of a family, his shares in the succession of property shall be his inherent portions plus fifty percent thereof."[67] However, the inheritance portion of a female successor "whose name is not registered in the same family registry shall be one-fourth of a male successor's portion".[68]

The phrase "female successor whose name is not registered in the same family registry" refers to the married daughter of the deceased person. When a woman marries, her family surname is not changed, but her registration is transferred to the husband's family.[69] Consequently, under the old law, a married woman had to accept only one-fourth of a male successor's portion.[70]

This was a significant example of sex discrimination in Korea, and it indicated the pervasiveness of male-orientedness in this society. However, the newly

[64] KCC, Art. 837, para. 2.
[65] Old version, Art. 837.
[66] KCC, Art. 1009.
[67] Old version, Art. 1009, para. 1.
[68] Old version, Art. 1009, para. 2.
[69] KCC, Art. 826, para. 3.
[70] Old version, Art. 1009, para. 2.

revised provision indicates that all successors have equal portion regardless of sex, marriage status or status as the next head of the family. It is an encouraging development that Korean inheritance law now states: "If there are two or more successors of the same rank, their shares in the succession shall be equally divided."[71]

G   CONCLUSION

This chapter has briefly reviewed the relationship between social change and the family law in Korea and how the 1990 family law reform as the legal responses to the social change has improved the status of women in Korea. This amendment weakened, but did not eradicate, the patriarchal character of Korean family law. The reform, however, was an important first step to protecting women from discrimination in their legal and social life. The efforts must be continued to realise a complete equality of both sexes through subsequent reforms in Korean family law.

[71] KCC, Art. 1009, para. 1.

7

Ireland: The Family and the Law in a Divided Land

KERRY O'HALLORAN

INTRODUCTION

The island of Ireland is divided into two cultural traditions and two jurisdictions. The separation of culture and land more or less coincide. The south is an independent Republic of 26 counties and Roman Catholicism is the cultural tradition of at least 90 per cent of the population. The north consists of six counties, is constitutionally a part of the United Kingdom and while approximately 60 per cent of the population belong to the Protestant cultural tradition the remainder are largely Catholics. The island and its inhabitants are thus divided almost exclusively into these two powerful cultural blocks.

This carefully contrived constitutional arrangement for cultural and territorial partition was achieved by adjusting borders, populations and electoral boundaries to maximise the political supremacy of the two main groupings in their respective territories on the island. It may be seen as essentially a colonial arrangement.

To understand how family forms on the island of Ireland have now come to stand as historical legacies of their separate cultural traditions we must first examine their past. We can then consider whether inherited family forms provide a suitable fit for modern family needs.

This chapter is in three Parts. Each holds focus on the three usual benchmarks of the law as it relates to marriage, children and property.

The first and largest Part is concerned with the history of the family in Ireland during the period when the island remained undivided by its present internal frontier. The second and briefest Part is also historical and is concerned with what happened to the law and structures of the family when the island was partitioned. The final Part identifies and compares some current characteristic differences between the island's two jurisdictions. From that comparison this chapter draws some conclusions about the extent to which present differences embody and perpetuate an historical legacy.

First Period

The island of Ireland was not always divided. Two successive legal systems provided unifying frameworks for the development of social institutions and structures, including those of the family.

The first period of legal unity commenced during the early centuries of the last millennium. The Brehon Laws[1] prevailed for at least 1,000 years and formed the legal bedrock for governing the social life within and between the patchwork of separate clans and their kingdoms which covered the length and breadth of the island. This period also saw that other great institution, the Roman Catholic Church, become rooted in Irish society. The clans were tied to their traditional family territories. They were autonomous social groupings and they were constantly feuding with each other. By the ninth century the Brehon Laws had evolved as a fully developed body of law, often administered by a nominal High King of Ireland, to govern disputes between clans and by clan chieftains to settle internal disputes. These laws applied throughout the island of Ireland and remained in place until destroyed by invading English armies.

Characteristics of the Brehon Laws included, first, the fact that marriage was not an indissoluble union.[2] Secondly, due to that fact, there were always large numbers of illegitimate children in the clan system. They were not disadvantaged; they were entitled to inherit equally with their legitimate siblings and there does not seem to have been any attached sense of stigma. Thirdly, the custom of "gavelkind" was integral to the Brehon Laws.[3] This was the practice whereby on the death of a clan member his land was divided equally among all the adult sons in the clan both legitimate and illegitimate. Fourthly, adoption[4] was very common under the Brehon Laws both as a means of reinforcing the collective strength of that social group and to demonstrate alliances between clans.[5] It was free of stigma and any child, whether legitimate or illegitimate, could be adopted and could then acquire rights of inheritance. Finally, foster care was well devel-

---

[1] See, for example, the account given of the Brehon Laws by F. Kelly, *Early Irish Law* (Dublin, Institute of Administrative Studies, 1988).

[2] There were 7 instances in which the Brehon Laws permitted a wife to legally separate from her husband. This looseness of the marriage tie continued in Ireland at least until Elizabethan times.

[3] For an account of this practice, see Robbins, *The Lost Children* (Dublin, Institute of Public Administration, 1980), at 2–3.

[4] The Irish word for adoption was *foesam* which simply meant "taking into protection". The clan system facilitated a practice of formal adoption—which relied on contracts, specified duties and payments.

[5] See H. J. Abramson, *Issues in Adoption in Ireland* (Dublin, the Economic and Social Research Institute, 1984), at 18. The author there refers to this early form of adoption in Ireland as "supplemented kinship" as distinct from what he terms "supplanted kinship" which he suggests characterises the modern form of adoption.

oped. The closed boundaries typical of the modern private nuclear family had no place in the Irish clan system.[6]

Under the Brehon Laws foster care[7] was largely "kinship fostering" whereby the extended family, or clan, would take care of its own. So, for at least a full millennium, this body of law provided the governing authority for shaping family structures and resolving family disputes throughout the island of Ireland. Then the family in effect was the clan. Public and private law were not readily distinguishable.

Second Period

The second period of legal unity resulted from successful conquest. The Brehon Laws and the social system of independent clans disappeared under the weight of foreign military rule.[8] As England consolidated its control, it extended the common law and statutory law to Ireland.

First, English rule brought with it legislation to enforce monogamous union for life as the only legal form of marriage.[9] Thereafter marriage could be ended only by annulment through the ecclesiastic courts or by divorce following a private act of Parliament.

Secondly, with the suppression of the Brehon Laws the relatively favourable position of illegitimate children was swept aside by a combination of common law principles, statutory law and assertion of Christian values in relation to marriage and to marital faithfulness.[10]

---

[6] Children were reared within a clan's extended family network. A sophisticated system of foster care existed which made provision for boys to be fostered until the age of 14 and girls until 17. Families would frequently make formal contractual arrangements to place a child for reasons of tutelage or for cementing allegiances with other families within the clan.

[7] Kelly *Op. cit.*, at 87–91. Strict rules were applied which required a foster child to be maintained according to his or her rank. The son of a king, for example, had to be supplied with a horse for riding. Again a foster child also had to be educated and trained appropriate to their rank; a well-bred girl, for example, would be taught sewing, cloth-cutting and embroidery skills while a girl of humbler origins would be taught basic cooking skills. Where one family was unable to care for a child, that responsibility would be assumed by another family within the clan and the expense of rearing the child would be borne by the clan. See also S. O'h. Innse, *Fosterage in Early and Medieval Ireland* (unpublished masters thesis, School of Law, Trinity College Dublin, 1960).

[8] In particular the many massacres and the destruction of the great monasteries by Cromwell in the middle of the 17th century did much to crush and suppress the Catholic identity of the Irish people. This suppression was reinforced by the deliberate policy of settling English Protestant families on Irish land under the protection of English armed forces. The process of colonisation was particularly effective in the north of the island.

[9] See Davies, *A Discovery of the True Causes*, 126. This was intended to regulate what was seen by Sir John Davies and others as the licentious behaviour of the Irish. By 1660, according to the contemporary writings of Geoffrey Keating in *The History of Ireland*, the marriage bond had become generally respected throughout Ireland.

[10] As H. B. Abramson has said "By the close of the 18th century, at any rate, the stigma of illegitimacy had taken a powerful hold on the cultural values and social system of the Irish people" (*op. cit.* at 15).

Finally, destruction of the monasteries and suppression of the Brehon Laws combined with the effects of war and plague to leave many Irish children destitute and without the protection of the defunct clan system. To cope with these problems the Poor Laws[11] of England were extended to Ireland. Kinship or private foster care was replaced by institutional or public care.

PART 2—PARTITION

The political, cultural and territorial division of the island of Ireland began in 1916 and was finalised in 1922. However, not until the Constitution of Ireland was established in 1937 as the overarching body of principles[12] governing the law in the 26 counties of the south did the development of the law relating to the family begin to deviate significantly from equivalent law in the six counties of the north.

The 1937 Constitution succeeded, more effectively than the frontier had done, in dividing the population of Ireland. It placed Irish family law in the 26 counties on an ideological basis. Its natural law ethos emphasised the indissoluble nature of marriage. It stressed the inalienable nature of parental rights and duties. It upheld the inviolable integrity of the marital family unit.[13] In particular, it declared the special position of the Roman Catholic Church. The cultural separation of the Roman Catholic population of the south from the Protestant population of the north became enshrined in law.

Thereafter, in the south, the constitutional ban on any legislation which might permanently impair the legal integrity of the marital family,[14] has presented an effective block on legislative initiative to any recognition of possible separate legal interests owned by the individual parties within the marital family. A marital family was ideologically defined and constitutionally protected as being more than the sum of its parts. When family breakdown occurred that unit was not legally divisible into autonomous sets of interests.

Thereafter, in the north, however, under Westminster initiated legislation, that was precisely the effect of bringing the results of family breakdown before the

---

[11] As represented by the statutes of 1703, 1838 and 1862 foster care was replaced by institutional or public care. The Poor Law era applied throughout the island and continued until the public interest in the care and welfare of children was replaced throughout Ireland by such legislation as the Guardianship of Infants Act 1886 and the Children Act 1908.

[12] See J. H. Whyte, *Church & State in Modern Ireland 1923–1979* (Dublin, Gill and Macmillan 1984); particularly ch. 2 'The Catholic Moral Code becomes enshrined in the Law of the State, 1923–37'.

[13] The Constitution abolished the Matrimonial Causes and Marriage Law (Ireland) Amendment Act 1870 and with it the civil proceedings for divorce. By Art. 41—The Family:

"3.1. The State pledges itself to guard with special care the institution of marriage, on which the family is founded, and to protect it against attack."

Also, see, Art. 41.3.2 which states "No law shall be enacted providing for the grant of a dissolution of marriage".

[14] See Art. 41. 3.1.

courts. The ethos of legal pragmatism defined the legislative and judicial approach to the difficulties associated with family breakdown. This permitted a more flexible and functional separation of a family's collective legal interests.[15]

PART 3—CURRENT FAMILY LAW AND STRUCTURES

For the past 75 years the island of Ireland has been divided into two jurisdictions.[16] The Roman Catholic cultural tradition of the 26 southern counties has developed and been consolidated under the natural law ethos of the 1937 Constitution. The Protestant cultural tradition[17] entrenched its political dominance in the six counties of the north for the first 50 years, ameliorated to a degree during the past 23 years by the legal pragmatism of direct rule from Westminster.

Now, the most characteristic differences in family law between the island's two jurisdictions are those which derive from one differentiating factor—namely, the *locus standi* of the marital family.[18] These differences can be seen in the following brief impressionistic survey of comparable legal responses to the same modern social pressures. But, while this deals with the effects of difference in substantive law, it must also be borne in mind that differences of process were

[15] Basically, the legal status of the family is defined differently in the two jurisdictions. In the south, there is a public law assumption that the status of 'family' is conferred by a marriage ceremony (Art. 41.3.1) that thereafter the integrity of the marital family unit in entitled to protection in law (*KC* v. *An Bord Uchtala* [1985] ILRM 302) and that any private rights of a party to that unit should not be exercisable so as to terminally damage that integrity. In the north, as elsewhere in the UK, the public law assumption is that status is now conferred more on 'parenthood' than on 'family', that the law will extend its protection primarily to the child in such a unit and that all parties hold private rights to enter into or leave that unit whether or not a marriage ceremony has been effected in respect of it.

[16] For a scholarly consideration of this period see Whyte, *Church & State in Modern Ireland 1923–1979* (Dublin, Gill & Macmillan, 1980).

[17] See, J. H. Whyte, *Interpreting Northern Ireland* (Oxford, Clarendon Press, 1990) for a thorough examination of the characteristics of Protestant culture in the north at this time.

[18] See, the Constitution, Art. 41—The Family:
"1.1. The State recognises the Family as the natural primary and fundamental unit group of Society, and as a moral institution possessing inalienable and imprescriptible rights, antecedent and superior to all positive law.
1.2. The State, therefore, guarantees to protect the family in its constitution and authority, as the basis of social order and as indispensable to the welfare of the Nation and the State."
The above and, in descending order of importance, the remaining provisions of Art. 41, Art. 42, the fundamental rights articulated in Arts. 40.1 and 40.3, together with the rights relating to religion in Art. 44, provide the body of constitutional provisions responsible for the legal elevation of the marital family unit. See A Shatter, *Family Law in the Republic of Ireland* (Dublin, Wolfhound Press, 1985), who identifies the following instances where a judicial response to constitutional provisions has given recognition to the distinctive legal standing of a marital family: fluoridation (*Ryan* v. *The Attorney General* [1965] IR 294); taxation (*Murphy* v. *The Attorney General* [1982] IR 241); homosexuality (*Norris* v. *The Attorney General* [1984] IR 36); succession (*O'B* v. *S* [1984] IR 316); spousal residence in the state (*Mohammed Abdelkefi and Susanne Abdelkefi* v. *The Minister for Justice* [1984] ILRM 138, also *The State (Bouzagou)* v. *Fitzgibbon Street Garda Station* [1986] ILRM 98); dissolution of marriage (*Murray & Murray* v. *The Attorney General & Ireland* [1985] ILRM 542); separation (*Dalton* v. *Dalton* [1982] ILRM 418); and foreign divorce decrees (*G* v. *G* [1984] IR 368).

also at work. The earlier availability in the north of comprehensive schemes of free legal aid and welfare benefits (particularly for unmarried mothers) provided its poorer citizens with a financial capacity to take decisions relating to legal status which were denied for some time to their counterparts in the south.

First—the Law Relating to Family Breakdown[19]

Divorce[20] in the south was prohibited by the Constitution[21] as a means of enforcing a legal definition of marriage as a life long monogamous union. The absence of divorce in the south has led to a great increase in recourse to nullity suits,[22] to foreign divorces and to very many situations where spouses simply choose to live apart, perhaps with new partners, but without any hope of regularising the legal status of their new domestic arrangements. In contrast, the availability of divorce in the north has resulted in very many legally reconstituted families.[23]

Secondly—the Law Relating to Assisted Conception

Abortion is illegal in both jurisdictions.[24] Contraceptives have a legally restricted availability in the south but are freely available in the north. The law relating to methods of artificially facilitating parenthood is, however, very different. In the north the UK legislation governing surrogacy arrangements applies and the full range of medically assisted treatments are available. In the south, the natural law ethos of the Constitution has prevented the introduction of equivalent legislative provisions.[25] The net result is that decisions about becoming a parent lie more

[19] See, T. Fahey and M. Lyons, *Marital Breakdown & Family Law in Ireland* (Dublin, The Economic and Social Research Institute, 1995). The authors estimate that Ireland has a much lower rate of marital breakdown than is the norm elsewhere in the western world but comment that the absence of divorce " . . . has not caused Ireland to have a lower marital breakdown rate than is found in southern Europe" (110).

[20] Divorce in the north has been available since its introduction throughout the island by the Matrimonial Causes and Marriage Law (Ireland) Amendment Act 1870.

[21] The Constitution abolished the Matrimonial Causes and Marriage Law (Ireland) Amendment Act 1870 and with it the civil proceedings for divorce. By Art. 41—The Family:
"3.1. The State pledges itself to guard with special care the institution of marriage, on which the family is founded, and to protect it against attack."

[22] See, P. O'Connor, *Key Issues in Irish Family Law* (Dublin, The Round Hall Press, 1988), Part 1 "Nullity", 1–71. The author notes the remarkable increase in the number of nullity petitions and in the creative judicial interpretation of the grounds in recent years. There can be no doubt that the law of nullity has been developed as a "modern" mechanism for coping with the historical legacy presented by the explicit constitutional ban on divorce.

[23] The availability of divorce was broadened by inclusion of grounds of desertion, cruelty and incurable insanity; and extended by the Matrimonial Causes (NI) Order 1978 to include no fault grounds. The 1991 census for Northern Ireland recorded 11,302 persons registered as divorced.

[24] In the north, abortion remains illegal; the Abortion Act 1967 applies only to England & Wales, though women requiring a termination are often routinely referred to clinics in England. In the south, the Constitution was amended in 1983 to prohibit the enacting of any law permitting abortion.

[25] Surrogacy arrangements are illegal in the south.

within the control of couples in the north than is the case with couples in the south.

Thirdly—the Law Relating to Illegitimacy

The primacy accorded to the marital family under the Constitution had the corollary of marginalising illegitimate children and their mothers.[26] For many years, until legislation explicitly addressed this inequity, the strong social stigma, together with a lack of legal status and lack of eligibility for welfare benefits, forced the surrender of many thousands of children in the south for adoption or for assisted emigration.[27] In the north, the sense of social stigma was itself probably sufficient to achieve the same end result.

Fourthly—the Law Relating to Child Care

The constitutional declaration regarding the inviolability of the marital family led to some specific differences in the development of child care. In the south, at least until the implementation of the Child Care Act 1991, there was no history of child care interventionist powers.[28] The parents of children judged to be at risk of abuse or neglect would be more likely to be offered a voluntary foster care[29] service rather than be faced with a compulsory long term care order.[30] In the north, the frequent use of compulsory interventionist powers is long established. Similarly, there has never been any equivalent in the south to the freeing for adoption orders used in the north by the statutory child care agencies to compulsorily place abused children for adoption. Again, while statutory child care agencies in the north had frequent recourse to wardship,[31] as a means of ensuring the protection of children, there was no comparable use of wardship in the south.[32] Basically, in the south, the Constitution established a firm legal

[26] See, e.g., *G* v. *An Bord Uchtala* [1980] IR 32 where Henchy J remarked that due to
"the central and fundamental position accorded by the Constitution to the family in the social and moral order, there is a necessary and inescapable difference of moral capacity and social function between parents or a parent within a family and the parents or parent of an illegitimate child."

[27] For a history of adoption law in the southern jurisdiction, see O'Halloran, *Adoption Law and Practice* (Dublin, Butterworths, 1992).

[28] This is a direct consequence of constitutional protection given to: parental rights; the integrity and autonomy of the marital family unit; the legal protection to which it is entitled; and the presumption that child welfare is best assured by care within his or her family of origin.

[29] See, R. Gilligan, *Foster Care for Children in Ireland* (Dublin, Trinity College, Occasional Paper No 2, 1990).

[30] See, R .Gilligan, *op. cit.*

[31] See O'Halloran, *Wardship in Northern Ireland* (Belfast, SLS, 1988). The governing principle in wardship was articulated by MacDermott LJ in *J* v. *C* [1970] AC 668 where he stated that in all cases concerning the welfare of the infant
" . . . the court shall regard the welfare of the infant as the first and paramount consideration."

[32] This was because of the constitutional difficulty in giving recognition to the principle that in welfare matters a child's best interests must be treated as the factor of paramount importance. Under

presumption that the care responsibility for a child should rest with that child's parents and the relevant agencies were very hesitant about challenging that presumption. In the north, however, the equivalent agencies were instead encouraged to give precedence to a child rescue approach.

Fifthly and Finally—the law Relating to Adoption

A distinctive jurisdictional difference in adoption law has been that in the south adoption was not available in respect of legitimate children nor was it available in circumstances where a natural mother refused her consent.[33] Therefore, in the north adoption developed not only as a private family law procedure but also as a public law option to provide homes for abused or neglected children despite parental resistance. In the south it remained virtually exclusively a private family law procedure. The constitutional bar on the adoption of legitimate children has led to adopters looking overseas for available children. The difference between the two jurisdictions in the numbers of foreign adoptions completed in recent years is very marked. It is estimated that in the south, such adoptions may have exceeded 3–4,000 in the past five years whereas in the north the comparable figure would be fewer than 50.[34]

CONCLUSION

This whistle stop tour of family law—across the island of Ireland and across the last two millennia—has noted certain characteristics from past legal systems which presently impact upon the family. From the period of the Brehon Laws at least two legacies are worthy of particular attention: first, from the legal fusion of clan and family we can trace the present success of foster and adoption placements within the extended families of the children concerned; secondly, in the legacy of "gavelkind" rather than primogeniture we can see the ruinous history of sub-divided farms so many of which are now barely viable as farming units. From the period of the Catholic Church's ascendancy perhaps the main legacy is the ideological basis for family law in the 26 counties—as evident in the lack of certain proceedings such as divorce, in the treatment of illegitimacy and in the

---

Arts. 41.1, 41.2 and 42.1 of the Constitution a marital child has the natural and imprescriptible right to belong, to be cared for and to be educated by his or her marital family. Judicial acknowledgement exists (see the comments of Walsh J in *G* v. *An Bord Uchtala* [1980] IR 32 at 76) to suggest that this right may override the statutory principle of the paramount welfare of the child—at least in disputes between a marital parent and third parties (see judgment of Finlay CJ in *In re JH* [1984] IR 599).

[33] Statute law introduced legal adoption to the north of Ireland in 1929 but this did not occur in the south until 1952. For a history of adoption law in the northern jurisdiction see O'Halloran, *Adoption Law in Northern Ireland* (Belfast, SLS, 1994).

[34] For statistical data comparing the use of adoption see O'Halloran, *Adoption in the Two Jurisdictions of Ireland* (Aldershot, Avebury, 1994).

cultural estrangement between the two jurisdictions. From the period of direct rule from England we can perhaps single out the legacy of a common law emphasis in family law which, with its concern for the individual's rights and duties, has conspired with monolithic cultural insularity to prevent recognition of the legal interests of minority groups.

This chapter has argued that in Ireland the nature and significance of current differences in the two jurisdictions arose from a process of colonisation—certainly by an imperial power and perhaps also by an imperious church. The consequences may now be clearly seen in the lack of fit between modern family needs and inherited family legal structures.

This brief historical survey reveals one particular area of resonance with the experience of South Africa. Legislating exclusively rather than inclusively for different cultural traditions is a defensive and ultimately negative approach to cultural differences. It is not merely divisive in itself but tends to nurture the growth of reinforcing ideologies and cements into place the respective hallmarks of cultural difference. These can then acquire icon status and prevent a flexible response to new social pressures. Also, divisions based on ideological differences tend to prevent, or unduly delay, a recognition of the rights of other discrete minorities existing within the same territorial boundaries. Thus, ethnic and racial minority groups together with such others as homosexuals, travelling people, disabled people, unmarried parents and of course women have all suffered from being either ignored, disadvantaged or discriminated against outright in both the jurisdictions of Ireland.

Looking back at the island of Ireland, from the perspective offered by the recent history of South Africa, two cultures are apparent which have a proven capacity to accommodate their differences and live together within a single common legal system. When separated, each instantly and deliberately set about strengthening and purifying their respective cultural models. The south became more Roman Catholic and the north more Protestant. Two cultural monolithic blocks developed: each becoming steadily more homogenous, each less able to cope with the other, unwilling to move away from their respective cultural reference points, assimilating the cultural identities of other minority groups and resistant to accommodating internally generated pressure for change. For at least the first 50 years after legal separation they seemed to concentrate mainly on pushing each other into becoming polarised cultural opposites. For the past decade or so things have been changing on the island of Ireland. Both jurisdictions seem to be recognising a need to respond in the same way to similar influences from the UN Convention on the Rights of the Child, the European Convention on Human Rights and Fundamental Freedoms, the Hague Conventions and to decisions taken by the European Court of Human Rights[35]. There are now emerging some clear indications of jurisdictional convergence. The most significant legislative step towards convergence came with the Family

[35] For example *Johnson v Ireland* (1987) 9 EHRR 203; *Dudgeon* v. *UK* (1981) 4 EHRR 149; *Morris v Ireland* (1991) 13 EHRR 186.

Law (Divorce) Act 1996 which gave the courts in the south of the island a restricted form of divorce previously only available in the north.

Perhaps, for the future of family law in South Africa as much as for on this island, the main lesson to be learned is the value of now looking out rather than in for the legal norms with a capacity to so inform the legislative framework that our laws may genuinely accommodate internal cultural diversity. A "rainbow nation state" is the goal of South Africa's political leadership. It may also be said to be the inspiration behind the European Union. The gradual harmonising effect of various conventions and rulings of the ECHR is serving to highlight the redundancy of certain historical legacies relating to the law and structure of the family within and between individual nations. A rapidly expanding EU, steadily building and consolidating a principled basis for transcending a millennium of divisive conflict between different cultural groups, offers an example and a challenge of equal relevance to both South Africa and to the island of Ireland.

8

Should and Can Family Law Influence Social Behaviour?

ANDERS AGELL

INTRODUCTION

Legislation can provide rules for solving social problems and conflicts between individuals. However, another aim of legislation can be to influence the *behaviour* of people. Even if legislators, either those who have drafted the laws or formed the majority vote in Riksdagen (the Swedish parliament), do not directly wish to influence social behaviour, legislation can have such an impact anyway.

The main issue in my presentation concerns the extent to which Swedish legislation during the past 30 years has been drafted with the *purpose* of influencing the structures for family building and for family life. The ability of legislation *actually* to influence social customs is a separate question. Social customs change with respect to technological, economic and other changes within society. However, legislation can certainly also be influential, at least as a complement to the other forces of change.[1]

Rapid and powerful social changes have influenced family life in recent decades. Presently, levels of gainful employment are to a large degree equal for men and women, married or single, with or without children. Since the end of the 1960s, for approximately the past 30 years, the structures for family building have changed dramatically. The number of marriages has dropped as a result of the increase in the number of non-married couples living together. A simple measure is the fact that almost 55 per cent of all children born in Sweden have unmarried mothers, most of which live with the child's father.

Relationships, with or without marriage, with or without children, have today a low degree of stability. Extrapolation of the latest divorce statistics gives the probability that 50 per cent of the marriages that are entered into today will end

---

[1] A general reference concerning Swedish political, legal and sociological development can be found in two books published in English. The authors, coming from the United States and England respectively, have studied the issues in an impressive way. See David Popenoe, *Disturbing the Nest. Family Change and Decline in Modern Societies* (Aldine de Gruyter, New York, 1988), and David Bradley, *Family Law and Political Culture, Scandinavian Laws in Comparative Perspective* (Sweet & Maxwell, London, 1996).

with divorce. On the other side, it can be noted that 50 per cent of all new marriages will last a lifetime.

The probability that an unwed pair will separate is, for different reasons, considerably higher than the divorce rate for married couples. According to the Central Bureau of Statistic's assessment, separations in 1991 affected 50,000 couples, of which 40 per cent were married and 60 per cent were unmarried. Separations affected 46,000 children, of which 37,000 children lived with both of their biological parents, while 9,000 lived in a reconstructed family, with a biological parent and his new partner.[2]

At the same time as the rate of divorce among married couples has increased, the rate of remarriage has also gone up. The risk for divorce in a second marriage is considerably higher than the risk for divorce in a first marriage. Thus, a person who breaks away from a relationship willingly seeks often a new relationship, but the statistical probability for stability in the next relationship is lower than that with the first attempt.[3]

It is certainly inevitable, for a number of reasons, that family stability is lower today that it was for 50 or 75 years ago. Family life and household work were then organised differently. Even if the laws concerning divorce have been rather liberal in Scandinavia since the 1920s, the dominant social values were more negative to divorce in earlier days. In addition, economic factors could make it difficult for a woman to break away from a bad marriage.

Permanently bad marriages should be dissolved, not least for the sake of the children. On the other hand, divorce and separation can be unnecessary in certain situations, or entered into too hastily. Family stability has a value even if everyone does not think so today. A functioning core family offers the best support for the personal and social development of children. In addition, the stability of a relationship is also of value for the man and the woman personally.[4] Even if we must accept social changes and new attitudes in individuals, today there exists reason to fear for the stability of the nuclear family in Sweden.

---

[2] Skilsmässor och separationer—bakgrund och utveckling ("Divorce and Separation-background and development"), Central Bureau of Statistic's (hereinafter "SCB") demographic report 1995: 1, 85, complemented with information orally given to the author that parents to 29,000 children have moved in together during 1991! Compare also tables 7.1 and 7.5 in the report concerning the varying risks for separation, for married and unmarried couples, with respect to children of various ages.

[3] The percent of remarriages in comparison to all marriages has risen from barely 4% in the 1920s and 1930s, to approximately 10% in the 1960s, and approximately 20% in the 1980s. In 1996 there were 35,000 marriages, of which 21.1% were remarriages.

[4] A very insightful analysis of the conditions for modern family life was presented by Lars Dencik, Professor of Social Psychology, in his essay, *"Familjen i välfärdsstatens förvandlingsprocess"* ("Family in the Welfare State's Changing Process"), *Dansk sociologi* ("Danish Sociology"), 1996, 57–82. Of great interest in the evaluation of relationships and children's growth is Torsten Husén's essay, "Home and School Relationships", as found in T. Husén, A. Tujnman and W. D. Halls, *Schooling in Modern European Society*, A Report of the Academia Europaea (Oxford, Pergamon Press 1991).

The changing family patterns in Sweden have their equivalents in the United States and in other countries in northern and central Europe.[5] Sweden, however, appears to be taking the lead.[6]

The Swedish legislator is of course not unaware of the influence legislation has. The famous 1969 Guidelines to the Committee on Family Law stated that legislation is one of the most important instruments society possesses "when it comes to meeting the wishes of individuals *or* as a link to development in new paths". There was no reason, according to the guidelines, "to refrain from using legislation regarding marriage and family as one of several instruments in seeking reform toward a society in which every individual can take responsibility for himself, without being economically dependent on those close to him, and where equality between men and women is a reality".[7]

Despite the mentioned goals, the legislators chose a different attitude with questions that could be considered either ethical or ideological. The Committee maintained, in its 1972 proposal, that legislation on marriage should not contain laws of a specific, ethical nature, since ethical viewpoints could vary and couples should be allowed to develop their relationships within their own individual assumptions and values.[8]

The Committee's proposals went so far as to suggest repealing the general guideline given in the marriage legislation stating that spouses owed each other *faithfulness and support*. The Committee viewed a legislated duty of faithfulness as an expression of an ethical value, and altogether too rigid to be a basis for a legal consequence. The proposal was not implemented.[9]

However, the laws expressly connecting legal consequences to a spouse's, or a parent's, more or less immoral or unethical behaviour, were repealed. That change had repercussions for the grounds for divorce, including the right to

---

[5] According to statistics from the Commission of the European Union, the probability for divorce within marriages entered into in 1995 varied with 8% in Italy, 12% in Spain, 17% in Greece, to 55% in Belgium (new divorce laws skewed the statistics), 52% in Sweden, 49% in Finland, 45% in Great Britain and 41% in Denmark. In the United States the equivalent statistic was 55%. For some countries, especially for Sweden, one has to add the high frequency of unmarried couples, and the higher frequency of separation in unmarried couples, as opposed to married couples.

[6] It is often assumed that Denmark experiences similar development in comparison with Sweden. The rates of marriage between the two countries have, however, possibly diverged in later years. According to the above-mentioned EU statistics, in Denmark in 1995, 6.6 marriages were entered into for every 1000 persons (the highest percentage in Europe), while in Sweden the rate was 3.8 (the lowest percentage in Europe).

[7] Official Reports Series of Swedish Legislative and Investigative Commissions (hereinafter "SOU") 1972: 41 *Familj och äktenskap* ("Family and Marriage"), 58. The Guidelines meant that the legislators had clearly chosen a new course compared to the aim of family cohesion, which characterized older legislation. Compare my essay "*Individ, familj, stat. Om värderingar i familjerättslagstiftningen under 1900-talet*" ("Individual, family, state. On values in the family law legislation of the 1900s", Svensk Juristtidning (hereinafter "SvJT"), 1981, 715 ff. The Guidelines, as well as the 1973 legislation on divorce, led to discussions within the Nordic Council regarding Sweden's position to Scandinavian cooperation. See the summary in *SvJT* 1971, 385, and compare Lidbom, *SvJT* 1973, 273 ff, with responses from the other Scandinavian countries given at 398 ff.

[8] SOU 1972: 41, 97, and especially 101.

[9] *Id.* at 100. According to the 1987 Code on Marriage (1 Ch. 2 §), spouses shall show each other, among other things, faithfulness and respect.

damages if the divorce was based on the fact that one spouse had deeply wronged the other, the right to alimony for a divorced spouse, and for custody of children.[10] Among the reasons for not giving guilt of a spouse legal consequences was that moral conceptions could vary. That viewpoint is not particularly convincing, however, since there exist certain basic norms for relationships within a family which even legislators should be able to support. Other and better reasons were given, however, as to why issues of guilt should not be given special legal consequences. It could be difficult to determine which spouse or parent in a deeper meaning has to bear the guilt for the difficulties that have arisen within the family. It could also deepen the conflicts that can arise in a divorce situation, and be to the disadvantage of the children, if the spouse's guilt can be a basis for various legal consequences.[11]

Now to my main issue concerning the desire of legislators to influence family structures and family life. I will more closely scrutinise three subissues concerning legislators' attitudes to the suitability of influencing behaviours with respect to what I call *family stability* (especially the stability of the nuclear family), *parental stability,* and *changing sex roles.*

FAMILY STABILITY

The principles expressed in the legislation, which I have already mentioned, have been seen to mean that the state should remain ideologically neutral to the question whether a man and woman marry, or live together out of wedlock. The choice between marriage and cohabitation has been understood as an *ethical*, or *ideological*, choice in which legislators should not be involved. In the Guidelines to the Committee, the head of the Justice Department stated that marriage should have a central place within family law, but that one should "try to ensure that the legislation affecting families does not contain regulations that could create unnecessary difficulties or unpleasantness for those who decide to have children and build families without marrying".[12] On the basis of this perspective, and with regard to the need for legal solutions for unmarried couples, legislation has been passed regarding cohabiting unmarried couples within several different areas. In areas regarding social benefits, taxes and various other issues, equal treatment of married and unmarried couples has been sought, at least in theory. Legislation has not gone as far with respect to the issue of unmarried couples' mutual property rights, since marriage is the entrance ticket to effecting those particular property rights. An unmarried partner has been given, however, through the

---

[10] See SOU 1972: 41, 184 (requisites for divorce), 191 (support and damages), and 209 (custody of children). Without being expressly stated in the law, a spouse's blameworthy behaviour can be assessed with respect to child custody in a determination of what is the best for the child's interest.

[11] Compare Swedish Government Bill (hereinafter "Proposition") 1973: 32, 89 (the proposal to the Riksdagen which was based on the proposals from the Committee on Family Law).

[12] See SOU 1972: 41, 58.

Cohabitees (Joint Homes) Act 1987, an economic claim against a portion of the house and household goods which the other partner has acquired for both partners' use.

In addition to avoiding an ethical stance, the Swedish legislators have apparently assumed that the state *cannot* influence an individual's decision to enter into marriage, unless the legislation is of a compulsory nature. The idea that legislators, and legislation, could *encourage* individuals to enter into marriage has not seriously been considered. Nor has the possibility been discussed that marriage as an institution can be meaningful for family stability.

Interest in supporting family stability has been generally lacking in Sweden over the past 30 years. A minor exception can be noted, however, in the conditions for granting divorce. The laws regarding divorce have since 1974 been based on the understanding that a spouse's unilateral wish to break up the marriage should, in principle, be respected. This perspective is rather natural in a society such as Sweden is today. At the same time, a requirement of a six-month waiting period from the date of filing of the petition for divorce to the date of the judgment granting divorce has been introduced to encourage family stability in special cases. The waiting period is required in cases where one spouse opposes the divorce, or if one spouse has custody of their own child.[13]

Within family law, and even in the question of pension rights, the importance of each spouse's economic independence has been stressed; in other words, women should be independent of men. This policy, which has a good basis with respect to women's independence and social security, has been successful in so far as women, generally, have been taking the initiative in divorce proceedings. Divorces have also been facilitated by social benefits created especially to benefit single-parent custodians. I refer particularly to state-paid child support advances. State-paid housing allowances to families with children, with special consideration in the case of a single parent, are also relevant. Public policy has not intended to reduce family stability, only to help the often-difficult economic situation of single parents, but in reality it certainly has had such an effect, although its extent is uncertain. These observations do not imply that support to single parents should be abolished or reduced, but they point to what can be seen as a dilemma for the legislator if family stability is considered desirable.

---

[13] These regulations can be found in the fifth chapter of the Code on Marriage. The waiting period, in reality, seems to play only a minor role. The issue deserves closer inspection. A related observation is that the authority responsible for the administration of the courts in Sweden, "Domstolsverket", has recently drafted a form for the petition for divorce. The form consists of one page plus explanations on the laws regarding divorce, custody and support. The purpose of the form is for spouses to be able to fill in the form, and jointly petition for divorce. See *Domstolsverket Information* no. 10/1997. The introduction of this simplified course of action, which enables spouses to file without the help of legal counsel, can be seen as an expression of the fact that questions on divorce are treated lightly in Sweden. The background to Domstolsverkets form is related to the regulations given in the new law on legal aid, Rättshjälpslagen (1996: 1619). According to the new law, legal aid in connection with divorce and related issues can only be given in cases where a special need exists, for example where issues are contested. In contrast to this, a special compensation guarantee is available, under which a less well-to-do spouse can petition for compensation of up to 5 hours work for a court-appointed executor of property division.

Legal conditions probably can only marginally counteract the high frequency of divorce. In this context, however, the use of family counselling is also of interest. Family counselling could prevent at least some unnecessary divorces. It is important that family counselling is available and used early by those couples wishing for help in salvaging their relationship.[14] The provision of good education by schools in the area of personal relationships is also important.

PARENTAL STABILITY

The goal of parental stability, that is, that a child should maintain contact with both parents, is sometimes explained by the idea that a marriage or cohabitation can be broken up, but parenthood exists for a lifetime. Since 1975, legislators have supported parental stability by creating the possibility for divorced parents, as well as unmarried parents living together or separately, to have joint legal custody of their children. Unmarried parents can now be granted joint custody through application to the authority responsible for registration of the population, that is, the tax authorities. For divorcing parents, joint custody continues automatically after the granting of the divorce, if neither of the spouses requests sole custody from the court.[15] Presently (January 1998), the Riksdagen is considering a proposal from the government that will go a step further in promoting joint custody of children to unmarried or divorced parents.[16] According to the proposal, the court can award joint custody even if one spouse opposes it, if the court finds that joint custody is in the best interests of the children. Another expression of the desire of parental stability is found in legislative changes that have facilitated *visitation rights* for the parent with whom the child does not habitually live.

Consideration for parental stability has also played a role in the regulations adopted in the Parental Code regarding so-called "cooperation talks" in cases where the parents contest custody of the children. The intention is good: parents will hopefully gain a better understanding of what is best for their children. The strong interest in achieving co-operation between separating parents, however, simultaneously illustrates the fact that there is *no* interest in supporting, for example through family counselling, family stability as such.

---

[14] The Committee on Family Law suggested that the courts be responsible for informing family counselling centres on petitions for divorce that have been filed, so that the centres would be given the opportunity to inform couples of their services. The proposal was never accepted, however, as family counselling centres were not available throughout the country during the 1970s. In 1995 the municipalities in Sweden were given the responsibility of insuring access to family counselling within each region according to s. 12a of the Law on Social Services.

[15] The rules recapitulated in this section can be found in the sixth chapter of the Code on Parents and Children.

[16] See Proposition 1997/98: 7 on custody and visitation rights.

I now come to the issue of sex roles and equality, an area in which the interest of legislators in changing social behaviour has been especially strong. The issue raises many questions unrelated to family law. However, it is important in modern family life that women and men are given the same opportunities. This presupposes that the traditional role of men should undergo a change.

Many legislative measures have had the express purpose of improving the position of women in the workplace. State-paid parental leave has been of great importance in allowing work and child-rearing to be combined. For a period of up to 12 months, state support replaces a large percentage of the income loss of the parent who stays home to take care of a child. This *parental insurance* contributed to the fact that Sweden, in the first half of the 1990s, had one of the highest birth-rates in Europe. The parental insurance also contributes to the fact that women wait until they are older to have children, assured that their wage levels will remain satisfactory. Parents are, according to the main principle, allowed to divide the months of social insurance between themselves. However, since 1995 one month is reserved for the father, and may not be used by the mother at all. The legislator has attempted, in other words, to influence the behaviour of fathers.[17]

The role of men has been noted also in family law, even if only symbolically. The First Chapter of the Marriage Code, section 2, states that spouses shall show each other faithfulness and that "They shall jointly take care of their home and children, and in consultation promote the best interest of the family". This regulation, enacted in 1978, expressed the attitude that previous generations' division of work within the home should no longer be followed, and instead that both spouses should take a direct and personal responsibility for home and children.[18]

Work in the home, as a major occupation in place of gainful employment, has generally been treated with ideological hostility by legislators as an out-dated lifestyle. In some respects, however, the legislation has given expression to a different estimation.

"The desire that a parent should be able to, in the best way possible, combine employment and the care of a child—and an increased presence with the child—was the motivation behind the 1978 legislation on *the right to parental leave* for the care of children, a step beyond those rights given by the law on state-paid parental leave.[19] The regulations, as found in the Law on Parental Leave (1995: 584), give among other things, a parent the right to reduce normal working hours by 25% to care for a child under the age of eight years.

---

[17] The regulations on parental social insurance are contained within the fourth chapter in the Law on Public Insurance (SFS 1962: 381 with later amendments).
[18] See SOU 1977: 37, 134, and Proposition 1978/79: 12, 180.
[19] See Proposition 1977/78: 104.

In 1981, legislation allowed a parent who stayed home to take care of a child under the age of three years to count 'caring years' added to years worked outside the home, as a basis for the right to *pension payments*. The changes in the law were motivated by the fact that the need of children for security and well being is influenced by parents' satisfaction with their lives. Parents should be able as far as possible, to choose how they will order their lives and the lives of their children."[20]

However, the attitude of legislators towards work in the home has generally been negative over the past 25 years. An expression of that attitude can be found in the legislative history of the 1978 regulations on child support and alimony. Previously, the Code on Marriage stated that a spouse could contribute to a family's maintenance through work in the home. That reference was removed, as it was considered to give the wrong signal. At the same time, it is clear that one spouse's contribution to the maintenance of the spouses and children can still consist of work in the home.[21] Despite this, the legislator did not wish to mention that in the written law.

Another example of hostility towards work in the home is found in the situation of a family with children which cannot live on the income of only one parent when the other parent stays home to take care of the children. This family is not entitled to social aid if the municipality can offer a day-care place for the children and the parent who wishes to stay home can find income-earning work. The need for social aid will then disappear. The underlying reasoning is that everyone who receives social aid should be at the disposal of the job market, ready to work. At the same time, municipalities can decide the type of support that is to be given. This is so even when the child is three to four years old, and even if it would be cheaper for the municipality to pay social aid than to offer a day-care place. The end result is that the municipalities, and not the parents, can decide if the parents should take care of their own children, or if the children should be left in day-care.[22]

A comparable hostility to work in the home can be found in other areas of social benefits. Legislation for a state-paid "child caring-allowance" enabling parents to stay home was enacted in July 1994. The objective of the subsidy was that parents should be given the choice to use the money either as payment for day-

[20] The regulations on "caring years" are contained within the eleventh chapter, s. 6a of the Law on Public Insurance and the above-given reasons can be found in Proposition 1980/81: 204, 36.

[21] See Proposition 1978/79: 12, 182, and SOU 1977: 37, 135, where the Committee on Family Law stated the reason for the removal thus: "With respect to the fact that it has become increasingly rare for one spouse, other than periodically, to entirely devote herself at such a work, we find that it is most suitable to not name such work in the home as a way to contribute to maintenance."

It should be noted that according to the regulations found in the seventh chapter of the Code on Parents and Children, child support is determined by proportionally dividing the economic needs of the child between the parents, with respect taken to each parent's net income (income remaining after deductions are made for taxes and for the parents' living expenses). Work in the home performed by the custodial parent is not particularly taken into consideration in this situation. In Germany, for example, the situation is different. This comparison does not indicate any opinion of mine.

[22] Of guidance here is a judgment from the Administrative Supreme Court (Regeringsrätten) mentioned in RÅ 1985 2:5.

care or for taking care of the children at home. Immediately after the 1994 election, the new government initiated a repeal of the law.[23]

The latest example of this same ideology, that is the opposition to work in the home, is found in the new regulations concerning income evaluation for housing subsidies for families with children. Traditionally, income evaluation has meant that the highest possible housing subsidy is reduced when the combined income of both spouses is over a certain threshold. In 1996, however, a new system was introduced based on each individual's income evaluation. The changes mean that a housing allowance is lower if one spouse has a lower income because he or she takes care of children in the home while the other spouse works full-time. The basic purpose behind these changes was expressed in the Proposition with the words: "The so-called work-platform should be strengthened".[24] In passing, it should be mentioned that the value of such a goal underlying income evaluation during a period of high unemployment is not self-evident.

DISCUSSION

The Swedish legislator has shown only a minor, if any, interest in *family stability*. The same conclusion can be drawn with respect to the issue of *marriage frequency*. In this regard, the stance has expressly been taken that legislation should be neutral as to whether individuals marry or decide to live together out of wedlock.

If the legislator has neither cared about marriage or family stability in the nuclear family, the issue of *parental stability* has been treated differently. Legislators have energetically tried to promote parental stability, unquestionably a worthy goal in itself. Legal joint custody can certainly give the parent who is not living with the child psychological satisfaction, and it hopefully can also facilitate the child's contacts with the parent. If, however, two parents already have difficulty co-operating with each other and are forced, as may become the case, to accept joint custody against their wishes, there is a risk that joint custody might only deepen the gulf between them. It will be a delicate task for the courts to avoid such outcomes.

The desire to change social behaviour through legislation has been strongest, however, regarding *sex roles*. There is, of course, no reason to object to increasing a parent's opportunities for combining work with child-rearing and family life. The expansion of day-care has played an important role in this respect. Many parents of young children, especially in cases of those holding specially qualified work positions, lead hectic lives with a constant shortage of time, as they cannot obtain help in the home on reasonable terms.

---

[23] For the history of this subsidy's enactment, and later repeal, see Proposition 1993/94: 148 and 1994/95: 61, respectively.

[24] See Proposition 1995/96:186, 29.

Here I touch upon the negative aspects of high social security contributions and taxes. The costs of home services are not deductable from the taxable income of the family in need of help. The family therefore needs to meet such expenses out of its net income when social security contributions and taxes have been paid. The family is also, in its turn, obliged to pay social security for any person employed for home service and that person has to pay income tax on the amount that he or she receives. As a result of these "tax wedges" only a small portion of the corresponding gross income of the family is left as a net income of the person performing the services. The issue on changing Swedish tax regulations for the purchase of household services is a debated political question that has special significance to a number of families with small children.

A survey conducted by the Central Bureau of Statistics shows that a large number of parents with small children wish to stay home for longer periods of time than that afforded them by the parental insurance.[25] The legislator has not taken this into consideration when discouraging work in the home by a parent. It is true that a woman, or a man, who devotes a longer period of time to solely taking care of children, or to work in the home, runs the risk in the future of ending up in a work-related economically disadvantageous situation. In my view, however, the fact that the state tries to hinder the possibility for parents to take care of their own children in the home interferes too much with the individual's freedom of choice.

The idea of neutrality to marriage or cohabitation is built, as I have mentioned, on the premise that the state should not attempt to influence the choice of the individual. There is, however, no empirical support for the view that people generally are ideologically opposed to marriage. Rather, the opposite is true. A well-known example of this is the dramatic increase in the number of marriages in 1989, directly before the right to a widow's pension in the social insurance system was effectively abolished. During one month, namely December 1989, almost 65,000 marriages were entered into, as compared to 2–3,000 marriages in the same month in previous years.[26] The marriage rush was motivated by the belief, in many cases wrong, that a woman could protect her right to a widow's pension if she were married by 31 December. If the new spouses were ideologically resistant to the idea of marriage, then their resistance was not very deep.

There certainly is a dominant social custom that a man and woman can live together outside marriage. People appear, without any deeper consideration, to be following a habit that began to play a noticeable role approximately 30 years ago,

---

[25] In the SCB survey (in Swedish), "Coping with work, children and family," close to 5,000 parents were interviewed during 1992 and 1993. The results were reported in SCB's demographic report 1994: 1. Table 5.7 on 30 shows that 45% of all men, and 37% of all women, would prefer subsidies to all families, enabling care in the home of children or choice in types of day-care. This alternative received larger support than each of the following alternatives: continued expansion of state-paid parental leave, shortening of working hours without income loss, and the continued expansion of child-care so that children under the age of eighteen months could receive a day-care place.

[26] Compare SCB's demographic report (in Swedish) 1995: 2.2, "Women's and men's lives: Part II, Relationship building and separation", 38 ff.

and thereafter has grown with formidable speed. Many couples appear to believe, nowadays, that it is unnecessary for them to marry, despite the fact that they often desire the legal consequences resulting from marriage in their own relationships.

The regulations applicable to marriage, however, have such a secular character that it is not necessary to see marriage as an especially ethical or ideological choice. Most citizens do not see it as such either. From a legal perspective, marriage is primarily the way to acquire access to various legal consequences. Although certain marriage regulations could be seen as ethical, why should not the legislator recommend marriage so that these rules are applied as often as possible?

The laws mandating a waiting period in a divorce proceeding, where there are children or where only one spouse wishes to divorce, can be seen as an expression of an ethical attitude. The law requires that a spouse, who wants to be divorced, should show some patience toward the other spouse or in the interest of the children. Unmarried but cohabiting couples have no such mandated waiting period when they decide to separate. Viewed in light of the children's interests, it is contradictory to apply a waiting period to a married couple, but to show no interest as to whether parents are married or cohabiting.

I believe that entering into a marriage can have at least some stabilising effect on a relationship. Through the marriage ceremony, a man and a woman promise to stay together. After the wedding, they should have a higher degree of mutual understanding on the character of their relationship than they had before. In the case of an unmarried cohabiting couple, it is not unusual for the man and woman to have different perceptions on that matter. This is reflected in the frequency with which people begin to live with one another outside marriage, without any long-term plans.

The development can have been to the disadvantage of family stability in the nuclear family. Simultaneously, there is in Sweden an extensive system of regulation over unmarried couples. Here again we see the dilemma facing the legislator: practical solutions of actual problems can have a negative influence in the long run, if they contribute to the decline in the rate of marriage and in family stability. Even if the legislation concerning unmarried couples solves practical problems, it is also accompanied by practical disadvantages. The Cohabitees (Joint Homes) Act leaves gaps in what should be considered socially desirable concerning the protection of the economically weaker partner, usually the woman.[27] In addition, the legislation on cohabitation in various legal areas creates complexities, for the individuals as well as for the authorities, since there are two partly similar and partly dissimilar systems of legal regulation concerning marriage and cohabitation respectively.[28]

---

[27] If neither partner acquired a home or household goods for the common use of the couple, the Act gives no basis for a an economic claim even in cases where one partner has dramatically increased his or her assets during the relationship, perhaps with the support of the other partner's contributions.

[28] Compare my conclusions in Äktenskap, samboende, partnerskap ("*Marriage, Cohabitation and Partnership*"), Iustus förlag, Uppsala 1995, 205.

In my view, it is possible, or even likely, that the decrease in the marriage rate and the weakening of the nuclear family in Sweden has been unintentionally promoted by legislation. The neutrality of ideology has given more radical signals than have been asked for by the population. It is difficult to believe that such a proclaimed attitude, as taken in the past 25 years by the legislator, has not influenced the attitudes of the citizens. Without seeing the issue ideologically, young people nowadays appear to have little understanding of the idea that formal marriage should have any special significance. The expansion of laws regulating cohabitation is in itself an incentive to cohabitation instead of marriage.

The Swedish legislator has made poor choices in regard to the effects of legislation on family patterns and family life. When it comes to the issues of family stability and the rate of marriage, the legislator has, with debatable reference to supposed ethical and ideological arguments, determined that one cannot, or should not, seek to influence social behaviour. In other words, the idea that family legislation can have a norm-building function has been entirely abandoned.

In the questions of parental stability and sex roles, the legislator has, on the other hand, through active steps, sought to influence individuals' life-styles. The interest in parental stability, however, can be seen as a surrogate for the lack of interest in stability within the nuclear family.

The desire to influence attitudes regarding sex roles cannot be criticised, as long as it is a question of facilitating women's ability to attain opportunities comparable to men's in the areas of employment and combining employment and family life. However, when it comes to the issue of work at home, legislators have failed to take into account the fact that a rather large number of parents desire for the opportunity to order their family life in a way that differs from that they are forced to have by existing legislation on taxes and social benefits. This lack of choice is debatable even if the contrary attitude is held by a majority of the people. The legislators' capacity to influence an individual's behaviour, at the cost of the freedom of choice, has been especially strong in Sweden through high taxes and social benefits affecting large groups of citizens. Moreover, a forced pattern of living can possibly also be a threat to family stability.

It should also be observed that the birth rate in Sweden has dramatically decreased during the period of high unemployment the country is now experiencing. It has gone from being among the highest in Europe to one of the lowest Sweden has experienced during the entire twentieth century.[29] This sudden change, in a time of high unemployment, can be seen as an entirely consistent consequence of the political strategy. Family life and the raising of children have been rendered so dependent upon employment and the fact that both parents have suitable incomes that it is natural that the birth rate has declined. I recall the words in the Guidelines to the Committee on Family Law, on the use of leg-

---

[29] According to information taken from Elisabeth Landgren and Brita Hoem, SCB's *Welfare Bulletin*, 2/1997, 18, the rate of fertility, the average number of children born to each woman, if birth rates remain the same as those in the pertinent years, has decreased from 2.1 in 1990 and 1991, to 1.6 in 1996.

islation as an instrument for "meeting the wishes of individuals or as a link to development in new paths". My review indicates that the legislator's own wish to develop new paths has weighed considerably heavier than the goal of striving to meet the wishes of individuals.[30]

[30] The diverging attitudes that have arisen in the development of these issues, especially with respect to work in the home, can be seen as a reflection of changing political majorities, an issue that I have chosen not to address here.

9

Family Law in Namibia: The Challenge of Customary and Constitutional Law[1]

M. O. HINZ

1 BACKGROUND

Namibia inherited its legal system from the previous colonial administration. The independence Constitution of 1990 dealt with this heritage in a double way. On the one hand, the Constitution was made the supreme law of the land, binding upon the three branches of government. The fundamental rights and freedoms, as enshrined in chapter three of the Constitution, are the indisputable yardsticks of all governmental acts. On the other hand, the Constitution provided for the law in force at the date of independence to remain in force until changed in accordance with the procedures set out by the Constitution.[2]

Not all statutory changes enacted in South Africa in the years before independence were extended to South West Africa by the South African government or the South West African administrative bodies.[3] The Divorce Act, 70 of 1979, which replaced the guilt principle in divorce law with the principle of "irretrievable breakdown of marriage" as ground for divorce is one piece of legislation which was not made applicable to Namibia. The Matrimonial Property Act, 24 of 1984, is another. This means those substantial achievements, such as the abolition of the common law concept of marital power of the husband over his wife and the unification of the matrimonial property law of white and black marriages did not affect Namibia.

The concept of marital power was only recently abolished in Namibia. Civil marriages, i.e. marriages in accordance with the Marriage Act, 25 of 1961, between *natives*[4] and conducted north of the so-called *police zone*[5] are automatically out of

[1] The chapter is part of research conducted by a project on the interface of constitutional and customary law (CoCuP), funded by the Volkswagen-Stiftung Hannover, Germany. CoCup is executed by the Legal Department of the Centre for Applies Social Sciences (CASS), Faculty of Law, University of Namibia.
[2] Art. 140—For common and customary law, the Constitution stipulates that common and customary law should only remain valid to the extent to which that law "does not conflict with this Constitution and any other statutory law" (Art. 66(1)).
[3] Namibian statutory law of persons and family law in compiled in Bekker, Hinz (1997).
[4] This is the language of the Native Administrative Proclamation, 15 of 1928, parts of which are still in force.
[5] Application of Certain Provisions in Chapter IV of Proclamation 15 of 1928 to the Area Outside

community of property, unless the parties to the marriage declare their wish to be married in community of property.[6] Civil marriages conducted within the police zone are automatically in community of property unless the parties decide otherwise by antenuptial contract.[7]

Indigenous family law has never been recognised to the level it deserves in view of the fact that it is the law governing most of the family relations.[8] Current terminology does not know customary law *marriages*, but customary *unions*.[9] Customary unions never enjoyed the status of recognised marriages.[10]

The Constitution changed this in so far as it referred twice to *marriages by customary law*.[11] But more importantly, the Constitution ended a long debate about the place of customary law within the Namibian legal order.[12] Customary law was recognised as part of the law of the land and at the same level as common law.[13] Neither the view of Roman-Dutch common law being the predominant law, nor the corresponding one of customary law being only subsidiarily applicable will stand constitutional tests. Common law and customary law represent distinct legal systems with the same degree of validity and recognition.

Law reform is nowhere easy going. Reform in family law is even more difficult than reform in other fields of law. Family law reform is value-burdened to the extent that inherent emotions very often restrict rational discourse.

However, developments all over the world show an increasing awareness of ill-determined gender relations, negatively affecting the functioning of society and its development. The constitutionalisation of legal systems created an advocacy platform to address issues of inequality in gender relations. Gender activists, women and men, have become an important potential of social and legal reform. Gender activism has created social movements that politics cannot ignore.

Looking at the Namibian situation, it can be noted that law reform under the auspices of the Law Reform and Development Commission[14] of the Ministry of Justice is very much occupied with family law reform. The Women and Law

---

the Police Zone, GN 67 or 1954, read with Prohibited Areas Proclamation, 26 of 1928. The area *north of the police zone* consists of the northern communal areas.

[6] S. 17(6) of the Native Administration Proclamation, 15 of 1928.

[7] There is also a difference in the administration of estates according to the race of the deceased.

[8] And this irrespective of the law chosen for the conducting of the marriage. Research in Owambo (Omusati, Oshana, Oshikoto and Ohangwena Regions) has shown that people marry under civil law, but nevertheless live their marriages according to customary law. The basic patterns of Namibian customary family law are contained in Becker, Hinz (1995b); see further Solomon, Becker, Kaishungu, Hinz (1994).

[9] Cf. s. 17(1) of the Native Administration Proclamation, 15 of 1928.

[10] See Becker, Hinz (1995), 13 ff.; Hahlo (1985), 32 ff.; Sinclair (1996), 207 ff.

[11] In Art. 4(3)(b) and Art. 12(1)(f).

[12] Cf. here *Ndsiro* v. *Mbanderu Community Authority*, 1986 2 SA 532 (SWA); *Pack* v. *Mundjuua*, 1989 3 (SA) 556 (SWA); *Kakujaha* v. *Tribal Court of Okahitua*, Supreme Court of South West Africa of 20 Mar. 1989 (unreported); see also Hinz (1997a), 86 ff.

[13] Cf. Art. 66 of the Constitution. See also Hinz (1997a), 12 ff.; and Bennett (1995), 11 ff.

[14] Established by the Law Reform and Development Commission Act, 29 of 1991.

Committee of the Commission has a continuous record of activities since the establishment of the Commission.[15]

After more than two years of intensive work, the Married Persons Equality Act, 1 of 1996, passed Parliament. A draft Maintenance Bill has been completed; a draft Rape Bill is almost ready for submission to Parliament.

2 FAMILY LAW AND THE NEW LEGAL ORDER

1 Aspects of the debate around the Married Persons Equality Act, or: the constitutional challenge

The reform philosophy behind the Married Persons Equality Act is very simple and straightforward.[16] As the marital power of the husband over his wife which restricted the wife's legal capacity to that of a minor person is an obvious violation of the equality provision of the Constitution (Art. 10), the concept of marital power had to be abolished.

The Women and Law Committee decided to tackle the issue of marital power as its first contribution to law reform as it appeared to be of priority and relatively easy to implement. In particular, women in business and married in community of property complained about their incapacity to become fully accepted members in their trades.

It was decided that the abolition should, at this point of time, only affect civil marriages. There were a number of reasons for this: the first was that marital power was a common law concept not necessarily having the same connotation under the various customary laws of Namibia. Secondly, abolishing customary law marital power would necessitate special research. To wait for this research, would have meant to delay the much-awaited reform. Thirdly, the abolition of marital power in civil law marriages would indeed influence most of the marriages in Namibia since the majority of people sooner or later in their marriage life contract a civil law marriage.[17]

The implementation of the abolition of marital power faced two difficulties. *Normal* difficulties in the sense that the concept of marital power showed many ramifications that had to be addressed. Should all transactions in marriages in community of property require mutual consent? If not, where should the line be drawn between transactions requiring consent and transactions where both spouses could act separately? When would a third party need protection? Was the common law with regard to undue enrichment enough to remedy certain

[15] Cf. the First and Second Annual Report of the Commission: Republic of Namibia (1992), (1993).

[16] See to this Republic of Namibia (1994) and Keulder (1996).

[17] Where (differently from Owambo, e.g.) marriage in church is not the primarily used marriage form, people very often enter into a marriage under customary law, but add a civil marriage later in order to have access to benefits attached to civil marriages (subsequent dual marriage).

situations; was the common law on household necessaries sufficient to cater for situations without mutual consent?[18]

The second type of difficulties came rather unexpectedly. Various corners of the Namibian society objected to the philosophy of the Bill, albeit not directly focusing on the constitutional issue of equality.

The concerns raised again and again centred around the abolition of the husband's marital power, the abolition of the husband's position as head of the family, and the new domicile formula abolishing the previous rule according to which the wife automatically acquired the domicile of her husband.

The Bill stipulated the following for the abolition of marital power (section 2(1)):

> "Subject to the provisions of this Act with regard to the administration of the joint estate—
> (a) the common law rule in terms of which a husband acquires the marital power over the person and property of his wife is hereby repealed: and
> (b) the marital power which any husband had over the person and property of his wife immediately before the commencement of this Act, is hereby abolished."

Section 2(1) of the Act reads accordingly.

Under *Effect of abolition of marital power*, section 3(b) of the Bill ruled "that the common law position of the husband as head of the family is abolished". The Act added to this a proviso

> "that nothing herein shall be construed to prevent a husband and wife from agreeing between themselves to assign to one of them, or both, any particular role or responsibility within the family."

The domicile formula of the Bill and accordingly accepted in the Act says (section 12):

> "The domicile of a married woman shall not—
> (a) by virtue only of the marriage; or
> (b) where applicable, by virtue of the provisions of Article 41 of the Schedule to the Recognition of Certain Marriages Act, 1991 (Act 18 of 1991),
> be considered to be the same as that of her husband, but shall be ascertained by reference to the same factors as apply in the case of any other individual capable of acquiring a domicile of choice."

Section 16 of the Bill determined that Part I (Abolition of marital power) and Part II (Provisions regarding marriages in community of property) would not apply to marriages by customary law. The Act exempted further Part IV (Provisions regarding marriages out of community of property) from application to customary marriages.[19]

---

[18] The Act contains 21 consequential amendments to other Acts.

[19] Thus leaving Part III (provisions regarding domicile of married women and domicile and guardianship of minor children) applicable.

The abolition of marital power was called an unhealthy western import, being against nature and the bible, anti-African, anti-customary, destroying traditional family life. The open line programmes of the Namibian radio were occupied with callers from all walks of life and full of all sorts of comments. "We cannot allow SWAPO (the governing party) to amend the bible", was a point made by one of the people who commented. The many interventions made by members of the Women and Law Committee and other supporters of the Bill remained unheard. A meeting of Kavango traditional leaders[20] raised concerns of the above-mentioned nature, but, at the same time, requested time to think through the proposed Act and to allow for a step-by-step implementation.

The most spectacular events, however, happened when the National Council discussed the Bill after its adoption by the National Assembly. The National Council decided to call for a Select Committee in terms of Article 74(2) of the Constitution in order to get input from the 13 regions of the country

> with regard to the envisaged legislation on equality of married persons, particularly on the concepts of marital power, domicile of married women as well as guardianship and custody of minor children."[21]

Hearings were held all over Namibia between 18 January and 3 February 1996. The summary conclusions and recommendations contain, *inter alia*, the following:

- The participants in the various hearings did not, according to the select Committee, appreciate the decision of the Law Reform and Development Commission to concentrate on the abolition of the common law concept of marital power (i.e. to leave customary law marriages to a later phase of reform). The Select Committee of the National Council, therefore, recommended that either appropriate research be conducted to allow for the harmonisation of all kinds of marriages in the envisaged Act, or to draft a separate Act to cater for customary law marriages.[22]
- On the question of *head of household*, the Select Committee submitted the following:[23]

  > "The Select Committee concluded that the common law position of the husband as head of the family has been overwhelmingly defended by both sexes. At the same time, they called for legal barriers that surrounded the wife's capacity to effect juristic acts to be removed. The Select Committee therefore recommends that the provisions contained in Part 1 of the Bill, with the exception of 3(b), be retained."

- In view of the new formula for domicile in marriage the Select Committee

---

[20] Held at Rundu from 26 to 27 May 1995, and facilitated by the Legal Department of the Centre for Applied Social Sciences.

[21] National Council (1996): Introduction.

[22] *Ibid.*, 2.1.

[23] *Ibid.*, 2.2.

"concluded that the concept of domicile of choice for a married woman is a source of much controversy. There are fears, real or imagined that, once this provision is allowed to be part of the law, it will disrupt harmony in marriages."[24]

In a more elaborated form, the National Society for Human Rights (NSHR) enhanced this disruption-of-harmony argument in view of the domicile formula in the draft Act. The NSHR even went so far to say that the new domicile rule was in violation of constitutional and international human rights law as it encouraged separation and not unity, thus being out of line with, e.g., Article 14(3) of the Constitution which defines family as the "natural and fundamental group unit of society" and calls for its protection "by society and the State". The NSHR argued:[25]

"By making express provisions for separate domicile for a married couple, the Bill seeks to promote or encourage family disunity, infidelity and immorality, which vices more often than not lead to the dissolution of the marriage itself and, in the final analysis, the destruction of the family. As such, the MPEB 'Married Persons Equality Bill' sends shudders through family solidarity and could reasonably be seen as not family-friendly.

Secondly, in light of separate domicile for a married couple, the ownership of material property, which such couple may jointly own, seems to be the only and sole incentive for marriage. After all, 65 percent of the Bill's core clauses deal only with property. Hence the MPEB is materialistically commercializing, rather than socializing, spiritualizing and moralizing the marriage!

. . .

Fourthly, . . . the Bill seeks to promote or to encourage the growth of single-headed households, of which female-headed households would be in the majority. Female-headed households are a key contributor to the feminization of poverty."

Some quotations from the debate in the National Assembly and the National Council may round up the report on the debate of the Married Persons Equality Act.[26] MP Maxuilili, National Assembly, had this to say:

"We are not allowed to change the status of men and women, at all. That is what God said, the woman must be subject to her husband as head. . . . That remains so and if Parliament of Namibia wants to change it, then we commit a serious sin. We are not going to change this because of women."

MP Hango, National Council, put on record:

"The move behind this is to legalize the women to ruin man in terms of property and run away after acquiring that property she was in need of, provided she is protected by law."

MP Hendjala, National Council, added:

"If you listen to the members of our community, you will realize that this Bill is supported by single women, by women who have problems in their families, and by those who know that they are not going to marry."

[24] National Council (1996): Introduction 2.3.
[25] National Society for Human Rights (1996), 4 ff.
[26] Quoted from Sister (1996).

An evaluation of these responses to the *challenge of constitutional law* will follow after the *challenge of customary law* has been outlined. However, it may be noted here that all the strong points made did eventually not prevent the Bill from being adopted. It appears that even the critics consented to the Act. All the provisions under attack became law; only the one on the head of household received a remarkable amendment.

2 The *Ooveta Dhoshilongo shOndonga* and the rights of widows in Owambo, or the challenge of customary law[27]

The *Ooveta Dhoshilongo shOndonga*, the self-stated Laws of Ondonga,[28] were first enacted in January 1989. They are not a codification which substitutes the orally transmitted laws and the laws established through the practice of the Ondonga courts. The *Ooveta* only contain those parts of the laws of Ondonga which the King's Council felt to be of particular importance, such as the provisions which outline the procedure for initiating a court case, for appeal, and for the transfer to higher courts, culminating in the hearing before the King's Council.

Some of the provisions of the *Ooveta* can only be understood in relation to the law, which applied before the *Ooveta* came into force. Section 9, for example introduced into the laws of Ondonga a significant protection for widows and the property belonging to the household of the widow and her deceased husband. While the widow, according to the law in force before the *Ooveta*, was restricted to her hut or the kitchen of the homestead (*elugo lyoshigumbo*) and thus the relatives were given ample opportunity to search the homestead and carry away whatever they liked, she now has the right to move freely in and around the homestead and hence to secure its integrity until the end of the mourning period. Distribution of property is allowed to take place only after a period determined by the amount of time needed to conduct the funeral as requested by custom.

Amendments to the 1989 *Ooveta* came into force on 20 August 1993. King Kauluma Eliphas of Ondonga officially announced the amendments to the Ondonga community. The changes to improve the gender balance and the protection of widows were the most important amendments.

The 1989 version of the *Ooveta* had already deviated substantially from the land inheritance concept linked to the matrilineal kinship system governing all Owambo communities. While widows, on the one hand, were allowed to remain on the land they occupied with their husbands, on the other, they had to pay for their staying according to the size of the land. With effect from the 1993 amendments the requirement of payments was removed from the *Ooveta*.

---

[27] This follows basically Hinz, Kauluma (1994), Hinz (1997a), 91 ff.; and Hinz (1997b).
[28] Cf. Elelo (1989) and (1994). The Aandonga are one of the seven Oshiwambo speaking communities of northern Namibia. The term *self-stated laws* was introduced to qualify the documents, but also to indicate that the respective laws were neither results of codifications nor products of restatements (Hinz, 1995a), 91).

The pre-1993 version of the *Ooveta* provided for a split payment for impregnating a girl. From the N$600.00 to be paid as compensation, an amount of N$400.00 was to be given to the girl, N$200.00 to the Fund of the Traditional Authority. After the 1993 amendments, the whole amount must be paid to the girl.

In cases of adultery, the 1989 version of the *Ooveta* justified the obligation of the woman involved to pay one head of cattle to the Fund of the Traditional Authority by referring to the woman as the person who "caused conflict between men by this crime". The 1993 amendment deleted these words.

The real revolutionary change in the matter of land inheritance requires some further explanation. Complaints about the hardship and injustice arising from the matrilineal inheritance system of the Owambo communities date far back. They originate in the substantial economic changes that drastically affected traditional societies and, in particular, matrilineal societies that are based on an economically balanced extended family structure for which cattle raising and small-scale agricultural subsistence production was essential. In societies where the individual accumulation of wealth was not a prominent feature, the fact that a wife and children were not the legal kin to the husband and the biological father, but, in the case of the children, only to the family of the mother, was acceptably compensated for by this relationship. The changes in the said balanced extended family structure did not only affect women, and, in particular, widows, but also children.

Further details on how the change of the *Ooveta* developed may be recalled in order to allow for a better understanding of this exercise in law reform. The author of this contribution happened to have a meeting with the Ondonga King's Council in November 1992. The reason for this meeting was to discuss the English translation of the *Ooveta* prepared by the author and another member of his research team. While going through the original and the translation, the author was unexpectedly requested to give his opinion on land inheritance. The opinion was given with reluctance. Nevertheless, the point was made that it was difficult to accept that a widow who had spent most of her life cultivating the field, and whose power and strength went into the soil, should be required to pay for the land on which she had lived with her husband and children. After a lengthy intensive discussion, the decision was reached to delete the requisition for payment from the *Ooveta*; widows should not only be allowed to reside on the land; they should be allowed to remain there without any payment.

The Women and Law Committee of the Law Reform and Development Commission decided to seek a special audience with the Ondonga King's Council to confirm the reported decision. This meeting took place on 19 May 1993. Comprehensive minutes of this meeting exist[29] and provide a very interesting illustration of the difficulties which were brought about by the move of the King's Council. However, the 1992 decision was eventually confirmed.

---

[29] See Women and Law Committee (1993).

The events at the King's Council of Ondonga were followed by the Customary Law Consultative Meeting of Owambo Traditional Leaders which took place from 25 to 26 May.[30] All seven Traditional Authorities of Owambo consented to enact the position of the Ondonga King's Council on the rights of the widows to remain on the land in their respective communities. This was, in particular, important for Oukwanyama,[31] the Traditional Council of which had issued its laws not long before.[32] The Laws of Oukwanyama contained provisions that reflected the legal position of widows and land in line with the laws of Ondonga before the change.

The King of Ondonga addressed the issue of widows and land on the national television programme at the invitation of the Women and Law Committee on 22 July 1993. Although further incidents of widows being removed from the land after the death of their husbands have been recorded (and been assisted in line with the change of the Owambo customary law), the overall evidence is that the new law has been accepted and implemented.

3 EVALUATION AND CONCLUSION

1 The lessons from the debate of the Married Persons Equality Bill

The lessons from the debate of the Married Persons Equality Bill occupied the Women and Law Committee in a number of review meetings. Could the debate have been avoided? What could have been done to assist the debate in becoming more informed and rational? Should emphasis have been laid on public awareness campaigns?[33] These and other questions were raised. The following evaluation will try to advance the understanding of the lessons from the debate.

As stated above, the objections against the Bill were never raised against the constitutional point of departure, the objections were rather packed in statements for the foundation of which a whole range of ideological justifications were employed: nature, bible, African tradition. Although some of the most awkward positions can be attributed to mere chauvinism, others are certainly expressions of serious concerns about the decreasing stability of family life and family life as a societal value.

The manner in which these concerns were expressed, however, did not allow argument. The language of the debate did not reach what lawyers would call a jurisprudential argument. Counter-explanations, according to which the reference to nature was as wrong as the one to the bible, were not even acknowledged.

---

[30] Documented in Elelo (1994), 75 ff.
[31] The largest of the seven Owambo communities.
[32] Cf. Hinz (1995), 89 ff.
[33] The consultations held prior to the submission of the draft Bill concentrated on technical questions, such as the consequences of the abolition of marital power for the practice of the banks, the administration of immovable property by the deeds registry etc. Cf. Republic of Namibia (1994), 3.

The nature of the references by the critics and the way in which they made their points is reminiscent of ideological approaches very often employed by protagonists of what has been described as *revitalisation movements*. The typical turn to a syncretistic language which even accommodates obvious imports: the Roman-Dutch concept of marital power (but also the concept of civil marriage as a whole) under African customary law, is a well known syndrome in ideology-building in times of uncertainty and transition.[34]

The immature blend of all sorts of ideological elements is not conducive to interpreting societal realities, and by doing so, to determine the role and function of law. Is it the task of the legislature to educate the public in how to live a moral married life? Certainly not by way of legislative acts, as this would violate the basic notion of the post-independence constitutional state as a *secular* state (Article 1(1) of the Constitution). The fact that many provisions of the Married Persons Equality Act deal with property issues does not mean that financial issues are the only ones that matter in marriage. What the Act envisages is to provide rules of justice for cases of conflict which may arise during marriage, but in particular, after the breakdown of marriage. Evidence shows that private autonomy is very often unable to achieve fair solutions. Therefore, it is even the constitutional duty of the state to intervene.

The debate arose as if people had unconsciously waited for the opportunity to speak out on deeply rooted problems. And indeed, the environment of the current family life and the tensions between contradictory family concepts, support the assumption that both constitute most disturbing concerns with serious (including psychological) consequences. The traditional family concept works on the notion that marriage is primarily an agreement between families and not the marrying individuals; the modern family concept holds the opposite: it is primarily an agreement between the marrying partners. Article 14(1) of the Constitution of Namibia speaks of the right to marriage, and Article 14(2) stresses the "free and full consent of the intending spouses" without even mentioning the link to the families behind the spouses-to-be, thus leaving the traditional customary law requirement of consent by the families to the discretion of the marrying partners.

Many marriages entered into under customary or quasi-customary conditions have been forced into "individualised" marriages by circumstances.[35] In many cases, the process of individualisation only affected one partner. In some cases,

---

[34] The German sociologist and anthropologist Mühlmann analysed the ideology-building process of *revitalisation movements* in his book *Chiliasmus und Nativismus* (1964, see in particular, 241 ff.); Haviland (1996: 384) defines *revitalisation movements* as social movements "often of a religious nature, with the purpose of totally reforming the society". The same author defines *syncretism* as an element in acculturation, "the blending of indigenous and foreign traits to form a new system" (432). The reference to the anthropology of revitalisation movements does not suggest that there is a revitalisation movement at work, but points to a theoretical framework that appears to be helpful in interpreting otherwise not understandable social facts. Hinz (1971, 180 ff.) developed the quoted approach further to interpret certain aspects of African political theory.

[35] Cf. the data collected in Katutura by Pendleton (1994), 79 ff.; see further Burman (1996).

the individualisation may have led to open debates between the spouses; in others, the individualisation has developed without the partners seriously taking note of it.

A further burdening factor can be identified with regard to marriages conducted in a matrilineal environment as still prevails in Owambo (and Kavango) communities. Matriliny does not die fast as evidence from many matrilineal societies shows.[36] Matrilineal societies change and adapt themselves to new conditions as could be illustrated above. However, they do not always change fast enough as to accommodate the wishes of some members of matrilineal societies.[37]

It is a generally accepted anthropological finding that societal structures in times of substantial transition easily suffer from the loss of values.[38] Whereas social structures in times of relative stability are covered by congruent value structures, this coverage loses its link when structures radically change. The new structures may have their own value coverage, but these values will not reach down to situations halfway between the two structures.

The *prima facie* disturbing picture of the debate about the Married Persons Equality Act can be seen to represent the confused value pattern in a period of radical transition. The reported discourse is unlikely to develop into a coherent (albeit not necessarily contradiction-free) set of topical constructs capable of guiding society and orienting societal actions. However, the Constitution and its vote for gender equality would be a major obstacle against this happening.[39]

2 The self-reform of the Owambo communities

The legal interpretation of the change of Owambo customary law is beyond the scope of this study.[40] The point of interest to pursue here is that the Owambo communities were able to agree upon a major inroad into their matrilineal system in order to adjust it to contemporary demands. The Owambo communities responded to the public outcry[41] about the fate of widows and children, the motion of Parliament to express concern, the word of the President of Namibia, the advice from outside. All this, however, should not be overestimated in view of the fact that eventually the communities themselves took the lead in reforming their law.

This example of law reform *from within* illustrates the state of maturity and responsibility of which traditional communities are capable. Law reform from

---

[36] See Tuupainen (1970), 94 ff., but also Peters (1997).

[37] This is, in particular, expressed by people who are working in the modern economic sector. Matrilineal inheritance law is very difficult to reconcile with the needs deriving from such activities.

[38] Cf. Haviland (1996), 421 ff.

[39] And this despite the fact that the *grundnorm*-quality of the Constitution itself is still far from being rooted in Namibian society.

[40] Cf. here D'Engelbronner (1997).

[41] Cf. Hinz, Kauluma (1994), 35.

within is a way to make law the people's law. Law reform from within can, in particular, assist in times of radical transition, as it does not impose reform measures because the national or international supreme legal instruments require the implementation of a legal provision. Law reform from within is cheaper than state-driven law reform, and it provides the best guarantee of acceptance and societal legitimacy.

3 CONCLUSION

Despite the debate that surrounded the Married Persons Equality Bill, the message of the Bill remained a very simple one: it took away an outdated concept of common law. It opened the way for women to move in society as any other human beings. It did not impose anything on anybody. Those who allegedly prayed that the Bill should not become law,[42] are still allowed to confer marital power on the husband and, more importantly, to live accordingly. Those who believe that marriage should have one domicile are free to contract the domicile they want. Those who think there should be one head of household may either appoint the man or the wife to such position.

For people committed to democracy, the debate about the Act was certainly more than disturbing. For people with a long-term vision of a future civic society, the debate was healthy. It was healthy not in the sense that the issues of the debate were resolved. There are already indications that the debate will be revived in full force when the above-mentioned Rape Bill will go public. This time, the intended statutory confirmation of the abolition of marital rape will be the point at hand. It is expected that basically the same arguments will be used by all sorts of advocates.

It is easy to go into an intellectual exercise to unwrap family law as not gender balanced and to design a new order without *lobolo* and polygamy, with all forms of living together enjoying legal status (or being forced into such, as others may way). It is likewise intellectually easy to plead for the deregulation of family law and make family relations a matter of contracting them according to the wishes of the partners.[43] Reality, however, must be measured in accordance with the potential to absorb innovations. Missionaries have unsuccessfully tried to rule out the order of matriliny and the concept of traditional marriage as a whole. The fact that nowadays the majority of marriages in Owambo are conducted in accordance with Christian rites, recognised as civil law marriages, did not stop the people from living their marriages as if they were conducted under customary law. Many people married in church, but nevertheless found ways and means to have semi-formalised so-called *second house* relationships, circumventing the ban on polygamous relationship.[44]

---

[42] So reported to the Committee.
[43] Cf. here e.g. Fineman (1995), 226 ff.
[44] Solomon, Becker, Kaishungu, Hinz (1994), 34 f.

Many outdated institutions in family law (general or customary) will die a natural death. Official reforms have their place where fundamental rights and freedoms are *directly* violated or endangered. Otherwise, instead of all-embracing and welfare and protection-driven reform strategies, individuals, families, and communities should be encouraged to define their personal and family life and their property. The Owambo communities, at least, are proof of the power communities have in taking matters in their own hands.

REFERENCES

BECKER, H., and HINZ, M. O. (1995), *Marriage and Customary Law in Namibia* (Windhoek, CASS).

BEKKER, S., and HINZ, M. O. (1997), *The Law of Persons and Family Law. Statutory Enactments and Other Material* (2nd edn., Windhoek, CASS).

BENNETT, T. W. (1995) *Human Rights and African Customary Law under the South African Constitution* (Cape Town, Juta).

BURMAN, S. (1996), "Researching the Living Law in Urban South Africa", in T. W. Bennett and M. Rünger (eds.), *The Ascertainment of Customary Law and the Methodological Aspects of Research into Customary Law: Proceedings of Workshop* (Windhoek, 1996, Law Reform and Development Commission), 66 ff.

D'ENGELBRONNER, F. M. (1997), "The People as Lawmakers. A Discussion of the Juridical Foundation of the Legislative Power of Namibian Traditional Communities", in M. O. Hinz, F. M. d'Engelbronner and J. Sindano (eds.), *Traditional Authority and Democracy in Southern Africa* (Windhoek, New Namibian Books).

ELELO (Elelo Lyoshilongo shOndonga) (1989): *Ooveta* (Oompango) Dhoshilongo shOndonga, Oniipa (Oshinyanyangidho shOngeleke ELCIN).

—— (Elelo Lyoshilongo shOndonga) (1994): *Ooveta* (Oompango) Dhoshilongo shOndonga—*The Laws of Ondonga* (2nd edn., Oniipa, ELCIN Press).

FINEMAN, M. A. (1995), *The Neutered Mother, the Sexual Family and Other Twentieth Century Tragedies* (New York/London, Routledge).

HAHLO, H. R. (1985), *The South African Law of Husband and Wife* (5th edn., Cape Town/Wetton/Johannesburg, Juta).

HAVILAND, W. A. 91996), *Cultural Anthropology* (8th edn., Forth Worth/Philadelphia *et al.*, Harcourt Brace College Publishers).

HINZ, M. O. (1971), *Die Vergangenheit als Utopie. Das traditionelle Argument in der politischen Theorie Schwarzafrikas* (Mainz/Bremen, Habilitationsschrift).

—— (1995), *Customary Law in Namibia: Development and Perspective. Documentation* (Windhoek, CASS).

—— (1997a), *Customary Law in Namibia: Development and Perspective* (3rd edn., Windhoek, CASS).

—— (1997b), "Law Reform from Within. Improving the Legal Status of Women in Northern Namibia", *Journal of Legal Pluralism and Unofficial Law*, 39, 69.

—— and KAULUMA, P. (1994), "Ooveta dhoshilongo shOndonga—Efalomo; The Laws of Ondonga—Introductory Remarks", in *Elelo* (1994), 9 ff.

KEULDER, C. (1996), *The Making of the Married Persons Equality Bill in Namibia: an Analysis of NGO and Parliamentary Contribution* (Windhoek, Department of Political and Administrative Studies, University of Namibia).

MÜHLMANN, W. E. (1964), *Chiliasmus und Nativismus. Studien zur Psychologie, Soziologie und historischen Kasuistik der Umsturzbewegungen* (Berlin, D. Reimer Verlag).

NATIONAL COUNCIL (1996), *Report by the Select Committee on the Married Persons Equality Bill* (Windhoek).

NATIONAL SOCIETY FOR HUMAN RIGHTS (1996), *The Married Persons Equality Bill as Passed by the National Assembly. The NSHR's Position (Revised)* (Windhoek).

PENDLETON, W. C. (1994), *Katutura: A Place Where to Stay* (Windhoek, Gamsberg Mcmillan).

PETERS, P. E. (1997), "Against the Odds: Matriliny, Land and Gender in the Shire Highlands of Malawi", *Critique of Anthropology* Vol. 17 (2), 189 ff.

REPUBLIC of NAMIBIA (1992), Law Reform and Development Commission, *First Annual Report* (Windhoek, Republic of Namibia).

—— (1993), Law Reform and Development Commission, *Second Annual Report* (Windhoek).

—— (1994), Law Reform and Development Commission, *Aspects of Family Law: The Abolition of Marital Power and Equalisation of Rights between Spouses* (Report No 1, Windhoek).

SINCLAIR, J. (1996), *The Law of Marriage* (Kenwyn, Juta), vol. 1.

SISTER NAMIBIA (1996), *Married Persons Equality Bill: What some of our Law Makers have to Say*, Sister Namibia, vol. 8, No. 1, 7.

SOLOMON, B., BECKER, HEIKE, KAISHUNGU, O., HINZ, M. O. (1994), *Improving the Socio-economic Situation of Women in Namibia: Kwambi, Mbalantu, and Uukwanyama Integrated Report*, Part 2 "The Legal Aspects" (2nd edn., Windhoek, NDT, FES, CASS).

TUUPAINEN, M. (1970), *Marriage in a Matrilineal African Tribe. A Social Anthropological Study of Marriage in the Ondonga Tribe of Ovamboland* (Helsinki, Academic Bookstore).

WOMEN AND LAW COMMITTEE (1993), *Record of the Proceedings Held between the Ndonga King's Council and the Women and Law Committee of the Law Reform and Development Commission held on Wednesday, 19 May 1993 at the King's Residence at 15H00* (Windhoek).

10

Changing Families and Changing Concepts: Reforming the Language of Family Law

ANDREW BAINHAM

I INTRODUCTION

It would not be an exaggeration to say that over the last decade English family law has been transformed.[1] The Family Law Reform Act 1987 removed some of the last remaining legal disadvantages attaching to children born out of wedlock;[2] the Children Act 1989 established a new and comprehensive children code;[3] the Child Support Acts of 1991 and 1995 abolished to a large extent the jurisdiction of the courts over child maintenance replacing it with a mathematical formulaic process to be applied by an administrative agency set up for the purpose;[4] and the Family Law Act 1996 has brought about a new regime governing domestic violence and occupation of the family home[5] to be followed by a wholly new divorce law abolishing fault and emphasising mediation.[6] The reforms of the substantive law and procedure have been radical and wide-ranging but they are not the focus of this chapter. Instead, it is concerned with the reformulation of the ideas and concepts which lie behind these changes.

[1] For a comparative study of the transformation of English family law alongside that of the United States, France, Germany and Sweden up to the end of the 1980s see Mary Ann Glendon, *The Transformation of Family Law* (University of Chicago Press, Chicago, Ill., 1987).

[2] Particularly in relation to equality of inheritance rights and legal procedures for securing maintenance from the father. The latter has been rather overtaken by the Child Support legislation of the 1990s but the principle of equality in the treatment of children born in or out of wedlock has been established.

[3] Adoption however remains largely outside, though related to, this code and is governed by its own legislation currently the Adoption Act 1976.

[4] The Child Support Agency. The rigidity of the original scheme of the 1991 Act lead to a public outcry which has been only partially ameliorated by the 1995 Act which in particular makes provision for "departure directions" in limited circumstances.

[5] Part IV, which was brought into force in Oct. 1997.

[6] The Act has generated extensive commentary. The best introductions are probably Roger Bird and Stephen Cretney, *Divorce: The New Law*, Family Law (1996) (on the divorce aspects) and Roger Bird, *Domestic Violence: The New Law*, Family Law (1996) (on the domestic violence aspects). Of particular assistance on the detailed provisions and the ideological aspects of the whole Act is Michael Freeman, *The Family Law Act 1996* (Sweet and Maxwell, 1996).

It is of course scarcely original or revolutionary to say that language is the tool of lawyers or that it is through language that the ideas and thinking of law reformers finds expression.[7] So it is not perhaps surprising that we find alongside these major reforms a no less striking abandonment of old terminology and the introduction of novel statutory concepts. Thus in the modern thinking parents have "responsibility"; children have "rights"; there is no more adultery (at least not officially); protection from domestic violence will depend no longer on being a spouse or cohabitant but on being an "associated person"; and the state must allegedly abide by a principle or philosophy of "non-intervention". And in an unusual development for English law,[8] the legislature has seen fit to express directly in a statute some general principles about family life to educate us all, for example, that "the institution of marriage is to be supported" and that cohabitants "have not given each other the commitment involved in marriage".[9]

The use of particular language more often than not reflects an ideological position with which individuals may agree or disagree. As everyone knows, statutory provisions require interpretation and it is through interpretation and comment that we reveal our own values and ideological standpoints. These, it is suggested, are often at odds with the original intentions of law reform agencies and even with the express statutory language itself. A primary aim of this chapter is therefore to explore the origins of a few of the more important conceptual changes and ideas currently in fashion. The intention is to demonstrate that there has often been something of a distortion of the original sources and that some widely accepted modern notions are of dubious pedigree. In family law, perhaps more than in most areas of law, the language which we use is of central importance. Mary Ann Glendon has warned that "mesmerised by the coercive power of law, we tend to minimise its persuasive and constitutive aspects".[10] This, it is argued, is especially so in a field of law in which coercion seldom works. Family law is inherently unenforceable in the traditional sense since it attempts to regulate intimate human relationships. Parents cannot ultimately be forced to see children or children to see parents and it is not possible, through a restrictive divorce law, to force a harmonious domestic relationship on the unhappy. If therefore family law is to have any real influence on family behaviour it is more likely to be at the conceptual level—through what it attempts to tell us about desirable or acceptable models of family life. The relationship between legal and social change is of course undeniably problematic. No-one has yet been able to demonstrate a con-

---

[7] For a very useful collection of essays dealing with the relationship between law and language see John Gibbons (ed.), *Language and the Law* (Longman, 1994). For an historical perspective on the history, symbols and languages of the common law tradition, see Peter Goodrich, *Languages of Law* (Weidenfeld and Nicolson, 1990).

[8] Unusual, since it is contrary to the common law tradition, but not to the civil codes of continental Europe, for the state to enunciate directly principles which are thought to represent normative family life. See Glendon, n. 1 above, chap. 3.

[9] S. 1(1)(a) and s. 41(2) Family Law Act 1996 respectively.

[10] N. 1 above, at 10.

vincing correlation between the two let alone which comes first.[11] The factors which bring about change in society are bound to be so infinite and variable that any attempt to demonstrate a direct causal link between societal change and law reform is doomed to failure. It is nevertheless quite possible to identify some blatant attempts at social engineering in the recent reform of family law. And it is equally evident that some of the interpretations of these reforms have been designed to push particular agendas. In short what we can see is an ongoing battle over what are appropriate "family values".

II NON-INTERVENTION OR NON-SENSE?

In a lecture given at Lancaster University in 1983, the late Sir Roger Ormrod[12] described and illustrated with examples from family law what he called the "Frankfurter process". He was referring to the process whereby a literary expression is converted into a legal formula and by constant repetition goes on to assume a wholly disproportionate significance. The late Frankfurter J had drawn attention to this phenomenon (hence the "Frankfurter process") in *Tiller* v. *Atlantic Coast Railroad Co.*[13] What he said was:

> "A phrase begins life as a literary expression. Its felicity leads to its lazy repetition, and repetition soon establishes it as a legal formula, indiscriminately used to express different, and sometimes contradictory, ideas."

Sir Roger, in his lecture, showed how something like this had been happening to the dicta of English judges so that, from comparatively modest judicial pronouncements, emerged the "one-third rule" regulating financial provision on divorce, the "*status quo* principle" of child custody, the "gross and obvious" formula governing the relevance of conduct to divorce settlements and the notion of the "clean break".[14]

This "Frankfurter process" has been at work on what is supposedly one of the central principles of the Children Act 1989—the so-called "no order" or "non-intervention" principle. The principle is given prominence in section 1(5) of the Act and, having the status of a general principle, applies throughout the Act. It provides:

> "where a court is considering whether or not to make one or more orders under this Act with respect to a child, it shall not make the order or any of the orders unless it considers that doing so would be better for the child than making no order at all."

[11] But Glendon points out that legal change often takes place where it is at least possible to say that there is a coincidence with changes going on in that society. *Ibid.*, ch.1.
[12] "Words and phrases and their influence on the law in practice" in *Essays in Memory of Professor F. H. Lawson* (ed. Wallington and Merkin) (1986). The lecture was the third Annual Lawson lecture. Sir Roger Ormrod was sometime Lord Justice of Appeal.
[13] 318 US 54 at 68 (1943).
[14] *Ibid.*, at 146–8.

The source of the principle is beyond doubt. It is three paragraphs of the Law Commission's *Report on Guardianship and Custody* published in July 1988.[15] The Commission was concerned primarily with court orders on divorce. It took the view that orders had been made in many cases as "part of the package" of divorce despite the fact that there was often no dispute between the parents. It thought that orders should only be made where they would be the most effective way of safeguarding or promoting the child's welfare.[16] The Commission also felt that this would accord with "the fundamental principle that local authority services for families should be provided on a voluntary basis and compulsory intervention confined to cases where compulsion itself is necessary".[17] The Commission's recommendations are faithfully translated into section 1(5). What the Commission did not say and what the statute does not say is that court orders are *presumed* to be unnecessary in either the private or public context. Indeed, quite the reverse is true. The Commission recognised that:

> "in many, possibly most, uncontested cases an order is needed in the children's own interests, so as to confirm and give stability to the existing arrangements, to clarify the respective roles of the parents, to reassure the parent with whom the children will be living, and even to reassure the public authorities responsible for housing and income support that such arrangements have been made."[18]

And it most certainly did not suggest that in public care proceedings there should be a legal presumption against the making of care or supervision orders. All the Law Commission proposed, and all the statute did, was to incorporate a piece of common sense—that if a court order is not useful and would not positively advance the welfare of the child there is no point in making it. Viewed in this way it is entirely consistent with the welfare principle, another central principle in section 1.[19]

This is not the interpretation which has been given to the provision by commentators who have repeatedly referred to the "no order principle" which they argue creates a presumption against orders[20] and there is evidence that this is the

---

[15] Law Com. Report No. 172 at paras. 3.2–3.4.
[16] Para. 3.3.
[17] Para. 3.4.
[18] Para. 3.2.
[19] But if it is taken to mean some broader policy or philosophy against interfering with parents' own arrangements post-divorce it is arguable that it conflicts with the welfare principle. See Andrew Bainham, "The Children Act 1989: Welfare and Non-Interventionism" [1990] *Fam. Law* 143.
[20] A perusal of the relevant sections of the English Family Law texts is instructive. Cretney and Masson in *Principles of Family Law* (6th edn. (1996) at 657 head their section "the no order principle" and go on to refer to "the new principle of non-intervention". Bromley and Lowe in *Bromley's Family Law*, 8th edn. (1992) at 345 head their section "the non-intervention principle" and state that the provision "reflects a basic philosophy of the 1989 Act, namely that of non-intervention . . . ". Standley in *Family Law* (1993) at 162 heads her section "the no-order presumption" and at 160 locates this "presumption" in an "emphasis in the Act . . . on self-determination for both parents and children with a policy of minimum state intervention". The most accurate section heading and following discussion, which sticks fairly closely to what the Law Commission intended, is that of Hayes and Williams in *Family Law* (1995) at 43. The heading is "No order unless better for the child" which is precisely what the Law Commission said and precisely what the statute says.

way it has been viewed by judges and legal practitioners and (one could add from personal experience) students relying on the many commentaries on the Act.[21] A more accurate epithet would have been the "no *unnecessary* order principle" which would not have implied as a starting point that an order is, or is not, likely to be unnecessary. This is the neutrality intended by the Law Commission but the phrase it must be conceded, though accurate, lacks style. So instead, the intended neutrality has been hijacked by the adoption and repetition of loaded language with a popular appeal and a certain ring to it. Sir Roger Ormrod appreciated the seductiveness of language and its role in securing general acceptance for a legal formula. He said:

"only a few literary expressions or descriptive statements give rise to formulas. Repetition is the mechanism which induces the metamorphosis. To lead to repetition the language must catch the eye or the ear and be easily memorised and quoted. The statement must be attractively phrased, i.e. felicitous. . . . To become established, it probably must also epitomise an idea for which there are receptive minds. This suggests an uncomfortable resemblance to successful advertising slogans."[22]

So it was that the notion of a "no order principle" had a receptive audience in the late 1980s. Yet more seductive was the notion of "non-intervention" and it is this latter expression which is perhaps more commonly used to describe the principle in section 1(5). Some have even seen in this modest little subsection a much wider non-interventionist *policy* or *philosophy* which would have as its aim to roll back the frontiers of the state and protect, as they would see it, the private realm of family life.[23] Thus the Children Act is portrayed as a predominantly "non-interventionist" statute. Leaving aside the rather obvious point that the intervention/non-intervention dichotomy is itself simplistic and unhelpful[24] there is nothing in the Law Commission's Report or in the actual words of the statute to justify so cavalier a view. But the Act appeared hot on the heels of the Cleveland debacle[25] and at the end of the Thatcher era in which it had become fashionable to lay into the state and to trumpet individualism. So with "receptive minds" and parrot-like repetition we now have a principle, policy and philosophy of non-intervention in defiance of the facts surrounding the history of the provision. One is reminded here of Tony Weir's caustic remark that "there is nothing much wrong with facts, except their inconvenience for theorists".[26]

---

[21] It must be conceded that the one of the texts concerned was written by the author of this ch. See Bainham, *Children: The New Law*, Family Law (1990) at para. 2.10 ff.

[22] Above n. 12 at 152.

[23] There is at least a flavour of this in the views of Bromley and Lowe and Standley, *supra* n. 20.

[24] Glendon, n. 1 above, at 307 and sources cited there.

[25] See *Report of the Inquiry into Child Abuse in Cleveland 1987* (HMSO, London, 1988) (Cmnd. 412).

[26] Review of H. Collins, *The Law of Contract* (1986) 45 *CLJ* 503 at 507.

III RIGHTS WITHOUT RESPONSIBILITIES
AND RESPONSIBILITIES WITHOUT RIGHTS

Another area in which there has been a good deal of theorising over the last decade is the proper characterisation of the legal relationship between parents and children.[27] In England, as elsewhere, there has been a palpable shift in emphasis away from the old idea that parents have proprietorial interests in their children towards the new thinking that their position is best seen as one of "responsibility".[28] Conversely, we now recognise much more openly that children have "rights".[29] This is not the place to enter into the jurisprudential arguments about the nature of "rights" or "duties/responsibilities" nor to go over yet again the substantive law of parent and child.[30] The present concern is with the use of particular language and the problematic questions which this may raise. There are two broad questions which perhaps need addressing. First, how sensible is it to say that a person has "rights" without "responsibility" or vice-versa?[31] And secondly, just because someone has "rights" or "responsibility" does it follow that someone else does not?

On the first question there is an important distinction between the work of the English and Scottish Law Commissions and the subsequent children legislation in those two jurisdictions.[32] For whereas the English accept only grudgingly (if at all) that parents have "rights" as well as "responsibility"[33] the Scots openly acknowledge the co-existence of both and to a degree spell out their content.[34] What then of children—if they have "rights" do they also have "responsibility"? This might appear a radical suggestion but legislation in quite a number of countries expressly acknowledges the existence of children's duties, especially to honour and respect their parents.[35] It is more than arguable that there is a case for

---

[27] An attempt to pull together some of the strands is to be found in Bainham, *Children: The Modern Law* (1993), ch. 3.

[28] The Children Act 1989 introduced a new central concept of "parental responsibility". For the thinking behind this see Law Com. Report No. 172 (1988) Part II.

[29] This is in part the result of international developments not least the adoption of the United Nations Convention on the Rights of the Child.

[30] For the author's views on this subject see *Children: The Modern Law*, Family Law (1993), ch. 3.

[31] The view that it is not sensible has been called, in the context of parenthood, the "exchange view". See on this K. J. Bartlett, "Re-Expressing Parenthood" (1988) 98 *Yale Law Journal* 293.

[32] See English Law Com. Report No. 172 at para. 2.4 ff. See Scottish Law Com., *Report on Family Law* (No. 135) (1992) Part II, especially at paras. 2.1–2.35. See also the English Children Act s. 3(1) and ss. 1 and 2 Children (Scotland) Act 1995.

[33] S. 3(1) Children Act 1989 contains what purports to be a definition of "parental responsibility" namely "all the *rights*, duties, powers, responsibilities and authority which by law a parent of a child has in relation to the child and his property" (emphasis added).

[34] Parental "responsibilities" are set out in s. 1 Children (Scotland) Act 1995 while parental "rights" are set out in s. 2.

[35] See Bainham, " 'Honour Thy Father and Thy Mother': Children's Rights and Children's Duties" in Gillian Douglas and Leslie Sebba (eds.), *Children's Rights and Traditional Values* (Dartmouth, 1998) at 93. Countries as disparate and geographically remote from each other as Croatia, Indonesia and Israel all make express provision for this duty.

the more open recognition of these duties as a concomitant of gathering legal independence especially for those "children" at the old end of the spectrum of minority. As to the second question, the concern is that the popular appeal and constant repetition of expressions like "children's rights" and "parental responsibility" is capable of creating an unbalanced view of the parent–child relationship. "Children are the ones with rights, not parents" captures the mood of the times but it is really quite illogical. There is no reason in logic for assuming that where two parties are in a legal relationship to one another they cannot have reciprocal claims and obligations. It would, for example, be an odd contract which did not recognise this. It is true that the parent–child relation is hardly a contractual one but there are surely dangers in portraying it as one with all the rights on one side and all the obligations on the other. But is this perhaps just semantics—does it really matter what language is used? It is suggested that it does and the issue which best illustrates the problem is arguably also that of greatest importance—contact.

Contact is now widely described as a right of the child *rather than* the right of the parent. How did we arrive at this position? What is generally regarded as the landmark judicial statement came in 1972 from Wrangham J in *M* v. *M (Child: Access)*[36] where he said:

> "what Willmer LJ meant was that the companionship of a parent is in any ordinary circumstances of such immense value to the child that there is a basic right in him to such companionship. I for my part would prefer to call it a basic right in the child rather than a basic right in the parent. That only means this, that no court should deprive a child of access to either parent unless it is wholly satisfied that it is in the interests of that child that access should cease, and that is a conclusion at which a court should be extremely slow to arrive."

So Wrangham J preferred to emphasise the interests of the child in preserving contact and this is quite consistent with the application of the welfare principle. But provided contact is not thought to be against the interests of the child, there is nothing in what Wrangham J said which would deny the independent interest or claim of the parent to contact with his or her child. Indeed, in the very same case Latey J said:

> "So what is this basic right in a parent to access to his or her child? It is I believe no more and no less than a fact of human experience and of common sense. . . . "[37]

Human experience and common sense do indeed dictate that contact be recognised as a *mutual* right or claim of parent and child, in each case subject always to the welfare principle. Such common sense evidently appealed to the House of

---

[36] [1973] 2 All ER 81 and 85. In another linguistic change English law now refers to "contact" rather than "access" and purports to make it "child-centred" by the wording of the relevant statutory provision. Thus the new contact order in s. 8 means "an order requiring the person with whom a child lives, or is to live, to *allow the child* to visit or stay with the person named in the order, or for that person and the child otherwise to have contact with each other" (emphasis added).

[37] *Ibid.*, at 88.

Lords in *Re K.D.*[38] and to the European Court of Human Rights which seems clearly to have invested contact with the status of a fundamental human right possessed by the parent.[39]

This has not stopped some English courts from viewing the contact question exclusively from the child's perspective.[40] Neither has it stopped commentators, most recently Smart and Neale, from challenging the proposition that contact is a fundamental right which the courts should attempt to enforce in the absence of a very good reason for not doing so.[41] The authors are arguing from the perspective that contact has become accepted as a basic right of the *child*, and enforced as such, but the effect of failing to enforce it, as the authors must be aware, would be felt particularly by parents, usually the so-called "absent fathers". Indeed it cannot be seriously doubted that the article is pushing a feminist agenda and that it is the interests of *mothers*, and not those of children, which preoccupy the authors. They are crudely equating the interests of women and children and setting them up in opposition to those of men.[42]

That said there is much in the article with which it is possible to agree. The authors acknowledge "that ongoing contact is, in many circumstances, highly beneficial for children and parents", and it is difficult to take issue with the argument that caution ought to be exercised in attempting to enforce contact in the minority of extreme cases in which the parent (usually the father) has been violent or abusive. It is also valuable to draw attention to the connection between the ideology and enforcement of family law. The difficulty is with their central argument that "the public and judicial treatment of contact has taken on an increasingly rigid and dogmatic form, which is becoming a harmful trend in family law". Two points about the relationship between the ideology and enforcement of contact can be made in response. The first is that the attempts by the courts over many years have shown how notoriously difficult it is to force contact on unwilling parents or children.[43] Thus it is the *expectation* or *presumption* of contact which is of much greater significance than its actual enforcement. This is reason enough for asserting the independent claims of children and parents to it. The law needs to find a way of setting out its ideological position which is not actually dependent on the machinery of enforcement.[44] And it is not helpful to

---

[38] *Re K.D. (A minor)(Access: Principles)* [1988] 2 FLR 139.

[39] *Hokkanen* v. *Finland* (1994) Publ. Eur. Ct. HR series A No. 229 A.

[40] See particularly the Court of Appeal's decision in *Re M (Contact: Welfare Test)* [1995] 1 FLR 274.

[41] Carol Smart and Bren Neale, "Arguments Against Virtue—Must Contact Be Enforced?" [1997] *Fam. Law* 332.

[42] The authors are quite explicit in regretting that the "old link between a child's welfare and the circumstances of the primary carer has thus been broken". *Ibid.*, at 334.

[43] But this has never stopped them from trying to do so. For a recent extreme example of this see *A* v. *N (Committal: Refusal of Contact)* [1997] 1 FLR 533 where the Court of Appeal upheld the judge's decision to commit a mother to prison for six weeks (originally suspended for six months) for flagrant breaches of the court's orders for contact between father and child. The mother had disputed the paternity of the child, in the face of DNA evidence, and steadfastly refused to allow contact.

[44] It is interesting to note that whereas in the *public* context parents (and certain other people) have the benefit of a statutory presumption of reasonable contact with a child in care (s. 34(1) Children

this process for contact to be conceptualised *solely* as a right of the child. But this is not to say that *attempts* at enforcement should not be made. The second point is that attempted enforcement lies somewhere between actual enforcement and doing nothing. The value of the attempt is not because it will necessarily lead to results in individual cases, but because of the broader message which this conveys that contact is generally desirable and beneficial for all concerned. The answer to Smart and Neale's rhetorical question—"Must Contact be Enforced?" is therefore "Yes", if by enforcement we mean the *attempt* to enforce since, to that extent, ideology and enforcement go hand in hand.

The contact debate also takes us back to the question about the connection between rights and duties. If contact is a right of both parent and child it must, by definition, also be a duty of each—subject always to the application of the welfare principle. Thus residential parents should be under a legal duty to allow it, non-residential parents to exercise it[45] and children to co-operate.[46]

None of this should be taken as an indication that the emphasis on children's rights is misplaced—it is merely that parents have them too. Indeed, there is every reason to believe that it will be necessary to go on asserting the language of children's rights. In a recent appeal,[47] in which the issue was whether a mother should be ordered to co-operate with the medical assessment of her terminally ill child for a liver transplant, Waite LJ said that it was:

> "not an occasion—even in an age preoccupied with 'rights'—to talk of the rights of a child, or the rights of a parent, or the rights of the court."

This was a difficult case with complicating factors[48] but, leaving aside the merits of the decision, it is not difficult to see why someone about to deny a life-saving opportunity to a child might find the language of rights inconvenient.

We should not leave the question of rights and responsibilities without reference to a curious twist to the debate about the legal position of unmarried fathers. The desirability or otherwise of giving an automatic and complete legal status to these men on proof of paternity has been long-running.[49] Ten years ago it was very much a minority view that "rights" should be automatically conferred on

Act 1989), in the *private* context there is no such *statutory* presumption although the practice of the courts over many years has effectively created one. The Scots, as usual, are more explicit. A parent is acknowledged to have a *right* "if the child does not live with the parent, to maintain personal relations and direct contact with the child on a regular basis" (s. 2(1)(c) Children (Scotland) Act 1995).

[45] This is the clear implication of the Scottish legislation which makes it a parental responsibility "if the child is not living with the parent, to maintain personal relations and direct contact with the child on a regular basis" (s. 1(1)(c)). The reciprocity of rights and responsibilities inherent in the Scottish scheme is thus clear.

[46] See the author's article on this, *supra* n. 35.

[47] *Re T (Wardship: Medical Treatment)* [1997] 1 FLR 502.

[48] The baby had had previous unsuccessful and distressing surgery at three weeks, the parents were both health care professionals with experience of caring for sick children and the parents had by the time of the appeal gone abroad where the father had obtained employment.

[49] The arguments against doing so are probably put most forcefully in Ruth Deech, "The Unmarried Father and Human Rights" (1992) 4 *JChL* 3, which may be usefully contrasted with M.-T. Meulders-Klein, "The Position of the Father in European Legislation" (1990) 4 *IJFL* 131.

the whole range of fathers involved.[50] But the Children Act reconceptionalised the position of parents generally playing up their "responsibility" and playing down massively their "rights". Since then opinion has begun to swing sharply behind recognition of an improved legal status for the unmarried father.[51] Is it too fanciful to speculate that the linguistic change may have played its part in this sea-change of opinion? In short, if parenthood is *primarily* seen as a matter of responsibility there is a rather strong case for encouraging, even requiring, all fathers to accept it. This is surely the thinking behind the child support legislation and is a view evidently shared by Butler-Sloss LJ who in *Re S (Parental Responsibility)*[52] put it this way:

> "It is important for parents to remember the emphasis placed by Parliament on the order which is applied for. It is that of duties and responsibilities as well as rights and powers. Indeed, the order itself is entitled 'parental responsibility'. A father who has shown real commitment to the child concerned and to whom there is a positive attachment . . . ought . . . to assume the weight of those duties and cement that commitment and attachment by sharing the responsibilities for the child with the mother."

Here then, perhaps, is an example of the influence on the judiciary of conceptual change and shifting ideology.

IV ILLEGITIMACY—DEAD OR ALIVE?

The controversy about unmarried fathers has been inextricably linked in England with the question of illegitimacy. The central issue has been whether it is possible to abolish the discriminatory status of illegitimacy without also equalising the legal position of "married" and "unmarried" fathers.[53] One thing has been clear since the late 1970s—that it is generally thought desirable to remove from children the discriminatory labelling and language of illegitimacy. The Law Commission signalled its priorities in this respect in 1979. In its *Working Paper* of that year it said:

> "It may be that the biggest discrimination suffered by a person born out of wedlock is the legal characterisation of him as 'illegitimate'."[54]

---

[50] The author was in that minority. See "When is a Parent not a Parent? Reflections on the Unmarried Father and his child in English Law" (1989) 3 *IJLF* 208.

[51] Many examples could be given of this trend but among the more important are the provision for unmarried mothers to share parental responsibility with fathers by agreement (s. 4(1)(b) Children Act 1989), the willingness of the courts to grant parental responsibility orders to "worthy" fathers and the decision of the European Court of Human Rights in *Keegan* v. *Ireland* (1994) 18 *EHRR* 342 where it was held that a "secretive" adoption process and failure to consult an unmarried father violated his right to respect for family life under Art. 8.

[52] [1995] 2 FLR 648 at 659.

[53] It should be noted that not everyone agrees with the use of the epithet "unmarried father". Stephen Cretney points out that many such men are in fact "married" but not to the mother. Thus "Charles II, King of England, enjoys a certain notoriety as the father of a number of illegitimate children; yet it would be absurd to describe him, in defiance of the facts, as 'unmarried'." See S. M. Cretney, *Elements of Family Law* (2nd edn., Sweet and Maxwell, 1992), at para. 11.22.

[54] Law Com. Working Paper on *Illegitimacy* (1979), para. 2.10.

When the legislation eventually came in 1987 the principle of removing stig-matising terminology from the law was given pride of place in section 1 of the Act.[55] The Scottish Law Commission had reached a similar view in 1984 that "the terms 'legitimate' and 'illegitimate' should, wherever possible, cease to be used as legal terms of art".[56] The Scottish Commission was also opposed to any alternative labels such as 'marital' and 'non-marital' which it felt could quickly take on old connotations. Both Commissions therefore opted for a formula which would enable any necessary distinctions to be drawn between *parents* and not between children and this is the intention of the legislation in both jurisdictions.[57] It has prompted the authors of one source book of English family law to adopt as one of their section headings the question—"illegitimate children or illegiti-mate parents"?[58] And it is a moot point whether the very status of legitimacy/ illegitimacy remains or has been removed.[59]

Fascinating though this question is in its own right[60] the issue here is why the attempt by the two Commissions and by Parliament to remove the stigmatising labelling of children has been such a spectacular failure on the ground. The pol-icy was crystal clear—that to refer to children as "illegitimate" had unacceptable connotations of illegality which ought not to be visited on them whatever the cir-cumstances of their birth. Returning to 1979 the English Commission clearly appreciated the force of legal language:

> "We believe that the law can help to lessen social prejudices by setting an example
> clearly based upon the principle that the parents' marital relationship is irrelevant to
> the child's legal position. Changes in the law cannot give the illegitimate child the ben-
> efits of a secure, caring, family background. They cannot even ensure that he does not
> suffer financially. . . . But they can at least remove the *additional* hardship of attaching
> an opprobrious description to him. . . . "[61]

[55] S1(1) provides:
   "In this Act and enactments passed and instruments made after the coming into force of this section, references (however expressed) to any relationship between two persons shall, unless the contrary intention appears, be construed without regard to whether or not the father and mother of either of them, or the father and mother of any person through which the relationship is deduced, have or had been married to each other at any time."

[56] Scot. Law Com., *Report on Illegitimacy*, No. 82 (1984), para. 9.2.

[57] Thus in both jurisdictions only the mother *automatically* acquires parental rights and responsi-bilities. See the English Children Act s. 2(2) and the Children (Scotland) Act 1995 s. 3(1)(b). This latter provision was contrary to the recommendations of the Scottish Law Commission. For fuller discussion see Elaine Sutherland, "Child Law Reform—At Last!" in A Bainham (ed.), *The International Survey of Family Law 1995* (Martinus Nijhoff, 1997) at 435.

[58] B. Hoggett, D. Pearl, E. Cooke and P. Bates, *The Family, Law and Society* (4th edn., Butterworths, 1996).

[59] The Scottish Law Commission certainly took the view that the Scottish reforms of the 1980s did not succeed in abolishing the status of legitimacy or illegitimacy. See Report No. 135, especially at para. 17.3.

[60] There is a view that once the bulk of discriminatory legal effects against a class of individuals has been removed, the preservation of a very small number of differentiating provisions does not add up to a "status". There is of course scope for argument about how much differentiation has to remain for a status to be acquired or preserved and it can be argued that *any* different treatment is sufficient.

[61] Working Paper No. 74 at para. 3.15.

Has there then been a concerted attempt to banish the labelling of children? In fact quite the contrary is true. It is not perhaps surprising that the 1987 reform should have had no impact whatever on the ultra-conservative tabloid press, though "love-child" is apparently now the preferred choice of epithet. Many examples could be given but a recent one appeared in the *Daily Mail* on 7 July 1997.[62] The subject of the piece was the so-called "love-child" of former Conservative minister Tim Yeo and a former Tory councillor. "Little Claudia-Marie is Tim's *second* illegitimate child. The first happened when he was a Cambridge undergraduate" we are told. What is rather more surprising is that law reporters, judges and academics do not seem to have done much better. The language of illegitimacy continues to be part of the legal vocabulary long after the 1987 reforms. It is indeed possible to find a number of post-1987 reported cases which even refer to "illegitimate" children in their titles. The most well know is probably *Re H (Illegitimate Children: Father: Parental Rights)*[63] decided by the Court of Appeal in April 1989 and returning again in November 1990 under the title *Re H (Illegitimate Children: Father: Parental Rights) (No. 2)*.[64] Other examples are *C v. S (A minor) (Abduction: Illegitimate Child)* and *H v. P (Illegitimate Child: capital provision)*.[65]

Re H (above) was essentially concerned with the status of unmarried fathers specifically to resist adoption of their children. When the Court of Appeal had to decide the matter the general principle in section 1(1) of the 1987 Act had been in force for some time and other provisions of the Act bearing particularly on the standing of fathers had been implemented ten days earlier.[66] Among these an amendment to the adoption legislation had replaced the statutory phrase "in the case of an illegitimate child whose father is not its guardian" with "in the case of a child whose father and mother were not married to each other at the time of his birth".[67] This presented the court with an early opportunity to underline the linguistic changes brought about by the Act and to give effect to the policy of distinguishing between fathers but not between children.[68] The opportunity was missed, the court referring to the "father of an illegitimate child".[69] Indeed, one wonders whether the judge at first instance had properly understood the policy of the 1987 legislation when he said "the purpose of the

---

[62] Article by Angela Levin under the title "Love, Loyalty and the Secret Daughter Tim Yeo still visits every month".

[63] [1989] 2 FLR 215.

[64] [1991] 1 FLR 214.

[65] [1990] AC 562 and [1993] Fam. Law 515 respectively.

[66] These provisions applied in particular to the construction of enactments relating to parental rights and duties already in force at the time of the passing of the 1987 Act. They included provisions in the child care and adoption legislation.

[67] S. 18(1) Adoption Act 1976.

[68] The author has in fact always been unconvinced by this distinction and would argue, along with the Scottish Law Commission, that the much better approach would have been to eliminate all distinctions between fathers as well. There is a curious artificiality about pretending that it is possible to distinguish between fathers but not thereby also differentiate between children.

[69] Above n. 63 *per* Balcombe LJ at 221.

Act was the conferring of . . . parental rights and duties" on "the deserving father of an illegitimate child".[70] Both the judge and Court of Appeal therefore continued to draw distinctions not merely between parents, but between children. Nor should it be thought that this was a unique occurrence confined to the immediate aftermath of the 1987 legislation. In the leading paternity case *Re F (A minor: Paternity Test)*,[71] decided by the Court of Appeal in 1993, we find Balcombe LJ referring again to "an application for a parental rights order by the father of two illegitimate children".[72] Yet more recently some of our most respected academic commentators have used the selfsame language. Stephen Cretney, in an admittedly amusing and memorable swipe at the new statutory period for consideration and reflection before divorce, speculates that some of those concerned may prefer "to spend their time in the far more pleasurable activity of conceiving— *necessarily illegitimate*—babies".[73] And Michael Freeman, reproducing the Cretney quotation doubtless because it is memorable, refers to the hardship that may be caused by an absolute waiting period including the hardship of being unable quickly "to remarry and *legitimate* children".[74] Most striking of all to a law teacher and examiner, though the evidence is purely anecdotal, are the countless essays and examination scripts written by law students in universities across the land which continue to refer to illegitimate children apparently oblivious to the reforms of the earlier decade.[75]

Faced with all this evidence it would seem that Glendon, commenting in 1989, was unduly optimistic when she wrote that the 1987 Act had "expunged the term 'illegitimate' from the law relating to children".[76] But suppose that a discriminatory *status* still exists. Is it not appropriate to continue with language which recognises this? There is a respectable academic argument that since the legislation did not repeal certain earlier legislation which invokes the concepts of legitimacy and illegitimacy, and since certain legal distinctions are still drawn between children born in and out of wedlock[77] we need to preserve differentiating language. This is essentially a technical argument which will appeal to lawyers but is unlikely to appeal much to anyone else. It is doubtful whether it is consistent with the

[70] The judgment of Judge Morton Jack in Slough County Court is quoted by Balcombe LJ, *supra* n. 64 at 219.

[71] [1993] 1 FLR 598.

[72] *Ibid.*, at 603 referring to the earlier case of *Re C (Minors) (Parental Rights)* [1992] 1 FLR 1 in which, incidentally, Waite LJ at 2 referred to the "right of a natural father of an illegitimate child to apply for a declaratory order . . . " Ward LJ was also at it in 1995 in the Court of Appeal decision in *Re S (Parental Responsibility)* [1995] 2 FLR 648 where he said at 652 that the "logic would have suggested that one should also sweep away any disability that remained vested in the father of the illegitimate child".

[73] "The Divorce White Paper—Some Reflections" [1995] *Fam. Law* 302 at 303 (emphasis added).

[74] "Divorce Gospel Style" (1997) *Fam. Law* 413 at 416 (emphasis added).

[75] The same scripts, incidentally, refer by the score to the "policy" and "philosophy" of "non-intervention" in the Children Act.

[76] N. 1 above at 269.

[77] Mainly in relation to citizenship, titles of honour and, of course, the child's relationship with his father. Perhaps the most readable account of the current state of the law is Cretney, above n53 especially at paras. 11.18–11.21.

letter of the 1987 reforms and it is certainly not consistent with their spirit. This is because the question of status in the real world is, it is suggested, intimately connected to the use of language. Society is more likely to believe that children can be illegitimate if the press and the media keep saying so. Law students are more likely to believe it if judges and academics say so. And so it is that despite the good intentions of the Law Commission and of Parliament illegitimacy is alive today in England not least because those with influence say it is.

V   THE FAMILY LAW ACT 1996—AN IDEOLOGICAL EXPERIMENT?

The Family Law Act 1996 is a more overtly ideological piece of legislation than most.[78] First, its final shape (incorporating both the reform of divorce and the law relating to violence and occupation of the family home) is largely the result of the ideologically inspired, yet misinformed, opposition of a few MPs on the far right who objected to what they saw as the extension of the rights of the married to the unmarried or, as they put it, "live-in lovers".[79] Hence the former Family Homes and Domestic Violence Bill 1995, which started life as an uncontroversial measure emanating from the considered work of the Law Commission,[80] was lost at the eleventh hour. The long-awaited reform of divorce law was similarly in jeopardy for a while and the government only succeeding in securing both reforms with opposition support and by making concessions to the extremists.[81] Secondly, and unusually for an English statute, section 1 sets out a list of "general principles" which are to be applied by the Court and "any person, in exercising functions under or in consequence" of those parts of the Act dealing with divorce and mediation.[82]

The general principles governing divorce are, as Michael Freeman has observed, not legal rules but stated ideals or objectives and behind these objectives lie values. He identifies the core values as "pro-marriage, pro-children and anti-violence".[83] One could add to this "pro-cost cutting".[84] Yet Freeman notes

---

[78] For two readable and succinct views of the changes, which comment on the ideological aspects of the legislation, see Michael Freeman, "England: Family Justice and Family Values in 1995" in the *International Survey of Family Law 1995*, above n. 57 and Gillian Douglas, "England and Wales: 'Family Values' to the Fore?" in A. Bainham (ed.), the *International Survey of Family Law 1996* (Martinus Nijhoff, 1998).

[79] In fact this opposition was deeply misguided since comparable, if not co-extensive, protection from violence was extended to cohabitants some 20 years earlier by the Domestic Violence and Matrimonial Proceedings Act 1976.

[80] Law Com. Report No. 207 on *Domestic Violence and Occupation of the Family Home* (1992).

[81] The best example of these concessions is the bizarre s. 41(2) which provides: "Where the Court is required to consider the nature of the parties' relationship, it is to have regard to the fact that they have not given each other the commitment involved in marriage."

[82] S. 1.

[83] *The Family Law Act 1996*, above n. 6, annotations to s. 1.

[84] S. 1(c)(iii) enunciates a general principle that marriages should be terminated "without costs being unreasonably incurred in connection with the procedures to be followed in bringing the marriage to an end".

that "the principles are important as much for what they imply and for what they do not say, as for what they actually state". Thus, while there is no doubt that the legislation is "pro-marriage" it is not at all clear that it is "pro-family". It enjoins the courts and others exercising functions under the legislation to have regard to the principles "that the institution of marriage is to be supported" and "that the parties to a marriage which may have broken down are to be encouraged to take all practicable steps, whether by marriage counselling or otherwise, to save the marriage". Yet there is no principle corresponding with that in section 43 of the Australian Family Law Act 1975 which requires the Family Court there to have regard to, *inter alia*, "the need to give the widest possible protection and assistance to *the family* as the natural and fundamental group unit of society, particularly while it is responsible for the care and education of dependent children".[85] Marriage is therefore the officially preferred form of family arrangement and the impression created is that families constituted outside marriage are inferior in some undefined way. This is a theme also underlying the part of the Act dealing with violence and occupational rights.[86]

Where divorce is concerned there needs to be a good deal of reading between the lines. The general principles repeat a central objective of the former divorce law "that a marriage which has irretrievably broken down and is being brought to an end should be brought to an end . . . with minimum distress to the parties and to the children affected" and (and this is new) "with questions dealt with in a manner designed to promote as good a continuing relationship between the parties and any children as is possible in the circumstances".[87] Beyond this the values informing the legislation are in part to be found in what has been removed. Fault has been abandoned as a basis for divorce and with it the very concepts of adultery, desertion and unreasonable behaviour to be replaced by nothing in particular. Gone too is the polarising and adversarial terminology[88] of "petitioner/respondent" and the two-stage divorce "decree" which will be replaced by the more neutral divorce "order". All this might suggest official approval for divorce, perhaps even acceptance of divorce as a right. But, taking the legislation as a whole, Freeman is correct to assert that it is in reality "anti-divorce".[89] The device chosen to convey what amounts to official disapproval of divorce is procedural complexity and built-in delay.[90] It will take substantially longer in future for the majority of people to obtain a divorce than under current procedures. The

---

[85] For an informative discussion of ideology and rhetoric in the Australian family legislation see Rebecca Bailey-Harris and John Dewar, "Variations on a Theme—Child Law Reform in Australia" (1997) 9 *CFLQ* 149.

[86] Freeman puts it this way: "So being married is better than not being married, marriage is a better arrangement than cohabitation, monogamy is preferable to polygamy, staying married is better than getting divorced, heterosexuality is on a higher plain than homosexuality", *op. cit.* at x.

[87] S. 1(c)(i) and (ii).

[88] The need to reform the terminology of the divorce process was identified as long ago as 1985 by the "Booth Committee". See the *Report of the Matrimonial Causes Procedure Committee* (HMSO, London, 1985), particularly at paras. 4.2–4.5.

[89] Above n. 74.

[90] For the details of the new procedure see Bird and Cretney, above n. 6.

mandatory waiting period, ostensibly for reflection and consideration and which will be extended for a further six months where there are minor children, has been said by Freeman to be the "expression of a moral diktat" or punishment for marriage failure.[91] The new divorce law, like the old, will be dominated by procedure—ironic given the attempt to push principles and ideology to the fore.

Part IV of the 1996 Act has also introduced some striking changes of terminology. Of these the most interesting is the novel concept of "associated persons".[92] The special remedy for protection from domestic violence[93] will now depend not on being the spouse or cohabitant of the aggressor (though in most cases the victim will be) but on being "associated" with him. Commenting on the new concept Freeman describes it as perhaps "the most suspect aspect of the domestic violence provisions" since it is being used "to restrict eligibility to seek remedies".[94] Thus, those who have had a sexual relationship, but never shared a household, are excluded as are victims of obsessional harassment from amongst others unrequited lovers. These "relationships" are in essence considered insufficiently "familial" or "domestic" but are likely to fall under the new protective mechanisms of the Protection from Harassment Act 1997.[95] But it is possible to take another view of this development. The notion of "associated persons" while admittedly not all-embracing takes a much broader view of family or domestic relationships than has ever been the case before.[96] There are in all seven categories and some of these are themselves extremely broad. "Relative" can surely never have been defined so widely.[97] Imagine your surprise at discovering that for these purposes you are a relative of your cohabitant's half-sister, uncle or nephew. And for the first time in English law (excluding commercial relationships) it is the fact of sharing a household which will trigger the availability of certain domestic remedies.[98] The new law will embrace amongst others gay and

---

[91] Above n. 4 at 416.

[92] Defined by S. 62(3)–(5).

[93] It is important to remember that the Act is only concerned with the *special* "familial" remedies previously in effect available only to spouse and cohabitants. Everyone, whatever the nature of their relationship, is protected to a degree from violence by the criminal law and the law of tort.

[94] *Op. cit.* at p. xii.

[95] The Act, which received the Royal Assent on 21 Mar. 1997 and which will be brought into force as soon as possible, creates, *inter alia*, a new criminal offence of "harassment" and a new civil remedy where there is an actual or apprehended commission of the offence. The details are beyond the scope of this article.

[96] There are seven categories in all *viz.* spouses and former spouses; cohabitants and former cohabitants; those who live or have lived in the same household; relatives; engaged and formerly engaged persons; parents and those with parental responsibility and parties to the same family proceedings.

[97] "Relative" is defined by s. 63(1) to mean:

"(a) the father, mother, stepfather, stepmother, son, daughter, stepson, stepdaughter, grandmother, grandfather, grandson or granddaughter of that person or of that person's spouse or former spouse, or

(b) the brother, sister, uncle, aunt, niece or nephew (whether of the full blood or of the half blood or by affinity) of that person or of that person's spouse or former spouse,

and includes, in relation to a person who is living or has lived with another person as husband and wife, any person who would fall within paragraph (a) or (b) if the parties were married to each other."

[98] The household sharing must under s. 62(3)(c) be "otherwise than merely by reason of one of them being the other's employee, tenant, lodger or boarder".

lesbian couples and household companions who are not "cohabiting" in the more traditional sense.[99] So one way of looking at the concept of "associated persons" is to view it not as restrictive of remedies but as an almost unique example of the extension of "domestic" remedies to many who have never before been regarded as having "quasi-familial" relationships. Although confined to protection from violence and molestation the new definition has the potential for re-opening the debate about the legal meaning of the family. And seen in this light it is almost certainly right that "stalkers" should be excluded and at least arguable that those whose relationship has been sexual, but not communal, should also be excluded.

Yet when we turn to the other aspect of Part IV relating to occupation orders we can certainly find there the use of restrictive definitions to limit the availability of remedies relating to use of a home.[100] Applicants are divided into the "entitled" and the "non-entitled" and there are further distinctions between "spouses" and "cohabitants", "former spouses" and "former cohabitants". If you are really unlucky you may find yourself being labelled a "non-entitled former cohabitant". What is not wholly clear from the new regime is whether these distinctions exist predominantly to emphasise the superiority of marriage over cohabitation or the superiority of possessing property rights over not possessing them. As Gillian Douglas astutely observes:

> "One cannot help but conclude that the result of these provisions is as much to stress Parliament's concern for the importance of property rights as it is to emphasise the importance of marriage. A cohabitant who is 'entitled' is to be treated in the same way as any other entitled applicant including, of course, spouses. This is because his or her property rights are to be protected by the courts. But a legislature really concerned to privilege marriage might have been expected to lay down extra protections for spouses *qua* spouses."[101]

Perhaps then the most striking feature of the Family Law Act 1996 is the ambivalence, even inconsistency, in its ideological base. It promotes no-fault, non-adversarial divorce yet incorporates procedures which will make it more difficult to get one; it claims to be in favour of marriage yet introduces a concept which, in one respect, will stretch the notion of what is familial way beyond the context of marriage or even heterosexual cohabitation, and a divorce process which is calculated to put off significant numbers of those who might otherwise have been inclined to marry; and while marriage and property rights are clearly though to be largely irrelevant to the question of protection from violence and molestation, they are considered highly relevant to the inextricably connected matter of occupying a home—and, even here, the weight to be attached to each is uncertain. None of this is all that surprising given that the Act is the product

---

[99] The concept of "cohabitation" has hitherto been confined to *heterosexual* cohabitation where the parties are said to be living together "as husband and wife". Thus, for example, heterosexual partners will be aggregated for the purposes of social security legislation whereas homosexual partners will not.

[100] S. 30 ff.

[101] Above n. 78.

of at least two very different influences—the considered work of the Law Commission over some years[102] and the misinformed intervention of the tabloid press and a small minority of extremists who needed to be placated to secure the survival of the legislation.

VI   CONCLUSION

The theme of this chapter has been the influence of changes in legal concepts and terminology as a means of conveying new ideas and new values in the development of family law. It has been a necessarily selective review and other examples easily spring to mind. The former concept of "voluntary care" has for example been replaced with the notion of "accommodated" children to emphasise the distinction between compulsory care and voluntary arrangements.[103] More recently the notion of joint or shared residence has gathered ground arguably for its symbolic affirmation of the post-divorce equality of parents which, it may be, sole residence coupled with contact might not achieve.[104]

It has been argued here that the constitutive effect of these conceptual changes is of considerable importance in an area of law which is difficult, if not impossible, to enforce through traditional enforcement mechanisms. The language used in family law statutes often reflects the objectives and values which lie behind a programme or agenda of law reform. The precise agenda or objectives can shift, as happened in the case of divorce and domestic violence where the Law Commission's carefully thought out objectives have to some extent been skewed in a quite different direction during the Parliamentary process.

Even where the language of the statute accurately reflects the intentions of the law reform agencies there can be a shifting of the agenda as the original objectives are distorted through inaccurate interpretation or deliberate misrepresentation. The principle that no *unnecessary* orders should be made in children cases becomes, before our very eyes, the "no-order principle", the "non-intervention" principle and, from there, a "policy" or "philosophy" about the relationship of the state to the family; the statutory emphasis on the "responsibilities" of parents leads to an illogical denial that they have "rights" and the attempt to remove the stigmatising language and status of illegitimacy fails as judges and commentators decide to ignore it. In this way what people *say* a statute means assumes an importance greater than what it actually says.

The device used by those with alternative agendas is the process identified by Sir Roger Ormrod and by Frankfurter J before him. And doubtless there will be

---

[102] On the domestic violence and occupation aspect Law Com. Report No. 207, *supra* n. 80. On the divorce aspects *Facing the Future*, Law Com. No. 170 (1988) and *Looking to the Future: Mediation and the Ground for Divorce* (1993) (Cm. 2424).

[103] S. 20 Children Act 1989.

[104] As to which see Caroline Bridge, "Shared Residence in England and New Zealand—A Comparative Analysis" (1996) 8 *CFLQ* 12.

plenty of opportunity for more of the same as the value-laden Family Law Act reaches the implementation stage. How seriously, for example, will those administering the new divorce law really take the injunction to push reconciliation when their experience will already have taught them the simple truth that reconciliation is for the vast majority a dead duck once a public step towards divorce has been taken? And how far are judges with 20 years' experience of being even-handed towards the married and unmarried really going to be prepared to drive a wedge between the two when it comes to applying the criteria for occupation orders?[105] It seems more than likely that the attempt to influence through the enactment of general principles will fail as surely as it did in the case of illegitimacy.

As we look to the future it is already evident that the evolving concept of "parenthood" is about to become a major battleground for those with conflicting values. Is being a "parent" about procreation, as the English child support legislation suggests,[106] or is it about performing the social role of a parent?[107] And, if the latter, why not simply confer "parental responsibility"[108] on those concerned as has been possible for many years? The answer may again be a linguistic one—that those acting out the role of social parents do not merely want the powers and duties of parents but want to *be*, or at least to be *called*, "parents". And perhaps that is why a female-to-male transsexual was not content merely to seek a residence order in relation to his cohabitant's child but insisted that he wanted to be registered and thereby accepted as the "father" of the child.[109]

It is a trifle depressing to come to the realisation that everyone—law reformers, parliamentarians, judges and academic commentators alike—use the language of the law to assert and uphold his or her own values and that there can never be a complete resolution to the problem of conflicts in fundamental beliefs. But we could all perhaps benefit from Sir Roger Ormrod's moral for judges:

> "You cannot avoid value judgments in these days so you had better use the proper scale of value, not one distorted by formulas or slogans."[110]

---

[105] Under the Domestic Violence and Matrimonial Proceedings Act 1976 the courts were required to apply the criteria in the Matrimonial Homes Act 1983 to applications by either the married or the unmarried. Now under the Family Law Act 1996 the criteria, and the maximum duration of orders, may differ depending on whether the applicant has or has not got a proprietary interest in the home is married, formerly married or merely a cohabitant or former cohabitant without any proprietary interest. The details are complex and beyond the scope of the current article. They are principally to be found in ss. 33, 35, 36 and 41 of the Act.

[106] Under the Child Support Act 1991 it is the fact of being a biological parent rather than a social parent (such as a step-parent) which counts for liability.

[107] It is now being argued that "parenthood" is today more about the *intention* to be a parent than the fact of procreation. See Chris Barton and Gillian Douglas, *Law and Parenthood*, (Butterworths, 1995), especially at 50–2.

[108] The concepts of "parenthood" and having "parental responsibility" are distinct in English law though, of course, they will frequently coincide in the same person.

[109] *X, Y and Z* v. *The United Kingdom*, judgment delivered by the European Court of Human Rights on 22 Apr. 1997.

[110] N. 12 at 152.

PART TWO

The Dynamics of Legal Assimilation of Changes in Social Norms

This Part examines how flexibility within the administration of the law has allowed legal systems to correspond to changes in social norms and structures. Rwezaura (Chapter 11) demonstrates how this has been achieved in Tanzania under processes threatened by official disapproval, while Kabeberi–Macharia and Nyamu (Chapter 12) show that, in Kenya, administrative means have been used to make the same accommodations. Stewart (Chapter 13) explains, from Zimbabwean examples, how the actual application of customary law can respond to perceived normative values not always recognised in official versions of customary law, suggesting difficult conceptual problems as to the nature of law itself. Dewar (Chapter 14) argues that the lack of consensus about family forms in western countries was accommodated by conferring wide discretion on judges, but that the more recent trend towards rules reflects not only a wish to improve the efficiency of family law administration, but also to implement a more uniform view of family living, frequently based on notions of rights between family members. Bailey-Harris (Chapter 15) provides an example of this occurring within the Australian context with respect to financial obligations after divorce, but Dewar himself and Bainham (Chapter 10) discuss another illustration: the growing policy of continued parenting of children by parents who have separated from one another. This attempt to retain, or construct, a form of family living when the "household family" is non-existent is examined more fully in Part Five. Family norms generally involve reciprocal expectations of support and this Part closes with a comparison by Jones-Pauly (Chapter 16) between Germany and Tanzania, showing the way in which legal systems respond (or in some cases fail to respond) to changing expectations of support between family members, but particularly the way in which comparison between European and African systems indicates possibilities of a *rapprochement* between modernistic individualism and "traditional" familial ideologies.

11

The Proposed Abolition of de facto *Unions in Tanzania: A Case of Sailing Against the Social Current*

BART RWEZAURA*

1. INTRODUCTION

In April 1994 the Law Reform Commission of Tanzania (LRC) recommended, *inter alia*, that section 160 of the Law of Marriage Act (LMA), be repealed because it constitutes "an unnecessary encroachment [on] the sanctity of marriage and [is] contrary to the spirit of the Law of Marriage Act" (Tanzania 1994, 33). Subsection (1) of the offending section enacts a statutory presumption of marriage in favour of reputed *de facto* unions that have subsisted for a minimum of two years. Subsection (2) states that once the presumption is rebutted, the woman cohabitant and the children born of that union become legally entitled to apply to the court for economic support from the male partner.[1] In these proceedings the court has similar jurisdiction as a divorce court, including the making of orders for the division of assets jointly acquired by the couple and the

* I wish to express my sincere thanks to all my friends and colleagues who read through an earlier draft of this paper and made helpful and encouraging suggestions. I particularly wish to thank Dr Wanitzek who also allowed me to use sources from our common research in Tanzania. Mrs C. O. Kaisi also deserves special mention for allowing me to use her unpublished LLM dissertation and Dr M. Mukoyogo, her LLM supervisor, who made the dissertation available to me.

[1] Subs. (1) of s. 160 states that: "Where it is proved that a man and a woman have lived together for two years or upwards, in such circumstances as to have acquired the reputation of being husband and wife, there shall be a rebuttable presumption that they were duly married." And subs. (2) of s. 160 further states that: "When a man and a woman have lived together in circumstances which give rise to a presumption provided for in subs. (1) and such presumption is rebutted in any court of competent jurisdiction, the woman shall be entitled to apply for maintenance for herself and for every child of the union on satisfying the court that she and the man did in fact live together as husband and wife for two years or more, and the court shall have jurisdiction to make order or orders for maintenance and, upon application made therefor either by the woman or the man, to grant such other reliefs, including custody of children, as it has jurisdiction under this Act to make or grant upon or subsequent to the making of an order for the dissolution of marriage or an order for separation, as the court may think fit, and the provisions of this Act which regulate and apply to proceedings for and orders of maintenance and other reliefs shall, in so far as they may be applicable, regulate and apply to proceedings for and orders for maintenance and other reliefs under this section."

determination of who is to have custody of the minor children. In 1971 when section 160 was enacted, it was widely recognised that *de facto* unions had become a social fact which the law could not ignore. Hence, the decision to extend to these unions the same legal consequences that follow a formal dissolution of a legal marriage. However, in so doing the legislature had indirectly raised and yet left open a number of important questions that have continued to engage the minds of judges.

Some of the difficult questions raised by section 160 LMA include the absence of any provisions in subsection 160(1) or anywhere else in the LMA as to the rights and responsibilities of the parties during cohabitation. Furthermore, no provision was made in case the cohabitants wished to be recognised as married without first seeking the rebuttal of the statutory presumption. Again, no legal rules were instituted to govern the distribution of property where one of the cohabitants died intestate before the validity of the relationship was tested in court. Such omissions, however, are easily explained when one examines the legislative history of section 160. The legislature seems to have been so concerned with ensuring economic protection to the woman cohabitant and her children that it spared no thought to these legal issues. Nonetheless, despite these statutory silences the High Court has now held a number of times that subsection 160(1) creates a form of marriage with the same legal effects as other forms of marriage provided for in the LMA. This development in the law, even though it remains somewhat incomplete, has generated hostility in certain influential circles. As the LRC warned in its report, "cohabitation should never be mixed up with issues of marriage. *De facto* arrangements may be considered elsewhere [but] not in the LMA" (Tanzania 1994, 33).

This chapter tells a story of how some judges in Tanzania have applied section 160 to deal with complex issues of legal pluralism and social change. I present here a case study of Tanzania's pioneering efforts to harmonise its plural systems of family law, inherited from the British colonial state. The chapter also describes various struggles for the control of women's labour and rights in children. At the same time I argue that the proposed repeal of section 160 is motivated by a misunderstanding of the main object of the LMA and its underlying social policy. Furthermore, this chapter argues that even if section 160 were repealed, such a measure would have little impact on social behaviour because *de facto* unions are a consequence of social forces that are much deeper and more enduring than law.

2. THE SPIRIT OF THE LAW OF MARRIAGE ACT

The term "spirit of the LMA" is used in this chapter to refer to two aspects of the LMA. The first is the main object of the Act and the second is the strategy by which the LMA seeks to achieve that main objective. With regard to the first, it is widely accepted that the LMA has two major goals, namely; to integrate and harmonise the various systems of personal law existing in Tanzania up to 1971, and, secondly, to introduce important reforms in the status of women and children. A careful reading of the LMA reveals that while it sought to unify the most significant areas of family law and to make certain reforms, it was also keen to avoid sudden and radical changes. For example, although the LMA enacted uniform rules to regulate key aspects such as initial capacity to marry, consent to marriage, property rights between spouses and compulsory judicial divorce, it also recognised the parties' right to celebrate a marriage in accordance with their personal laws. Furthermore, although marriage payments ceased to be a precondition to the validity of any marriage, the LMA did not prohibit parties from paying if they so wished. Today, such property exchanges are regarded as private contracts between the bride's family and that of the husband.

Furthermore, besides recognising polygyny, a measure intended to accommodate the interests of Muslim men and African traditionalists, the LMA also created a new form of civil polygynous marriage under its general provisions. Not only that, the LMA also permitted under certain conditions, the conversion of an existing monogamous marriage into a potentially polygynous marriage by a joint application of the parties (section 11 LMA). Even then, and perhaps as a trade off for the women, the LMA recognised the right of an existing wife to object to a proposed marriage of her husband to another woman on the ground, either, that her husband did not have sufficient means to support his existing family or, that the intended wife was otherwise unsuitable.[2] The LMA also recognised women's limited access to economic resources by stating that the primary obligation to maintain a wife is placed upon her husband (section 63 LMA). The wife's duty to maintain the husband arises only in exceptional circumstances.[3] On the other hand, while the LMA recognises the wife's right to own separate property, to sue and to be sued in contract and in tort, she is still presumed to have authority to pledge her husband's credit and indeed, she may even "borrow money in his name or use any of his money which is in her possession" to meet the family's basic needs (section 64(1) LMA). But LMA also provides that the wife's right to maintenance is forfeited where she "is living openly in an adulterous association" (section 64(3) LMA).

In short, the design and approach of the LMA reflects a policy inspired by caution, sensitivity and flexibility (Read 1972, 19; Rwezaura 1990, 157). The LMA represents an effort to move with the changing times but without totally losing touch with the prevailing community practices. While it enables individuals to "escape" from the restraints of their personal laws, it does not seek to "liberate" them from their customs or religious beliefs. In this sense the LMA

---

[2] According to s. 20(2)(b) (LMA) an objection to an intended marriage may be made by an existing wife, or one of the wives, to the registrar of marriages or registration officer on the ground that, "the intended wife is of notoriously bad character or is suffering from an infectious or otherwise communicable disease or is likely to introduce grave discord into the household".

[3] See LMA s. 63(b): "it shall be the duty of every wife who has the means to do so, to provide in similar manner for her husband if he is incapacitated wholly or partially, from earning a livelihood by reason of mental or physical injury or ill-health".

has a double mission. It aims at unifying personal laws while permitting a degree of pluralism and diversity. It is in many ways a provisional statute which requires periodic review and adjustment to meet the changing social conditions of Tanzania. In short, this is the spirit of the LMA which, during the last 25 years has provided the basis for judges to creatively develop a new family law for Tanzania. It is into this context that section 160 must be located along with the interpretation it has received from the courts.

3. BACKGROUND TO THE ENACTMENT OF SECTION 160 LMA

In its 1969 White Paper the Government stated that a practice had developed in Tanzania where couples were living together for many years and having children without being formally married to one another. That experience had shown that the woman cohabitant was the loser because the day the man got "tired of living with her he [would] drive her out of his house or leave her. Such a woman cannot sue the man for maintenance and her children are . . . illegitimate" (Tanzania 1969, 13). To remove such injustice it was recommended that "if a man cohabits with a woman for a period of more than two years, he would be presumed to have married that woman" (Tanzania 1969, 13). Given that *de facto* unions were now viewed as a social fact, the government could not ignore or show indifference to the injustice that was being perpetrated against women and children in these unions.

Although in 1969 there were no statistics showing the incidence of such unions, a later study has revealed that *de facto* unions are popular especially in urban areas. Thus in a sample of 126 men and 294 women, covering a period from 1971 to 1992, Kaisi found that 37 per cent of the respondents were living in *de facto* unions or had separated from such unions. Those who were formally married consisted of 48.6 per cent of the sample, while the widows and the never-married groups accounted respectively for 6.5 per cent and 5.8 per cent of the sample. As to the social and educational background of the parties to the *de facto* unions, Kaisi found that 43 per cent of the cohabitants were mostly white-collar employees with a minimum of secondary school education (Kaisi 1994, 129). Those aged between 21–30 years comprised of 33 per cent of the total sample, while 41 per cent were aged 31–40 years.[4] Although these data are by no means

---

[4] The 1985 European figures for *de facto* unions expressed as a proportion of all legally married couples were as follows: Sweden (19.9%), Finland (11.4%), Norway (10.8%) France (8.6%), Netherlands (7.7%), Great Britain (6.2%), Germany (4.7%), Austria (4.2%), Hungary (2.9%) and Italy (1.4%) See Prinz (1995, 75). The fact that the proportion of *de facto* unions in Tanzania far exceeds that of Sweden and of other European jurisdictions may be a consequence of how *de facto* unions are defined for the particular study and a result of the differences in the law and social conditions producing the European version of *de facto* unions. On the other hand, the Mozambique figure of 90% reflects a different kind of legal history whereby, the Portuguese colonial legal system neither recognised nor prohibited customary unions. Such non-recognition resulted in these unions being defined as "*de facto* unions" instead of valid customary marriages (Sachs & Welch 1990, 103).

representative of the whole country, they do offer a good indication of the extent to which *de facto* unions have spread in urban Tanzania. They also show that most cohabitants are young, educated and in white-collar employment.

Furthermore, and going beyond the figures, the Dar es Salaam study also uncovered a thick file of correspondence addressed to the office of the Registrar General containing many queries regarding what to do with several employees living in *de facto* unions who wished to be paid "married-person" allowances but had no marriage certificates.[5] Some of the employees had sworn affidavits showing that they were married. However, unlike in the neighbouring Republic of Kenya where these affidavits are reported to be widely used (Kabeberi-Macharia & C. Nyamu 1997, 15), such documents have not become popular because, among other reasons, they are not favoured by employers. At the Registrar General's Office, there was also "an endless list of women complainants" who had been abandoned by their male cohabitants for other women (Kaisi 1994, 141). The women believed that they were married under section 160 and had come to protest against their husbands expressed intention to marry other women. Some of these women had up to six children born in these *de facto* relationships.[6] One cannot dispute, therefore, that *de facto* unions, whatever class these might belong to (see below), have become part of the Tanzanian social fabric.

4. CLASSIFICATION OF *DE FACTO* UNIONS IN TANZANIA

Three general categories of *de facto* unions seem to be more frequently litigated in the courts. The first (i.e. *class one*) consists of customary unions that are considered irregular or incomplete because the essential customary procedures might have been started but not yet completed. And where such a union subsists for some years but without being regularised, customary law recognises it for certain limited purposes. In such cases the husband has no rights over his children. Such unions belong to the customary law system and date back to the pre-colonial era. They arise primarily from a failure to comply with the prescribed requirements for contracting a marriage under customary law as defined, not by state law, but by the woman's family. But such failure is not viewed as a serious irregularity in the same way as Western law views irregularity of ceremonies leading to marriage. The notion of a customary law marriage as a process has traditionally permitted the husband's family to complete the procedures over the years without incurring serious challenges on the status of the parties. In short, although *class one* can be broadly described as *de facto* union, it is not a result of a conscious decision by the parties not to contract a marriage. Rather, it arises from a failure

---

[5] These inquires came from public institutions such as the Tanzania Peoples Defence Forces, the Police, the Tanzania Harbours Authority, the Tanzania Railways Corporation, the Tanzania Posts and Telecommunication, the Insurance Corporation and the Tanzania-Zambia Railway Authority.

[6] According to Kaisi, the average period of cohabitation in her sample was 5.4 years (1994, 129).

by the parties or one of them to comply with the essential formalities leading to a valid customary marriage.

The second category of *de facto* unions (i.e. *class two*), consists of what may be called "modern" as well as "voluntary" *de facto* unions (Jessep 1992, 463). Unlike *class one*, these are consciously established, even though the partners may have differing conceptions of the nature of their relationship.[7] They are "modern" because they are not a result of an attempt to contract a customary marriage. Moreover, these unions exist as a result of a mutual agreement of the parties with little if any involvement of their respective families. Such unions are found not only in Tanzania but in most parts of Africa, particularly in the urban areas. Thus, Michael Bourdillon refers to "a new from of union in urban situations, in which a man and a woman live together although no bride-price is paid. Many Shona [people] reject the idea that such unions are properly to be called marriages; they are referred to as *mapoto* (i.e. pots), suggesting simply a convenient sharing of cooking arrangements" (1991, 320).[8] In short, although *class two* unions raise the question of fact whether parties or one of them have consented to being regarded as married, and if so, what form of marriage such a unions should be, in practice, section 160 provides room for any cohabitant to challenge such a presumption of marriage. As will be shown later, courts do not impose marriage on parties who can show that they regarded one another merely as boy and girl-friend. As to the form of marriage which is to be presumed by the law, such a question remains unresolved, hence the use of the term *section 160 marriage* in this chapter.

The third and final category, (i.e. *class three*), exist under circumstances where a party who is married under a civil or Christian form, purports to end such a marriage using extra-judicial procedure as provided under customary law. Thereafter, believing oneself to be free of a previous marital bond, he or she formally remarries under customary law. Although the second marriage is invalid under the general law, it is normally recognised as valid under the parties' customary law. To this class of unions must be added cases where the couple in similar circumstances, as noted above, rather than going through a second ceremony of marriage decides simply to cohabit with that other woman. Again another vari-

---

[7] For example, the male partner might assert that the woman is his girl-friend while the woman believes that she is his wife. In this connection, cases show a tendency for women claiming under s. 160 to cite a longer period of cohabitation while the men admit a shorter period. In some cases the women use their children's age to corroborate their story. See *Leticia Bagumba* v. *Thadeo Magoma & Anor.* (n. 11 below) where the man testified that between 1977 and 1980 he regularly had sexual intercourse with the appellant but that they were then staying separately. However, the woman contended at the trial that she and the man had started cohabitation together in 1976. Similar denials by men have been reported also in Kenya (Kabeberi-Macharia & Nyamu 1997, 12). Thus, as noted by Bledsoe, "[w]hen brought to court, cases involving disputes over marital statuses invariably end in a tangle of contradictory testimonies from numerous witnesses"(1980, 8). In these circumstances courts have to be alert to such manipulation of personal status and the possible motives underlying such conduct.

[8] Bourdillon further notes that although some of these *mapoto* unions might be transitory and short-term, many of them are relatively stable "lasting ten years and more, and involve a contractual arrangement which has been partially recognised by a Shona urban court" (Bourdillon 1991, 320).

ation to *class three* are unions where a monogamously married man, instead of first divorcing his first wife, purports to marry an additional wife under customary law.[9] Such practices are common in urban centres where working men, who also have homes in the rural areas, find it convenient to leave their first wives in the village as "farm managers" while they continue to work in the city, regularly sending money and presents and paying occasional visits to them. Such arrangements also provide a convenient relocation for school age children, away from the supposed "negative" urban influences. In a few instances one also finds some city dwellers who maintain two households, the first with a statutory wife and the second with a cohabitant or customary law wife. Here again, the second marriage is void but the parties or one of them may not be aware of this until there is a dispute.

It is clear that *class three* unions are a result of a conflict between the customary system, the religious system, and the general law system.[10] Thus, unlike *class two*, this category is a by-product of multiple systems of marriage law operating in a single jurisdiction and thus making it possible for individuals to switch between the various systems. Before the enactment of the LMA, divorce under customary law was by agreement between the spouses and their families, followed, in certain cases, by the refund of bridewealth. There was no need for a judicial divorce and no requirement for documentary proof of such divorce. Such an underlying cultural assumption may have led many couples married in Christian or civil forms to believe that their marriages could be terminated in the same way as other customary marriages. This impression was reinforced, in some cases, by the fact that irrespective of the form of marriage, parties were still expected to go through all the usual customary preliminaries including the transfer of bridewealth.

The use by parties of more than one system of law in contracting a marriage and the uncertainties in individual status that resulted from such choices are widely reported in sub-Saharan Africa. For example, Poulter found in Lesotho spouses who had "married one another both under the received law and under customary law" (1981, 34). Nhlapo has also reported a similar situation in Swaziland and how men move between the two systems of law to the great detriment of their women (1987, 125). In such cases the difficult question is first to determine the form of marriage that has resulted before its legal effects can be ascertained. In these circumstances parties remain for a very long time ignorant of their actual legal status under state law until one day a marital dispute or the

---

[9] *In the Matter of Mwanjesa Albert*, (DSM) High Court Probate & Admin Case No 23 of 1989, the deceased had two wives. The first was a church–wife and the other was either "just a cohabiter" (as noted in Kaisi) or probably a customary law wife. There were eight children from each of these unions (Kaisi 1994, 171).

[10] *In the Matter of S.R.H.*, (DSM) High Court Probate and Admin. Case No 222 of 1980, the deceased, a prominent Tanzanian politician, was previously married in accordance with Islamic law. He subsequently cohabited with another woman, a Christian, with whom he had two children. On his death intestate, the first wife successfully challenged the validity of the second union and was able to oust the two children from inheriting their father's property (Kaisi 1994, 170).

death of one of the parties (especially the husband) throws a dark shadow on the validity of their marriage.

5. THE EMERGENCE OF "SECTION 160 MARRIAGE"

I believe that if section 160 (LMA) had been given a restrictive interpretation as certain judges have done, it would have remained a simple device for securing division of family assets, maintenance of the female partner and custody of children. Fortunately, during the last 25 years, the true object of section 160 and how this object fits into the broader scheme of the LMA have emerged in the decisions of many High Court judges. It is important to stress here also that the birth of what may be called *section 160 marriage* has occurred as part of a wider process of judicial integration of the principles of English common law with those of African customary law.

1 A Presumed Marriage is a Legal Marriage

A number of High Court judges have expressed the view that subsection 1 of section 160 (LMA) creates a valid form of marriage in cases where the presumption is not rebutted. For example, in *Leticia Bagumba*,[11] Mwalusanya J held (in 1989) that by fulfilling the conditions laid down by section 160(1), the parties "were duly married by virtue of the doctrine of presumption of marriage". In this case the couple had lived together as husband and wife for over five years; had gained the reputation of husband and wife, and had not gone through any kind of marriage ceremony.[12] This was a *class two* union with no involvement of the couple's respective families. The main dispute between the parties was whether the woman had a right to remain in the family house which her male partner had sold to a third-party without the wife's knowledge or consent. Mwalusanya J held that in the context of a "presumed marriage", the wife enjoys the same rights as any married woman including the right to continue to reside in the matrimonial home until the marriage is judicially terminated.[13] The court

---

[11] *Leticia Bagumba* v. *Thadeo Magoma & Anor.*, (Mwanza) High Court Civ App. No. 8 of 1989 (unreported).

[12] This is the test applied by Nyalali, J (now CJ) in *Elizabeth Salwiba* v. *Peter Obara* [1975] LRT 52.

[13] S. 59 (LMA) states that where "any estate or interest in the matrimonial home is owned by the husband or by the wife, he or she shall not, while the marriage subsists and without the consent of the other spouse, alienate it by way of sale, gift, lease, mortgage or otherwise and the other spouse my be deemed to have an interest therein capable of being protected by caveat, caution or otherwise under any law for the time being in force relating to the registration of title to land or of deeds." And where this is done in contravention of the above restriction, then, unless the buyer had no notice of the other spouse's interests, "the estate or interest so transferred or created shall be subject to the right of the other spouse to continue to reside in the matrimonial home until—(a) the marriage is dissolved; or (b) the court on a decree of separation or an order for maintenance otherwise orders."

not only upheld the wife's claim but it also ordered maintenance for her and the children. This decision in effect resolves the issue of what rights and obligations such couples have during cohabitation or when they are temporarily living apart. There are several decisions of the High Court which support Justice Mwalusanya's interpretation of section 160(1). The remaining problem, however, is that the status of these couples remains doubtful until determined by a court of law.[14] Moreover, as noted above, and unless the parties agree in advance, it is difficult to determine precisely what form of marriage has resulted from such cohabitation. For, example, one cannot tell whether such unions are monogamous or polygynous.

Additional light can be shed on subsection (1) of section 160 by examining some of the cases where the presumption of marriage has been successfully rebutted. In *Elizabeth Salwiba* v. *Peter Obara*[15] the court held that "there was no evidence . . . which could show that the parties . . . had acquired a reputation of being husband and wife". The only witness called by the woman cohabitant to give evidence of cohabitation and repute was vague as to whether the parties had acquired the reputation of being married. Again in *Charles Ruyembe* v. *Mwajuma Salehe*,[16] where the cohabitants described themselves as "boy and girl-friend", Katiti J held that the presumption of marriage had been rebutted because "the life style of the girl and boy friend cannot be equated with that of husband and wife and doing so is a misallocation of dignity and respect". Therefore, in this case the parties had not acquired "the reputation of being husband and wife, to accommodate a presumption that they were duly married".[17]

Another line of High Court decisions lead to the conclusion that in cases where the presumption of marriage cannot arise, this has the result of effectively blocking the remedies or relief available under section 160(2). This is especially so where the parties lack the initial capacity to marry or where they have not cohabited for at least two years. Thus, in *Charles Ruyembe*[18] after stating the provisions of section 160, Katiti J added, albeit obiter, that "it should never be forgotten that the said subsection [i.e. 160(1)] does presuppose capacity to duly marry, as no presumption will be attached to associations of parties, of for instance, below

[14] In my view, s. 160 could be amended to permit parties to such unions to apply jointly for the registration of the marriage once they have fulfilled the conditions laid down by s. 160 LMA. At the moment one or both parties can apply to the court (s. 94 LMA) for a declaratory decree that they were validly married. However, such a remedy is hardly affordable by most couples and seemingly, it is only pursued when there is a marital problem. See *Yonathan Gwandenga* v. *Kastani Daniel*, (DSM) High Court Civil Appeal No 70 of 1994 (unreported), *per* Kyando J. In this case a man applied to the court to be declared a husband "by virtue of long cohabitation together, and secondly, and perhaps mainly, that he be given a share of the house". This is one of the very few cases where the man moved into his partner's house and sought to rely on s. 160 to secure division of assets.

[15] [1975] LRT 52.

[16] [1982] TLR 304.

[17] But having so held, Katiti J correctly made orders under s. 160(2), in this case, the custody of the child of the union. Therefore, the presumption may be heavy but it is not irrebuttable and in cases where one of the parties does not wish to be presumed married, there is room under s. 160(1) to maintain one's single status.

[18] N. 16 above.

marriage age. Nor will the sub-section apply if the parties are actually married [i.e. are incompetent to marry by reason of an existing marriage]".[19] In another High Court decision, Moshi J, held that "[i]f one of the parties lack the legal capacity to marry, the presumption would not even arise for they could never be duly married in the first place, and it would indeed be an error of law to suggest that the law can presume a marriage between parties who cannot marry because of lacking initial capacity to marry one another."[20]

In short, where parties fulfil the conditions laid down by section 160(1), and have initial capacity to marry, they will be presumed "duly married" until this presumption is rebutted. Where the presumption is not rebutted, they will remain married until the marriage is dissolved by a court of competent jurisdiction. Until then, the parties are legally entitled to all the rights and obligations enjoyed by any married couple. Evidently, a heavy burden of proof is upon a person alleging that the parties are not man and wife. Furthermore, according to the holding in *Elizabeth Salwiba*,[21] if the parties have not cohabited for at least a period of two years, the presumption under section 160(1) will not arise and section 160(2) will not apply.

2 The Origins of a "Section 160 Marriage"

The origins of *section 160 marriage* can be traced back to the early decisions on which judges have relied when interpreting section 160 LMA. They include *Sakala* v. *Elia*,[22] where it was held that notwithstanding failure to pay bridewealth, a valid marriage would arise "on the application of the common law principle that long cohabitation in the absence of evidence to the contrary raises a presumption that a marriage is valid". The court noted further that courts favour the common law principle of presumption of marriage because they are reluctant "to invalidate any marriage unless there are good and compelling grounds for doing so". In *Loijurusi* v. *Ndiinga*,[23] the High Court stressed again

---

[19] Although in an earlier paper (Rwezaura 1985, 179) I had argued that where parties lack initial capacity to marry, then s. 160(2) LMA should not apply, I am now of the opposite view that s. 160(2) does apply. But as I have argued elsewhere in this chapter, all cases of void ceremonies, where among other things, parties lack initial capacity to marry, ought to be governed separately under the nullity provisions of the LMA.

[20] *Thadeo Mutarubukwa* v. *Hermalinda Herman*, (Mwanza) High Court Civil Appeal No. 60 of 1991.

[21] N. 15 above.

[22] [1971] *High Court Digest* n. 257 In this case the husband applied for custody of children born during the marriage. The children's mother denied the existence of the marriage on the ground that the husband had not paid any bridewealth to her natal family. The lower court held for the wife but the husband successfully appealed to the District Court where it was held that, long cohabitation raises a strong presumption of marriage.

[23] [1971] *High Court Digest* n. 33. In this case the parties had cohabited for six years, the husband having not completed the payment of the whole bridewealth. Then the wife's natal family tried to break-up the cohabitation/marriage unless the husband paid the outstanding balance. The court held that the strong presumption in favour of the marriage had not been rebutted by the wife's natal family.

that it was "against public policy to interfere with the family . . . and courts of law all over the world are very loath to allow such interference". Referring to the English common law doctrine of presumption of marriage, Kwikima Ag J noted that the "Anglo-Saxon common law, to which our legal system is heavily indebted, accords particular regard to the sanctity of marriage. On that principle this court has held that even under customary law, prolonged cohabitation raises a presumption of marriage unless there are circumstances indicating the contrary."[24]

In both cases the appellate judges quoted with approval the 1944 decision of the Governor's Appeal Board in *Nyamakaburo Makabwa* v. *Makabwa Mabera Watila*,[25] where it was stated that:

> "when persons are living together as man and wife over a long period, and especially where there are children of the union, the Board would require the strongest possible evidence to rebut the presumption that the marriage was valid. It would require stronger evidence than that of the interested parties to confirm the assertion that no brideprice was paid and even if satisfactory proof was forthcoming that the brideprice has never been paid further evidence would be necessary from an independent source to establish the assertion that non-payment of brideprice necessarily involves the invalidation of the marriage."

In 1963 by virtue of Rule 5 of the Declaration of Customary Law, (GN No 279/63) bridewealth was declared no longer necessary for the validation of a customary marriage. This became the official customary law in most districts of Tanzania.[26] In 1971 the LMA further declared that "a marriage which in all other respects complies with the express requirements of this Act shall be valid for all purposes, notwithstanding any non-compliance with any custom relating to dowry or the giving or exchanging of gifts before or after marriage"(section 41 LMA). Moreover, under section 41(f), failure to register a marriage does not affect its validity. Following the amendment to the Judicature and Application of Laws Ordinance, the LMA attained an overriding status over customary law and Islamic law, thus completely eliminating the legal importance of bridewealth.[27] With these statutory changes in place the way was cleared for section 160 to enter the scene with a defined period of two years' cohabitation (not previously laid down under the common law) which enabled the courts to declare many unions (predominantly *class one*) as valid marriages.

---

[24] Ironically, the concept of "sanctity of marriage" is used here by Kwikima Ag J to uphold the validity of a *de facto* union while the LRC takes the opposite position that s. 160 is an "unnecessary encroachment on the sanctity of marriage". In my view, the comments of the LRC appear to be directed largely, if not exclusively, at *class three* unions while Kwikima J in this case refers to *class one*.

[25] Governor's Appeal Board No 7 of 1944.

[26] See GN 279/63 Rule No 5.

[27] S. 9(3A) of the Judicature of and Application of Laws Ordinance (Cap. 453) states that "notwithstanding the provisions of this Act the rules of customary law and the rules of Islamic Law shall not apply in regard to any matter provided for in the Law of Marriage Act, 1971".

Despite the statutory changes rendering bridewealth legally irrelevant to the validity of a marriage, the social importance of bridewealth was not greatly affected. In other words, parents continued to demand bridewealth before consenting to the marriage of their daughters. Young men and women, on the other hand, begun to question the traditional view of marriage as a union of families. Many rejected the choices made for them by their parents under a system of "arranged marriage" in preference to their own mates (Katapa 1994, 76–80). In this way section 160 seemed to have provided a site for social struggles between elders who are not willing to let their daughters be married to men who could not pay bridewealth. In some way, therefore, the effect of section 160 was to weaken parental authority, particularly in the sphere of spouse selection. Yet, as will be argued below, this is only one aspect of the many functions of section 160 in the overall working of the LMA. In the discussion that follows, it is argued that the presumption of marriage doctrine is an essential aspect of the overall strategy of the LMA.

6. SECTION 160: AN ESSENTIAL PART OF THE LMA SCHEME

This section examines four major areas showing how section 160 complements the LMA. The first is that it enhances the principle of individual consent to marriage by promoting autonomy and choice of spouse. Indirectly, section 160 undermines parental power and the custom of arranged marriages. Secondly, section 160 mitigates considerably the problem of unregistered customary marriages. Thirdly, it provides a means by which the economic contributions of cohabitants, especially the women, are recognised and protected. Fourthly, section 160 reduces the problem of illegitimacy of children, especially in view of the rising rate of *de facto* unions in Tanzania.

1 Principle of Individual Consent to Marriage

The principle of consent to marriage is central to the LMA. It is, for example, enshrined in section 9 which defines a marriage following closely Lord Penzance in *Hyde's case*.[28] Furthermore, section 16 (LMA) stipulates that "no marriage shall be contracted except with the consent freely and voluntarily given by each of the parties thereto". And, section 38 (LMA) provides that "[a] ceremony purporting to be a marriage shall be a nullity if the consent of either party was not freely and voluntarily given thereto".[29] So important is the principle of consent to marriage that even when the parties are already married, "no proceedings may

---

[28] See *Hyde* v. *Hyde & Woodmansee* (1866) LR 1 P & D 130, at 133.
[29] This is in contrast to the law in England after 1973 when lack of consent, previously a ground for making a marriage void, now makes a marriage only voidable. See s. 12(c) Matrimonial Causes Act 1973 and Bromley & Lowe (1992, 90).

be brought to compel a wife to live with her husband or a husband with his wife" (section 140 LMA). To enhance this principle the LMA also dispenses with parental consent to marriage when the parties have attained the age of 18 years. In effect, males are exempted totally from parental consent because 18 years is their minimum age for marriage. Prior to the enactment of the LMA the government announced that the minimum age for females was to be fixed at 15 years in order to comply with the UN recommendation and "to prevent the parents from removing their young daughters from school" for purposes of marriage (Tanzania 1969, 7). It has now been recommended by the LRC that the minimum age for both males and females be raised to 21 years; noting that "a girl below the age of 18 years may easily be coerced into marriage by greedy parents . . . ". Therefore, if this recommendation becomes law, parental consent to marriage will become legally irrelevant in Tanzania (Tanzania 1994, 25).

It seems to me that the process of transforming customary marriage into a union of individuals continues to derive support from the government. Moreover, and perhaps inevitably, such a social trend has come with a new form of domestic arrangement which cannot be separated from the notion of individual freedom to marry. It would have been naive for the legislature to encourage individual consent to marriage, remove the legal importance of bridewealth, support the weakening of and eventual abolition of parental consent to marriage, while at the same time closing its eyes to *de facto* unions which are to some extent a by-product of, or indeed, a consequence of individual choice. No doubt such choices are largely influenced by the current social and economic context of Tanzania but the law is also involved in providing favourable conditions for the exercise of such choices. In this connection, the responses of certain Dar es Salaam cohabitants confirm that *de facto* marriages are a product of social change. For example, when asked why they had not gone through a formal marriage ceremony, 40 per cent cited financial reasons; 28 per cent said they belonged to different religions and 13 per cent cited parental objection to the proposed marriage (Kaisi 1994, 130).

Therefore, although as noted above these responses are based on a small sample obtained from a highly urbanised part of the country, still they reflect a wider national trend. This is a trend whereby individual choice of spouse is taking precedence over the dictates of the wider family. In other words, these statistics support a well recognised movement away from the idea of marriage as a union of families to the modern ideal of a marriage as a union of the immediate parties with individual consent as the underlying principle (Sawyerr 1977, 115; Rwezaura 1995, 25; Armstrong *et al.* 1993, 314). In conclusion, section 160 has contributed to the process whereby parental power to influence or even to compel their children to marry particular people is on the decline. The recognition of *de facto* unions has also tended to dampen parental vigour to break their daughter's marriage on account of unpaid bridewealth. In the words of Kwikima Ag J, it is "against public policy to interfere with the family".[30]

---

[30] See *Loijurusi Ndiinga* (n. 23 above).

2 Mitigating the Problem of Unregistered Marriages

Customary marriages have a dismal record of registration in Tanzania. For example, in 1971 when the LMA came into force, 219 customary marriage were registered, compared to the figures of 8,778 (Christian); 2,023 (Islamic); 768 (Civil) and 153 (others). In 1983–84 the rate of registration was even more discouraging. There were 62 registered customary marriages compared to that year's national total 35,036 marriages, (broken down as follows: 14,447 Christian; 17,714 Islamic and 2,788 civil) (Tanzania 1994, 22). Yet the low rate of registration is not proof that customary marriages have become less popular. On the contrary, "investigation has revealed that customary law marriages are still being celebrated [in large numbers] but they are not registered" (Tanzania 1994, 22). As to the reasons why there is such a low rate of registration, the LRC has noted that customary marriages are not registered because the registration procedure is too cumbersome.[31]

I agree that whereas the registration procedure is cumbersome, it is also true that customary marriages continue in certain respects to retain their old nature as a process rather than an event. To understand how this happens, we need to look again at the way the LMA allocated space for marriages under customary law. As a harmonising and integrating statute, the LMA extended recognition to customary marriages without making their official registration a condition to their validity. More specifically, under the LMA (section 25) parties are free to contract a marriage in accordance with the rites of a community or communities to which they belong, provided that they comply with the essential provisions of the LMA. It is also provided under section 43 (LMA) that when such a customary marriage is contracted in the presence of a registration officer, such officer is required to take the necessary steps to register the marriage with the district registrar. And if such officer is not present at the wedding, (since attendance is not mandatory), then the parties to the marriage are obliged to apply for registration within 30 days of the marriage. And to encourage parties to register their marriage, it was further provided that an application for registration can be made after the prescribed time limit has elapsed. Yet despite such enlightened provisions, it has not been possible to improve the rate of registration.

As noted above, it is possible that a number of potential customary marriages do not begin as precise events such as do civil marriages. Rather, they begin less spectacularly as an elopement or a cohabitation which ultimately matures into a regular customary marriage, or indeed, into a church wedding. But some couples never make it to the proverbial alter and this has the effect of postponing the reg-

---

[31] I believe also that most rural communities do not have the time or inclination to travel a long way to register their marriage with a state official. It has been recommended therefore, by the LRC, that an official at a village level be appointed as the registration officer, to achieve greater efficiency in the registration process. In Mozambique the Family Law Project recommended the establishment of a mobile registration centre to enable a more efficient system of registration. See Sachs & Welch (1990, 103).

istration of the marriage almost indefinitely. The effect of all this is that although unregistered customary marriages are recognised, proving them legally can be time-consuming and costly. Moreover, the lack of documentary evidence often provides an incentive to the parties to dispute the existence of the marriage. Therefore, whereas the LRC's recommendation to improve the registration procedures is a very welcome step indeed, yet until this new procedure is operative, the number of cohabitants who require the legal protection offered by section 160 will continue to escalate.

3 Protection of Cohabitant's Economic Contributions

Many of the cases cited in this chapter have been instituted mostly by women petitioners seeking maintenance and/or division of jointly acquired assets. In the neighbouring Republic of Kenya, a recent study has shown that of the women cohabitants who applied for maintenance, the majority were mothers with young children (Kabeberi-Macharia & Nyamu 1997, 24). It should not be surprising then that section 160 is more readily used by women to protect their economic interests and those of their children. One of the reasons for such dependence is that women are traditionally entrusted with the care of young children in most African communities including Tanzania. Furthermore, women are also economically disadvantaged compared with their male counterparts. All this makes section 160 one of the few available means for women and children in *de facto* unions to access maintenance. On the other hand, section 160 also provides the means to distribute jointly acquired assets at the end of cohabitation.

However, it is regrettable that an accurate interpretation of subsection (2) of section 160 does not at the moment extend to *class three de facto* unions. Thus, in *Thadeo Mutarubukwa*, the application of a woman cohabitant who had lived with a man she thought was her husband for 25 years and had children in that union, lost her share of family assets because her second marriage was void. Similarly, nothing was given to the woman applicant in *Angelina Mutalemwa*.[32] Again this was a *class three de facto* union where the applicant and the respondent had cohabited for 21 years and had five children. There are indeed many such cases where women's contributions are not at all protected by the general law. It must be stressed once again that the lack of protection for *class three* unions seems to be part of a more fundamental shortcoming in the LMA. As the LMA stands now, it does not provide remedies for parties to a void marriage. According to section 94(2)(a) LMA any person may petition the court for a declaratory decree to determine the validity of a marriage ceremony. This jurisdiction, unfortunately, does not include the power to order maintenance or division of assets. Indeed, it is not certain whether the court has such power when making a decree of nullity in respect of voidable marriage. Thus, in

[32] [1978] LRT n. 44.

Amida Shabani[33] Kisanga J doubted whether section 114 could be read as granting the power to order division of matrimonial assets following a decree of annulment.

I sincerely believe that the time has come for the LMA to permit the application of section 114 (LMA) in all cases where the court grants a decree of nullity of marriage and a declaration in respect of a void ceremony. Were such an amendment to be made, courts would have power to do justice to most *class three* cohabitants who are at the moment caught in the unjust web of legal pluralism. Moreover, parties seem to be resorting to subsection (2) of section 160 because they have no other means of redress. If courts were given power to order ancillary relief following a decree of nullity, it would no longer be necessary to apply subsection (2) of section 160. It must be stressed here that although nullity jurisdiction originates from English family law, most world jurisdictions today, including the United Kingdom, have amended their family laws to empower courts to order maintenance and property adjustments when granting a nullity decree whether in respect of a voidable or a void marriage (Cretney 1992, 28; Bromley & Lowe 1992, 720). This suggestion is consistent with the LMA's policy of protecting the economic rights of women, many of whom honestly believe that they are legally married. Such an amendment would also harmonise the principles of customary law with those of the received English law.

4 Alleviation of Illegitimacy of Children

The law governing the legitimacy and guardianship of children in Tanzania requires a large dose of reform.[34] In its present form, Tanzania law governing children contravenes Article 2 of the United Nations Convention on the Rights of the Child which prohibits discriminatory treatment of children, *inter alia*, on ground of birth.[35] There are at least two parallel systems of law governing the status and guardianship of non-marital children in Tanzania. On the one hand, there is the Affiliation Ordinance (Cap. 279) received from England under which a single mother may obtain limited financial support for her child. An affiliation order merely establishes the paternity of a child but does not legitimate such a child. Moreover, even if the child's parents eventually marry one another, their

---

[33] See *Amida Shabani v. Alfani Mtenga* [1981] TLR 232.

[34] A number of interesting changes intended to improve the status of all children (including illegitimate children) have been proposed to the government recently by the LRC but these have yet to be widely debated and enacted (Tanzania 1997, 7, 59–88). Furthermore, unlike Uganda which has made an effort to update and integrate existing child law in line with its international obligations, the recent Tanzania proposals, if implemented, will add new provisions to existing laws on the child without making major reforms.

[35] Art. 2(1): "States Parties shall respect and ensure the rights set forth in the present Convention to each child within their jurisdiction without discrimination of any kind, irrespective of the child's or his or her parent's or legal guardian's race, colour, sex, language, religion, political or other opinion, national, ethnic or social origin, property, disability, birth or other status." Tanzania became a party to this UNCRC on 10 July 1991.

children born before that marriage remain illegitimate unless legitimated under customary law. Tanzania has no general law providing for the legitimation of children by a subsequent marriage between the children's parents. Finally, although in many jurisdictions now a child of a voidable marriage is legitimate and in specific cases children of void marriages are presumed legitimate, there are no such provisions in Tanzania. This situation alone produces a significant number of illegitimate children given that a number of couples cohabit first before formally contracting a marriage.[36]

Customary law, on the other hand, provides that non-marital children belong to the maternal side unless they are subsequently legitimated by payment of a customary fee. It also provides for legitimation of the child by the subsequent marriage of the parents but this rule is presumably inapplicable to couples who are not members of a given customary law community. The close link, therefore, between the legitimacy of children and bridewealth is visible in all disputes over rights in children, where the woman's natal family endeavours to challenge the validity of the marriage on the ground that bridewealth was not paid. Within this narrow context it can be argued, therefore, that subsection (1) of section 160 reduces the rate of illegitimacy.

Regrettably, even if section 160 were retained, there are other categories of children who are left out. They include children born to cohabitants whose unions cannot be legally presumed, (e.g. *class three* unions); children born in unions where the presumption has been rebutted; and non-marital children born of parents who are not cohabiting. It is within this context that the decision by certain High Court judges to extend to all children irrespective of birth the protection of section 125 LMA (providing for the welfare of the child principle) is a very welcome development in the law (Rwezaura 1994–5, 534). Yet judges, unlike the legislature, cannot make major changes in the law such as abolishing all the legal consequences of illegitimacy. In short, although the abolition of the distinction between marital and non-marital children is what is urgently required, it must be recognised, nevertheless, that at the present time, emergence of *section 160 marriages* has contributed significantly to the reduction of illegitimacy.[37]

5 Can the Presumption of Marriage Doctrine Outlive Section 160 ?

In this section I argue that the repeal of section 160 does not necessarily put an end to the common law doctrine of presumption of marriage. This is because such a common law rule has been part of Tanzania law since the British colonial

---

[36] Kaisi found a marriage register at a Roman Catholic Church in Dar es Salaam showing that between 1986 and 1992, a total of 120 couples had lived together as husband and wife before celebrating their marriages in Church (1994, 144 n. 3).

[37] The law of inheritance is currently under review and it is believed that the intended reforms will further narrow the gap between marital and non-marital children in the area of intestate succession. See Rwezaura (1994–5, 523 and Tanzania 1997, 69).

era. I have shown above that even before 1971 when section 160 was enacted, courts were already familiar with this doctrine. For example, there are several decisions of the High Court, such as *Nyamakaburo*, *Sakala* and *Loijurus*,[38] where judges have stated that the English common law doctrine of presumption of marriage had become part of Tanzanian law and was applicable not only to marriage under the general law, but also to customary law marriages. It seems that section 160 merely codified and refined an existing common law rule without necessarily replacing or repealing it. In the light of this argument, if section 160 were repealed without at the same time abolishing the common law presumption, the latter rule would continue to apply. And in the absence of section 160(1) judges would have to determine the appropriate length of cohabitation necessary to trigger such a presumption of marriage.

The next question might be how to make up for the repeal of section 160(2). In my opinion, all applications relating to *class three* unions, where a ceremony of marriage (however irregular) has taken place, or where the parties lack initial capacity to marry, ought be dealt with under sections 38–39 LMA governing nullity of marriage. As noted above, the LMA ought to be amended so that courts have power to determine child support and custody and to make financial orders for partners, and orders of division of assets, on granting a decree of or a declaration of nullity of marriage. However, such change in the law will not cover cohabitants who: (i) lack the initial capacity to marry; (ii) have not attempted to go through any ceremony of marriage; and possibly, (iii) do not consider themselves husband and wife. Those who fall in this latter group have two options. They can, if they belong to a customary law community, rely on Rules 93–97 of the Declaration of Customary Law (GN 279 of 1963), which empowers courts to order division of assets on the termination of a concubinage.[39] If they do not belong to a customary law community or do not wish to rely on customary law, then, the court can invoke the principles of equity which are part of the received law in Tanzania. Rules of equity are regularly applied in other common law jurisdictions including Britain to determine the property rights and interests of unmarried cohabitants.[40]

My final point is that if the above argument regarding the continued application in Tanzania, of the doctrine of presumption of marriage does not hold, the alternative is to rely on section 9(3A) of the Judicature and Application of Laws Ordinance (Cap. 453) which provides in effect that the rules of customary law and rules of Islamic law are applicable in all matters not specifically covered by the LMA.[41] Hence, if section 160 were to be repealed, parties to *class one* unions

---

[38] See, respectively nn. 25, 22 and 23 above.

[39] Rule 94 states that "if a man and a woman have started a common household together, the property which has been acquired by common effort [will be] divided as follows:-" Then follows details as to how this should be done.

[40] See for example, *Eves* v. *Eves* [1975] 3 All ER 768 and *Grant* v. *Edwards* [1986] 2 All ER 426 and more generally Bromley & Lowe (1992) at 555–84.

[41] See s. 9(3A) cited at n. 27 above. It follows that such rules would apply in any matter not covered by the LMA.

could rely the application of the doctrine of presumption of marriage as a principle of customary law basing on previous High Court decisions.

7. CONCLUSION

This chapter has shown that the incidence of *de facto* unions in Tanzania is in one sense a result of the interaction between plural models of marriage operating in a single jurisdiction. The first, and most dominant, is the concept of marriage contained in the English colonial marriage laws from which the LMA derived some of its basic principles. The essential features of this model include the concept of marriage as a voluntary union of two individuals, which is monogamous, a result of a formal and legally prescribed ceremony, indissoluble except by judicial fiat, giving rise to specific rights and obligations which are enforceable by the state legal system. The African traditional model, on the other hand, is grounded on the notion of marriage as a union of two families; it is polygynous; it results not from a single precise ceremony but from a long process of negotiations between families; it is consummated by the transfer of an agreed bridewealth (or part thereof) and can be open-ended at its inception though gradually attaining a more definite character, especially after the birth of children. Its termination is much like its formation, effected not by judicial decree, but extra-judicially through negotiations between the two families followed, in some cases, by a refund of a portion of bridewealth. Consequently, the termination of customary unions can be a process and a result of many years of living apart followed by the remarriage of the wife. As long as bridewealth is not refunded a marriage might endure and it is not unusual in some communities for a wife to return with new children to her old husband after having lived apart for several years (Wanitzek 1998).

In 1971 these two models were integrated by the LMA and came under the jurisdiction of the national legal system administered by judges trained in the English common law. The doctrine of presumption of marriage, borrowed from English common and, in existence before 1971, became codified and enacted as section 160 of the LMA. In its native jurisdiction this doctrine provided the much needed bridge between the old common law system of marriage and the then new statutory form of marriage introduced in 1753 (Parker 1990; Stone 1995). In this sense the doctrine of presumption of marriage ensured a smooth transition between the old and the new system. In Tanzania, as this chapter has shown, both before and after 1971 this doctrine also played nearly the same role of validating marriages that had not strictly complied with the prescribed procedures. But in another sense, the doctrine has also operated to enhance individual freedom while also undermining the notion of marriage as a union of families. By enhancing individual autonomy and choice, section 160 has tended to play the political function of weakening the power of elders to determine the marriage choices of their children. On the other hand, section 160 has also seemingly supported unions made outside the authority of the Christian church and to a lesser extent, outside the prescriptions of the Islamic faith. This has consequently provoked a certain forceful political backlash, leading to the call to repeal of section 160.

In my view, the proposed repeal of section 160 will have minimal effect on social behaviour because it is sailing against the social current. Having regard to the social and economic changes taking place in Tanzania today and the plural and transitional nature of our family law, it is difficult to imagine how our system of marriage can actually function without the lubricant that section 160 currently provides. Thus, rather than repealing this provision, it should, instead be refined along the lines suggested in this chapter. On the other hand, as I have noted above, the repeal of section 160 will not by itself result in the abolition of the old common law doctrine of presumption of marriage. Therefore, whatever may happen to section 160, courts might continue to perform their difficult task of harmonising the present plural systems of family law while also responding to the needs of a changing society.[42]

REFERENCES

ARMSTRONG, A., "Uncovering Reality: Excavating Women's Rights in African Family Law" (1993) 7 *International Journal of Law and the Family* 314–69.

BLEDSOE, C., *Women and Marriage in Kpelle Society* (Stanford University Press, Stanford, 1980).

BOURDILLON, M. F. C., *The Shona Peoples* (3rd edn., Mambo Press Harare, 1991).

BROMLEY, P. M., and LOWE, N. V., *Bromley's Family Law* (8th edn., Butterworths, London, 1992).

CRETNEY, S. M., *Elements of Family Law* (2nd edn., Sweet and Maxwell, London, 1992).

JESSEP, O., "De Facto Relationships and the Law in Papua New Guinea" (1992) 41 *ICLQ* 460.

KABEBERI-MACHARIA, J., and NYAMU, C., "Marriage by Affidavit: Developing Alternative Laws on Cohabitation", Paper presented at the 9th World Conference of the International Society of Family Law, 28–31 July 1997.

KAISI, C. O., *Women under Presumption of Marriage: A Critical Analysis of the Law, Practice and Social Implications of s. 160 of the Law of Marriage Act No 5 of 1971*, LLM Dissertation, Faculty of Law University of Dar es Salaam, Tanzania.

KATAPA, R. S., "Arranged Marriages" in Z. Tumbo and R. Liljestrom (eds.), *Chelewa Chelewa: The Dilemma of Teenage Girls* (The Scandinavian Institute of African Studies, Ostersund, 1994), at 76–95.

NHLAPO, T., "No Cause for Optimism: Bigamy and Dual Marriage in Swaziland" in A. Armstrong and W. Ncube (eds.), *Women and Law in Southern Africa* (Zimbabwe Publishing House, 1987).

[42] In July 1997 the Minister for Justice and Constitutional Affairs reported to the Parliament that the LRC proposals, including its recommendation to repeal s. 160, will be opened for wider public discussion in the near future. According to the Minister, considering that family law and the law of inheritance affect people's religious beliefs, cultures and human rights, it will be necessary to seek wider consensus within the community before definite statutory changes are finally presented to Parliament.

PARKER, S., *Informal Marriage, Cohabitation and the Law, 1750–1989* (Basingstoke, Macmillan, 1990).

POULTER, S., *Legal Dualism in Lesotho, A Study of the Choice of Law Question in Family Matters* (Morija Sesuto Book Depot, 1981).

PRINZ, C., *Cohabiting, Married, or Single* (Avebury, Aldershot, 1995)..

READ, J. S., "A Milestone in the Integration of Personal Laws: the New Law of Marriage and Divorce in Tanzania" (1972) 16 *Journal of African Law* 19–39.

RWEZAURA, B., "Presumption of Marriage in Tanzania" (1985) 18 *Verfassung und Recht in Ubersee* 169–79.

—— "Integration of Personal Laws: Tanzania's Experience" (1985) 1&2 *Zimbabwe Law Journal* 85–96.

—— "The Integration of Marriage Laws in Africa with Special Reference to Tanzania" in J. M. Abun-Nasr, U. Spellenberg and U. Wanitzek (eds.), *Law, Society, and National Identity* (Helmut Buske, Hamburg, 1990), 139–61.

—— "Tanzania: Building a New Family Law out of a Plural Legal System" in M. D. A. Freeman (ed.), *Annual Survey of Family Law* (1994–5) 33 *Journal of Family Law* 523–40.

—— with A. Armstrong *et al.*, "Parting the Long Grass: Revealing and Reconceptualising the African Family" (1995) 35 *Journal of Legal Pluralism and Unofficial Law* 25–73.

SACHS, ALBIE, and WELCH, GITA H., *Liberating the Law: Creating Popular Justice in Mozambique* (Zed Books, London, 1990).

SAWYERR, G. F. A., "Judicial Manipulation of Customary Family Law in Tanzania", in S. Roberts (ed.), *Law and the Family in Africa* (The Hague, Mounton, 1977), 115–28.

SOUTH AFRICA, *Harmonisation of the Common Law and the Indigenous Law (Customary Marriages)* Project No 90, Issue Paper 3, South African Law Commission, 1996, 5.

STONE, LAWRENCE, *Road to Divorce: A History of the Making and Breaking of Marriage in England* (Oxford University Press, Oxford, 1995).

TANZANIA, UNITED REPUBLIC OF, *The Government White Paper No 1 of 1969. Government Proposals on Uniform Law of Marriage* (Government Printer, Dar es Salaam).

—— The Law Reform Commission of Tanzania, *Report of the Commission on Law of Marriage Act (No 5 of 1971).* Presented to the Minister for Justice and Constitutional Affairs, April 1994.

—— *Hotuba ya Waziri wa Sheria na Mambo ya Katiba,* (The 1997/98 Budget Speech by the Minister of Justice and Constitutional Affairs to the Parliament of the United Republic of Tanzania) (Government Printer, Dar es Salaam, 1997), 59–88.

WANITZEK, U., "Bulsa marriage Law and Practice: Women as Social Actors in a Patriarchal Society" in W. Zips and van Rouveray van Niewaal, E.A.B. (eds), *Sovereignty, Legitimacy and Power in West African Societies: Perspectives from Legal Anthropology* (Munster, 1998) at 119–71.

12

Marriage by Affidavit: Developing Alternative Laws on Cohabitation in Kenya*

JANET KABEBERI-MACHARIA and CELESTINE NYAMU

A INTRODUCTION

Cohabitation unions are on the increase in Kenya, perhaps due to the reconfiguration of the family unit as a result of increased urbanisation, and increasing isolation of young people from their family networks. Those entering into cohabitation unions may or may not have the intention of regularising the union in future. This chapter examines a practice that has developed in relation to cohabitation in Kenya, which we have labelled "marriage by affidavit". The following scenarios explain our choice of this label.

Pati (a woman) and Chali (a man) have lived together for five years now. They are not officially married under any of the officially recognised systems of family law in Kenya. *Scenario 1*: Chali's employer offers a health insurance policy that extends coverage to employees' spouses. Chali would like Pati to be covered under the policy. Chali and Pati go to a lawyer, who draws up an affidavit, stating that Chali and Pati are married under one of the customary law systems in Kenya. They swear the affidavit jointly, and Chali presents it to his employer, and Pati is covered under the policy. *Scenario 2*: Chali holds a Kenyan passport. He would like Pati to accompany him on a job-related trip abroad, but Pati does not have a passport yet. It will take a shorter time to have her included in his passport as spouse, rather than make an application for her own passport. They go to a lawyer once again, and swear a joint affidavit of marriage, which Chali presents to the immigration officials, and Pati is included in his passport as spouse. *Scenario 3*: Pati feels that her position will be more secure if she includes Chali's last name on her national identity card, or changes her last name altogether to his. She feels that this will be helpful to her if, for example, Chali dies, and for purposes of succession, she needs to show she is his next-of-kin, and that

* The authors thank FIDA (Kenya) for allowing access to case records and Roselyn Mungai for excellent research assistance. Celestine Nyamu thanks Women and Law in East Africa with whom she interned when writing this chapter and the Ford Foundation for funding the internship.

even though they were not officially married, they considered themselves married. She files a deed of change of name, and attaches onto it an affidavit of marriage. Her national identity card now bears Chali's last name.

These are simply examples of some of the uses to which affidavits are being put by couples cohabiting without formal marriage. The scenarios refer to use of affidavits for specific and narrow purposes. It is also the practice, however, for couples to swear a general affidavit of marriage that suffices as proof of marriage for all types of purposes. This type of affidavit remains valid for one year. The legal basis for the swearing of affidavits generally is the Oaths and Statutory Declarations Act, chapter 15 of the laws of Kenya. The general affidavit is valid for a period of one year, while those affidavits sworn for a particular purpose are valid only for the purposes for which they are sworn. The effect of this is that the couple, or, as is sometimes the case, only the women, have to constantly swear a general affidavit every year to show that they are married. In reality many swear one affidavit which they fail to renew but continue to believe in its validity even after its expiry. It appears that the affidavit, since it is a document, is presumed to have the same effect as a marriage certificate.

By now, some readers will be wondering why people in these situations do not simply get married formally. There are several reasons why people may cohabit without getting married, but a common reason is the costs involved. Cost refers not only to the expenses of the marriage ceremony, but also the marriage payments (bridewealth) expected by the woman's family in many African communities. Several commentators have shown how the nature of marriage payments has changed, and how the combination of "traditional" expectations with contemporary wedding practices has made marriage ceremonies an extremely expensive affair.[1] Affidavits, therefore, offer an affordable alternative to some people.

We make three main arguments in this chapter. First, that the question of what counts as a marriage is more than simply a matter of definition, in two senses. In the first sense, it marks the boundary between those to whom the state will award certain benefits and those to whom it will not, based solely on the type of union involved. The practice of marriage by affidavit, whereby couples are able to access benefits that would otherwise be unavailable to them, brings out the distributive nature of defining marriage in legal systems. In the second sense, we refer to the contest to define a relationship in a particular way. At the point when an informal (undocumented) relationship breaks down, the manner in which it is defined will determine the rights and obligations of the parties involved. Thus, describing a relationship as "a marriage under custom" will yield different results compared to describing it as "a cohabitation union".

Our second argument is that the practice of "marriage by affidavit" presents a case study in the ways in which people living in a pluralistic legal system manip-

---

[1] See Janet Kabeberi-Macharia, "The Marriage of Wahito: Modernization of Traditional Marriage Laws in Kenya", Paper presented at the Critical Legal Conference, University of Warwick, Sept. 1994. See also Angeline Shenje-Peyton, "Balancing Gender Equality and Cultural Identity: Marriage Payments in post-Colonial Zimbabwe", 9 *Harvard Human Rights Journal*, 105–44 (Spring, 1996).

ulate boundaries between categories whose existence is taken for granted, for example the boundary between "customary" and "official". The prevalence of marriage by cohabitation, and the official nod of approval given to it by the use of affidavits, mocks the conventional view that there are only four (separate and distinct) systems of marriage in Kenya, and that marriage by cohabitation is some exception outside this set-up.

Our third argument is that as a practical matter, the widespread nature of this practice calls for some guidelines to protect vulnerable people in those relationships, such as women and children in need of support. The need for guidelines will emerge when we examine 95 cases dealt with by the FIDA (International Federation of Women Lawyers) women's legal aid clinic in Nairobi, Kenya. These cases are summarised in Tables 1 and 2 in Appendix 1.

B WHAT COUNTS AS A MARRIAGE IN KENYA?

1 Nature of Kenyan Family Law

At the official level, unions will count as valid marriages if they are created under any of four systems of family laws in Kenya, namely:

- Any of the various African customary law systems in Kenya;
- Hindu religious practice, provided for under the Hindu Marriage and Divorce Act (chapter 157 of the Laws of Kenya);
- Islamic religious practice, provided for under the Mohammedan Marriage and Divorce Act (chapter 156 of the Laws of Kenya); or
- The statutory system set up under the Marriage Act (chapter 150) and the African Christian Marriage and Divorce Act (chapter 151).

Multiple systems of family law therefore operate side by side.

This set-up has its roots in the British colonial policy of indirect rule. Briefly, indirect rule was the idea that British colonial "law and order" would be maintained, as far as practicable, through already existing "native" institutions in the colonies.[2] Thus, the customs of each group would operate (except with regard to criminal matters), as long as those customs were not "repugnant to justice and morality", a qualifier that is still retained in the statute books of several former

---

[2] For a detailed discussion on the policy of indirect rule, see H. F. Morris and James S. Read, *Indirect Rule and the Search for Justice: Essays in East African Legal History* (1972). See also Yash Ghai and Patrick McAuslan, *Public Law and Political Change in Kenya: A Study of the Legal Framework of Government from Colonial Times to the Present* (1970). Although the rhetoric was one of continuity, that these institutions would continue operating as they had always done, it is clear that they were substantially altered in a direct way by indirect rule. For further reading on this point see Sally Falk More, "Treating Law as Knowledge: Telling Colonial Officers What to Say to Africans about Running 'Their Own' Native Courts", 26 *Law & Society Review* 11 (No. 1, 1992); Martin Chanock, *Law, Custom and Social Order: The Colonial Experience in Malawi and Zambia* (1985).

British colonies.[3] Issues of family law therefore were firmly within the domain of custom, for the Africans, and, for the immigrant Hindu and Islamic communities (and any Africans who converted to Islam), within the domain of their respective religions.[4] English law of marriage only applied to English people living in the colony, until the enactment of the Native Christian Marriage Ordinance in 1902, which extended aspects of English law of marriage to those Africans who converted to Christianity. African customary family law, therefore, catered for the African who did not convert to either Christianity or Islam. This colonial family law set-up has remained relatively unchanged. Presently, the application of various customary and religious laws relating to marriage and family has a constitutional basis in subsection (4)(b) of section 82 of the Kenya constitution. Section 82 makes it unlawful for any law to treat people differently on the basis of "race, tribe, place of origin, . . . colour or creed . . . ". Subsection (4)(b), however, makes an exception to this prohibition, in the case of laws that make provisions "with respect to adoption, marriage, divorce, burial, devolution of property on death of other matters of personal law".[5] The different regimes of family law can therefore continue to apply, purportedly without offending the constitutional prohibition of differential treatment in section 82.

The application of the various customary and religious laws also has a basis in section 3 of the Judicature Act (chapter 8 of the Laws of Kenya).[6]

Efforts aimed at harmonising the various family law systems were carried out in 1969 through the establishment of a presidential commission. The Commission submitted its report in 1970, together with a proposed Marriage Bill. To date, the commission's proposals have not been implemented, and two attempts to enact the Marriage Bill have failed to survive the parliamentary process.[7]

A cohabitation union that has not been formalised under any of these four systems will also count as a valid marriage if a court issues a judicial declaration applying the English common law presumption of marriage. We discuss this in the subsection that follows.

---

[3] For example, in s. 3 of Kenya's Judicature Act, ch. 8 of the Laws of Kenya.

[4] In the contemporary legislation, both the Hindu Marriage and Divorce Act and the Mohammedan Marriage and Divorce Act expressly recognise that a Hindu or a Muslim can celebrate his/her marriage in accordance with their religion. A marriage certificate is given upon celebration of the marriage, which provides documentary proof of the validity of the union. Whereas matrimonial causes for Hindus are handled by the Matrimonial Causes Act, those for Muslims are handled by the Kadhi's courts which apply Islamic laws and principles.

[5] Constitution of Kenya (revised 1992).

[6] S. 3 of the Judicature Act sets out the sources of the Kenyan law. It lists the Constitution, Acts of the Kenyan parliament, English statutes of general application, African customary law, Islamic religious law, Hindu religious law, and received doctrines of the English common law and principles of equity.

[7] See *Report of the Commission on the Law of Marriage and Divorce* (Kenya Government Printer, 1968). On the failure of the Marriage Bills see Kivutha Kibwana, "Marriage in Equality and Dignity: The Status of Family and Marriage Law Reform in Kenya", in *Women and Autonomy in Kenya: Law Reform and the Quest of Gender Equality*, CLARION Monograph No. 1, 1994, at 416.

(i) Kenyan law on cohabitation

Kenyan statutory family law is silent on the issue of cohabitation unions. The law in this area has been developed by the judges, applying the English common law presumption of marriage. The English common law presumption of marriage is applicable in Kenya by virtue of section 3 of the Judicature Act, which allows for the application of the common law of England and the doctrines of equity in so far as they are relevant and suitable to the conditions of Kenya and its inhabitants. In developing criteria for the application of the English common law presumption of marriage, judges have relied, to a great extent, on English decisions.[8]

When a court applies the common law presumption of marriage, the effect is that the relationship is treated, for all intents and purposes, as a marriage. Some of the factors that a court will take into account when deciding whether to apply the presumption to a particular case include:

- Duration of cohabitation. Although there is no fixed period that will automatically give rise to a presumption of marriage, long cohabitation often gives rise to a presumption of marriage in favour of the party asserting it.[9]
- Whether there are children resulting from the relationship.[10]
- Whether the parties ever intended to get married officially.
- Whether they were reputed to be married. This factor is arguably based on the notion that marriage is a (public) matter of status (rather than contract) and therefore marriage has just as much to do with external perceptions as with the internal intentions of the parties.

Once a court decides to apply the presumption of marriage, the burden then is on the party denying the existence of the marriage to rebut the presumption. The presumption of marriage has been held to apply generally to Kenya irrespective of the personal law system of the parties involved. This means that the presumption will apply regardless of what religion they profess, or which

---

[8] Even the available and often-used pronouncements of English judges on this subject, however, are contradictory. See, for example, *Eves* v. *Eves* [1975] 3 All ER 768 where Lord Denning argued that in a cohabitation situation (especially where one party in the relationship is already married to another person) in strict law the woman has no claim on her partner whatsoever:

"She is not his wife. He is not bound to provide a roof over her head. He can turn her and her children out in the street. She is not entitled to anything from him for herself. All she can do is to go to court to seek an affiliation order against him for the maintenance of the children. If he does not pay, she may have great difficulty in getting any money out of him, even for the children. Such is the strict law."

In *Tanner* v. *Tanner* [1975] 3 All ER 776, however, Lord Denning categorically stated, 'I think he has a legal duty towards them. Not only the babies, but also towards the mother in order to fulfil his duty towards the babies, he is under a duty to provide for their mother too".

[9] See *Mary Njoki* v. *John Kinyanjui*, Kenya Court of Appeal, Civil Appeal No. 71 of 1984. In this particular case, however, despite 6 years of cohabitation, the court declined to apply the presumption of marriage in favour of the woman.

[10] It is clear that this is often a factor, even though Madan J, in the *Mary Njoki* case, observed, "[A]lthough a child or children would be an important factor in giving rise to a presumption of marriage, it is not a *must* [emphasis in original] in order to give rise to it" (at 16).

customary law system they are subject to, if at all. Wambuzi J in *Yawe* v. *Public Trustee*,[11] stated:

> "the presumption has nothing to do with the law of marriage as such, whether this be ecclesiastical, statutory or customary; this must be proved. The presumption is nothing more than an assumption arising out of long cohabitation and general repute that the parties must be married irrespective of the nature of the marriage actually contracted."

(ii) More Than a Matter of Definition: Cohabitation Cases and the Contest Over Description of Relationships

In the Kenyan context, the presumption of marriage has been invoked mostly in cases where the existence of a customary marriage is asserted by one party and denied by the other. Often, the party denying existence of the customary law marriage argues that the requisite rituals were not performed, and that therefore the relationship has no legal status. Kenyan courts did accept this argument in one reported case: *Case* v. *Ruguru*,[12] where the court rejected a woman's claim that a marriage existed in accordance with customary law, and ruled that there must be proof that all the formalities were complied with. There are however cases that show that even if proper rituals were not carried out, this fact alone does not invalidate a marriage. This was the decision in *Peter Hinga* v. *Mary Wanjiku Hinga*.[13] The appellant, after 14 years of cohabitation with Mary Wanjiku, underwent a Christian marriage ceremony with another woman. The Christian Marriage and Divorce Act (the statute under which he underwent the Christian ceremony) invalidates a marriage under the statute if any of the parties has a pre-existing customary law marriage with another person.[14] The respondent (Mary Wanjiku) had tried to stop the ceremony to no avail. In these proceedings, therefore, she was seeking both a declaration that there was a valid marriage between herself and the appellant, and maintenance for the children.[15] The appellant argued that "because *Ngurario* was not performed there was no customary law marriage and the children are illegitimate and are not therefore

---

[11] Court of Appeal of East Africa, Civil Appeal No. 13 of 1976. In this case the court considered the 9 years of cohabitation, children, recognition of the woman as "wife" by the relatives of the deceased, and written and oral declarations by the deceased that the appellant was indeed his wife. See also *Kizito Charles Machani* v. *Mary Rose Vernoor alias Rosemary Moraa*, Kenya Court of Appeal Civil Appeal no 61 of 1984. Platt JA stated, "It is undesirable to bastardize children or debar succession, after long periods of cohabitation and the birth of children".

[12] High Court Civil Case No. 652 of 1968. Reported in [1970] EA 55.

[13] High Court Civil Appeal No. 94 of 1977. Reproduced in Eugene Cotran, *Casebook on Kenya Customary Law* (1987), 62.

[14] The prohibition is contained in s. 37 of the Marriage Act (ch. 150), which applies to marriages under the African Christian Marriage and Divorce Act (ch. 151) by virtue of s. 4 of ch. 151 which states, "Except as otherwise provided in this Act, the provisions of the Marriage Act shall apply to all marriages celebrated under this Act."

[15] The number of children is not explicitly stated in the judgment. Miller J, evidently very angry with the man's conduct, refers to the children as "as many as half a football team", ranging in age from 13 to 5½ years. Eugene Cotran, *id.* at 62.

entitled to maintenance".[16] Miller J rejected this argument, observing that the man was "relying on a mechanical point in Kikuyu customary law so as to take advantage of the repeal of the Affiliation Act".[17] Thus, defining the union as a customary marriage rather than a cohabitation union made all the difference for these children.

In the 95 FIDA legal aid cases that we examined, there were 13 cases in which the parties disagreed on the description or nature of their relationship. All except two of these were cases where the women (FIDA clients) were claiming maintenance for their children (rarely would they claim maintenance for themselves). In these cases, the women insisted that the union was a (customary) marriage, but the men denied it, arguing that the women were merely girlfriends, not wives. When it became necessary to institute court proceedings, FIDA had to first petition the court to apply the common law presumption of marriage and issue a declaration that there was a valid marriage between the parties. Only then would it be possible to claim maintenance.

The contest over definition of relationships also occurs in the area of child custody. Two of the 13 cases mentioned above concerned custody. This time, it was the women arguing that the relationship was not a marriage, and therefore, that the men had no rights of custody over the children born as a result of the union. In these cases, the cohabitation period had been brief, the children were very young and the women were no longer dependent on the men or no longer wished to depend on them for the children's upkeep. It is unlikely that there are many cases of this nature, precisely because not many women will be in a position of not needing economic assistance in raising children.[18]

The contest over definition of relationships does not occur only between the parties to the relationship. It also, in some cases, involves third parties who stand to gain or lose if the relationship is defined in a certain way. The most prominent example is in matters of intestate succession, often upon the death of the male partner, who invariably has more property. The woman will assert her claim

[16] *Ngurario* refers to a component of the marriage ceremony under Kikuyu customary law.

[17] The Affiliation Act was a statute that enabled single mothers, upon proof of paternity, to claim maintenance for their children from the fathers of those children. The statute was repealed in 1969. For discussion on the Affiliation Act, and the issue of provision for children born to unwed parents generally, see Violet Mavisi and Anne Kyalo, "The Affiliation Act: A Case for its Reinstatement", in *Women and Autonomy in Kenya: Law Reform and the Quest for Gender Equality*, CLARION Monograph No. 1 (1994) at 89. In the case of *Kizito Charles Machani* v. *Mary Rose Vernoor alias Rosemary Moraa* (Kenya Court of Appeal, Civil Appeal No. 61 of 1984 (Nairobi)), the judges ruled that the man had child support obligations, despite the fact that there was an impediment to the application of the common law presumption of marriage between the parties. The impediment was that even though the parties had cohabited for five years, the cohabitation had taken place during divorce proceedings between the woman and a previous spouse, and therefore as she did not have legal capacity to contract another marriage, the judges could not presume a marriage between the parties.

[18] We did find one reported case, where a woman regained custody of her children after arguing successfully that there was no valid customary law marriage between herself and the children's father: *Zepporah Wairimu* v. *Paul Muchemi*, High Court Civil Case No. 1280 of 1970, reported in Eugene Cotran, *Casebook on Kenya Customary Law*, 52. As in the *Case* v. *Ruguru* decision mentioned above, the court relied on the absence of the *ngurario* ceremony to declare that there was no valid customary law marriage. Contrast these decisions to Miller J's decision in the *Hinga* case, also discussed above, refusing to invalidate a customary law marriage on a technicality.

to the property, on the basis that she is the deceased's wife. If the man's relatives do not support her claim, for whatever reason, they will argue that there was no marriage between her and the deceased, thus excluding her from the division of the property. They will either argue that they knew her only as a girl-friend of the deceased, or, as often happens, that they never knew her at all.

This was the setting in two cases in which the judges arrived at different results. In the first case, *Yawe* v. *Public Trustee*,[19] the court upheld the woman's claim against the deceased's relatives, relying on the woman's evidence that:

— the parties had lived together for nine years;
— they had four children together;
— the man's relatives had visited the couple severally at the house in which they cohabited; and
— the deceased had made oral and written declarations (on job applications) that the woman was his wife.

In second case, *Mary Njoki* v. *John Kinyanjui Mutheru & others*,[20] the deceased man's two brothers and two step-mothers challenged a decision by the Public Trustee to include the appellant as a beneficiary of the deceased estate. She claimed that she was the deceased's widow, having cohabited with him for six years, and that both his family and hers knew of and approved of the relationship. The deceased's relatives denied the fact of cohabitation and argued that they knew of her simply as one of the deceased's girlfriends, not as a wife. Although a dissenting opinion by Madan J found in favour of the woman on the basis of "long cohabitation and repute", the court's majority ruled in favour of the deceased's relatives, and reversed the 30 per cent share that had been apportioned to her by the Public Trustee.

The foregoing discussion illustrates that defining marriage has distributive consequences. As we mentioned in the beginning, this distributive aspect is evident both at the level of interpersonal contests to define relationships, and at the level of official choices on what types of relationships to accord official recognition. The *Chali* and *Pati* scenarios we posed in the beginning portray people strategising to avail their union of benefits that would otherwise be unavailable to them, unless they were formally married.

The next section shows how people manipulate the distinction between "law" and "custom", "official" and "unofficial" in order to access these benefits.

C MARRIAGE BY AFFIDAVIT: NEITHER CUSTOMARY NOR LEGAL

There is already evidence that the boundaries between the various systems of marriage and family law are not lived out in reality. For instance, most Kenyans

---

[19] Court of Appeal for East Africa, Civil Appeal No. 13 of 1976. Also reported in Eugene Cotran, *Casebook on Kenya Customary Law*, at 63.
[20] Kenya Court of Appeal, Civil Appeal No. 71 of 1984.

of African descent regulate their family relationships primarily through custom, howsoever defined, regardless of their religious affiliation. Thus, it is not uncommon to find among African Muslims the combined application of African customary law and Islam to regulate inter-personal relationships.[21] It is only in cases of those strictly practising Islam that we find that customary personal law has little or no application.

The way in which marriage ceremonies are conducted among Kenyan Africans in the contemporary setting provides further evidence of this fluidity of boundaries. Take the case of a couple who profess the Christian faith, planning to get married. In most cases, they will first get their families together for some form of familiarisation and negotiations, often (if not always) accompanied by marriage payments by the groom's family to the bride's family. This is (believed to be) done within the framework of the parties' customary law(s). Only then is the church ceremony conducted. In fact, some churches have developed the practice of satisfying themselves that the family negotiations have been carried out, and that there is agreement, before they can proceed with a wedding ceremony. In effect, even though the African Christian Marriage and Divorce Act is supposedly the only law that governs their marriage, the couple will have complied with an adaptation of multiple systems.[22]

The practice of marriage by affidavit goes further because it really does bypass all of the recognised systems of marriage and family law. This section focuses on how the practice manipulates one boundary in particular: the boundary between customary law marriage and "unofficial" cohabitation unions.

1 What is the difference between a customary law marriage and a cohabitation union, and does it matter?

A marriage celebrated under customary law is, essentially,

> "an alliance between two families, which alliance creates new reciprocal rights and obligations for the new spouses; new relationships between the spouses and their relatives and between the relatives of the spouses."[23]

Although customary law marriages are potentially polygamous, a man can only celebrate each marriage at a time. Usually, the marriage is accompanied by marriage payments.

---

[21] *Women and Law in East Africa* (WLEA-Kenya), Research Report on Inheritance Laws and Practices in kenya, edited by Okech-Owiti, Njeri Karuru, Winnie Mitullah and Kamau Mubuu (Nov. 1995).

[22] For further discussion of marriage procedures in the contemporary Kenyan scene, see Janet Kabeberi-Macharia, 'The Marriage of Wahito: Modernization of Traditional Marriage Laws in Kenya", Paper presented at the Critical Legal Conference, University of Warwick, Sept. 1994.

[23] Kabeberi-Macharia, J., "The Marriage of Wahito: Modernization of Traditional Marriage Laws in Kenya", Paper presented at the Critical Legal Conference, University of Warwick at 1.

Although marriage under customary law is recognised as one of the valid forms of marriage under Kenyan law, the marriages are not officially registered, and there are no official records of customary law marriages. This makes it necessary for a couple married under customary law to prove the existence of the marriage by means of an affidavit, every time documented proof of the official status of their union is required, for example, in any official dealing. The affidavit will usually indicate the particular customary law system under which they are married (i.e. which ethnic group's system), and the date on which the ceremony was held.

An affidavit containing an assertion that parties were married under custom is usually taken as *prima facie* evidence that they do, indeed, have a valid marriage. It is not usual practice for officials to go behind the affidavit to require further or more specific evidence of marriage. It is presumed that they have complied with their community's essentials of a marriage which may include marriage payments and agreement between the two families. Thus, here lies the appeal of the affidavit to couples cohabiting informally. All they need to do is allege marriage under custom, even though they never actually went through the recognised formalities of it. Thus, an affidavit of marriage sworn by a cohabiting couple will, more often than not, allege that the parties are married by virtue of customary law. This is because the very idea of swearing an affidavit of marriage is rooted in the practice of documentary proof of customary marriage.

The use of affidavits has been taken up by other couples who cohabit as man and wife, but do not want to undergo either a customary or civil ceremony, but at the same time want to enjoy the same "benefits" as those who have undergone either of the ceremonies. That way, they get to by-pass both customary and statutory civil law marriage requirements;[24] hence our argument that a new form of marriage has been shaped, that is "neither customary nor legal".[25] On the one hand, it is not custom in the terms of what the state considers sufficient to fulfil the prerequisites of a customary marriage, although it could be argued that it is custom, in the sense that a new custom is being shaped to respond to new circumstances, such as increased urbanisation, and isolation of young people from their family networks. On the other hand, it is not law either, in the sense that it is not a form of marriage recognised under any of the family law systems in Kenya, although it makes use of a legal form/artifact, in the form of the affidavit.

---

[24] They also do not have to rely on judicial application of the common law presumption of marriage. Since cohabitation unions are legally invalid under Kenyan law, until a court applies the common law presumption of marriage, cohabiting couples have, as a coping mechanism, come to rely on affidavits to legalize their unions.

[25] The phrase, "neither customary nor legal" is borrowed from the title of an article by Martin Chanock, "Neither Customary nor Legal: African Customary Law in an Era of Family Law Reform", 3 *International Journal of Law and the Family* 72–88 (1989). Chanock uses the phrase to show how custom, and therefore the distinction between custom and "law" is invoked, whenever there is an attempt to reform family law to improve the protection of women. This practice often "obscure[s] the realities of gender and generational conflict in modern Africa". Rather than focus our attention on discussing the nature or merits of the categories, he calls for an examination of the underlying power relations that every invocation of custom, or assertion of the distinction between "law" and "custom" seeks to preserve.

The line of distinction between customary law marriage and "unofficial" cohabitation is rather thin, and largely artificial in the contemporary setting. Rwezaura makes similar observations with respect to Tanzania: "the line between *de facto* unions and an irregular or incomplete customary marriage is often hard to draw".[26]

Although we pointed out that officials will rarely go beyond an affidavit that alleges marriage by customary law to require evidence of a ceremony, the courts do insist on precisely this kind of proof. The courts insist on detailed proof of the ceremony, and witnesses have to testify that the prerequisites of a customary law marriage were complied with. In addition to oral testimony, there has emerged a practice of referring to documented "sources" or compilations of marriage customs of the various groups in Kenya.[27] This rigid requirement for strict proof hardens the distinction between customary law marriages, and cohabitation unions. Since many people who seek affidavits of marriage only interact with administrative officials other than courts (see examples given in the opening scenario), they rarely need to worry about this strict level of proof. However, the reality of different levels of proof has produced interesting scenarios, with people describing their relationships differently in different settings, depending on the level of proof required in each setting.

The FIDA cases that we examined illustrate this point. At the outset, many women seeking remedies such as maintenance, and restraining orders in cases of violence, will indicate that they are married under custom. This is what the FIDA staff will enter on the client's data sheet under "type of marriage", and in all correspondence concerning the case. For cases in which it became necessary to file suit, however, the staff would require more detailed information, and it would turn out in some cases that even though the client believed herself to be married under custom, none of the procedures had been followed. In many cases, she did not have sufficient proof that would satisfy the court. The lawyers therefore decide that the claim has a better chance of success if it is based on "marriage by virtue of long cohabitation", rather than on customary law marriage. The court documents, therefore, describe the relationship as a cohabitation union. Reading the court papers alongside other documents in the file, you could just as well be reading about two different relationships.

This points to the absurdity of requiring a particular type of proof of customary law marriages that only looks at certain pre-determined criteria for proving an "authentic" customary marriage. Here we are referring to criteria such as that which was insisted upon in the *Case* v. *Ruguru* case discussed above, or the often-consulted compilation of various marriage customs in Eugene Cotran's books, and

[26] Bart Rwezaura, "The Proposed Abolition of *de facto* Unions in Tanzania: A Case of Sailing Against the Social Current", Paper presented at the 9th World Conference of the International Society of Family Law, Durban, South Africa, 28–31 July 1997, at 6.

[27] The source that is referred to very often is Eugene Cotran, *The Law of Marriage and Divorce: Kenya* (Restatement of African Law series, 1968).

reliance on precedent.[28] The court process and records, therefore, miss out on the reality of what people are doing now, and how they are shaping custom.[29] It forces people to fit themselves into categories which will make judicial sense, even when they believe their reality to be different, as the FIDA cases illustrate.

From a pragmatic standpoint, therefore, it might appear that "marriage by affidavit" is a good thing: it helps couples to gain access to benefits which would otherwise only be available to those whose unions have been recognised by law. The affidavit facilitates this for you without the technicalities and expenses involved in complying with requirements of a formal marriage, both under statute and customary law.[30] The benefits of marriage by affidavit, however, are not available to everyone. Even though we indicated that affidavits are affordable, it is also true that legal services generally are beyond the reach of the majority of Kenyans. The experience of various legal practitioners is that more and more people are making use of affidavits as proof of marriage. It is very telling, therefore, that among all the FIDA cases we examined, none mentioned the existence of an affidavit, or reported ever having used one for any particular purpose. The presence of an affidavit would definitely have strengthened a claimant's position, particularly in those maintenance cases where the men denied the existence of a marriage. FIDA serves low income women. For most of them, their experience with FIDA is also their first contact with legal services.

This implies that use of affidavits, is, to a certain extent, a class-specific practice. This conclusion may also be drawn from the nature of the purposes for which people are likely to seek an affidavit, namely accessing a partner's employment benefits, or obtaining a joint passport, although these are by no means the only purposes for which people seek affidavits of marriage.

There are other drawbacks to the practice of "unofficial" cohabitation generally, and we will discuss these in the next section.

D POSITION OF WOMEN AND CHILDREN IN NEED OF SUPPORT

We stated in the beginning that the widespread nature of the practice of "unofficial" cohabitation calls for some guidelines to protect vulnerable people in those relationships, such as women and children in need of support. This is evident from our discussion of the cases in which male partners attempt to escape maintenance obligations by denying the existence of a marriage. The women involved are caught by surprise.

---

[28] See Eugene Cotran, "Kenya: The Law of Marriage and Divorce", *Restatement of African Law Series* (1968); and *Casebook on Kenya Customary Law* (1987).

[29] There has been increased recognition of the need to view (as well as research and teach) customary law as a "dynamic living system" and to de-emphasise compilations/codifications and court precedents, whose effect is to present customary law as a "fixed" category. For one such view see Julie Stewart, chapter 13 of this volume.

[30] There is a possibility that cohabitation unions do exist among Hindus and Muslims, but this has yet to be investigated.

1 Mistaken belief in the legal status of cohabitation unions, and validity of the affidavit

There seems to be a common belief that if people are not married formally before a registrar or in church, surely their union must be considered a customary law union. Many women do not know or anticipate the legal consequences upon break-up of the relationship. In the FIDA cases, some clients, believing in the legal validity of their unions, informed the FIDA staff at the initial interview that they wanted remedies such as:

— divorce or dissolution of the marriage;
— "that the separation be made official";
— "that she be relieved of her obligations as a wife".

As regards the use of affidavits, there is also a common mistaken belief in the validity of the affidavit. Having been able to secure, by virtue of the affidavit, benefits which they would be entitled to only if they were officially married, couples (even those who were planning to eventually formalise their union) become complacent, and feel that there is no further need for documentation. They believe themselves to be married by virtue of that piece of paper that says that they are married. Most of the couples base their belief on the fact that *a lawyer* had drawn the affidavit which they swore *in the lawyer's presence*, thus lending validity to their union. They then proceed to live a married life and the woman often assumes the man's last name and they may have children together. What they do not know is that even where an affidavit exists, it cannot, by itself, establish the validity of a marriage. At best, it can be relied upon, even after it has expired, to show that the couple intended to get married, thus support a party's petition for recognition of a common law marriage.

The legal status of a union is usually not an issue, until after the union begins to crumble, or after one of the parties dies. At this point, they are surprised to find that they are not automatically entitled to remedies that are available to people married formally. They cannot obtain any remedy from the court, such as maintenance for themselves and the children, or get a share of the property acquired in the course of cohabitation unless the court first makes a determination on whether to apply the common law presumption of marriage. This is the unfortunate position that Mary Njoki found herself in, in the case of *Mary Njoki* v. *John Kinyanjui & others*, discussed above, when her deceased partner's relatives challenged her status as widow, and the Court of Appeal refused (Madan J dissenting) to apply the presumption of marriage in her favour.

2 Position of children

In 70 of the 95 FIDA cases reviewed, the disputes involved parties who had cohabited for 15 years or less, 32 of those had cohabited for five years or less. All but five of the clients in the cases reviewed had children. (Refer to Table 2 in Appendix 1.) These data point to the fact that breakdown in cohabitation unions is occurring mostly when children are young and dependent. Evidently the children are in a vulnerable position. The children are caught up in the contest to define the relationship to suit each party's interests. FIDA records show several children who were sent away from school for non-payment of fees while their parents were involved in the dispute. We are not making a claim that such non-provision for children's needs is a problem associated only with cohabitation. Similar problems occur even within subsisting formalised unions, as well as with regard to enforcement of child support orders after separation or divorce. The vulnerability of children in cohabitation unions, however, is exacerbated by the ambiguous legal status of their parents' relationship.

In Kenya, a man's child support obligations extend only to his children born within marriage or legally adopted by him. Thus, by denying the existence of a marriage, men are in a position to invalidate maintenance claims as well. Before the repeal of the Affiliation Act in 1969, it was possible to claim child support from the biological father, upon proof of paternity. The mother in this case was required to make an application for an order from the court for the education and maintenance of the child by the child's father. The primary concern of this Act was to make provision for the maintenance and education of a child born to unwed parents, and in no way made provision for the recognition of the relationship between the child's parents. The Act made provision for all children born to unwed parents, whether or not the parents were cohabiting. The Act was repealed in 1969 and has not been replaced to date.[31]

In such a legal setting, it is commendable that some judges have gone ahead to require child support, even in cases where it was not possible to presume the existence of a marriage between the child's parents. A case in point is *Kizito Charles Machani*, where Platt, Kneller and Gachuhi JJ upheld a man's obligation to maintain his children, even though it was impossible to presume a marriage between him and their mother. The judges could not presume a marriage because at the time when the parties cohabited, the woman was still in the process of dissolving a previous marriage, and did not have the legal capacity to enter into another marriage. Such progressive decision-making is laudable. Maintenance of children, however, should not be left entirely to judicial discretion, as the outcome may not always favour children. There must be definite guidelines, as is the case in Tanzania. Section 160 of Tanzania's Law of Marriage Act, provides that where a couple cohabits for two years or more, there is a rebuttable presumption of marriage, and any children of such union are considered legitimate and entitled to maintenance.[32] Even if the presumption is rebutted, if the woman

---

[31] For further discussion on the Affiliation Act, see Violet Mavisi and Anne Kyalo, "The Affiliation Act: A Case for its Reinstatement", in *Women and Autonomy in Kenya: Law Reform and the Quest for Gender Equality*, CLARION Monograph No. 1 (1994) at 89.

[32] Law of Marriage Act, No. 5 of 1971 (Tanzania). We thank Bart Rwezaura for providing us with this source.

can show, as a matter of fact, that she did live with the man for two years or more, the court will still have jurisdiction to:

"make order or orders for maintenance, and, upon application made . . . either by the woman or the man, to grant such other reliefs, including custody of children, . . . "

One irony in Kenyan statutory law is that children born to unwed parents are provided with a father's financial support only in the event of his death. The Law of Succession Act places an obligation on a father to make provision for his children born outside wedlock, by defining "child", for purposes of succession, to include:

"in relation to a female person, a child born to her out of wedlock, and in relation to a male person, a child whom he has expressly recognized or in fact accepted as a child of his own or for whom he has voluntarily assumed permanent responsibility, children of the deceased born either within or outside wedlock (for a female person) and in the case of a male person a child whom he has expressly recognized, or in fact accepted as a child of his own, or for whom he has voluntarily assumed permanent responsibility."[33]

One limitation with section 3(2), of course, is that in order for the child born out of wedlock to inherit his/her father's estate, the father must have acknowledged paternity, or undertaken responsibility of the child during his lifetime.

Akiwumi J, in *Irene Wayua Katua* v. *James Mutonga Mulege*,[34] discussed the irony in Kenyan law that the only time a man's duty of support to a child born out of wedlock is recognised is after the man dies. The respondent had refused to maintain two children who were born out of a cohabitation union between himself and their mother. Akiwumi J stated:

"There is a substantial question involved in this case and that is whether a father should during his lifetime be responsible for the maintenance of his infant children (albeit illegitimate) which he has had with his mistress. Whereas the position of such children after the death of their father is safeguarded by the Law of Succession Act, ironically no legislation exists to cover the former contingency (maintenance while the father is alive). Justice in my view requires that the children of a mistress should be maintained by their father during his lifetime and [they should] not have to wait until [after] his death before being protected."

Platt J made similar observations in the *Kizito Charles Machani* case:

"To whom should the young children otherwise look [during their father's lifetime]? Should the Plaintiff [father] die intestate, it would seem that those children of his by the Defendant would have a right to inherit under Part V of the Law of Succession Act."

The draft Children's Bill, which awaits discussion in parliament, offers a glimmer of hope for children born out of wedlock. Section 81 of this Bill provides:

---

[33] S. 3(2), Law of Succession Act, ch. 160, Laws of Kenya.
[34] Nairobi HCCC no. 3415 of 1988.

"Each parent of a child shall have a duty to maintain that child, by providing or paying for such accommodation, food, clothing, health care and education as is reasonable having regard to the parents' means and standard of living."

These duties and obligations of parents may be enforced by a court (sections 82 and 83), should the parent fail to maintain his or her child. The duty to maintain one's child is placed on all parents whether married, single or cohabiting.

E CONCLUSIONS

In view of the issues discussed, there is a strong case in favour of developing some definite criteria in the recognition of informal unions, on account of their prevalence and increasing acceptance in official circles (except perhaps in courts), as the practice of swearing affidavits demonstrates. The precarious position in which women and children are left after these relationships break down makes the need for such criteria even more urgent. We argue that there is need for at least four changes:

• Establish a rule that once it is shown that parties have cohabited for a specified period, say two years, as is the case in Tanzania, automatically a rebuttable presumption of marriage applies, and it is upon the party disputing the existence of the marriage to rebut the presumption. The party seeking to rely on the fact of marriage needs not prove anything in order to trigger the operation of the presumption, so long as the requisite duration of cohabitation is established. This approach is potentially protective of the interests of the parties such as children who should not have to rely purely on the discretion of a judge to determine whether or not they will be maintained by their parents. It would also protect a woman's entitlement to economic contributions that she makes to the relationship, by making it possible for her to petition for division of any property acquired during the relationship. The provision also gives a court jurisdiction to determine custody matters, just as it would in a formal divorce. Unfortunately in Tanzania, the Law Reform Commission has recommended that this provision be repealed, a measure that some commentators view as negative.[35]

• Where customary marriage is alleged, proof of compliance with formalities and procedures should not be the pivotal factor in deciding whether or not to recognise the existence of a marriage, or to apply the presumption of marriage rule. Evidence of a traditional ceremony could count as additional evidence, but in the contemporary setting, where people are constantly readjusting and adapting the requirements of customary marriage, it seems ridiculous to apply rigidly criteria such as those documented in Cotran's *Restatements of African Law*. Instead, there should be a flexible approach which pays attention to the intentions of the parties, and the justice of the case. Following the lead of

[35] Bart Rwezaura, chapter 11 in this volume.

Miller J in the *Hinga* case (where he rejected a man's attempt to rely on a technicality in Kikuyu customary marriage formalities to evade child support obligations), and that of Platt J in the *Machani* case, legal technicalities should not be permitted to render children destitute.

- We need a law that bases child support obligations on proof of paternity alone, regardless of the status of the relationship, between the child's parents. The case for reinstatement of the Affiliation Act, or a similar measure such as that proposed in section 81 of the draft Children's Bill, is definitely a strong one.
- Develop a criterion that recognises marriage only for a particular specified purpose, not generally. For example, we could say that all unions that have resulted in children will be presumed to be valid marriages, for purposes of determining issues of maintenance, custody and other issues relating to the children. Similarly, we could say that where the dispute between the cohabiting parties concerns property acquired (jointly) during the period of cohabitation, their rights in relation to that property should not rest on a judicial declaration that they were married "for all intents and purposes". Rather the focus should be on whether, for purposes of settling the property dispute, the property was acquired jointly, or could be treated as having been acquired for their joint use, as in the case of marital property.

There is currently a Task Force on the Review of Laws Relating to Women, operating under the Kenya Law Reform Commission. The mandate of the Task force is to propose the necessary changes in laws affecting women. The Task Force's proposals on marriage should exact specific legal provisions to regulate informal unions.

Table 1. Types of problems presented to FIDA (Kenya) by low income women in cohabitation unions between 1992–1997.

Nature of problem	No of cases in which it is reported
Maintenance for woman and children	60
Desertion + cases where woman is sent away from home	26
Physical violence	51
Abduction and custody	24
Inheritance	2

Note: a total of 95 cases were analysed. Most cases, however, raised multiple problems. For instance, a woman whose partner has deserted her and fails to support her financially may also report that he was violent toward her, and also seek maintenance for herself and any children of the union.

Table 2. Cases in relation to number of years of cohabitation (1993–1997)

Number of years	Number of cases (Total 86)
0–5 years	32
6–10 years	20
11–15 years	18
16–20 years	14
21–25 years	1
Over 25 years	1

Note: in nine out of the 95 cases analysed, the clients did not specify the duration of the cohabitation. All but five clients had children with their partners.

APPENDIX 2

Sample affidavits of marriage.
1. General Affidavit

REPUBLIC OF KENYA
THE OATHS AND STATUTORY DECLARATIONS ACT CAP. 15 LAWS
OF KENYA
AFFIDAVIT OF MARRIAGE

WE, _____ and _____ both of Post office Box number ____ NAIROBI, do hereby make oath and state as follows:

1. THAT we are adult male and female respectively and therefore competent to swear this affidavit.

2. THAT we are holders of identification card numbers ____ and ____ respectively copies whereof are hereto annexed and marked ____.

3. THAT in 1980 we, being Bachelor and Spinster respectively, got married under the Kamba customary law after undergoing all the necessary rituals precedent to such a marriage.

4. THAT we have lived in various places in Nairobi province and all who are acquainted with us know that we are man and wife.

5. THAT the said marriage has been blessed with two issues namely _____ born in December 1983, and _____ born in 1991.

6. THAT what is deponed herein is true to the best of our knowledge, information and belief.

SWORN at NAIROBI
This 21st day of July, 1994
by the said _____ and _____

BEFORE ME _____(lawyers' name and official stamp)
COMMISSIONER FOR OATHS

2. *An Affidavit for a Specific Purpose*

REPUBLIC OF KENYA
THE OATHS AND STATUTORY DECLARATIONS ACT CAP. 15 LAWS
OF KENYA
AFFIDAVIT OF MARRIAGE

WE, _____ and _____ both of Post office Box number ____ NAIROBI, do hereby make oath and state as follows:

1. THAT we are adult male and female respectively and therefore competent to swear this affidavit.

2. THAT we are holders of identification card numbers ____ and ____ respectively copies whereof are hereto annexed and marked ____.

3. THAT in March 1978 we, being Bachelor and Spinster respectively, got married under the Luhya customary law after undergoing all the necessary rituals precedent to such a marriage.

4. THAT we have between us six issues of marriage.

5. THAT we make this affidavit in support of our application for passports to enable us to fly to India to take our third child _____ aged 12 years for medical attention.

6. THAT it is vital to accompany the said child on the 10th of March when she is scheduled to fly out.

7. THAT what is deponed herein is true to the best of our knowledge, information and belief.

SWORN at NAIROBI
This 7th day of March, 1996
by the said _____ and _____

BEFORE ME _____ (lawyers' name and official stamp)
COMMISSIONER FOR OATHS

13

Why I Can't Teach Customary Law

JULIE E. STEWART*

EXPLAINING THE TITLE

From the outset it is important to note that my inability to teach customary law is not an absolute "can't" but a relative "can't". A more accurate, but less tantalising, title would have been: "Why I try not to teach customary law within a positivist general law framework".

TEACHING CUSTOMARY LAW

Historically within law curricula in the Southern African region the bulk of teaching on African customary law has tended to be on the captured and formalised versions that are recorded in the law reports, built upon and interpreted through an Anglo-Saxon or Roman Dutch law procedural and substantive law filter.

A different starting point for devising curricula is that customary law is a dynamic living system that has the capacity to enrich and inform the other systems of law with which it interacts within a given legal system. This requires a pedagogic approach that investigates the jurisprudence of custom. It postulates that customary law should be approached as a system of cohesive laws with underlying guiding principles that need to be identified, recognised as a source of jurisprudence and their content sensitively explored. It is to this latter approach that I have come to subscribe.

Thus whether or not I can teach customary law has become a matter of the content of what is to be taught and the sources from which that content is drawn. If the content is to be the positivist versions of customary law as captured in the textbooks on customary law and the precedents in the law reports then I am ethically bound to critique it at every turn. I can teach it in the technical sense; arguably that is a relatively easy task as it is pre-digested, ordered and

* Part-time Women and Law in Southern Africa Research Associate. I would like to extend my special thanks to the African Gender Institute, University of Cape Town, who provided the space, physical and mental, to enable me to work on this and other papers from April to June, 1997, as a member of their Associate Programme.

homogenised as a coherent set of hierarchical rules, usually arranged in accordance with pre-existing general law subject divisions. It is frequently presented as a sub-class of general law, either within specific subject areas such as Family Law, Delict, Property Law and Succession Law or as a single subject, Customary Law. In this version the relevant legislation, choice of law rules, procedural issues and substantive law "rules" teased out of the cases, across the whole gamut of recognised customary law topics, are addressed. There is, increasingly, less of this version of customary law to teach. Legislative intervention is consistently intervening in the construction of customary law to the point where if the matter is to be adjudicated in the courts it may well be regulated by statute, which by its very nature ceases to be customary even if it is a statute regulating or amending customary law.[1] So that a focus on this as African Customary Law is a misnaming of the content of the law, as once legislation intervenes the content is general law.[2]

Just as I can teach the Zimbabweanised Roman Dutch Law of Succession, so I could teach the "Roman Dutchised" Zimbabwean Customary Law of Succession, but it is not a version which accords with the customs and practices of the peoples of Zimbabwe. However this all begs the question as to what it is that ought to be taught.

THE NEED TO RE-SEARCH CUSTOMARY LAW

Reconsidering the thrust and content of syllabi for the teaching of customary law has its origins in the research into, and reconsideration of customary law as a dynamic living system of law that affects the lives of the majority of the population of Zimbabwe. Even where the general law is purportedly applicable in family, inheritance, land, environmental or other matters it is trite that the direct or indirect influence of local customs and practices affects the way in which such matters will be resolved (Dengu-Zvobgo *et al.* 1994; Ncube and Stewart 1995)

Section 1 of the Zimbabwe Customary Law and Local Courts Act defines "customary law" as:

> "[t]he customary law of the people of Zimbabwe, or any section or community of such people, before the 10th of June, 1891, as modified and developed since that date."

---

[1] The customary law (in the books) of inheritance in Zimbabwe, which forms the backdrop to this chapter, has since the chapter was written been significantly changed by legislative intervention. The Administration of Estates Amendment Act 6 of 1997, now prescribes how the intestate estates of persons to whom customary law is applicable shall be distributed. In general it is a reflection of the principles that underlie local customs and practices, however it is no longer customary law but statute. It is instantly ossified law. However it is reasonable to assume that many estates or substantial portions of estates will continue to be dealt with by families outside the bounds of the statute.

[2] It might be argued that my agenda will be overtaken by legislative intervention, even if this is to be the case the nature and form of legislative intervention needs to be informed by a thorough understanding of what is to be reformed. Arguably a thorough understanding and reinterpretation of custom might obviate legislative change.

Although the first part of the definition seems to refer to an ossified version of custom for which it would be difficult to obtain an accurate version of its 10 June 1891 content, there is room for recognition of custom's oft stated dynamism. In fact the section demands research into the development and modification of customary law since 1891. In other words there is a need to re-examine custom as an internal exercise as well as an external exercise.

National constitutions, legal systems and the mode and extent of the recognition of customary law create their own considerations of how customary law should and can be addressed as a system of law.

Section 89 of the Zimbabwe Constitution provides for the recognition of customary law, the effective extent of such recognition being regulated by other statutes, as is the purported content of the customary law to be applied by the courts. The current recognition statute, the Customary Law and Local Courts Act, Chapter 7:05, provides for the application of customary law as follows:

> "s. 3 Subject to this Act and any other enactment, unless the justice of the case otherwise requires –
> a) customary law shall apply in any civil case where—
>   i) the parties have expressly agreed that it shall apply; or
>   ii) regard being had to the nature of the case and the surrounding circumstances, it appears that the parties have agreed that it should apply; or
>   iii) regard being had to the nature of the case and the surrounding circumstances, it appears just and proper that it should apply;
> b) the general law of Zimbabwe should apply in any other case. . . . "

There are also statutes which prescribe that customary law or the customs and practices of the tribe or people to which a person belonged should govern a particular matter, such as section 68 of the Administration of Estates Act, Chapter 7:05;[3] the Customary Marriages Act, Chapter 5:07; section 12 of the Wills Act, Chapter 6:06; section 8 of the Communal Land Act, Chapter 20:04.

The processes to be followed in determining the content of customary law are prescribed by statute as with section 9 of the Customary Law and Local Courts Act, Chapter 7:06:

> "If a court entertains any doubt as to the existence of or content of a rule[4] of customary law relevant to any proceedings, after having considered such submissions thereon as may be made and such evidence thereof as may be tendered by or on behalf of the parties, it may without derogation from any other lawful source to which it may have recourse, consult reported cases, text books and other sources, and may receive opinions, either orally or in writing to enable it to arrive at a decision in the matter . . . "

---

[3] This s. has now been replaced by the provisions of s. 3 of the Administration of Estates Amendment Act 6 of 1997. A discussion of the effect of this amendment lies well beyond the scope of this chapter.

[4] "Rule" may have been an inappropriate word to use in this context; the preferable word would probably have been "principle" of customary law. (Rwezaura *et al.* 1995; Stewart *et al.* 1997 (Methodology)). It has been postulated that rule collection may have been a significant source of misconstruction of custom in that the end rules from general principles were collected rather than the underlying principles (Dengu Zvobgo *et al.* 1994).

The section is worded sufficiently broadly to permit the review of the content of custom.

Thus it can be argued that the Zimbabwean unified legal system is suitably constructed for a thorough review of the nature and form of one of its major component systems of law, customary law.

CUSTOMARY LAW REFORM: AN INSIDER JOB?

Putting customary law through the constitutional sieve, that is, determining whether it measures up to the criteria stipulated in Bills of Rights, is one way to reform customary law (Bennett 1995). However it still remains a reform of the customary law on the books. In the Zimbabwean context even this is not possible as customary law is a protected species. Section 23 of the Zimbabwean Constitution, as recently amended by section 9 of Act 14 of 1996, provides that there may not be discrimination in any written law or by a public authority on the grounds, of race, tribe, place of origin, political opinion, colour, creed or gender, except where such is necessary by reason of physiological difference between the genders.

The relevant portions of section 23, as amended, provide:

"(1) Subject to the provisions of this section—
   (a) no law shall make any provision which is discriminatory either of itself or in effect: and
   (b) no person shall be treated in a discriminatory manner by any person acting by virtue of any written law or in the performance of the functions of any public office or any public authority . . . "

However, this does not provide a basis for putting customary law through the constitutional sieve and ridding it of its supposed discriminatory elements as section 23(3) provides:

"Nothing contained in any law shall be held to be in contravention of subsection of (1)(a) to the extent that the law in question relates to any of the following matters—
a) adoption, marriage, divorce, devolution of property on death or other matters of personal law:
b) the application of African customary law in any case involving Africans or an African and one or more persons who are not Africans where such persons have consented to the application of African customary law in that case
   . . .
d) the according to tribes people to the exclusion of other persons of rights and privileges relating to communal land"

If customary law is to be reformed or revisited within the existing Zimbabwean constitutional and legal frameworks, using constitutional provisions is not the way, at present. Clearly other modes have to be found and, to some extent, this was a driving force behind the reconsideration of the content and form of customary law as a potentially dynamic part of the legal system which could be the source of its own transformation.

As a Women and Law in Southern Africa (WLSA) and Women's Law researcher my entry point into this terrain is determined by having to make grounded appraisals of women's experiences of the different versions of customary law and how these assist or hinder them to access resources (Ncube and Stewart *et al.* 1997b). After some preliminary forays into the field and analysis of findings it seemed clear that at least some of the customary law on the ground as used among the people was, surprisingly, consistent with notions of gender equity. So from the initial stages of the research process it was clear that this was a research and reform agenda that would bear fruit. There was also an appreciation that even if certain customs were problematic, at the very least one should have an understanding of the social and cultural milieu to be addressed if reform was to take place in accordance with human rights paradigms (Tsanga 1997).

OLD PRINCIPLES, NEW SOLUTIONS

The underlying hypothesis in this chapter is that customary law as captured and applied in the formal legal system began as little more than a collection of end result determinations as pronounced by tribal authorities or as generalisations about outcomes at the level of rules recounted to early researchers (Rwezaura *et al.* 1995; Armstrong *et al.* 1993). This hypothesis incorporates the notion that what may have been missed in these collection processes are the underlying social values that translate into general guiding principles that informed the decision-making processes of traditional judicial authorities (Dengu-Zvobgo *et al.* 1994). There has been a great deal written about those old collection processes and about the dynamism of custom, but often the critiques stop at that point (Bennett 1995). These critiques have to be transformed into research into the development of customary law at all levels, be it the courts, state administration or the versions current among the people. The findings from such research have to be turned into legal action. Students cannot be treated as the end consumers of the research product, they have to be skilled in doing, case by case if necessary, their own research into customs and practices on the ground.

RESEARCH, DIALOGUE AND REFORM: AN ILLUSTRATION

A meeting in 1996 between chiefs from different provinces and ethnic groups, Ministry of Justice officials and women's organisations held to discuss proposed amendments to the laws of inheritance in Zimbabwe illustrates the importance of sound background research into the jurisprudence that underlies custom.

The resolution of the discussion and the form that any amendments to the law might take turned on whether there were underlying principles that guided determinations in inheritance disputes or whether there was an irrefragable rule that the eldest son was his father's heir as held by the Supreme Court in cases such as *Mudzinganyama* v. *Ndambakuwa* S–50–93.

The President of the Council of Chiefs and Member of Parliament, Chief Mangwende, when asked whether there was the underlying principle of customary law in inheritance matters, replied that the overarching principle was that the family of the deceased, especially wives and children, but not excluding husbands, had to be provided for from the property previously within the command of the deceased person. There was universal agreement among the Chiefs present on this principle regardless of ethnic group. Where the difference lay was in the way that this could be accomplished.

Chief Mangwende saw the way in which this could be carried out to be by leaving the property in the hands of the surviving spouse. A married couple, regardless of the form of the marriage, was, in his view, a productive unit and there was no notion of division until after the surviving spouse had died. Formal status would be transmitted to the eldest son but the property and its daily management should remain with the surviving spouse, in this context the wife. There was an elderly chief, from the Gweru area, who could not accept that a woman would have the necessary managerial capacity and skills to carry out the tasks required. His view was that a son or a male relative needed to be in general control. However, even in his case, the underlying principle was not disputed, only the mode of its accomplishment. The rest of the chiefs, some 12 in all, subscribed to Chief Mangwende's approach to the matter but with room for variation depending on specific family situations. The principle had remained static. The best interests of the remnant family of the deceased person predominated, but the manner of its realisation was subject to constant pragmatic variation. The end result determinations are therefore likely to be different from era to era and place to place but this does not disturb the principle.

Asking what was the principle behind customary inheritance practices was a calculated risk. However, it was one that was informed as to the likely response to the question. Suffice it to say that this turned the tide of the meeting which was at risk of being bogged down in a plethora of demands for reform from the women and a cultural defensive stand from the men. The meeting then, to the surprise of many, redivided its alliances into women's organisations and the chiefs on one side and the "other" men defending patrilineal rule-oriented views of women's inheritance rights on the opposing side. This redivision proved critical in achieving reforms of the law that affirmed women's acknowledged customary entitlement to significant rights in their deceased husbands' estates.[5] The battle had been waged on a number of fronts. One was to transform the interpretations of customary law through the superior courts, the second to improve women's lot through legislative intervention.[6] The latter came first and was not to be quib-

---

[5] See s. 3 of the Administration of Estates Act, Amendment Act 6 of 1997.

[6] The legislative intervention does not obviate the need further to explore customary law in this area as there will still be estates to be handled and fought over that are governed by the previous law.

bled over because of the significant benefits conferred on widows. However it is now an un-customary reflection of customary principles.

In the empirical data generated by the WLSA research into inheritance there are similar examples that illustrate this principle-versus-rule construction of customary law. Families, chiefs and ordinary individuals in rural and urban Mashonaland and Matebeleland stated that the care and protection of the family of the deceased person was at the centre of customary practices of inheritance. In Nkayi in Matebeleland it was stressed that surviving spouses remained in control and possession of the family land allocation for their own benefit and that cattle would be made available to a widow for her own use. Cattle and other movable property, once the needs of the spouse had been satisfied, would be distributed in different proportions to the children according to need and according to whether they had received previous allocations of resources on marriage or for other purposes.[7] The youngest son of a deceased male might take over the duty of assisting his mother and seeing to her daily needs. The eldest son would inherit his father's status and overall responsibility for the family, but not the land allocation. This would ultimately pass to the youngest son. If the union was polygynous then it was the youngest son of the respective houses who would acquire the responsibility for assisting his mother and the eldest son of the most senior house would probably become the heir to his father's status[8] (Dengu-Zvobgo *et al.* 1994).

The Zimbabwe Supreme Court held in *Vareta* v. *Vareta* S–126–90 and later in *Mwazozo* v. *Mwazozo* S–121–94, reversing the decision in *Chihowa* v. *Mangwende* S–84–87, that a daughter cannot inherit from her father's intestate estate under either Ndebele or Shona customary law. However both Ndebele and Shona custom, on the ground, is far more pragmatic.

"One of my neighbours died and was survived by only female children. We distributed his many cattle and other property among his daughters. The brothers and other close relatives of the deceased decided on this and the rest of us and the community had no problems with it as it is our custom.—Headman Muziwapansi, Nkayi district, Matebeleland" (Dengu-Zvobgo *et al.* 1994).

In Bulawayo urban areas a discernible trend was for the family to try and arrange for the family home to be transferred to the surviving widow. This was usually not problematic until the matter was to be dealt with by the courts where the formal pronouncement would be made that the eldest son was the heir. Even where this took place, the son might be prevailed on to transfer the property to his mother. This was explained as being in accordance with custom.

In Mashonaland similar pragmatic processes were uncovered, where intestate heirs to commercial immovable property, appointed according to the provisions

[7] This is a good example of the fairness and equity principle among children. There is also a marked similarity to the Roman Dutch principle in inheritance matters of collation so as to ensure equitable distribution of an estate among the children of the deceased.

[8] Although it was pointed out that each family did things slightly differently, the principle remained firm.

of section 6A of the Customary Law and Primary Courts Act,[9] tried as far as possible not to disturb the occupation rights of widows, leaving them in occupation and control of commercial land holdings. Chief Mazungunye from Bikita, interviewed during the field research, stated that:

> "the essence of custom was to care for the family of the deceased, using the land or whatever resources were available . . . Thus the appointment of the heir, if one was to be appointed, had to focus on the welfare of the family rather than on some predetermined formula" (Dengu-Zvobgo *et al.* 1994).

Local customs and practices were, when applied in accordance with the underlying principles of customary law, not necessarily inimical to the rights of women. Rather, they were already in advance of the reform agendas.

EXPLORING LEGAL PLURALISM IN THE COURTS

It is argued in this chapter that there is a need to develop students research and analytical skills so that they can be part of the re-discovery and re-conceptualisation of customary law and its jurisprudence. However, a word of caution. It must not be assumed that rediscovery processes will always yield satisfactory results. Customs and practices have their inherent weaknesses and flaws. But at least an overarching jurisprudential approach broadens the scope for dialogue around both the "good" and the "bad" elements.

One research and analysis technique to be employed is to make internal comparisons of customary law norms between the higher and lower courts (Dengu-Zvobgo *et al.* 1994). Field research revealed that magistrates' courts which are charged with administering the intestate estates of deceased "Africans" frequently had a broader and more pragmatic approach to the distribution of such estates than the Supreme Court. Magistrates hearing disputes in terms of the then section 69 of the Administration of Estates Act, Chapter 301, through their discussions with the families of the deceased person, were alive to the nuances of local customary law and would make similar determinations to those outlined above. On some occasions these decisions were reversed on appeal by the Supreme Court in favour of eldest sons. However, there is evidence that many of these distributions were happily accepted by families and not appealed. It was also evident that the magistrates continued to apply the local customs and practices.

The Supreme Court continues to employ a constructed version of custom that has been built up through precedent and has not re-engaged with custom on the ground even though the customary law application and ascertainment statute makes it possible for this to take place.[10] However it rarely takes place. The

---

[9] S. 6A was later incorporated as s. 7 into the Customary Law (Application Act) Chapter 8:05. This Act has since been repealed by s. 10 of the Administration of Estates Amendment Act.

[10] See the discussion earlier in this ch. on s. 9 of the Customary Law and Local Courts Act, Chapter 7:05.

Supreme Court merely looks to what the precedent system has constructed as the customary law (Dengu-Zvobgo *et al.* 1994; Stewart and Ncube 1997).

The data that were emerging from court determinations alone raised questions as to the nature, form and content of the customary law. The crucial question then became whether the customary law as applied by the superior courts is an authentic version of custom that merits the authoritative treatment it receives? Was it an historical anachronism, ossified and inappropriate or perhaps a distorted creature that the senior judiciary applied for want of available alternatives?

LEGAL PLURALISM: A CRITICAL METHODOLOGICAL APPROACH

The convergence of research, analysis and teaching made it impossible to avoid the pervasiveness of legal pluralism and the significance of the reglementary power of semi autonomous social fields in inheritance matters (Falk Moore 1983). A research and teaching framework based on legal pluralism means that multiple skills had to be developed for our own use and then transferred to students. This framework combined normative analysis of the law, both general law and the formal aspects of customary law, and anthropological techniques in uncovering the customary norms at the level of the people. How these norms operated and were influenced by and influenced the law in its formal operation also had to be explored.

Procedural issues, it transpired, had to be considered simultaneously with those of the substantive content of custom as it operated on the ground. The composition of decision-making bodies within families was of critical importance as were the composition of chief's *dares*. Women's voices, although muted, were not absent from such councils. The role of *vatete* (senior women in the family— aunts), in Shona societies, was critical at all stages of inheritance decisions. Such women were often the source of family genealogies, and had the last word if not the final decision when it came to how estates should be divided and allocated. The same could be said of women in Ndebele societies.

Time frames for decision making were often protracted, especially in inheritance matters, with time for negotiation and exploration of options. A years moratorium between a death and a *kurova guva* ceremony or *umbuyiso* ceremony, at which distribution of substantive property and future plans for the widow were made, gave time for informed and careful decision making. What emerged from this procedural investigation was confirmatory evidence of the underlying concerns of these bodies for the remnant families of the deceased.

Apart from the juxtaposition of various official and formal versions of customs and practices, such as those advanced by the chiefs, there is a need to conduct a more broad based enquiry into the functioning and operation of customs and practices on the ground. A truly gender sensitive approach to the research process is a necessary prerequisite to uncovering customary jurisprudence, the next question technique and exploring the values that inform decisions is critical if an understanding of how customs and practices are shaped is to be realised. Likewise it is not enough to unpack just the content of custom. The procedural aspects, who participates in decision making, how decisions are made, are all vital elements in the reconceptualisation and reinterpretation process.

VALUES, NORMS, CUSTOMS, PRINCIPLES

One of the major criticisms of the earlier collections of customs was that the sources were elderly males in positions of power who colluded with the colonial governments and missionaries to exclude women and young males from power and resources (Chanock 1985; Rwezaura *et al.* 1995; Armstrong *et al.* 1993). Current attempts to review custom from a grounded perspective must avoid the possibility of similar criticisms and cast more widely for versions and interpretations of custom. As Holleman recounts, the official versions of custom may not accord with the actual application of the principles of customary law on the ground (Holleman 1973). Thus it is important to uncover the actual practices in the field, especially as they affect women. Interviews with persons who had experienced inheritance problems and inheritance non-problems generally triangulated with the views that were expressed by the chiefs and other local figures. Women's ways of manipulating the system and the processes also spoke to the entitlements women have and their ways of accessing them. Women's entitlements did not fit into the Hohfeldian rights framework but this did not make them any the less rights that were enforceable. (For a fuller discussion of this see Stewart 1997, Mbatha 1997)

However, it is not of itself sufficient merely to allege that a few interviews indicate that customs and practices have developed or evolved in a particular direction. There needs to be a systematic process through which the reconceptualisation of customary law is explored and its jurisprudence charted. Finding ways to triangulate the results from different sources in the field and build up holograms of customs and practices and their reflection of general principles is a key part of the new approach to teaching customary law. As each finding triangulates with the other perceptions and understandings of customs a hologram is built piece by piece from local values, through their translation into norms, practices and procedures and on into the more pervasive principles that imbue customary law and shape its jurisprudence.

Individuals, when "cross examined" on issues around inheritance, would describe what they considered from a cultural and family position to be important. Whether these same values emerged at the level of normative orderings of civil society was the next quest. If communities told you that "in our culture" the welfare of the wife and children in inheritance is paramount, this might be described as a value. If families, as a matter of practice, consistently administered estates in favour of women and children then the value was translated into action as a custom or a norm. In such situations community values were triangulating with norms and custom.

The next investigation was to determine whether further up the chain of adjudication within the customary frameworks it was possible to identify such values and norms at the level of principles that governed dispute resolutions. Chiefs, as discussed above, when asked how they would determine such issues, or had done so,[11] indicated that the primary concern was for the welfare of the children, in particular, and for the wife or wives of a deceased man, or in the case of women, for the children and the husband. Likewise magistrates at the lower end of the judicial scale, in constant touch with local customs and practices, were also responding to the principles of customary law that were located within the community.

Importantly, this was not just a few random findings but a whole process of triangulated findings as to the underlying principles of customary law across a wide spectrum of society and from different decision making fora. To continue uncritically teaching the Supreme Court's version of the customary law of inheritance, or for that matter without further research any area of customary law, would be unsupportable.

TEACHING CUSTOMARY LAW?

This chapter thus proposes that what ought to be focused on in teaching "customary law" are the methodologies to assist students, the future researchers and practitioners, to transcend the rule-bound versions of custom. An understanding of the gap between the customary law in the books and the dynamic situation sensitive versions of customs and practices that were found among the people also needs to be fostered. Students need to know how to broaden the parameters of the debates about custom with traditional leaders and the community at large beyond the oppression discourse to that of values. This is a liberating debate for all parties, as when the social value or customary principle is raised it is possible to ask: How would you deal with the needs of the family under particular circumstances? What if there is no son? What if the widow works in town and the couple had acquired the house together in an urban area? The "next question" technique is pursued with confidence and an informed dialogue conducted.

It was possible to calculate the risk, which at the time was a very significant risk, of asking the Chiefs what was the relevant principle of custom in inheritance matters because there was a background of knowledge and concomitant courage to dialogue, built up through an alternative construction of customary law to that in the minds of the Ministry of Justice officials. This is also a useful skill in the event that there is resistance to necessary transformative reforms of customary law and dialogue with the wider society is needed to "market" the reforms.

[11] This needed to be posed as a hypothetical question as Chiefs did not have jurisdiction in such matters. However that they would intervene in matters was common knowledge. Thus it was a concrete hypothetical question.

FINDING THE GATEWAYS

Having traversed the empirical field, the next methodological challenge becomes to channel the findings at their various levels back through the gateways of the law, into the courts, into the law reform processes and into the "textbook" constructions of the Customary law (Dengu-Zvobgo *et al.* 1994). It is here that the teaching has to re-engage with the field of "law games", while at the same time ensuring that the open-ended frameworks remain and that principles are the focus of the research process not ossified end product rules.

Students need to be guided in the process of constructing the arguments to present to the courts, the legislators and administrators as to why these new interpretations of customary law have credence and should and can displace the old ossified versions. At the level of formal "law games", identifying the legislation that allows for the admission of customary law is a key task. Further, the parameters for its admission have to be investigated and the skills to cast the admission and content arguments in appropriate formats have to be actively taught.

CONCLUSION

Thus, although in my teaching I cannot ignore the ossified Customary Law in the books, I am compelled to go beyond those versions and explore the underlying principles in the customs and practices of a people. Such an approach must also contain a section on the development of critical skills in the analysis of the customary law in its many locations and guises.

REFERENCES

ARMSTRONG *et al.* (1993), "Uncovering Reality: Excavating Women's Rights in African Family Law" (1993) 7 *International Journal of Law and the Family* 314–69.

BENNETT, T. W. (1995), *Human Rights and African Customary Law* (Juta, Cape Town).

CHANOCK, M. (1985), *Law, Custom and Social Order: The Colonial Experience in Malawi and Zambia* (Cambridge: Cambridge University Press).

DENGU-ZVOBGO *et al.* (1994) (DENGU-ZVOBGO, K. C., DONZWA, B. R., GWAUNZA, E. C., KAZEMBE, J. L., NCUBE, W., STEWART, J. E.), *Inheritance in Zimbabwe: Law, Customs and Practices* (SAPES Trust, Harare).

FALK MOORE, S. (1983), "Law and Social Change. The Semi-autonomous Social Field as an Appropriate Subject of Study", Chapter 2 in *Law as Process: An Anthropological Approach* (London: Routledge and Kegan Paul).

HOLLEMAN, J. F. (1973), "Trouble-cases and Trouble-less Cases in the Study of Customary Law and Legal Reform", *Law and Society Review* 585–609.

MBATHA, L. (1997), *Customary Land Allocation Processes Which are not Incompatible with the Constitution*, Seminar Paper, African Gender Institute Associate Programme Seminar Series, University of Cape Town, June 1997.

NCUBE, W., and STEWART, J. (eds.) (1995), *Widowhood, Inheritance Laws, Customs and Practices in Southern Africa* (WLSA, Harare, 1995).

—— (1997a) (NCUBE, W., STEWART, J. E., DENGU-ZVOBGO, K. C., DONZWA, B. R., GWAUNZA, E. C., KAZEMBE, J. L.), *Continuity and Change: The Family in Zimbabwe* (WLSA, Harare, forthcoming).

—— (1997b) (NCUBE, W., STEWART, J. E., DENGU-ZVOBGO, K. C., DONZWA, B. R., GWAUNZA, E. C., KAZEMBE, J. L.), *Paradigms of Exclusion: Women's Access to Resources in Zimbabwe* (forthcoming).

RWEZAURA *et al.* (1995) (RWEZAURA, B., ARMSTRONG, A., NCUBE, W., STEWART, J., LUTEKA, P., MUSANYA, P., CASIMIRO, I., MAMASHELA, M.), *Parting the Long Grass: Revealing and Reconceptualising The African Family; Journal of Legal Pluralism and Unofficial Law*, No 35/1995.

STEWART, J. (1997), *Rights, Rights, Rights: Women's Rights? Reconceptualising and Reconsidering Rights*, Paper presented at the African Gender Institute, Associate Seminar Series, University of Cape Town, June 1997.

—— and NCUBE, W. (1997), *Standing at the Cross Roads: WLSA and the Rights Dilemma, Which Way Do We Go?* (WLSA, Working Paper).

TSANGA, A. (1997), *Taking Law to the People: Experience of Zimbabwe*, D.Phil. Thesis University of Zimbabwe.

WEIS BENTZON *et al.* (1998) (WEIS BENTZON, A., HELLUM, A., STEWART, J., NCUBE, W., AGERSNAP, T.), *Pursuing Grounded Theory in Law: South–North Experiences in Developing Women's Law* (Tano, Oslo).

14

Reducing Discretion in Family Law*

JOHN DEWAR

INTRODUCTION

For nearly the last quarter century, family law in England and Australia has been marked by a heavy reliance on discretion vested in courts to deal with the consequences of marital or family dissolution. In this chapter, I want to suggest that a number of recent legislative developments in both jurisdictions, especially in the areas of children and property distribution, offer evidence of a trend away from discretion towards a more rule-based family law. After discussing some theoretical and methodological problems entailed in making this claim, I will present the evidence for it, and then go on to speculate as to its possible causes.

I confine my observations to England and Australia. Although there are important differences between them, I think they are comparable at the level of analysis I wish to pursue.[1] I think also that the trends that I am describing could be applied to other jurisdictions. Indeed, it is possible that Anglo-Australian family law[2] is in some respects trailing behind other jurisdictions in the reduction of discretion.[3]

In summary, my argument is that the heavy reliance on discretion encountered in both the Family Law Act 1975 (*Cth.*) and the Matrimonial Causes Act 1973 (*UK*) in their originally enacted forms reflected what I shall call "technocratic liberalism". I use this to denote, first, a belief in the ability of expert adjudicators, when armed with sufficient information, to make better decisions than would be possible if outcomes were to be specified in advance by rules; and second, a belief that it was impossible to frame any explicit normative or justificatory framework for resolving the consequences of divorce, either because there was no consensus for doing so, or because such matters were regarded as private

---

* An earlier version of this chapter was delivered at the Faculty of Law, University of Hong Kong. I am especially grateful to Stephen Parker for his comments on earlier versions. This chapter was published as an article in the Australian Journal of Family Law. The editors are grateful to Butterworths (Australia) for permission to include it in this volume.

[1] For an important point of divergence between the two jurisdictions, see n. 26, below.

[2] I borrow this term from S. Parker, "Rights and utility in Anglo-Australian Family Law" (1992) 55 *Modern Law Review* 311.

[3] Especially Scotland and New Zealand, both of which have enacted more rule-based statutes for the distribution of property on divorce: see further below.

and therefore beyond the reach of legislators.[4] As Katherine O'Donovan has put it, "[s]ince, in liberal society [which is ideologically attached to privacy], the law's role in personal relations is under attack it must retreat into discretion".[5]

More recently, however, there has been growing dissatisfaction with this technocratic liberalism and its associated discretionary regime, which has led legislators steadily to reduce the discretionary content of family law. I will suggest that the reasons for this are complex but can be arranged under two broad headings. The first has to do with the concern of government to reduce the costs associated with family breakdown. These costs are internal to the legal system, as well as external, either to the state or to the parties themselves. Concern to reduce both types of cost has led to growing use of rules: it is argued that a more rule-based legal framework will make cases easier to settle, and so reduce internal costs; and that the formulaic and rule-based nature of (for example) child support can be relied on to reduce the external costs of family breakdown to the welfare state.

The second arises from a growing interest in reviving questions of normative or justificatory frameworks governing the rights and obligations of family members to each other. This too has been associated with a shift to rules and away from discretion, because (as I shall argue later) there is an affinity between rights on the one hand and rules as their mode of normative expression. This shift towards rights/rules in family law in turn stems from a number of factors. One is the growing politicisation of family law in both jurisdictions, as evidenced by the growing number of lobby groups whose primary purpose is to press for changes in family law that grant increased recognition to the "rights" of whichever constituency they represent. The most vocal of these are fathers' rights groups.[6] Legislators have responded to these calls for rights; but the politicisation of family law stems also from lawmakers' own anxiety to use family law as a way of instilling family values back into the population at large in the face of a perceived crisis in the family itself. The traditional liberal reluctance to prescribe rules for proper family living through law, characteristic of technocratic liberalism, has been overcome. Instead, it could be said that we are moving slowly and uncertainly towards a "post-liberal" family law, in which prescriptive rules are more prominent.[7]

---

[4] See R. Ingleby, "Australian Matrimonial Property Law: The Rise and Fall of Discretion" in Bradbrook, Ellinghaus and Duggan (eds.), *The Emergence of Australian Law* (Melbourne UP, 1993), ch. 8; "Recent Australian Developments: Discretion Discredited" in Weitzman and Maclean (eds.), *Economic Consequences of Divorce: The International Perspective* (OUP, 1992).

[5] K. O'Donovan, *Sexual Divisions in Law* (Weidenfeld & Nicholson, 1985), 205.

[6] See R. Graycar, "Equal Rights *versus* Fathers' Right: The Child Custody Debate in Australia" in C. Smart and S. Sevenhuijsen (eds.), *Child Custody and the Politics of Gender* (Routledge, 1989), ch. 7; M. Kaye and J. Tolmie, "The Impact of Fathers' Rights Groups on Australian Family Law Reform", Paper delivered at the 9th Annual Conference of the International Society of Family Law in Durban, South Africa.

[7] S. Parker, "The Place of Conduct in Family Court Proceedings: Signs of Paradigm Lost", Paper delivered at the CLE/FLPA Family Law Residential, Sanctuary Cove, Queensland, Australia, July 1997.

The combined effect of this has been a more widespread use of the language of rights and responsibilities, and of their normative correlative, rules. But, as we shall see, the rights claims being put do not arise from an overarching conceptual model of family relations, but are more limited, competing and strategic. The original discretionary model has been steadily amended, but never entirely overhauled. As a result, these new rights claims are in potential conflict with each other. It is conflicts of this sort that a less discretionary family law will increasingly be called on to resolve.[8]

The trend towards reducing discretion in family law is one that has considerable significance. Not only does it affect the way in which family lawyers will set about their task of advising clients, or the way judges will decide cases (if, indeed, judges are still required under a more rule-based regime); it also points towards a reconfiguration of the relationship between the state and the family as mediated through law. The family is increasingly seen as the primary source of economic support for its members and as the means of their socialisation: and the shift to rules can be seen as part of this process, as a way of ensuring that the family properly discharges these functions.

The trend also raises some pressing and controversial questions of what the content of a more "rule-like" family law might be. For one consequence of the heavy reliance on discretion over the last 25 or so years has been to conceal the lack of public consensus over basic terms on which the law should intervene in personal relationships. This is partly because such consensus was hard to find, even 25 years ago; but it was also associated with a liberal politics that regarded such things as properly a matter for private decision-making rather than legislation. If it is now the case that discretion is being reduced, and that legislators are more confident in prescribing rules of proper familial behaviour, then we need to ask what vision of family relations is being established, or imposed, under a more rule-based regime.

RULES AND DISCRETION

Before proceeding to make the claim that family law is becoming less discretionary, it may be helpful to begin by clearing some conceptual and methodological ground. What, first of all, do we mean by discretion in law? For many, the essence of legal discretion is captured by the idea of a person with legal authority to make a decision having a choice between a range of outcomes. That power to choose may have been conferred explicitly by legislation; or it may have simply been assumed by the decision-maker, or may simply be an inevitable feature of making a decision at all.[9] Discretion of this latter, assumed or nondeliberate, sort is often said by both legal theorists and by legal sociologists to be

---

[8] J. Dewar, "The Normal Chaos of Family Law" (forthcoming).
[9] K. Hawkins, "The Use of Legal Discretion: Perspectives from Law and Social Science" in K. Hawkins (ed.), *The Uses of Discretion* (OUP, 1992), 11.

an essential part of a legal system. For legal theorists, for example, a central point of dispute has been the extent to which rules govern the outcomes of judicial decision. A major cleavage in modern legal theory is between, on the one hand, those who are sceptical about the power of rules in this respect, and for whom discretion, or choice, in adjudication is therefore inevitable and endemic, and, on the other, those who are not so sceptical about the power of rules to dictate judicial outcomes.[10] In legal sociology, the existence of discretion as an empirical fact has been regularly documented, leading to the now widely accepted proposition that there is a gap between the law as written and law as practised or enforced: discretion, or choice, exercised by human agents, is what fills the gap.[11]

For the purposes of this chapter, my interest is in discretion of the deliberately conferred sort, and with deliberative norm-making by legislatures. I want to suggest that the deliberately created normative content of family law is moving away from conferring legally authorised choice on decision-makers, and is instead seeking to constrain that choice by specifying outcomes more precisely in advance. Examples would be starting points of equal division of matrimonial property on divorce, formulaic calculations of child support liabilities, or the legislative expression of a child's "right" to contact with parents after parental separation.

In suggesting this, I do not wish to deny the sociological insight that there may be a gap between what is written as law on the one hand, and its actual effects on the other. In other words, I am not saying that a shift away from deliberately conferred choice at the level of legislated norms will eliminate that choice in practice;[12] nor, conversely, that deliberately conferred discretions have in the past resulted in choices actually being made. On the contrary, I want to draw on some empirical work currently being conducted in Brisbane[13] to suggest that the shift away from discretion may have a number of unintended consequences, and to suggest an interpretive framework for making sense of them. Nor do I intend to

---

[10] The extreme version of this scepticism is associated with the American Realists and, more recently, with CLS; a more moderate version is associated with HLA Hart's model of discretion as that which happens when the rules run out: see *The Concept of Law* (OUP, 1961), ch. 7. Perhaps the most ambitious attempt to deny discretion anything but a "weak" role in adjudication is that of Ronald Dworkin, for whom even apparently unconstrained choice will be constrained by a judge's duty to weigh and give effect to rights: see "The Model of Rules I" in *Taking Rights Seriously* (1977, Harvard), ch. 2. For a good summary of the arguments, see G. Fletcher, *Basic Concepts of Legal Thought* (OUP, 1993), ch. 3. For more detailed jurisprudential accounts, D. Galligan, *Discretionary Powers: A Legal Study of Official Discretion* (OUP, 1986); J. Bell, "Discretionary Decision-making: A Jurisprudential View" in Hawkins (ed.), *op. cit.*, ch. 3. For a discussion of CLS-derived rule scepticism in the context of family law, see S. Parker and P. Drahos, "Closer to a Critical Theory of Family Law" (1990) 4 *Australian Journal of Family Law* 159.

[11] See, for example, K. Hawkins, *Environment and Enforcement: Regulation and the Social Definition of Pollution* (OUP, 1984); A. Reiss, "Discretionary Justice" in D. Glaser (ed.), *Handbook of Criminology* (Chicago, 1974).

[12] The Full Court's decision in *B* v. *B: Family Law Reform Act 1995* (1997) 21 Fam. LR 676 is an interesting example of judicial interpretation preserving discretion in the face of legislation which could be interpreted as designed to reduce it: see further below.

[13] ARC Small Grant, "Parenting, Planning and Partnership: A Study of the Impact of the Family Law Reform Act 1995".

take sides in the jurisprudential debate about the impact of rules on adjudication. My observations are limited to the laws that are passed onto the statute books, and to offering explanations for what is happening at that level: but even this modest project can, I believe, tell us something useful about modern family law, and about contemporary state policy with regard to the family.

Another methodological point is that it is too simple to paint a picture of a flight from discretion to rules. Discretion and rules are sometimes portrayed as opposites locked into some zero sum relationship: the more discretion, the fewer rules, and vice versa. Most recent writing on rules and discretion avoids this crudity, partly because of a recognition of the "gap" that is likely to develop between norm and practice (rules may be applied in a discretionary way, choice may be constrained through rules of thumb or interpretive practice); but also because it is recognised that there are many more lawmaking techniques available than just rules and discretions, and that it is better to visualise a continuum or spectrum, with hard and fast rules at one end and unconstrained discretion at the other, with many intermediate points along the way.

Cass Sunstein has suggested that rules can be understood as "approaches to law that try to make most or nearly all legal judgments under the governing legal provision in advance of actual cases" and as exemplifying an approach to lawmaking under which a "wide range of judgments about particular cases will occur before the point of application".[14] This contrasts with "untrammelled discretion", which he characterises as "the capacity to exercise official power as one chooses, by reference to such considerations as one wants to consider, weighted as one wants to weight them".[15] Other devices, which lie somewhere between these two poles in terms of the extent to which they seek to constrain outcomes in advance, include presumptions, checklists of factors, general standards, guidelines, principles and analogies. Examples of each of these devices are readily found in family law: indeed, we might say that family law offers a particularly rich array of these different sources of law.

Using Sunstein's terminology, combined with the metaphor of a spectrum of lawmaking possibilities strung between rules and discretions, my argument is that modern family law legislation is characterised by a deliberate attempt to shift the normative content of family law towards the rule end of the spectrum, and so remove or constrain choice at the point of application or adjudication. The most common techniques employed have been those of presumptions, checklists, guidelines, factors or principles. So, there is no suggestion here of a sudden flip from discretion into rules.

It might also be helpful to be clear about why legislatures have in the past considered it necessary or convenient to confer discretions, in the sense just outlined, on decision-makers. In this context, I find Schneider's classification of

---

[14] C. Sunstein, "Problems with Rules" (1995) 83 *California Law Review* 953, at 961; see also *Legal Reasoning and Political Conflict* (OUP, 1996), ch. 2.

[15] *Ibid.*, 960.

deliberately conferred discretions useful. He distinguishes three types: rule-failure discretions, rule-building discretions and rule-compromise discretions.[16]

A rule-failure discretion is conferred where it is thought that the cases to be dealt with by the decision-maker cannot be provided for in advance by rules of any sort; rule-building discretions are conferred where the legislator could develop rules, but thinks that it would be better to leave the development of rules to the decision-makers as they go along; and rule-compromise discretion is granted where the legislators cannot agree on what the rule should be, and deliberately pass that responsibility to the decision-maker. This classification relates to the common arguments made in support of discretion in family law: that the circumstances of family life are so varied that it would be impossible to lay down rules in advance, and that discretion maximises the chances of doing justice in each case; and that it would in any case be difficult to agree what the rules should be, even if rules were thought desirable.[17]

Of course, it may not be easy, or even possible, to classify discretions as Schneider suggests: some discretions may have been conferred for "rule-failure" reasons, but may actually be used in practice for "rule-building"; and discretions may be conferred for more than one of these reasons. Nevertheless, this gives some clearer idea of why discretions might be conferred, and discretions in family law have been conferred for all three reasons.

With those methodological problems at least identified, if not resolved, I turn to the substance of what I want to say. I will deal first with the evidence for the proposition that there is a shift towards the rule end of the spectrum in family law. Then I will seek to offer some explanations. I shall conclude by offering a preliminary report of some relevant empirical work and use them to draw some conclusions about the way forward, drawing in particular on the concept of "acoustic separation" as a guide to how to create and target legislative norms in family law.

EVIDENCE FOR THE SHIFT

First the evidence. In both England and Wales, and in Australia, the framework for modern family law was created in the late 1960s or early 1970s. In England and Wales, the governing statutes were the Divorce Reform Act 1969 and the Matrimonial Proceedings and Property Act 1970, both of which were later consolidated into the Matrimonial Causes Act 1973.[18] In Australia, the main Act is

---

[16] C. Schneider, "Discretion and Rules: A Lawyer's View" in Hawkins (ed.), *The Uses of Discretion*, ch. 2

[17] See C. Schneider, "The Tension between Rules and Discretion in Family Law: A Report and Reflection" (1993) 27 *Family Law Quarterly* 229; E.Jackson *et al*, "Financial Support on Divorce: The Right Mixture of Rules and Discretion?" (1993) 7 *International Journal of Law and the Family* 230; R. Ingleby, "Australian Matrimonial Property Law: The Rise and Fall of Discretion" , above n. 3.

[18] The grounds of divorce, and some aspects of the law governing financial provision, will be altered when the Family Law Act 1996 is brought into force.

the Family Law Act 1975, which both reformed the substantive law and created the Family Court of Australia to hear family law matters reserved to the Commonwealth under the Australian constitution (and, subsequently, some that were referred to the Commonwealth by the States). Both Acts have been heavily amended since first enacted.

Although there are many important differences between the two Acts, there were some significant features or assumptions common to both jurisdictions: for example, it was assumed that the law could do little to affect divorcing behaviour, and that the primary role of the law was to set the terms of divorce;[19] that there would be public support for parties who were unable to afford their own legal costs; and a tacit willingness to accept that the financial cost of family breakdown was properly borne by the public purse through the welfare system. In both jurisdictions, the courts were given very wide discretion to set the terms of a divorce according to general standards requiring the courts to achieve certain loosely defined outcomes in the different circumstances of each case (eg, that arrangements for children were to be decided according to the child's welfare, or that the courts were to use their powers to redistribute property to achieve results that were "just and equitable" in the light of factors specified elsewhere in the legislation[20]).

In short, the legislation of a quarter of a century ago could be characterised as having been informed by the spirit of what I have termed "technocratic liberalism": that is, a reposing of faith in the ability of experts, when armed with sufficient information, to arrive at optimal solutions for the parties, with "optimal" for these purposes being cast in economic or therapeutic, rather than moral or ethical, terms; and a belief in limits to the state's role in prescribing clear ground rules for what were regarded as private decisions about how private lives should be lived.

It is this model, and the assumptions on which it was based, that have been modified in recent years.[21] In particular, there has been a tendency to reduce or constrict the discretionary features of this model, and to specify outcomes in much clearer terms. For example:

- the issue of child support, which under the 1970s model was determined as part of the overall picture of the party's finances on divorce, and so dealt with under the general standards just referred to, has been hived off from the court

---

[19] Both the relevant statutes refer to the promotion of reconciliation or the "buttressing of marriage" as general aims, but neither statute contains any significant provisions that contribute to their realisation.

[20] S. 79(2) FLA 1975 (*Cth*). Relevant factors are specified in s. 75(2) (spousal maintenance) and s. 79(4) (property distribution). In its original form, s. 25 Matrimonial Causes Act 1973 (*UK*) directed the court to exercise its powers while having regard to a number of factors, and to pursue the overall objective of seeking to place the parties in the position they would have been in had the marriage not broken down: see J.Eekelaar, *Family Law and Social Policy* (Weidenfeld, 1978) for discussion.

[21] The Family Law Act 1996 (UK) introduces a stronger element of "marriage saving" into the divorce law, largely by introducing the principle that a divorce is conditional on agreement over children and finances.

system and dealt with bureaucratically according to a strict set of rule-generated formulae, from which departures are permitted in only limited circumstances;[22]

• the division of assets on divorce is increasingly governed by firm rules or standards: in Scotland and New Zealand, for example, there is a more or less heavy reliance on presumptions of equal division;[23] similar starting points are increasingly appearing in US states,[24] and a starting point of equal division has been proposed in Australia;[25]

• decision-making about children after divorce is increasingly constrained: for example, many jurisdictions have introduced joint custody laws, or equivalents, under which both parents automatically retain some degree of legal relationship with their children no matter what court orders are made, so that what was once a matter of discretion has become a rule;[26] further, matters that were once dealt with in terms of children's welfare are now being cast in terms of children's "rights".[27] Increasingly detailed checklists now govern the courts' approach to children's welfare,[28] and there is growing use of general statements of objects or principle as an aid to the interpretation and application of family law legislation.[29] There are also proposals for even firmer rules about post-

[22] In Australia: Family Law (Amendment) Act 1987, Child Support (Registration and Assessment) Act 1988, Child Support (Assessment) Act 1989; in the UK, Child Support Acts 1991 and 1995.

[23] Family Law (Scotland) Act 1985; Matrimonial Property Act 1976 (NZ).

[24] L. Weitzman, "Marital Property in the US: Its Transformation and Division" in L. Weitzman and M. Maclean (eds.), *Economic Consequences of Divorce: The International Perspective* (OUP, 1992), ch. 5.

[25] Australian Law Reform Commission, *Matrimonial Property*, Report No.39; Family Law Reform (No. 2) Bill 1995; see R. Ingleby, "Recent Developments in Australia: Discretion Discredited" in Weitzman and Maclean, *supra*, ch. 4

[26] Children Act 1989 (UK); Family Law Reform Act 1995 (Cth), reforming Part VII of the FLA 1975 (*Cth*). This pattern is clearer in the UK, where, before the Children Act 1989, there was no rule of automatic joint guardianship, and where a non-custodial parent after divorce would have no formal legal link to a child unless a court order was framed so as to confer it, for example by joint custody. There was no rule requiring courts to make such orders, and orders for sole custody were common: see J.Dewar, *Law and the Family* (2nd edn., Butterworths, 1992), 353. The CA 1989 introduced the rule that both parents have parental responsibility for a child irrespective of any orders made by a court. The pattern in Australia is not so clear, given that before the new Part VII, each parent was automatically a "guardian" of a child: see the "old" s. 63F FLA 1975. The effect of the Australian changes may be more perceptual; although the idea that an order of custody exclusively to one parent terminated the custody of the other has now gone.

[27] S. 60B Family Law Act 1975 (Cth) (inserted by the FLRA 1995), which speaks of the child's "right" to contact with both parents; but see *B* v. *B: Family Law Reform Act 1995* (1997) 21 Fam. LR 676, in which the Full Court of the Family Court held that s.60B has not altered the fact that the child's best interests remain the primary criterion for resolving children's cases, including relocation or "move away" cases: "any question of presumption of onus has the potential to impair the inquiry as to what is in the best interests of the children" (at para. 9.59).

[28] S. 1(4) CA 1989 (*UK*); s. 68F FLA 1975 (*Cth*); in proposing such a checklist, the Law Commission referred explicitly to its settlement-promoting qualities: Law Com. Report No. 172, *Guardianship and custody* (HMSO, 1988), para. 3.18

[29] See s. 1 Family Law Act 1996 (*UK*), which sets out "general principles" to which the courts or anyone exercising power under the Act must have regard; and the new s. 60B FLA 1975 (*Cth*), which sets out the "objects and principles" underlying the new Part VII of that Act.

divorce arrangements, for example, that the child should live with the person who has been its primary carer up to that point.[30]

Taken together, these developments amount to a significant tilt away from the 1970s technocratic liberalism, and from a discretionary model towards something more constrained. Why?

SUGGESTED EXPLANATIONS

I want to suggest that the reasons for the shift towards the "rule-like" end of the spectrum can be grouped under two broad heads: (a) cost and efficiency; and (b) the greater weight attached to arguments of rights and equality as starting points for legal relations between family members. I will deal with these in turn.

Cost and efficiency

A system of family justice that relies heavily on judicial discretion is easily portrayed as expensive and inefficient. There are two ways in which this might happen.

(i) External costs

The first concerns what I have called external costs, that is, state expenditure on welfare benefits for family members following a relationship breakdown. During the 1980s, figures from both the UK and Australia showed that the discretionary system of redistributing finances on divorce was doing little to prevent women, especially those with dependent children, from becoming heavily reliant on welfare.[31] The judges clearly did not see themselves as the guardians of the public purse,[32] and there was nothing in the relevant legislation that required them to be so. Indeed, the emphasis in both Australian and English law, which required the judges to consider the desirability of a "clean break",[33] seemed to point the other way; and there was evidence that the judges were willing to take account of welfare benefits in the orders they made. In other words, judges seemed willing to assume that basic levels of financial support were properly a state, rather than family, responsibility. From the point of view of governments concerned to reduce welfare spending, this state of affairs could not be allowed to continue:

---

[30] See below.

[31] For Australia: P. McDonald *et al.*, *Settling Up* (AIFS, 1985) and M. Harrison *et al.*, *Paying for the Children* (AIFS, 1991); for England: Child Support White Paper, *Children Come First* (HMSO, 1992), vol. 2

[32] See, e.g., *Delaney* [1990] 2 FLR 457, where the court acknowledged that the availability to the wife of welfare benefits could reduce the husband's liability towards her; Australian courts also engaged in benefit maximisation: see S. Parker, "Rights and Utility" *op. cit.* at 313.

[33] S. 25A MCA 1973; s. 81 FLA 1975.

and the late 1980s and early 1990s saw the introduction in both England and Australia of child support schemes, both of which sought to shift the burden of financial support of children and their primary carers back to the family (usually the breadwinner father).

This is connected to the question of discretion versus rules in two ways way. The first is that if the objective of reducing welfare expenditure is to be achieved, choice has to be removed at the point of application. Instead, a judgement has to be made in advance about the financial outcomes of family dissolution in so far as child support and the costs to the state are concerned. Judicial discretion cannot be relied on to produce the right outcome, and is therefore replaced by rules.[34]

The second is that the child support schemes in both England and Australia are primarily bureaucratic rather than judicial. In Australia, the scheme is administered by a division of the Australian Tax Office; in England by the Child Support Agency, a "next steps" agency closely linked to the Department of Social Security. In both cases, the bureaucratic rather than judicial nature of the scheme was dictated by the need for processing and enforcement machinery that was beyond the capacity of the court system to provide; and if that system was to succeed in dealing efficiently with the large number of cases with which it was likely to be faced, the system had to be a rule-bound one requiring limited information, and excluding the need for the exercise of judgment (which, under a separation of powers argument, could in any case properly be seen as a task reserved to judges).

(ii) Internal costs

The second way in which discretion could be linked to expense and inefficiency is through what I have called internal costs, that is, the cost to the state of paying for disputes to be resolved, either directly through the funding of the court system, or indirectly through legal aid for litigants. A system of discretionary decision-making, it is argued, creates uncertainty about parties' entitlements and promotes party dependence on highly paid professional advisers.[35] It also creates an insatiable demand for information.[36] A discretionary system draws its legitimacy in part from the belief that it is capable of achieving better outcomes in individual cases through its sensitivity to the individual facts of each case: by the same token, if it is to fulfil that promise, a discretionary decision-maker must have all relevant information available. This can lead to considerable delays and tactical manœuvring as the parties seek to obtain information from the other side, or to deny the other side information they want. All of this, so it is said, creates

---

[34] The Australian scheme permitted departures from formula assessments from the outset; the English scheme did not, but has been amended to permit departures in certain cases: see Child Support Act 1995 (*UK*).

[35] See Australian Law Reform Commission, Report No. 39 *Matrimonial Property* (AGPS, 1987), para. 32.

[36] G.Davis *et al.*, *Simple Quarrels* (OUP, 1994), esp. at 259.

delay, clogs up the court system and makes it difficult for the parties to negotiate a settlement.

It also assumes that there will be a decision-maker who is capable of fine-
tuning their judgment in the light of all the information. But the reality is that
in the vast majority of cases, appearance before a judge is no more than a theoretical possibility: as many as 95 per cent of cases will be resolved by other means,
especially inter-party negotiation through the medium of solicitors. So, discretion is preserved, arguably, for the benefit only of a tiny minority of cases in
which it might be of some use: for the rest, it serves only to confuse matters and
to prolong disputes.

There are a variety procedural ways in which these problems of delay and
information-need could be dealt with. One would be for the court system to
adopt a more managerial approach to cases coming into the system (e.g., compulsory directions hearings, pre-trial conference, etc.); another would be to set
limits to, or standardise, the type and amount of information that can be sought.
All of this has been tried or is being considered, yet the burden on the courts
still seems to grow. So, there is increased interest in abandoning the discretionary
regime altogether and moving towards a set of firmer presumptions or starting
points as a way of promoting settlement and of deflecting parties away from
courts and lawyers. With firmer guidelines or rules, so it is argued, there will
be less demand for information and a clearer backdrop against which parties can
settle their disputes.

The settlement-promoting and cost-reducing qualities of rules or firmer guidelines have frequently referred to in recent discussions of family law reform. For
example, the Explanatory Memorandum accompanying the Family Law Reform
Bill (No. 2), a Bill introduced by the Labor government of Paul Keating which
would, in effect, have created a presumption of equal division of matrimonial
property on divorce, argued that:

> "the structured approach to the resolution of spousal maintenance and matrimonial
> property disputes laid down by the Bill should provide parties whose marriages have
> broken down with a clear and logical framework within which to discuss these issues,
> and facilitate their concluding agreements rather than depending on Court imposed
> solutions to their disputes, with a minimum of cost . . . This structured approach will
> enable the parties to predict more accurately the likely outcome of a court resolution
> of a particular dispute and assist them in their negotiations".[37]

The assumed connection between clear rules and settlement-promotion also
helps to explain recent changes to child law in both England and Australia.[38] In

---

[37] Family Law Reform Bill (No. 2) 1995, Explanatory Memorandum, paras. 2 and 3. Similar arguments were advanced by the Australian Law Reform Commission in Report No. 39, *Matrimonial
Property* (AGPS, 1987), e.g. at para. 303: the Commission, however, laid more emphasis on the need
for clarity of principle as an aid to public understanding, and for the avoidance of unrealistic expectations, rather than assuming a direct correlation between clearer rules and settlement: see, e.g., paras.
32, 64, 301, 302–4.

[38] See n. 22 above

both jurisdictions, an explicit policy of encouraging parents to agree arrangements for their children after divorce or separation was set against the background of a clearer framework of parental rights and responsibilities.[39] In both jurisdictions, it is now clear (in a way that it was not previously) that both parents automatically retain parental status, irrespective of any orders a court might make.[40] Previously, the position of the non-custodial parent was thought, either as a matter of law or of general perception, to turn on the orders that a court made. As a consequence of the new laws, there is now less scope for the operation of the welfare or paramountcy principle, because both parents are automatically presumed to retain what is now called parental responsibility no matter whether a court makes an order.[41] The reduction of discretion (or, at least, the reduction in the range of matters subject to discretionary standards) is therefore an integral part of a strategy of deflecting litigants from courts and legal advisers.[42]

I have argued, then, that the tendency to reduce discretion in the areas of child support, the financial consequences of divorce, and the law concerning parenting after divorce, can be understood, in part, as an attempt to address the perceived inefficiencies and costs entailed in a discretionary system. Those costs are either external (e.g., to the welfare system) or internal to the legal system itself. But before this process goes much further, I suggest that we need some empirical work to investigate whether the premise of much of this legislative activity is correct: namely, that the more "rule like" the law becomes, the less costly it is to resolve disputes and the more efficient the outcomes are likely to be in terms of public spending.[43]

For, as far as internal costs are concerned, there is no hard evidence that firmer rules make it easier to reach agreements; and as far as external costs are concerned, it is just possible that reduced discretion brings costs of its own in its wake. For example, it is becoming increasingly common in jurisdictions outside England and Australia to encounter rules or presumptions favouring equal division of property on divorce (as in Scotland or New Zealand). While this may lead to internally cost-efficient solutions arising through quicker settlement (although that hypothesis is as yet untested), it may entail external costs (eg, to the state) that a discretionary system could avoid: equal sharing of matrimonial property, for example, will normally mean immediate equal division of property, which will

---

[39] S. 60B FLA 1975; s. 1(5) CA 1989.

[40] See n. 26 above, for an explanation of the differences between England and Australia in this respect.

[41] See, e.g., s. 60B FLA 1975 (*Cth*) (as amended). Although, under the old Part VII FLA 1975 (*Cth*), parents previously were each guardians of their children, and were joint custodians (s. 63F FLA 1975), it was possible for one parent's status as custodian to be removed by an order granting custody exclusively to the other. Under the reformed Part VII, both parents retain what is now called parental responsibility irrespective of any court order regarding the practical arrangements for the child.

[42] This connection emerges from the Law Commission's Report No. 172, *Review of Child Law: Guardianship and Custody* (HMSO, 1988), Part IV.

[43] See R. Epstein, *Simple Rules for a Complex World* (1995) for an elaboration of this premise.

in turn normally mean sale, including of the family home. This could have all kinds of adverse consequences for children, especially if it means moving suburb or school, or to poorer quality housing; and it could even end up as a cost to the state in certain circumstances, for example, through rehousing.[44] A discretionary, outcome-oriented, system is arguably better equipped to avoid this—but may generate other external (and possibly internal) costs of its own.

Rights and equality

I have said that one of the sources of legitimacy for a discretionary system is its implicit claim that it is able to reach better results through its sensitivity to the facts of each case. Flexibility is needed to produce optimal outcomes, just as empirical research is needed to "fine tune" the law itself.[45] However, there is now growing scepticism of our ability to know what the best solution is likely to be in any particular case. This is partly because much decision making in family law concerns future as well as past events, and there is doubt about our ability to predict the future with any certainty;[46] but even if we were confident of that, there are also doubts about law's ability to translate the messages of the experts into results that are beneficial.[47] In short, there has been a tendency towards what O'Donovan has called "an abandonment of law's claims to knowledge".[48]

Instead, we are increasingly seeing a shift towards conceptualising family law as a means of giving effect to rights irrespective of consequences, or to specific *a priori* juridical models of family relations, rather than as being concerned to search for the most beneficial or welfare-maximising outcome. This has been characterised as a shift from a "utility" or "needs" model of family law towards a rights model, and it seems to be associated with greater reliance on rules, or at least, norms that come closer to the rules end of the spectrum.[49] There is, of course, no necessary connection with rights and rules: rules do a lot more than just confer, or give effect to, rights, just as rights can find expression by means other than rules. Nevertheless, to the extent that we think of rights as unqualified claims or guarantees, we can still identify some loose connection between a shift to rights thinking and a shift towards the rules end of the spectrum of norms.

---

[44] E. Jackson *et al.*, "Financial Support on Divorce: The Right Mixture of Rules and Discretion?" (1993) 7 *International Journal of Law and the Family* 230; C. Bridge, "Reallocation of Property after Marriage Breakdown: The Matrimonial Property Act 1976" in M. Henaghan and B. Atkin (eds.), *Family Law Policy in New Zealand* (OUP, 1992), 231.

[45] See, e.g., J. Eekelaar and M. Maclean, "Divorce Law and Empirical Studies—a Reply" (1990) 106 *Law Quarterly Review* 621.

[46] This sort of scepticism is voiced by R. Deech: "Divorce Law and Empirical Studies" (1990) 106 *LQR* 229

[47] E.g., M. King and C. Piper, *How the Law Thinks about Children* (2nd edn., Arena, 1995).

[48] K. O'Donovan, *Family Law Matters* (Pluto, 1993), 115.

[49] Jackson *et al.*, *op. cit.*; S. Parker, "Rights and Utility" *op. cit.* at 311.

I suggested earlier that the reasons for this shift in thinking are complex: that it stems not just from scepticism about the role of experts, or the ability of law to translate expertise; but also from the increasingly politicised nature of family law reform which translates into claims from various groups to increased recognition of "their rights".

The primary evidence for growing rights thinking in family law comes from the area of children's rights. Although the form and content of children's rights are still controversial questions, there are signs that they are being taken more seriously by legislators. A striking example of this comes from the new Part VII to the FLA 1975, discussed above. This opens with the declaration, taken almost directly from the UN Convention on the Rights of the Child, that children have a "right" to contact with both their parents.[50] The intention seems to be to reduce discretion by indicating a clear preference for one outcome (contact) over another (no contact), although the Full Court of the Family Court has not adopted this interpretation of the relevant provisions.[51]

It could be argued, however, that the increased emphasis on children's rights is at least consistent with greater recognition of the rights of the non-custodial parent: that the same shifts that have given greater recognition to children's rights have also strengthened the position of the non-custodial parent, usually the father by giving him greater control over the mother. For example, almost all respondents in research conducted in Brisbane into the effects of the new Part VII of the Family Law Act 1975 were clear that the legislation had substantially weakened the position of the primary carer. This bears out the suggestion that the legislation in both jurisdictions was as much a response to claims for fathers' rights as for those of children.[52]

Another instance of this shift towards rights thinking comes from the tendency to enshrine equality as the basis of legal relations between adults. This displaces discretion by adopting a starting point or presumption that gives expression to equality in a particular context. One example would be the notion of joint parental responsibility between parents after divorce, just discussed. Another would be the actual or proposed matrimonial property laws which make equal division of property the starting point, drawing explicitly on analogies with partnerships.[53] I have already suggested that this can be understood in part as a response to political claims for rights; but the ostensible justification offered (together with the efficiency arguments discussed above) is usually the intuitive justice of notions of equality, rather than any suggestion that equality leads to

---

[50] Art. 9 UNCROC and s. 60B FLA 1975 (as amended). Many aspects of the Convention have not been incorporated into Australian law.

[51] *B* v. *B: Family Law Reform Act 1995* (1997) 21 Fam. LR 676.

[52] Graycar, n. 4, above; J.Brophy, "Custody Law, Child Care and Inequality in Britain" in C. Smart and S. Sevenhuijsen (eds.), *Child Custody and the Politics of Gender* (Routledge, 1989), ch. 9.

[53] See nn. 23–5, above.

fairer or better results.[54] Indeed, most of the evidence, especially in the context of finances, is that equality can produce very unequal results.[55]

In addition to arguments of rights and equality, rules are increasingly appealed to for their virtues in protecting individuals from arbitrariness. Thus, one of the reasons given for introducing child support legislation was to ensure that like cases were treated alike: i.e., that all those with the same ability to pay should pay the same amount in child support (something which the discretionary system had conspicuously failed to manage).[56] Further, it is often suggested that children's cases should be decided according to a "primary carer presumption", according to which the care of a child would be assigned to the person who had been its primary carer up to that point. One of the reasons offered for this is that it would protect parents, and particularly mothers, from the normalising predations of "experts", and would protect mothers from conceding too much in negotiations over property for fear of losing their children.[57]

Thus, there is a growing interest in rules arising from their ability to confer or protect rights, to give clearer expression to the notion of equality as the juridical basis of family relations in law, and to protect individuals from arbitrariness or lack of bargaining power. Of course, none of this helps us to answer what rights should be conferred or protected, whether equality is an appropriate juridical basis for family law, or when difference or equality of treatment is to be preferred. If the movement towards rights is to continue, some of these questions will have to be addressed. One of the advantages of discretion, of course, is that it means that these difficult questions can be avoided.[58]

SOME EVIDENCE?

I have suggested that there are a number of factors pushing towards a more rule-like family law; and I have suggested that this shift towards a "post-liberal" family law has been superimposed on an earlier technocratic liberalism without any overall re-examination of family law's guiding principles. I am not going to suggest here how such a re-examination might proceed. Instead, I want to ask the more modest—and perhaps more technical—question of whether it is possible, at the level of legislative norm-making in family law, to construct a more coherent relationship between rules and discretion, or to make more coherent use of the

[54] ALRC, Report No. 39, *op. cit.*, at para. 363. There is no necessary connection between a shift towards rules and a shift towards equality: equality seems simply to have acquired a widespread purchase on law reform thinking. Other rules could be formulated; but it increasingly looks as though those wishing to oppose equality will be on the back foot in doing so.

[55] See Jackson *et al.*, *op. cit.*

[56] *Children Come First*, vol., para. 1.5

[57] M. Fineman, *The Illusion of Equality: The Rhetoric and Reality of Divorce Reform* (Chicago, 1991). The argument is made in stronger terms by the same author in *The Neutered Mother* (1996). See also C. Smart, "Power and the Politics of Child Custody" in Smart and Sevenhuijsen (eds.), *Child Custody and the Politics of Gender* (Routledge, 1988).

[58] Cf. Schneider, *op. cit.*, and especially his notion of "rule-compromise" discretion.

spectrum of law-making possibilities. In this context, I want to consider briefly some preliminary findings of research being conducted in Brisbane under the auspices of the Family Law Research Unit. What we have learned so far may have some bearing on the present discussion.[59]

The project is considering the practical impact of the new Part VII of the FLA 1975, which recasts the law concerning parenting after divorce in ways that I have already touched upon. In brief, the new Part VII introduced the concept of parental responsibility to replace those of guardianship and custody. Parental reponsibility is now shared between parents, irrespective of the care arrangements for the child. The legislation also introduced the notion of a child's "right" to contact with both its parents,[60] together with a series of new "parenting orders", called residence, contact and specific issues orders. It also requires the courts to have regard to any "family violence" as a relevant factor in deciding on the child's best interests.

In our research, we were interested to learn whether these changes have had any effect on the way in which lawyers, judges, registrars, court counsellors and mediators approach their various tasks; whether there has been any noticeable impact on the way disputes are settled or negotiated; and whether the changes have affected the outcomes arrived at, by whatever means. Our primary research technique was the semi-structured interview, which we transcribed for the purposes of analysis.

I offer only tentative conclusions here. The most important of these is that the impact of the new law seems to vary according to the respondent's proximity to the trial process. At the outer edge are solicitors: they see many couples who do not go anywhere near court. Moving in, we come to court counsellors, who see fewer people than solicitors do;[61] moving in again, we come to registrars, who deal with routine applications and directions preparatory to trial, and with consent orders; then we come to the trial experts, the barristers and, ultimately, the judge.

What we are finding is that respondents are reporting more impact of the new law the further they are from the trial process. Thus, solicitors were able to report quite a few changes to practice, while the barristers and judges reported comparatively few. In between, counsellors and registrars were seeing some changes, but not as many as solicitors. As one barrister in our sample put it:

> "[M]y suspicion is that the true impact of the legislation will be seen at solicitor level and not at barrister level . . . [and] there may have been significant cultural changes at solicitor level."

---

[59] This section was written at a time when only a small number of transcripts of the research interviews were available. The tentative conclusions presented here may need revision in due course.

[60] This "right" must now be read in the light of the Full Court's decision in *B* v. *B: Family Law Reform Act 1995* (1997) 21 Fam. LR 676, discussed at n. 27 above.

[61] But who also see some people whom solicitors do not, such as unrepresented litigants-in-person.

This appeared to be borne out by a solicitor, who, in answer to a question about the impact of the concept of shared parental responsibility, said:

"It has a big practical effect on the contact parent, because that's where all of these issues are coming from of more time: 'I want more time with the children so that we can share our parenting; I want to be consulted and discuss aspects of schooling, where the children are going to spend holidays, how will their medical treatment be dealt with, what decisions will be made if the child needs certain counselling or educational assistance of some sort'—they want to be part of all of those sorts of issues. So the concept of shared parenting is creating that perception in a contact parent. It's also creating enormous stresses and strains upon the residence parent, who is being put upon by the contact parent to say, 'You can't just get on with your life. You've got to answer back to me.' And that's creating some very serious problems that lead to the interims."

One hypothesis is that the closer one gets to trial, the more likely it is, by definition, that the disagreement is going to be intractable: and the disagreement will be over the "big" issues of residence or contact, or both. So, judges and barristers are still seeing these intractable conflicts over what remain essentially the same questions: namely, where the child is going to live and whether there will be contact with the non-resident parent and, if so, how much. Changes in terminology do not seem to have altered practice very much, if at all: the questions requiring resolution seem to be the same, and they are resolved in much the same way.[62]

However, the further away from the trial one gets, the more likely it is that parents agree over the big issues of residence and contact, which means that it's the smaller detail that needs to be sorted out: the frequency and nature of contact, schooling, and so on. Here, what seems to be happening is that the new language of shared parental responsibility, or perhaps the expectations generated by that change of language, are leading to an *increase* in disagreement over these subsidiary issues: as the quote above suggests, the non-resident parent is relying on his or her (formally) equal involvement in the child's life, and is trying to dictate to the other the exact terms under which the child will be brought up—how they will have their hair cut, which dentist they will go to, how many parties a week they can attend, etc. While not all of these disagreements are enough to warrant a court application, they are a live area of disagreement for some time.

So, there is evidence that the framework of shared parental responsibility, which was partly intended to promote agreement by creating a clear default rule and by reassuring the non-resident parent that they retained their status, has actually had the opposite result. It has opened up new areas for disagreement where none existed before.

I want to draw two conclusions from this. The first is the commonplace one that legislation rarely works as it is intended. But in this instance, the causes of that gap between intention and result are worth thinking about. I suggest it stems

[62] The most notable changes at the trial stage concerned the likelihood of contact being ordered (which was higher than before), and the likelihood that the custodial parent would be restrained from moving geographical location in the interests of maintaining contact with the other parent.

from the ambivalent nature of the shift to rules. The simultaneous pursuit of efficiency (by promoting party agreement) and the starting point of equality of parental rights, both of which I have suggested explain the push towards rules, are incompatible: the more rights are conferred, the more likely it is that there will be disagreement over their exercise. Making parents bearers of equal rights does not make them more agreeable. We have no hard evidence that this is creating more work for the court system than before, but we have some of anecdotal evidence that it is.

The second is what might be called the principle of variable reception. This comes in two versions. The first is that the same legislative message will have a variable impact on different actors according to their position in the family justice system. In this case, I have suggested that the main variable is proximity to the trial. In other words, the variable is structural, or outside the control of the respondent.

The second version of this principle is that the same legislative messages will be "heard" differently by different actors, regardless of their place in the system: for example, a number of respondents said that while they thought the reference to family violence in the welfare checklist merely confirmed pre-existing practice, and was therefore of little significance, they attached great weight to the child's stated right to contact with both parents. Other respondents, however, saw matters in precisely the reverse way: the family violence provisions were seen as a very important innovation, while the reference to contact was thought merely to confirm a trend that had been under way for some time. Gender seemed to be an important factor in determining the respondents' views.

In my conclusion, I will suggest ways in which the principle of variable reception, at least the first version of it, might be put to some good use. The second version, of course, points to the unpredictability of law's reception in practice, and simply underlines the fact that modern family law increasingly offers rhetorical resources for a number of different competing positions, without clearly prioritising one over the other. Using Galanter's phrase, family law could be described as "a second kind of politics".[63]

CONCLUSION: TOWARDS "ACOUSTIC SEPARATION"?

I have suggested that there are specific conditions producing a shift away from discretion towards rules in family law. In doing so, I have rehearsed some of the common arguments concerning the merits and demerits of both rules and discretion, but without so far taking any clear position on what I think the right

---

[63] "Law provides resources and opportunities for the pursuit of our competing commitments . . . But isn't that what politics is supposed to do? . . . Increasingly, some modern democracies—especially those committed to pluralism—rely heavily on this second kind of politics": M. Galanter, "Law Abounding: Legalisation around the North Atlantic" (1992) 55 *Modern Law Review* 1 at 23. See also my "The Normal Chaos of Family Law", forthcoming.

balance should be. That is possibly because my own view is unsurprising: namely, that there is room for both, and that we should seek to draw the best from each while avoiding, if we can, the worst.

To achieve this will require some more holistic thinking than has taken place hitherto. The process I have described, of a steady retreat from wide discretion, has really taken the form of a series of specific inroads into the framework established in the 1970s, rather than any coherent overhaul of the system as a whole. We have an essentially discretionary system, overlaid with some specific rule-like norms. There is no overarching conceptual framework, and, in particular, no coherent view emerging about the vices and virtues of particular normative types.

One suggested way forward comes from my very tentative conclusions from the Brisbane research. This is that we should acknowledge that there are different audiences for law, who, for reasons connected with their position in the family law "system", will interpret the same legal provisions in different ways: the first version of the principle of variable reception. If that is the case, then why not abandon the attempt to address all audiences at the same time and with the same message? Why not, instead, change the message, and the normative medium through which it expressed, according to the audience, and according to what might be best suited to promote whatever outcomes we deem desirable in that particular context? Thus, for example, judges could be left with wide discretions, because they can actually make use of them to fine tune outcomes in the small minority of cases that come before them; while those negotiating in private could be made to do so within a more rule like framework, so drawing on the efficiency-promoting virtues of rules (if, indeed, the hypothesis that rules have such a virtue turns out to be correct). This has been termed "acoustic separation": the idea that "legislatures should lay down rigid rules for the public—'conduct rules'—but that . . . [o]fficials might follow more flexible 'decision rules' that deviate from conduct rules and indeed that work as standards".[64] Something like this already operates in Australia under the child support scheme, where liability is calculated under a fixed formula, but where there is the possibility of departures from the formula result being ordered by a Review Officer or by a court.

But the problem may go deeper than this suggested solution suggests. For one thing, if we were to introduce firmer rules as a framework for private ordering, we would need to cement some agreement over what they should be. We may be a long way from that sort of consensus. For another, I hope it is clear from what I have said that the choice between rules and discretion is more than just a technical choice. It is a choice that is connected up to some wider questions of what Parker calls "ethical impulses" in the law[65] (for example, whether we want to see family law in terms of rights or utility, of fairness or efficiency), as well as to the

---

[64] Sunstein, "Problems with Rules", above, at 1007.
[65] "Rights and Utility", above n. 2.

material conditions under which family law operates (especially internal and external costs, the judicial or bureaucratic nature of family justice and the evolving relationship between the family and the state). This means that the question of the appropriate balance between rules and discretion has to be seen in the light of those wider considerations.

15

Equality or Inequality within the Family? Ideology, Reality and the Law's Response

REBECCA BAILEY-HARRIS

INTRODUCTION

The discourse of formal equality has received some fresh impetus in the context of current family law reform. The model of rule equality between adult partners in the family underpins developments such as the vigorous promotion on both sides of the globe of private ordering in dispute resolution, further reduction in the role of spouse maintenance, and the paradigm of joint parental involvement with children following separation. However, the formal equality model is open to the criticism that it rests on generalised assumptions which fail to take adequate account of the realities of inequality which commonly exist during the currency of individual relationships and to which the breakdown of those relationships gives rise. Focusing on financial provision, this chapter will advocate a more pro-active role for private law in equalising as between the adult parties the effects of a relationship and its breakdown. Family law rules of maintenance and property division should have two aims. First, where parties have assumed different roles by mutual agreement within a committed relationship, the law's evaluation of their respective contributions should reflect the ideology of equality. Secondly, the law should intervene to redress any inequalities which the relationship has created in the parties' capacities to access the economic market. Private family law will fail to promote true equality if it retreats into generalised concepts of formal equality and restricted state intervention in the consequences of its family breakdown.

A pro-active role for family law in adjusting the economic consequences of family breakdown is necessitated by the combined operation of a number of factors. Role-division of adults during the currency of their relationship—largely but not exclusively the allocation of child-rearing responsibilities—affects both current and future earning capacity. The effect of the role-division adopted during a relationship is rendered more acute when its breakdown occurs against the background of a harsh economic climate and, in particular, high unemployment. The capacity of an individual to realise the ideal of financial independence from a former partner by achieving optimum self-support is commonly restricted. This is compounded by a reduced role for state support through social security. Fogarty J has highlighted the potential for equality during a relationship to be transformed into inequality on its breakdown:

"On separation, the partnership, and the division of responsibilities which it produced, come to an end. . . . However, the world outside the marriage does not recognise some of the activities that within the marriage used to be regarded as valuable contributions. . . . Post-separation, the party who assumed the less financially rewarded responsibilities of the marriage is at an immediate disadvantage. Yet that party often cannot simply turn to more financially rewarding activities. Often, opportunities are no longer open . . . "[1]

If a relationship has been characterised by violence, it is by its nature one of inequality.[2] A violent relationship is necessarily one of power imbalance between the individuals concerned. The disempowering effects of violence may impede not only the victim's capacity to operate within society generally (including the employment market) but also to access the legal system and therefore to realise her rights.[3] A legal system which fails to take violence seriously will further compound disempowerment. In terms of the parties' respective contributions to the relationship, those of the perpetrator may properly be regarded as unequal to those of the victim.[4]

Equalisation in economic terms of the effects of a relationship is a right created by the relationship itself and one to which both parties are equally entitled upon its breakdown; a more proactive role for financial provision law should be viewed (positively) as realising the legitimate rights of individuals rather than (negatively) as reinforcing dependency.[5] Such a role is not gender-specific, since it focuses on how the role-division within a particular relationship has affected the parties' respective financial positions. Nevertheless, it should be acknowledged that in current social conditions a family relationship is more likely to have adversely affected the woman's financial position than the man's, at least where children are concerned, and so women are more likely as a class to benefit from the adjustive regime, at least in the short term.

What specific steps should the private law of financial provision take to be more pro-active in redressing inequalities between the parties when a relationship has ended? This chapter will advocate two, although others are available.[6] First, maintenance awards should take greater account of labour market condi-

---

[1] *Waters* v. *Jurek* (1995) 20 Fam LR 196 at 199–200.

[2] See e.g. R. Graycar and J. Morgan, *The Hidden Gender of Law* (Federation Press, 1990); ALRC Report No 69: Part 1: *Equality Before the Law: Justice for Women* (AGPS, 1994), paras. 2.30.9.4.

[3] ALRC Report No 67 Interim: *Equality Before the Law: Women's Access to the Legal System* (AGPS 1994), paras 1.4, 2.8, 2.9, 2.22, 3.2.

[4] J. Behrens, "Domestic Violence and Property Adjustment: A Critique of No-fault Discourse" (1993) 7 *AJFL* 9. This issue is further discussed later in this chapter.

[5] A. Diduck and H. Orton, "Equality and Support for Spouses" (1994) 57 *MLR* 681 at 686.

[6] For instance, increased powers to adjust pension rights. In England, see Matrimonial Causes Act 1973 (UK), ss. 25B–25D, inserted by the Pensions Act 1995 (UK); Family Law Act 1996 (UK), s. 16; White Paper, *The Treatment of Pensions on Divorce* (Cm 3345, HMSO, 1996); *Pension Sharing on Divorce: Reforming Pensions for a Fairer Future*, DSS, June 1998.

tions and the difficulties facing those who wish to re-enter the workforce at optimum capacity. Secondly, the division of property should (i) give full recognition to the value of non-financial contributions to a relationship (ii) retain and give appropriate weight to "prospective" considerations, i.e. any disparity in the parties' respective financial positions, present and future, and (iii) take account of any violence within the relationship. It is acknowledged that these strategies may further erode the "clean break" policy, but that policy may itself be productive of injustice and may be rendered unrealistic or unattainable by economic conditions. It is also accepted that these strategies necessitate the retention of judicial discretion in the adjustive regime, in particular in relation to assessment of prospective considerations and in relation to violence in the context of contributions made to the relationship. Whilst the exercise of judicial discretion has in the past been criticised as a vehicle for conscious or unconscious gender-bias,[7] it is hoped that a new spirit of enlightenment on gender issues is now abroad amongst the judiciary, fostered by a receptiveness to feminist writings and by recent educational programmes. Moreover, future reforms should aim to structure the exercise of discretion to render the underlying principles more transparent and hence to lead to greater predictability in outcomes and to promotion of settlements.

This chapter will draw principally on the Australian experience in recent years to consider whether the law of financial provision has adopted an active role in redressing inequality. Marriage breakdown will be the primary focus. It is timely in Australia to re-open debate on the principles of financial provision in this context, since the appearance of a fresh Bill to amend Part VIII of the Family Law Act 1975 (Cth) seems imminent. The chapter will conclude by asking whether the debate should be broadened to consider whether the law should adopt a more active role in redressing inequalities arising from relationships other than marriage.

SPOUSE MAINTENANCE

It has commonly been predicted that the already limited role of spouse maintenance payments will be further restricted—or even abolished—in future. Yet such a development is by no means a foregone conclusion. The opposite could occur, i.e. a revival of spouse maintenance, if spouse maintenance payments after marriage breakdown were viewed as one method of equalising the economic effects of the relationship, at least until the wider framework of social and economic inequalities between men and women is remedied. Eloquent advocates of this approach include O'Donovan[8] and Diduck and Orton. To quote the latter authors:

[7] R. Graycar and J. Morgan *op. cit.*, *supra* n. 2, at 130 ff; M, Neave, "From Difference to Sameness—Law and Women's Work" (1992) 18 *MULR* 768; ALRC Report No 69 Part II: *Equality Before the Law: Women's Equality* (AGPS 1994), paras. 2.27–2.32.

[8] "Principles of Maintenance: An Alternative View" (1978) 8 *Fam. Law* 180; "Should All Maintenance of Spouses be Abolished?" (1984) 45 *MLR* 424.

"Along with true equity in employment and pay and affordable good quality child care, an adequate valuation of domestic work would mean that it would not be necessary that each partner play exactly the same role in wage earning . . . Roles in marriage could be adopted based on the partners' actual interests and skills. Maintenance on divorce would still sometimes be necessary . . . but it would no longer overwhelmingly be women who require it and it would not result in economic disadvantage for the recipient. Maintenance would be seen as a right, expected and earned . . .

We would suggest . . . that . . . 'private' family law reform remains an important feminist strategy . . . Law must deal with the society it has helped to create . . . in the short term . . . thousands of women do enter into and leave the status-based contract of marriage, with all of its ideological baggage, and support law must play its part in alleviating their poverty . . . "[9]

In Canada the celebrated decision in *Moge* v. *Moge; Women's Legal Education and Action Fund (Intervener)*[10] in 1993 "set the stage for a considerable increase in the number of spouse maintenance orders . . . and the amounts awarded".[11] In that case maintenance was awarded to an ex-wife who had the capacity for a degree of self-support, to compensate for the economic disadvantages which she had suffered as the result of the parties' role division during the marriage. The essence of the majority's approach has been summed up in this way:

"The court noted the reduced earning capacity experienced by many women in the long term as a result of interruptions in workforce participation due to child-rearing responsibilities, and observed also that these sacrifices sometimes embellished the earning capacity of the other spouse. L'Heureux Dubé J, for the majority, regarded it as a goal of the spousal support provisions in Canadian law that the parties should share equitably in the economic consequences of the marriage and its breakdown. In calculating the economic disadvantages . . . which have resulted from the role-division within the marriage, the court should consider . . . loss of future earning power, loss of seniority, missed promotions, lack of access to . . . pension plans, the effects of having outdated educational qualifications . . . The longer the marriage lasted, and the closer the economic union, the greater would be the presumptive claim to equal standards of living upon dissolution."[12]

Has the influence of *Moge* been felt in Australia? Has the Family Court of Australia, within the framework of the existing legislation, itself undertaken the development of a more active role for spouse maintenance orders in redressing economic inequalities? Its capacity to do so is admittedly constrained by the existing case law, which gives spouse maintenance a residual role where proceedings for property division are also in issue,. Thus the usual practice is to consider spouse maintenance last, and the quantum of a property order is often said to render a maintenance order unnecessary.[13] Nevertheless, important statements of

---

[9] "Equality and Support for Spouses" (1994) 57 *MLR* 681, 686–7.
[10] (1993) 99 DLR (4th) 456.
[11] (1994) 8 AJFL 2.
[12] *Ibid.*
[13] See e.g. *Clauson* v. *Clauson* (1994) 18 Fam. LR 693; *Whitely* v. *Whitely* (1996) 20 Fam. LR 590; *W* v. *W* (1996) 21 Fam. LR 343; *Parshen* v. *Parshen* (1996) 21 Fam. LR 199.

principle were made by the Full Court in *Mitchell* v. *Mitchell*,[14] particularly concerning judicial notice of employment conditions, which might be utilised in promoting an expanded role for spouse maintenance orders in Australia. In a marriage lasting 27 years the wife was a registered nurse and the husband a barrister. She did not practise her profession full time after the children were born, although she took some part-time employment. Her claim for spouse maintenance was dismissed by the trial judge, who held that she did not meet the requirements of section 72 of the Family Law Act 1975 because *inter alia* she should have made greater efforts to secure appropriate employment. Her appeal was allowed and the case remitted for rehearing. To quote from the judgment, which bears much of the stamp of *Moge*:

> "Importantly, and particularly in more recent times, there is the notorious circumstance that there is a significant gap between theory and reality for employment, especially for people in middle age, lacking experience and confidence, and who have been out of the skilled work-force for many years, and in the context of current high employment. Loss of security, missed promotion opportunities, loss of retraining in developing skills in an increasingly skilled workforce . . . particularly in times of high unemployment, are notorious circumstances of which the court must take notice and apply in a realistic way . . . Like Canada, Australia has a body of research indicating that mothers who are the primary carers of children inevitably drop out of the paid workforce and consequently suffer financial deprivation which is exacerbated by marriage breakdown . . . In our view there are significant advantages in the court being able to take judicial notice of research concerning the economic consequences of marriage and its dissolution."[15]

The Full Court thought it unlikely that the wife in this case would be successful in obtaining appropriate employment:

> "In the ultimate, this could only be finally determined by enquiries and applications by the wife. But her age, her legitimate needs, the standard of living enjoyed by the parties during the course of the marriage, and the husband's professional skills and prospects of high earnings . . . suggest that any additional employment she obtains would be unlikely to meet those needs . . . [T]he husband has a capacity to meet a reasonable maintenance order."[16]

However, these important statements of principle seem to have failed as yet to promote any significant change in the pattern of spouse maintenance orders in Australia. The reported case law since 1995 does not reveal any discernible increase in the use of orders under section 74 of the Family Law Act 1975 (Cth) to redress economic inequalities.[17] We shall see in the next section of this chapter that this pattern is also discernible in relation to property division under section 79: strong statements of principle by the Full Court are not always followed by a consistent change in practice.

[14] (1995) 19 Fam LR 44.
[15] *Id.*, at 61–2.
[16] *Id.*, at 63.
[17] Nor does anecdotal evidence of practice.

Whatever the drawbacks of judicial activism as the vehicle for reform, legislative interest in reform of the principles of spouse maintenance has in recent years been strikingly absent. The Family Law Reform Bill (No 2) 1995 (Cth) which lapsed due to a federal election contained no significant proposals for reform of the principles of spouse maintenance.[18] It is unclear whether the principles of spouse maintenance are likely to be addressed in the future legislative reforms of Part VIII of the principal Act foreshadowed by the Attorney-General. Rumours (admittedly unsubstantiated) have circulated of possible further curtailment of entitlement. In the writer's view this would be a totally retrograde step and one completely antithetical to the role of private law in redressing inequality.

PROPERTY DIVISION

Property division is another vehicle for equalising the economic effects of marriage and its breakdown. The current system of property division under section 79 of the Family Law Act 1975 (Cth) gives the court a wide discretion to make such order as is appropriate; the exercise of discretion takes account both of a wide range of contributions (financial and non-financial) to the marriage as well as of present and future needs (the "prospective component").[19] The width of judicial discretion and the process of evaluation have been consistently stressed in the case-law since the decision of the High Court of Australia in *Mallet* v. *Mallet*[20] in 1984 and any *legal principle* of half shares, even as a starting point, has been disclaimed.[21] Three issues in relation to property division must be considered when assessing the law's capacity to redress inequalities arising from marriage: the value accorded to non-financial contributions in the evaluation process, the use made of the "prospective component" as a means of equalising disparity in the parties' financial positions, and the relevance of violence.

Justice of outcome in property division on marriage breakdown will be not be achieved if the legal process fails to accord equal value to financial and non-financial contributions made by spouses to a joint enterprise during the currency of their relationship. The pattern of decisions of the Family Court of Australia the latter 1980s was criticised on the basis of the exercise of conscious or unconscious gender-bias, manifesting itself in this context as the systematic undervaluing of non-financial as compared with financial contributions to a marriage,[22] particu-

---

[18] Apart from a provision that when an order is made by consent, consideration by the court of the s. 75(2) factors should not be mandatory—reflecting a principle of restricted judicial scrutiny of financial agreements and a corresponding retreat from legal paternalism, consistent with the generalised assumptions of formal equality referred to in the introduction of this chapter.

[19] Family Law Act, s. 79(4).

[20] (1984) 156 CLR 605.

[21] *Ferraro* v. *Ferraro* (1992) 16 Fam. LR 47; *Georgeson* v. *Georgeson* (1995) 19 Fam. LR 302; *Harrison* v. *Harrison* (1996) 20 Fam. LR 322.

[22] See n. 7, *supra*.

larly in "deep pocket" cases involving substantial business assets.[23] However, a change in the dicourse of the court at appellate level is clearly discernible from the early 1990s onwards. A past tendency to undervalue non-financial contributions was recognised,[24] and in *Ferraro* v. *Ferraro* in 1992 the Full Court showed increased sensitivity to

" . . . an evolving social background which gives greater emphasis to the equality and partnership concepts in a marriage and, no doubt, this evolutionary process will continue. *Dawes* and *Harris* illustrate the shift towards a greater societal recognition of the worth of domestic labour . . . "[25]

In *Waters* v. *Jurek* in 1995, Fogarty J in the Full Court stated that:

"This court values different kinds of contributions equally while the marriage subsists."[26]

Further important statements of principle from the Full Court followed in *McLay* v. *McLay*[27] in 1995. The outcome of the case was that the wife received 40 per cent of assets totalling $9 million. The judgment of the Full Court described the task of evaluating "the disparate contributions to which s. 79(4) refers and the translation of those into monetary terms" as an "onerous" one.[28] Whilst acknowledging the discretionary nature of the exercise, the judgment nevertheless advocated the utility of the Full Court providing guidelines. It spoke of:

"a practical recognition of the circumstance that in many marriages each party contributes in ways which might be described as the normal way in our society and that in any qualitative evaluation of those matters the likely outcome is one of equality . . . In many cases any assessment of the facts readily makes it clear that an outcome of equality . . . is most likely and that a lengthy trial in which those facts are examined in detail will produce no different result."[29]

But has the persuasive rhetoric of these appellate decisions been followed by a real change in the pattern of subsequent case law? Have grand statements of principle been reflected in practical outcomes? *Ferraro* itself was criticised[30] for the result not measuring up to the rhetoric (the wife ultimately received only 37.5 per cent of overall assets worth $11 million). It is true that a number of decisions of the Family Court from the mid-1990s show non-financial

---

[23] See e.g. *Lawler* v. *Lawler* (1988) 12 Fam LR 319; *Gamer* v. *Gamer* [1988] FLC 91–932; *Aldred* v. *Aldred* [1988] FLC 91–933; H. Charlesworth and R. Ingleby, "The Sexual Division of Labour and Family Property Law" (1988) 6 *Law in Context* 29.

[24] This approach can be traced back to *Dawes* v. *Dawes* (1990) 12 Fam. LR 599 and through *Harris* v. *Harris* (1991) 15 Fam LR 26.

[25] (1992) 16 Fam. LR 1 at 47.

[26] (1995) 20 Fam. LR 190 at 200.

[27] (1995) 20 Fam. LR 239.

[28] *Id.*, at 248.

[29] *Id.*, at 249–50.

[30] R. Chisholm, *Butterworths Australian Family Law Bulletin* No 106 (Jan. 1993), 17.

contributions made during[31] the marriage accounting for a more generous percentage of property division under section 79; it is not uncommon for financial and non-financial contributions made by the parties in a "traditional" division of roles to be assessed as equal. Illustrations of this fairer attitude to role-division during marriage include *Best* v. *Best*,[32] *Kessey* v. *Kessey*,[33] *Clauson* v. *Clauson*, [34] *Gould* v. *Gould*,[35] *MacGregor* v. *MacGregor*,[36] *Alexovski* v. *Alexovski*,[37] *Elsey* v. *Elsey*,[38] and *W* v. *W*.[39] Nevertheless, one may question whether a system of property division which vests such a wide discretion in the court is inherently capable achieving consistency in the equal recognition of financial and non-financial contributions. Other reported decisions post-*Ferraro* reveal a less generous evaluation of non-financial contributions and continue to stress both the width of discretion and the task of actual evaluation which the current legislation imposes on the court.[40]

The preferable approach to securing proper recognition of non-financial contributions in a consistent way is a *legislative* structuring of the exercise of discretion through clearer articulation of statutory principles. That means the enactment of a statutory principle that the parties' respective contributions to the relationship (financial and non-financial) are presumptively to be treated as equal, subject only to clear exceptional circumstances. This approach has already been strongly advocated, through the enactment of a principle of half shares of property as a starting point, both by the Australian Law Reform Commission in two of its references (*Matrimonial Property* in 1994 and *Equality Before the Law* in 1994[41]) and by the Joint Select Committee in 1992.[42] The exception must be narrowly formulated if the statutory reformulation is both to introduce greater certainty in the law and to serve an educative function in achieving community acceptance of the equal value of the differing roles assumed by partners within the family. However, as is discussed below, violence within a relationship should properly be included in the formulation of the exception. The lapsed

---

[31] Allowance is made for substantial contributions brought into a marriage by one party, subject to the "erosion" principle: *Way* v. *Way* [1996] FLC 72–702; *MacGregor* v. *MacGregor* (1996) 21 Fam. LR 57; *Elsey* v. *Elsey* (1996) 21 Fam. LR 249. Similarly, credit is given for contributions after separation: see e.g. *Bartlett* v. *Bartlett* (1996) 21 Fam. LR 267.

[32] (1993) 16 Fam. LR 973.

[33] (1994) 18 Fam. LR 149.

[34] (1994) 18 Fam. LR 693.

[35] (1995) 20 Fam. LR 1.

[36] (1996) 21 Fam. LR 57

[37] (1996) 20 Fam. LR 894.

[38] (1996) 21 Fam. LR 249.

[39] (1996) 21 Fam. LR 343

[40] See e.g. *Money* v. *Money* (1884) 17 Fam. LR 814; *Harrison* v. *Harrison* (1996) 20 Fam LR 322; *Whitely* v. *Whitely* (1996) 20 Fam. LR 590; *Bartlett* v. *Bartlett* (1996) 21 Fam .LR 267; *Beneke* v. *Beneke* (1996) 20 Fam. LR 841.

[41] ALRC Report No 39 (AGPS, 1987), para. 363; ALRC Report No 69 Part 1: *Equality Before the Law: Justice for Women* (1994), Rec. 9.6.

[42] *Report on Certain Aspects of The Operation and Interpretation of the Family Law Act* 1975(Cth) (AGPS, 1992), para. 8.95.

Family Law Reform Bill (No 2 1995 (Cth) contained a statutory statement that:

"In proceedings for a property order, the court is to assume, as a starting point, that the parties to a marriage have made equal contributions to the marriage as a whole . . ."[43]

The provisions of the lapsed Bill could be criticised for their complexity and for the weakness of the presumption of equality, i.e., that the starting point was subject to too many exceptions.[44] A new Bill, when introduced, must state the presumption of equality with clarity and transparency and avoid undermining it by treating routine matters as exceptions.

A "prospective component" in the principles governing property division is in principle a valuable tool in equalising the economic effects of marriage and its breakdown, since it allows the court (resources permitting) to make a further adjustment of assets to allow for disparity in the parties' financial positions on breakdown which stem from the role-divisions adopted during marriage and which is not adequaltely addressed by the quantum of property division based on contributions.[45] This component inevitably necessitates the retention of an element of judicial discretion. However, this tool will not be effective if courts are unwilling to make sufficient adjustment under this component where real disparity exists between the parties' financial positions. In past years decisions of the Family Court of Australia were open to criticism for the very small adjustments to property orders made under section 79(4)(d)–(e) (encompassing the section 75(2) considerations) of the Family Law Act 1975 (Cth). A "loading" in favour of the economically disadvantaged spouse in the range of only 5–15 per cent was common.[46]

However, here too decisions of the Full Court evidence a change of discourse in recent years through vigorous statements that the prospective component potentially has a real role to play in redressing financial inequalities which manifest themselves on the breakdown of marriage. In 1995 Fogarty J observed in *Walters* v. *Jurek* that:

"There is no doubt that the centre of gravity in the determination of property cases has, especially in more recent times, moved to the evaluation of the s 75(2) factors and the significance of that has been heightened because of recent Full Court decisions which have emphasised those provisions and indicated that they should be given real rather than token weight".[47]

In *Clauson* v. *Clauson*[48] the Full Court in allowing the wife's appeal increased

---

[43] Cl. 86C(1).

[44] Family Law Reform Bill (No 2) 1995 (Cth), cll. 86C(2).

[45] A need for further adjustment may not arise because of the size of award made to a party by reason of contributions: see e.g. *Whitely* v. *Whitely* (1996) 20 Fam. LR 590.

[46] See e.g. *Penza* v. *Penza* [1988] FLC 91–949; *Abdo* v. *Abdo* (1989) 12 Fam LR 861; *Shaw* v. *Shaw* (1989) 12 Fam. LR 806; *Goodwin* v. *Goodwin* (1990) 14 Fam. LR 801.

[47] (1995) 20 Fam. LR 190.

[48] (1994) 18 Fam. LR 693.

the section 75(2) adjustment of a property award in her favour from 15–25 per cent, referring to "the enormous disparity in the income and income earning capacities" of the parties and noting that:

" . . . in most cases the most valuable 'asset' which a party can take out of the marriage is a substantial, reliable, income earning capacity".[49]

It was expressly recognised that in the past artificially delineated boundaries have been imposed on the scope of awards under the prospective component of section 79. *Waters* v. *Jurek*[50] is another example of the vigorous statements of principle by the Full Court. Both parties were psychiatrists and high earners although the husband more so than the wife. The Full Court refused to disturb an adjustment of $50,000 in the wife's favour to take account of the disparity in the parties' incomes, notwithstanding that her lower income had not been directly attributed to family commitments. More general remarks made in the judgments reveal the change in judicial attitude and an express recognition of the role of financial provision in achieving equality on marriage breakdown:

"In some cases, an adjustment is called for because it would be unjust for the roles and activities of a party, which were recognised until separation, and which largely determined or influenced the personal development of that party and the arrangements made between the parties, to suddenly count for little, while those of the other party, which were of equal significance during the marriage, to now have a far greater financial impact outside the home—in circumstances where it was the joint decision of the parties that be the way in which they conduct their affairs . . .

This court values different kinds of contributions of the parties equally while the marriage subsists. It would be inconsistent with the equality which that position recognises not to take into account the transformation which the termination of the relationship results in, at least in terms of the capacity for present and future income generation."[51]

But have these statements of principle at appellate level produced much real change in the way in which judges and practitioners approach the prospective component in property division? As with any discretionary jurisdiction generalisations are difficult to make since cases inevitably turn on their own facts. Arguably they have not; here again, rhetoric is not matched by substantive outcome. In the later 1990s there are instances of substantial percentages of adjustment made under the prospective component of property division, such as *W* v. *W*[52] (40 per cent), although the high percentage is usually attributable to particular facts rather than to general economic conditions (in *W* v. *W* the wife was disabled). However the general pattern of reported case law in the past five years does not reveal consistently higher percentages of adjustment being made under

---

[49] *Id.*, at 709.
[50] (1995) 20 Fam. LR 196.
[51] *Id.*, at 199–200, *per* Fogarty J.
[52] (1996) 21 Fam. LR 343.

the prospective component of section 79 to remedy inequality.[53] Here again, there may well be a need for reform to be effected through clearer articulation of principle by statute. In the first place it is essential that the prospective component of property division be retained in a new Bill proposing amendments to Part VIII of the Family Law Act 1975 (Cth). This has been consistently recommended in the past both by the Australian Law Reform Commission[54] and by the Joint Select Committee.[55] It formed part of the Family Law Reform Bill (No 2) 1995 (Cth) which later lapsed due to the election.[56] However, past recommendations and proposed legislative provisions have done little more than reiterate the existing formulation of the section 75(2) factors as the content of the prospective component in property division. It can be argued that more is needed in the new statute: an express statement that the purpose of this component is to take account of disparity and thus to redress inequality. The statute should also state clearly that the evaluation of disparity reqires not only a consideration of the role-division assumed by the parties during the marriage but also of the state of the current employment market. It is hoped that the drafters of a new Bill will heed this message.

The law's response to violence within the family has in recent years been identified as an issue central to society's promotion of equality between men and women.[57] Whilst there is now widespread acceptance that the effects of violence should be recognised and acknowledged across a range of family proceedings and not confined to the realm of injunctions and protection orders, the issue of whether violence should be relevant in financial proceedings nevertheless remains controversial. It is commonly perceived as raising the question whether violence can be taken into account without re-introducing wholesale considerations of conduct, inappropriate in the context of a system of no-fault divorce. In a seminal article published in 1993 Julia Behrens argued that "the courts have retreated behind no fault discourse to strike out allegations of violence"[58] and that there are "strong normative arguments for allowing the fact of violence against women in the home to benefit women in financial proceedings".[59] It is in principle possible to regard violence as a negative contribution to family welfare under section 79(4)(c) of the Family Law Act 1975 (Cth) in its current form, or as creating dis-

---

[53] It is common for the extent of the disparity in the parties' financial position to be minimised (see e.g. *Bartlett* v. *Bartlett* (1996) 21 Fam. LR 267; *Alexovski* v. *Alexovski* (1996) 20 Fam. LR 898 and for the practical difficulties of making a substantial loading under the prospective component to be emphasised: see e.g. *Elsey* v. *Elsey* (1996) 21 Fam. LR 249.

[54] Report No 39, *Matrimonial Property* (AGPS 1987), paras. 373–82.

[55] *Report on Certain Aspects of the Operation and Interpretation of The Family Law Act* (AGPS 1992), Rec. 74.

[56] Cl. 86D.

[57] ALRC Report No 67 Interim: *Equality Before the Law: Women's Access to the Legal System* (AGPS, 1994), ch. 3; ALRC Report No 69 Part II: *Equality before the Law: Women's Equality* (AGPS 1994), chs. 2 and 3; R. Graycar "The Relevance of Violence in Family Law Decision-Making" (1995) 9 *AJFL* 58.

[58] "Domestic Violence and Property Adjustment: A Critique of No-Fault Discourse" (1993) 7 *AJFL* 9 at 13.

[59] *Id.*, at 9.

parity (of empowerment) relevant under the section 75(2) component of property division. This thesis has proved controversial: the ability of courts to "sever" the consideration of violence from that of behaviour generally has been questioned, as has the freedom of courts to develop such jurisprudence—particularly where the violence has seemingly had no direct effect on the victim's financial position—within existing statutory provisions, given the clear pattern of past authority.[60] Nevertheless, in *Doherty* v. *Doherty* (1995)[61] the Full Court awarded the wife 65 per cent of the property, taking account both of contributions and the section 75(2) factors. Baker J in the Full Court commented that:

> "Although the domestic violence . . . related to a relatively small period of time . . . nevertheless . . . his Honour would have been entitled to have found that because of the appellant's conduct, the respondent's contribution as homemaker was increased and the appellant's similar contribution diminished as a consequence."[62]

Whilst this case is significant in being the first where violence was consider in principle to be relevant to contributions made to a marriage, it nonetheless remains a fairly isolated example[63]. If the relevance of violence in this context is to be assured, then legislative change is needed.

The Australian Law Reform Commission recommended in Report No 69 Part 1: *Equality Before the Law: Justice for Women* that the statutory formulation of circumstances in which the court should depart from equal division of property as the starting point should include an express reference to the impact of violence on past contributions and future needs. This recommendation was not adopted in the drafts of the Family Law Reform Bill (No 2) 1995, an omission which drew criticism from Behrens.[64] The objective of the recommendation is almost certainly not achieved by the amendment to section 43 of the Family Law Act 1975 (Cth) effected subsequently by the Family Law Reform Act 1995 (Cth), which adds to the general principles to be considered in *all* proceedings "the need to ensure safety from family violence". Should the amendment to property provisions advocated by Behrens and the Australian Law Reform Commission be made in the new Bill reforming Part VIII of the Act, or are the objections voiced by Murray and others persuasive? The present writer's view is that the amendment is desirable.The equation of violence with inequality provides one key. If violence within marriage is one of the clearest indicators of inequality, and if the objective of financial provision law is (as this chapter has advocated) the redressing of inequality, then logic demands that violence be taken into account in property division. Another justification lies in human rights analysis. Violent

---

[60] K. Murray, "Domestic Violence and the Judicial Process—Should it Change Direction?" (1995) 9 *AJFL* 26 at 34–36.

[61] (1995) 20 Fam. LR 137.

[62] *Id.*, at 141.

[63] See also *In the Marriage of Mirando* (1997) 21 Fam.LR 841; *In the Marriage of Kennon* (1997) 21 Fam.LR 1.

[64] J. Behrens, "Violence in the Home and Family Law: An Update" (1995) 9 *AJFL* 70 at 72–3; J. Behrens, "Ending the Silence, But . . . " (1996) 10 *AJFL* 35 at 45.

behaviour within a marriage should be treated differently from, say, adultery because (a) freedom from violence is a basic human right to which all persons are entitled, whether married or not; and (b) adultery—unlike violence—has no meaning outside the definition of marriage. The inclusion of violence as a factor relevant in property division can serve both a normative and an educational function in the elimination of violence.

CONCLUSION

This chapter has argued that, whilst the Family Court of Australia at appellate level has in recent years delivered admirable statements of principle which could have provided the impetus for a more proactive role for maintenance and property orders in redressing inequality, those statements of principle have in practice failed to produce marked changes in the pattern of subsequent case law. Legislative amendments are necessary if the private law of financial provision is to fulfil this role, and, since a new draft of a Bill to amend Part VIII of the Family Law Act 1975 (Cth) is expected, these issues require urgent debate.

Whilst the immediate priority is reform of the principles of financial provision on marriage breakdown, one may nevertheless ask whether the debate should be widened at some time in the future. Should the more proactive role for the law which this chapter advocates be confined to formal marriage or extended also to cohabitation? If the latter, should both heterosexual and homosexual relationships be included? Those who argue that the legal rules determining the consequences of marriage should be distinctive invoke on the one hand the public nature of that commitment which entry into that relationship exclusively entails, and on the other the apparent injustice of assimilating the institutional norms all family forms in a diverse society where individuals have deliberately exercised freedom of choice.[65] However, the contrary view is more persuasive.[66] The content of a legal rule should be determined by its functional context; the function of the law of financial provision is identical for all couples, whatever the status of their relationship: to redress the economic inequalities between the parties which have arisen from the relationship. Furthermore, to deny unmarried couples of whatever sexuality the protection of an adjustive financial regime afforded to their married counterparts is discriminatory and runs contrary to the support of a variety of different family forms required in a pluralist society. The same model of maintenance and property division regime should apply to all cohabitation relationships (subject to a minimum duration), whether formalised by marriage or not. Moreover, that adjustive regime should be operated in the positive way

---

[65] NSWLRC *Report on De Facto Relationships* (1993), para. 6.67; *Report of the Select Committee on Certain Aspects of the Operation and Interpretation of the Family Law Act 1975* (AGPS 1992), paras. 10.42–10.43.

[66] R. Chisholm, O. Jessep and S. O'Ryan, "De Facto Property Decisions in NSW: Emerging Patterns and Policies" (1991) 5 *AJFL* 241, 246, 266; R. Bailey-Harris, "Law and the Unmarried Couple: Oppression or Liberation?" (1996) 8 *C&FLQ* 137.

advocated in this chapter, to redress inequalities arising from de facto relationships as well as from marriage. Australian law, though in advance of some other countries, at present fall far short of this ideal, and the future task of law reform is therefore a challenging one. Even in states and territories where a full adjustive regime of financial provision has been created in recent years for relationships outside marriage (New South Wales, Victoria, the Northern Territory, the Australian Capital Territory and South Australia) the statutory model adopted to date in most cases impedes the courts from fully redressing financial inequalities resulting from the roles the parties have assumed during the relationship.[67] Entitlement to maintenance is more limited than in the case of spouses,[68] is rarely awarded or is not available at all.[69] The principles of property division in New South Wales, Victoria and the Northern Territory lack a "prospective component" on the face of the statute,[70] an omission not remedied by the bold interpretation made by some judges of "just and equitable" to include consideration of disappointed expectation and reliance interests.[71] Nor has the express inclusion of violence within a de facto relationship as a factor relevant to assesment of the parties' contributions or needs to date even been canvassed. The question of a half-shares strating point in property division has received scant attention.[72] Problematical as it may seem in the current political climate in Australia, and notwithstanding the practical difficulties inevitably caused by the existence of different regimes in the various States and Territories, debate on the principles of financial adjustment between de facto partners deserves, in the interests of equality, to be reopened.

[67] R. Bailey-Harris, "Financial Rights in Relationships outside Marriage: A Decade of Reforms in Australia" (1995) 9 *Int. J of Law and the Family* 233 at 240–53.

[68] De Facto Relationships Act 1984 (NSW), ss. 27, 30; De Facto Relationships Act 1991 (NT), ss. 26, 30 ; Domestic Relationships Act 1994 (ACT), ss. 19, 22. See also Maintenance Act 1967 (Tas.), s. 16.

[69] The legislation in Victoria and South Australia provides only for property division.

[70] De Facto Relationships Act 1984 (NSW), s. 20; Law of Property Act 1985 (Vic.), s. 285; De Facto Relationships Act (NT), s. 18. By contrast the Domestic Relationships Act 1994 (ACT) makes express reference to prospective factors (s. 15(1)(d)), and the De Facto Relationships Act 1996 (SA) adds "other relevant matters" without specifying what they are.

[71] See e.g. *Dwyer* v. *Kaljo* (1992) 15 Fam. LR 645; *Parker* v. *Parker* (1993) 16 Fam. LR 863; *Kemp* v. *King* (1995) 20 Fam. LR 265; but cf. *Green* v. *Robinson* (1995) 18 Fam. LR 594; *Wallace* v. *Stanford* (1995) 19 Fam. LR 430.

[72] R. Bailey-Harris, "Property Disputes in De Facto Relationships" in Cope (ed.), *Equity: Issues and Trends* (Federation Press, 1995), 181 at 200–12.

16

The Law and Morality of Support in the Wider Family in Germany and Tanzania: Changing Perceptions of Family Forms

CHRIS JONES-PAULY

INTRODUCTION

In an unreported Tanzanian suit Zainabu Maulidi, a Muslim woman, brought an action against her two cousins, Jumanne Rashidi and Mhando Rashidi, each over 60 years of age.[1] The two elderly men had been born in and lived all their lives in the family home which Zainabu had inherited, along with other houses, from her father. She petitioned the courts for eviction of the two elderly men from the family home so that she and her daughter could enjoy exclusive use of the premises. She also said—without specifying the nature of the conflicts—that her cousins had become quarrelsome and made life for her and her daughter unbearable. The trial magistrate's court denied her petition on the ground that eviction of her close relatives who had no other place to go would be unfair. Zainabu appealed to the High Court, which reversed the decision on the ground that the learned magistrate was presiding over a court of law and not of morals. The Court gave Zainabu the right to possess the house without restraint.

This case can, in my opinion, be analysed as a kind of "norm claim", that has to do with how the law is to handle the morality of expectations of relatives when they seem to compete with the bundle of legal rights assigned to the nuclear "conjugal" family.[2] In other words, marriage creates legally relevant material obligations between the contracting parties and their first generation of offspring that can continue long beyond the life of the marriage itself.[3] The relatives

---

[1] Civil Appeal 31/1987, High Court of Tanzania at Dar es Salaam; Civil Application 12/1991, Court of Appeal of Tanzania.

[2] John Griffiths, "The General Theory of Litigation—a First Step", 5 (2) *Zeitschrift für Rechtssoziologie* (1983), 145–201, 164.

[3] S. M. Cretney et al., *Principles of Family Law* (6th edn., London, Butterworths, 1997), especially 425; (the impossibility at common law for a couple to contract out of the husband's obligation to support his wife); 439 (obligation of husband's second wife or cohabitant to work). The Tanzanian

outside this core "conjugal" family remain—in contrast to divorced partners—related to one another for life, but have material and moral claims that the law does not always regard as so morally pressing as to enforce.[4] The law has to decide whether to make their claims subordinate to, or equal to, those of the nuclear family.

THE LEGAL CHOICE DEBATE: INDIVIDUALISM VS SOLIDARITY

How the law makes its choices depends on a larger debate that gets put in terms of individualism versus solidarity, and solidarity can mean either solidarity among the extended family, or the larger societal solidarity.[5] For some there is no question of choice. The societal forces have so "evolved" that we are too advanced into the age of individualism to talk of solidarity. The popular press in Europe for the young educated élite blares out boldly that our way of life is individualistic, and that means each takes her/his own life in hand, that we live in the postmodern society where the ego stands at the centre. Each wants to have her/his own money, liberties, and experiences. The motto is "I" instead of "We".[6]

Law of Marriage Act, No. 5 of 1971, makes such maintaintenance incumbent on the man as a matter of principle and on the woman only in case of incapacity of the man (s. 63), and allows a court to order post-divorce maintenance only for special reasons (s. 115, proviso and (2)).

[4] Tanzanian Disabled Persons (Care and Maintenance) Act No.3 of 1982 provides in s. 14(1) that *all relatives* of a disabled person shall be obliged all together to provide maintenance according to their means. "Relative" means lineal ascendants (parents) or descendants (children) and any persons required under custom to take care of the disabled, and "disabled" includes elderly persons who cannot take care of themselves due to old age (s. 2). The problem of elderly persons not being maintained can vary from region to region. For example, where there are permanent crops grown, e.g. coffee and bananas, the old persons can survive for themselves without arduous cultivation, but where annual crops dominate, as in Tabora, the elderly have problems surviving because the cultivating is too strenuous for them (Interview with Resident Magistrate, Tabora, Sept. 1996). Old parents have been known to complain officially to Welfare Officers about relatives not looking after their "welfare", but do not appear to be prepared to go to court about the matter (Interview, Regional Welfare Officer, Songea, Aug. 1996). See C. Jones, "Menschenrechte und Landfrauen in Tansania" [Human Rights and Rural Women in Tanzania], 1 *Frauen in der einen Welt*, 1995, 86–99 on an elderly woman who came into conflict with her nephew for having sold clan land and used the proceeds to maintain herself. See also B. A. Rwezaura, "Changing Community Obligations to the Elderly in Contemporary Africa", in John E. Eekelaar, *et al.*, *An Aging World. Dilemmas and Challenges for Law and Social Policy* (Oxford, Clarendon Press, 1989), 113–31, n. 15. Moroccan law goes even further and punishes children who are negligent towards any of their ascendant relatives (parents to great-great grandparents) (Zkik Said, *La Répresssion de l'Abandon de Familie en droit marocain* (Rabat, Arabian Al Hilal, 1994), 7).

[5] E.g. in Sweden, where the Government appears to regard each as an individual and bases solidarity not on smaller units of extended families, but requires contributions from each and every to a collective pot made available to all in the society (Anders Agell, University of Uppsala, Lecture on Swedish Law, Third Regensburger Symposium for European Family Law, 24–26 Oct. 1997, Regensburg, Germany, to appear in *Beiträge zum europäischen Familienrecht* (Bielefeld, Gieseking Verlag).

[6] UNICUM, *Das Hochschulmagazin* [University Magazine], Mar. 1996, Ich statt wir, on the book by U. Beck *et al.*, "Eigenes Leben" [Your Own Life] (München, Beck Verlag, 1995), 28. See also H. Marcuse, *Ideen zu einer kritischen Theorie der Gesellschaft* [On a Critical Theory of Society] (Frankfurt a. M., Suhrkamp, 1969).

Concentrating on the "I" means to emphasise one's bodily uniqueness. For that one needs money to improve one's outward appearance, not necessarily for raising one's prestige by supporting other relatives.[7] The scholarly literature also harmonises with the tune of individualism and observes the same forces of "evolution" affecting African societies.[8]

Contrapuntally there are voices in favour of effecting family solidarity.[9] Some socio-psychoanalytical studies have recognised that individualism is leading to feelings of loneliness and the realisation that industrial society is so interdependent that going it alone is no longer possible.[10] But the ideal solidarity is not in the form of a deformed parasitic relationship among individuals,[11] meaning, some have to play the role of the powerful educated master and others the role of the weak small ignorant servant.[12] Family solidarity in this sense is not a revival of the original meaning of the ancient Roman *familia*, the collection of servants, spouse(s), children plus other relatives all under the authority of the family head.[13] Nonetheless, the notion of non-parasitic solidarity still reserves a place for individualism, for the individual retains the freedom to make decisions on an equal basis with the other family members. The sociologists, however, are showing that the material basis of the highly touted freedom and mobility of individuals in European society is financial solidarity among the extended family (primarily among lineal relations, but also inclusive of collateral relations).[14] In some instances this allows parents to limit the exercise of individual decision-making,[15] in other instances it enables the individual to widen choices. It has been established in a study of over 2,200 young persons recently that

[7] UNICUM, "Männer glauben Geld allein mache sexy . . . Wolfgang Joop über Parfum, Perfektion und Persönlichkeit" [Men think money alone makes one's sexy . . . Wolfgang Joop on perfume, perfection and personality], Mar. 1996, 20.

[8] Diane Kayongo-Male *et al.*, *Sociology of the African Family* (London, etc., Longman, 1984, Third Impression 1991), ch. 3; B. A. Rwezaura, "The Changing Role of the Extended Family in Africa", in M. T. Meulders-Klein *et al.*, *Famille, Etat et Sécurité Economique d' Existence*, Vol. I— *Famille* (Brussels, E. Story-Scientia, 1988), 167–85.

[9] Example from the popular press: "Wir können von Afrika noch lernen. Von den Werten in der zivilisierten Welt und der Dritten Welt" [We can still learn from Africa. On Values in the civilized [sic] World and the Third World], *Die Welt*, 29 Dec. 1995 (Pressespiegel 1/1995, 7).

[10] Horst E. Richter, *Lernziel Solidarität* [Learning Solidarity] (Hamburg, Rowolt, 1974), 69.

[11] Richter, 29.

[12] *Ibid.*, 18.

[13] Michael P. Einbinder, "Comments: The Legal Family—A Definitial Analysis", 13 *Journal of Family Law* (1973–4), 781–801, 781.

[14] Laszlo A. Vaskovics *et al.*, *Familienabhängigkeit junger Erwachsener und ihre sozialen Folgen* [Social consequences of family dependence of younger adults] (Forschungsforum der Otto-Friedrich-Universität Bamberg, Heft 3, 1991, 87–91); "Innerfamiliäre Transferbeziehungen zwischen den Generationen" [Inter-familial transfer relations between the generations], in Rainer Silberstein *et al.*, *Jungsein in Deutschland. Jugendliche und junge Erwachsene 1991 und 1996* [Being young in Germany. Youth and young adults in 1991 and 1996] (Opladen, Leske and Budrich, 1996), 317–29.

[15] E.g. in Austria and Germany, where the law allows the parents to determine to which university their child goes if they are paying for the fees, but Austrian law does give more chance to the child to contest the parents' decision (Susanne Ferrari, University of Graz, Austria, Lecture on Austrian Law, Third Regensburger Symposium for European Family Law, 24–26 Oct. 1997). In the Vaskovics Study, 50% of 29 year olds felt that their parents intervene too much in their life (Vaskovics, DFG Forschungsbericht 2, Intergenerative Transferbzeihungen, Sept. 1994, 40).

characteristic of post-modern society is the fact that 75 per cent of all adult persons between 18 and 28 years of age receive help of some kind from parents.[16] Almost half of them (48 per cent) are totally dependent (i.e. what they earn is below the poverty line) on parental support (59 per cent for the age group 18–21; 46 per cent for 22–24-year-olds; and 41 per cent for the years 26–28). The marriage rate is 16 per cent. About half live with their parents. Multiple institutional features account for this trend: longer educational and qualifying times, military conscription, growing number of single-parent households, difficulties getting a life-long job, and unemployment plus more time needed to requalify at one's own expense when made redundant. The support given is material (i.e. monetary) or non-material (e.g., washing clothes, cooking, doing repairs, shopping, cleaning up, taking care of grandchildren). This phenomenon of dependency means that parents are faced with an ever lengthening pressure to give support to their children and eventually to turn to their own ascendant and collateral relatives for a supplementary support network.[17] The greater the unemployment, the greater the readiness of the ascendant family to help. Almost 25 per cent of the parents were found to be living dangerously near the poverty line because of supporting their adult children. When less well off parents have several children seeking educational qualifications at the same time, the older young adults tended to forego higher education in order to help finance their younger siblings. Even among the well-to-do, when the adult young person is financially independent, 9 per cent of the parents still give help. While such arrangements do not correspond to the modernist values of individualism, they are normal in post-modern societies.[18] In German society only a minority of all adults (42 per cent) are able to live solely from their own wage earnings.[19] The results of the large German study do not deviate much from those of a small informal survey that I conducted among pre-university adult high schoolers in southern Tanzania with ages ranging from 18 to 34 (the vast majority being between 19 and 23). They were dependent on family help for fees, transport and personal costs, with mother and father as the leading source, then brothers and sisters, and finally mothers and brothers.[20]

---

[16] Vaskovics, 1991; Silberstein, 1996.

[17] The study mentions a network covering two or more generations (Vaskovics, DFG Forschungsbreicht. Intergenerative Transferbeziehungen in der Familie: Problemstellung und theoretische Konzeption der Studie, Arbeitsbericht I, Sept. 1994), 5). Unfortunately, the study did not include expressly an investigation of help from grandparents and aunts/uncles, for these persons are well known to play an important role in our daily life in Germany, especially in semi-rural areas (Observations of the author; for the 1980s see Margret Dieck, "Long-Term Care for the Elderly in the Federal Republic of Germany", in Teresa Schwab (ed.), *Caring for an Aging World* (New York, etc., McGraw-Hill, 1989), 96–161, 142–3).

[18] Charlotte Höhn *et al.*, "The Changing Family in the Federal Republic of Germany", 9 *Journal of Family Issues*, Sept. 1988, 317–35, 334, differentiating between modern and post-modern.

[19] "Einkommensquelle" [Sources of income], *Göttinger Tageblatt*, 1/10/1996, 6.

[20] Informal survey (74 participants coming from Iringa, Mbeya, and Songea), Songea, Tanzania, Sept. 1996 and May 1997.

All in all, help from ascendant or collateral kin over two or more generations is given beyond the call of duty.[21] The readiness to help confirms the extended family as a source of help that has always functioned despite the culture of individualism. It is there to call upon whether need arises or not. The motives are surely mixed—a sense of a moral obligation together with self-interest to secure inheritance or to facilitate socio-ritual gatherings (communion, birthdays, etc.). Recent attention to this from sociologists[22] has given rise to cautions against the ideologisation of family typology. There is a re-examination of the "myth" that urbanisation and industrialisation destroy the extended family.[23] There is the critique that the extended family as "typically" African is a creation of European evolutionary ideology that typifies the European family form as "conjugal" and places it at the apex of an evolutionary societal pyramid, ignoring the factual and historical diversity in family forms and relationships.[24] The attention being given since the late 1980s to the extended family may, however, be a function of individualism, that is, as more adult children dare to assert themselves as individuals—individuality encompassing the equal right to be heard—and exercise their rights to challenge authority figures by bringing their parents to court (in the case of Germany) or state authorites (as in the case of Tanzania[25]) to demand support for financing professional requalification, the state is pressed to decide whether the moral contours of kin support should be extended or ignored or even restricted.

LEGAL SITUATION

Just as there is no consensus on whether the dominant value of our times is individualism or solidarity, and whether solidarity should come from the extended (close[26] or distant) family or society at large, the law is also wrought with controversies. This part deals with the relevant case law in Germany and Tanzania in a comparative study on how the law treats extended family support.

[21] See FamRZ, 1997, 675 (OLG Hamm, 1 May 1996) on an 83-year-old married lady alienating her property to her nephew so as to keep it out of the hands of her drunkard husband.

[22] For Germany: Vaskovics, 1991, *op.cit.*; Silberstein, 1996, *op. cit.*

[23] For Great Britain: *Janet Finch, Family Obligations and Social Change* (Cambridge, Polity Press, 1989), 85.

[24] For Africa: Eliso Macamo, *The Study of the African Family in Western Social Science*, Master's Thesis (unpublished), Polytechnic of North London, Faculty of Environmental and Social Studies, Oct. 1991, 23–4, 29. Cf. a colonial description of differing family practices in East Africa as "deviations"—due to personality of clan head—and not part of diverse patterns (Bernhard Ankermann, "Ostafrika" [East Africa] (*Das Eingeborenenrecht* [Native Law], ed. Erich Schultz-Ewerth, Stuttgart, Strecker u. Schröder, 1929), 60).

[25] Interview with Welfare Officers, Tabora and Songea Districts, Tanzania, Aug. and Sept. 1996, on a few cases of children complaining about their parents not paying school fees. The problem was resolved by compromise. The schools agreed to accept in lieu of money a bag pro year of the parents' harvested maize.

[26] I.e., collateral first degree and lineal first and second degree.

Germany

The law divides maintenance basically into two categories: (1) covering the running costs of living together, and (2) covering the costs of a specific person. Those falling in the first category are entitled to unconditional support. They include a minor child of direct descendent who cannot work to earn her/his own living and a married adult who does not wish to earn her/his own living, e.g. a spouse. In the second category fall adults or near-adults who qualify as "relatives", people who could establish their own homestead by virtue of age or being married. Support for them is subject to various conditions, and therefore more controversial.

It is only the lineally extended family that is of key relevance to the German law (deriving from the received Roman law). For only kin who are related lineally are obliged to support one another, that is, parents, children, and grandparents and grandchildren to the nth degree are required to support one another.[27] The duty is enforceable under two conditions: (1) if the kinsman or -woman is in need and unable to maintain him/herself; and (2) if the relative giving the support is not thereby at risk of falling into need her/himself. If for example, the parents have only enough for themselves and nothing for their children, then the grandparents have to help.[28] The law in this case corresponds to sociological reality, which is that not only in cases of necessity, but even where financial difficulties arise, 50 per cent of families expect help from parents, especially those of the wife.[29] A short word on in-laws: each adult child is responsible for her/his own parent, not the in-law parent, unless of course the adult children live in community of property, which would carry the costs of support for ascending or descending in-laws.[30]

What is of interest is the hierarchisation of the lineal relatives who are obliged to help, correlating with the hierarchy of inheritance (the children [and spouse if any] exclude other relatives). First in the line of duty are the adult children, then the grandparents, next the great-grandparents and so on up the line. This is in contrast with what is implied in the Tanzanian Act,[31] which obliges all relatives

---

[27] S. 1601 German Civil Code (BGB). This is in contrast to the Swiss law which until recently made brothers and sisters responsible for supporting one another (Dokumentation: 3. *Regensburger Symposium für Europäisches Familienrecht: Unterhaltspflicht unter Verwandten im europäischen Vergleich* [Report on the Third Regensburger Symposium on Family Law: Maintenance for Relatives— European Comparisons, 24–26 Oct. 1996, FamRZ, 1996, 1529–30).

[28] S. 1603(2) of the German Civil Code (BGB).

[29] Gerhard Richter, "Rechtspolitische Erwägungen zur Reform des Unterhaltsrechts nach S. 1601 ff. BGB" [Legal-Political Considerations for Reforming Maintenance Laws in S. 1601 ff of the Civil Code], FamRZ, 1996, 1245–50, 1246.

[30] Joachim Gernhuber, "Die Schwägerschaft als Quelle gesetzlicher Unterhaltspflichten. Zugleich ein Beitrag zum allgemeinen Eherecht und zum Ehegüterrecht" [In-Laws Obliged to Give Support and on the Law of Marriage and Community Property in General], FamRZ 1955, 193–200; Gernhuber *et al.*, *Lehrbuch des Familienrechts* [Textbook on Family Law] (4th edn., München, C. H. Beck'sche, 1994), s. 45 III, 672–3.

[31] Disabled Persons (Care and Maintenance) Act No. 3/1982, s. 14(1) that requires every relative to help according to her/his means.

simultaneously to make what contributions they can to support ageing relatives too feeble to support themselves. Even my informal survey of high schoolers in southern Tanzania indicates that when the parents cannot meet all necessary costs, then relatives pool what resources they can, so that there is in effect a proportional sharing of obligations. This simultaneous obligation has been deemed by some in Germany incompatible with the notion of the German family,[32] while other jurists have demonstrated that reality is not represented by the isolated nuclear family but by a supporting network of relatives and godparents.[33] The only sharing foreseen in the German law is when there are, for example, two pairs of grandparents obliged to support, when the duty to support would be split between them.[34]

There is also a set hierarchy of relatives entitled to support in case the relative obliged to give support has a small income: first the minor unmarried children and the spouse (who are on the same footing[35]), then minor married children and adult children, then the divorced spouse, the cohabiting mother (of the child born out of marriage), then the grandchildren, the parents, grandparents, great-grandparents, etc. In reality, well-off self-sufficient adult children tend to fulfil simultaneously two duties towards relatives: the educational costs of adult children and the old-age home costs of elderly parents, known as the "sandwich" generation. There does not at the moment appear to be much sympathy for this generation.[36]

Collateral relatives such as brothers and sisters are cut out of the maintenance scheme either as needy recipients or as persons potentially responsible for maintaining their minor nieces and nephews. They belong to that group of relatives whom one is morally—not legally—obliged to help. This seems to be a carry-over of the early Prussian code which had required siblings of the first decree to give at least emergency support for siblings who were totally unable to take care of themselves.[37] In contemporary legal practice, however, they can be important indirectly for purposes of support. For example, if the putative father of a child has died before the establishment of the paternity, the brother of the deceased can be ordered to take a blood test to help establish the paternity of the child.[38]

---

[32] Gernhuber *et al.*, *Lehrbuch des Familienrechts* (1994), *op. cit.*, s. 45 V, 679.

[33] Richter, FamRZ 1996, *op. cit.*, 1246. My experience confirms this. For example, when the uninsured house of a relative burned down, several members of the extended family responded to a written request for contributions of help proportional to their resources.

[34] S. 1606(3) of the Civil Code (BGB).

[35] This position is being doubted as morally doubtful by some family court judges, who believe that due to the vulnerability of minors, they should have priority—when the resources are limited—over a spouse who as an adult can work (Interviews, Sept. 1997).

[36] Richter, FamRZ, 1996, *op. cit.*, 1249; FamRZ, 1996, 1494 (LG Osnabrück, 20 Mar. 1996), in which the adult son had to pay for the old-age costs of his mother and could not argue that he would not be able to then buy as many new clothes and go to as many cultural activities as before.

[37] *Allgemeines Gesetzbuch für die preussischen Staaten* [General Code for Prussian States] (Berlin, 1791, Nachdruck, Frankfurt a.M., Keip Verlag, 1985), Vol. II/3, Second Part, Third Chapter on Rights and Duties of the Other Family Members, s. 15.

[38] Interview, Oct. 1996, Gutachterin (Expert) of the Institut für Rechtsmedizin, University of Göttingen, Germany.

And if the deceased be established as the father, then the grandparents are liable for the maintenance. Collateral relatives, such as a niece or nephew can also be of help when an aunt, for example, wishes to prevent property falling into the hands of her drunkard husband.[39]

One of the more controversial areas of turning a moral expectation into a legal obligation relates to grandparents. There is a controversial discussion going on about whether a grandparent can be held to make contributions to the upkeep of a grandchild when the mother of the child is on social welfare. The courts have up to now normally decided that moral expectations that grandparents should support grandchildren can be transformed into obligations under certain conditions. For example, if the grandmother allows the child to live in her house along with the mother and the grandmother can still live quite comfortably, then she should be obliged to help.[40] The same has applied to step-fathers (or mothers).[41] There is no clear consensus on the extent to which equity allows the law to enforce the moral expectations on the contemporary grandparent generation.[42] On one hand, courts have held grandparents liable for advancing court costs in a maintenance suit brought by a minor child when the adult mother and her child live with the grandparents.[43] On the other hand, courts have refused even to have parents advance court costs for an adult child who is still a student dependent on the parents and not yet earning her/his own money.[44]

Adult daughters who have children without being married are also cause for discussion. Demographical studies show that most women in Germany, unlike in France,[45] believe that they are morally expected to refrain from working in order to take care of their children during the first three years of the child's life.[46] This means that someone has to take care of mother and child. The law makes the father of the child primarily responsible for maintaining mother and child for three years.[47] His obligation to her and their child takes precedence over the

---

[39] As in the case of FamRZ, 1997, 675 (OGL Hamm, 31 May 1996), where an 83-year-old with a property other than the house in which she and her husband lived, alienated the property to her nephew reserving for herself the right of usufruct, because she feared that her drunkard husband would eventually squander the property.

[40] NJW 1996, 2880 (BVerwG, 29 Feb. 1996); Richter, FamRZ 1996, *op. cit.*; Gerd Brudermüller, "Solidarität und Subsidiarität im Verwandten Unterhalt—Überlegungen aus rechtsethischer Sicht" [Solidarity and Support in Maintenance of Relatives—Ethical/Legal Considerations], FamRZ 1996, 129–35, 129 on the social welfare law that exempts grandparents from repayment to the Welfare Office for welfare payments to relatives.

[41] NJW 1960, 1267 (BVerwG, 10 Jan. 1960).

[42] Brudermüller, FamRZ 1997, *op. cit.*, 134 on proposals to end the ascendant obligations.

[43] FamRZ 1997, 681 (OLG Koblenz, 9 Sept. 1996).

[44] FamRZ 1997, 694 (KG, Berlin).

[45] Frédérique Ferrand (University of Lyon), Lecture on French law, Third Regensburger Symposium on European Family Law, 24–26 Oct. 1996, to appear in *Beiträge zum europäischen Familienrecht* (Bielefeld, Gieseking Verlag).

[46] Arbeitsstelle für Frauenseelsorge der Deutschen Bischofskonferenz, Frauen und Kirche. Anmerkungen zu einer Allensbacher Repräsentativuntersuchung [German Bishops Conference, Women and Church, Remarks on the Allensbacher Representative Study], Düsseldorf, 1994.

[47] Civil Code (BGB), s. 1615 l (2).

obligation to help ageing needy parents. But, if he is married, and cannot meet all the costs, his primary duty is to all of his children within and without the marriage, and then to his spouse, leaving the unmarried mother of his child to turn to her relatives. Some parents object that they should be expected to support their daughter, especially if she has interrupted her studies, for which they were paying, because of pregnancy. It could be argued that the daughter is the cause of her own dependency.[48] Still, several courts have decided that the parents have to accept the more compelling moral expectation that a mother shall be able to choose not to work in the early years of her child's life. But such support of the mother should not last beyond 18 months after the birth.[49] It is hoped that the recent extension of the father's obligation to maintain the mother of his child from one to three years will relieve somewhat the parents. Again, the courts allow themselves flexibility in terms of legally enforcing a moral expectation, in this case, of mothers of very young children. In this process it has also expanded the circumstances in which a family member unable to earn a living is entitled to assistance from other relatives. Another category of adult children which sometimes has to rely on parents is the adult divorced daughter or son who has custody of the children and therefore needs to keep the family house. In the case of newly built houses or restored old inherited houses, there is a often a lifetime mortgage that still has to be paid after divorce. If the departing partner now has to support a second spouse and all the children involved and cannot keep up mortgage payments, the house may have to be sold. In order not to disrupt the life of their grandchildren, the grandparents may buy the house.[50]

It is precisely this expansion of what is an acceptable cause of inability to stand on one's own that now bedevils the courts in several support suits brought by unemployed adults and students who, believing that if they take both a vocational and an academic qualification their chances for finding employment are better, undergo longer qualifying periods than the post-war generation.[51]

The kind of support that the German law requires an adult lineal relative(s) to give to another adult relative should be in a material form, i.e. money, and be at least sufficient for subsistence.[52] Only exceptionally can the relative be

---

[48] S. 1611 of the Civil Code (BGB) relieves relatives of support if the needy relative has become dependent because of her/his own immorality (e.g. criminal activity or severing ties with the family); Cf. Dieter Schwab, "Familiäre Solidarität" [Family Solidarity], FamRZ 1997, 521–8, 526; FamRZ, 1995, 475 (BGH 25 Jan. 1995), where the divorced father was chastised for not having the moral right under s. 1611 to condemn his daughter's coolness towards him when he himself had not even congratulated her on her 18th birthday.

[49] Gernhuber *et al.*, Lehrbuch (1994), *op. cit.*, s. 45 II. 3, 669; FamRZ 1996, 1493–4 (OLG Hamm, 5 Mar. 1996—3 UF 319/95).

[50] While published cases contain orders to have the matrimonial home sold, the fate of the house afterwards and the involvement of the parents is hard to trace. The parents are taking over the mortgage in the divorces of two of my neighbours.

[51] Interview in Hameln, Germany, Dec. 1996, with two wage-earning household servants, each 60 years old, who had started working at the age of 14, and whose adult children finished pre-university school at age 21, but now at ages 30 and 35 have only part-time jobs.

[52] S. 1612(1) of the Civil Code (BGB).

required to give support in a non-material form.[53] Recognising the social reality that the length of compulsory education plus professional qualifying time stretches long into adulthood, the law obliges relatives to pay for the costs of an appropriate education.[54] If it is the parents who are financing the education, then they have a choice, either to give the adult child money or board and lodging at home free of charge.[55] Grandparents can only give money. Most families willingly support their adult children as the recent studies on dependency mentioned above show. The majority of young adults up to 30 years of age receive material and non-material support from their parents, including the 9 per cent who do not even need help. Cases demonstrating the types of conflicts arising out of this obligation abound. The reasons for the conflicts are many: for example, more awareness of the human right of children to develop a personality independent of parents' expectations, a rapidly changing market that leads young adults to changes of direction, the rise in divorce or dissolution of partnerships, and cases where a parent, dissatisfied with custody or visiting arrangements, threatens to reduce payments.[56] The courts are asked to solve the question of what is an "appropriate" amount and duration of support demanded by the law. Should a second qualification be financed because it is more likely to insure a job (e.g. in eastern Germany, where the former GDR qualifications are no longer recognised[57])? Is it worth supporting further studies because of a past record of failing exams? Should the parents' decision to offer board and lodging be conclusive? The courts are not unanimous in their answers to these difficult questions. Some are strictly of the view that the person who holds the purse strings also calls the tune, and adult children refusing to stay home go empty-handed.[58] The value upheld there is the individualism of the parents who want to assert control over their own resources over the individualism of the adult child who wants to follow her/his interests. Other courts hold the adult child responsible for making decisions independently. As one court noted, an adult child has to take responsibility for making the decision which qualification to take and not follow a particular course of study just to satisfy the wishes of the parents.[59] Other courts

[53] This applies to the urban majority. For rural families working on family farms that cannot be divided up it is different. The adult daughter or son who takes over the farm has to allow the ageing parent to stay in the farmhouse and fulfill various immaterial obligations. See C. Jones, "Menschenrechte für tansanische Landfrauen" [Human Rights for Tanzanian Rural Women], 1 *Frauen in der einen Welt*, 1995, 86–99, 98.

[54] S. 1610(2) of the Civil Code (BGB).

[55] S. 1612(2) of the Civil Code (BGB).

[56] FamRZ 1995, 475 (BGH 25 Jan. 1995); FamRZ, 1995, 957 (OLG Düsseldorf).

[57] Gregor C. Biletzki, "Der Anspruch auf Finanzierung einer weiteren Ausbildung nach ss. 1601, 1610 II BGB" [The Right to Having a Second Professional Qualification Financed under ss. 1601, 1610 II of the Civil Code], FamRZ, 1996, 777–81, 778.

[58] Stephan Buchholz, "Zum Unterhaltsbestimmungsrecht der Eltern gegenübner volljährigen Kindern nach s. 1612 II BGB" [The Right of Decision of Parents in Matters of Support under s. 1612 II of the Civil Code], FamRZ 1995, 706–13, 708; Heinz Schroers, "Zum 'Recht' auf Ausbildungsunterhalt eines volljährigen Kindes durch Naturalunterhalt" [On the "Right" of the Adult Child to Immaterial Support Regarding Educational Costs], *Der deutsche Rechtspfleger* 1996, 271–5.

[59] FamRZ 1997, 694 (OLG Frankfurt/M., 4 Oct. 1996).

seek a compromise between the economic interests of the parents and the right of the child to determine her/his life-style so that neither dominates the relationship.[60] As one court noted, the Civil Code obliges adult children and parents to be considerate to one another.[61] The case involved the refusal of the divorced father of the adult daughter, who was not living with him or the mother and who had poor results in earlier educational attempts, to help finance her further education. The court appealed to tolerance and compromise: " . . . when the parents' relationship remains intact, they are often generous in striving to help their children get qualified and are prepared to accept temporary set-backs and mistakes in choosing what suits them. Divorce shouldn't make any difference."[62] This is a particularly good example of the law balancing solidarity and individualism by applying the moral expectations of tolerance and patience treating individualism not as matter of one's right excluding another's right, but as a matter of each articulating their rights and interests, but then finding what the parties have in common, namely, as in the case of the duty to pay educational costs, a well-educated adult earning a decent living.[63]

The phenomenon of the law recognising the family as a network of relatives co-operating to help the weaker members to obtain an education or raise the child of an unmarried daughter pales somewhat when the worlds of business and family overlap. Family debts involve difficult questions of morality and fairness. In one case[64] the question was whether an adult son should be held liable for his pledge to act as surety for a loan to the family business managed by the father. The father had taken on an investment credit of over a million Marks for the family business. At the time he was paying for the university education of his 25-year-old son who was studying engineering. The son, along with his other three brothers, was expected to join the family business and to enjoy a good income shortly after joining. The bank making the loan to the father's business accepted the son—with his brothers—as surety on the basis of his potential earning capability. Two years later the business went bankrupt. The bank made the sons liable for repayment of the loan. The student son contested, arguing that it was immoral of the bank to have accepted him as surety, given that he had no large income at the time he gave his pledge and no business experience, and that the immorality of this action nullified his pledge of surety. The appellate court agreed with him. Even if there was no evidence of the father pressuring his student son to sign as surety, one cannot expect young inexperienced adults who are dependent financially and emotionally on their parents to make an objective

---

[60] Buchholz, FamRZ, 1995, *op. cit.*, 709.

[61] S. 1618a (BGB).

[62] FamRZ 1997, 694–6 (OLG Hamm, 4 Jan. 1996).

[63] Sweden, however, has decided not to mix financial concerns and moral concerns in personal relationships. Families are not responsible for educating their adult children. The larger society provides for loans which the adult child can decide to take out to finance professional education (Anders Agell, University of Uppsala, Third Regensburger Symposium on European Family Law, 24–26 Oct. 1996, *op. cit.*).

[64] FamRZ 1997, 153–6 (BGH).

independent assessment of the father's ability to keep the business flourishing. In other words the banks should rely only on family persons for surety who at the time are in fact independent, that is, on a par with the family member who wishes to charge the family network with a financial burden, and should not rely on the future potential of those supported by the family network. Here the courts are applying a principle that has been well appreciated in an African context, where a court disallowed a creditor's claim against family members whose family property had been pledged by the family head.[65]

To summarise this section of the chapter, the widespread sociological phenomenon of dependent adults has given rise to German law recognising the family as a network that has to co-operate and be considerate of one another as individuals acting in solidarity in order to help weaker members to become independent who in turn are to help other weaker members. The law of support has not been interpreted restrictively. It has been broadened by making the wider moral expectations of family members legally enforceable. In the law of debts under certain circumstances, however, it remains restrictive.[66]

Tanzania

In Tanzania there are two main statutes regulating family support: the Marriage Act and the Disabled Persons Act. The Law of Marriage Act[67] regulates maintenance relating essentially to the nuclear conjugal family: the partners and the children. The provisions in section 116, however, allow the courts to look beyond the core family. The amount of the maintenance, if awarded at all, is conditioned on the means and needs of the parties and the courts may take into account the custom practised by the community (communities) of the spouses. This could mean that if the woman's community is accustomed to accepting her back in her father's homestead, where she will be taken care of, then she can expect less or no alimony from her partner. If a particular Muslim community is accustomed to practising sunnah injunctions,[68] it could be that either partner receives support from lineal relatives obliged to help under Islamic injunctions. Such amounts would be taken into account. Thus there is no fixed statutory hierarchisation of who is obliged to support and who receives support. This correlates with the non-hierachised inheritance systems to which most people are accus-

---

[65] *Kasumu Aralawon* v. *Yesufu O. Aromire and Elo Aiyedun*, 15 Nigeria Law Reports 90 (1940).

[66] S. 31 of the Konkursgesetz [Bankruptcy Act] allows the creditors to get at assets that the insolvent has alienated to close in-laws or relatives in the lineal or collateral line. See Michael App, " 'Nahestehende Personen' im Sinne des neuen Insolvenzrechts und ihre Stellung im neuen Insolvenzrecht und Gläubigeranfectungsrecht", FamRZ 1996, 1523–5.

[67] Act No. 5 of 1971.

[68] Some maintenance rules are laid out in the Ministry of Justice's Statements of Islamic Law (G.N. 222 of 27 June 1967), which is hardly used. The key to the application of what is customarily practised or believed to be practised is the test of how a person leads her/his life (Judicature Act and Application of Laws Ordinance, cap. 453, s. 9).

tomed: near or distant lineal or collateral relatives are not excluded from the inheritance by the conjugal family. The law realistically reflects a network of material and non-material debts ever-changing according to the fortunes of close and distant family members. In Germany it is left up to the courts, as illustrated above, to integrate into the fixed hierarchised system of statutory law the reality of family networking.

The second major statute governing maintenance is, as already mentioned, the Disabled Persons (Care and Maintenance) Act.[69] The definition of relatives of a person unable to work because of injury or old age or disease expressly names the lineal lines of first degree (parents and child) who are obliged together to support. If they are not to be found or have died or are themselves disabled, then "any person" in the community from where the disabled comes is obliged to give support if such community customarily so requires of such persons.[70] The definition is broad enough to cover in-laws or "social" relatives[71] of whom the community has moral expectations. The local community under the auspices of the local government is in addition obliged to provide facilities of support.[72] This seems to have been an answer to the various reports of murders of older persons accused of being witches, and no relative would be expected morally to take care of a witch.[73] The statutory emphasis on children taking care of the aged parent along with the person who would customarily be obliged to give support appears to be changing the parameters of the solidarity network. The question of the exact nature and extent of a child's obligation to support the parent seems to have been subsumed up to now under questions of inheritance, rights of residence, rights to keeping part of the refunded marriage gift, usufructuary rights to land, etc. Life when schematised looks somewhat like this: each child, minor and adult, belongs to the father. The conjugal relation is a temporal interruption. While it lasts, the husband supports the wife, unless he is indisposed, in which case she supports him. If the relation terminates (or a series of consequent relations terminate), each reverts to seeking support from her/his father (often in the form of farm land allocations). Father is a broad term, a leadership term, i.e. the one to whom one goes to settle conflicts, and can include whoever succeeds to the "fathership", better expressed as "seniorship", such as an older sister,[74] brother or uncle. In such a scheme there is no direct obligation on the old

[69] Act No. 3 of 1982.

[70] S. 2, Definitions; s. 14.

[71] Peter G. Forster, "Anthropological studies of kinship in Tanzania", in Colin Creighton *et al.* (eds.), *Gender, Family and Household in Tanzania* (Aldershot, etc., Avebury, 1995), 70–117, 82.

[72] S. 16.

[73] Interview, Sept. 1996, with Welfare Officer, Tabora, on a few instances of older women and men who wander from the village to the town because they have been accused of being witches, whom no relative wants to come near. See also M. C. Mukoyogo, *Ethical, Legal, Human Rights Cases in Tanzania 1983–1994*, Dar es Salaam, unpublished research report, on superstitious beliefs, 2.

[74] P. H. Gulliver, *Neighbours and Networks: The Idiom of Kinship in Social Action amongst the Ndendeuli of Tanzania* (London, University of California Press, 1971); Jan J. Konter, *Changing Marital Relations among the Nyakyusa, Rungwe District, Tanzania*, Seminar "New Directions in African Family Law", Leiden, 30 Sept.–4 Oct. 1974, 19.

parents, especially an older father. An old father relies on his polygamous rights to obtain support from a young woman who can work his fields;[75] an old mother, if divorced or single, relies on her father;[76] if widowed, she lives with her in-laws or her children.[77] This scheme of not addressing the question of a duty to support a family member head on is compatible with the common law[78] approach which tends to regard each adult as independent with rights to autonomy (e.g. the historically infamous testamentary rights) and charity as a purely voluntary matter.

By grafting the clear obligation of children towards their parents on to the schema of marriage, divorce, custody, land and inheritance rights, in addition to the obligations of other family members, the Disabled Persons Act has introduced the element of need or financial difficulty. How the courts relate need to the functionings of the family network and how the family members themselves do so can differ, as a recent case illustrates. A widow objected to the clan decision to have the brother of her husband appointed as administrator of the estate. The brother opposed her application, arguing that her appointment would contravene custom and tradition. He would be in a better position to consider (more objectively?) all the interests of all the family survivors of the deceased. The High Court favoured the widow and gave her the responsibility of administration. It said custom had to be reconsidered. Women are just as good as men. Furthermore—perhaps, the crowning social argument—"she knows the needs of her children best".[79] It was not clear in the judgment whether the applicant widow was the only widow, or whether only her children and not those of another woman were involved.[80] Although in the case the question of needs was important for the decision, the legal problems were framed around issues of "custom", "tradition", "extended family" versus "reason", "modern human rights", "nuclear family". Presumably, the judge felt that the widow would return to the clan, direct the discussions on the distribution and eventually negotiate an agreement on the actual distribution that would meet the autonomous rights of heirs.

[75] B. A. Rwezaura, "Changing Community Obligations to the Elderly in Contemporary Africa", in John M. Eekelaar (ed.), *An Aging World. Dilemmas and Challenges for Law and Social Policy* (Oxford, Clarendon Press, 1989), 113–31, 117–18; in the 1970s divorced or widowed elderly men in Germany tended to marry younger women who could perform household tasks: see Margaret Dieck in Teresa Schwab, 1989, *op. cit.*, 136.

[76] Such as in the case of *Bernardo Ephrahim* v. *Holaria Pastory and Anor.*, Civ. App. 70/1989, High Court, Mwanza, in which an elderly woman inherited land bequeathed to her from her father.

[77] M. K. Rwebangira, *The Status of Women and Poverty in Tanzania, Socio-Economic Growth and Poverty Alleviation in Tanzania*, 14–20 May 1995 (Arusha, Dar es Salaam, SIDA), 16; typical also of Germany in the 1970s (Margaret Dieck in Teresa Schwab, 1989, *op. cit.*, 137).

[78] See William Holdsworth, *A History of English Law* (London, Methuen/Sweet and Maxwell, 1981), Vol. X, 272 ff., Vol. III, 530; John Eekelaar, *et al.*, "The Evolution of Private Law Maintenance Obligations: the Common Law", in M. T. Meulders-Klein, *et al.* (eds.), *Famille, État et Sécurité économique d'existence*, Vol., I (Bruxelles, E. Story-Scientia, 1988), 137–48.

[79] *Habibu M. Kumkana* v. *Mariam Kumkana*, High Court, Dar es Salaam, Civ. App. 33/1995.

[80] Cf. *In re Effiong Okon Ata—Abassi Okon Ekpan* v. *Chief Elijah Henshaw and anor.*, 10 Nigeria Law Reports 65 (1930), at 66: "The grounds on which the English Courts have usually preferred the widow are quite inapplicable to a system of polygamy . . . " Today the children of a widow in Europe can compete equally with the children of a concubinate widow.

Going back to the extended family for a decision on the distribution is not always an easy matter. For the most important issue in the setting of the family "council" seems to be the totality of need within the close and distant family and the prioritization of needs.[81] Discussion and oversight of the family network is directed by the person holding the "fathership" or "seniorship". Much discipline is required to take into account and hierarchise all needs. Such a process differs from German law's regulation of needs which hierarchises persons, i.e. some family member will exclude others if there are insufficient resources. Instead, the process in Tanzania involves hierarchising the needs and the potential to contribute productively. The threat from the state law that one person's needs within the family might exclude discussing and prioritizing the totality of needs may lead to panic grabbing[82] and abuse of the authority of the "fathership"/"seniorship".

Re-examining the cases involving a network of relatives in the light of the question of need can change one's perception of the competition between the nuclear and the extended form of family and between the morality of support and the right to autonomous enjoyment of property. One such case is that of Zainabu, which I cited earlier. The constellation of her circumstances is not uncommon. For example, Joha left the house which she owned and in which she had been living to the two daughters of her uterine brother, who had nine children.[83] Joha had been residing in the house with her two nieces up until she died. The two nieces continued to live in the house for the next 20 years. During this time Joha's relatives did not bother to open probate of her estate, which consisted only of the house, for it was agreed that the house would remain family property. However, when probate was finally opened, Joha's granddaughter contended that the house was no longer part of Joha's estate, since it had been bequeathed to the two nieces, and she offered evidence of a will and a deed of gift. The administrator contended on behalf of all the other children of Joha's uterine brother that the property was still part of the estate since Joha, a Muslim, could not deprive the totality of her relatives of two-thirds of her property. She could make a bequest of up to only one-third of the property. The court found the will was only a confirmation of the inter vivos gift that had been previously executed. The court sealed its arguments with the remark that even if Joha had violated the limits of bequest, it would have been immoral to deprive the two nieces of the premises. For 20 years the other relatives had acquiesced in their staying there.

[81] Stefan Arnold, "Land Tenure, Labour and Migration in Rural Tanzania. The Example of the Zahabu Family in Ngulwi Village (Usambara Mountains)", in Robert Debusmann *et al.* (eds.), *Land Law and Land Ownership in Africa* (Bayreuth, African Studies Series, 1996), 113–30, 121 and 128. See discussion on defining need in Janet Finch, 1989, *op. cit.*, 195 ff.

[82] For recent examples of "grabbing" see Mukoyogo, *op. cit.*, 10–20. "Grabbing" is not new. See judgment of a colonial District Officer on order of damages to punish the rash action (D. Connelly, District Commissioner, Bukoba, Rhodes House, Oxford, MSS.Afr. s. 1678, Judgment, 2 Mar. 1962 (estate of Felix Lugakingira), 15).

[83] *In the Matter of the Estate of the late Joha Bint Silaha and in the Matter of the Application for Letters of Administration by Ramadhani A. Kidaga*, High Court, Dar es Salaam, Probate/Admin. Cause 21/1992.

The two apparently needed the place more than the others. It was morally unfair to expel relatives who expected—unlike tenants—that their housing needs were met for life. If the court had pursued need as a legal issue and not as an unsaid premise, it would have had to take into consideration Quranic injunctions such as that the poor should also be given part of an estate and that probate administrators should perform their duty as if they had left an enfeebled (needy) family behind.[84]

In another case between two brothers the dispute involved determining whether there was a tenancy or family relationship. Mohamed had bought a house in partnership with his sister and put his brother in it and allowed him to live there free of charge "because he was his brother".[85] Then Mohamed started building another house. As he wanted money for that, he sought to sell the house where his brother lived. The parents disapproved and gave him cash. Several years later, he needed money again and wanted to raise it by selling the house where his brother stayed. The brother resisted and gave him cash. Later Mohamed tried to actually sell the house. The brother resisted, claiming that by giving cash to Mohamed, he had bought the house from him. The lower courts were of differing opinions about whether a sale had been effected. The High Court said that the one brother residing in the house had bought out his brother and now owned the house. So Mohamed could not sell it. One can infer from the opinion of one of the lower courts that it felt that the money given to Mohamed by his relatives was intended to help him out financially and not necessarily to buy out his rights in the house. For if the parents' payment to him did not entitle them to own the house, then why should the payment from the brother? The family network apparently was attempting to keep the house within the family by meeting the needs of one of its members who had met the housing needs of another member. If the court had raised the issue whether this was a dispute over the needs of the family network or a sale agreement, then it would have clarified some ambiguous points, e.g., had the brother the right to sell out the partnership rights of the sister? Had the parents an interest in the house because of monies they had given to the brother? Were the monies paid equivalent to the market value of the house? Instead the court perceived the dispute as a transaction between two autonomous individuals without taking into account whether the brother had raised an expectation that he had augmented the capital base of resources of the family network and would not unilaterally diminish it.

Keeping a house intact as a resource for a family network was the background issue of another case involving a widow and her step-daughter.[86] Habiba was an old woman living with her step-daughter. She was the second wife of the deceased and the step-daughter and her brother were the offspring of the first wife. On the advice of the local Muslim community, the lower court gave Habiba, as a widow, the right to own one of the rooms in the house and to let it for

[84] Al Nisa' (4: 8–9).
[85] *Maulidi Ally Uyaga* v. *Mohamed Uyaga*, High Court (n.p.), Civ. No. 104/1992.
[86] *Mariam Daudi* v. *Habiba Yusuf*, High Court (Dodoma), Civ. App. 62/1977.

income if she wanted, plus her Quranic share of ⅛ of the value of movables, including a sewing machine. This solution appears to have been compatible with both the rule that customarily[87] allows a widow to stay on with her husband's family and the Islamic injunctions that tolerate co-tenancy in lieu of division of the property substance.[88] The step-daughter was aggrieved and claimed that the entire house left by her father was now her own property. The High Court decided to award the widow her Quranic share of ⅛ of the entire estate and send the case back to the trial level to determine the value of the estate, implying that the award of one room in the house did not seem to square with a precise ⅛ share. Again if the court had identified the needs of the parties as a legal issue, it could have evaluated the solution of awarding an income generating room in the house and allowing the widow to create with the other heirs a joint lien on any income from the room. The result would have been that the step-daughter need not fear having to sell the house to raise monies to pay off[89] the old widow and the widow would have an ongoing source of support.

Thus, to return to the *Zainabu* case, in which the heiress wanted to evict her two old cousins, the High Court—ruling against the relatives—was thinking in terms of the legal apportionment of autonomous shares. The District Court—awarding the relatives a place to stay—was thinking in terms of a moral expectation that compels kin who were not in financial difficulty to refrain from rendering relatives in need even more vulnerable.

The latter position of the District Court is more in line with the results of the small survey I made in southern Tanzania among young adults about whether they agreed with the Disabled Persons Act obliging adult children and relatives to support aged relations. The overwhelming majority agreed that this is morally supportable because the aged are in need, because each of us becomes old and because one wants to show gratitude. Spreading the burden among all kin is important.[90] Need of the ageing relative is conditioned, however, on inability to work. As long as one has the physical ability to work s/he cannot expect to be supported, though one can expect voluntary gifts from one's children. About 9 per cent disagreed outright, coming closer to the point of view of the High Court. In their view, family support should not be enforced legally against adult relatives. Old people were feared and thought useless, a burden on the able-bodied

---

[87] Local Customary Law (Declaration) Order, G.N. No. 279, published 28/6/1963, First Schedule, s. 66A, Suppl. 2, Tanganyika Gazette, Vol. XLIV, No. 36, 28 June 1963.

[88] See C. Jones, "Reforms in the Islamic Legal Judicial System and the Sharia Inheritance and Family Law in Tunisia", 7 *Jahrbuch für afrikanisches Recht*, 1993 (published 1995), 3–23, 19. For an example of recognition of the custom of the Indian Muslim community in Malawi not to fragment their property see In *re Osman Hussein*, 1923–60 The African Law Reports Malawi 276 (1954).

[89] Same considerations in *Salima Mzee* v. *Hindu Salum*, High Court, Dar es Salaam, Civ. App. 109/1993, in which the daughter of the deceased sought her share in a house that the deceased had inherited with her sisters and one of the solutions proposed was to put at the disposal of the other heirs four rooms in the house.

[90] One response noted that working adult children should be held primarily responsible; if there were no children, then the relatives should be obliged.

struggling poor masses of the country and care for the ageing was seen to be the duty of the larger solidarity embodied in the state.[91]

This consensus on support for the aging generation correlated with the responses on the image of the family and its function. The overwhelming majority have positive experience of the close extended family form (consisting mostly of collaterals first and second generation and lineals up to third generation) in terms of financial and non-material help. About 34 per cent had been sent to live with other relatives for such reasons as discipline, death of a parent, or a change in a parent's workplace. The main picture of the wider extended family (inclusive of clan) is that it is expected to settle quarrels among family members, to discuss how best to solve individual problems, and to give disciplinary warnings against misconduct (e.g. a drinking problem). The second function relates to work needs. On the farms, especially in the harvesting and weeding seasons and for clearing land, the family meets to decide on a schedule for allocation of work. If there is a harvest surplus, a collective decision is made about whether to plough back the proceeds into the land (e.g. purchasing fertilisers) or into a business. If family members have rural or urban businesses, it is expected that kin will support with their labour (e.g. marketing the produce) wherever they are residing. The survival of this extended family support depends sometimes on whether the person holding the "fathership"/"seniorship" is at the location; when s/he is far away in an urban area and has refused to delegate someone, it falls apart. Honesty and enforcing honesty among the relatives is also significant. Most responses about the extended family as a source of material support, paying debts for insolvent family members, school fees or emergency help in case of famine, were cautious and differentiated. A few mentioned that if a member of the family wants to pay off a debt, s/he is allocated land from the family holdings so that they can produce for themselves and pay off the debt directly or repay those family members who have advanced monies or materials. Only one mentioned that land would be sold in order to help the insolvent. Otherwise, there is a clear expectation among all that each adult is responsible for her/his own living costs and debts, but help from extended kin is morally expected in the case of certain unavoidable debts and living costs. These include school fees,[92] the marriage gift, financial difficulties because of loss of a spouse, government debts, debts left by an insolvent deceased, and hospital debts. The amounts of contribution are voluntary, each according to his/her ability.[93] For family ceremonies, all members are expected to make some contribution. If the debt is not inevitable, the family members can take pity and help out without expectation of repayment, but with

---

[91] It would be interesting to undertake a survey among the old relatives to ask whether they wish to be supported, for some individuals do not wish to be seen as a burden.

[92] For an historical example of the tensions in the close extended family over the payment of school fees, see judgment by colonial District Officer setting a precedent by ordering a trust for school fees in a Haya case of inheritance (D. Connelly, District Commissioner Bukoba, *op. cit.*, Rhodes House, Judgment, 2 Mar. 1962, 15 and 17).

[93] One can imagine that quarrels would arise about who is more able to give larger contributions, but this was not mentioned in the responses.

a stern warning that the debtor learn how to handle borrowings. The family members can also decide whether their contributions should be repaid. When it comes to a family member's need for capital for a business, most agree that the kin are obliged to help. Depending on the terms of agreement reached in the family meeting, the profits can be split as part of a kind of joint enterprise or the recipient pays back each his/her contribution but keeps the profits.[94]

A few respondents from small (defined as four or less children) nuclear-type families with only one or two collaterals of the same generation as the parents (e.g. one uncle), noted that the family does not look to distant kin or the clan for help in farming. Rather the family changes the nature of its agricultural work. It tries to avoid intensive farming and goes in for livestock. Parents cover the debts of their adult children without support from other relatives, but only after receiving a detailed explanation.

The descriptions of the kin meetings give the impression that only those who are present are bound or can bind morally, but that it could be regarded in some clans as an affront to family unity if a member refuses to attend. Not all those attending are allowed to be part of the discussion (or in one family, take part in voting on who shall lead the meeting). Women, for example, as described in only four responses, are under restriction. In one family, women are excluded from the meetings; in another they join the discussion if it concerns them. In another instance if the father of the conjugal family is absent, the mother substitutes for him, and finally, in one family women participate in the discussion very actively and on an equal basis. In only one response was it mentioned that close neighbours are also part of the family discussions especially in regard to emergency debts and work allocations.

Legal recognition of the extended family form as a forum for settling quarrels and distributing resources is most obvious in the courts' probate practices. As seen in the above case of Kumkana's widow who sought and won letters of administration of her deceased husband's estate, the brother defended himself with the argument that the clan had chosen to propose him.[95] If there is no objection, the courts are informed of only the final decision of the family meeting. The courts are not bound in law to accept the family's decision, but in practice they acknowledge the social reality and confirm the candidate put forth. Unless a family member raises serious objections or the results are manifestly unjust, the courts tend not to probe into the details of the meetings and the reasons for the

---

[94] In case of losses arrangments would be presumably negotiated. On "negotiating" family relationships see Janet Finch, 1989, *op. cit.*, 235–6.

[95] *Habibu M. Kumkana* v. *Mariam Kumkana*, High Court, Dar es Salaam, Civ. App. 33/1995. Same arguments brought by the brother of the deceased before the trial court, which appointed him instead of the widow in *Isabela Mbundu* v. *Richard Mbundu*, High Court, Dar es Salaam, Civ. App. 67/1994. Elders' intimations at the funeral were mentioned in *Catherine M. Mhagana* v. *Janet G. Mhagama*, High Court, Songea, Civ. App., 2/1994. In probate cases in the Primary and District Courts the magistrates and court chairpersons accept written or oral protocols of the family meetings as evidence of who the heirs were and their shares, e.g. *Probate and Administration No. 6/1994*, Mlingoti Primary Court, Tunduru (mother of deceased selected to administer the estate for daughter-in-law and grandchildren).

decisions taken on who should be the heirs, what their shares should be and who should administer the estate. If there is objection, the courts tend not to ask what factors lead a member to go to court, or why this member is dissatisfied.[96] Hence, the result as in the Kumkana case above is that a court, while asking for tolerance of women's participation and even leadership at the family council, does not usually wish to intervene too much. There is no investigation of whether the councils have met the minimum standards of fairness[97] and whether evaluation of need as made at a council should be a legal issue in court. This laissez-faire approach may recede in time, as recent litigation initiated by women forces courts to think more about moral issues that would have also been raised in family council meetings. A surviving daughter[98] and two widows[99] objected to the exclusive appointment or co-appointment of a nephew and brothers, respectively, as administrators on the grounds that the clan did not look at the character, reputation, and impartiality of the men it recommended or determine whether the men were trustworthy, cooperative, responsible, interested in the welfare and needs of the surviving conjugal or concubinate family.[100]

To summarise this section, the close and distant extended family plays a very important part of moral expectations in Tanzania in regard to inheritance distribution, land allocation, and raising capital for family business. The integrity of the family council making the decisions depends on its assessing and hierarchising the needs of the relatives fairly. Thus, succession to the resources left behind is generally seen as a matter of need/support and is not to be treated as a matter of an absolute inheritance right by virtue of relationship alone. The nuclear family form is not necessarily smothered by the extended family. Its members can decide to what extent they wish to support or obtain support from the extended family, and the extended family members hold the nuclear family responsible for their own non-inevitable debts. Courts, however, are geared towards supporting the individualisation process by awarding exclusive rights and do not make need a legal issue *per se*. Nor do they tend to supervise the internal workings of the family meetings called to settle quarrels. As a result the tension between the nuclear conjugal family form and the extended family form grows.

[96] On breaking away as an option to consensus, see C. Jones, "Rezeption europäischen Rechts in Malawi und Botswana: Die Rolle der afrikanischen Informanten, Richter und Rechtsassessoren" [Reception of European Law in Malawi and Botswana: The Role of African Informants, Juges and Assessors], 29 *Verfassung und Recht in Übersee*, 1996, 347–74, 358–9.

[97] Using, for example, analogies with examples from administrative law, e.g. *Ridge v. Baldwin*, [1964] AC 40; *Breen v. Amalgamated Engineering Union (now Amalgamated Engineering and Foundry Workers Union) and ors.*, [1971] All ER 1148 (CA).

[98] *Pili Lukaye v. Mohamed J. Lukaye*, High Court, Tabora, Civ. App. 39/1994.

[99] *Isabela Mbundu v. Richard Mbundu*, High Court, Dar es Salaam, Civ. App. 67/1994; *Deusdedith Bachubila v. Jenerosa Ngaiza*, High Court, Tabora, Civ. App. 17/1994.

[100] Magistrates' Courts Act, No. 2 of 1984, Fifth Sched., s. 2(b), requires the Primary Courts when using its discretion to appoint an administrator to name a "reputable impartial" person. This is in line with a description from the German colonial era of the practice of several Wahehe families of choosing as the main administrator the most diligent unselfish person who would administer the properties in the interest of the entire family and indeed augment the resource base (Bernhard Ankermann, Ostafrika (as part of *Das Eingeborenenrecht*, ed. Erich Schultz-Ewerth), 1929, *op. cit.*, 288).

Its resolution may depend on the courts focusing more specifically on moral expectations concerning needs of relatives.

CONCLUSIONS

My basic aim in comparing family support in an European and an African country was to show that the nuclear family form as the epitome of modernisation/ westernisation[101] and the extended family form as the epitome of anti-modern tradition polarises positions unnecessarily. Different family forms have always existed side by side, though the demographic spread of any one form and the reasons for the existence of any one form differ over time. For example, there have always been single-parent families, the reason in the past being widowhood perhaps more frequently than unmarried father- or motherhood.[102] Today the reasons are due more to not wanting to be regulated with the automatically imposed mixture of material and non-material duties that "marriage" brings. The various family forms are not autonomous of one another. They have always competed and yet they will always need one another.[103] Many a nuclear family cannot exist without the extended family in Germany and many an extended family in Tanzania has expectations of the nuclear family that it not burden the relatives with unnecesssary debts. What does change is how the law perceives family and the moral expectations its members have on one another for support. By dint of many forces legal perceptions are being compelled to change. Such forces include the longer periods of the adult life taken by education and deepening financial troubles due to rising costs of living, unemployment, decline in self-employment or self-production as land ownership patterns change, and women objecting to being silenced in the name of family authority. Courts are not unanimous in accepting a change in the law's perceptions of family and the moral expectations on its members for support. The law is still struggling to find ways to draw the boundaries of interdependence between the nuclear and extended family forms. I have suggested in this chapter one way, *viz.* by making needs the key legal issue and hierarchising needs in terms of moral expectations rather than hierarchising persons obliged to and persons entitled to support. In the course of steering a clear course, the law has, I believe, to avoid two pitfalls: first, not to fall victim to the ideology that westernisation/urbanisation destroys the extended family and that the conjugal family is at the apex of an evolutionary pyramid; and secondly,

---

[101] Cf. Sabitha Jithoo, "Fission of the Hindu Joint-Family in Durban", 2 *University of Durban-Westville Journal*, 1975, 55–62, 57.

[102] See for example the case of an unmarried mother at the end of the last century in Germany who fought her way up to the appellate level for her right to give her male child a feminine name, and the practice in the 18th century of allowing children of men in concubinate relationships to carry the name of the father in C. Jones, "'Mami, darf ich Bo heissen?': Staatliche Bestimmung über Geschlechterordnung und Kulturidentität" ["Mama, may I have the name Bo?": State Control over Sexual and Cultural Order], 1 *Frauen in der einen Welt*, 1997, 46–71, 53 and 59.

[103] Janet Finch, 1989, *op. cit.*, chs. 5 and 6.

to avoid perceiving individualisation as a process of autonomisation that polarises extended and nuclear families. It is especially the process of individualisation as a social agent of change that courts should consciously identify and try to understand. If the law perceives individualisation of rights as a process of autonomisation, it could lead to further polarisation between the extended and nuclear forms of family.[104] If the law sees individualisation in terms of the moral expectation that each has an equal right to be heard and to consideration[105] concerning needs—and women are in the forefront of this approach—then there may be a better chance for reconciliation of the two forms of family.

---

[104] For interesting conceptualisations of family tensions at various levels see Isak A. Niehaus, "Disharmonious Spouses and Harmonious Siblings. Conceptualising Household Formation among Urban Residents in Qwaqwa", 53 *African Studies* (1994), 115–35; and Edward D. Breslin *et al.*, "A 'Proper Household'—exploring household and community dynamics in South Africa", *PLA Notes*, No. 28, Feb. 1997, 4–8.

[105] On a Norwegian approach see David Cheal, *Family and the State of Theory* (New York, etc., Harvester Wheatsheaf, 1991), 113.

PART THREE

The State and Pluralism

This Part opens with Freeman's examination of the concepts of relativism and pluralism (Chapter 17). The immediate context is the co-existence of a variety of familial traditions within a state. Atkin and Austin (Chapter 18) discuss the way New Zealand law is now being affected by concepts originating in Maori tradition and human rights norms. De Koker (Chapter 19) explains how African customary law became ossified in the South African "official" version and Zaal (Chapter 20) draws attention to the problems which arise when inadequately trained state officials exercise jruisdiction over traditions which are alien to them. Sloth-Nielsen and van Heerden, followed by Goolam (Chapters 21 and 22), illustrate the opportunities and problems opened out by the recognition of pluralism within the 1994 South African constitution. Wardle (Chapter 23), Lund-Andersen (Chapter 24) and Steyn (Chapter 25) explore the problem of pluralism within the context of same-sex unions. While it may be that in some cultures the word "marriage" is too imbued with the concept of heterosexuality to be transferrable to same-sex unions, that does mean that the norms associated with it should not be transferrable if they would reflect norms held by the people involved themselves. This Part concludes with an account by Katz (Chapter 26) of the changing attitude of the state in the United States towards the conduct of parents towards their children. Although the earlier *laisser-faire* attitude, grounded in a religious perspective about family life, has given way to greater state supervision, there is still no duty on the state to compensate victims of its failure to supervise.

17

Cultural Pluralism
and the Rights of the Child

MICHAEL FREEMAN

INTRODUCTION

In 1968 a man went to a doctor in South London for medical treatment of a venereal disease. He introduced his young wife to the doctor and let it be known that
he had already taken her to a clinic to be fitted with a contraceptive appliance.
The doctor was concerned and reported the matter to the police who brought a
complaint to the juvenile court that she was in need of care because she was being
exposed to moral danger.[1] The couple were Nigerian Muslims:[2] he was in his
mid-twenties and she was at most 13, but may have been as young as 11. They
had married in northern Nigeria shortly before coming to England. The court
made a "fit person order"[3] under the Children and Young Persons Act 1963 and
the girl was admitted to the care of a local authority. The reasons which
prompted the court to conclude that she was in moral danger are encapsulated
in the following statement:

> "Here is a girl, aged 13, or possibly less, unable to speak English, living in London with
> a man twice her age to whom she has been married by Muslim law. He admits having
> had sexual intercourse with her at a time when according to the medical evidence the
> development of puberty had almost certainly not begun. . . . He further admits that
> since the marriage . . . he has had sexual relations with a prostitute in Nigeria from
> whom he has contracted venereal disease. In our opinion a continuance of such an asso-
> ciation, notwithstanding the marriage, would be repugnant to any decent-minded
> English man or woman. Our decision reflects that repugnance".[4]

This decision was reversed on appeal by the Divisional Court. The Lord Chief
Justice, Lord Parker, conceded that it was possible to hold that a validly married
wife was in moral danger, but he refused to accept that the girl in this case was.
He said:

> "I would never dream of suggesting that a decision by this bench of justices, with this
> very experienced chairman, could ever be termed perverse: but having read that, I am

---

[1] *Alhaji Mohamed* v. *Knott* [1969] 1 QB 1.
[2] They were domiciled in Nigeria.
[3] Fit person orders were replaced by care orders in 1969.
[4] Above, n. 1, 15.

convinced that they have misdirected themselves. When they say that 'a continuance of such an association notwithstanding the marriage would be repugnant to any decent-minded English man or woman', they are I think, and can only be, considering the view of an English man or woman in relation to an English girl and our Western way of life. I cannot myself think that decent-minded Englishmen or women, realising the way of life in which this girl was brought up, and this man for that matter, would inevitably say that this is repugnant. It is certainly natural for a girl to marry at that age. They develop sooner, and there is nothing abhorrent in their way of life for a girl of 13 to marry a man of 25. . . . Granted that this man may be said to be a bad lot, that he has done things in the past which perhaps nobody would approve of, it does not follow from that that this girl, happily married to this man, is under any moral danger by associating and living with him. For my part, as it seems to me, it could only be said that she was in moral danger if one was considering somebody brought up and living in our way of life and to hold that she is in moral danger in the circumstances of this case can only be arrived at, as it seems to me, by ignoring the way of life in which she was brought up, and her husband was brought up".[5]

The Divisional Court held that the marriage was entitled to recognition by the English courts. It followed from this that the husband was not committing the offence of unlawful sexual intercourse[6]—unlawful meant outside marriage.[7]

The case, understandably, provoked considerable controversy. The *Daily Express* was outraged. So was Baroness Summerskill who initiated a debate in the House of Lords.[8] The decision was branded as racist, a failure by white institutions to protect a vulnerable black child. Olive Stone thought the case "disturbing"[9] and Ruth Deech believed its "practical consequences would be disastrous".[10] It led Ian Karsten to call for a minimum age to be prescribed for recognition purposes.[11] But other commentators welcomed the decision. It showed a willingness to embrace the customs and culture of another society.[12] What was "moral danger" was being tested by the morality of the culture to which the couple belonged. The decision was seen to be consonant with an acceptance of moral pluralism.[13]

Whichever stance one adopted, the case had troubling features. An analysis of Lord Parker's judgment reveals prejudices and misconceptions galore, not least a concern that this understanding of Islamic culture in Northern Nigeria may not have been very deep, assumptions and biases filling in gaps in his knowledge base. It is not clear what evidence, if any, was given to either court about the life realities of Muslim Nigeria.

---

[5] Above, n. 1, 15–16.
[6] Sexual Offences Act 1956, s. 6(1) (intercourse with a girl under 16).
[7] Cf. *R. v. Chapman* [1959] 1 QB 100 (on the interpretation of s. 19(1) of the 1956 Act).
[8] *Hansard*, HL, vol. 290, cols. 1321–3.
[9] *Family Law* (MacMillan, 1997) 40.
[10] "Immigrants and Family Law" (1973) 123 *NLJ* 110, 111.
[11] "Child Marriages" (1969) 32 *MLR* 212, 215–16.
[12] Brenda Hoggett, *Parents and Children* (Sweet & Maxwell, 1977), 110.
[13] M. D. A. Freeman, *The Legal Structure* (Longmans, 1974), 48.

About the same time as *Mohamed* v. *Knott* was going through the courts, the question arose in a different context in *R. v. Derrivierre*.[14] A West Indian father was charged with an assault upon his 12-year-old son occasioning him actual bodily harm. The boy had been disobedient and the father punished him by punching him a number of times in the face. English law provides a defence to the crime of wilfully assaulting a child[15] if the purpose is chastisement and the punishment is moderate and reasonable.[16] The father was given a six-month term of imprisonment for what the Deputy Chairman of the Inner London Quarter Sessions described as a "brutal attack". On an appeal against sentence the Criminal Division of the Court of Appeal upheld the decision and set out the broad principle involved:

"Standards of parental correction are different in the West Indies from those which are acceptable in this country; and the Court fully accepts that immigrants coming to this country may find initially that our ideas are different from those upon which they have been brought up in regard to the methods and manner in which children are to be disciplined. There can be no doubt that once in this country, this country's laws must apply; and there can be no doubt that, according to the law of this country, the chastisement given to this boy was excessive and the assault complained of was proved. Nevertheless had this been a first offence, and had there been some real reason for thinking that the appellant either did not understand what the standards in this country were or was having difficulty in adjusting himself, the Court would no doubt have taken that into account and given it such consideration as it could".[17]

In fact Derrivierre had a previous conviction for assaulting his daughter only a year before and thus had already received a fair warning of the unacceptable nature of this type of behaviour in England. But the case does show a willingness by English courts to take supposedly different standards of another culture into account in sentencing.[18] More recently, in a child care case,[19] the practices of a mother who was by origin Vietnamese were judged against the "reasonable objective standards of the culture in which the children have hitherto been brought up",[20] though the judge was careful to add, "so long as these do not conflict with our minimal acceptable standards of child care in England".[21] But, of course, the judge heard no evidence of what the "reasonable objective standards" of rural Vietnam were, though he was convinced that the mother's disciplinary

---

[14] (1969) 53 Cr.App.Rep. 637.

[15] See Children and Young Persons Act 1933 s. 1(7).

[16] As to which see Lord Cockburn CJ in *R. v. Hopley* (1860) 2 F & F 202. See further P. Newell, *Children Are People Too* (Bedford Square Press, 1989). On the religious roots see P. Greven, *Spare the Child* (Vintage Books, 1992). Echoes of this can be detected in M. Straus, *Beating The Devil Out of Them: Corporal Punishment in the American Family* (Lexington Books, 1994).

[17] *Op. cit.*, n. 14, 638–39.

[18] On which matter see S. M. Poulter, *English Law and Ethnic Minority Customs* (Butterworths, 1986), 271–4.

[19] *Re H* [1987] 2 FLR 12.

[20] *Ibid.*

[21] *Ibid.*

measures were unacceptable in that culture too. Neither *Derrivierre* nor *Re H* (the Vietnamese case) provoked the interest or the controversy which *Mohamed* v. *Knott* fuelled. But that is hardly surprising, given our ambivalence to questions of the physical chastisement of children.[22]

These extended case studies are but two examples of the problem posed when legislation comes up against the practices of another culture.[23] It is a problem well known to drafters of international conventions and the two examples drawn from England could be added to by reference to confrontations in other countries. But the temptation to document such examples will be resisted and I will focus on two international conventions instead.

Seventy-five years ago the International Labour Organisation adopted a convention fixing the minimum age for admission of children to industrial employment.[24] Article 2 of this states:

"Children under the age of fourteen years shall not be employed or work in any public or private industrial undertaking, or in any branch thereof, other than an undertaking in which only members of the same family are employed".

For most Western States the age of 14 was accepted. But the Commission on Children's Employment, responsible for preparing the Labour Conference, met strong objection from countries in Asia where child labour under the age of 14 was—indeed still is—widespread and where the financial resources for implementing rapid change did not exist. "Should modifications of the Convention be allowed in the case of those countries with special climatic and industrial conditions?", asked Sir Malcolm Delevinge of the United Kingdom.[25] A trades unionist from Britain, Margaret Bondfield, was in no doubt that such exceptions were unacceptable but a compromise at her initiative was effected. Speaking of what became Article 6 of the Convention, she said:

"With regard to one of the main objections, namely the nature of the Indian industries. We have carefully drafted this amendment to exclude all those industries that could be considered purely native industries or that are small industries. It is especially drafted to refer only to those industries which are being modelled on Western ideas, which are to some extent under control of factory legislation and which are mainly supervised by Western people".[26]

---

[22] This came to the fore yet again in Britain in 1994 over the question of the moral propriety and legality of a childminder smacking a child in her care. See *London Borough of Sutton* v. *Davis* [1994] 1 FLR 737. It has now been "resolved" by Government Guidance permitting a childminder to smack, but only where a parent gives consent (*The Times*, 3 Dec. 1994).

[23] On scarification see *R.* v. *Adesanya*, *The Times*, 16 and 17 July 1974 (and S. Poulter, "Foreign Customs and The English Criminal Law" (1975) 24 *ICLQ* 136); on West African fostering practices see *Re O* (1973) 3 Fam. Law 40, *Re E O* (1973) 3 Fam Law 48 and *Re A* (1978) 8 Fam. Law 247. Also interesting is *Re H* [1978] Fam. 65 (returning a battered Pakistani child of 4 to her parents who were returning to Pakistan).

[24] See Philip Veerman, *The Rights of The Child and The Changing Image of Childhood*, Martinus Nijhoff, 1992 ch. XIII.

[25] League of Nations, *International Labour Conference*, First Annual Meeting, 96.

[26] *Idem.*

And so Article 6 declares boldly that Article 2 "shall not apply to India" and then sets a lower age (12) below which children are not to be employed in factories "working with power and employing more than ten persons" or in mines, transport or the docks. India continued to raise reservations, in particular relating to the "difficulties which local customs would place in the way of organising adequate primary education".[27] In the event India did not ratify this Convention though it did ratify (in 1921) another ILO Convention adopted in 1919 on the prohibition of nightwork.[28] The 1919 Convention on minimum age has been replaced by one adopted in 1973.[29] This states that every State Party is to undertake progressively to raise the minimum age for admission to employment or work "to a level consistent with the fullest physical and mental development of young persons".[30] Developing countries are, nevertheless, still allowed to specify a minimum age for employment at 14 years.[31] The UN Convention on the Rights of the Child recognises the right of the child to be protected from economic exploitation and from performing hazardous work or work likely to interfere with education[32] but no minimum age is specified.

But it is another Article of the UN Convention to which attention must now turn. Article 24, dealing with health and health services, confronts the issue of cultural difference in paragraph 3. This states:

"State Parties shall take all effective and appropriate measures with a view to abolishing traditional practices prejudicial to the health of children."

There are many traditional practices which may harm children but no one is in any doubt that one practice in particular is targeted by this provision *viz.* female circumcision[33]. This is prevalent in wide areas of the world:[34] takes a number of forms[35] and infibulation—genital mutilation of the grossest kind—is particularly common in the Sudan, Somalia, Ethiopia and Mali. At least three

---

[27] *International Labour Review*, vol. III, nos. 1–2, July–Aug. 1921, 16.

[28] Convention 6 (it is reproduced in Veerman, *op. cit.*, n. 24, 420). India did originally ask for preferential treatment on this Convention too: so did Japan and Belgium (whose request to except the glass industry was rejected by the Conference).

[29] ILO Convention No. 138 (reproduced in Veerman, *op. cit.*, n. 24, 484).

[30] Art. 1.

[31] Art. 2(4). They must state a reason or alternatively agree to renounce "the right to avail itself of the provisions in question as from a stated date" (Art. 2(5)). India by the Child Labour (Prohibition and Regulation) Act 1986 has prohibited those under 14 working in certain hazardous employments and regulated their working conditions in certain other employments.

[32] Art. 32. States Parties must provide a minimum age for employment and provide for penalties or other sanctions to ensure effective enforcement. (Art. 32(2)(a) and (c)). On India see Myron Weiner, *The Child and the State in India* (Oxford University Press, 1991).

[33] Delegates of Canada, the UK and the USA were in favour of formulations of the Art. that would have referred specifically to female circumcision. See D. Johnson, "Cultural and Regional Pluralism in the Drafting of the UN Convention on the Rights of The Child" in M. Freeman and P. Veerman, *The Ideologies of Children's Rights* (Martinus Nijhoff, 1992), 95, 109–10.

[34] See Alison Slack (1988) 10 *Human Rights Quarterly* 437. See also Stephen James (1994) 8 *Bioethics* 1.

[35] See Efua Dorkenoo and Scilla Elworthy, *Female Genital Mutilation: Proposals for Change* (Minority Rights, 1992) Efua Dorkenoo, *Cutting the Rose* (Minority Rights, 1994).

Western countries have legislated against it,[36] including the United Kingdom in 1986,[37] and France has prosecuted and imprisoned parents involved in it. Nevertheless, in formulating Article 24, paragraph 3 caution had to be taken. Senegal, for example, warned that a more direct condemnation would force the practice underground.[38]

Four examples have now been used: child marriages, child labour, female circumcision and corporal chastisement practices. Of female child circumcision more will be said. But at this stage attention must turn to the concept of cultural pluralism and its justification. And pluralism must be distinguished from two other political ethical theories, relativism and monism (or universalism).

CULTURAL PLURALISM

The fact of cultural pluralism was known as early as the Greek historian, Herodotus,[39] and it is traced through Montaigne,[40] Vico,[41] Hume[42] and Montesquieu[43] (who perhaps was the first to try to explain cultural difference). But it is to twentieth-century anthropology that we must look for articulation of the concept.[44]

Pluralism is a theory about the sources of value (as are relativism and monism).[45] Pluralists believe that there are many reasonable conceptions of a good life and many reasonable values upon which the realisation of good lives depend. There are conflicts among reasonable conceptions of a good life as well as among reasonable values. Political ethics needs to cope with these conflicts, to attempt to surmount difficulties caused by the incompatibility and incommensurability of values whose realisation is thought to be essential. Where values are

---

[36] The UK has the Prohibition of Female Circumcision Act 1986. There is also legislation in the USA (The Female Genital Mutilation Act of 1993, HR 3247). This is discussed in *Berkeley Women's Law Journal* 206 (1994).

In France there is no specific law but the violence involved in circumcision brings the activity within a more general proscription. The recent *Gréon* case in France, which led to a one year suspended sentence, promoted an outcry (see *Guardian*, 17 Sept. 1994).

[37] For the view of social workers towards it see Lynn Eaton, "A Fine Line", *Community Care*, 21–27 July 1994, 16. See also Bryan Hartley, *Archives of Diseases in Childhood* (1994).

[38] And pointed to son preference as another harmful traditional practice.

[39] See his *Persian Wars* ("if one were to offer men to choose out of all the customs in the world such as seemed to them the best, they would examine the whole number, and end by preferring their own") (Book 3, Ch. 38).

[40] See C. Geertz, "Anti Anti-Relativism", 86 *American Anthropologist* 263 at 264.

[41] *The New Science* (1744).

[42] See, in particular, his "A Dialogue" in *Enquiries concerning Human Understanding and concerning the Principles of Morals* (ed. L. A. Selby-Bigge, revised by P. H. Nidditch, Clarendon Press, 1975), 324.

[43] *The Spirit of The Laws* (1748).

[44] In particular to Franz Boas (see e.g. "The Mind of Primitive Man", 14 *Journal of American Folklore* 1 (1901)), Ruth Benedict, *Patterns of Culture* (Houghton Mifflin, 1934) and Melville Herskovits, *Cultural Relativism: Perspectives in Cultural Pluralism* (Random House, 1972).

[45] And see Charles Larmore, "Pluralism and Reasonable Disagreement", 11(1) *Social Philosophy and Policy* 61, 64 (1994).

incompatible—for example a belief in equality of the sexes and a belief that men are superior—the realisation of one value must exclude the other. Values are incommensurable where there is no measuring rod by which they can be compared.

Incommensurable values need not necessarily be incompatible, and where they are not they can co-exist. If values were only incommensurable the problem would not be too great—a vision which allowed for and requited discrete but compatible conceptions of the good life is not beyond the scope of imagination. It is the incompatibility of values that constitutes the stumbling-block.

Pluralists accept that conflicts among values can be resolved by appealing to some reasonable ranking of the values in question. They acknowledge that a plurality of reasonable rankings also exists.

MONISM

Monism or universalism,[46] by contrast, is committed to there being an overriding value or set of values and, if the latter, a ranking scheme on the basis of which values can be compared in a way that all reasonable people would find acceptable. Pluralists object to monism because they cannot accept the idea that there is an overriding value, that there is some consideration which always takes precedence over all other considerations. Monism also overlooks those cases of moral conflict where no standard can legitimately claim a monopoly of the truth (the issue of abortion[47] is the best example of this). Where pluralists and monists agree is in accepting the need for a reasonable method of resolving conflict.

RELATIVISM

Pluralists also reject relativism. Pluralism may have emerged out of relativism and the two are often confused.[48] Pluralists and relativists agree that there are no overriding values, that all values are conditional, that there is a plurality of incompatible and incommensurable values. They agree on the need for conflict resolution. But relativists go beyond pluralism and think that all values are conventional. Relativism emerged in reaction to cultural evolutionism, which was European and often racist.[49] As Hatch puts it: "It goes without saying that people who were thought to be the least cultured were also thought to be the least

---

[46] There are different models of monism, ranging from the Platonic "Idea of The Good" (see his *Republic*, 504–9) and to different versions of utilitarianism, using in its simplest model a felicific calculus (see Jeremy Bentham, *Introduction to the Principles of Morals and Legislation*).

[47] And see Ronald Dworkin, *Life's Dominion* (Harvard University Press), 1993.

[48] Joseph Raz claims not to know what cultural pluralism is (see "Moral Change and Social Relativism", 11(1) *Social Philosophy and Policy* 139 (1994)); *Ethics in the Public Domain* (Clarendon Press, 1994) chapter 8.

[49] G. W. Stocking Jr., *Race, Culture and Evolution* (Free Press, 1968).

intelligent and the darkest in pigmentation".[50] When cultural relativism emerged in the first third of this century it was seen as a challenge to racist, Eurocentric notions of progress.[51] Cultural relativism, like pluralism, is a theory about the way evaluations or judgments are made. But to the relativist, "evaluations are relative to the cultural background out of which they arise".[52] So to Ruth Benedict, one of the founders of relativism, tolerance is a key element of cultural relativism;[53] and to Herskovits it is necessary to recognise the "dignity inherent in every body of custom".[54] The philosopher Charles Taylor talks of the presumption of the equal worth of cultures.[55]

The attractions of relativism are difficult to ignore. It is rooted in egalitarianism, in liberalism, in modernism. It belongs perhaps to a disenchanted vision of the world.[56] It is anti-assimilationist, it is anti-imperialist, it is hostile to ethnocentrism.[57] It is sympathetic to, and would wish to protect, the traditions and rights of indigenous peoples.[58] It has the value also, in a sort of Millian way,[59] of enhancing the prospects of achieving moral knowledge, though this presupposes the possibility of real communication across cultures and this is not always possible.[60]

Relativists regard all values as the products of the customs, practices and beliefs which have as a matter of fact developed within a particular tradition. They deny that any value has any authority, epistemological or moral, outside of this cultural context. They deny that conflict between values belonging to different traditions can be settled in any reasonable way, because, so they argue, what is reasonable is itself a product of particular cultures. And so they demand of us that we ask not whether social practices like child marriage or female circumcision, or for that matter purdah, suttee or polygamy, are justified by the moral considerations that we find cogent, but rather whether they are sanctioned by the relevant social understandings of the cultures within which they are practised.

But, if that means that a culture can only be judged by endogenous value judgements, and that moral principles which derive from outside that culture

---

[50] E. Hatch, *Culture and Morality: The Relativity of Values in Anthropology* (Columbia University Press, 1983), 26.

[51] Alison Dundes Renteln, *International Human Rights: Universalism Versus Relativism* (Sage, 1990).

[52] *Per* Melville Herskovits, above, n. 44, 14.

[53] Above, n. 44, 37. See also Hatch, *op. cit.*, n. 50, 99–100.

[54] *Man and His Works* (Alfred A. Knopf, 1947), 76.

[55] *Multiculturalism and "The Politics of Recognition"* (Princeton University Press, 1992), 72.

[56] Charles Larmore so characterises it (above, n. 45, 71).

[57] See Abdullahi, A. An-Na'im, "Religious Minorities Under Islamic Law and The Limits of Cultural Relativism", 9 *Human Rights Quarterly*, 1 (1987).

[58] See Will Kymlicka, *Liberalism, Community and Culture* (Oxford University Press, 1989). See also Alan Gewirth, "Is Cultural Pluralism Relevant To Moral Knowledge?", 11(1) *Social Philosophy and Policy* 22, 35 (1994).

[59] See J. S. Mill, *On Liberty* (1859).

[60] But see Chandran Kukarhas, "Explaining Moral Variety", 11(1) *Social Philosophy and Policy* 1, 18 (1994).

have no validity, morality has become a slave to custom,[61] the "ought" has relinquished any transcendental power that it may have had to critique the "is". However, if, as Amy Gutmann has argued persuasively in a recent article, "cultural relativists agree that there can be standards for judging justice that are independent of social consensus, then they give up the distinctive premise of cultural relativism".[62] I would argue that they must. The argument for any practice must be more than that the practice exists. A culture which permits child marriage or female circumcision must be able to support these practices by a stronger argument, or series of arguments, than that there is—if, indeed, this is the case— social consensus. An examination of the social understandings within the culture may reveal that there is no social understanding at all or that there are conflicting understandings, misunderstandings or inconsistencies. Often, it will reveal that the so-called dominant understanding is in reality the understanding of the dominant.[63] Many cultural practices when critically examined turn on the interpretation of a male élite, with a consensus having been engineered to cloak the interests of a section of the society.[64]

Both monists and pluralists disagree. Monists because they believe that a practice can be judged by an overriding value: pluralists because they claim that there are values independent of the context of the culture in question to which we can reasonably appeal in settling conflicts. There is surely no dispute that there are certain needs which do not vary either temporally—they are historically constant—or culturally—they are the requirement of people everywhere. This does not mean that there are not differences in the ways in which these needs are met. There is a need for food: not a need for meat and two vegetables.[65] There is a need for shelter but it does not have to be a semi-detached house. Nor are these needs only physiological. There are psychological needs too: for comfort, affection, companionship. There are social needs: for order, security, dignity, respect, privacy. There are minimum requirements of human welfare. They must be met whatever the conception of what constitutes a good life and regardless of what other values are upheld in any particular culture.[66]

It is easy to distinguish this model of pluralism from one of relativism. Relativists do not acknowledge these primary values and therefore fail to see that

---

[61] In *On Liberty*, J. S. Mill wrote of the "despotism of custom".

[62] "The Challenge of Multiculturalism in Political Ethics", 22 *Philosophy and Public Affairs*, 171, 177 (1993).

[63] *Ibid.*, 176.

[64] Stephen A. James argues persuasively that this is the case with female circumcision in African societies. See "Reconciling International Human Rights and Cultural Relativism: The Case of Female Circumcision", 8 *Bioethics*, 1, (1994).

[65] And the need is for food as nutrition. Food may have secondary purposes such as the fulfilment of religious obligations. This is not addressed by Michael Walzer in *Spheres of Justice* (Basic Books, 1983), 8 ("If the religious uses of bread were to conflict with its nutritional uses . . . it is by no means clear which should be primary"). Only a relativist could say this: it is crystal clear that the religious use of bread is of secondary importance to its use as nutrition. Nutrition is a basic, primary value: religion (cf. John Finnis, *Natural Law and Natural Rights* (Clarendon Press, 1980)) is not.

[66] And see John Kekes, "Pluralism and The Value of Life", 11(1) *Social Philosophy and Policy*, 44, 49 (1994).

there are standards independent of a particular culture by which it can be judged. It is less easy to distinguish it from monism, but it is a different claim for primary values may conflict with each other, in which case it may become necessary to put the conflict into its cultural context to determine which, if either, should prevail. The contribution that the achievement of the particular value makes to the life of the individual concerned may also be significant: which of two values, for example, enhances the goal of his or her "good life".

RESPONDING TO THE CASE STUDIES—RELATIVISM

We may return now to the examples used at the beginning of this essay: child marriages, corporal punishment practices, child labour and female circumcision. The relativist would situate each of the case studies into its cultural context and would, I would argue, be impotent to offer any real critique. It is surely one of the limitations of a belief in cultural relativism that it can lead us to conclude that "anything goes". A consequence of this is that we lack the ammunition to protect the individual against the group. The challenge of rights is easily snuffed out. We are forced to condone practices which we find repressive or intolerable because we are told that is only our opinion and had our enculturation been into the culture we are now criticising our opinion would be different. The relativist has little to offer the child either by way of protection or empowerment, any more I suggest than it could have offered Jews living in Nazi Germany or blacks in South Africa under apartheid.[67]

THE MONIST RESPONSE

The monist response is more positive. It points to there being an evaluative consideration, an overriding value, which trumps all other considerations. It may take the form of a categorical imperative,[68] a harm principle[69] or a principle of generic consistency,[70] or many other forms.

The epistemic relevance of these may be questioned. Certainly, a relativist might observe the use here of conceptions of reason and rationality firmly rooted within Western Enlightenment culture; there are other conceptions of "reason"

---

[67] Renteln, *op. cit.*, n. 51, believes that relativism is "out of favor" mainly because of this supposed impotence (67). J. Cook described relativism as "nihilistic": see "Cultural Relativism as an Ethnocentric Notion" in R. Beehler and A. R. Drengson (eds.), *The Philosophy of Society* (Methuen, 1978), 289.

[68] As with Immanuel Kant.

[69] As with John Stuart Mill (and see *op. cit.*, n. 59).

[70] As with Alan Gewirth, *Reason and Morality* (University of Chicago Press, 1978). See also "The Epistemology of Human Rights", 1(2) *Social Philosophy and Policy*, 1 (1984), and, briefly, above, n. 58. Deryck Beyleveld, *The Dialectical Necessity of Morality: An Analysis and Defence of Alan Gewrith's Argument To The Principle of Generic Consistency* (Unveristy of Chicago Press, 1991) is a sustained defence.

to which other cultures appeal including myth, religious faith, intuition and tradition. Why, it may be asked, should alien reasoning processes be admitted when cultural practices external to the culture are ruled irrelevant? This is not unreminiscent of the debates about the relevance of human rights language to non-Western traditions.[71] And there are parallel debates about the meaning of childhood in different cultures and political economies.[72]

The response of the monist to our four examples would depend upon the overriding value or values chosen. Abstracting values from international human rights norms[73] would lead to condemnation of female child circumcision,[74] would result in castigation of countries which permitted child labour and would give no unequivocal answers on the other two matters. The UN Convention on the Rights of the Child has nothing to say on marriages of the very young and whether it allows corporal punishment at all depends upon how Article 19 is interpreted.[75]

THE PLURALIST APPROACH

To the pluralist the practices found in the case studies at the beginning of this chapter have to be looked at both in terms of primary values and the cultural context in which the individuals concerned lived. If one takes preservation of physical integrity to be a primary value then even situating this within relevant cultural contexts leads to a condemnation of child female circumcision. Apart from ritualistic circumcision, where the clitoris is merely nicked and there is little mutilation or long-term damage, the term "female circumcision" is a euphemism which has only the remotest similarity with male circumcision in terms of its physical effects. The practice has been described by Alison Slack as follows:

> "The practice can be broken down into four basic forms that vary in degrees of severity. The first, and least severe form, is . . . ritualistic circumcision. . . . . The second form is simply called circumcision or 'sunna' by the Muslims. This involves the removal of the clitoral prepuce—the outer layer of the skin over the clitoris, sometimes called the 'hood'; the gland and body of the clitoris remain intact. Occasionally, the tip

---

[71] See e.g. Josiah A. M. Cobbah, "African Values and the Human Rights Debate: An African Perspective", 9 *Human Rights Quarterly* 309 (1987); Donna E. Arzt, "The Application of International Human Rights Law in Islamic States", 12 *Human Rights Quarterly* 202 (1990); Ann Mayer, *Islam and Human Rights Trdition and Politics* (Westview Press, 1992).

[72] See Philippe Ariès, *Centuries of Childhood: A Social History of The Family* (Jonathan Cape, 1962); Barbara A. Hanawalt, *Growing Up In Medieval London: The Experience of Childhood In History* (Oxford University Press, 1993); Rex and Wendy Stainton Rogers, *Stories of Childhood: Shifting Agendas of Child Concern* (Harvester Wheatsheaf, 1992).

[73] See John O'Manique, "Universal and Inalienable Rights: A Search for Foundations", 12 *Human Rights Quarterly*, 465 (1990).

[74] Using the Universal Declaration of Human Rights, Art. 25 (and 15). And see further James, *op. cit.*, n. 64, 12–22.

[75] But a case can be put that it would proscribe it, as Sweden, amongst other countries, has done.

of the clitoris itself is removed. Sunna has been equated with male circumcision, because the clitoris itself is generally not damaged.

A third, and more harsh form of the practice, is called excision or clitoridectomy. This is the most common form and involves the removal of the gland of the clitoris—usually the entire clitoris—and often parts of the labia minora as well.

Finally, the most severe form of the practice is infibulation . . . , where virtually all of the external female genitalia are removed—removing the entire clitoris and labia minora—and, in addition, much or most of the labia majora is cut or scraped away. The remaining raw edges of the labia majora are then sewn together with acacia tree thorns, and held in place with catgut or sewing thread. The entire area is closed up by this process leaving only a tiny opening, roughly the size of a matchstick, to allow for the passing of urine and menstrual fluid. The girl's legs are then tied together—ankles, knees and thighs—and she is immobilized for an extended period varying from fifteen to forty days, while the wound heals".[76]

Often one of the harsher forms of the practice occurs, even though a milder type was intended because the girls struggle due to the blunt instruments used and the lack of anaesthesia. The instruments used range from kitchen knives, old razor blades, broken glass and sharp stones to scalpels: the wounds are frequently treated with animal dung and mud to stop the bleeding. The practice occurs most often on young girls between the ages of 3 and 8. It is primarily found in areas where there is considerable poverty, where hunger, insanitary conditions and illiteracy are rife, and where there is little in the way of health care facilities. It is also pertinent to note that the economic and social status of women characteristically is low where female child circumcision is prevalent.

The practices are supported by a number of arguments. The control of female sexuality is the central justification.[77] It prevents wantonness and preserves the virginity of a future bride.[78] Where infibulation has taken place, the girl has to be "re-opened" surgically so that her husband may have sexual intercourse with her, reassured that he is the first to have done this. The preservation of virginity is essential for determining a woman's social position in these societies and in some areas the value of a prospective bride is based on the size of the infibulated opening.[79] There is a belief also that female circumcision is a religious imperative:[80] thus the belief is widely held among Muslims that the practice is scripturally mandated by the Koran.[81] Although the practice is often supported by

[76] "Female Circumcision: A Critical Appraisal", 10 *Human Rights Quarterly* 437, 441–2 (1988). See also Efua Dorkenoo and Scilla Elworthy, *op. cit.*, n. 35; K. Brennan, "The Influence of Cultural Relativism on International Human Rights Law: Female Circumcision as a Case Study", VIII *Law and Inequality* 367 (1989); K. Boulware-Miller, "Female Circumcision: Challenges To The Practice as a Human Rights Violation", 8 *Harvard Women's Law Journal* 155 (1985).

[77] Lawrence P. Cutner, "Female Genital Mutilation", 40(7) *Obstetrical and Gynecological Survey* 438 (1985).

[78] See Slack, *op. cit.*, n. 76, 445.

[79] *Ibid.*, 446.

[80] The practice does not exist in the teachings of any formal religion. Slack, *op. cit.*, n. 76, 446 notes it is practised amongst Jews in Africa, but this is not correct. The Falashas in Ethiopia may have practised circumcision.

[81] See Asma A. El Dareer, *Woman, Why Do You Weep?* (Zed Press, 1982), 71.

Muslim leaders, there is no mention of either excision or infibulation in the Koran. Female circumcision is supported by these leaders as being a positive "sunna", or tradition, one that serves to attenuate sexual desire in women.[82] Muslim men in Africa hold uncircumcised women in contempt. One of the worst insults in Muslim Africa is to be called "Son of an uncircumcised mother".[83]

Justification of the practice also finds support in a number of myths including the belief that the clitoris represents the male sexual organ and, if not cut, will grow to the size of a penis,[84] that females are sterile until excised, the operation being thought to increase fertility, that the operation is a biologically cleansing process that improves the hygienic and/or aesthetic condition of female genitalia.[85] There is also the argument that the adherence to the tradition of female circumcision amounts to a right to cultural self-determination and that the pursuit of this right brings psychological benefits to women. Research in Sudan, Egypt and Nigeria suggests that the importance of tradition[86] is the most significant of justificatory arguments for the practice, and that the support amongst women for the tradition is hardly less than that by men.[87]

These justifications can be examined utilising the cultural pluralist framework that I have offered. That there is a violation of physical integrity, at least in the case of clitoridectomy and infibulation, is incontestable. To the monist or universalist that is the end of the question. But the cultural pluralist must go on to ask how important a value physical integrity is to women in Sudan or Somalia, particularly when its preservation may lead to their being social outcasts. If an analogy may be given, it is clear that life is a primary value, but we can all think of circumstances, being in a persistent vegetative state for example, when we would not wish to continue to live. A PVS condition may constitute life but hardly a "good life".

What this overlooks is the age of those who undergo female circumcision. They are for the large part very young children in no position to give informed consent. And yet the operations carried out upon them may severely and

---

[82] Directing it, so it is said, to "the desirable moderation" *per* Marie Bassili Assaad, "Female Circumcision in Egypt: Social Implications, Current Research, and Prospects for Change", 11(1) *Studies In Family Planning* 5 (1980). Hanny Lightfoot-Klein nevertheless found that sexual desire and pleasure were experienced by the majority of women subjected to the most extreme form of circumcision, in spite of their being culturally bound to hide these experiences. ("The Sexual Experience and Marital Adjustment of Genitally Circumcised and Infibulated Females In the Sudan", 26 *Journal of Sex Research* 375 (1989). See also her *Prisoners of Ritual, An Odyssey Into Female Genital Mutilation In Africa* (Haworth Press, 1989).

[83] Raqiya Haji Dualeh Abdalla, *Sisters In Affliction: Circumcision and Infibulation of Women in Africa* (2ed Press, 1982), 84.

[84] Nayra Atiya, *Khul-Khaal: Five Egyptian Women Tell Their Stories* (Syracuse University Press, 1982), 11.

[85] Note, "Female Circumcision", *The Lancet*, 12 Mar. 1983, 569.

[86] Robert A. Myers *et al.*, "Circumcision: Its Nature and Practice Among Some Ethnic Groups in Southern Nigeria", 21 *Social Science and Medicine* 584 (1985); El Dareer, *op. cit.*, n. 81, 141 ff.; Atiyo, *op. cit.*, n. 84, 11.

[87] El Dareer intervied over 4,500 adults in Sudan: 82.6% of women approved of circumcision regardless of the type and 87.7% of men approved the practice.

irreversibly affect their future sexual experience. It may lead to their having difficulty with childbirth. There is an increased risk of sterility. Many are afraid of sex or can experience little enjoyment from sexual relationships. These are potential harms and will occur in the future. There are immediate harms too: severe pain, shock, infection, scarring, bleeding, even death.[88] According to a UNESCO report, emotional reactions "may present themselves as chronic irritability, anxiety, depressive episodes, conversion reactions or frank psychosis".[89] Circumcision is thus within the understanding of the cultures which legitimate the practice dysfunctional. Even so were it practised on adult women with their full and informed consents, we might be inhibited from attacking it (though whether the House of Lords, the final court of appeal in the United Kingdom, would find similar hesitation in the light of its condemnation in *Brown's case*[90] of sado-masochism may be doubted). We allow breast implants and even gender reassignments,[91] and both are carried out by the national health service. Were girls purportedly to consent to circumcision we might still employ, what I have defended elsewhere, as "liberal paternalism", to protect them from the consequences of actions that will prevent them subsequently enjoying rationally autonomous adulthood.[92] But here we have a situation where many of the girls concerned cannot consent, but it seems that looking at their circumcision as adult women would have done so. There are real dilemmas here which cannot be avoided them by resorting to relativism, for then there would be no debate, or by seeking the refuge of monism, for this would impose a decontextualised overriding value. It would be comforting to rest in the moral certitudes of monism but this study has shown the fragility of the moral determinacy for which it stands.

How is then the cultural pluralist to respond? The answer lies in subjecting the practice to an internal critique, in deconstructing the arguments that are used to support it. The arguments in the case of female circumcision are, it will be recalled, four-fold. It is claimed as a control on female sexuality. Whilst there can be little doubt that it reduces sensitivity and responses to stimulation, it offers no guarantee that a woman has not had sexual experiences and, indeed, even infibulation is no guarantee: an unmarried woman can have sexual intercourse and then be re-infibulated immediately before her marriage to disguise this fact from her husband.

It is supposedly based on religion, but there is no evidence for this and at least a suspicion that it is an elitist religious fraud perpetrated by a clerical oligarchy on vulnerable women.

---

[88] Slack, above., n. 76, dicusses these at 450–5; Dorkenoo and Elworth, above., n. 35, do so at 8–10.

[89] *Draft Report of the Working Group on Traditional Practice Affecting The Health of Women and Children*, UN Doc. E/CN.4/H.C.42/1985, 12 Sept. 1985, 13.

[90] [1993] 2 All ER 75.

[91] Though we do not grant much in the way of rights to transsexuals: see *Corbett* v. *Corbett* [1971] P. 83, and *Rees* v. *UK* (1986) 9 EHRR 56.

[92] *The Rights and Wrongs of Children* (Frances Pinter, 1983).

It rests also upon sexual myths and these—such as that the clitoris is a masculine feature and will grow to the size of a penis need to be shown for what they are. If features of the other sex need to be removed is there any move in any of these societies to excise male nipples?

And, as for the supposed benefits, it has already been shown that, to the contrary, there are physical and psychological harms which surely outweigh any social or cultural benefits.

It would be easier to empathise with the arguments put if there were not in addition a suspicion that the cultural values upheld by the practices depicted here were not the values of a section of the society rather than the whole of it. Of what value are the norms of a community when they are directed at a group at best devalued but more likely excluded from it? It is concerns such as these which lead me to ask whether in a clash between the value of physical integrity and the value of cultural identity, the latter can possibly prevail.[93]

It also leads me to conclude—though it has not been necessary to discuss the question in this paper—that, using similar reasoning processes, it would not be difficult to show that in a similar clash over ritualistic male circumcision it would be the latter value, namely cultural (or religious) identity that would prevail.

On the other case studies set out at the beginning of this chapter, much briefer answers must be given. The cultural pluralist is likely to come to the same conclusion on child marriages as the Divisional Court did in *Mohamed* v. *Knott*. But s/he would need a deeper understanding of the cultural context than it would seem the English courts had.

The cultural pluralist's response to child labour in the developing world would require greater tolerance of the problems attendant on poverty, a greater understanding of the global economy and a more sophisticated approach to the relationship between child labour and education questions than is often found, but a conclusion not dissimilar from that in the UN Convention is likely to result from these deliberations.[94] On punishment practices s/he could be more categorical: there can be no reason for tolerating excessive punishment in the name of cultural difference; there is no cultural tradition or identity at stake. Of course, it would be so much easier if we knew what such punishment was different from.

---

[93] Attacks on the practice of male circumcision have been launched by eminent thinkers like Alice Miller. There is also an organisation called NOHARMM in the United States (National Organization to Halt The Abuse and Routine Mutilation of Males). See also Denise Winn, "A Campaign to Save The Foreskin", *The Independent*, 20 Apr. 1993. But see Michael Freeman, (1998) *Br. J. Urology* (forthcoming).

[94] Cf. Myron Weiner, *The Child and the State in India: Child Labor and Education Policy in Comparative Perspective* (Oxford University Press, 1991) with Olga Nieuwenhuys, *Children's Lifeworlds: Gender, Welfare and Labour in The Developing World* (Routledge, 1994). See also her review of his book in 2 *Int. Journal of Children's Rights* 205 (1994) and his article in 2 *Int. Journal of Children's Rights* 121 (1994).

A CONCLUDING COMMENT

I have set out in this chapter three approaches that may be adopted towards cultural conflict and children's rights. I reject cultural relativism because it renounces normative judgement. The moral determinacy of monism offers blanket solutions but fails to address cultural difference. Cultural pluralism, a via media perhaps between two extremes, situates values within cultural context and offers dialogue and change. Nothing can provide solutions to the difficult cases thrown up by the ways different societies treat children, but cultural pluralism does, I believe, offer a challenge. It is one that those concerned with children, their welfare and their rights, must take up.

18

Family Law in Aotearoa/New Zealand: Facing Ideologies

WILLIAM R. ATKIN and GRAEME W. AUSTIN

I. INTRODUCTION

To speak of ideology[1] and family law in Aotearoa/New Zealand in the same breath would seem to many to be somewhat odd. Family law in Aotearoa/New Zealand has, during the latter part of the twentieth century, exhibited characteristics which suggest that it is a decidedly *non*-ideological enterprise. Where individual statutory regimes allow, its focus is on particular problems arising for particular families and family members. Dominating family law discourse[2] is the theme that it is a peculiarly human branch of the law which responds humanely to individual human problems. Its *non*-ideological posture is supported in two ways: first, by broad, largely unfettered discretions, in the exercise of which decision makers simply "respond" to the facts before them and secondly, by the adoption of "neutral" principles, such as the "equality" between spouses in matrimonial property divisions.[3] Neither appears ideological. Rather, these positions appear to be either scientific or enlightened.[4]

---

[1] Professor Eagleton observes, "Nobody has yet come up with a single adequate definition of ideology. . . . [T]he term 'ideology' has a whole range of useful meanings, not all of which are compatible with each other. To try to compress this wealth of meaning into a single comprehensive definition would thus be unhelpful even if it were possible." T. Eagleton *Ideology: An Introduction* (Verso, 1991), 1. In *Literary Theory: An Introduction* (Blackwell, 1983), 210, Eagleton referred to ideology as being "the link or nexus between discourses and power", a characterisation adopted by Martha Fineman in *The Neutered Mother, the Sexual Family and Other Twentieth Century Tragedies* (Routledge, 1995), 20–4. In this chapter, we understand "ideological aspects" of family law in Aotearoa/New Zealand as referring to those aspects of the law which, with differing degrees of obviousness, pursue identifiable policy aims and agenda.

[2] The phrase "dominant discourse" is borrowed from M. Fineman, "Dominant Discourse, Professional Language and Legal Change in Child Custody Decision Making" (1988) 101 *Harv. L Rev.* 727.

[3] It should be acknowledged that some areas of family law have in recent years adopted a far *less* discretionary approach than had been considered appropriate in previous decades. The Child Support Act 1991, with its rigid formula assessment and the narrow scope allowed for departure orders, is a notorious example. See generally, W. R. Atkin "Financial Support: The Bureaucratization of Personal Responsibility" in M. Henaghan and W. R. Atkin (eds.) *Family Law Policy in New Zealand* (OUP, 1992), 210; and W. R. Atkin "Child Support in New Zealand Runs into Strife" (1994) 31 *Houston L Rev.* 631. For discussion of similar trends in Australian family law, see S. Parker "Rights and Utility in Anglo-Australian Family Law" (1992) 55 *Mod. L Rev.* 311, 325.

Our chapter has the following structure. In Part II we examine some of the claims made about and within modern family law[5] in Aotearoa/New Zealand as to its ideological neutrality. We suggest that too ready acceptance of this perspective makes it particularly difficult to evaluate critically much of what comprises the content of modern family law. This provides the framework for the discussion in Part III of selected recent developments in New Zealand family law. In the context of decisions involving the placement of children, we detail two classes of case in which it has been argued that various judicial discretions should be limited by factors which do not appear on the face of the relevant statutes. The first involves arguments based on human rights norms; the second involves claims based on Maori customary law.[6]

II. "MODERN" FAMILY LAW IN AOTEAROA/NEW ZEALAND

The aptness of the phrase "'modern' family law" is immediately apparent when one foregrounds its modernist aspirations. Broadly understood, the founding concerns of modernity are the separation of expert knowledge from opinion, discovery of and reliance on abstract truths without reference to transcendental authority and the separation of fact from opinion and politics.[7] Much of what characterises family law in the latter part of the this century is the result of a long process of debunking and rejection of principles which derive ultimately from decidedly *pre*-modern, Judaeo-Christian traditions. The natural order of things, according to these traditions, was reflected in a number of rules and principles, including the common law doctrine of *femme covert* and those associated with paternal hegemony in areas such as child custody law. The rules, judicial statements and procedures of modern New Zealand family law indicate, on the surface at least, just how much of a departure from these principles there has been.

[4] For comment on the "neutrality thesis" pursued in recent family law scholarship, see S. Parker and P. Drahos "Closer to a Critical Theory of Family Law" (1990) 4 *Aust. J of Fam. L* 159.

[5] In this chapter, we use the phrase "modern family law" to refer to a period after the first wave of significant changes occurred in family law in Aotearoa/New Zealand. Perhaps the most significant event was the creation of the New Zealand Family Court system under the Family Courts Act 1980. Family Courts are a distinct branch of the New Zealand District Courts whose creation was recommended in a significant report on the New Zealand judicial system: Beattie (Chmn.) *Report of the Royal Commission on the Courts* (Gvt. Print, 1978). The creation of the Family Court system was contemporaneous with other significant statutory changes, including the Family Proceedings Act 1980 and the Guardianship Amendment Act 1980. A slightly earlier initiative was the Matrimonial Property Act 1976 which introduced a system of deferred community of property for married spouses. For the perspective of the current President of the Court of Appeal on these changes, see the comments of Richardson J., as he then was, in *Slater* v. *Slater* [1983] NZLR 166 (C.A.). See further, Part II, below.

[6] See generally, J. Metge (Dame) and D. Durie-Hall, "Kua Tutuu Te Puehu, Kia Mau Maaori Aspirations and Family Law" in M. Henaghan and W. R. Atkin *Family Law Policy in New Zealand* (OUP, 1992), 54.

[7] See generally M. Davies *Asking the Law Question* (Sweet & Maxwell/Law Book Co., 1994), 219 ff.; D. J. Haraway *Modest Witness@Second Millennium* (Routledge, 1997), 24–5.

Those who read New Zealand child custody judgments will be reminded of this. Section 23 of the Guardianship Act 1968, which contains the rule that the welfare of the child must be the first and paramount consideration in matters of custody, access and guardianship,[8] lists factors which judges are *not* permitted to take into account when making decisions about children. Parental conduct may be considered "only to the extent that such conduct is relevant to the welfare of the child".[9] Presumptions based on gender are specifically outlawed.[10] The wishes of the child need be considered only "to such extent as the Court thinks fit, having regard to the age and maturity of the child".[11] Peppering child custody judgments are judicial statements to the effect that the Family Court deals "with human feelings, not any arid question of fact or law" and "will respond to the human situation in any case which comes before it".[12] Results in child custody decision are said to be "personalised" to meet the circumstances of the particular cases.[13] Outcomes are "tailored" to meet the individual circumstances of the families who come before the Court.

These developments are consistent with the view that modern child custody law has eschewed much of its legal content. Judge B. D. Inglis Q.C., a leading New Zealand family law jurist, captured the point with his observation in 1964 that "[f]ew areas of the law are less suited to formal legal treatment than those relating to the custody and guardianship of children".[14] New Zealand child custody law has travelled a long way from the common law rule that fathers have an absolute right to the custody of their children[15] and from the rules of thumb and

---

[8] The Infants Guardianship and Contracts Act 1887 required that, when making a child custody determination, the Court should have regard to "the welfare of the infant, and to the conduct of the parents, and to the wishes as well of the mother as of the father." This provision had been borrowed from English legislation, the Guardianship of Infants Act 1886 (UK). The provision remained in the same form in s. 6 of the Infants Act 1908 The paramountcy principle was first enshrined in New Zealand legislation with the Guardianship of Infants Act 1926, following a similar change made by the Westminster Parliament the previous year.

[9] Guardianship Act 1968, s. 23.

[10] Guardianship Act 1968, s. 23(1A).

[11] Guardianship Act 1968, s. 23(2).

[12] *Tiller* v. *Esera* 26 Apr. 1989 unrep., Family Court, Wellington F.P. 085.016.89.

[13] *Spence* v. *Spence* (1984) 3 NZFLR 347, 350; *Kidd* v. *Kidd* 3 May 1991 unrep., Family Court Hastings, F.P. 021.128.89.

[14] B. D. Inglis Q.C. in "Custody" (1964) 1 *NZULR* 310, 310. Of course, these observations are not unique to New Zealand. See, for instance, the statement of Lon Fuller that, in the child custody area, a Court is not "[n]ot applying legal rules at all, but is exercising an administrative discretion which by its nature cannot be rule bound". L. Fuller "Interaction Between Law and its Social Context" (1971 item 3 of unbound material for students, University of California at Berkeley) cited in R. H. Mnookin "Child Custody Adjudication: Judical Functions in the Face of Indeterminacy" (1975) 39 *L. and Contemp. Problems* 226, 255.

[15] See, e.g., the comments of Bowen LJ in *Re Agar-Ellis* (1883) 24 Ch. 317, 337–8: "Then we must regard the benefit of the infant: but it is to be remembered that if the words 'benefit of the infant' are to be used in any but the accurate sense it would be a fallacious test to apply to the way the Court exercises its jurisdiction over the infant by way of interference with the father. It is not the benefit of the infant as conceived by the Court, but it must be the benefit to the infant having regard to the natural law which points out that the father knows far better as a rule what is good for his children

presumptions which fettered the judicial discretion in the early part of the twentieth century.[16] Judge Inglis' comment anticipated a period of intense interest in what the social sciences could offer to the area. In the 1970s judges told us that deliberations in the area were based on "an enormous increase in our knowledge and understanding of human nature and behaviour and the forces that shape it".[17] The work of Goldstein, Freud and Solnit, particularly that concerning the "psychological parent principle",[18] was influential in Aotearoa/New Zealand,[19] as it had been elsewhere.[20] At the beginning of the 1980s amendments to the Guardianship Act 1968 increased the role of non-legal personnel. Specific provision was made for psychiatric, medical or psychological reports to be prepared in respect of any child who is the subject of an application under the Act.[21] With the introduction of the New Zealand Family Court system, and its accompanying counselling services, the hope was, and continues to be, that most disputes over the custody of children would be "resolved" by a counselling process with only the most entrenched disputes going to a full judicial hearing.

The legal principles governing child custody appear neutral and judicial activity appears to be untrammelled by ideological content. The semblance of ideological neutrality has been achieved by the diminution of its legal content. Decision-makers simply respond—neutrally and naturally—to the facts before them. To criticise the direction of modern family law in Aotearoa/New Zealand is thus to criticise sensitivity to the unique characteristics of individual families' situations.

than a Court of Justice can." The English common law of child custody was recognised as being part of New Zealand law in *J. H. and L. J. Thomson (Infants)* (1911) 20 NZLR 168, 169–73. Despite statutory changes which emphasised the welfare of the child, beginning with The Infants Act 1908, some New Zealand judges persisted with the view that the father's rights were paramount. See, e.g., *In re X and Y, Infant Children of A and B* (1912) 14 GLR 668, 669 where Edwards J commented: "The law upon this question is quite clear. At common law the father had the exclusive right to the custody of his children. That right still remains, but it is now, by the Infants Act 1908, made subject to the control of the Court." This analysis persisted as late as *Palmer* v. *Palmer* [1961] NZLR 702, 709 (C.A.) where Gresson P noted that the "statutory provisions leave a residue of the common-law right in a father".

[16] An example of one such rule was the presumption that a mother who was "guilty" of adultery was not suited to have custody of or access to her children. See *Fleming* v. *Fleming* [1948] GLR 220 (C.A.). These rules are discussed in G. Austin, *Children: Stories the Law Tells* (Victoria U Press. 1994), ch. 3.

[17] *Hall* v. *Hall*, 22 Aug. 1977 unrep., Supreme Court, Auckland Registry 614.77; *B* v. *B* [1978] 1 NZLR 285, 289. See also, M. Henaghan, "Judicial Attitudes in the Use of Expert Evidence in Custody Proceedings" (1978) 4 *Otago L Rev.* 262; C. Jackson "Custody: Specialist Evidence" in *The Rights of the Child and the Law* (Conference Papers, N.Z. National Commission for the International Year of the Child, 1979); on file with authors: G. P. Davidson, "Counsel for the Child and Psychological Expert Witnesses in Custody and Access Cases" [1980] *NZLJ* 177, 177.

[18] J. Goldstein, A. Freud and A. J. Solnit, *Beyond the Best Interests of the Child* (Free Press, 1973).

[19] *S* v. *E* (1981) 1 NZFLR 73; *McKewen* v. *McKewen*, 12 Dec. 1985 unrep., District Court, Christchurch F.P. 009.811.81; *M* v. *M*, Apr. 1988 unrep., Family Court Palmerston Nth. F.P. 054.318.87 (specific date of the judgment illegible).

[20] See generally, R. E. Crouch, "An Essay on the Critical and Judicial Reception of *Beyond the Best Interests of the Child*" (1979) 13 *FLQ* 49 and the sources cited therein.

[21] Guardianship Amendment Act 1980, s 17.

In this chapter, we wish to highlight some of the problems which we consider accompany the characteristics of family law in Aotearoa/New Zealand. First, there is very little deep questioning of the aims and purposes of family law. This is hardly surprising. The suggestion that family law might be "for" anything is inconsistent with the dominant view that it is ideologically neutral. In general, it is to be observed of Anglo jurisprudence that, whereas discussion of the purposes, policies, or aims of discrete areas of law enjoys a central place in the literature,[22] in family law such analyses tend to lie on the margins.[23] Secondly, and more importantly, because family law is not clear about its own purposes, we are left with a body of law which deals awkwardly with other, external ideas and agenda. In the following section we explore a few areas where family law in Aotearoa/New Zealand could improve the way that ideological issues are addressed.

III. NEW ZEALAND FAMILY LAW—IDEOLOGICAL CONTENT

a. Human Rights in Child Custody and Access Decisions

In domestic law in Aotearoa/New Zealand, the mandate for the increased attention given to the United Nations Convention on the Rights of the Child is to be found in the Court of Appeal decisions in *Tavita* v. *Minister of Immigration*[24] and *Puli'uvea* v. *Removal Authority*.[25] *Tavita* involved an application for judicial review of the Minister of Immigration's decision to execute a deportation warrant. At the centre of the case was a New Zealand born child whose Western Samoan father was to be deported. In an interim decision, the Court of Appeal held that certain international agreements, including the UN Convention and the International Covenant on Civil and Political Rights may fetter the Minister's discretion. The Minister was required to reconsider his decision, taking into account relevant principles relating to, *inter alia*, family privacy which are articulated in these documents.[26] The Court of Appeal's decision is notable for Cooke P.'s response to the argument that the Minister and the government officials were "entitled to ignore the international instruments." He commented: "That is an

---

[22] Numerous examples could be cited here. See, e.g., the discussion of the purposes of tort law which appears in S. Todd (ed.), *The Law of Torts in New Zealand* (2nd edn., Brooker's, 1997), 32.

[23] See, e.g., J. Dewar, *Law and the Family* (2nd edn., Butterworths, 1992), a text whose theoretical stance made it a somewhat uncharacteristic addition to family law literature.

[24] [1994] 2 NZLR 257.

[25] [1996] 3 NZLR 538.

[26] The comparable decision of the Australian High Court in *Minister for Immigration and Ethnic Affairs* v. *Teoh* (1995) 128 ALR 353 approached a similar question in a slightly different manner. A majority of the Court held that Australia's ratification of certain international treaties, including the UN Convention, provided a sufficient basis to give rise to a legitimate expectation that administrative decision-makers would act in conformity with relevant principles in these documents and that any party whose interests would be adversely affected by a decision-maker not so acting would be entitled to a hearing.

unattractive argument, apparently implying that New Zealand's adherence to the international instruments has been at least partly window-dressing."[27]

In a 1996 decision, *Puli'uvea* v. *Removal Authority*, a differently constituted Court of Appeal was required to cover similar ground to that traversed in the *Tavita* decision. Delivering judgment for the court, Keith J held that in the course of administrative decision-making it was not necessary to make explicit reference to the text of any international document. However, the court clarified a critical point that was left open in *Tavita*. Although the decision-maker did not need to make specific reference to international documents such as the UN Convention, the "substance" of the relevant international obligations has become a mandatory relevant consideration in administrative decisions in the immigration area[28] which may negatively affect children's lives.

We are not concerned here with the administrative law issues raised by these cases. Our interest is more with their influence in the rather more workaday world of custody and access decisions. The decision of Fraser J in *H* v. *F*[29] illustrates how the UN Convention may be taken into account. The case involved three children, aged 11, 10 and 9. They had been brought up by their parents in an Exclusive Brethren community. When the parents began experiencing marital difficulties, they placed the children in the custody of grandparents and an unmarried aunt, all of whom were deeply involved in the Church community. After reconciling, and deciding that they would leave the Church, the parents sought return of their children. The grandparents refused, maintaining that it would not be in the best interests of the children to leave the Church. There was evidence suggesting that the children wished to remain.

Fraser J thought that the parents and the grandparents both presented "compelling" cases for custody of the children. In exercising his discretion, he considered that he was entitled to take into account the impact of the tenets, doctrines and rules of society. It was legitimate, in his Honour's view, to look to the UN Convention as a source for these principles. He was, however, faced with a tension between key provisions of the Convention. Whereas Article 14 requires States Parties to respect "the right of the child to freedom of thought, conscience and religion"[30] a decision to allow the children to remain with the grandparents

---

[27] It is noteworthy that the Court of Appeal was influenced in its decision by two decisions of the European Court of Human Rights which were based on Art. 8 of the European Convention for the Protection of Human Rights and Fundamental Freedoms. See *Berrehab* v. *Netherlands* (1988) 11 EHRR 322 and *Beljoudi* v. *France* (1992) 14 EHRR 801.

[28] See also *Elika* v. *Minister of Immigration* [1996] 1 NZLR 741, where Williams J noted that the interests of New Zealand-born children are a consideration which is required to be taken into account pursuant to the International Covenant on Civil and Political Rights and the UN Convention on the Rights of the Child but held that the interests of children were not to be considered the paramount consideration.

[29] (1993) 10 FRNZ 486.

[30] A comparison may be made between the New Zealand litigation and two cases in the Supreme Court of Canada, *Young* v. *Young* (1993) 49 RFL (3d) 117 and *Droit de law Famillie 1150* (1993) 49 RFL (3d) 317, which considered the relationship between child custody and access law and the guarantees relating to freedom of conscience and religion contained in the Canadian Charter of Rights and Freedoms.

would have been inconsistent with other articles. Justifying the decision to return the children to the grandparents, His Honour said:

> "It may be noted that there are respects in which the views held by the Exclusive Brethren fellowship are incompatible with principles formulated in the Convention, for example, freedom to seek and receive information and ideas of all kinds (art 13), freedom of association (art 15), the accessibility of higher education to all on the basis of capacity (art 28), and education being directed to the preparation of the child for responsible life in a free society in the spirit of . . . tolerance and friendship among all people and . . . religious groups (art 29)."

Other New Zealand judges have adopted the view that "[i]n the exercise of its discretionary powers in matters covered by the Convention the Court may need to take account of the terms of the Convention".[31] One has gone so far as to comment that reference to UN Convention may be "essential".[32] This is a far-reaching suggestion. The phrase, "matters covered by the Convention" appears to encompass a broad range of issues: custody, access, guardianship, care and protection being merely the more obvious candidates. Others are: medical decisions, school suspensions, child support, and matrimonial property divisions.

The increasing relevance of human rights in child custody and access matters is suggested by the High Court decision in *B* v. *JM*, a decision of Ellis J, in May 1997.[33] In July 1993 the Family Court made an order granting interim custody of four children to the mother. A special condition was imposed with respect to the youngest child, born 1985, that she was to have no contact with her maternal grandfather. The child had complained that the grandfather had sexually abused her. The grandfather was subsequently tried and acquitted. By 1995, the mother and the grandfather wished that the child's contact with the grandfather be resumed. The mother did not wish to apply to the Court herself, as she feared that this would reopen the custody dispute with the father. The grandfather relied on section 17 of the Guardianship Act 1968, the governing statute, which provides that an application for review of a custody, access or guardianship order may be brought by "any person affected by the order." One difficulty with the grandfather's application was that under the 1968 Act, grandparents are not permitted to apply for access, although grandparents are permitted, with leave, to apply for custody.[34] Notwithstanding the former prohibition, Ellis J allowed the grandfather's application to proceed. In His Honour's view, as the grandfather was allowed to apply for custody, "surely he can apply to vary a custody order obtained by [the mother]".[35]

Ellis J considered himself to be "fortified in his conclusions" by certain sections of the New Zealand Bill of Rights Act 1990 and by the importance accorded

---

[31] *In re the S Children* [1994] NZFLR 971, 977 (Judge B. D. Inglis Q.C.).

[32] *Re the W Children* (1994) 12 FRNZ 548 (Judge P. von Dadelszen).

[33] [1997] NZFLR 529, on appeal from *M* v. *M* (1996) 14 FRNZ 102 (Judge Frater).

[34] Except where a parent, being the grandparent's child, has died. See Guardianship Act 1968, s. 16.

[35] [1997] NZFLR 529, 531.

to the family in Article 23 of the International Covenant on Civil and Political Rights. The New Zealand Bill of Rights Act 1990, whose wording was significantly influenced by the Canadian Charter of Rights, states in its preamble that its purposes include "affirm[ing] New Zealand's commitment to the International Covenant on Civil and Political Rights." It is not "higher law" empowering courts to strike down inconsistent legislation. Rather, it provides a canon of construction. Where an ambiguity in the construction of a statute may be resolved consistently with the rights and freedoms declared in the 1990 Act, that interpretation is to be preferred.[36] Ellis J invoked sections 17 (right to freedom of association) and 27 (right to observance of the principles of natural justice) of the Bill of Rights Act 1990 in support of his view that the grandfather should have standing to bring proceedings to review the interim custody order. He said: "It is easy to formulate a grandfather's ordinary social intercourse with his granddaughter as part of his freedom to associate with those he chooses and that he should have the right to be heard by the Family Court which deprives him of that freedom."[37] With respect to Article 23 of the International Covenant on Civil and Political Rights, Ellis J observed: "The family naturally includes members of an extended family according to the social customs of the community. In New Zealand that includes grandparents. Again, my view of s 17 [of the Guardianship Act 1968] is in harmony with this international instrument."[38]

The judgment in *B* v. *JM* is remarkable for what it does not address. The inability of grandparents—as well as other parties outside the nuclear family—to apply for access under the Guardianship Act 1968 might have been viewed as reflecting a clear policy that the immediate family should not be vulnerable to "interference" by "outsiders" by way of an application for access. Whatever one may think of this policy, and it has been subject to criticism,[39] it is at least arguable that Parliament considered that providing this degree of security for family arrangements is consistent with the welfare of children. However, in its determination to constitutionalise the issues, to view them in terms of consistency with human right norms such as the right to an individual's freedom of association, the judgment fails to consider what might be good for families and children, or, more precisely, what family and children centred policies Parliament may have been promoting through the interrelationship between the particular provisions of the Guardianship Act 1968.

The point here is not to evaluate the two positions—*viz.* respecting the grandfather's freedom of association and the policy reflected in the prohibition against broad access rights. Rather, it is to suggest that the use of human rights norms

---

[36] New Zealand Bill of Rights Act 1990, s. 6: "Wherever an enactment can be given a meaning that is consistent with the rights and freedoms contained in this Bill of Rights, that meaning shall be preferred to any other meaning."

[37] [1997] NZFLR 529, 532.

[38] [1997] NZFLR 529, 533.

[39] See generally, J. Metge (Dame) and D. Durie-Hall, "Kua Tutuu Te Puehu, Kia Mau Maaori Aspirations and Family Law" in W. R. Atkin and M. Henaghan *Family Law Policy in New Zealand* (OUP, 1992), 54, 69.

in family law decisions requires careful scrutiny. Without decrying the influence of human rights norms in family law *per se*,[40] we wish to raise two caveats. First, there is the issue of resources. During a time of fiscal constraints,[41] it may be questioned whether advocates' time and the resources of clients and the Family Court system should be devoted to framing intricate arguments based on human rights norms. Many of the rights in the UN Convention on the Rights of the Child, for instance, are qualified by reference to the interests of the child, reasonable limitations, and concepts such as public order and morality. Much work may need to be done to ascertain the precise meaning and scope of these rights. It must be questioned whether the Family Court is the appropriate place for this kind of analysis to occur.

Secondly, as the analysis in *B* v. *JM* indicates, there is the risk that increased recourse to human rights norms will finesse the issues raised in individual cases in particular ways. In *B* v. *JM*, the issue of standing became an issue concerning the right to freedom of association rather than of the welfare of the child and family. At a policy level, this may or may not be appropriate. At the very least, it should be debated. However, as we suggest earlier in this chapter, policy debate in this branch of family law is discouraged by its very structures and by the principles underlying it. If child custody and access decisions are perceived to be based simply on a judicial response to the "facts" of the cases, albeit a response informed by the social science data available to the Court, no footholds are provided from which ideological positions—such as promotion of civil and political rights—can be analysed.

b. Maori Customary Law

An important ideological challenge to the neutrality of New Zealand family law comes from the indigenous Maori population. Here it is important to distinguish between Maori customary law and mainstream family law which is found in numerous statutory regimes and common law principles and the institutional structures such as the Family Court. Although there have been many specific New Zealand innovations, the pedigree of the latter may be traced to its British origins. Maori have their own traditions and customary laws which pre-date and have developed since colonisation. As the following discussion indicates, there is as yet a considerable degree of incoherence in the way in which mainstream law approaches ideological challenges whose source is Maori customary law. Three questions arise: (1) is there a direct place for customary law in mainstream

---

[40] The UN Convention on the Rights of the Child may prove to be a particularly strong advocacy tool for interest groups and NGOs which wish to bring children's issues to the attention of government. See generally, G. W. Austin, "Children's Rights in New Zealand Law and Society" (1995) 25 *VUWLR* 249.

[41] See Harding "Financing the Family Court—Are there Storm Clouds Gathering?" in *The Family Court Ten Years On* (NZ Law Society, Wellington, 1991).

family law? (2) are there other more subtle ways in which custom can be recognised? (3) how should courts respond when faced with disputes involving children whose parents and loved ones are from different racial groups?

1. Direct recognition of Maori customary law

Because New Zealand family law is mostly statutory, where legislation has addressed the validity of customary concepts there is little scope to argue a contrary position. For example, in traditional Maori society there was no formal ceremony of marriage but validity of the marriage was assured by public expression of whanau (family) approval. Approval rather than actual cohabitation was the key to validity.[42] The imported law for a while accepted marriages according to Maori customary law. However, with the passing of the Maori Purposes Act 1951, customary Maori marriages were stripped of their legal status within mainstream statutory frameworks. Today, customary marriages—without the added extras of licences and registration—are treated as *de facto* relationships. Despite this, a possible exception emerged in one case which examined whether a couple who were married only according to custom could adopt a child. Under the Adoption Act 1955, an adoption order can be made in favour of two "spouses". In a somewhat non-conventional treatment of the issues, Judge Boshier in *Re Adoption by Paul and Hauraki*[43] held that "spouses" could refer to parties to a *de facto* relationship and he was influenced by the existence of the customary marriage. Arguably the decision is anomolous.[44]

The conventional approach to Maori customary law can be seen more authoritatively when we consider adoption. Section 19(1) of the Adoption Act 1955 states:[45]

> "No person shall hereafter be capable or be deemed at any time since the commencement of the Native Land Act 1909 to have been capable of adopting any child in accordance with Maori custom, and except as provided in subsection (2) of this section, no adoption in accordance with Maori custom shall be of any force or effect, whether in respect of intestate succession to Maori land or otherwise."

This provision came under the scrutiny of the Court of Appeal in *Whittaker v. Maori Land Court of New Zealand*.[46] In 1943 the Maori Land Court made a succession order in respect of the intestacy of the applicant's grandmother. The applicant's mother, Ngawini, whose adoption in 1892 according to Maori customary law had never been registered, was not provided for. The question was

---

[42] See "Husband and Wife" in *The Laws of New Zealand* (Butterworths, 1995), para. 10.

[43] [1993] NZFLR 266.

[44] Unless the statute expressly provides for the contrary, the term "spouse" and similar words will be taken to refer to legally married parties: "Husband and Wife" in *The Laws of New Zealand* (Butterworths, 1995), para. 113.

[45] Subs. (2) preserves for certain purposes the validity of customary adoptions made before 31 Mar. 1910 so long as they were registered with the Maori Land Court.

[46] [1997] NZFLR 707. The High Court decision is reported at [1996] NZFLR 163.

whether the customary adoption should have been recognised. The Court of Appeal noted the chequered legal history of customary adoptions which in fact vacillated in and out of recognition at various different times. Nevertheless, the current law overrode this history and operated retrospectively. Ngawini's adoption, valid some years and not valid other years, could not today be recognised. Though sympathetic to the claim, the Court of Appeal was constrained by the clear words of the current legislation:[47]

"the relevant legislative provisions have fluctuated from one position to the reverse without apparent attention being given to all the circumstances which might arise. In the result, Ngawini's adoption, and with it the present claim, however meritorious it may be, simply "falls through the cracks" of the successive enactments."

2. Recognition through the Treaty of Waitangi/Te Tiriti o Waitangi

The Treaty of Waitangi/*Te Tiriti o Waitangi* is a fundamental constitutional document signed by the Crown and Maori tribes in 1840.[48] It provided some legitimacy for the colonial government but also purported to preserve for Maori chieftainship ("*te tino rangatiranga*") over their traditional land and fishing rights, along with their "*taonga*" or "treasures". To what extent can customary law and/or mores be imported into family law via an argument based on the Treaty?

Where Parliament has expressly addressed an issue, as we have seen it has done with marriage and adoption, there is little or no likelihood of an argument based on the Treaty succeeding. As noted earlier, much family law is less direct and incorporates judicial discretion. In *R* v. *R*,[49] the New Zealand High Court rejected the argument that the Treaty/*Te Tiriti* was relevant to a custody dispute arising under the Guardianship Act 1968. There the father had claimed that patriarchal rights over his child had been preserved by the Treaty. Tipping J adhered to the view that parliamentary law, rather than the Treaty/*Te Tiriti*, was paramount and applied the statutory principle that the welfare of the child is paramount. It must be added that Tipping J considered that the father had a particularly poor case on the merits. The judgment does not reach the issues of whether the Treaty/*Te Tiriti* could in any event be interpreted as the father proposed and whether Maori customary law might have developed towards a more flexible approach.

---

[47] *Ibid.*, 713. The changing fortunes of Ngawini's legal status are spelt out by the Court of Appeal as follows: "Successively there were periods when the parent/child relationship between Meriana [the mother] and Ngawini was recognised by law (1892–1901), was recognised by law contingent upon registration (1902–1909), was of no legal effect (1910–1927), was contingently of full force and effect (1927–192) and was of no legal effect (1930 onward). That the legislature should vacillate on the status of a child in this way is as surprising as it is regrettable. While it may have reflected intermittent concern for potentially abusive claims to interests in land, it also wrought injustice in this case."

[48] The Treaty of Waitangi/Te Tiriti o Waitangi is more fully discussed in Atkin and Austin, "Cross-cultural Challenges to Family Law in Aotearoa/New Zealand" in Lowe and Douglas (eds.), *Families Across Frontiers* (Martinus Nijhoff, 1996).

[49] (1990) 6 FRNZ 232.

The latest authoritative word on the subject came up with a novel twist. In the High Court appeal decision in *BP* v. *D-GSW*[50] the Maori mother of a child born in July 1996 wanted the child adopted. She had four other children born to her existing partner, but the father of the latest child was another man serving time in prison. One of the reasons for the adoption was to preserve the longer-term relationship with her current partner. However, she faced an application for custody and guardianship from her own mother, ie the child's grandmother, who wanted to protect the child's indigenous rights to be raised by the whanau. She based the claim on *te tino rangatiratanga* in Article 2 of the Treaty of Waitangi/*Te Tiriti o Waitangi*. For many Maori, grandparents have special roles in the upbringing of children and this was doubtless also in the background of the grandmother's argument. The mother countered with the argument that she had been badly brought up by her mother and and that her decision to have the child adopted was partly to ensure in her own mind that her child would have a happy family environment. Allegations by the grandmother that this decision was driven by the mother's allegedly violent partner were rejected by the lower court as unfounded and this finding was upheld by the High Court in the appeal. The mother, the courts accepted, was making a free choice about the child's future. The adopting mother was Maori but not from the same *iwi* (tribe) as the mother and grandmother.

The Family Court Judge in the Court below had dismissed the grandmother's application. Judge B. D. Inglis Q.C. thought it difficult to interpret the Treaty in the way advanced, expressing his view that "anyone who seeks to rely on the Treaty of Waitangi in a case under the Guardianship Act is entering a legal minefield".[51] Article 2, he opined, does not preserve customary rights in respect of children and furthermore, Article 3 confers the Crown's protection on "all the ordinary people of New Zealand" and gives them "the same rights and duties of citizenship as the people of England". In contrast to the grandmother's stance, Article 3 gives the child the right to have her welfare treated as paramount and gives the mother the right to consent to adoption.[52]

While the High Court agreed with the decision not to grant custody to the grandmother, its reasoning differed. No mention is made of Article 3 of the Treaty/*Te Tiriti* but the position of the Treaty appears, on analysis only initially, to be given greater status than hitherto thought:[53]

"We are of the view that since the Treaty of Waitangi was designed to have general application, that general application must colour all matters to which it has relevance, whether public or private and that for the purposes of interpretation of statutes, it will have a direct bearing whether or not there is a reference to the Treaty in the statute. We also take the view that the familial organisation of one of the peoples a party to the

---

[50] [1997] NZFLR 642 per Gallen and Goddard JJ. The Family Court judgment of Judge Inglis Q.C. is reported as *B* v. *M* [1997] NZFLR 126.
[51] *Ibid.*, 137.
[52] *Ibid.*, 137.
[53] [1997] NZFLR 642, 646.

Treaty, must be seen as one of the taonga, the preservation of which is contemplated. Accordingly we take the view that all Acts dealing with the status, future and control of children, are to be interpreted as coloured by the principles of the Treaty of Waitangi."

The court also referred to Article 4 of the draft Declaration of Indigenous Peoples 1993, emphasising the right of indigenous peoples to maintain and strengthen their political, economic, social and cultural characteristics as well as their legal systems.

If the Treaty is to "colour" the law dealing with children, what does this really mean? The grandmother argued that Maori custom should be *dominant* in determining what is in the best interests of a Maori child, but the High Court rejected this argument:[54]

"We do not think it is helpful to consider the question in terms of domination or primacy. Few cases involving the welfare of a child are as clear as that."

The judges saw Maori concepts of family, genealogy and nurturing practices as "a starting point" applicable to all statutory provisions on children but having said that, they then held that everything was subsumed within the concept of the welfare of the child:[55]

"We emphasise therefore, that the child holds the central position within the context provided by the concepts of family to which reference has been made. That means that the child's interests will not be subordinated to the interests of any other member of the family or whanau, nor will the interests of the child be subordinated to those of the whanau as a whole. In addition, the ability of the whanau itself and the caregivers within the whanau, must be assessed with regard to the particular circumstances of the case and the needs of the child itself. It cannot be assumed that in all cases the standards and values accepted by traditional society from which the child comes will be preserved or available within the whanau to which reference must be made."

Drawing the threads together, the judges said:[56]

"We reject therefore, any concept that the whanau as a whole or individual members of it, or that the mother or father of the child, have rights which can subordinate the interests of the child itself."

Part of the grandmother's case was that, when decisions are made about a child, the *whanau* (family) should be consulted. While the High Court largely agreed with this in principle, the judges considered that the matter had been preempted by the mother's decision to consent to the adoption, a decision she was legally entitled to make. Because of the mother's "very clear decision" about adoption, "the genuineness of her belief that the appellant [grandmother] should not undertake the upbringing of her baby",[57] and the undesirability of upsetting

[54] *Ibid.*, 648.
[55] *Ibid.*, 653.
[56] *Idem.*
[57] *Ibid.*, 654.

the present bonding with the adopting parents, the High Court was not prepared to grant custody to the grandmother.

The case shows that New Zealand courts will not accept arguments based on Maori customary law without careful scrutiny. It also illustrates the obvious point that when faced with competing ideologies judges must inevitably give priority to one over the other. Within the one set of procedings there were perceived tensions between Maori customary law, children's interests, and, perhaps, the rights of mothers. The position of the two Maori women—the mother and the grandmother—contrasted markedly. Perhaps most importantly for present purposes, *BP* v. *D-GSW* does little to clarify the law. While the Treaty and hence custom are "a starting point" and "colour" our interpretation of legislation affecting children, the umbrella concept of the welfare of the child with all its discretion and imprecision remains foremost in the assessment of what should happen to a child.

The lack of clarity might have been anticipated from the outset. Arguments based on the Treaty of Waitangi/*Te Tiriti o Waitangi* are, by their very nature, political. Further, they are based, tacitly in some instances, on a growing body of legal principles related to the recognition of the Treaty within mainstream law.[58] As noted in Part II the posture adopted by much of the law relating to the placement of children is that it is neutral, non-legal, value-free. The grand statements of the High Court about the Treaty/*Te Tiriti* and about Maori practices begin to look as though they were driven by "political correctness" in an area where "politics" is otherwise eschewed. While not wishing to minimise the real complexities of cases such as *BP*, we might perhaps surmise that it is a further ad hoc response to varying ideologies confronting the courts.

3. Room for Compromise?

We have seen that even within Maori families there may be conflict about the right way to care for children. In *BP* v. *D-GSW* the clash was partly at a personal level but it is also possible that there will be significant differences of attitude between different *iwi* (tribes). The difficulties can be even more acute where one parent is Maori and the other is European. Is there any way of finding a compromise between these competing forces? As the case of *T* v. *F*[59] illustrates, judges will mine the relevant legislation in order to reach a compromise.

T v. *F* concerned a baby girl born to a European mother and a Maori father. The mother had placed the girl for adoption. In earlier proceedings,[60] the father had unsuccessfully sought custody in order to avoid the child's being divorced from her Maori heritage. The court was influenced by the fact that the father had not seen the child nor had he contributed to her support. He had also had seven *de facto* relationships in five years. In the later proceedings, after the girl had been with the adopting parents for 10 months, the Maori grandparents, who

---

[58] See generally, P. McHugh, *The Maori Magna Carta* (OUP, 1991).
[59] (1996) 14 FRNZ 415.
[60] *Re Baby "C"* [1996] NZFLR 280.

were deeply involved in Maori cultural affairs, sought custody and guardianship. Judge Inglis said that there is no presumption favouring blood relatives.[61] He also noted that the child's ancestry was in fact predominantly European but from the Maori point of view this is not crucial: any Maori ancestry is enough for *tikanga Maori* to become important for the child. On the other hand, the judge emphasised that both sides of a child's ancestry must be acknowledged:[62]

" . . . in this day and age, it has to be recognised that this child's feet stand astride two cultures. It is not for this Court to say that one is better for this child than the other. Rather it is for a Family Court to say that the child should be offered the best of both. The welfare of the child comes first . . . for this child of dual ancestry both sides of that ancestry are important to her and . . . in her upbringing neither is to be diminished at the expense of the other without good reason. For when the child reaches maturity and is able to make her own choices, her upbringing in both cultures will give her the opportunity to decide which course she wants her life to take."

How then could the child enjoy both cultures when the natural mother did not want the child brought up by the father or his family? Judge Inglis weighed up the evidence and decided that the grandparents who were elderly and did not know the child should not succeed in their custody application. However, he then proposed that they might be made "additional guardians" of the child, a power which would not be exercised lightly and only if there were concrete advantages for the child.[63] The additional guardianship role could be tailored to the particular needs, so that it does not interfere with the adopting parents normal day to day nurture of the child but could be geared to fostering grandparent/grandchild relationships and introducing the girl to her Maori heritage. Such an appointment was put on hold in this case as the adopting parents had not been heard on the issue but it is obvious that the judge saw it as a mechanism through what was otherwise an awkward bind.

Is the approach in *T* v. *F* a sound one? From the grandparents' point of view, they may have felt sold short. But the judge referred to the law as "a blunt instrument"[64] and hoped that over time with sensitivity the parties would make the relationships work. On the other hand, what if the court had granted the order in favour of the grandparents? The natural mother would feel distressed and deeply concerned about her baby's future. She obviously had concerns about the involvement of the father. Are her choices and values to be forgotten in order to achieve some other goal which she does not share? And do the adopting parents who have been the girl's family for 10 months suddenly drop out of the scene? None of these questions allow for easy solutions. Indeed, the reluctance of key branches of modern family law in Aotearoa/New Zealand to address questions of policy or ideology directly suggests that none is likely to be found.

---

[61] (1996) 14 FRNZ 415, 419.
[62] (1996) 14 FRNZ 415, 421.
[63] S. 8, Guardianship Act 1968.
[64] (1996) 14 FRNZ 415, 428.

IV. CONCLUSION

In this chapter, we have noted the supposed neutrality of family law—its desire to decide cases, especially those involving children, according to the individual circumstances of the particular case. This desire almost inevitably however disguises the underlying reality and comes under assault as parties invoke the more general ideologies which form part of their circumstances. Modern examples we have addressed are human rights norms and indigenous people's claims.

When many of the key areas of modern family law are examined, instead of a body of integrated ideals, policies and agenda, we find a considerable degree of incoherence. In part, this is due to the nature of the discipline. Its concern is, after all, the regulation of intimacy and intimate relationships in all their many varied forms. However, another part of the reason may also be found in the structures and rules of modern family law in Aotearoa/New Zealand—structures and rules which, we suggest, engender a reluctance to face ideologies.

19

African Customary Family Law in South Africa: a Legacy of Many Pasts*

JEANNE Y. DE KOKER

1. INTRODUCTION

The legal status and future of African customary family law in the South African legal system is at a crossroads. Constitutional recognition of both African customary law[1] and the right to equality[2] brought the debate about the compatibility of African customary law and human rights principles to a head in South Africa. One school of thought regards African customary law as a patriarchal, male dominated system which is highly discriminatory towards women[3] and incompatible with human rights. Consequently this school regards many of the central rules of African customary law as unconstitutional. Another school argues that African customary law and its rules and customs are protected by the right to culture, which is also enshrined in the Constitution. Many proponents of this school of thought argue that "official" African customary law is a rigid, distorted version of living African customary law and that the latter, pure version of the system is compatible with the constitutional right to equality.[4]

* This chapter resulted from another paper read at and participation in a conference entitled "Gender and colonialism" hosted by the University of the Western Cape during January 1997. The research was completed at the School of Oriental and African Studies, University of London. The financial support of Vista University and the hospitality of the School are gratefully acknowledged.

[1] Ss. 30 and 31 of the Bill of Rights recognise the right to language and culture as well as the right of cultural, religious and linguistic communities to enjoy and maintain their culture. S. 39, which regulates the interpretation of the Bill of Rights, provides explicitly that the Bill of Rights does not deny the existence of any other rights or freedoms that are recognised or conferred by common law, customary law or legislation to the extent that they are consistent with the Bill. Explicit provision for the recognition and application of African customary law is also made in the chapter dealing with traditional leadership in s. 211. Subject to the Bill of Rights, the Constitution therefore provides a firm basis for the future application of African customary law.

[2] The Constitution of the Republic of South Africa Act 108/1996, s. 9.

[3] Certain marriage customs which, according to this school, perpetuate the suppression of women are frequently mentioned as African customary law customs which violate human rights.

[4] For a discussion of and different opinions on the debate see *inter alia* Bennett 1995, 80; Bekker 1994, 440–1; Nhlapo 1994, 52; and Kaganas and Murray 1994, 410–12.

In order to address the debate successfully in a South African context an historical perspective of the development of African customary law, in particular "official" African customary law, in South Africa is required.

This chapter aims to provide such a perspective. The history of the recognition and application of African customary law in South Africa will first be outlined briefly. Then the chapter will proceed to discuss selected aspects of the South African history with specific reference to their respective influences on the development of "official" African customary law.[5]

2. THE DIFFERENT FORMS OF AFRICAN CUSTOMARY LAW DISTINGUISHED IN SOUTH AFRICA

This chapter focuses on the development of "official" African customary family law in South Africa. Therefore, it is necessary to clarify the use of the terminology.

Three forms of African customary law are distinguished in South Africa today: "Autonomic" [also referred to as "living" or "non-official"] African customary law, "official" African customary law and "academic" African customary law.[6]

The content of the different forms of African customary law, particularly that of "official" and "non-official" African customary law, differs.[7] "Official" African customary law is embodied in legislation and acknowledged in law reports and government papers.[8] It is a rigid set of written rules which are applied in the official courts and state bureaucracy in South Africa. This form of African customary law is generally regarded as a distortion of "living" African customary law.[9] "Living" African customary law, on the other hand, is a fluid and dynamic legal system, practised by the people and applied in various traditional and informal tribunals.[10] "Academic" African customary law is mainly distinguished for teaching purposes.[11] It is a flawed mixture of "official" and "non-official" African customary law which is presented to students in order to introduce them to the dichotomy of modern African customary law. The existence of these different forms of African customary law are regarded as one of the results of colonialism.[12]

---

[5] The chapter will focus on the development of African customary family and marriage law.

[6] Sanders 1987, 406; Bennett and Peart 1991, 49–50.

[7] Sanders 1987, 406–7; Nhlapo 1991, 136–7; Bennett 1991, 18–19, 1994, 122; Bennett and Peart 1991, 49–50; Bekker and Maithufi 1992, 48; Roberts 1984, 3; Chanock 1989, 72; and Njere 1994, 412. For a discussion on the difference between "official" and "non-official" African customary law, see Bekker and Maithufi 1992, 47–60.

[8] Sanders 1987, 406; Suttner 1984, 51.

[9] Sanders 1987, 406–7, 409; Nhlapo 1991, 136–7; Bennett 1991, 18–19; Church 1995, 295; Bennett and Peart 1991, 49–50, 1994, 122; Bekker and Maithufi 1992, 48; Roberts 1984, 3; and Chanock 1989, 72.

[10] Bennett 1991, 49–50; Sanders 1987, 409.

[11] Bennett and Peart 1991, 50.

[12] Sanders 1987, 406; Nhlapo 1991, 136–7; and Bennett 1991, 18–19.

The author is of the opinion that "official" African customary law, in particular "official" African customary family law, is the end product of various social, economic and political influences. It is in fact a legacy of many pasts. As it is not possible to investigate and discuss all the aspects of South African history which influenced the development of "official" African customary law in detail in a piece of this nature, this chapter will focus on and explore the effect of Dutch and British Colonialism on the development of "official" African customary family law.

3. AFRICAN CUSTOMARY LAW IN SOUTH AFRICA FROM 1652 TO 1997: A BRIEF HISTORICAL OVERVIEW

1 The status of African customary law under the rule of the Dutch East India Company

A new period in the history of Southern Africa began as a fleet of the Dutch East India Company (VOC), the *Drommedaris*, the *Goede Hoop* and the *Reijger* anchored in Table Bay in April 1652.[13] The instructions from the Dutch East India Company to the Commander of the new settlement, Jan Van Riebeeck, were clear: as the Directors of the Dutch East India Company had no interest in creating a Dutch Colony and the reasoning behind the settlement was purely commercial, the sole purpose of the settlement was to provide a provisioning station for the ships of the company.[14] However, by 1658 the settlement had become a colony.[15]

The first European inhabitants of the Cape were subjects of the United Netherlands. As such they were subject to Dutch law[16] in so far as it could find practical application in the Cape.[17] Due to its unique circumstances, very little of the Dutch law could, however, find such practical application in the Cape. Despite this fact, Dutch law formed a basis for and greatly influenced the laws and legal practice of the Cape.[18]

During the years of Dutch colonialism, contact between the colonists and the indigenes related mainly to trade and service[19] and neither the Hottentots nor the Khoi troubled the colonists significantly.[20] Consequently, the Company had been

---

[13] Muller 1986, 18.

[14] Fouché 1963, 114–15; Böeseken 1986, 20; Fredrickson 1981, 28; Elphick 1979, 10; Giliomee and Elphick 1979, 365–6; and Keegan 1996, 15.

[15] Fouché 1963, 122; Fredrickson 1981, 28–30.

[16] Which would also include Batavian legislation.

[17] Wijpkema 1934, 9; Fouché 1963, 119.

[18] Wijpkema 1934, 13, 18, 58.

[19] Fredrickson 1981, 29; Penn 1989, 2; Freund 1984, 55; and Elphick 1979, 10.

[20] The expansion of the "colony" into the interior was, however, not completely devoid of conflict. The Khoi and the San, to a greater extent, resisted the moving of "trekboere" (pioneers) into the interior. Their resistance was, however, apart from the resistance during 1738 to 1740, insignificant. See also Penn 1989, 8–9; Böekeseken 1986, 61; and Elphick 1979, 3.

indifferent to the Hottentots and Khoi. This led to a situation in which the legal position of the indigenous people of the Cape was ambiguous. On the one hand the Dutch East India Company termed them a free people and left them in general to act as they chose toward each other and did not attempt to govern the personal relations of the indigenes.[21] On the other hand, in 1672 the Council of Justice established its jurisdiction over Khoikhoi, who by culture, domicile and associations could be regarded as subjects of the colony rather than of a traditional chief, and over independent Khoikhoi involved in disputes with Europeans or slaves.[22]

In theory, therefore, the Khoikhoi were allowed to practise their legal system(s). In practice, however, the greater part of the Khoikhoi community in the Western Cape was integrated into the European society and subject to Dutch law,[23] with the result that very little of the indigenous legal system(s) was actually applied and implemented. The Dutch never clearly abolished the Khoikhoi's legal system, nor did they provide for its application in the Dutch legal system. A legal *fiat* resulted from this inconclusive situation—one which would have a far-reaching effect on the status of indigenous law and indigenous peoples in South Africa in the future.

2 The Cape Colony before the annexation of the Transkeian territories (Cape Colony proper)

When Britain occupied the Cape Colony proper the British administration was opposed to the recognition of African customary law, as it was dismissed by the early missionaries and colonial officials as a barbarous and inferior system of law.[24] Consequently, Roman-Dutch law as modified by legislation was retained as the only system of law governing the people living within the Colonial boundaries. African customary law received no formal recognition[25] as a legal system in the Colony proper.[26] A small concession to the existence of African customary law as a legal system was the promulgation of the Black Succession Act 18 of 1864 which regulated intestate succession.[27]

The colonial government could, however, not ignore the adherence of the African people to African customary law indefinitely. Consequently, despite their negative opinion of African customary law, the colonial administration devised a legal system in terms of which African customary law was afforded partial recog-

---

[21] Elphick 1979, 10; Theal 1922, 117, 381; and Elphick and Shell 1979, 116.
[22] Elphick 1979, 13, 18.
[23] See section 4 *infra*.
[24] Bennett 1994, 122, 1995, 61; Kaganas and Murray 1994, 16; and Ncube 1991, 59.
[25] In practice, however, African customary law was recognised and applied in the north-eastern territories of the colony.
[26] Bekker 1989, 1–2.
[27] Bekker 1989, 3; Van Niekerk 1990, 37.

nition. This entailed, in essence, the recognition of what they regarded as the less offensive rules of African customary law.[28] The partial recognition was linked to a policy of indirect rule which enabled the colonial government to utilise existing indigenous institutions to enforce and administer colonial rule in South Africa.[29] Native courts, empowered to adjudicate African customary law disputes, were incorporated into the formal legal system.[30]

The status of African customary law in the former territory of the Cape Colony proper remained unchanged until 1927, when the Black Administration Act[31] was promulgated.[32]

3 The Transkeian territories

The Transkeian territories, the region between the Kei River and Natal, were remote and sparsely populated by whites. A well-structured and organised indigenous community existed in this region. As a result, African customary law gained its first recognition in nineteenth century South Africa as a proper legal system in the Transkeian territories.[33] However, only certain rules of African customary law were recognised. Certain institutions of African customary law were prohibited and the application of a rule of African customary law was made subject to the condition that it should be compatible with the general principles of humanity observed throughout the "civilised" world.[34]

4 Natal

By the mid-nineteenth century African customary law had acquired some recognition in Natal.[35] Tribal leadership was restored and African customary law recognised in so far as it was not repugnant to the general principles of humanity observed throughout the "civilised" world.[36] In 1898 the laws regarding the administration of civil law in respect of Africans were consolidated in the Courts (Blacks) Act.[37] In terms of this Act the chiefs' courts, magistrates' courts and the specially constituted Black High Court, had original jurisdiction in all cases in

---

[28] Kaganas and Murray 1994, 16.
[29] See Crowder in Eze 1984, 9.
[30] Olivier *et al.* 1995, 190; Bennett 1991, 18–19; and Bennett and Peart 1991, 2
[31] Act 38/1927.
[32] Bekker 1989, 4; Van Niekerk 1990, 38.
[33] Van Niekerk 1990, 38; Bekker 1989, 4.
[34] Van Niekerk 1990, 38.
[35] Bennett 1985, 43, 1995, 62. For a discussion on Lord Theophilus Shepstone's implementation of the policy of "indirect" rule in Natal see Walker 1963, 358–9.
[36] Ord. 3/1849.
[37] Act 49/1898.

which the parties were Africans. The Act provided that all civil cases, except in certain stated situations,[38] were to be tried under African customary law.[39]

5 The Voortrekker Republics

In the Voortrekker Republics of Transvaal and the Orange Free State a policy of non-recognition was followed at first. In the Orange Free State only very limited jurisdiction was given to chiefs in the Witsieshoek area and African customary unions received specific recognition in the Thaba'Nchu Reserve. African customary unions were only afforded formal recognition in the remainder of the Orange Free State in 1899.[40]

Until 1885 the law of the land was applied to Africans in the Transvaal.[41] Law 4 of 1885 recognised the application of African customary law in civil disputes in the latter republic where the parties involved were Africans. This recognition was, however, again subject to the condition that the law had to be in accordance with the general principles of civilisation known throughout the civilised world.[42]

6 The Black Administration Act 38 of 1927

In 1927 the Black Administration Act was promulgated. This was a decisive event in the history of the recognition and application of African customary law in South Africa.[43] The aim of the Act was to introduce a more rational structure to African legal affairs and to bring about uniformity in the administration and application of African customary law in South Africa.[44]

The Black Administration Act presented an official version of certain rules[45] of African customary law to be applied by the central courts and the bureaucracy. It also repeated the condition that other rules of African customary law could only be applied in so far as they were not repugnant to the principles of public policy and natural justice.[46] The Act furthermore created a divided court struc-

---

[38] The Courts (Blacks) Act 49/1898, s. 80. The exceptions were the following: if it was specifically provided otherwise by law, if it would result in manifest injustice or if the laws, customs and usages were repugnant to the settled principles and policy of natural equity. Cases arising out of types of transactions which were foreign to traditional African customary law were also adjudicated in terms of colonial law.

[39] Bekker 1989, 6.

[40] Law 26/1899.

[41] Van Niekerk 1990, 39.

[42] Van Niekerk 1990, 39.

[43] Bennett 1991, 19.

[44] Bennett 1991, 19; Van Niekerk 1991, 39.

[45] The Act regulated the constitution and jurisdiction of special courts for the hearing of suits and proceedings between Africans, the consequences of civil marriages between Africans and succession to the estates of deceased Africans.

[46] Black Administration Act 38/1927, s. 11(1).

ture: one set of "special" courts for Africans, with the power to apply African customary law and another general court system for European people.[47]

7 The 1993 (interim) Constitution[48] and the 1996 (final) Constitution[49]

Although the 1993 (interim) Constitution[50] did not address the recognition of African customary law as a legal system comprehensively, it contained a sufficient number of references to ensure the application of African customary law. Constitutional Principle XIII, for instance, provided for the recognition and application of African customary law by the courts in terms of the final Constitution.[51] This principle, section 181(2) (which provided for the regulation of African customary law by legislation) the provisions regarding traditional authorities, the transitory clause contained in section 229 and certain provisions of the Bill of Rights confirmed that African customary law has been accepted as part of the South African legal system.[52]

The 1996 (final) Constitution also recognises African customary law. Sections 30 and 31 of the Bill of Rights recognise the right to language and culture as well as the right of cultural, religious and linguistic communities to enjoy and maintain their culture. Section 39, which regulates the interpretation of the Bill of Rights, provides explicitly that the Bill of Rights does not deny the existence of any other rights or freedoms that are recognised or conferred by common law, customary law or legislation to the extent that they are consistent with the Bill. Explicit provision for the recognition and application of African customary law is also made in the chapter dealing with traditional leadership. Section 211 in this chapter states the following:

"(1) The institution, status and role of traditional leadership, according to customary law, are recognised, subject to the Constitution.
(2) A traditional authority that observes a system of customary law may function subject to any applicable legislation and customs, which includes amendments to, or repeal of, that legislation or those customs.
(3) The courts must apply customary law when that is applicable, subject to the Constitution and any legislation that specifically deals with customary law."

[47] Olivier *et al.* 1995, 198 and Nhlapo 1994, 50. In 1986 the separate court system for blacks was to a large extent abolished by the Special Courts for Blacks Abolition Act 34/1986.
[48] Constitution of the RSA 200/1993.
[49] Constitution of the RSA 108/1996.
[50] Constitution of the RSA 200/1993.
[51] The 1993 (interim) Constitution contained a number of principles which provided guidelines for the drafting and evaluation of the final Constitution.
[52] Bekker 1994, 440; Bennett 1994, 122; Nhlapo 1994, 51–2; De Koker 1996, 97; Lourens 1994, 856–9; and Church and Edwards in Hosten *et al.* 1995, 1249. In terms of the interim Constitution African customary law is recognised subject to the provisions of the Bill of Rights. Therefore, the exact position of African customary law in the legal order and its compatibility with a human rights regime, particularly the position of women in African customary law, is a matter for debate. In this regard see Bekker 1994, 440–7; Bennett 1994, 122–30.

Undoubtedly the Constitution provides for the recognition and application, subject to the Bill of Rights, of African customary law in the future South African legal system.

4. THE INFLUENCE AND EFFECT OF DUTCH COLONIALISM

When exploring the influence and effect of Dutch Colonialism on the development of African customary law, it should be noted from the outset that this was, or rather, was intended to be, colonisation of a different type. As stated before,[53] the settlement at the Cape had no other purpose than to serve as a provisioning station for the ships of the Dutch East India Company. The Dutch had no interest in acquiring more land than that which was necessary to maintain and protect their fort and garden.[54]

The contact with the indigenes mostly took place on a commercial level. Trade with the Khoi was a major concern of the early Dutch commanders. The Khoi provided much needed fresh meat in exchange for copper, tobacco and iron. Due to the company's dependence on the Khoikhoi for supplies, it was a crucial policy of the Company that the Khoi were a free people, who were not to be conquered nor enslaved.[55]

Be that as it may, the arrival of the Dutch East India Company at the Cape had disastrous effects on the socio-economic situation of the indigenous communities of the Cape and consequently, on their legal system(s). The Company set in motion a process during which the Khoikhoi were gradually subordinated and assimilated into the Dutch society.[56]

Contact with the European community resulted in the breaking up of the traditional social structure of the Khoikhoi. Displaced from their pastures by the European farmers and attracted by the comparative security and stability of European farm life, many Khoikhoi families and clans were integrated into the colonial society and economy. Many of the Hottentots lost their tribal distinctions and lived as dependants of farmers, or wandered about the country, taking service occasionally as they felt disposed. The Khoi was a source of labour in pastoral regions and they were incorporated as servants and clients into the society.[57] By the first decade of the eighteenth century the traditional order of the Khoi in the South-western Cape had disintegrated beyond recall.[58]

[53] Para. 3.1 *supra*.

[54] Fouché 1963, 114–15; Böeseken 1986, 20, 49; Fredrickson 1981, 28; Elphick 1979, 10; Keegan 1996, 15; and Giliomee and Elphick 1979, 365–6.

[55] Theal 1922, 94, 117; Elphick and Giliomee 1979, 365–6; Fredrickson 1981, 29–31; Freund 1984, 55; and Elphick 1979, 9, 10.

[56] Theal 1922, 381; Keegan 1996, 26; and Elphick 1979, 19. This process of socio-economic suppression and degradation of non-Europeans in South African continued well into the 19th century. See De Kiewiet 1979, 857.

[57] Elphick 1979, 19; Keegan 1996, 15, 20, 24–6; Muller 1986, 89–90; Penn 1989, 4; Freund 1979, 220; 1984, 55; and De Kiewiet 1937, 3. With regard to alienation of land, see also Fouché 1986, 123–7; Böeseken 1986, 33; and Theal 1922, 37.

[58] Elphick 1979, 21.

Integration into European society resulted in the diminishing rights and status of the Khoikhoi. Although, in general, there was little discrimination in law against free people of colour,[59] the social order was never colour-blind.[60] A tendency to treat free Blacks as a separate status group from the free burghers grew in the eighteenth century.[61] This subtle racial stratification, combined with the Europeans' superior attitude toward the "heathen savages", and their marital and domestic arrangements,[62] led to the subordinate status of the Khoikhoi in colonial society. Gradually the native population turned into the proletariat, governed by laws which restricted their liberties rather than widening their opportunities.[63]

Furthermore, the displacement of the Khoikhoi and their assimilation into European society caused the economic inferiority of the group.[64] In the last 18 years of the Company's rule, the tribal system of the Khoikhoi had virtually disappeared. Many of the Hottentots were impoverished and possessed no cattle. They were integrated into the colonial community in a subordinate position as servants.[65] The Cape consequently developed into a multi-racial society dominated by colonists and one in which labour was largely unfree and the preserve of people of non-European origin.[66] Inexpensive manual labour, in particular, came to be regarded as the exclusive role of Black people and the destiny of the indigenous peoples of the Cape.[67]

The effect of Dutch colonialism on African family law lies not so much in its direct contact with and effect on the system,[68] but in the socio-economic effect of Dutch colonialism on the lives of the indigenous people of the Cape. Interaction with an alien European society exacerbated the weaknesses of the Khoikhoi society and in part led to its disintegration.[69] It turned the indigenous people into servants, established a culture of "otherness" with regard to non-Europeans and laid the foundation on which South African society's notion of white supremacy was built.[70]

---

[59] At least until the 18th century.

[60] Keegan 1996, 23–4; Penn 1989, 17; and Fredrickson 1981, 87–8. For a discussion of the racial divide in the Cape during the early 19th century see Bickford-Smith 1987, 32 ff.

[61] Free Blacks were compelled to carry passes whenever they wished to leave town for more than a few days. See Keegan 1996, 24–6; and Guelke 1989, 43.

[62] Van den Boogaart 1982, 47–8, 54.

[63] De Kiewiet 1937, 3. See also Keegan 1996, 26–7 and Guelke 1989, 44.

[64] De Kiewiet 1937, 3; Keegan 1996, 26.

[65] Muller 1986, 89–90.

[66] Keegan 1996, 15.

[67] Elphick 1979, 35.

[68] The Dutch only had contact with the Xhosa at the very end of the Dutch East India Company's rule.

[69] Elphick 1979, 18–19, 22, 33–4.

[70] Keegan 1996, 292; Coetzee 1994, 64; and Guelke 1989, 40.

5. BRITISH COLONIALISM AND AFRICAN CUSTOMARY FAMILY LAW

The first British conquest of the Cape in 1795 marked the beginning of an extended period of British rule in South Africa.[71] This period had a profound impact on African customary law in South Africa. The policy of "indirect rule" and partial recognition of African customary law adopted by the British during this period directly influenced the development of African customary family law in South Africa. Specific consequences of British rule such as legal dualism and the "invented tradition" of African customary law will be discussed in greater detail in this chapter.

1 Dualism and the partial recognition of African customary law

As stated earlier,[72] the British regarded African customary law as a barbarous, primitive and inferior legal system. They could not, however, abolish African customary law and impose their own legal system on the African population as they feared a hostile reaction from the indigenous communities.[73] They also lacked the necessary finances and manpower to enforce a European legal system on an unreceptive population.[74] This led to the adoption of a policy of "indirect rule" and linked to it, a selective recognition of the rules of African customary law.[75] As a result South Africa to this day has a dual legal system:[76] both the law of the land and African customary law is recognised and applied within the borders of the Republic.[77]

The term "legal dualism" refers to the existence and recognition of two legal systems within one territorial area.[78] It generally also implies equal recognition of the legal systems. Equality was, however, not part of South African legal dualism. Throughout South African legal history recognition of African customary law was only partial. It was never treated as the equal of the law of the land.[79] Instead, in terms of the dual legal system devised by the British, African customary law was recognised as a subservient system, subordinate to the dominant

---

[71] Apart from the period of Batavian rule from 1803 to 1806.

[72] See section 3.2 *supra*.

[73] Bennett 1985, 39; Kaganas and Murray 1994, 16; Olivier in Sanders 1990, 41; and Simons 1968, 32.

[74] *Ibid.*

[75] See the discussion in section 3.2 *supra*. See also Bennett 1991, 2; Kaganas and Murray 1994, 16; Seidman in Currie 1994, 146; Allot 1984, 56–7; Armstrong *et al.* 1993, 231–2; and Ncube 1991, 6.

[76] Ncube 1991, 59.

[77] Although there are numerous African customary legal systems which apply in South Africa, the author views the position in South Africa as a "dual" legal system in which the system of African customary law as a whole co-exists with the law of the land.

[78] Bennett and Peart 1983, 145; Van Niekerk 1990, 34; Van Reenen 1996, 80; and Church and Edwards in Hosten *et al.* 1995, 1249.

[79] Bennett 1994, 122; Church and Edwards in Hosten *et al.* 1995, 1249; and Nhlapo 1995, 49.

law of the land.[80] In terms of the South African dual legal system, the relationships of Europeans were governed by the law of the land while the family relationships of the indigenous population were regulated by African customary law.[81] The application of African customary law was, however, subject to European interpretations and views of natural justice and public policy. It could only be applied if it did not expressly conflict with legislation and if it was not, in the opinion of the judges and officials who supervised its administration, "repugnant to justice, equity and good conscience" or "natural justice and morality".[82]

The partial recognition of African customary law and its subordinate position led to its marginalisation from mainstream legal studies and practice. It became a neglected part of South African law. It was seldom studied as post-graduate level and received little attention until the 1980s.[83] The neglect of African customary law affected the development of African customary family law in many ways. For instance, African customary family law developed into a system of family in terms of which women occupied a subordinate position, a situation which went unnoticed for a long time.[84] Furthermore, the neglect of African customary law affected the ability of the system to adapt to and develop along with the changes in social and legal conditions.[85]

2 "Official" African customary family law[86] and the status of women

The "official" African customary family law of today grants women a particularly subjugated and subordinated position in the family. In terms of the main source

[80] Van Niekerk 1990, 34. Church and Edwards in Hosten *et al.* 1995, 1249. The "law of the land" denotes the hybrid South African legal system which consists of Roman, Dutch and English law. See Church and Edwards in Hosten *et al.* 1995, 1248; Van Niekerk 1990, 35–6 and Bekker 1991, 12.

[81] Kaganas and Murray 1994, 16–17; Allot 1984, 58; and Armstrong *et al.* 1993, 321–2. For a brief discussion of legal dualism in Zimbabwe see Stewart *et al.* in Stewart and Armstrong 1990, 166–8.

[82] Allott 1984, 58; Bennett 1991, 129; Dlamini in Sanders 1990, 2; Elias 1962, 101; Olivier in Sanders 1990, 42; Peart 1982, 99; Van Reenen 1996, 81; Church and Edwards in Hosten *et al.* 1995, 249; Olivier *et al.* 1995, 208; and Read 1972, 175. The provision regarding compliance with natural justice and public policy is generally known as a so-called "repugnancy clause". In South African legislation the "repugnancy clause" is contained in s. 1(1) of the Law of Evidence Amendment Act 45/1988 which reads as follows: "Any court may take judicial notice of the law of a foreign state and of indigenous law in so far as such law can be ascertained readily and with sufficient certainty: Provided that indigenous law shall not be opposed to the principles of public policy and natural justice: Provided further that it shall not be lawful for any court to declare that the custom of lobola or bogadi or other similar custom is repugnant to such principles." In practice the clause has, to a large degree, fallen into disuse. See Bennett 1994, 130; and Bekker 1994, 443. For a comprehensive discussion on the discretion to apply African customary law and the application of the repugnancy clause see Knoetze 1996, 147 ff.; and Peart 1982, 99–116 respectively.

[83] Bennett 1991, 18; Kaganas and Murray 1991, 17.

[84] Kaganas and Murray 1994, 17.

[85] SALC 1996, 2.

[86] The term "family law" denotes more than the concept of family law as that branch of private law which regulates the relationship between the spouses as well as that between parents and children and the relationship of the family with other members of society: Cronjé 1994, 129. It also denotes rules relating to the legal status of women in a family and matters of succession.

of "official" African customary family law, the Black Administration Act,[87] women in African customary law are perpetual minors. African women are under the guardianship of their fathers or guardians until they enter into a customary marriage. From that moment their husbands are deemed to be their legal guardians.[88] A married woman's property is controlled by her husband as she is regarded as a minor.[89] The status of married African women as minors effectively prevents them from owning property and denies them full contractual and legal capacity.[90] Where the Black Administration Act does allow for the full legal capacity of women, it is limited to the performance of legal acts in relation to leasehold and ownership and is framed as an exception.[91]

Section 23 of the Black Administration Act limits a testator's testamentary capacity by prescribing the application of the African customary rules of succession. The section specifically provides that "all movable property belonging to a Black and allotted by him or accruing under Black law or custom to any women with whom he lived in a customary union, or to any house, shall upon his death devolve and be administered under Black law and custom".[92] In terms of African customary law of succession women cannot inherit as a principle of male primogeniture is followed.[93] Furthermore, the Act prescribes that quitrent land in tribal settlement devolves "upon one male person" in accordance with the prescribed tables of succession.[94]

The subordinate position of women in terms of African customary law is in stark contrast with the status of their sisters in terms of the law of the land. Major changes were made to the status of women under the law of the land during the past 50 years,[95] whereas the status of women in African customary law remained mostly unchanged.[96] For instance, the law of the land was amended in 1993 to the effect that both parents are equal legal guardians of children born from a valid marriage.[97] The position according to African customary law however, remained

---

[87] See section 3.6 *supra*.

[88] Act 38/1927, s. 11(3)(b).

[89] Bennett 1991, 325–8.

[90] Robinson 1995, 461–2; Kaganas and Murray 1994, 17. For a discussion of the position of women with regard to divorce see Simons 1968, 211–13.

[91] The capacity of an African woman to perform such legal acts is determined "as if she were not subject to Black law and custom". See Act 38/1927, s. 11A. For a general discussion of the efficacy of s. 11A see Robinson 1995, 462.

[92] S. 23(1).

[93] Bekker 1989, 273; Chanock 1991, 64.

[94] S. 23(2).

[95] With the promulgation of the Marital Affairs Act 37/1953, the Marriage Property Act 88/1984, the General Fourth Law Amendment Act 132/1993 and the Guardianship Act 192/1993.

[96] The 1943 amendment to contractual capacity and *locus standi in iudico* ito s. 11(2)(b) is one of only a few amendments which have been made to the capacity of women in African customary law since 1900. Only in 1988 the Marriage and Matrimonial Property Law Amendment Act 3/1988 made the whole of the Marriage Property Act 88/1984 applicable to Africans. The marriage property regime was however only changed in favour of women who entered into civil or Christian marriages: Bennett 1995, 81.

[97] Ito the Guardianship Act 192/1993.

unchanged. Consequently, the husband of a customary marriage is still the legal guardian of children born from such a marriage.[98]

3 African customary law as an "invented tradition"

The recognition of African customary law, albeit partially, entailed that colonial administrators, officials and courts had to apply African customary law. The application of African customary law presupposed knowledge of the legal system. This presented a practical problem. The courts were mainly[99] staffed and run by white officials who had only superficial contact with the communities from which the law was derived. They lacked an intimate knowledge and understanding of African customary law and had to rely mainly on oral and secondary written sources of African customary law.

Rules of customary law were adduced by calling expert witnesses and by attaching people whom the colonials regarded as having first hand experience of customary law as assessors to the courts to give advice when questions involving African customary law arose. African customary law proved in evidence was derived from oral or written sources. Witnesses and assessors were usually male elders from the communities concerned. The colonial administration and courts relied heavily on the male elders as the local leaders in order to ascertain the content of African customary law because they regarded them as the custodians of traditional African customary law. Written evidence was mainly derived from textbooks and manuals which were compiled by missionaries, traders, colonial officials and anthropologists. Gradually from a stock of precedents, a general body of customary law was built up[100] and thus "official" African customary law was created.[101]

In the process of incorporating African customary law into the formal legal system it was transformed to comply with the requirements of the dominant western legal culture. Indigenous institutions were described in terms of European legal concepts and the social contexts of rules were regarded as rather unimportant.[102] For example, European interpretations or explanations of African customary law turned levirate marriage into widow inheritance, an explanation which caused women to be regarded as property. The African system of property "rights" was translated into a concept of women being unable to own property.[103] Rather than adjusting to the law they applied, the colonial courts changed

---

[98] The position is being reconsidered by the SALC ito of project 90 (the harmonisation of the common law and indigenous law). Guardianship of parents is referred to in para II.1 of Issue art. 3.

[99] At least until native courts were established and even then it was still the case.

[100] Bennett 1985, 18, 1991, 19; Sanders 1987, 406–7.

[101] See Bennett 1985, 18, 1991, 19, 1995, 63; Sanders 1987, 406–6; Roberts 1984, 1; Fitzpatrick 1984, 23–4; Chanock 1977, 80–91, 1989, 72–88; Freund 1984, 3; Armstrong *et al*. 1993, 324–5; and Eze 1984, 9.

[102] Sanders 1987, 407; Bennett 1985, 22; and Fitzpatrick 1984, 20.

[103] Armstrong *et al*. 1993, 325.

the law to suit them.[104] This process of "inventing" a "tradition" of "official" African customary law created a distorted version of African customary law which was claimed to be a body of rules which represented a genuine pre-colonial tradition or a continuing evolution of social norms.[105] In reality, this body of law reflected the preconceptions and biases of its translators.[106]

The "invention" of a "tradition" of African customary law had a profound impact on the status of women in African customary law.[107] The process was infected by the desire of colonialists and African males alike to legitimise new types of power and to induce new forms of societal behaviour.[108]

African men were the main primary sources of African customary law. Inevitably the version of African customary law that emanated from these sources could not avoid being distorted or at the very least, being skewed, by their male perspectives when giving evidence. During the colonial period African males would have been particularly influenced by the struggle by women and young people to escape from the patriarchal system.[109] All the parties involved in this struggle sought to engender the support and power of the colonial government.[110] It was the men who succeeded in acquiring the authority of the colonial state in customary legal matters.[111] In order to strengthen their waning powers over the traditional community, they expounded a rigid and distorted version of African customary law.[112] Their version, greatly influenced by the elders' anger and frustration at their loss of political power and the challenges they faced from the women and the younger generation, was fed into the colonial court system and became "official" African customary law.[113]

Thus African men used their unique position during the colonial period to present a version of African customary law in terms of which they had power and control over women. This version coincided with the views and perceptions of the male colonialists regarding the position of women in society. They therefore accepted this version and afforded it formal status.[114] According to Bennett and Vermeulen "official" African customary law can be viewed as a corruption of indigenous law, a compromise between certain African power brokers and the dominant White power structure.[115]

---

[104] Sanders 1987, 407; Bennett 1985, 22; and Fitzpatrick 1984, 20.

[105] Bennett 1985, 46, 1995, 63–4; Roberts 1984, 1; Nhlapo 1995, 217; and Bennett and Vermeulen in Currie 1994, 146.

[106] Bennett and Vermeulen 1980, 260ff.; Fitzpatrick 1984, 20; and Bennett 1995, 61.

[107] Armstrong *et al.* 1993, 325; Currie 1994, 151.

[108] See Eze 1984, 9; Chanock 1989, 72, 80; Armstrong *et al.* 1993, 324–7; and Kaganas and Murray 1994, 20.

[109] Armstrong *et al.* 1993, 325; Chanock 1982, 57.

[110] *Ibid.*

[111] *Ibid.*

[112] Armstrong *et al.* 1993, 325.

[113] Armstrong *et al.* 1993, 325; Chanock 1982, 57.

[114] This version of African customary law reflected the interests of the traditional authorities and the colonial administration. See Armstrong *et al.* 1993, 326–7; Kaganas and Murray 1994, 20; and Chanock 1989, 76.

[115] Bennett and Vermeulen 1980, 217, 219 as interpreted by Robinson 1995, 460.

The product of the co-operation between the colonialists and African elders is an "invented tradition". It does not represent the legal system which actually applied in the indigenous communities but rather the views of the colonial government and the male elders on the ideal legal system.[116] Tradition wad distorted and frozen and became the object of purposive manipulation.[117]

6. THE INVENTED LEGAL SYSTEM OF AFRICAN CUSTOMARY FAMILY LAW

Dutch and British colonialism and all its ramifications[118] left a particularly unenviable legacy to women living under African customary law. The "invented tradition" of African customary family law forms a significant source of oppression, subordination and discrimination against women.[119] This is especially so when the legal system is viewed in combination with economic and social factors which operate to the disadvantage of women.[120]

The "invented tradition" of African customary law presents African customary law as a static, unchanging set of rules. Customary law, by definition, is susceptible to constant change, changing in accordance with changing behaviour, attitudes and circumstances.[121] "Official" African customary law, however, is portrayed as a rigid set of rules which do not change to adapt to a changing environment.

The Black Administration Act 38 of 1927 affords a good example. This Act was drafted in the first part of this century when the socio–economic situation differed greatly from the present. This Act is antiquated and anachronistic.[122] It does not reflect the role and function of women in the society of today.[123] Yet, the courts still apply this Act and still rely on the authority of past precedents and outdated ethnographies.[124]

Despite the fact that the modern role of African women expands far beyond the narrow confines imposed by their status under "official" African customary law, an old, out-dated and skewed version of African customary family law is still preserved.

[116] Bennett 1995, 63; Roberts 1984, 1; Fitzpatrick 1984, 23–4; Chanock 1977, 80–91, 1989, 72–88; Armstrong *et al.* 1993, 324–5; and Eze 1984, 9.

[117] See Eze 1984, 9; Chanock 1989, 72, 80; Armstrong *et al.* 1993, 324–7; Kaganas and Murray, 1994, 20; and Fitzpatrick 1984, 24.

[118] *Inter alia* labour migrancy, the development of the money economy, urbanisation and loss of land. Chanock 1989, 78, 1991, 63; and Krige 1981, 193.

[119] It is a system in terms of which *inter alia* men are allowed to marry more than one wife, women have very little legal and property-holding capacity, spouses are not equal guardians of the children born from the marriage and the grounds for divorce available to women differ from the grounds available to men. See further Bekker 1997, 21 ff. and Robinson 1995, 457 ff.

[120] Armstrong *et al.* 1993, 327; Currie 1994, 146; Romany 1996, 861; and Kaganas and Murray 1996, 16.

[121] Bennett 1985, 92 and keegan 1996, 292.

[122] Armstrong *et al.* 1993, 327.

[123] Bennett 1985, 23; Chanock 1991, 63.

[124] Bennett 1985, 23.

7. CONCLUSION

Clearly, the development of African customary family law in South Africa was influenced by a number of social, economic and political factors. The system is indeed a legacy of many pasts. The question which now confronts South Africa is whether we are going to make a clean break with this history, as we did on other terrains of South African society, and establish a new, modern general system of family law based on the values of human dignity, equality, non-racialism and non-sexism?[125] Or, are South Africans going to allow the history of the past centuries to dictate the status of women in South Africa in the twenty-first century too? If the latter option is chosen, the legacy of the past will not only be the legacy received by the present generation but also become a burdensome inheritance for future generations.

REFERENCES

ALLOTT, A. N. (1984), "What is to be done with African Customary Law?", *Journal of African Law* 56
—— (1970), *New Essays in African Law* (London: Butterworths).
ARMSTRONG, A. *et al.* (1993), "Uncovering Reality: Excavating Women's Rights in African Family Law", *International Journal of Law and the Family* 314.
BEKKER, J. C. (1989), *Seymour's Customary Law in Southern Africa* (5th edn., Cape Town: Juta).
—— (1991), "Interaction Between Constitutional Reform and Family Law", *Acta Juridica* 1.
—— (1994), "How Compatible is African Customary Law with Human Rights?", *Journal for Contemporary Roman Dutch Law* 440.
—— and MAITHUFI, P. (1992), "The Dichotomy Between 'Official Customary Law' and 'Non-official Customary Law'", *Journal for Juridical Science* 47.
BENNETT, T. W. (1985), *The Application of Customary Law in Southern Africa* (Cape Town: Juta).
—— (1991), "The Compatibility of African Customary Law and Human Rights", *Acta Juridica*. 18.
—— (1994), "The Equality Clause and Customary Law", *The South African Journal on Human Rights* 122.
—— (1995), *Human Rights and African Customary Law* (Cape Town: Juta).
—— and PEART, N. S. (1983), "The Dualism of Marriage Laws in Africa", *Acta Juridica* 151.
—— (1991), *A Sourcebook of African Customary Law for Southern Africa* (Cape Town: Juta).
—— and VERMEULEN, T. (1980), "Codification of Customary Law", *Journal of African Law* 206.
BICKFORD-SMITH, V. (1987), "Commerce, Class and Ethnicity: Cape Town at the Advent of the Mineral Revolution", *Social Dynamics* 32.

[125] Founding provisions of the Constitution of the Republic of South Africa 108/1996, s. 1.

BÖESEKEN, A. J. (1986), "The Arrival of Van Riebeeck at the Cape", "The Settlement under the Van der Stels", and "The Lure of Africa", in C. F. J. Muller, *Five Hundred Years. A History of South Africa* (Pretoria: Academica).

CHANOCK, M. (1977), "Neo-traditionalism and the Customary Law in Malawi", *African Law Studies* 80.

—— (1982), "Making Customary Law: Men, Women, and Courts in Colonial Northern Rhodesia", in M. J. Hay and M. Wright, *African Women and the Law. Historical Perspectives* (Boston: Boston University Press).

—— (1985), *Law, Custom and Social Order* (Cambridge: Cambridge University Press).

—— (1989), "Neither Customary nor Legal: African Customary Law in an Era of Family Law Reform", *International Journal of Law and the Family* 72.

—— (1991), "Law, State and Culture: Thinking about 'Customary Law' after Apartheid", *Acta Juridica* 52.

CHURCH, J. (1995), "Constitutional Equality and the Position of Women in a Multi-cultural Society", *The Comparative and International Law Journal of South Africa* 289.

—— and EDWARDS, A. B. (1995), "Introduction to Indigenous Law and the Comparative Method", in Hosten *et al.*, *Introduction to South African Law and Legal Theory* (Durban: Butterworths).

COETZEE, C. (1994), "Visions of Disorder and Profit: The Khoikhoi and the First Years of the Dutch India Company at the Cape", *Social Dynamics* 35.

CURRIE, I. (1994), "The Future of Customary Law: Lessons from the Lobolo Debate", *Acta Juridicia* 146.

CRONJÉ, D. S. P. (1994), *The South African Law of Persons and Family Law* (Durban: Butterworths).

DE KIEWIET, C. W. (1937), *The Imperial Factor in South Africa* (London: Cambridge University Press).

—— (1963), "Social and Economic Developments in Native Tribal Life", in E. A Walker (ed.), *The Cambridge History of The British Empire* (London: Cambridge University Press).

DE KOKER, J. T. (1996), "Die bestaanbaarheid van *lobolo* in 'n nuwe Suid-Afrikaanse regsbedeling", *Journal for Juridical Science* 75.

DLAMINI, C. R. M. (1990), "The Future of African Customary Law", in A. J. G. M. Sanders (ed.), *The Internal Conflict of Laws in South Africa* (Durban: Butterworths).

ELIAS, T. O. (1962), *British Colonial Law* (London: Stevens & Sons Ltd).

ELPHICK, R. (1979), "The Khoisan to *c.* 1770", in R. Elphick and H. Giliomee (eds.), *The Shaping of South African Society, 1652–1830* (Cape Town: Maskew Miller).

—— and GILIOMEE, H. (eds.) (1979), *The Shaping of South African Society, 1652–1820* (Cape Town: Maskew Miller).

—— and SHELL, R. (1979), "Intergroup Relations" Khoikhoi, Settlers, Slaves and Free Blacks", in R. Elphick and H. Giliomee (eds.), *The Shaping of South African Society, 1652–1830* (Cape Town: Maskew Miller).

EZE, O. C. (1984), *Human Rights in Africa* (Lagos: Nigerian Institute of International Affairs and Macmillan Nigeria Pty Ltd).

FITZPATRICK, P. (1984), "Traditionalism and Traditional Law", *Journal of African Law* 20.

FOUCHÉ, L. (1963), "Foundation of the Cape Colony", in E. A. Walker (ed.), *The Cambridge History of the British Empire* (London: Cambridge University Press).

FREDRICKSON, G. M. (1981), *White Supremacy. A Comparative Study in American and South African History* (Oxford: Oxford University Press).

FREUND, W. M. (1979), "The Cape under the Transitional Governments, 1795–1814", in R. Elphick and H. Giliomee (eds.), *The Shaping of South African Society, 1652–1830* (Cape Town: Maskew Miller).

—— (1984), *The Making of Contemporary Africa. The Development of African Society Since 1800* (London: Macmillan Education).

GILIOMEE, H., and ELPHICK, R. (1979), "The Structure of European Domination at the Cape, 1652–1820", in R. Elphick and H. Giliomee (eds.), *The Shaping of South African Society, 1652–1830* (Cape Town: Maskew Miller).

GUELKE, L. (1989), "The Origin of White Supremacy in South Africa: An Interpretation", *Social Dynamics* 40.

HARLOW, T. (1963), "Cape Colony", in E. A. Walker (ed.), *The Cambridge History of the British Empire* (London: Cambridge University Press).

HOSTEN *et al.* (1995), *Introduction to South African Law and Legal Theory* (Durban: Butterworths).

HAY, M. J., and WRIGHT, M. (eds.) (1982), *African Women and the Law: Historical Perspectives* (Boston: Boston University Press).

JAMES, W. G., and SIMONS, M. (eds.) (1989), *The Angry Divide: Social and Economic History of the Western Cape* (Cape Town: David Philip).

KAGANAS, F., and MURRAY, C. (1991), "Law, Women and the Family: The Question of Polygyny in a New South Africa", *Acta Juridica* 116.

—— (1994), "Law and Women's Rights in South Africa: An Overview", *Acta Juridica* 1.

—— and —— (1994), "The Contest Between Culture and Gender Equality under South Africa's Interim Constitution", *Journal of Law and Society* 409.

KEEGAN, T. (1996), *Colonial South Africa and the Origins of the Racial Order* (Cape Town: David Philip).

KNOETZE, E. (1996), "The Discretion to Apply Customary Law", *Obiter* 146.

KRIGE, E. J. (1981), "Summary and Conclusions", in E. J. Krige and J. L. Comaroff, *Essays on African Marriage in South Africa* (Cape Town: Juta).

—— and COMAROFF, J. L. (1981), *Essays on African Marriage in South Africa* (Cape Town: Juta).

LIEBENBERG, S. (1995), *The Constitution of South Africa from a Gender Perspective* (Cape Town: Community Law Centre of the University of the Western Cape in association with David Philip).

LOURENS, J. (1994), "Inheemse reg: aard en inhoud in terme van die Grondwet", *De Rebus* 856.

MORRIS, H. F. (1979), "The Development of Statutory Marriage Law in Twentieth Century British Colonial Africa", *Journal of African Law* 37.

—— and READ, J. (eds.) (1972), *Indirect Rule and the Search for Justice* (Oxford: Clarendon Press).

MULLER, C. F. J. (1986), "Introduction. Domestic Strife and International Warfare", in C. F. J. Muller (ed.), *Five Hundred Years. A History of South Africa* (Pretoria, Academica).

—— (ed.) (1986), *Five Hundred Years. A History of South Africa* (Pretoria: Academica).

NCUBE, W. (1991), "Dealing with Inequities in Customary Law: Action, Reaction and Social Change in Zimbabwe", *International Journal of Law and the Family* 58.

NHLAPO, T. R. (1991), "The African Family and Women's Rights: Friends or Foes?", *Acta Juridica* 135.

—— (1994), "Indigenous Law and Gender in South Africa: Taking Human Rights and Cultural Diversity Seriously", *Third World Legal Studies* 49.

—— (1995), "Cultural Diversity, Human Rights and the Family in Contemporary Africa: Lessons from the South African Constitutional Debate", *International Journal of Law and the Family* 208.

—— (1995), "African Customary Law in the Interim Constitution", in S. Liebenberg, *The Constitution of South Africa from a Gender Perspective* (Cape Town: David Philip).

NJERE, S. (1994), "Law and 'Othering'", *Responsa Meridiana* 398.

OLIVIER, N. J. J. (1990), "The Judicial Application of African Customary Law", in A. J. G. M. Sanders (ed.), *The Internal Conflict of Laws in South Africa* (Durban: Butterworths).

—— *et al.* (1995), *Indigenous Law* (Durban: Butterworths).

PEART, N. S. (1982), "Section 11(1) of the Black Administration Act no 38 of 1927: The Application of the Repugnancy Clause", *Acta Juridica* 99.

PENN, N. (1989), "Land, Labour and Livestock in the Western Cape during the Eighteenth Century", in W. G. James and M. Simons (eds.), *The Angry Divide: Social and Economic History of the Western Cape* (Cape Town: David Philip).

READ, J. (1972), "Customary Law under Colonial Rule", in H. F. Morris and J. Read (eds.), *Indirect Rule and the Search for Justice* (Oxford: Clarendon Press).

ROBERTS, S. (1984), "Introduction—Some Notes on 'African Customary Law'", *Journal of African Law* 1.

ROBINSON, K. L. (1995), "The Minority and Subordinate Status of African Women under Customary Law", *South African Journal on Human Rights* 457.

ROMANY, C. (1996), "Black Women and Gender Equality in a New South Africa: Human Rights Law and the Intersection of Race and Gender", *Brooklyn Journal of International Law* 857.

ROSS, R. (ed.) (1982), *Racism and Colonialism. Essays in Ideology and Social Structure* (The Hague: Martinus Nijhoff Publishers).

SANDERS, A. J. G. M. (1987), "How Customary is African Customary Law?", *Comparative and International Law Journal of South Africa* 405.

—— (ed.) (1990), *The Internal Conflict of Laws in South Africa* (Durban: Butterworths).

SIMONS, H. J. (1968), *African Women: Their Legal Status in South Africa* (Evanston: Northwestern University Press).

SOUTH AFRICAN LAW COMMISSION (1986), *Marriage and Customary Unions of Black Persons* (Pretoria: Government Press).

—— (1996), *Harmonisation of the Common Law and Indigenous Law (Customary Marriages)* (Pretoria: Government Press).

SUTTNER, R. (1984), "The Social and Ideological Function of African Customary Law in South Africa", *Social Dynamics* 49.

STEWART, J. *et al.* (1990), "The Legal Situation of Women in Zimbabwe", in J. Stewart and A. Armstrong (eds.), *The Legal Situation of Women in Southern Africa* (Harare: University of Zimbabwe Publications).

—— and ARMSTRONG, A. (eds.) (1990), *The Legal Situation of Women in Southern Africa* (Harare: University of Zimbabwe Publications).

THEAL, G. M. (1922), *History of South Africa, Vol. iv—Before 1795* (London: George Allen and Unwin).

VAN DEN BOOGAART, E. (1982), "Colour Prejudice and the Yardstick of Civility: The Initial Dutch Confrontation with Black Africans, 1590–1635", in R. Ross (ed.), *Racism and Colonialism. Essays in Ideology and Social Structure* (The Hague: Martinus Nijhoff).

VAN DER VYVER, J. D. (1982), "Human Rights Aspects of the Dual System Applying to Blacks in South Africa", *Comparative and International Law Journal of South Africa* 306.

VAN NIEKERK, G. (1990), "Indigenous Law in South Africa—A Historical and Comparative Perspective", *Codicillus* 34.

VAN REENEN, T. P. (1996), "The Relevance of Roman(-Dutch) Law for Legal Integration in South Africa", *Fundamina* 65.

WALKER, E. A. (ed.) (1963), *The Cambridge History of the British Empire, Vol. xiii* (London: Cambridge University Press).

20

Language, Culture and the Detritus of Apartheid: Understanding and Overcoming Secondary, Systemic Abuse in South African Child Care Proceedings

F. NOEL ZAAL

1. INTRODUCTION

The phrase, "child care proceedings", in this chapter should be understood as meaning legal proceedings which arise because of a discovery of a child who appears to be a candidate for removal into alternative care with the involvement and assistance of professional persons designated by the state. In other words, this chapter provides a discussion of care proceedings as commonly understood and as arising where a child appears to have been subjected to abuse, neglect or bereavement or is for any reason beyond the control of those who currently serve as her/his guardians. More specifically, what this chapter provides is a critical overview of the law of South African care proceedings from a perspective which is intended to be of interest to an international audience. As will be seen, conclusions can be drawn from the South African experience which may be most valuable for those who influence policies and law reform in other nations.

At first glance, it might appear that South Africa possesses one particularly impressive resource, namely, specialised children's courts which cover the entire country with a network of relatively small territorial jurisdictions. It is true that the South African children's courts are indeed highly specialised in that they offer a narrow, although important, range of services for children. They assess children for possible removal into alternative care, they finalise adoption and foster-parent applications and they can grant consent to marry to a person under 21 who does not have a guardian available to provide such consent. That is the sum of their work. The apparently complete geographic coverage in small jurisdictions has been achieved by the simple expedient of enacting that every South African magistrates' court shall be a children's court for the area of its jurisdiction.[1] From this it can already be seen that the degree of specialisation which has been

[1] S. 5(1) of the Child Care Act 74/1983.

achieved is in some respects more apparent than real. It is ordinary magistrates, and not specially trained officers, who conduct children's court inquiries.

From an historical point of view, it is worth noting that the concept of a national network of children's courts came from an earlier, more creative, period in the development of South African legislation. It pre-dated the accession to power of the Nationalist Government and the era of high apartheid. In 1913, the concept of "a child in need" appeared in section 34 of the Children's Protection Act.[2] By 1937, the "child in need" had been considerably refined into a comprehensive legal definition of a "child in need of care" which was fully delineated with detailed sub-definitions in section 1 of the Children's Act 31/1937.

Chapter One of that same 1937 Act set up an impressive infrastructure of specialised children's courts which was intended to protect all children found to be "children in need of care" as defined by section 1.[3] In view of what subsequently happened, it is interesting to note that a special effort was made in the 1937 Act to ensure that the body of adjudicative officers who sat in the children's courts would include "native commissioners" who would have specialist expertise when it came to assisting black children.[4] Apparently alive to the problem of cultural or linguistic barriers which might interpose between adjudicating officers and black children in need of alternative care, the drafters of the 1937 Act included an extremely broad definition of court assessors that would allow for any person, including a black person who was even without professional qualifications, to sit with the commissioner when a children's court matter was decided.[5]

One would not wish to exaggerate the better qualities of an infrastructure produced by what was of course then very much a minority-dominated, neo-colonial society.[6] However, the awareness of the need to bridge cultural and linguistic barriers, the setting up of specialised children's courts, and the whole concept of the "child in need of care", gave South African child care law a progressive, modern approach that might well have been the envy of many other nations in the 1930s and 1940s.

Yet another resource made available for the children's courts in 1937 was one or more "children's court assistants" who would be available to generally assist the court and, for example, help with the leading of evidence and represent one or several parties at a court hearing. The impression which one derives from reading the 1937 Children's Act is that it was composed by knowledgeable persons who felt that children of all races were sufficiently important to deserve the

---

[2] Act 25 of 1913.
[3] See ss. 2–7 of the Children's Act 31/1937.
[4] See s. 3(5) of Act 31/1937.
[5] See the definition of an assessor in s. 5(2) of Act 31/1937.
[6] Between 1938 and 1942 (and possibly longer) children of colour who were taken in as being "in need of care" in the city of Durban were locked into "blacked-out cells 18 feet by 10 feet with an open lavatory in one corner as the only furniture and stinking to high heaven" pending a hearing in the children's court. See the article "Durban's 'Gaol' for Little Children" *The Natal Daily News*, Thursday, 24 Sept. 1942 at 1 col. 3 and 5 cols. 1–2.

allocation of relatively expensive and substantial resources whenever it became necessary to hold an inquiry into their circumstances.

2. THE PERVERSION AND EROSION OF RESOURCES ALLOCATED FOR CHILD CARE PROCEEDINGS IN THE APARTHEID PERIOD 1948–94

The network of South African children's courts was maintained in most jurisdictions with the appearance of a non-racial system serving the interests of all children during the apartheid era between 1948 and 1994. However, the work of these courts did not continue unaffected.

In January 1960 Mr B. J. Vorster, who was then Deputy Minister of Social Welfare, attempted to pilot through Parliament a drastic provision which would have allowed for the forcible removal of any child from a parent or guardian if the child had been classified differently from the parent or guardian under the Population Registration Act 30/1950.[7] This terrible perversion of child care law would in some cases have replaced the child in need of care consideration with a purely racial criterion designed to break up supposedly transracial familial units. Fortunately, fear of international condemnation caused the Government to abandon this clause, although it was replaced five years later with a less extensive racial prohibition.

In 1965, the Children's Act was amended with the addition of new section 35(2)(c). In this section, it was laid down that:

"A child shall not be placed in the custody of any person whose classification in terms of the Population Registration Act, 1950, is not the same as that of the child except where such person is the parent or guardian of the child."

In order to understand the full reach of this provision, one needs to note that parents or guardians would have been discouraged from using the apparent exception in their favour because if either the child or they had been classified as white, then they would be opening themselves to criminal prosecution under section 15 of the Immorality Act, which prohibited sexual intercourse between white persons and others.

On 19 June 1991, the law affecting transracial child placements was made more subtle by an amendment to the Child Care Act.[8] In place of an express prohibition which was unhelpful to South Africa's international image, a new section 40(b) of the Child Care Act now required children's courts to "have regard to the religious and cultural background of the child concerned and of his parents as against that of the person in or to whose custody he is to be placed or

---

[7] Cl. 1(x)(j) of the Children's Bill of 1960. See *Government Gazette* No. 6347 [vol. CXCIX] of 8 Jan. 1960. For critical discussion see Frederick Noel Zaal, "The Ambivalence of Authority and Secret Lives of Tears: Transracial Child Placements and the Historical Development of South African Law" 18(2) *Journal of South African Studies* (1992) 372 at 389–90.

[8] See *Government Gazette* No. 13311 of that date.

transferred".[9] This continued to serve the primary purpose of ensuring that white children would not be placed with adoptive and foster parents of colour and that generally physical appearance would remain an important consideration in child placements. Unfortunately, in the post-apartheid era, this provision has simply been retained without any clarification of South African policy in regard to transracial placements of children.[10] For many conservative officials in our legal and welfare infrastructure, it thus continues to be "business as usual" when it comes to using racial differences as a barrier to placements. In post-apartheid South Africa, there needs to be more debate and a formulation of clearer criteria.

The "child in need of care" concept survived alongside the original 1965 racial bar. It remained the ground for removing children into State care in the Children's Act 33/1960 which replaced the Children's Act of 1937.[11] But the entirely child-centred approach which it required was something which sat uncomfortably with a government which was, as has been shown, prepared to subject the best interests of children to racial and political considerations. When a new Child Care Act was drafted in 1983, the "child in need of care" ground was therefore entirely removed in favour of an archaic parental fault-based approach to child care proceedings. When the new Act was discussed in parliament, the Minister of Health and Welfare is reported to have declared:

> " . . . I think that the time has come for us to tell an incompetent parent, without beating about the bush, that his child is in need of care because he is an incompetent parent, and that action should be taken against these unfit parents for the sake of the child."[12]

Thus began an era in which the efforts of social workers to conduct reconstruction services were often hampered because it was necessary to reach a formal finding that a parent was unfit or unable to be a caregiver before that parent's child could be even temporarily removed from her care.[13]

Yet another unfortunate development during the apartheid era was that, as the South African Government put its "homeland" system into effect, children's courts tended to stop functioning in many homeland jurisdictions. This was due to a lack of resources within the homelands, an inability to keep on providing the necessary specialist legal expertise, and partial collapses of the welfare infrastructure which the children's courts depend on.[14]

---

[9] For critical discussion of this provision see Zaal, n. 7 above, at 397–9.

[10] For critical discussion see generally Noel Zaal, "Avoiding the Best Interests of the Child. Race-Matching and the Child Care Act 74/1983" (1994) 10 *South African Journal on Human Rights* 372.

[11] See s. 30 of the Children's Act 33/1960.

[12] *Republic of South Africa House of Assembly Debates* (*Hansard*) 9 May 1983, Second Reading of the Child Care Bill, col. 6559 at col. 6561.

[13] For criticism of this approach under the Child Care Act, see generally Noel Zaal, "Child Removal Procedures Under the Child Care Act: Some New Dangers to Contend With", 105 *South African Law Journal* 224 (1988).

[14] This information was obtained from interviews which the author conducted with the following children's court commissioners: Mr B. M. Mchunu (Emnambithi, 7 May 1996); Mr T. J. Mohohlo (Ditsobotla, 9 May 1996); and Ms A. Gela (Enzibeleni, 30 May 1996).

Aside from its imposition of a fault approach in place of a child-centred approach to grounds for removing children into state care, the Child Care Act 74/1983 is in other respects a seriously flawed piece of legislation. It fails to give children who are old enough and otherwise capable even the basic right of speaking at child care proceedings to which they are subject. Except in the case of an adoption order, it fails to allow parties the right of an appeal. Yet another major weakness of the Child Care Act is that it allows the children's courts only a very limited role. Once a children's court has ordered that a child be placed in an institution, that child falls entirely under the power of officials acting for the Minister of Welfare and Population Development. The children's court has absolutely no power to alter or rescind its order in the light of changed circumstances.

One of the more cynical amendments to the Child Care Act which made it even worse was the amendment to section 15 in 1991 which permitted the Minister of Welfare and Population Development arbitrarily to alter the type of placement ordered by the children's court, or even permits him not to bother to implement the order at all.[15] The unfortunate result of this amendment is that children sometimes languish in places of safety for the full period of the children's court order without ever being placed in the institution designated by the court.[16]

Yet another serious blow to the quality of child care proceedings in South Africa was the decision taken by the Department of Justice in 1992 to remove social workers from their positions as children's court assistants in the children's courts.[17] Since the social workers were not replaced by anyone else, the result of their removal was to leave court clerks and the children's court commissioners in a situation of having to share the duties of the assistants in addition to their own normal duties. In different research projects, I have interviewed more than a hundred children's court commissioners, and more than three-quarters of them complained to me about the ethically difficult situation which they often face when they have to act as the person who provides pre-inquiry advice to the parties, subsequently elicits evidence at the inquiry and then gives a decision as the adjudicating officer.

One may wonder why the Nationalist Government passed such an inadequate piece of legislation as the Child Care Act and then proceeded to water down its provisions even further with the types of amendments that have been referred to. This government was clearly not keen to spend more than the bare minimum on child care proceedings. To a large extent, it is the children of poor persons, and thus in South Africa the children of persons of colour, who have to rely most heavily on State intervention when alternative care arrangements have to be

[15] See s. 15(5)(a) and (b) of the Child Care Act as added by s. 6(b) of Act 86/1991.

[16] Interview with Mr D. S. Rothman, commissioner of the Durban children's court, 24 Feb. 1995. See also H. M. Bosman-Swanepoel and P. J. Wessels, *A Practical Approach to the Child Care Act* (1995), 47.

[17] Department of Justice Circular 1/2/2/3/5 of 1992. For criticism of this step see C. R. Matthias, "Are We Making Progress? The 1996 Child Care Bill and Some Fundamental Aspects of Practice and Procedure in the Children's Courts" (1996) (32) *Social Work/Maatskaplike Werk* 242 at 243.

made. This may explain the lack of priority accorded to care proceedings and the attitude that children's courts were relatively unimportant, merely quasi-curial forums. By contrast, in 1987, the very year in which the Child Care Act of 1983 was finally implemented, the government provided very expensive and sophisticated resources for children from wealthier families whose parents could afford to get divorced in the then supreme courts, as opposed to the less expensive black divorce courts. A national network of specialised family advocates was set up to represent the interests of these children from the wealthier classes.[18]

It must be concluded that, during the apartheid era, not only was little priority accorded to children's courts and child care proceedings, but the limited resources available were drastically reduced.

3. THE PRESENT SITUATION

In post-apartheid South Africa, there are some serious problems which subvert the effectiveness of the children's courts. The courts themselves are still, to a large degree, staffed by the persons who were the commissioners during the apartheid era. These commissioners have never received specialist training for their role. The vast majority are regular magistrates who do children's court cases on an occasional basis. This means that relatively few of them know how to inculcate a children's rights approach as enjoined in section 28 of the South African Constitution by relating to the child and encouraging the child to feel that her wishes are an important factor. It also means that they have little understanding of the methodologies of social work and thus do not always work effectively with the investigative social workers whose evidence is often such an important component in child care inquiries.[19]

The majority of commissioners are white English and Afrikaans speakers. Many of the black children who appear before them are most comfortable with an indigenous African language which the commissioner does not speak. The solution which is used in this situation is for the commissioner to make use of the services of a court interpreter. As Mr K. G. T. Kutshwa (commissioner at Idutywa, former Transkei) stated:

> "Using an interpreter makes the children's court proceedings more complex and artificial for the child. It distances the child, who does not understand the strange process of everything being repeated in another language."

Interviews with black social workers who appear regularly in the children's courts revealed further problems with using interpreters. One difficulty is the fact that the interpreters are not trained to communicate in a non-adversarial way that

---

[18] See generally the Mediation in Certain Divorce Matters Act 24 of 1987.

[19] See Carmel Matthias and Noel Zaal, "Can We Build A Better Children's Court? Some Recommendations For Improving the Processing of Child-Removal Cases" [1996] *Acta Juridica* 51 at 54–6.

will not worsen an already dysfunctional parent–child relationship. And they also sometimes go beyond the bounds of their duties. As an example of this, a social worker cited an interpreter interposing moralistic and judgemental condemnation of a parent in between his translating at an inquiry which she attended.

Another cited a case in which the interpreter persistently attempted to set up a date with the mother of a child whilst he was supposed to be translating remarks of the commissioner. In both of these cases the commissioners were blissfully unaware of the translators' derogations because they were unable to speak the indigenous African language concerned.

Perhaps an even more serious problem which arises where the commissioner cannot speak the language of the child is that she may miss subtle but important nuances in evidence. Mr B. M. Mchunu (children's court commissioner at Emnambithi, Kwazulu-Natal) gave the example of a case where he had been trying to establish whether there had been child abuse committed by a parent. The interpreter had translated some remarks of the child as: "That day I could not understand what the teacher was saying at school". What the child had actually said in Zulu was: "That day I left home feeling terrible physical pain which was so severe that I could not concentrate on what the teacher was saying at school". Clearly, the original statement pointed in the direction of possible parental abuse, whereas the interpreter's version did not. The fact that the majority of our commissioners cannot communicate with African children in their own indigenous language is a matter for serious concern. The fact that they are linguistically out-of-touch with such children is obviously compounded by the fact that apartheid has helped to ensure that they are culturally out-of-touch with the child's indigenous social norms as well.

The cultural and linguistic chasm which obtrudes between most commissioners and black children could at least to some extent be bridged if children were provided with legal representatives who understood their home language and culture. Unfortunately, my field research indicates that, in practice, children are represented in less than 1 per cent of all matters which go before the children's courts.[20] And even where children do occasionally have a lawyer, this lawyer is, in the great majority of instances, not particularly effective in what is clearly a specialised form of advocacy.[21]

The continuing unavailability of a right of appeal in most cases means that there has been relatively little scrutiny of the work of children's court commissioners by any higher courts. This is an unhealthy situation which is conducive to short-cuts and wrongful practices, and it is clearly not in the best interests of the children who appear before the children's courts.

---

[20] See F. N. Zaal, *Do Children Need Lawyers in the Children's Courts?* (University of the Western Cape, 1996), 37–8.
[21] *Id.*, at 38–9.

4. REFORMS THAT ARE REQUIRED

In the post-apartheid era, some steps have already been taken, but considerably more are required. After a confused process in which no fewer than six short-lived draft versions of Bills appeared between February 1995 and November 1996, an Act to amend the Child Care Act was finally promulgated on 22 November 1996.[22] This amending Act is due to be implemented in October 1997. One of its most significant effects will be a return to the "child in need of care" ground as the basis for removing children from their guardians.

The other major change that will be produced by the amending Act 96/1996 is to allow for a child to have legal representation in any children's court proceedings if the commissioner decides that this will be in the best interests of the child.[23] Children will even be given the right to request the commissioner to appoint a legal representative.[24] The new rights in regard to legal representation as produced by Act 96/1996 were clearly an attempt to move into line with section 28(1)(h) of the Constitution which provides that a child may have a legal practitioner assigned to her, at State expense, "in civil proceedings affecting the child if substantial injustice would otherwise result". Unfortunately, the grounds provided by both section 28(1)(h) of the Constitution and the pending new section 8(A) of the Child Care Act are far too vague. Neither the substantial injustice nor the best interest tests provide sufficient guidance to allow for a rational prioritisation of the types of children's courts cases or the types of indicators that should allow a particular child to receive legal representation at state expense in a situation where the funds available for this are very limited. Also, with these vague grounds, the legislature has simply passed the buck to its corps of mainly untrained commissioners where it should have provided them with a list of at least some indicators.[25]

What other reforms are urgently needed? A reduction of the network of children's courts should be seriously considered. Many of the commissioners whom I interviewed do fewer than half a dozen cases a year. Typically of most third-world countries, the vast majority of the South African jurisdictions are non-urban and financial resources are limited. Therefore, it does not make sense that there is supposed to be a children's court in every small magisterial district.

---

[22] Act 96/1996: See *Government Gazette* No. 17606, vol. 377 of 22 Nov. 1996. For a discussion of the draft Bills, see generally Julia Sloth-Nielsen and Belinda van Heerden, "Proposed Amendments to the Child Care Act and Regulations in the Context of Constitutional and International Law Developments in South Africa" (1996) 12(2) *South African Journal on Human Rights* 247. For a discussion of the Act, see Julia Sloth-Nielsen and Belinda van Heerden, "The Child Care Amendment Act 1996: Does it Improve Children's Rights in South Africa?" (1996) 12(4) *South African Journal on Human Rights* 649.

[23] S. 8(A) of the Child Care Act as added by the Child Care Amendment Act 96/1996.

[24] *Id.*, s. 8(A)(1).

[25] For a suggested list of such indicators, see F. N. Zaal, "When Should Children Be Legally Represented in Care Proceedings? An Application of Section 28(1)(h) of the Constitution" (1997) 114 (II) *South African Law Journal* 334 at 343.

There is no reason why one children's court centre should not serve four adjoining magisterial districts. These courts could then be staffed with properly trained, child-oriented and linguistically selected adjudicating officers. The demographic consequences of apartheid will facilitate this because the rigid division of our population groups has left the situation that certain mother-tongue languages still tend to predominate amongst children in many of our magisterial districts. This should make deployment of commissioners with the appropriate language skills easier. We should also return to the 1937 idea of scope for lay assessors to sit with commissioners in any case where additional linguistic or cultural empathy with the child is required. In setting up properly-staffed children's courts, priority needs to be given to those former "homeland" districts where children's courts presently do not function at all.

In terms of providing appropriate legal representation for children in care proceedings, the least expensive way to do it properly in a third-world context is to appoint full-time child advocates who can serve several adjoining children's courts. To have such persons as salaried employees will be far less expensive than employing private lawyers on a case-by-case basis, often with the result that someone appears who is not sufficiently knowledgeable.[26] Also, this measure will help to fill the gap left by the removal of professionally qualified children's court assistants. The steps proposed here may be worthy of consideration in other countries, particularly third-world nations, because they will not only increase efficiency and specialisation, but will keep costs to a minimum.

Insofar as the scope of the work of the South African children's courts is concerned, it is essential to drastically reduce the sweeping ministerial powers that presently place the child completely under the control of a civil service bureaucracy that is not accountable in any way once the children's court has issued its judgment in a particular case. The children's courts must be given the power to alter their judgments in the light of changed circumstances. Children who are in institutions must be given regular access to the children's courts so that they can report any changes in their situation or any malpractices or abuses of basic rights to which they have been subjected. The best way to achieve this is to require the children's court to have a monitoring hearing during every six months that a child remains placed by it in a an institution. As has been suggested earlier, children's courts must also be made subject to a broad right of appeal by any party who wishes to argue that a decision reached by a children's court was not in the best interests of the child.

---

[26] The full-time child advocates should nevertheless be completely independent of children's court commissioners, and their availability should not preclude the appointment of a private legal representative where the child requires this and the financial resources are available. In both the USA and the UK it has been found that there is a risk of expending substantial sums of money on legal representatives who do not have sufficient expertise in the specialised field of child care proceedings: see R. F. Kelly and S. H. Ramsey, "Legal Representation for Parents and Children in Child Protection Proceedings: Two Empirical Models of Accusatorial Processes and a Proposal for Reform" (1985) 89 *Dickinson Law Review* 605 at 606; and Judith E. Timms, *Children's Representation: A Practitioner's Guide* 193 (1995).

These steps will also prepare the way for the setting up of a network of specialised family courts as has been envisaged by the Department of Justice.[27] Care proceedings must be preserved as a specialised and properly supported component of family courts when these are set up.

Finally, no discussion of child care proceedings would be complete without making the point that the quality of attention which children receive in those unfortunate cases where they must, perforce, spend time in State institutions is of critical importance. In South Africa these services, in many cases, need considerable upgrading. Of particular concern are the basic facilities, the training of staff, and the provision of reconstruction services designed to heal dysfunctional child–parent relationships so the child may be returned as quickly as possible to her family.[28]

5. CONCLUSION

In conclusion, it is clear that the provision of specialised children's courts to deal with child care proceedings was a most significant development in 1937. That this concept survived the erosions of the period of intensive apartheid is most fortunate. At the present time, the South African children's courts are under a new threat of a very different kind. They may lose their specialist role as a result of being combined with juvenile courts or subsumed within a family court system. What renders them more vulnerable to removal as a separate curial network is their present ineffectiveness in many cases. However, it has been argued in this chapter that, even if a family court system is introduced, the concept of specialist care-proceedings courts should be preserved—perhaps as a component within the family court system. Regardless of whether children's courts become part of a family court network or not, there are important and cost-effective reforms which need to be implemented as a matter of urgency if South African care proceedings are to have a significantly positive effect upon the lives of the many children who need to have not just a meaningless single appearance, but a constructive, ongoing relationship with judicial officers in whom they can confide.

It is essential that adjudicating officers in children's courts or their future equivalent be carefully selected. They need to have both a knowledge of appropriate areas of black-letter law and an ability to interact effectively with children and dysfunctional families. Such interaction will generally only be possible where the adjudicating officer understands the cultural norms of the child and can speak directly to parties in the language with which they are most familiar. Even where these basic requirements are met, there will still be problematic cases where parties, and particularly the child, will need legal representation. In an environment

---

[27] For proposals in this regard see *A National Plan of Action for the Children in South Africa and the Role of the Department* (Dept. of Justice Publication LD390396 of 1996), 15–16.

[28] See Matthias and Zaal, n. 19 above, at 59–60 for some further discussion.

where financial resources will always be scarce, specific guidelines for the provision of state funding for legal representation must be promulgated. Where cases fall within these guidelines, the least expensive and most effective way for the state to provide representation at care proceedings would be in the form of full-time, salaried child advocates who serve several adjoining jurisdictions.

In order to a facilitate constructive relationships between adjudicating officers and children in need of care, current South African law needs to be drastically revised in order to give the court at which care proceedings were initiated, and not welfare civil servants as at present, the power and duty to monitor the progress of the child—especially whilst the child remains in an institution of any kind. Appeals from and other possibilities for a curial altering of the initial court order must be facilitated in the interests of the child through the promulgation of enabling legislation. Rather than finally destroying the children's courts, the South African legislature should move to realise the withered dream of 1937. As has been suggested in this chapter, effective care-proceedings forums can be achieved at relatively little cost and are worth preserving as a specialist entity.

21

*Signposts on the Road to Equality: Towards the New Millennium for Parents, Children and Families in South Africa**

JULIA SLOTH-NIELSEN and BELINDA VAN HEERDEN

"Itself a country where considerable political and socio-economic movement has been and is taking place, South Africa occupies a distinctive position in the context of developments in the legal relationship between family members and between the state and the family. Its heterogeneous society is 'fissured by differences of language, religion, race, cultural habit, historical experience and self-definition' and, consequently, reflects widely varying expectations about marriage, family life and the position of women in society."[1]

1 INTRODUCTION

The last few years have seen the development by government and other state bodies of an entirely new body of literature and documentation on child and family law issues in South Africa. The first part of this chapter will describe briefly key aspects and dimensions of these developments, and attempt to illustrate the magnitude of the impending revolution in child and family law which they herald. In doing so, we will necessarily consider the socio-historical background to these innovations, in order to draw links between seemingly disparate endeavours. Through identification of these links, and of several broad themes illuminating the relationship between social and political change and legal development, we conclude by analysing the implications for the future shape of South African child and family law. Our overall thesis will be that this changing legal regime is

* An earlier version of this chapter appears as "Putting Humpty Dumpty back together again: Towards Restructuring Families' and Children's Lives in South Africa" (1998) 115 SALJ 156. The financial assistance of the University of Cape Town Subsistence and Travel Grants Committee is gratefully acknowledged by Belinda van Heerden, while that of Radda Barnen (Swedish Save the Children Fund) is gratefully acknowledged by Julia Sloth-Nielsen.
[1] June Sinclair, *The Law of Marriage Vol.* 1 (1996), 7.

destined dramatically to influence the conceptual and substantive construction of "childhood", "parenthood" and "the family" in South African society.[2]

2 THE STATE OF PLAY TO DATE

Usually, dicussions of this nature would commence with the required standard discussion of the new constitutional environment introduced by the adoption of the 1994 Constitution,[3] followed by the mandatory reference to the ratification by South Africa of the United Nations Convention on the Rights of the Child (1989) ("CRC") and the Convention on the Elimination of All Forms of Discrimination Against Women (1979) ("CEDAW"), whereafter the next step would be an analysis of the extended provisions affecting women, children and families in the 1996 Constitution.[4] This route being by now rather well-trodden, we will assume that our readership is au fait with the broad picture, and begin our story after the honeymoon has ended.

1 Legislation

The period under discussion from 8 May 1996[5] until the end of November 1997 has seen the promulgation of at least seven pieces of legislation which we identify as being legal responses relevant to our discussion. First, the Births and Deaths Registration Amendment Act 40 of 1996[6] makes allowance for the first time for children born of African customary unions and of marriages by religious rites (e.g. Muslim and Hindu rites) to be registered at birth as "legitimate" children. Although this is only of formal significance and does not affect the substantive legal status of such children, it does lessen the potential stigma attached to "illegitimate" birth. Perhaps more importantly, it can also be regarded as the first step towards the elimination of legal discrimination between the different marriage forms prevailing in this country.[7]

---

[2] Our main intention is to chart legislative and other policy developments situated within the parliamentary sphere. We therefore do not consider case law in any detail. Furthermore, as our goal is to highlight broad themes and trends, we do not always provide a critique of the substantive detail of the individual documents or provisions discussed.

[3] Constitution of the Republic of South Africa Act 200 of 1993.

[4] Constitution of the Republic of South Africa Act 108 of 1996.

[5] The date on which the "final" South African Constitution was adopted by the Constitutional Assembly. After certification by the Constitutional Court later in 1996, the Constitution of the Republic of South Africa Act 108 of 1996 was promulgated on 18 December 1996 and finally came into force on 4 February 1997.

[6] Which came into force upon promulgation on 5 September 1996.

[7] See also in this regard the recent South African Law Commission, *Discussion Paper on Customary Marriages* (Discussion Paper 74, Project 90 *The Harmonisation of the Common Law and the Indigenous Law*, August 1997). The most important recommendation made by the Law Commission in this Discussion Paper is that customary unions must be given full legal recognition as valid marriages, subject to compliance with a minimum set of essential requirements (the consent of the spouses being

The Divorce Amendment Act 95 of 1996[8] is another apposite example: in short, by the introduction of a new section 5A into the Divorce Act 70 of 1979, a divorce court now has the power to refuse to grant a decree of divorce if it appears that one or both of the spouses must, according to the precepts of their religion, also obtain a religious divorce, until and unless the necessary steps to obtain such religious divorce have been taken. As Ashraf Mahomed contends, this legislation "disempowers manipulative parties from using certain inequitable and patriarchal precepts of their religions to deny innocent parties (mainly women) their full and unencumbered freedom and individual human rights".[9]

The process was taken a step further in the Child Care Amendment Act 96 of 1996.[10] Not only did this Act (like the Births and Deaths Registration Amendment Act) replace the discriminatory term "illegitimate child" with the less objectionable term "child born out of wedlock", but it also introduced a new definition of "marriage". Here, the innovation is the inclusion of African customary unions and marriages "concluded in accordance with a system of religious law subject to specified procedures"[11] as legally recognised marriage forms for the purposes of the principal Act (i.e. the Child Care Act 74 of 1983).

In addition, the 1996 Amendment Act ushers in significant shifts in emphasis in four key areas of child law and policy.[12] Section 2[13] makes it possible for children now to have legal representation in children's court proceedings, if needs be at state expense. Formerly, no mechanism existed empowering commissioners of child welfare to arrange the appointment of a legal representative for a child who was the subject of an enquiry in the children's court, even where clear conflicts between (for example) parents and children necessitated child advocacy. The new possibility of appointing a legal practitioner to represent a child in such cases represents a clear attempt to recognise the child's autonomy, as research appears to indicates that it is precisely in the context of parent/child and

the key requirement): see Report, paras. 3.1.9 and 4.2.10. Further far-reaching recommendations are that parties to customary marriages should have equal capacities and powers of decision-making, that both such parties should have full capacity to acquire, own and possess property and that full ownership in individual acquisitions should be recognised by legislation: see Report, paras. 6.2.2.20–21 and 6.3.1.16.

[8] Which came into force upon promulgation on 22 Nov. 1996, following the recommendations of the South African Law Commission in its *Report on Jewish Divorces* (Project 76, October 1994).

[9] Ashraf Mahomed, "The Divorce Amendment Act 95 of 1996: A Case of Doctrinal Entanglement and a Step Closer to the Legitimate Democratisation of Religion" 1997 *De Rebus* 495 at 496. Cf. also *Ryland* v. *Edros* [1996] 4 All SA 557 (C).

[10] Promulgated in Nov. 1996, but at the date of writing not yet in operation.

[11] S. 1(d).

[12] For a fuller discussion of the background to, and content of, this amending legislation, see Julia Sloth-Nielsen and Belinda van Heerden, "Proposed Amendments to the Child Care Act and Regulations in the Context of Constitutional and International Law Developments in South Africa" (1996) 12 *SAJHR* 247, "The Child Care Amendment Act 1996: Does It Improve Children's Rights in South Africa?"(1996) 12 *SAJHR* 649, and "New Child Care and Protection Legislation for South Africa? Lessons from Africa" (1997) 8 *Stell LR* 261.

[13] Inserting a new s. 8A into the principal Act.

family disputes in children's court proceedings that the independent voice of the child must be heard.[14]

Improvements were also effected in regard to the provisions of the Child Care Act covering the reporting of child abuse. The pool of persons obligated to report child abuse has been widened to include teachers and persons employed by or managing children's homes, places of care or shelters.[15] Thirdly, the Amendment Act inserted a definition of "shelter" and a corresponding definition of "children in especially difficult circumstances",[16] concepts which are entirely novel in legislative experience in this country. The assumption by the state of some responsibility for the basic welfare needs of specifically disadvantaged groups of children (through the new possibility of state subsidisation of shelters) illustrates the emergence of a paradigm shift in the public/private law divide in the sphere of child support, traditionally regarded as entirely parental or family responsibility.

The last landmark in the Child Care Amendment Act for the purposes of this discussion concerns the criteria for the removal of children from parental care. When the Act comes into operation, the primary ground for the removal of children will (once again[17]) be the concept of the "child in need of care", as evidenced by factors such as abandonment, physical or mental neglect, abuse or ill treatment (physical, emotional or sexual) or uncontrollability.[18] Until this change comes into effect, it is usually necessary first to prove parental unfitness or incapability in order to establish a ground for removal.[19] Mirroring the common law position of familial rights with regard to children (e.g. parental rights to impose reasonable chastisement upon children and to control a child's association with other persons), the present legal framework in the Child Care Act therefore reflects a philosophy of children as the objects of parental control, parents generally being deprived of such control only upon proof of "wrongdoing" or "inadequacy". The new order, rather, shows an increasing awareness of children as

[14] See Art. 12 of CRC, and further Noel Zaal, "When should Children be Legally Represented in Care Proceedings? An Application of Section 28(1)(h) of the 1996 Constitution"(1997) 114 *SALJ* 334 and *Do Children Need Lawyers in the Children's Courts?* (Publication of the Community Law Centre, University of the Western Cape,1997). However, in the recent case of *Fitschen* v. *Fitschen* (C) Case No. 9564/95 (as yet unreported), in which the plaintiff's counsel argued that the children's viewpoint (in a custody dispute) should be conveyed to the court through an intermediary or court appointed legal representative, Van Reenen J rejected this contention, on the basis that: "the children's preferences—which were not called into doubt—as well as the reasons for these preferences, were placed fully before the court by the two clinical psychologists and the weight which should be attached thereto was properly debated . . . " (our translation). Interestingly, the ultimate order did *not* give effect to the expressed wishes of either child.

[15] S. 15, amending s. 42 of the principal Act.

[16] Ss. 1(f) and (c) respectively.

[17] The Children's Act 33 of 1960, which preceded the present Child Care Act, also encapsulated this criterion, and was regarded by many as being ahead of its time in this regard (see M. J. C. Olmesdahl, *Discretion, Social Reality and the Best Interests of the Child*, Inaugural Lecture, University of Natal, Durban 1986). But, it must also be pointed out that many of the indicators which could give rise to a finding under the 1960 Act that a child was in need of care were couched in the paternalistic and moralistic tones of that era.

[18] Ss. 5(b) and (c), amending s. 14(4) of the principal Act.

[19] Child Care Act 74 of 1983, s. 14(4)(b).

individuals; as bearers of rights independent of the family structure and, therefore, worthy of state intervention on their own account. It is our contention that this has potentially important implications for the boundaries of the relationships between children, parents and the state.

Our fourth example in the area of legislation is the recent accession by South Africa to the Hague Convention on the Civil Aspects of International Child Abduction (1980), which Convention became part of our domestic law on 1 October 1997.[20] The import of accession to this Convention lies in the designation of a state organ (the Central Authority[21]) with powers and functions designed to protect children internationally from the harmful effects of their wrongful removal or retention (usually by their parents), and to provide procedures to ensure their prompt return to the state of their habitual residence. The Convention also attempts to secure protection across international borders for rights of access, particularly of non-custodian parents. Once again, this exemplifies a trend towards an increasing blurring of the boundaries between private and public domains in the family law arena, with a concomitant focus on the protection of the rights of children at the expense of unfettered parental control.

The rights of children to make decisions for themselves finds its most striking expression in the Choice on Termination of Pregnancy Act 92 of 1996.[22] In terms of section 5(3), a pregnant "minor" (defined in section 1(vi) as a female person below the age of 18 years, with no minimum age limit) has the right to decide to terminate her pregnancy within the constraints imposed by the Act, *without* the consent of her parents or guardian. Although she must be advised to consult her parents, guardian, family members or friends, termination of her pregnancy (if necessary at state expense) may not be denied should she choose not to consult them or should they oppose her decision. Indeed, even a married women (of any age) does not require the consent of her husband or of anybody else to terminate her pregnancy within the provisions of the Act.

Although overtly linked to the reproductive autonomy provisions in the 1996 Constitution,[23] these termination of pregnancy provisions also have a different relevance. They epitomise the demise of parental control and decision-making in an area of vital importance, with a corresponding amplification of the child's right to self-determination. Additionally, it can be pointed out that this Act provides further evidence of state intervention in traditionally private family matters (as regards children's relationships with their parents and relationships between

---

[20] See the Hague Convention on the Civil Aspects of International Child Abduction Act 72 of 1996 (date of commencement 1 October 1997). In terms of Art. 38 of the Convention, the entire text of which is incorporated as a Sched. to Act 72 of 1996, the accession will only be effective between South Africa and those other Contracting States which declare their acceptance of our accession.

[21] In terms of s. 3 of the Act, the Central Authority for the Republic is to be the Chief Family Advocate. Certain practical aspects required by the implementation of the Convention in South Africa will be regulated in terms of Regulations issued by the Minister of Justice under s. 5 of Act 72 of 1996, which regulations were published in *Government Gazette* 18322 of 1 Oct. 1997.

[22] Which came into operation on 1 February 1997.

[23] See s. 12(2)(a) of Act 108 of 1996.

spouses *inter se*), stemming from the dominant current concerns about "the values of human dignity, the achievement of equality, security of the person, non-racialism and non-sexism" (as set out in the Preamble to Act 92 of 1996). These benefits now apparently outweigh common law notions of the autonomy of the family, patriarchal concepts of the husband as head of the family, and the traditional subordination of women and children to male decision-making.

There have also been some interesting developments regarding the commencement of pregnancy, specifically in the area of the rights to assisted reproductive techniques. Until 17 October 1997, an artificial insemination procedure (as defined in the Human Tissue Act 65 of 1983) could only be performed by a medical practitioner on a married woman, and then only with the written consent of her husband.[24] This provision was challenged by three unmarried women, all of whom were desirous of being recipients of donor sperm.[25] Approaches by these women to the Minister of Health and to the Human Rights Commission resulted in the amendment by the Minister of Health of the offending regulations on 17 October 1997.[26] In a significant step forward for both reproductive autonomy and non-discrimnination on the basis of marital status, unmarried women now qualify for artificial insemination procedures, including the receipt of donor sperm, on exactly the same basis as their married counterparts.

The last example of legislative reform is possibly less obviously linked to the "traditional" family and child law terrain. The South African Schools Act 84 of 1996[27] intends "to set uniform norms and standards for the education of learners at school and the organisation, governance and funding of schools throughout the Republic of South Africa".[28] As is now widely known, this Act, together with the National Education Policy Act,[29] was also the vehicle for the prohibition and criminalisation of corporal punishment in all public and private schools[30] in this country. Under the common law, the parental right of reasonable chastisement could be delegated by parents to educators and others in loco parentis. In our view, therefore, the Schools Act too represents an intrusion upon parental rights (specifically, the right of parents to delegate their powers of chastisement), and additionally serves as another example of the shrinking sphere of influence of "the family" as a site of entirely private concern.

---

[24] See Reg. 8(1) of the Regulations Regarding the Artificial Insemination of Persons, and Related Matters, issued by the Minister of Health under s. 37 of the Human Tissue Act on 20 June 1986.

[25] See *FEMINA* magazine (Nov. 1997) at 88.

[26] See Government Notice R1354, published in *Government Gazette* 18362 of 17 Oct. 1997.

[27] Which came into force on 1 January 1997.

[28] See the Preamble to the Act.

[29] Act 27 of 1996.

[30] But not yet in children's institutions: see s. 53(1) of the Child Care Act 74 of 1983, read with Reg. 32 of the Regulations issued in terms of s. 60 of the Act (Government Notice R2612 in *Government Gazette* 10546 of 12 Dec. 1986). However, it is likely that this aspect will be addressed with the pending redrafting of South African child care legislation (South African Law Commission Project 110, *Review of the Child Care Act, 1983*). Both authors of this chapter have been appointed to this project committee.

2 Bills and Draft Bills

A number of bills and draft bills have been published which, at the time of writing, are in various stages of passage in the parliamentary process, and which give further clues as to the future direction of South African child and family law. We highlight two examples in particular, which we perceive to be especially relevant to the changing conception of "childhood", "parenthood" and "family". The first is the Natural Fathers of Children Born out of Wedlock Bill.[31] This document originated in the South African Law Commission July 1994, *Report on the Rights of a Father in respect of his Illegitimate Child* (Project 79), and gained momentum through the landmark decision of the Constitutional Court in the widely publicised Lawrie Fraser case.[32] At common law, it is the mother of an extra-marital child who is the sole guardian and custodian of such child. The father has no inherent rights in respect of the child, but is theoretically obliged to share with the mother the parental duty of support—although it rarely works out this way in reality and mothers of extra-marital children generally bear the full burden of child support and child rearing.[33] In recent years, there has been a spate of litigation by fathers seeking access to their extra-marital children, culminating in the 1995 decision of the Supreme Court of Appeal in *B* v. *S*.[34] This case confirmed the father's lack of inherent rights under common law, but at the same time clarified his locus standi to approach the court for an order granting him certain rights such as access if this is in the best interests of the child in question.

The Bill, in its present form, does not materially alter the common law position with regard to access to and custody and guardianship of extra-marital children, despite possible expectations[35] that a different outcome would have been justified by the equality provisions of the 1996 Constitution[36] and by those articles of CRC which prohibit discrimination against children on the grounds of, *inter alia*, birth or parental marital status, and which entrench the child's right to know and be cared for by both parents, irrespective of their marital status.[37] In our view, the retention of the *status quo* (as it were) stems from a consciousness of the particularly vulnerable position of single mothers in our society and the intention not to exacerbate their already tenuous socio-economic and legal position. However, where there *will* be a diminution of the maternal position is

[31] Bill 68B of 1997, as amended by the Parliamentary Portfolio Committee on Justice after public hearings (during October 1997) on Bill 68 of 1997.

[32] *Fraser* v. *Children's Court, Pretoria North and Others* 1997 (2) BCLR 153 (CC). For a more detailed discussion of the judgment of Mahomed DP in this case, see Julia Sloth-Nielsen and Belinda van Heerden, "New Child Care and Protection Legislation for South Africa? Lessons from Africa", n. 12 above.

[33] See Sandra Burman and Eleanor Preston-Whyte, "Assessing Illegitimacy in South Africa" in *idem* (eds.), *Questionable Issue: Illegitimacy in South Africa* (1992), ix at xiv–xvi.

[34] 1995 (3) SA 571 (A). See also *T* v. *M* 1997 (1) SA 54 (A) in this regard.

[35] For example, by fathers' lobby groups: see, for one viewpoint, David Van Onselen, "TUFF—the Unmarried Fathers' Fight" 1991 *De Rebus* 499.

[36] S. 9 of Act 108 of 1996.

[37] See, for example, Arts. 2, 7, 9 and 18.

in respect of adoption, because the Bill introduces the requirement (for the first time) that the natural father be given reasonable written notice of any intended adoption of his extra-marital child.[38]

While the Bill, therefore, does not signal a shift of power between state and parents, it does to a certain extent imply a changing balance of power (at least in legislative theory) between the natural parents of extra-marital children *inter se*.[39]

Furthermore, the Bill contains provisions for enquiries and reports by the Family Advocate to inform a court's decision in any application governed by the Bill, as well as the specific requirement that the court have regard to the attitude of the child in relation to such applications, and new limitations designed to protect the privacy of children (and other parties) in these proceedings.[40] In this, we once again detect the emergence of the "child" as a separate role player in what was previously regarded as primarily inter-parental domain (admittedly with the High Court holding a "watching brief" in its capacity as upper guardian of all minor children within its area of jurisdiction).

The second Bill relevant to this discussion is the Draft Bill on Surrogate Motherhood,[41] which was circulated for public comment by a parliamentary *ad hoc* select committee in June 1995. In November 1996 the select committee published an interim report, the contents of which are still under discussion. But from this interim report, recent media statements made by the chairperson of the select committee and the June 1997 parliamentary debates pertaining to the issue,[42] it is clear that the "conservative" view of "family" and "parenthood" apparent in the Draft Bill is no longer endorsed. The latest views hold that it is not advisable to allow only married women to be surrogate mothers, nor should commissioning parents necessarily be restricted to heterosexual married couples. The rights of gay and lesbian partners to make use of surrogacy arrangements[43] is firmly on the agenda, as is also the question whether the surrogate mother should have the right to abort (or refuse to abort) the child, irrespective of the

---

[38] Cl. 6. Unfortunately, it is not possible at this stage to predict the exact extent to which this requirement will impact upon mothers' autonomy concerning placements of their extra-marital children: all the details about how, when, by whom the notice must be given and so on have been left for prescription by the Minister of Justice by means of a notice in the *Government Gazette*. As the Bill provides further that the notice to the father may be dispensed with, *inter alia*, if the children's court is satisfied that the natural father cannot be identified, there may be more than a little inducement for mothers to avoid the implications of the legislation by concealment of the identify of the father. Given the importance of the issues to be prescribed by notice in the *Gazette*, it is noteworthy that, subsequent to the public hearings mentioned above, a clause requiring the submission by the Minister of these "prescriptions" to Parliament prior to their publication in the *Gazette* was inserted in Bill 68B of 1997, apparently in response to concerns expressed by many of the interest groups who participated in the public hearings.

[39] As well as clarification of the paramountcy of the "best interests of the child" principle in disputes between these parents.

[40] See cll. 2(4)(d), 3 and 5.

[41] First published as Sched. A to the South African Law Commission *Report on Surrogate Motherhood* (Project 65, 1993).

[42] Debates of the National Assembly (Hansard) (Wednesday, 18 June 1997), 4045–72.

[43] Underpinned by rights to equality and to reproductive autonomy, as enshrined in the 1996 Constitution (ss. 9 and 12(2)(a)).

wishes of the commissioning parent or parents. Some of these recent ideas contrast strongly with the earlier approach, which intended to confine the option of surrogacy to legally married spouses, which regarded surrogate motherhood as a "last resort alternative" available only where the commissioning wife was medically unable to give birth to a child, and which permitted only married women (or divorcees or widows) who have already given birth to at least one child to act as surrogate mothers. Therefore, the likelihood exists that any final legislation on surrogacy will encompass a much broader concept of parenthood and family than that evident in the Draft Bill. And, although it is well known that surrogacy arrangements, both formal and informal, are *de facto* a reality in South Africa, the prospect of regulatory legislation on this issue also supports our broad thesis of increasing state supervision of the traditionally "domestic" sphere.

Apart from the above considerations, there is another dimension. One strand of our overall contention relates to the increasing recognition of African values and traditions in developing South African family and child law and policy. (We have already referred, in preceding sections, to new definitions of "marriage".) The chairperson of the select committee sums this up in relation to the surrogacy debate as follows: "Surrogacy is practised within all black groups on an informal basis. Many cultures demand that a child be born of a marriage and people desire genetically-linked children. In many customs the elders get together to arrange for someone to give birth for an infertile woman. It also happens that a man is found to assist where a husband is infertile."[44]

3 Policy documents and reports

These are so numerous and varied, that we have had to select only a few to illustrate our general themes. First, the question of domestic violence. Following a prior Issue Paper, the South African Law Commission published (in February 1997) a *Discussion Paper on Domestic Violence*[45] pertaining to improvements to the Prevention of Family Violence Act 133 of 1993. At issue are numerous defects in the scope and effectiveness of the procedures set up by the 1993 Act intended to deal with the problems of domestic violence. We have to recognise that, at root, the process of law reform in this sphere is linked to better protection of women and children in the legal system, in the context of a patriarchal society in which violence against vulnerable groups is pervasive and often "invisible". With this in mind, the Discussion Paper addresses the broadening of the protection envisaged in the Act to include new categories of victims who are parties to domestic relationships, such as persons of the same *or opposite* genders who live or have lived together in marital-like relationships, parties to dating and engagement relationships and persons who share or have shared the

---

[44] *Weekend Argus*, 5/6 July 1997.
[45] Discussion Paper 70, Project 100.

same household.[46] Courts granting domestic violence interdicts will be empowered to impose special conditions to protect children, and the possibility of maintenance, custody and access orders being granted simultaneously with interdicts is being mooted.[47]

Independent of the proposed changes mentioned above, a potential widening of the concept of domestic violence is envisaged, as "including, but not limited to" physical or sexual abuse or threats of such abuse, intimidation, harassment and destruction of property. It is also noteworthy that the violence in question can consist of a single act or a number of acts which form part of a pattern of behaviour "even though some or all of these acts, when viewed in isolation, may appear to be minor or trivial".[48]

Obviously, the Discussion Paper is relevant to the emerging legal recognition of different family forms. The broadened definition of "domestic relationship" better reflects the reality of plural family structures in South Africa, which in turn provides the context for enhanced protection for victims of "family" violence. Not only does the present priority afforded to this proposed legislative reform show the policy shift towards improving access to justice for women and children, but it is also our contention that the more flexible concepts of domestic relationships *and* of violence presently under discussion point to two things: a state unwillingness to make protection conditional upon either recognised first world legal family constructs, or to limit protection with the erection of artificial barriers to justice inherent in limited legal definitions of "domestic violence". The import of the Discussion Paper, in its preparedness to "enter the private home" in order to uphold constitutional rights to human dignity and physical integrity, is also significant in the context of our present discussion.

Perhaps somewhat unrelated to the above matter is the next issue, which pertains to a new system of juvenile justice presently under investigation and discussion (see the South Africa Law Commission *Issue Paper on Juvenile Justice*).[49] The key reason why we regard this as being part and parcel of the pending revolution referred to in our introduction is because this Issue Paper forges clear links between criminal justice and other formerly discrete areas of child law, such as child care and protection. It has even been informally mooted that any juvenile justice legislation that emerges from this project should be drafted in such a way as ultimately to form an integral part of an entirely new and comprehensive children's code. This would remove juvenile justice firmly from the traditional

---

[46] At present, the protection afforded by Act 133 of 1993 is only available to "parties to a marriage", defined as "including a man and a woman who are or who were married to each other according to any law or custom and also a man and a woman who ordinarily live or lived together as husband and wife, although not married to each other" (s.1(2)), and to children living with such parties or living with either of them.

[47] A further recommendation is to the effect that the Family Advocate may be drawn in when domestic violence orders are made.

[48] See Recommendation 10, para. 3.10.41 of the Discussion Paper.

[49] Project 106, Issue Paper 9, May 1997.

criminal justice (public law) arena, and place it squarely within the general body of law (statutory and common) dealing with children and families.

The Issue Paper also raises a number of concerns to which we have already alluded: legislative priority for children and children's rights, an emphasis on family preservation and restorative justice, and some recognition of the difficulties associated with family disintegration and the need to encourage the support of children by a much wider pool of potential care-givers. The *Issue Paper on Juvenile Justice* follows on a comprehensive policy review of the residential child care system, which culminated in a draft policy document accepted by Cabinet in February 1997. The *Interim Policy Recommendations* of the Inter-Ministerial Committee on Young People at Risk lay the foundation for an overhaul of placements of children in a variety of institutional settings, and focus future policy on family reunification and community-based models of care and care-giving.

The notion of "care-giver" has hitherto played a limited role in the common law of parent and child. It has been mainly relevant as a factor in the exercise of the judicial discretion in custody disputes between married or divorced parents, and has not explicitly emerged in legislation to date. However, some of the documents and legislative proposals which we have discussed introduce or prefigure such a concept. One important question that arises concerns the future legal relevance of this notion.[50]

This notion has recently gained some public prominence in the context of state maintenance grants (the new child support grant). In the debate which has ensued since the release of the *Report of the Lund Committee on Child and Family Support* (August 1996) and the subsequent publication, in September 1997, of the Welfare Laws Amendment Bill 90 of 1997, the criteria of payments for child support to "primary care-givers" have just begun to be focused, not only on the amounts to be paid and various other concerns, but also on the conceptual analysis and implications of formalising in law the role of a "primary care-giver" as a new player. In the recent Transkei case of *Nguza* v. *Nguza*,[51] the following comments were made apropos the concept "care of a child": "The concept of 'care' is an elastic one. It may, at one end of the scale in a particular case, embrace custody and, at the other end, entail a temporary entrusting of the welfare of a child to another for a matter of minutes. It does not require a continuous physical proximity to the child and indeed situations where more than one person in different places from each other may be simultaneously 'in care of' a child are also easily envisaged. . . ."[52]

As has been pointed out by researchers in both South Africa and other African countries, the most striking characteristic of the physical care of children in these countries is fluctuation and movement, with children often being placed

---

[50] See unpublished *Summary of Proceedings of Seminar on the Concept of the "Primary Care-Giver" in New South African Legislation*, Community Law Centre, University of the Western Cape, Aug. 1997.

[51] 1995 (2) SA 954 (Tk).

[52] At 958 F–G.

temporarily or permanently with someone other than the biological parent, and staying with a range of persons for differing periods of their childhood.[53]

On a purely practical plane, therefore, it would be overly simplistic to assume that the "primary care-giver" is necessarily synonymous with a natural parent; yet, contrarily, the idea of linking material economic benefits to a person other than such a parent requires clear criteria and some degree of administrative sophistication. The apparent primary aim of the new child support grant (which will replace state maintenance grants for mothers and children) is to ensure that the basic material needs of children are met. Although it is clear that these needs are satisfied only in the context of a adult (usually woman) care-giver or care-givers, the Lund Committee signals the change in emphasis with the adage "follow the child".[54] But the Lund Committee Report provided no basis for determining the identity of the primary care-giver, particularly in situations where a child resides temporarily or permanently apart from its natural parents.

Granting the natural parent (usually the mother) primacy in determining the identity of the adult recipient of the child support grant holds many attractions: it strengthens the position of mothers, and would be perceived as promoting the goals of gender equality recently endorsed by our constitutional court. If, as Kriegler J pointed out, "the notion . . . that women are to be regarded as the primary care givers of young children is a root cause of women's inequality in our society",[55] then, by implication, giving mothers the final say in accessing limited economic state resources enhances their societal power.

If, on the other hand, the state were to attempt to determine empirically the de facto care-giver position,[56] i.e. take "follow the child" at face value, then there are obvious consequences relating to resulting state intervention in effectively reconstructing "a family" for the child. There may well be unintended consequences for the legal and social rights of the natural or biological family.

The original Welfare Matters Amendment Bill 90 of 1997 emanating from the Department of Welfare which attempted to give legislative definition to the primary care-giver principle showed evidence, though, of some retreat from the apparent initial tenets of the Lund Committee Report: the Bill retracted from a wider and more open factual assessment of identifying the primary care-giver as the person who physically attends to the basic daily needs of the child, supplanting this with what is essentially a biologically-linked test.[57] A coalition of

---

[53] See e.g. Alice Armstrong, "School and Sadza: Custody and the Best Interests of the Child in Zimbabwe" (1994) 8 *Int J of L and the Fam.* 151 at 170; Vivienne Bozalek, "Contextualising Caring in Black South African Families" (1998) 5 *Social Politics: International Studies in Gender, State and Society*, Lund Committee Report Ch. 2.

[54] See Lund Committee Report 84. Unfortunately, the precise meaning of this "central theme" is not fully explored in the Report or the recommendations.

[55] *The President of the Republic of South Africa and Another* v. *Hugo* 1997 (6) BCLR 708 (CC) at para. 80; see also para. 38 (*per* Goldstone J), para. 93 (*per* Mokgoro J) and para. 110 (*per* O'Regan J). Cf. *Brink* v. *Kitshoff NO* 1996 (4) SA 197 (CC) at para. 44.

[56] The grants systems are notorious in their vulnerability to manipulation and wide-scale fraud.

[57] Including the parent of the child, the grandfather, grandmother, brother, sister, uncle or aunt of the child. In addition, the Minister may designate certain other relatives by blood or marriage for

non-governmental organisations argued that the limitations inherent in restricting the "legal" definition of the primary care-giver to biologically related persons failed to reflect the reality of child care arrangements in contemporary South Africa, and would unnecessarily restrict the availability of the grant. In response to these concerns, the Parliamentary Portfolio Committee on Welfare and Population Development ultimately made amendments to the original version, *inter alia* substituting the biologically-linked definition of a primary care-giver with one based on much more objective criteria, as proposed at a seminar on "The Concept of the 'Primary Care-Giver' in New South African Legislation" held in August 1997.[58]

The final document we have selected is the Department of Justice Draft Discussion Paper entitled "Gender Policy Considerations", released for public consultation on 20 June 1997. This document reflects an attempt by the Department to make explicit the role of women and children as "consumers of justice" and as fully-fledged participants in the legal profession and in the Department itself. Based on the recognition that it is women "who have been most disempowered in formal structures such as the legal system",[59] the document addresses such matters as violence against women, sexual offences, the enforcement of private maintenance obligations, the harmonisation of religious and customary family law with the common law and family law reform in general. The policy document details strategies to implement key provisions of CEDAW such as the "elimination of discrimination of women in all matters relating to marriage and family relations".[60]

Arguing that the legal profession itself "in all of its manifestations" should "become truly representative of the South African community", the document also proposes numerous changes, not only to the structure of law degrees and the content of legal curricula, but also to court structures and procedures which are designed to improve women's experiences of and access to justice. It is not unimaginable that these strategies will, at a different level, have a more substantive transformative effect on the existing power relationships within families and between families and the state.[61]

---

inclusion within the pool of potential primary care-givers: see the Welfare Laws Amendment Bill 90 of 1997, cl. 3(h), read with cll. 1(a) and (b).

[58] See n. 50 above. The amended definition of "primary care-giver" now reads as follows:
  " 'primary care-giver', in relation to a child, means a person, whether or not related to the child, who takes primary responsibility for meeting the daily care needs of the child, but excludes—
    (a) a person who receives remuneration, or an institution which receives an award, for taking care of the child; or
    (b) a person who does not have an implied or express consent of a parent, guardian or custodian of the child" (see cl. 3(h) of the Welfare Laws Amendment Bill 90D of 1997).

[59] See the Presentation by Deputy Minister M.E. Tshabalala-Msimang MP at the launch of the Discussion Paper on 20 June 1997 at 9.

[60] Art. 16. See the Draft Discussion Paper, 16–17.

[61] For example, if maintenance courts are rendered more woman-friendly and responsive to women's real needs, then mothers will have more financial clout against the fathers of their children and less need to rely on state support.

3 CONCLUSION: PARENTS, CHILDREN AND FAMILIES
IN THE NEW MILLENNIUM?

In detailing the legal and policy developments of the past 18 months or so, we have attempted to illustrate a number of broad themes which we perceive to be "directional", in the sense that they appear to indicate the path ahead for the development of a new legal context for child and family law.

First, we have hinted at the priority evidently being accorded women's and children's issues in the sphere of legal reform, and the corresponding drive to address the historical "invisibility" of the interests of both these groups.[62] It is notable that both family law and child law, which were formerly accorded inferior status by comparison to other areas,[63] have attracted increased political and legal attention, and that the discourse is no longer as male-dominated as it was in the past.[64] Both these, and the actual content of some of the reforms to we have alluded, point to greater recognition of "the family" as a site of public concern.

Secondly, it is hardly necessary to spell out the implications for personal law of such recent events as the ratification of international treaties, the adoption of the 1996 Constitution and the new culture of equality in South Africa. These have already, as pointed out in the survey, contributed definitively to the ambit and scope of the law reforms and proposals discussed. We have in consequence already moved some way from the patriarchal, discriminatory and male-dominated family law system of the past,[65] and are beginning to grapple with the Africanisation of our law and the concomitant recognition of plural marriage systems and different family forms which this entails. Also, the debate on surrogacy and the inclusion of non-heterosexual relationships in the South African Law Commission *Discussion Paper on Domestic Violence* point to practical instances

---

[62] See the Department of Justice Draft Discussion Paper (n. 54 above) 1: "The reality is that women have largely been rendered invisible in the legal system . . . the laws upon which they must rely have historically been formulated and applied by men and are not informed by the genuine needs of women."

[63] Such as commercial and contract law. Sinclair alludes to "family-law syllabuses and a body of academic writing largely confined to the explication of the black-letter rules that govern the relationship of family members *inter se*" (n. 1 above, at 4) which in our view may be a contributory factor in the past lack of vitality and consequent relative unimportance of "The Law of Persons" and "The Law of Marriage". It is not without significance that at most universities these courses form part of the first year law curriculum. By contrast, subjects such as "Tax Law" and "Corporation Law" are traditionally presented to senior law students. Another indicator of the inferior status of family and child law is obviously the low standing of courts serving (primarily) women's and children's interests: children's courts, maintenance courts and Black divorce courts as prime examples. And, despite the ongoing debate about the desirability of umbrella family courts (which commenced in the late 1970s), we still have no finality on this proposed forum, yet recent years have seen the establishment of a highly successful specialised commercial court in Gauteng.

[64] See e.g. the recent Constitutional Court decisions in *The President of the Republic of South Africa and Another* v. *Hugo* and *Brink* v. *Kitshoff NO*, n. 55 above.

[65] See Felicity Kaganas and Christina Murray, "Law and Women's Rights in South Africa: An Overview" 1994 *Acta Juridica* 1–38.

where the law is inclining towards the recognition of "gay" or same-sex relationships.

Thirdly, we have drawn together some examples which signal the emergence of "the child" as an autonomous bearer of rights, albeit along with some diminution of parental power. The proposed creation of a new juvenile justice system, the child-focused removal criteria in the 1996 Child Care Amendment Act and the provisions of the Choice on Termination of Pregnancy Act are examples in point. In the children's rights arena, South Africa is also attempting to eliminate past inequalities between different groups of children—and the "rights" of their natural parents.

Finally, we have been struck by recent endeavours to address the inaccessibility of the legal system for women and children, and to marry law reform with a deeper and more nuanced understanding of the realities of daily existence for the majority of women and children in this country, not only as regards the specific issues discussed above, but also as a general point of departure informing policy-making and legislative reform. As South Africa enters the new millenium, the themes we have highlighted will undoubtedly reshape public and private law responses to the needs and fundamental rights of children, parents and families.

POSTSCRIPT

More than 6 months have passed since November 1997, which was the end of period under discussion in this chapter. A number of important developments that have taken place in South Africa during this time are worthy of mention in a brief postscript.

The inexorable march of the parliamentary process has seen the promulgation (on 12 December 1997) of the Natural Fathers of Children Born out of Wedlock Act 86 of 1997, as well as the promulgation (on 19 December 1997) of the Welfare Laws Amendment Act 106 of 1997. While the content of both Acts is substantially the same as that of the bills which preceded them, only the latter Act has at the time of writing been put into operation (on 1 April 1998). Publication of all the details relating to the requirement of notice to the natural father of the intended adoption of his extra-marital child is still awaited, and the Natural Fathers Act is still inoperative. Furthermore, the Regulations that were published (in *Government Gazette* 18771 of 31 March 1998) to accompany the Welfare Laws Amendment Act have been severely criticised as unduly restrictive and potentially unworkable in practice. Officials receiving applications for the child support grant have to determine the existence of a long list of factors relevant to both the primary care-giver, and to the income of the household of which such primary care-giver is a member. This determination is complicated by the rather vague definitions of "household" and of "household income", and by the fact that the qualifying household income levels differ depending on whether the primary care-giver and the child concerned live in a urban or rural area, or in a informal dwelling (defined as "a house which is, whether partly or wholly, without brick, concrete or asbestos walls"). Initial studies (in June 1998) appear to indicate that, although some applications for the child support grant have been received, no grants are actually being paid out yet, and that enormous difficulty is being experienced in the practical implementation of this legislation.

Another Act which commenced operation on 1 April 1998 is the Child Care Amendment Act 96 of 1996, together with substantial amendments to the Regulations under the Child Care Act of 1983. Not only do the amended regulations (published in *Government Gazette* 18770 of 31 March 1998) prohibit corporal punishment as a form of discipline by foster parents and in children's residential facilities (including shelters for street children), but they also introduce other significant improvements to the care, protection and development rights of children in such facilities. Another new regulation of potentially great importance to children involved in children's court proceedings spells out in considerable detail a variety of cicumstances in which legal representation, at State expense, must be provided for a child who is involved in any such proceedings. Unfortunately, however, neither this new regulation (Regulation 4A), nor the corresponding section of Act 96 of 1996 dealing with legal representation for children (section 2), came into operation together with the rest of the Act and the amended Regulations. Legal representation for children caught up in proceedings under the Child Care Act therefore remains a promise which has not yet matured into reality.

The most significant development in the intervening period has, in our view, been the release (on 12 May 1998) by the South African Law Commission of its *First Issue Paper on the Review of the Child Care Act* (Issue Paper 13, Project 110). The Issue Paper does not merely traverse traditional concerns of child care and protection, but opens up a broad ranging discussion concerning the child's place in the family, community and society at large. It is indeed true that a large part of the Issue Paper focuses on the Child Care Act, highlighting aspects which have proved to be problematic in practice or which appear to be outdated in the light of modern international developments in the sphere of child and family law. However, the document foreshadows a much wider review of legislation, common law and customary and religious laws affecting children. The discussion addresses in considerable detail the special needs of children in difficult circumstances, including children affected by HIV/AIDS, street children and children with disabilities. It also tackles such thorny issues as alternative technologies, gay and lesbian family rights, and transracial and transcultural adoptions. Finally, the Issue Paper emphasises the interplay between different legal regimes concerning children and their rights in a variety of settings, such as within the family, in schools and day care centres, in residential care facilities, in the court process, and in the labour market. In so doing, it provides further evidence of our contention that the themes highlighted in this chapter are in the process of reshaping child and family law in South Africa, causing what has traditionally been regarded as the domain of private law to emerge increasingly into the public law arena.

22

Constitutional Interpretation of the "Best Interests" Principle in South Africa in Relation to Custody

NAZEEM GOOLAM*

1. CONSTITUTIONAL INTERPRETATION IN SOUTH AFRICA

Section 39 of the Constitution provides:[1]

"(1) When interpreting the Bill of Rights, a court, tribunal or forum
    (a) must promote the values that underlie an open and democratic society based on human dignity, equality and freedom;
    (b) must consider international law; and
    (c) may consider foreign law.
  (2) When interpreting any legislation, and when developing the common law or customary law, every court, tribunal or forum must promote the spirit, purport and objects of the Bill of Rights.
  (3) The Bill of Rights does not deny the existence of any other rights or freedoms that are recognized or conferred by common law, customary law or legislation, to the extent that they are consistent with the Bill."

The values of human dignity, equality and freedom must thus permeate the interpretation process. According to Froneman J[2] "[c]onstitutional interpretation in this sense is thus primarily concerned with the recognition and application of constitutional values and not with a search to find the literal meaning of the statute".

One of the values of an open and democratic society is that the values of all sections of society must be taken into account and given due weight. Indeed, Sieghart points out that "the hallmarks of a democratic society are pluralism, tolerance and broad-mindedness".[3] In this respect, and particularly in the context

---

* The author wishes to thank Prof. T. Nhlapo of the SA Law Commission for his assistance.

[1] The Interpretation Clause.

[2] *Matiso and Others* v. *Commanding Officer, Port Elizabeth Prison and Others*, 1994 (3) BCLR 80 (SE) at 87H.

[3] *The International Law of Human Rights* (Clarendon Press, New York, 1983), at 784–91.

of this paper, a number of other constitutional provisions merit enunciation. First, the preamble to the constitution declares:

"We, the people of South Africa,
Believe that South Africa belongs to all who live in it, united in our diversity."

Secondly, subsection 3 of the equality clause[4] provides:

"The state may not unfairly discriminate directly or indirectly against anyone on one or more grounds, including race, gender, sex, pregnancy, marital status, ethnic or social origin, colour, sexual orientation, age, disability, religion, conscience, belief, culture, language and birth."

Thirdly, section 10 provides that everyone has inherent dignity and the right to have their dignity respected and protected. Fourthly, section 31[5] of the constitution provides:

"(1) Persons belonging to a cultural, religious or linguistic community may not be denied the right, with other members of that community—
    (a) to enjoy their culture, practise their religion and use their language; and
    (b) to form, join and maintain cultural, religious and linguistic associations and other organs of civil society.
 (2) The rights in subsection (1) may not be exercised in a manner inconsistent with any provision of the Bill of Rights."

Finally, in terms of section 185, a Commission for the Promotion and Protection of the Rights of Cultural, Religious and Linguistic Communities is to be established as a state institution supporting constitutional democracy. The primary objects of the Commission are:

(a) to promote respect for the rights of cultural, religious and linguistic communities;
(b) to promote and develop peace, friendship, humanity, tolerance and national unity among cultural, religious and linguistic communities, on the basis of equality, non-discrimination and free association; and
(c) to recommend the establishment or recognition, in accordance with national legislation, of a cultural or other council or councils for a community or communities in South Africa.

In the context of family law or personal law issues, the aforementioned constitutional provisions will, undoubtedly, play a significant role in the process of interpretation. The values of human dignity, equality and freedom are uppermost in these provisions and it is these values which must, as stated earlier, permeate the interpretation process.

In a very recent judgment of the Cape Supreme Court,[6] Farlam J analysed the significance of these values in the context of South African family law. Commenting on an Appellate Division decision of 1983, *Ismail* v. *Ismail*,[7] in

---

[4] S. 9.
[5] Cultural, Religious and Linguistic Communities.
[6] *Ryland* v. *Edros*, 1997 (1) BCLR 77 (C).
[7] *Ismail* v. *Ismail*, 1983 (1) SA 1006 (A).

which the court had decided that the recognition of a potentially polygamous union celebrated according to the tenets of the Islamic faith was contrary to public policy, Farlam J stated that the basis underlying the decision in the *Ismail* case—and a long line of cases that had preceded it—was the notion that the monogamous concept of marriage was fundamental to our society. It was considered that the recognition of polygamous unions would undermine the status of marriage. Marriage and family laws had been designed primarily for monogamous relationships. While a polygamous union might be consistent with the tenets of the Islamic faith, it was considered entirely foreign to society's then prevailing notion of a conjugal relationship and was thus regarded as void on grounds of public policy.

In Farlam J's view, the question which now arose was whether it could be said, since the coming into operation of the Interim Constitution, that a contract concluded by parties arising from a marriage relationship entered into by them in accordance with the rites of their religion and which was, in fact, monogamous, was "contrary to the accepted customs and usages which are regarded as morally binding upon *all* members of our society" or was "fundamentally opposed to *our*" principles and institutions, as had been reasoned in earlier decisions.

Farlam J concluded that a positive answer to this question would run contrary to the spirit of the Constitution and that it was quite inimical to all the values underlying the Constitution for one group to impose its values on another and that courts should only brand a contract *contra bonos mores* if it is offensive to those values which are shared by the community at large, that is by all right-thinking people in the community, and not only by one section of it.[8] In the *Ismail* case, he said, the views of only one group of our plural society had been taken into account. Farlam J added that the principle of equality and the principle of tolerance and accommodation are important values underlying the bill of rights.[9]

It is against this background and in this spirit, the spirit of the values underlying the bill of rights, that a multicultural approach to the interpretation of the "best interests" principle in South Africa should be analysed.

2. THE WESTERN/EUROPEAN PERSPECTIVE

In a number of early South African decisions, the courts declared that in all cases involving decisions about the custody of children, the main or paramount consideration would be the interests or welfare of the children.[10] However, the court did not explain what would constitute the best interests of a child nor did it

---

[8] Above n. 6, at 90.
[9] *Ibid.*
[10] *Fletcher* v. *Fletcher*, 1948 (1) SA 130 (A) at 145; see also *Segal* v. *Segal*, 1971 (4) SA 317 (C) and *French* v. *French*, 1971(4) SA 298(W).

mention any particular factors/criteria which should be considered in the enquiry. The guiding principle was then that each case would be decided on its own merits, taking into account the facts and surrounding circumstances of the case.

However, In 1994, the court, in *McCall* v. *McCall*,[11] for the first time, listed a detailed set of criteria/factors which should inform the choice of what is best for the child. King J stated:

> "In determining what is in the best interests of the child, the Court must decide which of the parents is better able to promote and ensure his physical, moral, emotional and spiritual welfare. This can be assessed by reference to certain factors or criteria which are set out hereunder, not in order of importance, and also bearing in mind that there is a measure of unavoidable overlapping and that some of the listed criteria may differ only as to nuance. The criteria are the following:
>
> (a) the love, affection and other emotional ties which exist between parent and child and the parent's compatibility with the child;
>
> (b) the capabilities, character and temperament of the parent and the impact thereof on the child's needs and desires;
>
> (c) the ability of the parent to communicate with the child and the parent's insight into, understanding of and sensitivity to the child's feelings;
>
> (d) the capacity and disposition of the parent to give the child the guidance which he requires;
>
> (e) the ability of the parent to provide for the basic physical needs of the child, the so-called "creature comforts", such as food, clothing, housing and the other material needs—generally speaking, the provision of economic security;
>
> (f) the ability of the parent to provide for the educational well-being and security of the child, both religious and secular;
>
> (g) the ability of the parent to provide for the child's emotional, psychological, cultural and environmental development;
>
> (h) the mental and physical health and moral fitness of the parent;
>
> (i) the stability or otherwise of the child's existing environment, having regard to the desirability of maintaining the *status quo*;
>
> (j) the desirability or otherwise of keeping siblings together;
>
> (k) the child's preference, if the Court is satisfied that in the particular circumstances the child's preference should be taken into consideration;
>
> (l) the desirability or otherwise of applying the doctrine of same sex matching, particularly here, whether a boy of 12 . . . should be placed in the custody of his father; and
>
> (m) any other factor which is relevant to the particular case with which the Court is concerned."
>
> In every case, a court would thus have to make an objective assessment within the particular framework of its specific circumstances.[12]

The most striking and fundamental differences between the Western/European approach and the African approach are twofold: first, Western society,

---

[11] 1994 (3) SA 201 (C) at 205.

[12] Palmer, "The Best Interests Criterion: An Overview of its Application in Custody Decisions Relating to Divorce in the Period 1983–1995" [1996] *Acta Juridica* 98 at 102.

and Western philosophy in general, places great emphasis on the individual, while African society and philosophy stresses the importance of the group, the idea of communitarianism; and secondly, in relation to the family, Western social values are founded on the nuclear unit, while the extended family is the basis of African socio-cultural beliefs. This, then, leads us to consider . . .

3. THE AFRICAN PERSPECTIVE

In an African extended family, the individuals and the families are not autonomous. Van Niekerk explains:[13]

"The concept of human rights as natural, inherent, inalienable rights held by virtue of the fact that one is born a human being remains a creation of Western civilization and is foreign to indigenous law. In indigenous societies rights are assigned on the basis of communal membership, family status or achievement."

On the distinction between individual rights and group rights, Heyns[14] adds:

"The glorification of the individual hardly fits in with a world view in which the group is of fundamental importance and a culture in which duties also play a prominent role. In fact, this is where the indirect influence of the traditional African emphasis on groups [in] African constitutions become apparent. The explicit recognition of duties in African human rights instruments is in fact a different way of expressing respect for the role of the group."

Bearing this in mind, what then is the African perspective on the "best interests" principle? In African society, submission to the will of the parent—particularly the father—is highly valued and is considered to be an essential virtue to be cultivated in a child.[15] The duty of the child's submission to the father is based on the idea that parents make decisions which will be in the best interests of the child. But does the principle really exist in African societies? Nhlapo thinks not. He writes:[16]

"According to the Roman Dutch common law the overriding principle in child law is that the interests of the children are paramount. The same cannot be said of customary law. Rules of affiliation, fostering, custody and guardianship all appear to serve interests other than those of the child. But this is not to suggest that the interests of

---

[13] *The Interaction of Indigenous Law and Western Law in South Africa: A Historical and Comparative Perspective* (1995) at 261; See also Bekker, "Human Rights and Customary Law" (1997) 1 *The Human Rights and Constitutional Law Journal of Southern Africa* 21.

[14] "Where is the Voice of Africa in our Constitution?", Occasional Paper No. 8, Centre for Human Rights, University of Pretoria (1996), at 6.

[15] Belembaogo, "The Best Interests of the Child—The Case of Burkina Faso", in Alston (ed.), *The Best Interests of the Child Reconciling Culture and Human Rights* (Clarendon Press, Oxford, 1994), at 209.

[16] "Biological and Social Parenthood in African Perspective: The Movement of Children in Swazi Family Law", in Eekelaar and Sarcevic (eds.), *Parenthood in Modern Society* (Kluwer Academic Publishers, The Netherlands, 1993), at 47.

the child are deemed to be irrelevant. Rather, there exists a presumption that those interests will best be served if the strong rights of fathers and their lineage over children are not lightly interfered with, for it is by '*belonging*' [my emphasis] that a child is best protected."

Nhlapo concludes that, at least amongst the Swazi people, the best interests of the child are seen as encapsulated in the concept of "belonging". The position is not dissimilar in Zulu law, according to which a child belongs to the guardian of his mother, which is always a male person. As a result of the agnatic principle, the custody of a child is always awarded to the family head of his/her mother. At the death of the head of the family, all the inmates of the family are subject to his successor. If the successor is too young to take control of the affairs of the family, the child will remain in the custody of a male relative of his/her father's family.

Closely interrelated to this concept of "belonging" is the *duty to care* for family members, which lies at the heart of the African social system and is emphasised as a fundamental value in the African Charter on Human and Peoples' Rights.[17] Paragraph 4 of its preamble urges state parties to pay heed to "the virtues of the African tradition and the values of African civilization" while chapter 2 provides a list of duties that individuals, including children, owe their families and society. In addition, Article 29 of the Charter states that each person is obliged "to preserve the harmonious development of the family and to work for the cohesion and respect of the family; to respect his parents at all times, to maintain them in case of need".[18]

Onora O'Neill goes so far as to reject the concept of children's rights in favour of attributing appropriate obligations to adults and others responsible for the care of children.[19] Katherine O'Donovan, too, is very critical of children's rights due, *inter alia*, to the adversarial element they introduce.[20] She advocates an alternative approach based on "an expanded legal concept of *trust*" under which "care of the infant's person" would be held in trust by adults who would then be liable for breaches of trust.

In the final analysis, whereas the interests of the child have preference to that of its parents in Western culture, the welfare of the extended family predominates in African society. Whereas in Western culture, the emphasis is on the individual, autonomy of the child and on the concept of "rights", in African society the emphasis is on the community/group, on the concept of "belonging" and on the concept of "duties".

Robinson's study[21] of the Maori people in New Zealand exhibits the existence of a marked similarity between the plurality of family law systems in South Africa

---

[17] Bennett, *Human Rights and African Customary Law* (Juta and Co. Ltd, Cape Town, (1995), at 6.

[18] *Ibid.*

[19] "Children's Rights and Children's Lives", in Alston, Parker and Seymour (eds.), *Children, Rights and the Law* (Oxford University Press, Oxford, 1992).

[20] *Family Law Matters* (Pluto Press, London, 1993), at 100–5; see also Alston, above n. 15, at 22.

[21] "Multi-Kulturaliteit en die Familiereg: Enkele Gedagtes oor die Posisie in Nieu-Seeland" (1996) 7 *Stellenbosch Law Review* 210.

and that of New Zealand. In 1989, the New Zealand legislature adopted the Children, Young Persons and Their Families Act[22] in order to accommodate Maori culture, values, ideas and beliefs regarding the protection of children and young persons. This legislation was preceded by two reports on the issue, which appeared in 1986 and 1988 respectively. The former, entitled *Puao-Te-Ata-Tu, Report of the Ministerial Advisory Committee on a Maori Perspective for the Department of Social Welfare*, contains a clause in which the idea set out represents a mirror-image of the approach in African society. It reads:[23]

> "The child was not the child of the birth parents, but of the family, and the family was not a nuclear unit in space, but an integral part of a tribal whole, bound by reciprocal obligations to all whose future was prescribed by the past fact of common descent . . . the children had not so much rights as duties to their elders and community. It was a community responsibility."

4. THE ISLAMIC PERSPECTIVE

The primary sources of Islamic Law (*Shari'ah*) are the Holy *Qur'an* and the *Ahadith* (sing. *hadith*), the latter being the sayings and exhortations of the Prophet Muhammad (on whom be peace). Although Almighty God does not directly address the question of custody in the *Qur'an*, the following verse[24] is often quoted as authority:

> "The mothers shall give suck to their offspring for two whole years, if the father desires to complete the term. But he shall bear the cost of their food and clothing on equitable terms. No soul shall have a burden laid on it greater than it can bear. No mother shall be treated unfairly on account of her child nor father on account of his child" (2: 233).

There are a number of Prophetic sayings relating to the issue of custody. Two illustrations are given here. First, a woman once complained to the Prophet that upon divorce, her husband wished to remove her young child from her custody. The Prophet commented: "You have the first right to the child as long as you do not marry."[25] Secondly, on a different occasion a woman again complained that her husband wanted to take her son away from her, although her son was a source of great comfort and warmth to her. Her husband simultaneously denied her claim over the child. The Prophet said: "Child, here is your father and here is your mother; make a choice between the two as to whom you prefer."[26] The son took hold of his mother's hand and they dispersed.

Following upon the direction and spirit of the first *hadith*, all four Sunni schools of thought—the Hanafi, Maliki, Shafi'i and Hanbali—as well as the Shia

---

[22] Act 24 of 1989.
[23] Above n. 21, at 211.
[24] Surah Al-Baqarah (Chapter on Women) 2, verse 233.
[25] Sunan Abu Dawud, Kitab at Talaq (Vol.2) 616.
[26] Above n. 25, at 617.

school hold that the mother, whether she is separated or living with her husband, has the prior claim to the custody of the child.

In terms of Islamic law, both males and females must comply with two important conditions to be eligible for custody. First, they must be sane and of the age of majority, and secondly, they must have the ability to raise the child. This second condition entails, *inter alia*, protecting the child both physically and morally as well as looking after the interests of the child.[27] In addition to these conditions, a female custodian (*hadina*) should not marry someone whom the child is not prohibited from marrying, in terms of Islamic law. This condition is based on the saying of the Prophet, "You have the first right to the child as long as you do not marry".[28] Jamal Nasir explains that although the tradition would imply that the mother, and *a fortiori*, any other female custodian, would lose the right to custody of the child once she has remarried, regardless of her husband's relation to the child, it is not interpreted so sweepingly. The Hanafis and Malikis restrict the marriage that deprives the mother of her right to custody to that with a relative who is not prohibited from marrying the child.[29] For example, if the mother marries a cousin of the child, she forfeits her prior right of custody, whereas if she marries the child's uncle, she retains that right.

As stated earlier, there is no express direction in the *Qur'an* on the question of custody. Arab and Islamic countries, in their modern legislation on the issue, have, however, upheld the spirit of the Prophetic sayings and the approaches of the Sunni and Shia schools of thought. Inherent in the spirit of the Prophetic traditions and the various schools of law is the principle of the "best interests" of the child, the welfare of the child. A few illustrations suffice.

Article 20 of the Egyptian law on Personal Status of 1929[30] provides that the right of a woman to custody of her children shall cease on the attainment of the age of 10 years in the case of a male child and 12 years in the case of a female child. After the child has reached that age the *qadi* can order that the child continue in such custody until the male child reaches 15 and the female child gets married, if he is satisfied that the welfare of the child so demands. The Article grants the mother the prior right to custody—in terms of the *hadith* of the Prophet—and then awards custody in accordance with the Hanafi school of thought.

The Islamic Family Law (Federal Territory) Act of 1984 in Malaysia provides, in Article 84, as follows:

"(1) The right of the hadinah [female custodian] to the custody of a child terminates upon the child attaining the age of seven years in the case of a male and the age of nine years in the case of a female—but the court may, upon application by the hadinah, allow her to retain custody of the child until the attainment of the age of nine years in the case of a male and eleven years in the case of a female.

[27] Nasir, *The Islamic Law of Personal Status* (Graham and Trotman, London, 1986), at 178.
[28] See above n. 25.
[29] Above n. 27, at 179.
[30] As amended by Law 100 of 1985.

(2) After termination of the right of the hadinah the custody devolves upon the father, and if the child has reached the age of discernment (*mumaiyiz*), he or she shall have the choice of living with either of the parents, unless the court otherwise orders."

How have the courts in Islamic countries approached the issue? This chapter looks very briefly at the Pakistani and Malaysian approaches.

In Pakistan, the courts have developed the presumption that the minor's welfare lies in granting custody in accordance with the personal laws of the minor. In the case of *Atia Waris* v. *Sultan Ahmad Khan*,[31] Mahmud J stated:

"In considering the welfare the court must presume initially that the minor's welfare lies in giving custody according to the dictates of the rules of personal law, but if circumstances clearly point that his or her welfare lies elsewhere or that it would be against his or her interest, the court must act according to the demand of the welfare of the minor, keeping in mind any positive prohibitions of the personal law."[32]

In this case, custody was given to the paternal grandparents so as to ensure that the minor was raised as a Muslim, despite the positive rule of Muslim law— all four Sunni schools of thought are *ad idem* on this rule—which states that if the mother is found unsuitable to have custody of her female child, the custodial right devolves on the maternal grandmother.[33] However, the same court, some six years later, in the case of *Zohra Begum* v. *Latif Ahmad Manawwar*[34] stated that it is permissible for the courts to differ from the rules of custody as stated in textbooks on Muslim law because there is no *Qur'anic* injunction on the point and courts, which have taken the place of *qazis*, can, therefore, reach their own decisions by the process of *Ijtihad* (individual reasoning).[35] It would thus be permissible to depart from the rules if, on the facts of a particular case, its application would prejudice the welfare of the minor.

There have been a number of cases decided in the Shariah Courts of Malaysia on the issue of the custody of children. In one of the leading cases, *Nooranita bte Kamaruddin* v. *Faeiz bin Yeop Ahmad*,[36] the Shariah Appeal Committee, after referring to the Prophetic sayings on the right to custody,[37] as well as leading authorities such as Imam Al-Shafi'i and Syed Sabiq, concluded that:

"(1) The primary consideration in all cases of custody under the Islamic law is that the right of the child over whom custody is claimed must be given preference to the right of the persons claiming custody, as the purpose of custody is for the interest and welfare of the child and not for the interest and welfare of the parties contending for custody.

(2) Based on this legal principle of the Shariah and having considered all the facts of the case, including the reluctance of the child herself to choose between the father

---

[31] 1959 PLD (WP) Lah 205.
[32] Above n. 31, at 214.
[33] Pearl, *A Textbook on Muslim Personal Law* (Croom Helm, London, 1987), at 93.
[34] 1965 PLD (WP) Lah 695; See also *Fahmida Begum* v. *Habib Ahmad*, 1968 PLD Lah 1112.
[35] See Iqbal, *The Reconstruction of Religious Thought in Islam* (Khitab Bhavan, New Delhi, 1981).
[36] (1989) 2 *Malayan Law Journal* CXXIV.
[37] See above nn. 25 and 26.

and her mother, the Appeal Committee is of the opinion that it is to the welfare and interest of the child that she should continue to stay with her father, a situation which has existed for over four years, even though the mother-appellant could not be blamed for the delay in the hearing of the appeal."

5. CONCLUSION

The preamble to South Africa's constitution declares that "South Africa belongs to all who live in it, united in our diversity". However, until quite recently, and understandably so, the interpretation of the "best interests" principle—and family law issues in general—in South Africa has been very eurocentric in nature.

If the values that underlie an open and democratic society based on human dignity, equality and freedom are to be truly promoted and respected in South Africa, then judges, mediators and cultural council's commissioners will have to take into account the culturally diverse nature of our society. In this regard, the approach of Farlam J in *Ryland* v. *Edros*[38] is not only appropriate, but highly commendable. He concluded that it was quite inimical to all the values underlying the constitution for one group to impose its values on another.

It is in this spirit that the constitutional interpretation of what is in the best interests of the child, not only in relation to custody, but in all matters relating to the child, should be approached in a multicultural society such as ours.

REFERENCES

ALSTON, P. (1994), "The Best Interests Principle: Towards a Reconciliation of Culture and Human Rights" in P. Alston (ed.), *The Best Interests of the Child Reconciling Culture and Human Rights* (Oxford, Clarendon Press).

BAINHAM, A. (1994), "Religion, Human Rights and the Fitness of Parents", *Cambridge Law Journal* 39.

—— (1995), "Family Law in a Pluralistic Society", 22 *Journal of Law and Society* 234.

BEKKER, J. C. (1997), "Human Rights and Customary Law", 1 *The Human Rights and Constitutional Law Journal of Southern Africa* 21.

BELEMBAOGO, A. (1994), "The Best Interests of the Child—The Case of Burkina Faso" in P. Alston (ed.), *The Best Interests of the Child Reconciling Culture and Human Rights* (Oxford, Clarendon Press).

BENNETT, T. W. (1995a), *A Sourcebook of African Customary Law for Southern Africa* (Cape Town, Juta and Co. Ltd).

—— (1995b), *Human Rights and African Customary Law* (Cape Town, Juta and Co. Ltd).

DEVENISH, G. E. (1997), "The New Constitution and the Interpretation of Statutes—Some Preliminary Ideas and Explanatory Thoughts", 1 *The Human Rights and Constitutional Law Journal of Southern Africa* 3.

---

[38] See above n. 6.

DE VILLIERS, B. (1993), "The Rights of Children in International Law: Guidelines for South Africa", 4 *Stellenbosch Law Review* 289.

EEKELAAR, J. (1994), "The Interests of the Child and the Child's Wishes: The Role of Dynamic Self-Determination" in P. Alston (ed.), *The Best Interests of the Child Reconciling Culture and Human Rights* (Oxford, Clarendon Press).

GOONESEKERE, S. (1994), "The Best Interests of the Child: A South Asian Perspective" in P. Alston (ed.), *The Best Interests of the Child Reconciling Culture and Human Rights* (Oxford, Clarendon Press).

HAHLO, H. R. (1985), *The South African Law of Husband and Wife* (Cape Town, Juta and Co. Ltd).

HEYNS, C. (1996), "Where is the Voice of Africa in our Constitution" (Occasional Paper No. 8., Centre for Human Rights, University of Pretoria).

IQBAL, M. (1981), *The Reconstruction of Religious Thought in Islam* (New Delhi, Khitab Bhavan).

JONES, S. (1992), "The Ascertainable Wishes and Feelings of the Child", 4 *Journal of Child Law* 181.

MAHMOOD, T. (1987), *Personal Law in Islamic Countries* (New Delhi. Academy of Law and Religion).

McGOLDRICK, D. (1991), "The United Nations Convention on the Rights of the Child", 5 *International Journal of Law and the Family* 132.

MNOOKIN, R. (1975), "Child-Custody Adjudication: Judicial Functions in the Face of Indeterminacy", 39 *Law and Contemporary Problems* 60.

—— (1985), *In the Interest of Children: Advocacy, Law Reform and Public Policy* (New York, W. H. Freeman and Co.).

NASIR, J. J. (1986), *The Islamic Law of Personal Status* (London, Graham and Trotman).

NHLAPO, R. T. (1993), "Biological and Social Parenthood in African Perspective: The Movement of Children in Swazi Family Law" in J. Eekelaar and P. Sarcevic (eds.), *Parenthood in Modern Society* (The Hague, Kluwer Academic Publishers).

O'DONOVAN, K. (1993), *Family Law Matters* (London, Pluto Press).

O'NEILL, O. (1992), "Children's Rights and Children's Lives" in P. Alston, S. Parker and J. Seymour (eds.), *Children, Rights and the Law* (Oxford, Oxford University Press).

PALMER, A. (1996), "The Best Interests Criterion: An Overview of its Application in Custody Decisions Relating to Divorce in the Period 1985–1995", *Acta Juridica* 98.

PARKER, S. (1994), "The Best Interests of the Child—Principles and Problems" in P. Alston (ed.), *The Best Interests of the Child Reconciling Culture and Human Rights* (Oxford, Clarendon Press).

PEARL, D. (1987), *A Textbook on Muslim Personal Law* (London, Croom Helm).

RAHMAN, J. (1980), *A Code of Muslim Personal Law* (Karachi, Islamic Publishers).

ROBINSON, J. (1996), "Multi-Kulturaliteit en die Familiereg: Enkele Gedagtes oor die Posisie in Nieu-Seeland", 7 *Stellenbosch Law Review* 210.

SIEGHART, P. (1983), *The International Law of Human Rights* (New York, Clarendon Press).

SLOTH-NIELSEN, J. (1995), "Ratification of the United Nations Convention on the Rights of the Child: Some Implications for South African Law", 11 *South African Journal of Human Rights* 401.

VAN NIEKERK, G. J. (1995), *The Interaction of Indigenous Law and Western Law in South Africa: A Historical and Comparative Perspective*, LL.D. Thesis, University of South Africa.

23

Same-Sex Marriage and the Limits of Legal Pluralism

LYNN D. WARDLE

INTRODUCTION

Legal pluralism has become a very significant concept in legal scholarship in recent years. It is not only an accepted fact of formal legal structure in many legal systems, but it also is widely embraced as a valid and useful theoretical construct by scholars in legal anthropology, legal sociology, and jurisprudence. Legal pluralism is a particularly relevant concept for students of African law and legal systems. African nations have had extensive experience with formal as well as functional legal pluralism.

Legal pluralism also has become very popular with advocates of various proposed legal policy changes, who try to capitalise upon the popularity of the rhetoric of pluralism. In particular, advocates of the legalisation of same-sex marriage have asserted pluralism-based arguments to support their cause, claiming that legalising same-sex marriage is required by inclusive, pluralistic values and that it is impermissibly discriminatory for a legal system to refuse to permit same-sex couples to formally (legally) marry. The appeal to pluralism by advocates of same-sex marriage may seem superficially attractive, but it is flawed in many respects. The basic defect is the failure to recognise the limits of legal pluralism.

In this chapter I will attempt to show that proposals to legalise same-sex marriage exceed the limits of legal pluralism. Before offering that analysis, I will describe the concept of legal pluralism, I will review some of the lessons learned from the African experience with legal pluralism, I will summarise the global effort to legalise same-sex marriage, and I will review the pluralism arguments for same-sex marriage. I will conclude with a word about the importance of rediscovering and reestablishing the value of marriage in our laws and cultures.

LEGAL PLURALISM

Legal pluralism has both factual and theoretical dimensions. The "fact of pluralism", to use John Rawls' term,[1] refers to "the diversity of the conceptions of the

[1] John Rawls, *Political Liberalism* (1993) 192.

good that we find in a liberal society".[2] Thus, legal pluralism "is 'characterized by the presence in one social field of more than one legal order.'"[3] To legal anthropologists and sociologists, legal pluralism is based on the notion that "the legal order of all societies is not an exclusive, systematic and unified hierarchical ordering of normative propositions depending on the state, but has its sources in the self-regulatory activities of the multifarious social fields present in society".[4] "The basic idea is that there are multiple sources and types of regulation that operate outside the legal system of the nation state and that are recognized by its members as binding."[5] Legal pluralism is linked to and sometimes used interchangeably with "legal polycentrism", which is the concept that law is "engendered in many centres—not only within a hierarchical structure—and consequently also as having many forms".[6] While recognition of the ubiquitous nature and importance of legal pluralism is relatively new,[7] "[l]egal pluralism or legal polycentricity are not new phenomena. Aspects of legal pluralism probably exist and have existed in most legal cultures".[8] Nor is legal pluralism waning. Legal pluralism grows as "more and more varied social areas are being subject to legal regulation".[9]

The *theories* of legal pluralism go beyond recognition of multiple sources of law in society and attempt "to reform state law so as to give an adequate recognition of this pluralism within the system of state law".[10] Pluralism theories seek to legitimate conflict and division which proponents consider the sources of liberty

---

[2] Chantal Mouffe, "Democracy and Pluralism: A Critique of the Rationalist Approach", 16 *Cardozo L. Rev.* 1533, 1534 (1995).

[3] Anne Hellum, "Actor Perspectives on Gender and Legal Pluralism in Africa" in *Legal Polycentricity: Consequences of Pluralism in Law* (Hanne Petersen & Henrik Zahle (eds.), 1995), 13, 15.

[4] "Preface", in *Legal Polycentricity: Consequences of Pluralism in Law* (Hanne Petersen & Henrik Zahle (eds.), 1995), 8.

[5] Anne Hellum, *supra* n. 3, at 15.

[6] *Id.* See also Inger-Johanne Sand, "From the Distinction between Public Law and Private Law—to Legal Categories of Social and Institutional Differentiation, in a Pluralistic Legal Context:, in *Legal Polycentricity: Consequences of Pluralism in Law* (Hanne Petersen & Henrik Zahle (eds.), 1995), 85, 88 ("By *legal polycentricity* is often meant that the legal system of one country does not have one, but many centres of interpretation, application and enforcement, even if there is only one formal and general court system."). Other relativistic theories include *perspectivism, antifoundationalism, antiessentialism,* and *postmodernism,* all of which posit that "there is no objective reference point, separate from culture and politics, available to distinguish truth from ideology, fact from opinion" or law from politics. These philosophies "challenge [ ] the idea that ideals like justice and equality refer to anything at all, except as particular cultures come to define them": Eric Blumenson, "Mapping the Limits of Skepticism in Law and Morals", 74 *Tex. L. Rev.* 523, 527 n. 7, & 528 (1996).

[7] John Griffiths, "Legal Pluralism and the Theory of Legislation—With Special Reference to the Regulation of Euthanasia" in *Legal Polycentricity: Consequences of Pluralism in Law* (Hanne Petersen & Henrik Zahle (eds.), 1995), 201 (20 years ago, few scholars understood the significance of legal pluralism).

[8] Sand, *supra* n. 6, at 88.

[9] *Id.* at 85. *See also id.* at 90 ("[T]*he increasing legal pluralism that we can observe . . . is primarily a result of the increasing social and functional differentiation taking place in society . . .* Legal pluralism is cognitively connected to social changes . . . ").

[10] Syrya Prakash Sinha, "Legal Polycentricity" in *Legal Polycentricity: Consequences of Pluralism in Law* (Hanne Petersen & Henrik Zahle (eds.), 1995), 31, 48.

and equality.[11] Professor Chantal Mouffe describes three theories of pluralism. The mildest he calls *liberal pluralism*, of which John Rawls is the most well-known exponent. Rawls argues for a "reasonable pluralism", where differences are relegated to the realm of private matters, but there is harmony as to public core ideals except for unreasonable persons—who, by definition, can be excluded.[12] The second variety, which Mouffee favors, *radical pluralism*, empha-sises the "ineradicable character" of power and pluralism;[13] Mouffee believes in universal principles, basic human rights, "[b]ut this universality is conceived as a horizon that can never be reached. Every pretension to occupy the place of the universal, or to fix its final meaning through rationality, must be rejected. The recognition of undecidability is the condition of existence of democratic politics. . . . The notion of the 'constitutive outside' forces us to come to terms with the idea that pluralism implies the permanence of conflict and antagonism."[14] The third kind of pluralism, *extreme pluralism*, values equally all differences and does not distinguish among those that should and should not exist, and, because it is blind to power relations, refuses "to attempt to construct a 'we,' a collective iden-tity that articulates the demands found in the different struggles against subor-dination".[15]

Among legal scholars, legal pluralism and related perspectivist theories have achieved widespread influence. They are " 'as dominant in legal theory [today] as any paradigm was in the past.' "[16] "The concept of law has become polycen-trical."[17]

LEGAL PLURALISM IN AFRICA

While legal pluralism is a relatively recent jurisprudential construct, scholars and students of African legal systems have long been acquainted with the practical concept of pluralism because "in most parts of Africa peoples of different ethnic, cultural, and religious groups live within one and the same political unit under different systems of law".[18] The concept of legal pluralism originally developed

---

[11] Mouffe, *supra* n. 2, at 1533, 1534.

[12] *Id.* at 1537–8; see also *id.* at 1542 (reasonable citizens "probably have very different, even con-flicting, conceptions of the good, but those are strictly private matters and they do not interfere with their public life").

[13] *Id.* at 1536.

[14] *Id.* at 1544.

[15] *Id.* at 1535.

[16] Blumenson, *supra* n. 6, at 531.

[17] Henrik Zahle, "The Polycentricity of the Law of the Importance of Legal Pluralism for Legal Dogmatics", in *Legal Polycentricity: Consequences of Pluralism in Law* (Hanne Petersen & Henrik Zahle (eds.), 1995), 185, 198; see also Griffiths, *supra* n. 7, at 201 (it is now generally recognised in legal sociology and legal anthropology that "law everywhere . . . is fundamentally pluralist in char-acter", and anyone who does not concede that point "is simply out of date and can safely be ignored").

[18] Denis V. Cowen, "African Legal Studies—A Survey of the Field and the Role of the United States" in *African Law, New Law for New Nations* (Hans W. Baade, (ed.), 1963), 9, 14; see also Lloyd Fallers, "Customary Law in the New African States" in *African Law, New Law for New Nations*

as a means of understanding the effect of the imposition of European law on what was called "indigenous law" of colonised societies.[19]

Family law was the most significant body of law in which legal pluralism was cultivated in Africa. Why did colonialists allow legal pluralism in family law? Perhaps, in part, it was because of their perception that family law as basically "private", and beyond the proper scope of regulation by "public" law.[20] Also, at the practical level, family relations of the indigenous population probably did not matter much to them. The dominant faction of colonialists were concerned primarily with other matters (mostly economic); the governing faction of conquering colonialists attempted to govern as efficiently as possible, and that meant to disturb the existing social order as little as possible (to disturb it only so far as necessary to allow them to extract disposable wealth without sacrificing their own personal security). Changing existing family law customs is not a low-impact undertaking, and because ideas about family relations are close to the heart, forced family law change can incite passionate opposition—which may significantly interfere with the extraction of wealth.[21] The importation of western laws (including family laws) was done primarily for the convenience of the conquerors, who saw no need to impose them upon of the local populations.

In the long run, wealth and security in society are closely tied to family relations and family structure. If the dominant colonists' vision had not been shortsighted, they might have undertaken on utilitarian grounds to replace indigenous, customary family laws with their own culture's version of family law in order to facilitate their long-term exploitation of the conquered peoples and territories. Fortunately, however, they overlooked the long-term social perspective.

Because of the multiplicity of cultures, even today, in the post-colonial era, legal pluralism still flourishes in African nations.

> "A common feature of most African legal systems is the coexistence of imported general law on the one hand and the customary and religious laws of the various ethnic and religious groups on the other. The form of legal pluralism which we find in most African countries is a colonial creation.
>
> . . .
>
> Upon independence, many African governments, as part of their nation-building strategy, undertook various measures in order to unify their dual legal systems. The aim was to eliminate the race, class and gender discrimination which was embodied in the dual colonial legal system where imported general law applied to the white population while customary laws, which regard African women as minors under male guardianship, applied to the blacks. Customary law and general law have, in spite of

(Hans W. Baade (ed.), 1963), 71, 72 (describing "congeries of traditional polities—some tiny clusters of a few villages, others great kingdoms numbering their subjects in the millions—thrown together by European diplomacy in the nineteenth century . . . ").

[19] Sinha, *supra* n. 10, at 47.

[20] See generally Sand, *supra* n. 6, at 92–5.

[21] Cowen, *supra* n. 18, at 17 ("Some branches of law are more deeply and emotionally involved with the life and culture of a people than others and hence more resistant to sudden and radical change by legislative fiat. This is the case, for example with family law. . . . ").

these efforts, to a large extent continued to coexist as separate legal orders within the national legal systems."[22]

Cultural diversity and legal pluralism can still produce profoundly centrifugal pressures in modern African nations. For example, Professor R. T. Nhlapo has written insightfully about the conflict between feminist advocates of gender equality and proponents of special protection for traditional laws and cultural institutions in the recent drafting of the Constitution of South Africa.[23] That exemplifies the broader tension between "proponents of modernism" and protectors of cultural traditions and institutions who fear the former "will swamp them on [their] march towards recreating the world in the image of the West".[24] Professor Nhlapo has noted that "the call for the abolition or supplanting of customary law is invariably made by people whose knowledge of the subject is no deeper than that of the missionaries of a century ago".[25]

THE GLOBAL MOVEMENT TO LEGALISE SAME-SEX MARRIAGE

No nation of the world permits same-sex marriage today, but the trend of legal developments in several trend-setting (affluent) nations seems to be moving in that direction. In December 1996, a trial court in the American state of Hawaii ruled that the state had no compelling reason to deny marriage licences to same-sex couples, and ordered the state to issue marriage licences to same-sex couples who apply for them.[26] That ruling has been appealed to the state supreme court, and the order has been stayed pending appeal. Just months after the ruling, the Hawaii legislature passed an amendment to the state constitution which, if ratified by the people of Hawaii in November 1998, will effectively overturn the basis for the court's ruling that the denial of same-sex marriage constitutes constitutionally impermissible sex discrimination.[27] Nevertheless, it is possible that the people of Hawaii (who overwhelming and consistently oppose legalizing same-sex marriage[28]) could be forced by their state supreme court to issue marriage licences for same-sex marriages, at least temporarily.[29] No other jurisdiction has

---

[22] Hellum, *supra* n. 3, at 15.

[23] Thandabantu Nhlapo, "Cultural Diversity, Human Rights and the Family in Contemporary Africa: Lessons from the South African Constitutional Debate", in *Families Across Frontiers* (Nigel Lowe & Gillian Douglas (eds.), 1996), 237.

[24] *Id.* at 244.

[25] *Id.* at 245. Nevertheless, he defends the universal human rights premise in modern African legal systems, and argues that claims of cultural immunity should be refuted: *id.* at 251.

[26] *Baehr* v. *Miike*, No. 91 Civ. 1394 (Haw. Cir. Ct. Dec. 3, 1996), 23 Fam. L. Rep. (BNA) 2001 (3 Dec. 1996).

[27] Hawaii H.B. 117 (1997).

[28] Voters strongly oppose gay unions, Honolulu Star-Bulletin, 24 Feb. 1997, at 1 (currently 70% of those polled oppose legalising same-sex marriage; 20% favour it; opposition has grown about 12% and support fallen 12% during four years).

[29] In *Baehr* v. *Lewin*, 852 P.2d 44 (1993), the Hawaii Supreme Court rejected the claim that the "right to marry" protected by the Hawaii Constitution extends to same-sex couples and held that there is no "fundamental constitutional right to same-sex marriage" because such relationship is not

yet legalised same-sex marriage, but the Dutch Parliament reportedly has instructed the government to draft a bill legalising same-sex marriage and submit it this summer.[30]

A number of related legal developments in other jurisdictions also point toward the eventual acceptance of same-sex marriage or a similar legal status. Since 1989 Denmark,[31] Norway,[32] Sweden[33] and Iceland,[34] have all enacted legislation authorizing the formal registration of same-sex "domestic partnerships" and extending to such relationships essentially all of the economic and many of the non-economic legal incidents of marriage.[35] After a decision by the national supreme court, the legislature in Hungary has legalised common-law same-sex live-in companionship for purposes of recognising their mutually-owned purchases and acquisitions.[36] In the Netherlands, the Second Chamber of Parliament has already enacted Scandinavian-style domestic partnership legislation and it is expected to gain final approval within a few months.[37] Finland also is expected

"rooted in tradition" or "at the base of all our civil and political institutions": *id.* at 55, 57. However, a plurality concluded that Hawaii's marriage licence law facially "discriminates based on sex against the applicant [same-sex] couples" on account of gender, in apparent violation of the state constitutional provisions protecting equality: *id.* at 57–62. The late 1996 ruling in *Baehr* v. *Miike* was on remand from this decision. If the Hawaii Supreme Court affirms the trial court decision in *Miike* before November 1988, same-sex marriage could be legalised before the people get to vote on the constitutional amendment. While the amendment, if passed, could effectively undo the supreme court decision, the same-sex couples who married in the interim could pose a significant political and legal dilemma. For a discussion of the *Baehr* case, see Lynn D. Wardle, "A Critical Analysis of Constitutional Claims for Same-Sex Marriage", 1996 *BYUL Rev.* 1.

[30] Rex Wockner, "Dutch Gays Will Have Two Ways to Get Hitched", *ILGA Euroletter* 49 (Apr. 1997) ("The majority in Parliament is for gay marriage," said Henk Krol, editor of Holland's largest gay publication, *De Gay Krant*.") (A Scandinavian-type domestic partnership bill has passed the Second Chamber of the Parliament by more than two-thirds majority and the First Chamber, which reportedly checks only for procedural problems, is expected by the end of the year).

[31] Danish Registered Partnership Act, No. 372 (7 June 1989). See generally Linda Nielsen, "Family Rights and the 'Registered Partnership' In Denmark", 4 *Int'l J L & Fam.* 297 (1990); Marianne H. Pedersen, "Denmark: Homosexual Marriages and New Rules Regarding Separation and Divorce", 30 *J Fam. L* 289 (1991–92). I am indebted to Prof. Linda Nielsen of the University of Copenhagen and Judge Svend Danielsen for information they have provided.

[32] The Norwegian Act on Registered Partnership for Homosexual Couples, Act No. 40 of 30 Apr. 1993. I am indebted to Prof. Peter Lödrup of the University of Oslo for material.

[33] Law Regarding Registered Partnership of 23 June 1994 (Bert Andersen, trans. 1995). See also Deborah M. Henson, "A Comparative Analysis of Same-Sex Partnership Protections: Recommendations for American Reform", 7 *Int'l J L & Fam.* 283, 287–8 (1993). I am indebted to Prof. Anders Agell of the University of Uppsala for useful information.

[34] Law on approved cohabitation, Arts. 1–9 (12 June 1996) (Kristjan Matiesen trans. 1996); see generally" Iceland Gives Gay Marriages Legal Stamp", Reuters World Service, 27 June 1996 (Icelandic legislature has legalised "gay marriage" following Denmark, Norway and Swedish precedents).

[35] Certain restrictions commonly are imposed on same-sex domestic partnerships that do not apply to heterosexual marriages, such as the requirement that at least one of the partners be a citizen or resident national of the country. Likewise, limitations on joint custody, adoption, artificial insemination, state-church weddings, and exemption from marital status under international treaties, are common. See generally Nielsen, *supra* n. 31, at 300.

[36] Year of 1996, XLII Law §§ 1–3 (21 May 1996) (Stuard Schulte transla. 1996). See also "Hungary's Gays Welcome Law on Rights as First Step", Reuters World Service, 22 May 1996.

[37] Rex Wockner, *supra* n. 30; Steffen Jensen, "Partnership Law in the Netherlands", *ILGA Euroletter* 51 (July 1997).

to approve a similar bill soon.[38] The legislatures of Spain, Luxembourg, Switzerland, Belgium, Germany, Italy, France and Brazil also have been considering domestic partnership registration bills.[39] The Hawaii legislature recently enacted a law allowing many unmarriageable couples (including but not limited to same-sex couples) to register as "reciprocal beneficiaries" entitled to some of the economic incidents of marriage,[40] and a few American localities also give some employment benefits to same-sex domestic partnerships.[41] In a number of cities around the world, same-sex couples can obtain official-but-legally-ineffective certificates, licences, or registrations that symbolise official approval of same-sex relationships.[42] One American state Governor has proposed that the state "get out of the business" of regulating marriage, and leave that to private (religious) regulation.[43]

More broadly, the new Constitution of South Africa forbids discrimination on the basis of sexual orientation, and is believed by some to lay the foundation for the legalisation of same-sex marriage there.[44] Discrimination on the basis of sexual orientation has been outlawed in at least ten other nations.[45] The European

---

[38] See Jon Henley, "Scandinavian 'Backwater' Sets New Standard", *Guardian*, 24 June 1995 at 16.

[39] International Lesbian and Gay Association, *ILGA Euroletter* 45, Nov. 1996 See generally Janet McEvoy, "Gay Marriages Throw Europe's Gaze on to Gay Agenda", Reuters North American Wire, 21 June 1996; Paul Vlaardingerbroek, "Marriage, Divorce, and Living Arrangements in the Netherlands", 29 *Fam. LQ* 635 (1995); Peter Tatchell, *Europe in the Pink: Lesbian and Gay Equality in the New Europe* (1992), 123.

[40] Hawaii Legislature HB 118 (1997). This law is being challenged in court by employers.

[41] The Lambda Legal Defense and Education Fund, Inc. reported that by mid-1996, 35 municipalities, 11 counties, 3 states, 5 state agencies, and 2 federal agencies extended some benefits to, or registered for some official purposes, same-sex domestic partnerships: Lambda Legal Defense and Education Fund, Inc., National Overview Of Jurisdictions And Companies That Recognize And/Or Provide Benefits To Domestic Partners of Employees—as of June 26, 1996—(copy in author's possession). Press-Enterprise (Riverside, Cal.), 21 Mar. 1997, at B01 ("While same-sex marriages are banned in California, a San Francisco city ordinance has recognized 'domestic partnerships' since 1991. Gay and lesbian couples may participate in a symbolic civic 'wedding ceremony' if they register as 'domestic partners.' They also have visitation rights in hospitals, shared health plans for city employees and bereavement leave for city employees if a domestic partner dies").

[42] Alex Duval Smith, "Mayors Spark Gay Row", *Guardian*, 26 Sept. 1996 at 10 (6 arrondisements of Paris issue certificates of cohabitation to same-sex couples); *Marriage Digest*, 28 May 1996 (same-sex couples who wish to register their domestic partnership with the city of West Hollywood, Calif., may now do so via the Internet); "San Francisco Oks Symbolic Gay Marriages", *Chi. Sun-Times*, 30 Jan. 1996, at 16; "Overseas News", *The Times*, 31 Jan. 1996 (New York allows symbolic marriage ceremonies for same-sex couples).

[43] Bruce Dunford, "Hawaii Lawmakers Pondering Whether to Legalize Gay Marriage", Associated Press, 21 Jan. 1996 (1996 WL 4407590, 3 of 10).

[44] See David Beresford, "ANC Liberal Reform Stuns South Africa : New Legislation on Abortion and Gay Rights is Proving Unpopular", Observer, 21 July 1996 at 22 (The new South African Constitution forbids discrimination on the basis of sexual preference, but does not recognize same-sex marriage). See generally Doug Ireland, "Remembering Herve: Defense of Marriage Act", *The Nation*, 24 June 1996 at 6 (asserting that South Africa, like Scandinavian countries, already recognizes same-sex unions).

[45] According to one ILGA report, the countries include Canada (Human Rights Act was amended in 1996 to forbid discrimination based on sexual orientation and is applicable to federally regulated employers, landlords and services including the federal government, banks, broadcasters, the telephone and telecommunications industry, railways, airlines, shipping and inter-provincial transportation); Denmark (sexual orientation is in the anti-discrimination clause of its Penal Code applicable to

Parliament has passed a resolution calling for equal rights for gays and lesbians.[46] The United Nations Human Rights Committee also has ruled that laws prohibiting homosexuality among consenting adults violate Article 1 of the International Covenant on Civil and Political Rights, and that the prohibition of discrimination on the basis of "sex" in Articles 2(I) and 26 of the ICCPR includes discrimination on the basis of sexual orientation.[47] The European Court of Human Rights has ruled that the right to privacy protected by Article 8 of the European Convention protects the right of consenting adults to engage in consensual homosexual sodomy.[48] While globally many jurisdictions still prohibit homosexual behaviour, nearly all European and slightly more than half of the American states have decriminalised some consensual adult sodomy.[49] These

public and private employment); Finland (the Penal Code was amended in 1995 to include sexual orientation among the grounds protected from discrimination in offering public or commercial services and the Constitution bans discrimination on the basis "characteristic of an individual", which the government interprets to include sexual orientation); France (Penal Code and Code of Labor prohibit discrimination based on sexual orientation); The Netherlands (Penal Code bans discrimination on basis of "heter- or homosexual orientation", Constitution also prohibits discrimination, and sexual orientation is considered a protected ground under the clause "or any other ground whatsoever"); New Zealand (Human Rights Act prohibits discrimination on the basis of sexual orientation and applies to employment, education, access to public places, provision of goods and services, and housing and accommodation); Norway (Penal Code prohibits discrimination based on sexual orientation in the provision of goods or services and in access to public gatherings, and bans hate speech directed at sexual minorities); Slovenia (Penal Code since 1995 has punished anyone who "denies someone his human rights or fundamental freedoms including sexual orientation"); Spain (Penal Code of 1995 declares the right to express one's sexual orientation a fundamental freedom, bans discrimination in housing, employment, public services, and professional activities based on sexual orientation, and punishes hatred and violence directed against homosexual persons and organisations); Sweden (forbids commercial organisations to discriminate on the grounds of homosexuality). International Lesbian and Gay Association, *ILGA Euroletter* 47, Feb. 1997.

[46] *Id.* European Parliament, Resolution on Equal Rights for Homosexual and Lesbians in the European Community (A3–0028194) (8 Feb. 1994). See also 1996 "Resolution on the Respect of Human Rights in the European Union" (A4–0223/96). See generally Bea Verschraegen, *G'leich Gerschlechtiliche "Ehen" (Same Sex "Marriage")* (Jarrett Dunlap trans. 1994).

[47] *Toonen* v. *Australia*, UN Human Rights Committee, case No. 488/1992 (1994); see also Elizabeth Mcdavid Harris, "Comment, Intercourse Against Nature: The Role of the Covenant on Civil and Political Rights and the Repeal of Sodomy Laws in the United States", 18 *Hous. J Int'l L* 525 (1996). See generally David A. Catania, "Note, The Universal Declaration of Human Rights and Sodomy Laws: A Federal Common Law Right to Privacy for Homosexuals Based on Customary International Law", 31 *Am. Crim. L Rev.* 28, 319–20 (1994) (reporting that the Human Rights Commissioner in Australia has asserted that it violates the ICCPR for Tasmania, but no other states in Australia, to prohibit homosexual consensual sodomy)

[48] *Dudgeon* v. *United Kingdom*, 45 Eur. Ct. H.R. (Ser. A), (1982) 4 EHRR 149 (challenging law prohibiting homosexual sodomy in Northern Ireland, though it was not prohibited in England, Wales and Scotland); *Norris* v. *Ireland*, 142 Eur. Ct. H.R. (Ser. A), (1991) 13 EHRR 186 (ruling that Ireland's homosexual sodomy prohibition violated of Art. 8 and invalidating Ireland's law); *Modinos* v. *Cyprus*, 7/1992/352/426, (1994) 16 EHRR 485 (invalidating Cyprus' anti-sodomy law under Art. 8); *Toonen* v. *Australia*, UN Human Rights Committee, Case. No. 488/1992 (1994), reportedly in 1 *Privacy Law and Policy Reporter* 50 (1994). See generally David A. Catania, *supra* n. 47, at 315–20; James D. Wilets, "Pressure From Abroad", (A.B.A. Section of Individual Rights & Respons.) Human Rights, Autumn 1994, at 22.

[49] More than 20 American states criminally prohibiting sodomy. "Constitutional Claims", *supra* n. 29 at 8, n. 13; *id.* at 55–60. Nearly 90 nations reportedly still prohibit consensual adult homosexual relations. International Lesbian and Gay Association, ILGA Euroletter No. 46 (December 1996) (the

reforms do not necessarily signal approval of same-sex marriage, but they represent public acceptance and are used by gay and lesbian advocates to lay the foundation for the legalisation of same-sex marriage.

Of course, same-sex marriage claims have been rebuffed much more often than they have been accepted. The overall global picture shows overwhelming support for exclusively heterosexual marriage. No legislature of any jurisdiction in the world has yet approved of same-sex marriage. Many jurisdictions (including most of the American states and Congress) have recently enacted laws denying legal recognition to same-sex marriage from other jurisdictions.[50] Likewise, in the past 25 years, dozens of lawsuits have been filed in the USA seeking judicial legalisation of same-sex marriage, and all of these except only one (the *Baehr* case in Hawaii) have failed as other courts unanimously have rejected judicial recognition of same-sex marriage.[51] Virtually all international conventions that describe marriage have defined it as the union of a man and a woman.[52] Polls have repeated found that the people in America oppose legalising same-sex marriage.[53] Nevertheless, there *seems to be* a trend in affluent countries toward legalisation of same-sex marriage or extending some equivalent legal relationship to gay and lesbian couples.

International Gay and Lesbian Human Rights Commission reports that 86 nations ban male homosexual conduct, and 44 also bar female homosexual behaviour).

[50] In the past 18 months, Congress and the legislatures of more than half of the American states have enacted legislation forbidding recognition of same-sex marriage. See generally Marriage Law Project, "Bills Concerning Same-Sex Marriage, 1997 Legislative Update", 16 June 1997 (available at http://www.pono.net). Likewise, Poland's new constitution defines marriage as between a man and a woman, thus constitutionally barring same-sex marriage. Agence France Presse, 22 March 1997.

[51] See "Constitutional Claims", *supra* n. 29 at 9–10, nn. 22–6, and *id.* at 56–7 nn. 252, 253 (identifying more than a dozen different lawsuits seeking marital status for same-sex unions). See also *Storrs* v. *Holcomb*, 1996 WL 379613 (NY Sup.Ct. 1996).

[52] See Universal Declaration of Human Rights, Art. 16 ("Men and women of full age, without any limitation due to race, nationality or religion, have the right to marry and to found a family."); [European] Convention for the Protection of Human Rights and Fundamental Freedoms, 213 UNTS 222, entered into force on 21 Sept. 1970, 20 Dec. 1971 and 1 Jan. 1990 respectively Art. 12 ("Men and women of marriageable age have the right to marry and to found a family, according to the national laws governing the exercise of this right"); American Convention on Human Rights, OAS Treaty Series No. 36, 1144 UNTS 123 entered into force on 18 July 1978, reprinted in Basic Documents Pertaining to Human Rights in the Inter-American System, OEA/Ser.L.V./II.82 doc.6 rev.1 at 25 (1992) Art. 17 ("the right of men and women of marriageable age to marry and to raise a family shall be recognized"); Habitat II Conference, Istanbul, Turkey, 3–14 June 1996, The Habitat Agenda (http://www.undp. org/un/habitat/agenda/ch-2.html) ("Marriage must be entered into with the free consent of the intending spouses, and husband and wife should be equal partners. The rights, capabilities and responsibilities of family members must be respected."). See also Hong Kong Bill of Rights Ordinance, 30 ILM 1310, 1318 (Effective 8 June 1991) ("The right of men and women of marriageable age to marry and to found a family shall be recognized.").

[53] *Portland Oregonian*, 19 April 1997, at A01 (1997 WL 4165366) (Mar. 1996 Gallup poll shows Americans oppose same-sex marriage 68-to-27); Associated Press, 19 Aug. 1996 (Lou Harris Poll reports 63–64% of Americans oppose legalising same-sex marriage; 10–11% favour); *supra* n. 28 (70% of Hawaiians oppose legalising same-sex marriage); *Fresno Bee*, 25 May 1997 at E6 (1997 WL 3904007) (1996 *Los Angeles Times* poll found Californians oppose legalising same-sex marriage 60-to-31); but see *Irish Times*, 10 Aug. 1996, at 10 (1996 WL 11037747) (Germans favour legalising same-sex marriage 48-to-42).

Perhaps one reason there *seems to be* a trend toward same-sex marriage is because the legal literature is overwhelmingly one-sided. Virtually all of the law review literature that has addressed the issue has been written by advocates of same-sex marriage. For example, between January 1990 and January 1996 American law reviews published 72 articles, notes, etc. about same-sex marriage; of those, at least 67 advocated or supported same-sex marriage while only one clearly opposed same-sex marriage.[54] The ideological ecosystem of the typical American university is hostile to the expression of criticism of gay and lesbian social initiatives. Scholars who have dared to express opposition to same-sex marriage and other gay/lesbian proposals have encountered animosity ranging from collegial rudeness to student demonstrations, slashed tyres, and efforts to have them fired.[55] Likewise, the popular media in the United States and other affluent nations is disproportionately supportive of same-sex relationships. Under these circumstances, the appearance of a pro-same-sex marriage trend is not surprising.

LEGAL PLURALISM ARGUMENTS FOR SAME-SEX MARRIAGE

Advocates of same-sex marriage frequently invoke the concept and language of pluralism in arguing for the legalisation of same-sex marriage.[56] Some argue that

---

[54] "Constitutional Claims", *supra* n. 29, at 18–20. Two of the remaining pieces opposed all marriage (same-sex and heterosexual), while the other two were ambivalent: *id.*

[55] *Id.* at 21–2; Marianne Moody Jennings, "Same-sex Marriage Critic Punished by Intolerance", *Ariz. Repub.*, 28 July 1995, at H3 (professor of legal and ethical studies had tyre ruined, calls for firing when she wrote column against same-sex marriage); Scott Wiener, "Homophobia Cannot Be Tolerated", *Harvard L. Record*, 29 Apr. 1994, at 11 (protest against and excoriation of Oxford Prof. John Finnis at Harvard Law School).

[56] See generally William N. Eskridge, Jr. and Philip P. Frickey, "The Supreme Court 1993 Term: Foreword: Law As Equilibrium", 108 *Harv. L. Rev.* 26, 94 (1994) (in gay rights cases the Supreme Court should override majoritarian qualms in the interest of pluralism); David Helscher, "*Griswold* v. *Connecticut* and the Unenumerated Right of Privacy, 15 *N. Ill. UL Rev.* 33, 60 (1994) (failure to recognise right to engage in homosexual practices is no longer legitimate in pluralistic world); Matthew Coles, "Equal Protection and the Anti-Civil-Rights Initiatives: Protecting the Ability of Lesbians and Gay Men to Bargain in the Pluralist Bazaar", 55 *Ohio St. LJ* 563, 574–5 (1994) (arguing that anti-gay-rights laws violate the Equal Protection Clause because they preclude gays and lesbians from participating in the political process); William N. Eskridge, Jr. and Gary Peller, "The New Public Law Movement: Moderation As A Postmodern Cultural Form", 89 *Mich. L Rev.* 707, 737 (1991) (pluralism has invited inclusion of gays in civil rights movement); Nadine Strossen, "Recent U.S. and International Judicial Protection of Individual Rights: A Comparative Legal Process Analysis and Proposed Synthesis", 41 *Hastings LJ* 805, 881(1990) (European Convention agencies have declared that the "hallmarks" of a democratic society are tolerance and pluralism. The application of these criteria to homosexual conduct was a significant factor leading it to invalidate laws criminalising such conduct in the *Dudgeon* and *Norris* cases); Marjorie Maguire Shultz, "Contractual Ordering of Marriage: A New Model for State Policy", 70 *Calif. L. Rev.* 204, 248 (1982) (The refusal to allow same-sex marriage "reflects a hesitancy to pursue fully the implications of pluralism" and "only as the state abandons a policy that mandates one correct form of intimacy" can privacy and autonomy have meaning."); *id.* at 333 ("Any system which attempted to impose standardized rules, even where those rules reflected more modern and desirable goals like sexual equality, would not sufficiently respect the pluralism and privacy of intimate values nor allow for the planning and self-definition of goals posited by this Article as vital to an effective system of marriage regulation. The essential point is that in intimacy no one can say what is 'right' except the parties involved.").

they merely want to "expand" the old-fashioned definition of marriage to include loving, committed non-traditional couples such as gay and lesbian couples.[57] Some make the pluralistic, assimilative assertion "that '[g]ays and lesbians are raised in the same culture as everyone else. When they settle down they want gold bands, they want legal documents, they want kids'."[58] Others make a related claim that the pluralistic value of tolerance requires legalisation of same-sex marriage. Another variation of the pluralism theme is the argument that allowing heterosexual couples to marry while denying marriage to same-sex couples violates the principle of equality under law. Advocates of same-sex marriage frequently compare their cause to the struggle for racial equality, and argue that it violates the principle of equality to forbid same-sex marriage just as it does to forbid interracial marriage. Other pluralists argue that same-sex marriage is essential to gender equality.

SAME-SEX MARRIAGE AND THE LIMITS OF LEGAL PLURALISM

There are obvious flaws in each of these pluralistic arguments for same-sex marriage. For example, the pluralistic tolerance argument confuses tolerance with preference. Relations and conduct may be legally categorised in three ways—as "prohibited", "tolerated" or "preferred".[59] Marriage is the classic example of a *preferred* relationship. It is one of the most highly-preferred, historically-favoured relations in the law.[60] Thus, the claim for same-sex marriage is not a claim for mere tolerance, but for special preference. The pluralistic principle of tolerance does not justify legalization of same-sex marriage because marriage is much more than a *tolerated* relation, it is a legally a *preferred* status.

Likewise, the racial discrimination analogy ignores the crucial distinction that race is unrelated to any legitimate purpose the law could have for distinguishing

---

[57] Paul Royal, The Right to Say 'I Do' The Legality of Same-Sex Marriage", 20 *L & Psychol. Rev.* 245, 251 (1996); Anne M. Burton, "Gay Marriage—A Modern Proposal: Applying *Baehr* v. *Lewin* to the International Covenant on Civil and Political Rights", 3 *Ind. J Global Legal Stud.* 177, 196 (1995) (commending Hawaii court for expanding definition of marriage); Kevin Aloysius Zambrowicz, Comment, "'To Love and Honor All the Days of Your Life': A Constitutional Right to Same-Sex Marriage?", 43 *Cath. UL Rev.* 907, 950 (1994) (encouraging courts to expand the definition of marriage to include same-sex couples); Jennifer L. Heeb, Comment, "Homosexual Marriage, the Changing American Family, and the Heterosexual Right of Privacy", 24 *Seton Hall L Rev.* 347, 368 (1993) (arguing that the judiciary must expand the definition of marriage to include gay and lesbian couples); Mary P. Treuhart, "Adopting a More Realistic Definition of Family", 26 *Gonz. L Rev.* 91, 92, 100 (1990–1) (advocating expansion of definition of marriage and family to include more non-traditional relationships).

[58] Christine Jax, "Same-Sex Marriage, Why Not?", 4 *Widener J Pub. L* 461, 482 citing Eloise Salholz, "For Better or For Worse", *Newsweek*, 24 May 1993, at 69 (quoting Eric Marcus).

[59] Bruce C. Hafen, "The Constitutional Status of Marriage, Kinship, and Social Privacy—Balancing the Individual and Society Interests", 81 *Mich. L Rev.* 463, 546–7 (1983); Bruce C. Hafen and Jonathan D. Hafen, "Individual Autonomy, Student Rights, and the U.N. Convention on Rights of the Child DeJure vs. De Facto Autonomy for Children" 69 *St. John's L Rev.* 601, 653–6 (1995).

[60] See *supra* n. 52. Other conventions (particularly dealing with women and children) plainly assume the cross-gender nature of marriage.

between two persons regarding marriage; but homosexual relations directly concern the fundamental purposes of marriage laws. As General Colin Powell put it: "Skin color is a benign non-behavioral characteristic. Sexual orientation is perhaps the most profound of human behavioral characteristics. Comparison of the two is a convenient but invalid argument."[61]

Similarly, the gender equality pluralism argument not only confuses interpersonal sexual conduct with personal sexual gender as legal classifications, it overlooks the fact that heterosexual marriage is the oldest gender-equality institution in the law. The requirement that marriage consist of both a man and a woman emphasises the absolute equality and equal necessity of both sexes for the most fundamental unit of society. It recognises the indispensable and equal contribution of both genders to the basic institution of our society.[62]

More fundamentally, pluralism arguments for same-sex marriage ignore the conceptual limits of legal pluralism. Advocates of same-sex marriage are "trapped in a Kelsenean dream", to borrow the phrase of Anna Christensen, where they erroneously believe that they can create social order out of moral chaos by merely enacting positive laws.[63] Like the most rigid legal positivists, advocates of same sex marriage embrace "the myth about the 'law-maker' and the 'legal system'" that is based upon an erroneous "impression of the origin, content and structure of law. . . . It hides the fact that the central elements of a legal order cannot be 'invented' by a law-maker, but must be rooted in a normative practice."[64] Shared normative values are "the basic element in what we call society."[65]

Advocates of same-sex marriage make the pluralistic flaw of believing that if they can get the label of "marriage" for their gay and lesbian relationships, they will magically acquire the socially and individually beneficial characteristics associated with marriage for millennia. That is very strange thinking.[66] Abraham Lincoln once lampooned the flaw of this thinking with a homespun story: he asked how many legs a dog would have if you counted a tail as a leg. To the response "five legs," Lincoln said, "No; calling a tail a leg doesn't make it a leg."[67]

---

[61] See Gen. Colin L. Powell, Letter to Representative Patricia Schroeder, 8 May 1992, in David F. Burrelli, *Homosexuals and U.S. Military Personnel Policy*, 14 Jan. 1993, at 25–6; see also "Gays in the Military, Hearing of the Military Forces and Personnel Subcomm. of the House Armed Serv. Comm." (Statement by Joint Chiefs of Staff Chairman Colin Powell), *Fed. News Serv.*, 21 July 1993, at 26.

[62] See "Constitutional Claims", *supra* n. 29, at 83–8.

[63] Anna Christensen, "Polycentricity and Normative Patterns", in *Legal Polycentricity: Consequences of Pluralism in Law* (Hanne Petersen & Henrik Zahle (eds.), 1995), 235, 239.

[64] *Id.* at 236.

[65] *Id.*

[66] It is ironic that gay and lesbian critics who often chide their opponents for trying to "legislate morality" seek to radically transform the essential normative characteristics of their relationships by have the legislature (or judiciary) label them "marriages".

[67] See generally J. Bartlett, *The Shorter Bartlett's Familiar Quotations* (1961), 218d cited in Stephen A. Newman, "Baby Doe, Congress and the States: Challenging the Federal Treatment Standard for Impaired Infants", 15 *Am. JL and Med.* 1, 15 (1989).

The relationship between two persons of the same sex is fundamentally different from heterosexual "marriage" because men and women are fundamentally different. Marriage is unique. No other companionate relationship provides the same great potential for benefiting individuals and society as the life-time covenant union of a man and a woman. That is why only committed heterosexual unions are given the legal status of marriage. It is not the marriage certificate, label, or legal status that makes the heterosexual marital relationship uniquely beneficial to individuals and society, but is the nature of the relationships itself that is so valuable, and that is why such unions are given the preferred legal status (and label) of *marriage*. Pluralistic arguments for same-sex marriage are simply self-alienating.[68] Their thesis of relational equivalence is a simplistic notion that fails to recognise that "something more complex is going on than can be explained" by saying "my sexual preference is as good as your sexual preference".[69]

Same-sex unions do not match the contributions to society that are made by heterosexual marriages. The public purposes for which marriage has been created are best achieved by cross-gender unions; same-sex unions fail to promote those social interests in any comparable degree. Heterosexual marriage provides, *inter alia*, (1) the best setting for the safest and most beneficial expression of sexual intimacy; (2) the best environment into which children can be born and reared (the profound benefits of dual-gender parenting to model intergender relations and show children how to relate to persons of their own and the opposite gender are lost in same-sex unions); (3) the best security for the status of women (who usually take the greatest risks and invest the greatest personal effort in maintaining families); (4) the strongest and most stable companionate unit of society (and thus the most secure setting for intergenerational transmission of social knowledge and skills); (5) a functional and historic basis for social stability that same-sex marriage would undermine; and (6) the best seedground for democracy and the most important schoolroom for self-government. From the perspective of these social interests underlying marriage, same-sex unions are not equivalent to heterosexual marriages.

A related conceptual flaw of the pluralistic arguments for same-sex marriage is that "antagonistic principles of legitimacy cannot coexist within the same political association without questioning the political reality of the state".[70] As Professor Christensen has written: "The very notion of Legal Polycentricity forms a sharp contrast to the notion of law as a legal system—a system which like all other modern systems must be free from internal contradictions and thus

---

[68] Jeremy Waldron, Review Essay, "On the Objectivity of Morals: Thoughts on Gilbert's Democratic Individuality", 80 *Calif. L Rev.* 1361, 1376 (1992) (Moral relativism is self-alienating; a moral relativist is "a person who could not take his own side in an argument.").

[69] See generally *id.* at 1381. The relativistic thesis offers no solution for a world of multiple cultures: *id.* See also Blumenson, *supra* n. 6, at 550 ("[T]he relativist idea of local truth makes little theoretical or practical sense. The practical problem is that the relativist alternative lacks the resources to provide anything more than the baseless choice of procedural dogmas.").

[70] Mouffee, *supra* n. 2, at 1539.

cannot have more than one centre. . . . A significant amount of legal thinking has been aimed at depicting and thus forming the law into a *legal system* with no internal contradictions."[71] Ideologically, same-sex marriage cannot long coexist with the belief that marriage reflects and embodies something fundamental and inherent in the complementary natures of men and women.

Historically, legal pluralism also had its limits. For example, "[t]he indigenous law was subjugated to the European law by such devices as the repugnancy principle which limited the application of local custom within the bounds of what the European rulers called natural justice, equity, and good conscience, or the inconsistency principle which disallowed local custom if it conflicted with the enacted law."[72] Even theoretical legal pluralism has limits.[73] The limit of *liberal pluralism* is "reasonableness"; it simply excludes "unreasonable persons".[74] The limit of *radical pluralism* is "differences . . . constructed as relations of subordination" which, Mouffee argues "should not exist" and "should be challenged by [ ] radical democratic politics".[75] Pluralism theories promotes pluralism *qua* pluralism as a value, thus establishing an external, non-relativistic moral preference. Indeed, all of the pluralism theories promote values (such as tolerance, liberty, democracy, multicentricity, or equality) which constitute self-defeating, nonpluralistic limits.[76] Invariably there are and *must be* some non-pluralistic limiting standards—traditionally protection of fundamental values, strong public policy, or *ordre public*, and these standards provide a sound, just, proven basis for rejecting relativist claims for same-sex marriage.

CONCLUSION: DEVALUING MARRIAGE

The recent increase in claims for same-sex marriage may be the logical sequel to the disintegration of marriage as the basis for the family. It probably is not merely coincidental that the movement for same-sex marriage has erupted about a generation after the legalisation of unilateral no-fault divorce in America, the liber-

---

[71] Christensen, *supra*, n. 63, at 235.

[72] See generally Sinha, *supra* n. 10, at 47.

[73] *See* Roel de Lange, "Divergence, Fragmentation, and Pluralism" in *Legal Polycentricity: Consequences of Pluralism in Law* (Hanne Petersen & Henrik Zahle (eds.), 1995), 103, 115–16 (noting five limits on toleration—self-preservation of the state, preservation of its "fundamental norms," compliance with international treaties, the degree of consensus withing a given community, and the closed-ness of the community).

[74] Mouffee, *supra* n. 2, at 1539. As Mouffee shows, this means that "liberal pluralism" is based on "circular argumentation: political liberalism can provide a consensus among reasonable persons who by definition are persons who accept the principles of political liberalism": *id.*

[75] *Id.* at 1535.

[76] Blumenson, *supra* n. 6, at 543 ("If all moral truths have only local validity, we have an insoluble dilemma about "whose truth we should privilege in practice . . . Any standard we choose violates the fundamental premise of relativism"). Waldron, *supra* n. 68, at 1371 ("[S]imple relativism is self-refuting since it makes the nonrelativist proposition that tolerance is the objectively proper attitude to have toward the moral judgments of other societies").

alisation of divorce in other western nations, and the de-stigmatising of giving birth to children out-of-wedlock in affluent countries.

The first generation of children of no-fault divorce has now come of age. Approximately 25 million children in America experienced the divorce of their parents in the last quarter-century.[77] One of the most common consequences of divorce is to deprive children of regular association with their fathers. Many children of divorce are effectively abandoned by, or withheld from, and feel distanced from their fathers. Likewise, the number of American children born out of wedlock has quintupled in the last 30 years, now approaching one-third of all childbirths annually in the USA, and over one million children are born into homes without a father each year.[78] Between 1960 and 1990, the proportion of children living in the USA with a never-married parent increased more than 700 per cent, and more than one-half of all American children are said to spend part or all of their childhood years living separated from at least one of their parents.[79]

It should come as no surprise that some of these victims of alternative relationships may be drawn to homosexual relationships. A boy's perception that he has been abandoned by, is displeasing to, or is distanced from his father seems to be one of the factors associated with male attraction to homosexual behaviour.[80] A girl's ruptured relationship with her father is known to directly influence her later ability to relate to and maintain an intimate emotional commitment with a man.[81] The loss of a father (today primarily through divorce) is associated with higher risk that someone will turn to homosexual behaviour.[82] Parental separation is "associated with a measurably increased incidence of homosexuality [in the children]."[83]

---

[77] Every year from 1970 until 1995 there have been approximately (usually more than) 1,000,000 children involved in divorces. Lynn D. Wardle, "No-Fault Divorce and the Divorce Conundrum", 1990 *BYUL Rev.* 79, 144.

[78] *Vital Statistics of the United States*, vol. 1, at 190, Table 1–76 (1989).

[79] See Louis S. Richman, "Struggling to Save Our Kids", *Fortune Magazine*, 10 Aug. 1992; see also William J. Bennett, "The Index of Leading Cultural Indicators", Mar. 1993, at 14–16.

[80] See, e.g., A. Dean Byrd, "A Developmental Model of Male Homosexuality: The Greg Louganis Story", in *Toward a Further Understanding of Homosexuality*, Collected Papers from the NARTH Annual Conference, 29 July 1995, at 13; Charles W. Socarides, *Homosexuality, A Freedom Too Far* (1995) 87–114; Jeffrey Satinover, "The Complex Interaction of Genes and Environment: A Model for Homosexuality", in *Toward a Further Understanding of Homosexuality*, Collected Papers from the NARTH Annual Conference, 29 July 1995 at 200–1; William F. Greer and Vanik D. Volkam, "Transitional Phenomena and Anal Narcissism Controlling the Relationship with Representations of the Mother and the Father: The Transference in a Case of Latent Homosexuality" in *The Homosexualities and the Therapeutic Process* (Charles W. Socarides and Vanik D. Volkam (eds.), 1991).

[81] William S. Appleton, *Fathers and Daughters* (19891), 31, 40, 63, 65, 108 (psychiatrist's random interviews with women reveals that "fathers leave a profound mark" upon adult women, *id.* at x, and fathers have a "profound influence" on women's long-terms relationships of intimacy with men: *id.* at 133).

[82] Thomas E. Schmidt, *Straight & Narrow* (1995) 144–6.

[83] Jeffrey Satinover, *Homosexuality and the Politics of Truth* (1996), 107; *id.* at 108 (one study found children separated from one or both parents were over represented by a factor of 1.5 to 2.0 in the population of youth being treated for gender disturbances).

Thus, the quest for same-sex marriage today is at least partially the result of part of our society having given up on their marriages a generation ago. For a quarter-century our laws have undervalued the magnificent service given by ordinary husbands and wives, moms and dads, aunts, uncles, stepparents, grandparents, and brothers, and sisters—by ordinary families founded on the relationship of a husband and wife. We have taken that for granted. We tend to overlook the ordinary husbands and wives who live lives of quiet, magnificent commitment and service to their spouses, children, grandchildren, parents, and siblings. The law must rediscover and remember that marriage is the safest relationship in which adults may express their deepest intimacies and develop their individual and interdependent identities, and it also is the oldest and surest method of providing committed parents for children, and providing altruistic care for extended families.

We do not have to have perfect marriages to produce very good benefits for ourselves, our children and society. That is important to remember, because a perfectionist's perspective can distort and magnify problems in marriage and families, making us prone to conclude prematurely that couples or families with problems are hopeless, label them "dysfunctional", and give up on them (troubled marriages and struggling families) too easily.

Claims for same-sex marriage challenge us and our entire generation to remember the importance of the institution of marriage. We need that challenge. For too long our societies have taken marriage and the family for granted. It is time to rediscover and retell the story of the worth of this most common but most essential and most beneficial unit of society. It is time to reaffirm marriage and to reject the unsound pluralistic arguments for same-sex marriage.

24

Cohabitation and Registered Partnership in Scandinavia: The Legal Position of Homosexuals

INGRID LUND-ANDERSEN

INTRODUCTION

As the first country in the world, Denmark introduced in 1989, the registered partnership for two persons of the same sex.[1] The registration of a partnership carries the same legal consequences as marriage, with a few exceptions. In the field of family law, Denmark became a pioneer.

The main purpose of the legislation was political: the only way towards full social acceptance was to give homosexual couples the same legal framework as married couples. The legislation was used as an instrument to change attitudes. Registered Partnership Acts, similar to the Danish Act, have since been introduced in Norway,[2] Sweden[3] and Iceland.[4]

This chapter provides an overview of the legislation on registered partnership in Scandinavia and Iceland—in particular I will examine the provisions for married couples which do not apply to the registration of a partnership: civil or church marriage ceremonies, adoption of a child and artificial insemination or fertilisation outside the body. In this spring the question of a church ceremony for registered partners and access to artificial insemination has been debated in

---

[1] The Danish Registered Partnership Act No. 372 of 7 June 1989. See Linda Nielsen, "Family Rights and the Registered Partnership" in (1990) 4 *Denmark, International Journal of Law and the Family* 297–307 and Marianne Højgaard Pedersen, "Denmark: Homosexual Marriages and New Rules Regarding Separation and Divorce", (1991/92) 30 *Journal of Family Law* 290.

[2] Act No. 40 of 30 Apr. 1993 relating to Registered Partnership. See translation of the Bill submitted by the government to the Storting in Dec. 1992 in "The Norwegian Act on Registered Partnerships for homosexual couples", The Ministry of Children and Family Affairs, Oslo, Norway, Aug. 1993 and Peter Lødrup, "Registered Partnership in Norway", *The International Survey of Family Law* (1994), 387–94.

[3] The Registered Partnership (Family Law) Act 1994:1117. See Åke Saldeen, *The International Survey of Family Law* (1994), 441–2.

[4] Law on Registered Cohabitation no. 87/1996. See David Thór Bjorgrinsson, "General Principles and Recent Developments in Icelandic Family Law" *The International Survey of Family Law* (1995) 225–6.

Denmark and there has been great interest in repealing these exceptions from the Danish Registered Partnership Act.

1. REGISTERED PARTNERSHIP

1. Social and cultural background

The introduction of registered partnership in Denmark has its background in the social and cultural traditions in the country. Denmark—and the other Nordic countries—are modern welfare states based on social democratic ideas. Since the early 1970s, equality of the sexes has been one of the main concerns. In Denmark there is a long tradition of societies and interest groups which often have contacts with one of the many political parties[5] represented in the Danish Parliament (at the moment nine parties). The state religion is Protestantism, but only a minority of the population is religiously active.

As early as 1948 the National Danish Organisation for Gays and Lesbians was founded. The organisation began to become more visible in the late 1960s when the student movement led to a more liberal attitude to sexuality. Thus, in 1968 censorship on pornography was removed. In 1984 the organisation put forward a proposal for legislation on homosexual partnership. The same year, two members of the organisation became members of a commission to study the legal, social and cultural conditions of homosexuals.[6]

In 1986 the commission issued a report on death duty[7] in which the commission suggested that the surviving partner of a homosexual couple should pay the same duty as the surviving spouse. A low duty would give the surviving partner—who had been unable to marry—better possibilities of maintaining the joint home and continue at the same standard of living. The same year an amendment to the law of death duty was carried through in Parliament.[8]

Before the commission published its final report in 1988[9] a Partnership Bill was introduced in Parliament, in January 1988, by the Social Democrats, the Socialist People's Party and the Social Liberals. The commission completed its report. The majority—six members—could not support the idea of a registration system. The minority—five members—were in favour of a Partnership Act.

In Parliament the legislators were given a free vote and the Bill was passed by 71 votes to 47. As in Denmark, the debate in Norway and Sweden has been emotional, both in the press and in Parliament.

---

[5] A political party which gets at least 2% of the given voters will achieve at least four members in Parliament.

[6] The commission was appointed by Parliament after a proposal by parties outside the Conservative Government.

[7] Report No. 1065/1986: Homoseksuelle og arveafgift (Homosexuals and death duty).

[8] Act. No. 339, 4 June 1986.

[9] Report No. 1127/1988 Homoseksuelles vilkår (The Conditions of Homosexuals).

2. Statistical Research in Denmark

Denmark has five million inhabitants. About 5 per cent of the population is purely homosexual, but only a small number have a registered partnership.

Table 1. Persons in registered partnership 1 January 1990–1996

	In registered partnership		Dissolved by cancellation		Dissolved by death		Total
	men	*women*	*men*	*women*	*men*	*women*	
1990	518	122	1	—	1	3	645
1992	1400	491	26	22	61	6	2006
1994	1777	704	105	79	130	14	2809
1996	2050	961	198	147	210	21	3587

From 1 January 1990 to 1 January 1996, a total of 3,587 persons have been registered, 345 persons have dissolved a partnership and 231 partners have died.[10] The number of men (2,458) is more than double the number of women (1,129). Most of the persons are 25–54 years old. In comparison about 31,000 marriages are contracted and about 12,000 marriages are dissolved annually; 16 per cent of marriages contracted in 1990 were dissolved over the period 1990–6 and 1 per cent of the spouses had died.

Before the Partnership Act was adopted, 57 per cent of the Danish population was in favour of the legislation. The figure has increased to 64 per cent since 1990. Only around 30 per cent is against the legislation. Those most sympathetic are younger people, academics and women.

3. The legislation in Denmark, Norway, Sweden and Iceland

The main principle in the Registered Partnership Act is that the registration of a partnership provides the rights and benefits of marriage apart from a few exceptions. Thus, rules in which a spouse is defined by sex will not be extended for registered partnerships.

1. Residence and nationality

A partnership may only be registered provided that one or both of the parties has his permanent residence in Denmark and is of Danish nationality. These conditions should prevent Denmark from becoming a new Las Vegas. The provision is the same in the other Nordic countries, which means that, for example, two

---

[10] See Denmark's Statistical Office 1995.

Swedish nationals living in Denmark may not contract a registered partnership in Denmark. This is in contrast to marriage, where two foreigners, who are in the country for a short period, can enter into a marriage.

A registered partnership, contracted in one of the Scandinavian countries or Iceland, will have full legal consequences in any of the other countries. Before the partners acquire domicile abroad outside Scandinavia and Iceland, they should check the legal effects of registration in the new country. Some countries will not recognise registered parthership at all, referring to the principle of *ordre public*.

2. Church ceremony

The rules governing civil or church marriage ceremonies will not apply to registered partnerships. In particular, religious political parties and religious groups generally have been against registered homosexual partnerships.

In Denmark the bishops have set up a committee to consider "Registered partnership, cohabitation and blessing". The committee published its report on 21 May 1997. The conclusion was that the committee could not find any fundamental objections to introducing a ceremony in the church for homosexuals. The Bible should be read in the light of the culture in our time. The committee has outlined three different forms for blessing and one of them is similar to a church ceremony after a civil marriage. However it should be left to the clergymen to decide whether they wish to give a blessing to a homosexual couple.

The committee's report has been criticised by the right wing of the national church. In its opinion marriage is the bond between man and woman and homosexual relationships are in conflict with the Bible's general ethical norms. The 12 bishops in Denmark have different attitudes to the proposals from the committee and the report will be discussed at the Bishops' Conference in October 1997.

3. Adoption and custody

The parties in a registered partnership cannot adopt a child. According to the Danish Act the provisions of the Danish Adoption Act regarding spouses do not apply to registered partners. The legislators considered it best for a child to have a mother and a father and that children should not be brought up in registered partnerships. Consequently, registered partners in Denmark and Sweden cannot have joint custody of a child. The legal situation in Iceland is different as registered partners automatically have joint custody if one of the partners has sole custody at the time of registration. In the case of dissolution of the partnership, the biological parent will automatically obtain sole custody.

As regards the adoption of foreign children, it would create great problems in the country of the child's origin if registered homosexual partners were to be allowed to adopt a child together. The wording in the Danish and Norwegian provisions is the same and no form of adoption will be permitted for registered partners. The adoption of a stepchild is also prohibited. According to the Swedish Act registered partners may neither jointly nor individually adopt children.

In my opinion the adoption of a stepchild should be allowed.[11] In these cases it is a question of safeguarding the conditions for a child who already lives in a homosexual partnership, e.g. give the child the right to inheritance. Often the child has only one of its biological parents, because one of the parents is deceased or the mother has refused to give the authorities the identity of the father. When a single parent moves in with a new partner the special social benefits to parents living alone with their child will be withdrawn and the new partner will in practice become the child's breadwinner. Thus, it is inconsistent that the partner— for ideological reasons—cannot acquire legal obligations towards the stepchild.

In this spring, five members of the Parliament in Iceland have presented a Bill which allows registered partners to adopt a stepchild.

4. Artificial procreation

It is stated in the Swedish Partnership Act that the Insemination Act (1984: 1140) and the Fertilization outside the Body Act (1988:7 11) do not apply to registered partners. The legal situation is the same in Denmark, Norway and Iceland.

In Denmark, no legislation existed until 27 May 1997, when a Bill on artificial procreation was carried through Parliament.[12] One of the main topics was whether single women and lesbians should have access to insemination. After a passionate debate in Parliament the members were given a free vote.

The majority voted against access to artificial procreation for people other than married couples and cohabitants. For lesbians, childlessness is not an illness but is a result of choice of way of life. Further, a child has a right to have both a mother and a father. So, access to insemination for lesbians would not be in the best interests of the child but would only accommodate the wishes of lesbians.

The Danish Minister of Health had recommended that single women and lesbians should have access to insemination. The spokesman from the Social Democratic party was of the opinion that the "father-mother-child ideal" was too narrow in 1997. During the debate in Parliament she said: "I know children living in nuclear families where they are not treated well and I know children who live in homosexual families and are very happy. The world today is manifold".[13] Lesbians cannot be prevented from being inseminated privately with sperm which has not been controlled for dangerous diseases, e.g. AIDS. Therefore, the minority in Parliament felt that it would be in the best interests of the child to focus on health reasons and not on morality. The new legislation on artificial procreation must be revised within two years. The spokesman from the Social

---

[11] See also in Norway Asbjørn Strandbakken in *Jussens Venner* (The friends of Law) (1993), 343–4 and in Sweden Anders Agell in *Äktenskap, samboende, partnerskap* (Marriage, Cohabitation and Partnership) (1995), 250–1.

[12] Act No. 460, 10 June 1997.

[13] See *Politiken*, 28 May 1997.

Democrats has announced that she will work for the easing of the restrictions on insemination.

The new rules enter into force on 1 October 1997. Until then it is legal for lesbians to be inseminated in private clinics but not at hospitals. There is already a "queue" of lesbian couples who want insemination in private clinics before 1 October. The Organisation of Gays and Lesbians is investigating the possibilities of establishing its own sperm bank.

2. THE LEGAL SITUATION FOR HOMOSEXUAL COUPLES WHO HAVE NOT REGISTERED THEIR PARTNERSHIPS—DIVISION OF PROPERTY

Until the passing of the Registered Partnership Act in Denmark in 1989, it was not clear whether the legal situation for cohabitants of the same sex was the same as for cohabitants of the opposite sex. Today the legal status will be the same.

The present legal situation in Denmark, Norway, and Sweden illustrates three different approaches to solving the important problems in property relations upon dissolution of unmarried cohabitation. In Denmark, the courts have introduced a legally constructed model based on an *enrichment principle*. Upon termination of the relationship, the financially weaker party has been awarded a modest compensation against the party who is better off, e.g. because the financially better party has achieved an unjust enrichment at the expense of the other party.[14] A cohabitant has no legal right to take over a residential property or household goods which belong to the other party. If the cohabitants have had joint household for at least two years and live in a rented flat, the cohabitant, who has not rented the flat, may be entitled to take over the flat when special reasons so indicate.

In Norway, work in the home is considered to contribute to co-ownership of the assets and a system of *joint ownership* has been established which is the same for spouses and cohabitees. If the economy has been mixed it can also lead to co-ownership. This means that in most families, the family home will be owned by both parties.[15] When a household community ceases to exist, the rights of the household members are regulated by Act No. 45 of 4 July 1991. The provisions apply when the parties have lived together for at least two years, or when they have, have had, or are expecting, a child together. According to the rules, special or strong reasons can indicate the right to take over a residential property or part of a residential property which belongs to the other party, or the right to take over, or acquire, part of ordinary household goods.

In Sweden, The Cohabitees (Joint Homes) Act 1987[16] lays down that all property, acquired for joint use in the common home during the relationship, is to be

---

[14] See Ingrid Lund-Andersen, "Moving Towards an Individual Principle in Danish Law", (1990) 4 *International Journal of Law and the Family* 338–9.

[15] *Id.*, at 339.

[16] SFS 1987: 232.

divided equally upon termination of the relationship. The rules correspond to those applicable to spouses with community property.[17] The cohabitant most in need of the dwelling or household goods is entitled to receive this property or to take over the joint dwelling on the basis of a tenancy. The Act is applicable to homosexual cohabitants.[18]

The legal situation in Norway and Sweden gives the financially weaker party more protection than the party can obtain under the Danish judicially constructed model. In this context it is surprising that Denmark was the first country in the world to introduce the registered partnership. The reason for this is that in 1980 the Danish Marriage Committee claimed that special legislation for unmarried cohabitees would create a second-class marriage and would give a false sense of security and that marriage framed family life better than any other legal regulation.

3. THE LEGAL SITUATION OF HOMOSEXUALS OUTSIDE THE NORDIC COUNTRIES

In many countries all over the world the legal status of same-sex relations is under discussion. (Further information on this is provided in Chapters 23 and 25).

Most interesting is the development in The Netherlands.[19] In March 1996 the majority in the Second Chamber of Parliament was prepared to vote for making marriage available to homosexuals. Marriage would automatically establish a legal filiation link between a child and his, or her, mother's partner. However, the cabinet was opposed to the idea. First, the Netherlands would be the first country in the world to take this step. Secondly, the cabinet was against homosexual couples having a right to adopt.

On 4 December 1996 the Second Chamber voted to accept a proposal on registered partnerships.[20] The proposal is on its way through the First Chamber and is expected to come into force on 1 January 1998. The proposal differs from the legislation in Scandinavia and Iceland on one crucial point: it allows *heterosexual couples* to register.[21] Further, the procedure is open to Dutch nationals and European Union nationals and nationals of the EFTA lawfully resident in The Netherlands. The registration is to have the same effect as marriage apart from the relationship to any children living with one of the partners.

In the United States, the right of lesbians and gays to marry has been brought to court.[22] In May 1993 the Hawaii Supreme Court ruled that the state constitution may prohibit the denial of same-sex marriage.

---

[17] *Id.*, at. 339. See also Mary Ann Glendon, *The Transformation of Family Law* (1989), 275–6.

[18] Cf. Homosexual Cohabitees Act of 1987, SFS 1987: 813.

[19] See Caroline Forder, "Re-thinking Marriage, Parenthood and Adoption", [1995] *The International Survey of Family Law*, 360–1.

[20] The following description is based on information from Caroline Forder, The University of Maastricht.

[21] The conditions for registration are similar to the requirements of marriage.

[22] See legislative considerations for American reform Deborah M. Henson, "A Comparative Analysis of Same-sex Partnership Protections: Recommendations for American Reform" (1993) 7

In Canada, advocates for homosexual couples have achieved some limited success in gaining recognition for their relationships.[23] In a lower court decision, which has not been appealed, a lesbian partner of a biological mother was permitted to adopt her child. The judge concluded that discrimination on the basis of sexual orientation is prohibited by the Charter, a view affirmed by the Supreme Court in the case of *Egan* v. *Canada*.

4. CONCLUSION

In the Nordic countries, social and cultural conditions are very similar. Therefore, it was obvious that the Danish initiative on Registered Partnership would be followed in the other Nordic countries. At present, the legal status for homosexuals is being debated in Finland and legislative reforms are expected.

The main purpose of the legislation on registered partnership was to change attitudes to homosexual relationships. The recent debate in Denmark illustrates that the legislation has served its purpose. Within a few years it is likely that registered partnerships may be contracted in a church and that lesbians may obtain artificial insemination in Danish hospitals. If so, stepchild adoption and joint custody should be allowed for registered partners.

The next step would be to permit homosexuals to enter into marriage, as has already been discussed in The Netherlands and Hawaii. The Registered Partnerships Act could be repealed and substituted by a prohibition against homosexuals adopting foreign children. Further, clergymen should have the freedom to deny marrying a homosexual couple.

International Journal of Law and the Family 282–313 and Martin D. Dupuis, "The Impact of Culture, Society and History on the Legal Process: An Analysis of the Legal Status of Same-sex Relationships in the United States and Denmark", (1995) 9 *International Journal of Law and the Family* 86–118.

[23] See Martha Bailey and Nicholas Bala, "The Supreme Court on the Nature of the Family and Spousal Support and Other Developments" [1995] *The International Survey of Family Law* 88–91.

25

From Closet to Constitution: The South African Gay Family Rights Odyssey*

ELSA STEYN

INTRODUCTION

Sexual orientation, and in particular homosexual[1] orientation, has never been far from the mind of the South African legislature. From being a ground for persecution, however, it has evolved into one of the prime human rights concerns in our fledgling democracy. Briefly put, South Africa has transfigured itself from a draconian outpost of Calvinist morality into a world-leader in the gay rights field.[2] Sexual orientation is now entrenched in the Constitution[3] as an enumerated ground of non-discrimination. This constitutes a major policy change based on an altered perception of social reality. It is significant enough in the Western context, but for an African state this type of libertarian jurisprudence is unheard of. It is not yet clear what the influence of this clause will be in the South African context, but it is certain to accentuate the underlying homophobia which reigns supreme on the Southern African subcontinent as a whole.

* An abbreviated version has appeared in [1998] 1 *Journal of South African Law* 97. I acknowledge the financial assistance of the Centre for Science and Development towards this research. The views expressed in this publication are those of the author and are not necessarily to be attributed to the Centre for Science and Development.

[1] In this chapter the words "homosexual", "gay" and "gay and lesbian" will be used interchangeably. Gays and lesbians can be defined as persons who have an erotic disposition towards their own sex: Cameron "Sexual Orientation and the Constitution: A Test Case for Human Rights" [1993] *SALJ* 450, 452. Unless the context demands otherwise, "gay" refers to both male and female homoerotic behaviour. It also encompasses bisexuals. Lind points out that bisexuals suffer exactly the same discrimination as homosexuals when they choose to live as homosexuals (through criminalisation) or to formalise homosexual relationships (in the field of family rights): Lind, "Sexual Orientation, Family Law and the Transitional Constitution" [1995] *SALJ* 481, 486. In other words, society censures them as soon as they opt for anything but a heterosexual lifestyle. On the use of the word "gay", see Ricci, "Of Gay Rights and the Pitfalls of the 'PC': A polemic" in Gevisser and Cameron (eds.), *Defiant Desire, Gay and Lesbian Lives in South Africa* (1994), 311, 312–13.

[2] In 1991 Amnesty International decided to treat the criminal prohibition of sexual acts between two people of the same sex as an infringement of human rights. It was accordingly one of the first organisations to congratulate the South African government on the inclusion of a clause prohibiting discrimination on the basis of sexual orientation. This is indicative of an increasing world-wide trend to view homosexuality as a human rights issue: Dunton and Palmberg, *Current Africa Series—Human Rights and Homosexuality in Southern Africa* (1996), 39.

[3] The Constitution of the Republic of South Africa, 108 of 1996.

This chapter will trace the course of gay rights in South and Southern Africa, with the emphasis on gay family rights.

1. THE POSITION IN SOUTH AFRICA PRIOR TO THE INCEPTION OF THE INTERIM CONSTITUTION IN 1994

South African society has long been characterised by a strong degree of hostility towards homosexuals and homosexual conduct. Far from it being mere moral disapproval, however, the South African legislature and judiciary entrenched a system of "sexual policing" in terms of which homosexual conduct was prosecuted and homosexuals were denied basic human rights.[4]

This treatment was historically founded, for Roman law expressly prohibited "unnatural practices" between men and barred homosexuals from public office, whilst Roman-Dutch law permitted only heterosexual acts directed to procreation and punished anything outside this purview.[5] Accordingly, in terms of our common law, sodomy and other "unnatural offences" between men are punished.[6] There have been several attempts to bring lesbian behaviour under the purview of the law,[7] but these invariably brought about mass mobilisation on the gay front and collapsed.[8] One instance of lesbian conduct is punishable: in terms of the 1988 Immorality Amendment Act the prohibition on "immoral and indecent acts" was extended to those between women and girls under 19.[9]

By far the most contentious piece of legislation was the 1969 amendment to the Sexual Offences Act,[10] to include the infamous "men at a party" clause, which criminalised any "male person who commits with another male at a party any act which is calculated to stimulate sexual passion or to give sexual gratifi-

---

[4] "In fact, far from being a political irrelevancy, sex has been an important area of concern for successive generations of National Party governments. Racist legislation and iron-fisted rule have, since the earliest days of National government, gone hand in hand with an obsessive interest in sexual policing. This policing has been based on the values of Christian Nationalist apartheid ideology: the need to keep the white nation sexually and morally pure so that it had the strength to resist the black communist onslaught": Retief, "Keeping Sodom out of the Laager: State Repression of Homosexuality in Apartheid South Africa" in Gevisser and Cameron, n. 1 above, 100.

[5] Cameron, n. 1 above, 453.

[6] It is not clear which male–male sex acts will still be held criminal: mutual masturbation has been punished (see e.g. *S* v. *V* 1967 2 SA 17 (E)), but our courts appear loath to expand on these categories. See Cameron, "'Unapprehended Felons': Gays and Lesbians and the Law in South Africa" in Gevisser and Cameron, n. 1 above, 91 and the cases cited there.

[7] "It is very doubtful whether any so-called 'unnatural act' in private between consenting adult females constitutes a criminal offence in modern South African criminal law; certainly there is no record of a prosecution ever having been brought": *S* v. *H* 1995 1 SA 120 (O) 127. Also see Lind, n. 1, 481 n. 3.

[8] See Gevisser, "A Different Fight for Freedom: A History of South African Lesbian and Gay Organisation from the 1950s to 1990s" in Gevisser and Cameron, n. 1, 14, 34–7 and 60–1.

[9] The heterosexual age of consent is 16, as opposed to 19 for homosexual acts. See Cameron, n. 6, 91–2. This would obviously constitute discrimination on the basis of sexual orientation in terms of s. 9 of the Constitution.

[10] 23 of 1957.

cation", with "a party" being defined as "any occasion where more than two persons are present".[11] This was intended to enable police to enter private homes and crack down on homosexuals with the full force of legislation.[12] Previously statutory offences could only be committed in public.[13]

Perhaps the most telling sign of change in societal perceptions of homosexuality is to be found in the judiciary's attitude to homosexuality. In 1956, 30 men were arrested on charges of indecent assault after a police swoop of the Durban Esplanade, a notorious cruising-place. Handing out sentences ranging from six to 15 months, the magistrate declared: "your type is a menace to society and likely to corrupt and bring about degradation to innocent and unsuspecting, decent-living young men and so spell ruin to their future . . . ".[14] This contrasts starkly with the approach in *S* v. *H*[15] where the court stated:

> "There is a growing body of opinion, in South Africa as well, which questions fundamentally the sociological, biological, religious and other premises on which the proscription of homosexual acts between consenting adult men which takes place in private, have traditionally been based."[16]

The court went on to criticise the phrase "normal heterosexual relationships" as employed in *S* v. *M*[17] on the basis that it "implies that homosexual relationships are abnormal in a sense other than the mere fact that they are statistically in the minority" and concluded:

> "In my respectful view the use of the word 'normal' in this context is unfortunate, as it might suggest a prejudgment of much current psychological and sociological opinion which is critical of various conventions and assumptions regarding human society. It may also suggest a wrong line of enquiry when coming to re-evaluate the status of homosexual relationships. I would suggest that a more fruitful legal enquiry might be directed at concepts of privacy and autonomy and the issue whether private sexual intimacy *per se* between consenting male adults can ever cause harm to society any more than private heterosexual intimacy between consenting adults."[18]

[11] In terms of the Immorality Amendment Act 57 of 1969.
[12] Visser "The 'Third Sex' Act" [1970] *South African Law Journal* 87, 90. Compare, however, the progressive interpretation of this clause by the court in *S* v. *Matsemela en 'n Ander* 1988 2 SA 254 (T) where the court held it to be meaningful that the offence is committed at a party, i.e. in the presence of a third person. According to the court this indicates that the legislature intended restricting the common-law "unnatural offences" rather than extending them.
[13] Retief, n. 4, 101–3. See also Gevisser, n. 8, 31–5 and Cameron, n. 6, 92.
[14] Gevisser, n. 8, 18.
[15] 1995 (1) SA 120 (C).
[16] At 122.
[17] 1990 (2) SACR 509 (E).
[18] At 124.

2. THE ORIGINS OF THE "SEXUAL ORIENTATION" CLAUSE

The enumeration of "sexual orientation" as a ground of non-discrimination in the South African Constitution is a counter-reaction to the long denial of gay consciousness under the old regime. Gay rights form part of the broader spectrum of human rights that were negated by the apartheid system. The Nationalist government's divisive strategy that was so integral to the concept of apartheid proved to be a crucial link in the subsequent development of human rights awareness and gay consciousness.[19]

The Gay Association of South Africa (GASA) was avowedly apolitical, in order to escape further state censure for aligning themselves with the anti-apartheid liberation struggle. Two momentous events impacted on the gay rights movement by linking gay rights with the liberation struggle: first, the Delmas Treason Trial in 1986 where anti-apartheid activist Simon Nkoli was charged with treason and publicly came out of the closet,[20] and secondly the trial of conscientious objector Ivan Toms, where the military used his homosexuality as the basis of a smear campaign.[21] These events had a twofold impact: it showed gay rights activists that they needed a political agenda and it prompted the African National Congress (ANC) to include gay rights on its agenda.[22]

In 1991 the lobbying work of the Organisation of Lesbian and Gay Activists (OLGA) led to the inclusion in the ANC's draft Bill of Rights of a clause outlawing discrimination on the basis of sexual orientation.[23] This clause also found

[19] See Gevisser and Cameron, "Introduction" in Gevisser & Cameron, n. 1, 4–5. Also compare the submission made by Archbishop Desmond Tutu to the Constitutional Assembly in which he advocated retention of the sexual orientation clause in the final Constitution: "The apartheid regime enacted laws upon the religious convictions of a minority of the country's population, laws which denied gay and lesbian people their basic human rights and reduced them to social outcasts and criminals in their land of birth. These laws are still on the Statute Books awaiting your decision whether or not to include gay and lesbian people in the 'Rainbow People' of South Africa. It would be a sad day for South Africa if any individual or group of law-abiding citizens in South Africa were to find that the Final Constitution did not guarantee their fundamental human right to a sexual life, whether heterosexual or homosexual": quoted in Dunton and Palmberg, n. 2, 37.

[20] See Nkoli, "Wardrobes: Coming Out as a Black Gay Activist in South Africa" in Gevisser and Cameron, n. 1, 249.

[21] See I. Toms, "Ivan Toms is a Fairy? The South African Defence Force, the End Conscription Campaign, and Me" in Gevisser and Cameron, n. 1, 258.

[22] See Gevisser, n. 8, 55–8. Simon Nkoli was subsequently acquitted, but had already spent two years in jail before being charged. Ivan Toms was sentenced to 18 months' imprisonment for refusing to do army camps. These events provided the impetus for liberation-oriented international gay organisations and anti-apartheid movements to introduce the issue of gay rights to the ANC.

[23] Albeit not in the primary protective clause. See Fine and Nicol, "The Lavender Lobby: Working for Lesbian and Gay Rights within the Liberation Movement" in Gevisser and Cameron, n. 1, 269–73 and Gevisser, n. 8, 70. OLGA was affiliated into the United Democratic Front, "the broad-based coalition of grassroots movements that led the anti-apartheid struggle in the 1980s" in 1989: 75. Other important figures include human rights advocates Edwin Cameron, Albie Sachs and Kadar Asmal, all three of whom currently hold influential positions: Cameron as our sole openly gay judge of the High Court; Sachs as judge of the Constitutional Court and Asmal as Minister of Water Affairs in the Government of National Unity. It should be noted that the last two are human rights activists who have championed the cause of gay rights in the ANC in spite of their own heterosexual orientation. See Lessik "South Africa's Gay Rights" *San Francisco Bay Guardian*, 22 May 1996

its way into the proposals of the Inkatha Freedom Party and the Democratic Party.[24] The National Party went along with the proposal of the Law Commission that lesbians and gays should be seen as a "natural group" and that discrimination on the basis of a "natural characteristic" should be prohibited.[25] This raised the question whether the courts would view homosexuality as a natural characteristic when considering the oblique protection provided by this proposed clause. In addition, the clause would only have vertical application—hence preventing discrimination by the state, but not by other parties.[26]

In December 1993 South Africa adopted an Interim Constitution which included "sexual orientation" as expressly prohibited ground of discrimination.[27] This clause was retained as an enumerated ground of non-discrimination in the Bill of Rights enshrined in the new Constitution that was adopted on 8 May 1996.[28] South Africa consequently became the first country in the world formally to protect freedom of sexual orientation as a basic human right in its Constitution.[29]

(http://www.sfbayguardian.com/Politics/96_052296world.html; 11 June 1996) and Mills, "South Africa's gays have much to celebrate—Constitution ensuring freedom is the only one of its kind in the world" *http://www.otago.ac.nz/qrd/world/africa/south_africa/summary.of.lgb.situation-10.07.94* (11 June 1996).

[24] Cameron, n. 1, 465–70.

[25] A "natural group" is one with characteristics that the members do not choose themselves. This represents a major policy shift on the side of the Nationalist government who had for decades actively persecuted people on the basis of their perceived choice to lead a perverse (i.e. homosexual) lifestyle.

[26] See Cameron, n. 6, 95.

[27] This was largely due to the carefully orchestrated professional lobbying of the Technical Committee by the National Coalition for Gay and Lesbian Equality(NCGLE), an umbrella body of 73 disparate groups who, in the words of Stychin, followed an "insider strategy", consisting of "[i]ntensive lobbying of politicians, carefully constructed written submissions, skilfully orchestrated public statements by the Coalition, as well as a highly 'professional' 'rational', and 'moderate' approach": "Constituting Sexuality: The Struggle for Sexual Orientation in the South African Bill of Rights" [1996] *Journal of Law and Society* 455, 477. Also see Hayward "History of the Equality Clause" *Equality* May 1996, 2.

[28] Only the African Christian Democratic Party (ACDP) opposed the clause and it has but a small electoral basis. See Stychin, n. 27, 473–7 for the approach followed by the ACDP and the reasons for its "defeat". For more on the Bill of Rights debate in South Africa, see Dunton and Palmberg, n. 2, 34–8. In his professorial inauguration at the University of the Witwatersrand, Cameron described sexual orientation as a moral focus in the constitution-making process: "There is little cost to the majority if non-discrimination against gays and lesbians is to be entrenched, except the disavowal of ignorance and irrational prejudice. Conversely, the claims of the gay and lesbian minority to be protected under law are strong: their history of oppression and their still vulnerable position place them uniquely at the mercy of the majority": , n. 1, 471. For the various provisions entrenched in the interim and final Constitutions, see Heaton "A Comparison of the Bills of Rights in the Interim and Final Constitutions" [1997] *De Rebus* 331.

[29] Canada has since adopted Bill C–33 which amended the Human Rights Act to prohibit discrimination on the basis of sexual orientation in all matters under federal jurisdiction. However, this is an unentrenched federal act that only applies to matters under federal jurisdiction. Only once the Canadian Charter of Rights and Freedoms is amended, will the right to freedom of sexual orientation have the same impact as the South African one. The Canadian courts have long read "sexual orientation" into the Act, but have so far refused to recognise family rights on this basis.

3. SEXUAL ORIENTATION AND THE CONSTITUTION

The Bill of Rights is located in the second chapter of the Constitution and enshrines the values of "human dignity, equality and freedom".[30] Human dignity is entrenched by section 10; section 9 protects the right to equality and freedom is guaranteed *inter alia* by sections 12 (freedom and security of the person), 15 (freedom of religion, belief and opinion), 16 (freedom of expression) and 18 (freedom of association). Also of relevance is the privacy provision in section 14.

Clearly the central concept here is the one of equality. Sixteen different grounds of non-discrimination are enumerated, including "gender", "sex", "marital status" and "sexual orientation".[31] The clause has both vertical and horizontal application[32] and there is a presumption that discrimination on the enumerated grounds is unfair.[33] Yet this does not give rise to an absolute right of non-discrimination: section 9 only prohibits "unfair" discrimination and rights may legitimately be limited in terms of section 36.[34] In addition, vague concepts such as "discrimination" and "equality" leave much room for interpretation, equality usually being interpreted as only prohibiting distinctions which are not based on reasonable and objective justification.[35] On the other hand, the legal standing of gays and lesbians in South Africa is greatly enhanced by the fact that the Constitutional Court is empowered to review the constitutionality of parliamentary legislation.[36] In the absence of such power a constitutional anti-

[30] S. 7(1).

[31] S. 9(3). Dunton and Palmberg, n. 2, 42 distinguish between "enumerated bans of discrimination with explicit reference to sexual orientation" and "specific national laws outlawing discrimination on the grounds of sexual orientation". The South African measure is the farthest reaching example of the former category, whilst Norway, Sweden, the Netherlands, Israel, Canada, Denmark, Finland, Slovenia, France, Ireland, New Zealand and several USA states have enacted such national laws.

[32] S. 9(4). See Wolhuter, "Horizontality in the Interim and Final Constitutions" [1996] *SA Public Law* 512 and Jeffery, "The Dangers of Direct Horizontal Application: A Cautionary Comment on the 1996 Bill of Rights", Feb. 1997 *The Human Rights and Constitutional Law Journal of Southern Africa* 10.

[33] S. 9(5).

[34] S. 36 states:

"(1) The rights in the Bill of Rights may be limited only in terms of law of general application to the extent that the limitation is reasonable and justifiable in an open and democratic society based on human dignity, equality and freedom, taking into account all relevant factors, including —

    (a) the nature of the right;

    (b) the importance of the purpose of the limitation;

    (c) the nature and extent of the limitation;

    (d) the relation between the limitation and its purpose; and

    (e) less restrictive means to achieve the purpose.

(2) Except as provided in subsection (1) or in any other provision of the Constitution, no law may limit any right entrenched in the Bill of Rights."

[35] Waaldijk and Clapham (eds.), *Homosexuality: A European Community Issue* (1993), 78–9. See the discussion by Dunton and Palmberg, n. 2, 42. The South African Constitution employs vague concepts such as "unfair discrimination" and "in a society based on human dignity, equality and freedom".

[36] There is no such power in Luxembourg or the Netherlands, and only limited power in Belgium, Denmark and France: Dunton and Palmberg, n. 2, 42.

discrimination clause will not necessarily be the best guarantee against legal discrimination, entrenchment and judicial control being the key to ensuring the efficacy of a Bill of Rights.

The application of the Bill of Rights to any given matter before the court has two elements: first, the provisions in the Bill of Rights have to be interpreted in order to determine the contents of each; and secondly these provisions have to be applied to the facts before the court. Rautenbach identifies four steps in this procedure:[37]

(1) The court determines (i) who the bearers of the right in section X are and (ii) whether D is such a person. This would include all natural persons, as a juristic person cannot have a sexual orientation. The clause explicitly states that "everyone" is entitled to equal treatment by the law.

(2) The court determines (i) what conduct and interests are protected by section X and (ii) whether such conduct and interests pertaining to D have been impacted on. It is not possible to generalise in this regard. The court has to determine protected conduct and interests with reference to the particular right in question. Thus it will be necessary to interpret the terms "equality" and "sexual orientation" here.[38]

(3) The court determines (i) who are bound by section X and what their obligations are towards the bearer of the right, and (ii) whether E is such a person and whether E has not fulfilled his obligations towards D. The Constitution binds all organs of state, the courts and natural and juristic persons.[39] Contrary to the Interim Constitution, the Constitution therefore clearly has both vertical and horizontal application. In addition, section 7(2) places a positive duty on the state to "respect, promote and fulfil the rights in the Bill of Rights". This means that it is not sufficient for the state merely to abstain from limiting rights in an unconstitutional manner.[40]

(4) The court determines (i) what requirements are laid down for the legitimate limitation of the right guaranteed in section X and (ii) whether the factual limitation of D's right by E was in compliance with these requirements. "Law" includes statutory law, common law and customary law. Hence the common law definition of a marriage as a heterosexual union will count as a limitation for the purposes of section 36(1). The phrase "to the extent that the limitation is reasonable in an open and democratic society based on human dignity, equality and freedom" means that a specific balance has to exist between the limitation and the purpose

---

[37] *Algemene Bepalings van die Suid-Afrikaanse Handves van Menseregte* (1996) 30.

[38] Lind, n. 1, 492–3 argues in favour of the Aristotelian concept of equality in terms of which equals should be treated equally, and unequals unequally. This invalidates the argument that gays and lesbians suffer no discrimination, as they are free to marry somebody of the opposite sex, but make a lifestyle choice not to do so. Hence the court has to take cognisance of their "different" sexual orientation and treat them accordingly.

[39] S. 8. This puts paid to the principle of parliamentary sovereignty, which formed one of the pillars of the apartheid regime.

[40] See Rautenbach, n. 37, 66.

of the limitation.[41] In terms of section 36(1) five factors have to be considered, in particular:

(a) The nature of the right. What is protected by the right and how important is the right in an open and democratic society?[42]

(b) The importance of the purpose of the limitation. What is the purpose of the limitation and how important is that limitation in an open and democratic society?[43]

(c) The nature and extent of the limitation. How does the limitation affect the protected interests and conduct?[44]

(d) The relation between the limitation and its purpose. Could the limitation in fact protect the purpose and, if so, to what extent?[45]

(e) Less restrictive means to achieve the purpose. Are there other ways in which the purpose could be achieved more or less as effectively and that would limit the right to a lesser extent?[46]

Four distinct sources come to mind for the purposes of interpreting a clause in the Bill of Rights: the text of the Constitution;[47] the South African history on human rights and the drafting of the Constitution;[48] an investigation into the purpose of the guarantee;[49] and international and foreign law.[50] It seems obvious that the existing common law and statutory law will also play a role here.

---

[41] See Rautenbach, n. 37, 102. In dealing with the concept of "reasonableness" the Canadian court held in *R* v. *Oakes*, 26 DLR (4th) 200 that two considerations were important in this regard: (i) the limitation should serve a sufficiently important purpose which outweighs the right itself, and (ii) the means employed for that purpose should not extend further than necessary to achieve that object: see Lind, n. 1, 496.

[42] See Rautenbach, n. 37, 105.

[43] *Ibid.*, 106.

[44] *Ibid.*, 107.

[45] *Ibid.*, 109.

[46] *Ibid.*, 110.

[47] For the purposes of the grammatical and systematical approaches. In terms of the grammatical approach the linguistic meaning of words and concepts is determined; the systematical approach implies that a clause is interpreted within the framework of all the provisions of the act and the existing legal order. It is clear that none of these approaches can be used in isolation. See *ibid.*, 37–8.

[48] For the purposes of the historical approach. According to this approach the court looks at the circumstances surrounding the adoption of the clause and the meaning imputed to the clause by the drafters of the act.

[49] The "purposive" approach is the Canadian version of the teleological approach, which looks at the underlying purpose and objectives of the clause. In *S* v. *Makwanyane* 1995 6 BCLR 665 (CC), 1995 3 SA 391 (CC) President Chaskalson referred with approval to this approach as expounded by the Canadian court in *R* v. *Big M Mart Ltd* (1985) 13 CRR 64, (1985) 18 DLR (4th) 321: see Rautenbach, n. 37, 39.

[50] For the purposes of the comparative approach. In terms of s. 39 the court must consider international law and may consider foreign law when interpreting the Bill of Rights. The court will only be bound by international law if South Africa is a signatory. Several international human rights documents entrench marriage and family rights as fundamental rights, e.g. the Universal Declaration of Human Rights (1948), Art. 16; the International Covenant on Civil and Political Rights (1966), Art. 23; the International Covenant on Economic, Social and Cultural Rights (1966), Art. 10; the African Charter on Human and Peoples' Rights (OAU: 1981), Art. 18; the European Human Rights Convention (1950), Art. 12; and the European Social Charter (1961), Art. 16: see De Villiers, Van Vuuren and Wiechers, *Human Rights: Documents that Paved the Way* (1992). The court may look at

Since our courts have not yet had occasion to apply this section to (alleged) discrimination on the basis of sexual orientation, this remains a theoretical exercise. However, it can be argued that the phrase "justifiable in an open and democratic society based on human dignity, equality and freedom" should present a compelling reason for our courts to endorse homosexual and heterosexual relationships equally.[51]

4. THE (POTENTIAL) IMPACT OF THE "SEXUAL ORIENTATION" CLAUSE IN SOUTH AFRICAN LAW

One of the ten "challenges" in the Gay and Lesbian Manifesto drafted by the Gay and Lesbian Organisation of the Witwatersrand (GLOW) and used for the annual Johannesburg Pride March is for the law to "recognise longstanding lesbian and gay relationships by giving them all the benefits afforded heterosexual couples".[52] This may well become a legitimate claim in terms of section 9.[53] Yet this is not the only claim being made by gay rights activists. Cameron lists the following potential effects of constitutional protection:[54]

• The decriminalisation of gay sex acts, by abolishing the common law crimes of sodomy and "unnatural sexual offences", as well as section 20A of the Sexual Offences Act[55] ("men at a party");[56]
• A uniform age of consent for hetero- and homosexual acts;[57]

any foreign legal system: Rautenbach, n. 37, 9. Of particular value would be American, West-European and Canadian case law. African states with comparable case law include Botswana, Zimbabwe and Namibia.

[51] Lind, n. 1, 499.
[52] See Gevisser, n. 8, 74.
[53] Dunton and Palmberg, n. 2, 41 distinguish between four levels of gay rights, from minimum to maximum:
    (a) Decriminalisation of sexual acts between women and men of the same sex, providing that the acts take place between consenting adults, without offending public indecency.
    (b) Freedom of expression when it comes to speaking and writing in public about homosexuality, without offending public indecency.
    (c) Legal protection against discrimination on the grounds of sexual orientation.
    (d) Recognition of equal rights for gay and lesbian relationships as compared with heterosexual relationships.
[54] N. 1 above 470–1.
[55] 23 of 1957.
[56] Cf. the following *dictum* in *S* v. *H* 1995 1 SA 120 (C) 129: "A broad consensus on eliminating discrimination against homosexuality appeared from the various draft bills issued by various groups during the South African constitutional negotiations, indicating a likelihood that this will be entrenched in a new constitutional dispensation. If this were to happen, it is difficult to see how common-law or statutory offences which proscribe private 'unnatural acts' between consenting adult men can escape being struck down."
[57] However, in 1980 the French Constitutional Council refused to equate the difference in age limits there on the basis that they were acts of a different nature. The French legislature later implemented equal age limits. That is also the position in Belgium, the Netherlands, Portugal and Spain. Other countries with unequal age limits include the United Kingdom, Greece and Ireland. See Dunton and Palmberg, n. 2, 42–3.

- Legislative enforcement of non-discrimination, particularly in the fields of employment, tenancies, provision of public resources, and insurance;[58]
- Rights of free speech, association and conduct—with regard to permissible publications and equal rights of commercial association;[59]
- Formal recognition of permanent domestic partnerships which implies partner benefits in pensions, medical aid, immigration and insurance; rights of intestate inheritance; fair assessment of fostering abilities in regard to adoption and child care; and legal standing to act on behalf of a partner who has lost the capacity to make conscious choices,[60] either automatically, or through a "living will" or power of attorney.[61]

5. SEXUAL ORIENTATION IN THE BROADER AFRICAN CONTEXT

In 1992 Benny Alexander,[62] then Secretary-General of the Pan-Africanist Congress (PAC) described homosexuality as "un-African" and part of "the spin-off of the capitalist system".[63] This seems to be the prevalent opinion of many African leaders on the matter,[64] and even the ANC has fallen prey to militant homophobia: in 1987 ANC National Executive Committee Member Ruth Mompati described lesbians and gay men as "not normal" and continued, "I cannot even begin to understand why people want lesbian and gay rights".[65] Homophobia also formed the foundation of Winnie Mandela's defence in her 1991 assault and kidnapping trial.[66]

[58] Also see Lind, n. 1, 494.

[59] This would include the right to dress in drag: punishable up to now if there was the necessary criminal intent to disguise: see Cameron, n. 1, 471. This right is seriously infringed by the judgment in *Van Rooyen* v. *Van Rooyen*, 1994 2 SA 322, where the judge laid down a number of rules as to how the couple had to behave in front of children: see 6.4 below.

[60] Particularly relevant because of the AIDS epidemic.

[61] Cameron is not necessarily in favour of gay marriage: "The right to 'marry' should properly be confined to the traditional heterosexual institution generally associated with the procreation and parenting of children": Cameron, n. 1, 467. This is criticised by Lind, n. 1, 499 who feels that the law should reflect the diversity of family life in South Africa. Also see the debate on gay marriage at 6.3 below. Note in this regard Stychin's conclusion that gay rights activists such as Cameron deliberately followed a moderate approach in the constitution-making process to avoid alienating the politicians: see n. 27 above.

[62] Now known as "Khoisan !X".

[63] See Gevisser, n. 8, 71.

[64] Cf. Zimbabwe Parliamentarian Mrs Tungamirai: "It might be culture in the western world but [it is] not our culture here. We would like to be proud of our identity as Zimbabweans" quoted in Dunton and Palmberg, n. 2, 14. Kenyan President Daniel Arap Moi has expressed the same sentiment: see Dunton and Palmberg 24.

[65] *Capital Gay* (London) 18 Sept. 1987, quoted by Fine and Nicol, n. 23, 270.

[66] See Holmes, " 'White Rapists make Coloureds (and Homosexuals)': The Winnie Mandela Trial and the Politics of Race and Sexuality" in Gevisser and Cameron, n. 1, 284. Mandela was tried for the kidnapping and assault of 4 youths who she claimed were removed from the Orlando West Methodist Manse to protect them from sexual abuse by the presiding priest, Reverend Paul Verryn. Verryn was subsequently cleared of these allegations at the Richardson trial and had already been cleared by a local community enquiry and a formal church investigation: 286. Also see Johnson, "Priest survives Public Trial of Faith", *Weekly Mail & Guardian* 6 June 1996.

The argument diametrical opposite to this perception of homosexuality as a Western "disease" is articulated by Gevisser as follows:

"Gay Africanism, a discourse only in the very early stages of development in South Africa, maintains that it is the censure of homosexuality that is a colonial import, brought to this continent by missionaries, and that there is irony to the fact that latter-day Africanists have assimilated this Judeo-Christian biblical propaganda and reconstructed it as pre-colonial African purity."[67]

Dunton and Palmberg identify four main contentions underlying African homophobia: homosexuality can easily be conflated with offences such as bestiality, pædophilia and the marketing of pornography;[68] homosexuality is a sickness;[69] homophobia is an unnatural perversion that goes against God;[70] and homosexuality is a Euro-American perversion that is foreign to Africa.[71]

Perhaps it is best illustrated with reference to the Zimbabwe International Book Fair (ZIBF) saga.[72] In 1995 the Gays and Lesbians of Zimbabwe (GALZ) were prohibited from participating in the Zimbabwe International Book Fair (ZIBF), ironically themed "Human rights and justice". Their stand had originally been accepted by ZIBF but under increasing governmental pressure the trustees reneged at the last minute out of fear that the fair would be disrupted.[73] In his opening speech at the book fair the president of Zimbabwe, Robert Mugabe, launched a stinging attack on homosexuals, saying:

[67] Gevisser, n. 8, 72–3. An interesting example of this is the statement by Namibian Finance Minister Helmut Angela that "homosexuality is an unnatural behavioural disorder which is alien to African culture. It is a product of confused genes and environmental aberration. In Judeo-Christian culture, it has generally been perceived as sinful" cited in Dunton and Palmberg, n. 2, 29. See also the evidence cited by Gevisser of African homosexual activity that exists independently of the migrant labour system and that is entrenched in traditional tribal hierarchy, such as the Lovedu Rain Queen in the Northern Transvaal who keeps up to 40 wives: 72. Regarding Namibia, Dunton and Palmberg refer to research conducted by Kurt Falk over a 10 year period early in this century which found evidence of homosexuality in all cultural groups and lesbianism in most: 30.

[68] N. 2 above, 24. Cf. Mugabe's speech at the opening of the 1995 Book Fair "If we accept homosexuality as a right, as is being argued by the association of sodomists and sexual perverts, what moral fibre shall our society ever have to deny organised drug addicts or even those given over to bestiality the rights they claim and allege they possess under the rubrics of 'individual freedom' and 'human rights' . . . ?" quoted in GALZ "Sexual Orientation and the Zimbabwe Government" http://www.icon.co.za/~stobbs/more.htm (11 June 1997).

[69] N. 2, 28, 40. See e.g. the statements by prominent Namibian officials that gays and lesbians should be "operated on to remove unnatural hormones" and "homosexuality is a mental disorder which is curable through long-term treatment and as new technological applications emerge", cited in Dunton and Palmberg 29. In 1993 the World Health Organisation removed homosexuality from its list of diseases. The US Psychiatry Association had already deleted homosexuality from its handbook of mental disorders in 1973 and Sweden took it off its lists of diseases in 1979.

[70] N. 2 above, 36, 40. Not all African religious leaders condemn homosexuality, though. See e.g. the submissions made by Bishop Mmutlanyane Moqoba (Methodist Church) and Archbishop Desmond Tutu (Anglican Church) to the Constitutional Assembly in support of the sexual orientation clause (cf. n. 19 above), quoted in Dunton and Palmberg 37.

[71] N. 2 above, 24. See also Stychin, n. 27, 472–3 and Menaker "South Africa: Fighting for Gay and Lesbian Rights" *Women's Feature Service* http://www.igc.apc.org/wfs/stories.html (11 June 1997).

[72] For a comprehensive discussion, see Dunton and Palmberg, n. 2, and GALZ, n. 68.

[73] On the trustees' position, see String, "We Agonised about Excluding Zim's Gays", *Mail & Guardian* (Johannesburg), 18 Aug. 1995.

"I find it extremely outrageous and repugnant to my human conscience that such immoral and repulsive organisations, like those of homosexuals who offend both against the law of nature and the morals of religious beliefs espoused by our society, should have any advocates in our midst and even elsewhere in the world."[74]

Despite immediate international condemnation,[75] Mugabe subsequently persisted in making homophobic statements such as "I don't believe they should have any rights at all"[76] and "It degrades human dignity. It's unnatural and there is no question ever of allowing these people to behave worse than dogs and pigs."[77]

In 1996 ZIBF refused to bow to governmental pressure and allocated a stall to GALZ. The Board of Censors then banned GALZ from exhibiting in terms of section 17(1) of the Censorship and Entertainments Control Act.[78] GALZ took the matter to the High Court which declared the order invalid on the basis that the censorship board could not ban materials it had not seen. The court also dismissed the government's attempt to lodge a counter-appeal against the judgement.[79] GALZ was accordingly allowed to exhibit, but its stand was subsequently thrashed by a homophobic mob.[80] Under Zimbabwean common law "unnatural sexual acts" are illegal, with penalties ranging up to ten years" imprisonment.[81]

---

[74] Dunton and Palmberg, n. 2, 9; GALZ, n. 68.

[75] E.g. by Amnesty International in a statement released on 31 July 1995, "70 US Congressman Sent a Letter of Condemnation to Mugabe" (available at http://mail.icon.co.za/~stobbs/usletter.htm) and South Africans demonstrated outside the Zimbabwean Trade Mission in central Johannesburg. Mugabe was unrepentant: "Let the Americans keep their sodomy, bestiality, stupid and foolish ways to themselves, out of Zimbabwe . . . Let them be gay in the US, Europe and elsewhere . . . They shall be sad people here." quoted in Dunton and Palmberg, n. 2, 13; GALZ, n. 68. Other countries who reacted to the continued homophobic campaign include the Netherlands, Norway and Sweden: see Dunton and Palmberg 16 and "Zim's Gay Policy Meets with Foreign Resistance" *Weekly Mail & Guardian* (Johannesburg), 5 Jan. 1996.

[76] SAPA, *BBC Summary of World Broadcasts*, 3 Aug. 1995, quoted in Dunton and Palmberg, n. 2, 10.

[77] Reuters, *The Herald* (Harare), 12 Aug. 1995, quoted in Dunton and Palmberg, n. 2, 12; GALZ, n. 72.

[78] CAP 10: 04. This move violated s. 23 of Zimbabwe's constitution, which prohibits discrimination on any ground and Arts. 18 and 26 of the UN International Covenant on Civil and Political Rights to which it is a signatory: IPS Correspondents in Harare "No Place for Gays", *Mail & Guardian* (Johannesburg), 25 July 1996. The ZIBF consequently denied GALZ a stall at the Book Fair: see "Gays Barred from Zim Book Fair", *The Citizen* (Johannesburg), 30 July 1996 and "Censors Board Bans GALZ from Bookfair" *The Herald* (Harare), 30 July 1996.

[79] See GALZ, "Zimbabwe Press Statement form Clayton Wakeford to Kevan Botha: GALZ will be seeking legal counsel this morning and intends to put in an application to the High Court of Zimbabwe to overturn this prohibition order" http://www.mail.icon.co.za/~stobbs.docugalz.htm (11 June 1997); "Report July 26, 1996 from Harare by Clayton Wakeford to Kevan Botha" http://www.mail.icon.co.za/~stobbs.docugalz.htm (11 June 1997); "Gays Take Government to Court", *The Star* (Johannesburg), 30 June 1996; "High Court Victory for Zimbabwe Gays", *Business Day* (Johannesburg), 1 July 1996 and "Gays Ignore Book Show Ban", *The Star* (Johannesburg), 25 July 1996.

[80] There are indications of government involvement in this attack. In any event, GALZ was denied police protection and the government did not condemn the violence. For an in-depth discussion of the 1996 Book Fair, see Dunton and Palmberg, n. 2, 17–23. Homophobia seems rampant in Zimbabwe society at large: cf. "Zimbabweans Blame 'Gay Immorality' for Drought", *Business Day* (Johannesburg), 2 Oct. 1995.

[81] See Dunton and Palmberg, n. 2, 13; GALZ, n. 68. Botswana's penal code also proscribes homosexuality: see Dunton and Palmberg 33.

All this is relevant to South Africa, both for geographical and economic reasons: South Africa is Zimbabwe's neighbour and primary trade partner. It is to be expected, therefore, that the South African approach to sexual orientation as a fundamental human right will impact significantly on Zimbabwe, or at least cause friction between the two countries.

6. THE ROAD AHEAD: GAY FAMILY RIGHTS

1. Decriminalisation of consensual sexual relations in private

The decriminalisation of consensual sexual relations in private is relevant for the purposes of family law for two reasons: first, the state can hardly afford a gay relationship any protection when the very expression of that relationship is deemed to be an offence, and secondly, the criminalisation of homosexual conduct often provides the basis for denying gays and lesbians some other right, such as custody of or access to their children.[82] Dunton and Palmberg make the important point that "[c]riminalisation of homosexuality has been invoked to justify a wide range of human rights violations against lesbians and gays".[83]

In South Africa homosexual acts between men will remain illegal until the relevant provisions are found to be unconstitutional or scrapped from the books. It is unlikely that the common law offences such as sodomy will still be recognised by our courts in the light of the Constitution.[84] A good indication of this is provided by the reasoning of the Cape Provincial Division in *S* v. *H*,[85] where the court reviewed the conviction and sentence to 12 months' (suspended) imprisonment of a 23-year-old man on a count of sodomy. The court referred to the proposed "sexual orientation" clause in the Constitution and cautioned that "[i]f this were to happen, it is difficult to see how the common-law or statutory offences which proscribe private 'unnatural acts' between consenting adult men can escape being struck down".[86] It was also emphasised by the court that public opinion has changed in this regard and that "principles of equality, privacy, autonomy and the absence of public harm militate strongly against criminal proscription of such acts."[87] Accordingly the court set aside the sentence and

---

[82] Cf, Lind, n. 1, 489: "while much homosexual conduct is illegal, it is unlikely that a children's court would approve the attempt of a homosexual person to adopt a child, particularly if an acceptable alternative is available".

[83] N. 2 above, 44. Cf. Stychin, n. 27, 465: "Sodomy laws have become a national myth which serves to regulate extra-legally all 'deviant' sexual conduct and which legitimizes an anti-gay animus."

[84] Perhaps this will also open up the way for a redefinition of "rape" to encompass forced intercourse perpetrated on men—currently rape is defined in terms of "sex", i.e. the perpetrator has to be male and the victim female.

[85] 1995 1 SA 120 (C). This decision was made before the Constitution was implemented, but the court took notice of the fact that "sexual orientation" was a protected ground of non-discrimination in the proposals of all the major parties.

[86] At 129.

[87] At 128.

replaced it with a nominal one of caution and discharge, saying that "at the present time a custodial sentence is not an appropriate sentence for consensual, adult, private sodomy taking place under circumstances which pose no threat to any legitimate societal interest".[88]

An international perspective may be instructive here. Europe has long been in favour of the decriminalisation of consensual sexual relations in private: homosexuality is decriminalised in most European countries, with the notable exception of Romania[89] and the European Court of Human Rights has ruled on several occasions that sodomy laws violate "the right to privacy" entrenched in the European Convention for the Protection of Human Rights and Fundamental Freedoms.[90] This also seems to be the position of the United Nations Human Rights Committee, who ruled in 1994 that the Australian state of Tasmania violated the privacy and non-discriminatory provisions of the International Covenant on Civil and Political Rights (ICCPR) with its sodomy law.[91]

In *Bowers* v. *Hardwick*,[92] on the other hand, the United States Supreme Court rejected the claim that gays were entitled to protection against sodomy laws.[93] Arguments in favour of the decriminalisation of homosexual conduct have largely been based on two grounds in the States: privacy, which failed in the *Bowers* case, and the right to dignity and equal protection. In terms of the latter, discrimination on the basis of sexual orientation is untenable, since sexual orientation is "a matter of indifference morally and constitutionally".[94]

The Southern African subcontinent is unequivocal about the matter: while Swaziland and Lesotho do not criminalise homosexuality,[95] homosexual acts

---

[88] At 129. The question of constitutionality was also raised in *S* v. *A* 1995 2 BCLR 153 (C), but the court found it inapplicable to the matter at hand as the dispute was not centred around consensual sex. See Rautenbach, "*S* v. *A* 1995 2 BCLR 153 (K): Sodomie en die grondwet" [1995] *South African Journal of Criminal Justice* 344.

[89] Which led to the naming of Romania as "the most homophobic country in Europe": Dunton and Palmberg, n. 2, 41. Amnesty International's first gay prisoners of conscience were two men convicted of homosexual offences under the draconian laws of Romania. A 1996 parliamentary initiative contained jail sentences of up to 3 years for consensual homosexual acts in private, and 5 in public: see "Homosexuality Voted a Crime", *Sydney Star Observer*, 19 Sept. 1996, 6 and "Sex Sanctions", *New Zealand Express*, 10 Oct. 1996, 11.

[90] See Dunton and Palmberg, n. 2, 44.

[91] *Nicolas Toonen* v. *Australia*, UN Hum. Rts. Comm., No 488, UN Doc. CCPR/c/50/D/488/ 1992. See Dunton and Palmberg, n. 2, 44. The prohibition against homosexual sex has since been repealed: GayLawNet, "GayLawNews: Tasmania Repeals Law" http://www.geocities.com/ WestHollywood/3181/news.html (11 June 1996).

[92] 478 US 186 (1986).

[93] See Cameron, n. 1, 463–4.

[94] Cameron, n. 1, 464. He identifies three premises which need to be accepted before the argument will hold water: (a) that sexual orientation, and consensual conduct expressing it, do not in themselves justifiably evoke *social* censure (whatever divergent moral view one may hold about it); (b) that homosexual orientation is not in itself evidence of illness or depravity; and (c) that orientation (homosexual or heterosexual) is or should be an indifferent factor in the distribution of social goods and services and the award of social opportunities.

[95] Dunton and Palmberg, n. 2, 41. However, Swaziland Prime Minister Dr Sibusiso Dlamini has condemned homosexuality as an "abnormality and sickness" and Tribal Chief and Former Prime Minister Prince Bhekimpi stated: "Homosexuality is regarded as satanic in Swaziland. Therefore, I am forced to evict all gays and lesbians in my area" GayLawNet "GayLawNews: Swaziland Group

between men are illegal in Angola, Botswana, Mozambique, Malawi, Namibia, Tanzania, Zambia and Zimbabwe.[96]

2. Formal recognition as a "family", i.e. family benefits

Gays and lesbians are currently denied family benefits on the basis that they are not legally married.[97] This involves twofold discrimination in terms of section 9 of the Constitution: discrimination on the bases of marital status and sexual orientation.

A whole range of benefits are relevant here:[98]

- Partner benefits in pensions;[99]
- Partner benefits in medical aid and medical insurance coverage;[100]
- Immigration;[101]
- Insurance;
- Rights of intestate inheritance;
- The legal standing to act on behalf of a partner who has lost the capacity to make conscious choices, either automatically, or through a "living will" or power of attorney;
- Spousal privilege;

Forms" http://www.geocities.com/WestHollywood/3181/di970406.html (11 June 1997). The formation of GALESWA, Swaziland's first gay and lesbian association, has been condemned by Parliament and several church groups: Greyvenstein, "Gay leier lug standpunt, glo afgedank" *Beeld*, 25 Mar. 1997.

[96] Dunton and Palmberg, n. 2, 33, 41. On Zimbabwe, see GALZ, n. 72.

[97] See e.g. Daniels "Better Work Practices Sought for Homosexuals", *The Star*, 13 June 1997. Currently only a few large institutions recognise gay partners: the University of the Witwatersrand (Wits), Rhodes University, the Universities of Fort Hare, Zululand, Cape Town and the Anglo American Corporation. Even then it does not completely exclude discrimination—Wits, for instance, requires that the couple have been together for at least 5 years before any benefits are granted and they have to prove a joint bank account and a shared household. The same does not apply to married couples. See Steynberg "Wits se gay pare kry ook siekefonds-voordele", *Beeld*, 17 Mar. 1997, 12. Litigation is currently being undertaken against two further institutions to force them to recognise gay partners: Escom and the South African Police.

[98] See Cameron, n. 1, 471, Mosikatsana, "The Definitional Exclusion of Gays & Lesbians from Family Status" [1996] *South African Journal on Human Rights* 549, 556 and De Vos, "Same-sex Marriage, the Right to Equality and the South African Constitution" [1996] *SA Public Law* 354, 360.

[99] South African law recognises gay spouses for the purposes of the Special Pensions Act of 1996 in terms of which gay spouses are recognised after 5 years' cohabitation. The Act is of very limited application though, providing pensions only for Struggle veterans. In Canada the seminal case is *Egan v. Canada* (1995) 124 DLR (4th) 609 where the definition of "spouse" in the Old Age Security Act RSC 1985 was challenged in terms of the equality principle in s. 15 of the Canadian Charter of Rights (which guarantees non-discrimination on the basis of sex, but not sexual orientation). On the basis of the procreation-argument the majority held that the applicants had not suffered discrimination on the basis of their sexual orientation, as the distinction between heterosexual and homosexual couples was not based on an irrelevant personal characteristic. For a discussion, see De Vos, n. 98, 366–8, 376–8.

[100] See n. 97 above.

[101] See Silver, " 'Til Deportation Do Us Part: The Extension of Spousal Recognition to Same-sex Partnerships" [1996] *South African Journal on Human Rights* 575.

- Fair assessment of fostering abilities in regard to adoption and child care;[102]
- A claim to a division of property on breakdown of the relationship;[103]
- Support after breakdown of the relationship;
- Delictual actions for dependant's relief;[104]
- Wrongful death actions;
- Bereavement leave;[105]
- Protection against domestic violence.[106]

Apart from the Constitution, the new Labour Relations Act (LRA) plays a role in this regard: the Basic Conditions of Employment Bill in the LRA has a progressive definition of family, meaning that any person who cohabits with an employee is family. This is the broadest definition of family in our law up to date and encompasses a variety of relationships previously ignored, such as same-sex couples, customary and religious marriages, and members of the extended family (grandparents, aunts and uncles, and the like) who are dependent on the employee for maintenance.

---

[102] See 4 below.

[103] South Africa's first gay "divorce" recently came before the Transvaal Provincial Division, but was settled out of court at the insistence of the presiding judge, Deputy-President Van Zyl. The settlement amounted to a near equal split of the "joint" estate. See Jurgens "Battle Lines Drawn as the First Gay 'Divorce' Goes to Court", *Sunday Times*, 1 June 1997; Sapa, "Battle over Money Erupts after Gay Lovers Fall Out", *The Star*, 3 June 1997; Hattingh, "Pta-gays 'skei': g'n skikking nog bereik", *Beeld* 3 June 1997; Pretoria Correspondent, "Court Hears of Rings, Marriage Vows in Gay 'Divorce' Case", *The Star*, 4 June 1997; Hattingh, "Gay paar se 'huwelikskontrak'", *Beeld*, 4 June 1997, 3; Own Correspondent, "Judge Fails to Persuade Gays to Settle Differences after Split", *The Star*, 5 June 1997; Jonker, "Derde poging van gay paar in Pta om oor bate-verdeling te skik, misluk", *Beeld*, 5 June 1997; De Lange, "Judge Relieved as Gays Settle Split", *Citizen*, 6 June 1997; Sapa, "Out-of-court Settlement in Gay 'Divorce'", *The Star*, 6 June 1997; Hattingh, "Gay paar van Pta verdeel hulle bates", *Beeld*, 6 June 1997.

[104] In terms of the Compensation for Occupational Injuries and Diseases Act 130 of 1993 the heterosexual cohabitant of a workman can claim compensation for loss of maintenance. The same does not yet apply to homosexual partners. This is a typical example of legislation being drafted with an underlying presumption of heterosexuality. However, this phenomenon may sometimes work to the advantage of gay and lesbian couples: e.g. the Insolvency Act 24 of 1936 treats heterosexual cohabitants as spouses for the purpose of the insolvency of one of them. The same does not apply to lesbian and gay couples. Lind, n. 1, 491–2 n. 60 argues convincingly that this is an instance where heterosexuals could avail themselves of the sexual orientation clause.

[105] In *Attorney-General* v. *Mossop* (1993) 100 DLR (4th) 658 the Supreme Court of Canada decided by a margin of 4 to 3 that "immediate family" did not extend to a homosexual partner for the purpose of bereavement leave claimed in terms of a collective agreement.

[106] In terms of the Prevention of Family Violence Act 133 of 1993 a heterosexual cohabitant is treated as a spouse, but not a homosexual one. Clark, "Cold Comfort? A Commentary on the Prevention of Family Violence Act" [1996] *South African Journal on Human Rights* 587, 597 proposes that the definition of a domestic relationship be widened to include "persons in a range of family and inter-personal relationships such as homosexual relationships, and relationships where the parties do not live together". A good prototype to follow would be the 1996 New Zealand Domestic Violence Act that extends protection to a range of persons including homosexual couples, extended family members and dating couples. The Act further prohibits physical, sexual and psychological abuse and carries a maximum jail sentence of two years: Gummer and Van Wetering, "Fighting on the Home Front", *New Zealand Express*, 15 Aug. 1996, 6 (http://www.geocities.com/WestHollywood/3181/ne_pert.html; 11 June 1997).

3. Marriage

The possibility of a successful judicial challenge to heterosexual marriage has been opened up by the Constitution.[107] While it is true that South African family law currently makes no provision for same-sex marriage,[108] it is clear that all legislation has to be interpreted and that the common law has to be developed in order to "promote the spirit, purport and objectives of the Bill of Rights".[109] In other words: the court is authorised to develop the common-law concept of marriage to provide for homosexual marriage.

In this quest it will be necessary for the court to consider sections 9 and 36, as discussed above.[110] Restricting the marriage institution to heterosexual couples seems to be a clear case of unfair discrimination as envisaged by section 9. The real question is whether this right may be legitimately limited in terms of section 36. In this regard it is argued that the exclusion of same-sex marriage will fail the proportionality requirement since recognition of same-sex marriage will not decrease or threaten heterosexual marriage (and therefore procreation) and the sole function of the exclusion is to "deny the benefit of the law for an already disadvantaged group in society".[111] Furthermore, recognition of same-sex marriages will involve little cost to society.[112]

De Vos stresses that a challenge to the existing marriage norms will only be successful "if the courts can be convinced that social institutions, such as marriage and sexual identities themselves, are mutable, changing and unessential in nature".[113] Changing perceptions of social reality will play a big role in this regard, as the courts come to realise that homosexuality is no longer regarded by the community at large with the jaundiced eye of the past.[114] Yet the greater public tolerance of homosexuality should not be taken as a sign that public opinion goes so far as to embrace the concept of same-sex marriage.

One must be careful though, not to argue that same-sex couples may not be allowed to marry as it goes against public morality at large. It has to be determined whether the Constitution affords them the opportunity to do so. In *S* v.

---

[107] Mosikatsana, n. 98, 555 argues that the courts should seize this opportunity to play an activist role to challenge "the racism, cultural chauvinism, patriarchy and homophobia of the dominant culture" that reflects "the values and interests of the white, middle-class, middle-aged, heterosexual male".

[108] The *locus classicus* here is *W* v. *W* 1976 (2) SA 308 (W) where the court held that the marriage of a post-operative transsexual was invalid on the basis that the operation did not change the plaintiff into a female, and a valid marriage could only be contracted by parties of the opposite sex. Also see Lind, n. 1, 486 n. 27.

[109] S. 39(2).

[110] See 3. Sexual orientation and the Constitution.

[111] Grant, "Comments and Cases on Same-sex Marriage" [1996] *South African Journal on Human Rights* 568, 572–3.

[112] See Cameron, n. 1, 471.

[113] N. 98 above, 382.

[114] On cultural diversity and value pluralism in our emerging democratic society, see Mosikatsana, n. 98, 550–1.

Makwanyane,[115] which dealt with the constitutional legitimacy of capital punishment, President Chaskalson pointed out that constitutionality is not determined by the opinion of the majority of South Africans, but by what is allowed in terms of the Constitution. He went on to say:

> "Public opinion may have some relevance to the enquiry, but in itself, it is no substitute for the duty vested in the Courts to interpret the Constitution and to uphold its provisions without fear or favour. If public opinion were to be decisive there would be no need for constitutional adjudication. The protection of rights could then be left to Parliament, which has a mandate from the public, and is answerable to the public for the way its mandate is exercised, but this would be a return to parliamentary sovereignty, and a retreat from the new legal order established by the 1993 Constitution. By the same token the issue of the constitutionality of capital punishment cannot be referred to a referendum, in which a majority view would prevail over the wishes of any minority. The very reason for establishing the new legal order, and for vesting the power of judicial review of all legislation in the courts, was to protect the rights of minorities and others who cannot protect their rights adequately through the democratic process. Those who are entitled to claim this protection include the social outcasts and marginalised people of our society. It is only if there is a willingness to protect the worst and the weakest amongst us, that all of us can be secure that our own rights will be protected."[116]

A possible solution is presented by Lind, who argues in favour of a distinction between the family as a moral institution and its legal counterpart.[117] This would dispense with the argument that the heterosexual family has to be protected as it forms the basis of our society.[118] Whilst society could still censure relationships in the social sphere according to public morality, it would allow for state recognition of relationships worthy of legal protection. Most of the inherent benefits of marriage are purely secular and have no foundation in morality, e.g. immigration, dependants' actions and taxation benefits.[119]

In the final analysis three possibilities present themselves:

1. Equal marriage rights

Gays and lesbians may have a stronger claim to equal marriage rights in South Africa than anywhere else in the world: not only are we the only country to

---

[115] 1995 6 BCLR 665 (CC), 1995 3 SA 391 (CC).

[116] Para. 88.

[117] Lind, n. 1, 482–5. He states: "Marriage in law is something other than merely a moral institution. It serves a larger, more diverse, community, with different, often peculiarly secular, needs."

[118] Cf. De Vos, n. 98, 381: "Marriage has been constructed to advance three intertwined goals: procreation; the providing of an environment for raising the children; and the relationship between the partners themselves, referred to as the 'relational' interest. It is impossible to demonstrate that the ban on same-sex marriage will advance any of the aims set out above (although some might argue that same-sex marriage will not necessarily promote these goals), unless one believes that there is something inherently wrong, abnormal or dangerous about same-sex relationships."

[119] Taxation benefits are not applicable in the South African context, as the Income Tax Act 58 of 1962 no longer distinguishes between married and unmarried persons.

entrench freedom of sexual orientation in our Constitution, but there is no constitutional clause protecting the family in its traditional guise, such as section 6 of the German Constitution.[120]

De Vos[121] argues that we should utilise section 9 to move away from an essentialist view of marriage as an immutably heterosexual institution towards a constructionist one in terms of which "marriages should change as subordinated groups identify their own oppression and decide to resist it".[122] Hence "the social construction of marriage in any given society is fluid and mobile, and change is inevitable".[123]

The following objections are typically raised against same-sex marriage and will have to be considered by the courts:[124]

- The essence of marriage is its heterosexual nature;[125]
- Same-sex marriage is morally reprehensible and must be outlawed to protect family values and traditional ethical notions;[126]
- Same-sex marriages will violate religious freedom;[127]
- Same-sex marriage will infringe on other individual rights;[128]
- The recognition of same-sex marriage will indicate approval of homosexuality at large;[129]
- Marriage is the natural and desirable form for procreation and the rearing of children;[130]

[120] Stychin, n. 27, 458–9 points out how role-players in the constitutional debate, such as the Coalition for Gay and Lesbian Equality and the Technical Committee downplayed the transformative character of constitutionalism in the context of sexual orientation; eg on the subject of politicians' fear of gay marriages and adoptions the Technical Committee argued "first that rights were necessarily limited, and, second, that the scope of the equality guarantee was a matter for judicial interpretation".

[121] N. 98 above, 368–76.

[122] 371.

[123] 371.

[124] See De Vos, n. 98, 364–6 and Grant, n. 111, 573.

[125] The desirability of this dominant conception of marriage as a heterosexual, monogamous, consensual union is itself being questioned. Mosikatsana, n. 98, 554 argues that "South African society fits the description of hegemony given by the Marxist theorist Antonio Gramsci where a dominant concept of reality is diffused throughout society with the result that the interests and control of the dominant class is maintained by norms and perceptions that have been internalised by all classes".

[126] In *Rees* v. *United Kingdom* (1987) 9 EHHR 56 and *Cossey* v. *United Kingdom* (1991) 13 EHHR 622 transsexuals claimed relief on the basis of Art. 12 of the European Convention on Human Rights (the right to marry). The European Court for Human Rights dismissed both petitions, holding that the Convention sought to protect traditional marriage as the basis of the family and homosexual relationships fall outside of the scope of traditional marriage. See Grant, n. 111, 569 for a critique.

[127] Grant, n. 111, 573 points out that churches have never been forced to marry couples contrary to the tenants of their religion. There is no reason why this will change.

[128] Grant, n. 111, 573 equates this with racist and sexist prejudices: regardless of his/her individual position, an employer is simply not allowed to discriminate on this basis. Hence it is a necessary limitation of his/her individual rights.

[129] Of course, this depends on the vantage point of the speaker. Destigmatisation of homosexuality is a powerful nonmaterial benefit to be gained through recognition of gay relationships. See Grant, n. 111, 570–1.

[130] E.g. in *Layland* v. *Ontario (Minister of Consumer and Commercial Relations)* (1993) 104 DLR (4th) 214 the Canadian court refused to grant a gay couple a marriage licence on the basis that

- If homosexuals are allowed to marry and raise children, the children will turn out to be homosexuals;[131]
- Gays and lesbians are free to marry a person of the opposite sex. It is their own choice not to do so.[132]

All of these reflect a heterosexist bias that may be difficult to justify in terms of the Constitution. It is clear that the courts will need to position themselves in the individual autonomy/public morality debate, for the purposes of which a look at the international position may be useful.

Internationally the concept of gay marriage has been making headway. Hawaii may soon become the first state to issue marriage licences to same-sex couples if the government's appeal against the Circuit Court's decision to uphold the Supreme Court's ruling in the controversial case of *Baehr* v. *Miike*[133] is unsuccessful.[134] In response several American states have pushed through legislation restricting marriage to a heterosexual union and federal legislation has been enacted to define a marriage as a heterosexual union for federal purposes.[135] At the same time gay rights groups are lobbying several states for (increased) recog-

procreation is the main purpose of the marriage institution. Mosikatsana, n. 98, 560 rightly criticises this approach on two grounds: heterosexuals who do not wish to procreate are allowed to marry and it is perfectly possible for lesbian couples to have children by means of artificial insemination. Also see Grant, n. 111, 569, 573.

[131] This objection is dealt with below at 4.

[132] Cf. *Layland* v. *Ontario*, n. 130, 223: "The law does not prohibit marriage by homosexuals, provided it takes place between persons of the opposite sex. Some homosexuals do marry. The fact that many homosexuals do not choose to marry, because they do not want unions with persons of the opposite sex, is the result of their own preferences, not a requirement of the law." This runs contrary to the generally accepted view that homosexuality is not a matter of choice. See Cameron, n. 1, 460; Grant, n. 111, 568–9.

[133] 1996 WL 694235 (Haw. Cir. Ct., 1 st Cir. Dec 3, 1996) (Formerly *Baehr* v. *Lewin*) 852 P2d 44 (Hawaii 1993).

[134] In *Baehr* v. *Miike* the Supreme Court of Hawaii was approached by three same-sex couples to decide on the constitutionality of the state's refusal to grant them a marriage licence. The court rejected their first ground, based on violation of their right to privacy, but upheld the second, namely that the refusal discriminated against them on the basis of their sex contrary to the provisions of art. I, s. 5 (the Equal Protection Clause) of the Hawaii Constitution (1978). See the case discussions by De Vos, n. 98, 378–80 and Mosikatsana, n. 98, 561–3. The government has appealed against the decision and is proposing to amend the constitution to exclude same-sex marriages. The plan involves a referendum on a type of rights-and-benefits package for same-sex couples as a trade-off. Even if the bill is passed, however, it is still possible that the Supreme Court will overturn the referendum and amendment as unconstitutional and legalise same-sex marriage. See "Hawaii Deal Scuttles Wedding Plans", *Sydney Star Observer*, 24 April 1997; "Marriage Law Standoff", *Melbourne Star Observer*, 18 April 1997; and "Landmark Hawaii Ruling on Gay Marriage", *Melbourne Star Observer*, 6 December 1996, 1 (http://www.geocities.com/WestHollywood/3181/ne_pert.html; 11 June 1997).

[135] The Defence of Marriage Act (DOMA), which also allows states to pass legislation prohibiting same-sex marriages contrary to the Full Faith and Credit Clause of the Constitution which would have meant that other states have to recognise same-sex marriages concluded in Hawaii. See "Defence of Marriage Act Passed", *Sydney Star Observer*, 12 September 1996, 4 (http://www.geocities.com/West Hollywood/3181/ne_pert.html; 11 June 1997). 20 US states have so far passed laws restricting marriage to heterosexual couples: Alaska; Arizona; Arkansas; Delaware; Georgia; Idaho; Illinois; Kansas; Maine; Michigan; Missouri; Mississippi; North Carolina; Oklahoma, Pennsylvania; South Dakota; South Carolina; Tennessee; Virginia; and Utah.

nition of same-sex relationships and gay families are gaining ground through the extension of family benefits to same-sex partners.

Europe has also had its share of controversy: the topic of gay marriage has been debated in Netherlands for the past couple of years and is currently being investigated by the Kortmann Commission, which is expected to report back to Parliament in September 1997.

Although our courts are not bound by either American or Dutch law, they are certain to take note of these developments when the time comes to consider an equal marriage rights issue.[136]

A factor that is also certain to influence the gay marriage debate is the divergence of opinion in gay and lesbian circles on whether equal marriage rights are desirable at all.[137] Those opposed to marriage argue that it is a heterosexist institution that requires conformity to heterosexual norms such as monogamy and patriarchy. Exercising the right to marry will therefore reinforce marriage as an oppressive institution.[138] Marriage rights activists argue that homosexual marriage will be regarded as a "second class marriage", which means discrimination against them on the basis of their sexual orientation. Probably the most compelling argument in favour of same-sex marriage is the one based on public legitimacy, in terms of which "recognition of same-sex marriage would help to 'normalise' the status of these relationships, thus both stabilising the relationships themselves and potentially eliminating some of the fears and prejudices surrounding homosexuality in the society at large".[139]

2. Registered partnerships

A second option would be the more limited homosexual marriage-option, which typically involves a type of registered partnership that is recognised by the state and accorded a range of legal effects. Such systems are currently in place in Denmark,[140]

---

[136] In terms of s. 39 of the Constitution. See n. 50 above.

[137] See generally De Vos, n. 98, 357–60. He advocates an approach that follows both long- and short term strategies: "The official acknowledgement that lesbians and gay men form important, positive, useful personal relationships may need to precede rights and entitlements being offered on a different basis", 360. Hence the first step is to gain official recognition of same-sex relationships which emulate heterosexual ones, and then to work for institutional change from within the system.

[138] Mosikatsana, n. 98, 557. This is counterbalanced by the "subversive" argument, formulated as follows by De Vos, n. 98, 358: "They contend that their position is not assimilationist, despite their claim to be treated the same as heterosexual couples, but rather, that their inclusion within the family will radically transform the nature of, and subvert the traditional gender roles within, the institution."

[139] De Vos, n. 98, 358.

[140] Since 1989, in terms of the Registered Partnership Act 372 of 1989, which extends to same-sex couples the same status as married couples, bar the right to adopt children, artificial conception technology and church weddings. See Mosikatsana, n. 98, 564–5; Wockner "Dutch Gays May Marry by Year 2000", *Capital Q* 14 Mar. 1997, 5 and "Danish Gay Couples Tie the Knot", *Melbourne Star Observer*, 15 Nov. 1996, 5 (http://www.geocities.com/WestHollywood/3181/ne_pert.html; 11 June 1997). See also Chapter 24 of this volume.

Greenland,[141] Norway,[142] Sweden,[143] Iceland[144] and Hungary[145] and are being considered in Belgium, France,[146] the Netherlands,[147] Switzerland,[148] Finland,[149] the Czech Republic,[150] Spain,[151] Brazil[152] and the State of Hawaii.[153]

The problem here is that such partnerships do not promote equality as envisioned by section 9 of the Constitution.[154] It may be possible to justify the limitation of legal recognition in terms of section 36.

[141] Wockner, n. 140. Access to adoption, artificial conception technology and church weddings is excluded.

[142] Since 1993: Dunton and Palmberg, n. 2, 43. Access to adoption, artificial conception technology and church weddings is excluded: Wockner, n. 140.

[143] Since 1995: in terms of the Partnership Act 1117 of 1994, which followed on the Homosexual Cohabitees Act 813 of 1987. Homosexual couples are granted the same legal protections as heterosexual cohabitants, but not all the benefits of marriage—e.g. they do not acquire joint parenting or adoption rights. Mosikatsana, n. 98, 563–4. Access to artificial conception technology and church weddings is also excluded.

[144] Since 1996. Like the previous 4 countries, Iceland grants all matrimonial benefits excluding access to adoption, artificial conception and church weddings. However, partners can obtain joint custody of each other's biological children: Wockner, n. 140. Also see "Iceland Recognises Gay Marriages", *Brother Sister*, 13 June 1996, 6 (http://www.geocities.com/WestHollywood/3181/ne_pert.html; 11 June 1997).

[145] Since 1996: Dunton and Palmberg, n. 2, 43. Hungary legalised common-law gay marriage on a mandate from the Constitutional Court but excluded the right to adopt: Wockner, n. 140. Also see "Hungary Marriage Law Due", *Capital Q*, 17 May 1996, 5 (http://www.geocities.com/West Hollywood/3181/ne_pert.html; 11 June 1997).

[146] The Socialist Party introduced a domestic partnership bill that would create "social-union contracts" in the National Assembly on 3 Feb. 1997. See "Partnership Bill Introduced", 14 Feb. 1997, 5 (http://www.geocities.com/WestHollywood/3181/ne_pert.html; 11 June 1997).

[147] See "Netherlands to Act", *Melbourne Star Observer*, 17 Jan. 1997, 5 and "Netherlands Marriage Proposal", *Sydney Star Observer*, 19 Dec. 1996, 6 (http://www.geocities.com/WestHollywood/ 3181/ne_pert.html; 11 June 1997). The proposed law will grant registered couples all the rights and benefits of marriage (particularly the same pension, social security rights, inheritance rights and enforcement of alimony on break-up) except access to adoption.

[148] See "Swiss Partner Legislation Stalled", *Adelaide Gay Times*, 30 Aug. 1996, 7 (http://www.geocities.com/WestHollywood/3181/ne_pert.html; 11 June 1997). The Swiss parliament granted the government a mandate to investigate the legalisation of same-sex relationships in June 1996, but action still has to be taken.

[149] See "Fins Consider Partnership", *Melbourne Star Observer*, 21 Mar. 1997, 5 and "Finland Partnership Bill Introduced", *Adelaide Gay Times*, 21 June 1996 (http://www.geocities.com/West Hollywood/3181/ne_pert.html; 11 June 1997). The proposed measure corresponds to those in place in Denmark, Norway, Iceland, Sweden and Greenland.

[150] Dunton and Palmberg, n. 2, 43.

[151] See "Spanish Partner Bill Loss", *Capital Q*, 27 Mar. 1997, 5 and "Spain Drafts Partnership Law", *Brother Sister*, 26 Dec. 1996, 6 (http://www.geocities.com/WestHollywood/3181/ne_pert. html; 11 June 1997).

[152] See "Break-through in Brazil", *Melbourne Star Observer*, 13 Dec. 1996, 5 and "Church Accepts Partnership Law", *Melbourne Star Observer*, 15 Nov. 1996, 5 (http://www.geocities.com/West Hollywood/3181/ne_pert.html; 11 June 1997). The proposed bill grants same-sex couples spousal rights regarding property, inheritance, health benefits, loans and immigration, but excludes adoption rights.

[153] See n. 134 above.

[154] Mosikatsana, n. 98, 566. Also see Sinclair, *The Law of Marriage* (Vol. 1) (1996) 299–300 and Grant, n. 111, 573.

3. *No official recognition of same-sex unions*

In the third instance it is possible to retain the *status quo*, though there seems to be general consensus that the "sexual orientation" clause will necessitate some recognition of same-sex relationships.

This approach implies that gays and lesbians will have to take care of their own position through such mechanisms as contracts, living wills and powers of attorney. It is very unsatisfactory, since there is great uncertainty regarding the enforceability of such arrangements and they are open to legal challenges from the extended family.[155] Even if valid, these can only account for material benefits.

4. Parenting rights

The problems surrounding gay parenting rights are manifold and varied.[156] For gays and lesbians who already have children from a previous heterosexual relationship, discrimination on the basis of their sexual orientation means losing custody and/or access rights.[157]

Internationally, there are a number of different cases that have dealt with this matter: in 1995 a North Carolina court removed two sons from the custody of their father on the basis that they had been exposed to "improper influences" that could damage them emotionally and socially in living with him and his male lover. The judgment was subsequently overturned by a State Court of Appeal, finding no evidence for that conclusion.[158] In the South African context it is informative to refer to the seminal case of *Van Rooyen* v. *Van Rooyen*[159] where the court dealt with the access rights of a (practising) lesbian mother to her minor children who were approaching their teens. The court explicitly rejected the idea that "the relationship created on the basis of two females" could be called a family[160] and

---

[155] Mosikatsana, n. 98, 557.

[156] Neville John, " 'Pretended Families': On Being a Gay Parent" in Gevisser and Cameron, n. 1, 342 identifies the following: the difficulty of becoming a gay parent; the higher cost of life insurance exacted by insurance companies when they find out about their client's sexual orientation makes it harder to provide for children in the event of early death; the child is likely to be confronted by societal prejudice and homophobia; and it is problematic to explain the nature of a homosexual relationship to a child when relationships are defined in heterosexual terms by society at large. John's version of a family consists of his lover Matthew, his son James, and James's mother, Anne, a lesbian who lives on the other side of a pair of semi-detached houses. James has a room in both units and moves freely between them.

[157] See Lind, n. 1, 488 on the commonplace distortion of a homosexual person's parental rights.

[158] "Gay Dad to Retain Custody of Sons", *Capital Q*, 18 Oct. 1996, 5 (http://www.geocities.com/WestHollywood/3181/ne_child.html; 11 June 1997).

[159] 1994 (2) SA 325. The case was decided before the interim Constitution came into effect on 27 Apr. 1994, which may account partly for the narrow position taken by the court.

[160] At 326J. Cf. the Supreme Court of Canada in *Attorney-General* v. *Mossop*, n. 105, at 676: "The appellant here argues that 'family status' should cover a relationship dependent on a same-sex living arrangement. While some may refer to such a relationship as a 'family', I do not think it has yet reached that status in the ordinary use of language."

attacked a statement by the family counsellor that homosexuality is no longer regarded as a mental illness or a sin.[161] This was followed by a diatribe on the "wrong signals" to which the children would be exposed in a lesbian household.[162] The outcome was an extremely intrusive order, effectively forcing the mother to choose between her (lesbian) lifestyle and unencumbered access to her children.[163] In a fairly similar judgment the Virginia Supreme Court removed Sharon Bottoms's 5-year-old son on the basis that her lesbian lifestyle made her an unfit mother and awarded custody to her mother.[164]

Gays and lesbians who want to adopt children are confronted by several difficulties. Joint adoptions are impossible in terms of section 17(a) of the Child Care Act,[165] in terms of which only married couples may adopt jointly.[166] It is impos-

[161] "I accept the former but nobody has brought that in issue so I do not know why she comments on that. As to whether it is a sin, I defer to her view but perhaps I would prefer to leave that to the Heavenly Father to decide" at 327F.

[162] "The signals are given by the fact that the children know that, contrary to what they should be taught as normal (that it is male and female who share a bed), one finds two females doing this and not obviously for reasons of lack of space on a particular night but as a matter of preference and a matter of mutual emotional attachment. That signal comes from the fact that they know the bedroom is shared. It is detrimental to the child because it is the wrong signal. . . . The wrong signals are given when, if that is true, the applicant wears male underclothes apart from male apparel. The signals come when there are signs of emotional attachment, not only by kissing and hugging as counsel argues, but by the way of speaking, the words of endearment used, the manner in which there is a glance": 329J–330B. The underlying philosophy here is that children will be influenced to form homosexual identities themselves. This is not borne out by research, which has so far found no significant deviation in the gender-role identity of children raised in same-sex households: see Lind, n. 1, 497 and the evidence cited there. In addition, it is a circuitous argument, since the children's homosexual parents were not influenced to lead a heterosexual lifestyle by the heterosexual households in which they were raised. Brits, "Toegang tot kinders, lesbianisme en die konstitusie" [1994] *Tydskrif vir die Hedendaags Romeins-Hollandse Reg* 710 points out that the divorce itself already constituted potentially confusing behaviour and that there is no evidence that the "wrong signals" sent by a lesbian household would aggravate the position.

[163] "Firstly, the applicant can live in whatever way she likes. She has an interest in that and I think the Court should try to respect and protect the interest as well. But, insofar as the interests of the children require it, she will have to make the choice between persisting in those activities or part thereof and having access on a wider basis than would otherwise be permitted. The choice, as in regard to her bedroom life, is hers. She cannot, however, make a choice which limits what should be appropriately done in regard to the children": 329F–G. The court order comprises regulations such as the following: during weekend visits the two women may not share a bedroom; for longer visits during school holidays they may not "share the same residence and/or sleep under the same roof"; and the mother has to "prevent the children being exposed to lesbianism or to have access to all videos, photographs, articles and personal clothing, including male clothing, which may connote homosexuality or lesbianism." According to Brits, n. 163, 712 these regulations have impractical consequences, serve to humiliate the mother and her partner and could be disadvantageous to the children.

[164] Bottoms recently abandoned a three-year fight to get the decision overturned: "Bottoms Gives Up Fight", 23 Aug. 1996 5 (http://www.geocities.com/WestHollywood/3181/ne_child.html; 11 June 1997).

[165] 74 of 1983.

[166] S. 17(a). This is also the position in countries that allow registration of same-sex relationships: see 2 above. British Columbia recently became the first state world-wide to enact a law specifically legalising adoption by same-sex couples: "Victory in Vancouver", *Melbourne Star Observer*, 13 Dec. 1996, 5 (http://www.geocities.com/WestHollywood/3181/ne_child.html; 11 June 1997). In terms of s. 17(b) it is possible for one partner to adopt a child as a single parent, but that would not establish any bond between the child and the other partner. Lind cautions in this regard that due to societal

sible for a gay or lesbian person to adopt his/her partner's child, as the Act determines that such a child may only be adopted by the parent's "spouse".[167] Single parent adoptions are possible, but in the past a person's sexual orientation often disqualified him/her from being considered as adoptive or even foster parent.[168] Where the adoption is successful, it still means that the other partner will have no access rights to that child if the relationship is terminated, even though they may have had a shared family life for a substantial period of time.

Biologically another option is open to lesbians: alternative forms of reproduction. In terms of South African law, artificial insemination[169] is only available to married couples[170] and self-insemination is illegal.[171] Even if they succeed, there will be no family relationship between the non-biological mother and the child.[172] This means no right of access to the child if the relationship is terminated, irrespective of how long the child knew her as "mother";[173] no duty to contribute towards the child's maintenance,[174] even where conception was a joint decision;

prejudice against gay parenting "[g]ay individuals who wish to adopt as single persons would be wise to hide both their sexual orientation and their relationships from the courts": n. 1, 489.

[167] S. 17(c). In all other cases the biological bond between parent and child will be severed. Hence it is not possible for a child to legally have two mommies or daddies.

[168] See De Vos, n. 98, 362–3 and Lind, n. 1, 489. There are indications that the welfare organisations have mellowed somewhat in this regard. See e.g. Duvenhage, "Lesbian Couple Gets First Official Adoption", *Weekly Mail & Guardian*, 11 August 1996, and Van der Westhuizen, "Kan homoseksuele pare kinders aanneem?", *Beeld*, 23 Aug. 1994. Queensland recently decided to ban single men and lesbian couples from fostering children: Clacher, "QLD to Ban Gay Foster Parents", *Melbourne Star Observer*, 29 November 1996, 3 (http://www.geocities.com/WestHollywood/3181/ ne_child.html; 11 June 1997).

[169] Lind, n. 1, 490 strongly objects against the use of the word "artificial", stating that there is nothing artificial about fertilisation once it has taken place. He uses the phrase "alternative technologies of reproduction".

[170] Reg. 8(1) (GN R1182 in GG 10283 of 20 June 1996) issued in terms of the Human Tissue Act 65 of 1983. S. 37(1)(e)(vii) (as amended by s. 25(d) of the Human Tissue Amendment Act 51 of 1989) empowers the responsible minister to issue regulations regarding artificial insemination. The countries that allow registration of same-sex relationships also ban access to artificial conception technologies. South Australia and Tasmania grant same-sex couples and single women access to IVF so long as infertility is evident: "No IVF Ban on Single Women & Gay Couples in South Australia", *Adelaide Gay Times*, 4 April 1997, 3, and "IVF Access in Tasmania", *Melbourne Star Observer*, 21 March 1997, 3, but Victoria restricts the opportunity to heterosexual couples, irrespective of their marital status: Pollard "Victoria Bans Lesbian IVF", *Sydney Star Observer*, 24 April 1997, 5 (http://www.geocities.com/WestHollywood/3181/ne_child.html; 11 June 1997).

[171] Regulation 3 GN R1182 in GG 10283 of 20 June 1986. In terms of this regulation only a medical doctor may effect artificial insemination.

[172] See Lind, n. 1, 490. A New York Family Court judge has allowed two lesbians to cross-adopt each other's daughters, conceived by using the same sperm donor: "Adoption Breakthrough", *Melbourne Star Observer*, 14 February 1997, 5 (http://www.geocities.com/WestHollywood/3181/ ne_child.html; 11 June 1997).

[173] Our common law allows visitation rights to grandparents and other family members where the circumstances warrant it, but so far not even the biological father of an illegitimate child can claim visitation rights on this basis. Hence it will be very difficult for the non-biological lesbian "mother" to persuade the court that she is entitled to visitation rights on the basis of the common law.

[174] In a landmark decision a New South Wales court ordered a lesbian woman to pay a lump sum of more than $150,000 to her former lover as child support for two children conceived by means of artificial insemination during the subsistence of the relationship: Magnusson, "Dyke Appeal! 'Partner is Straight' says Lesbian", *Melbourne Star Observer*, 9 Feb. 1996, 1 (http://www.geocities.com/West Hollywood/3181/ne_child.html; 11 June 1997).

and if the biological mother dies, her partner will not automatically become the child's guardian.

In this regard the Canadian case of *Re the Adoption by K and B*[175] is informative. Four lesbian couples jointly approached the court for the adoption of seven children conceived by means of artificial insemination during the subsistence of the relationships. They were faced by the same problems that same-sex couples encounter in South-Africa. In terms of the Child and Family Services Act[176] adoption is possible by either a married couple or a single person. The latter provision opens up the possibility for gay and lesbian adoptions, but as in South Africa all biological bonds between the birth mother and the child are terminated unless the child is adopted by the mother's spouse. The Ontario Provincial Division ruled that the definition of "spouse" as "a person of the opposite sex" in terms of the Human Rights Code is in conflict with the equality provision in the Canadian Charter of Rights and Freedoms and determined that homosexual partners qualify as spouses for the purposes of adoption under the Child and Family Services Act. The court's approach should provide good guidance to our courts when dealing with such a matter: apart from similar adoption provisions there, we share a common constitutional context. In fact, it should be much easier for a South African court to come to the same conclusion, as we need not work with an analogous ground of discrimination—sexual orientation is a specifically enumerated ground of non-discrimination in terms of section 9.[177]

Surrogate motherhood remains the primary way for a gay man to have a child that is genetically related to him.[178] The position regarding surrogate motherhood is still very problematic in South Africa.[179] Such a contract will almost certainly be held to be *contra bonos mores* and unenforceable. This means that the parties will have to work through an adoption agency—which again raises the problem of the couple not being able to adopt jointly.[180] Surrogate motherhood for commercial gain will certainly be out of the question, as trade in babies is not allowed. Hence it boils down to a normal open adoption where the mother knows the adoptive parent but may not receive any financial gain in the process.

When formulating judicial policies on all of these, the first and primary consideration must remain the best interests of the child in question, which are "of

[175] (1995) 31 CRR (2D) 151 (Ont Prov Div).

[176] RSO 1990, c C11.

[177] For a comprehensive case discussion, see Mosikatsana, "Comment on *The adoption by K and B, re* (1995) 31 CRR (2D) 151 (Ont Prov Div)".

[178] Lind's claim that this is the sole way of effecting such offspring (n. 1, 490) does not take into account the possibility of private agreements between lesbians and gay men to have a joint child, such as is evidenced by Neville John's story. See n. 156 above.

[179] See, generally, Clark, "Surrogate Motherhood: Comment on the South African Law Commission's *Report on Surrogate Motherhood* (Project 65)" [1993] *SALJ* 769 and Tager, "Surrogate Motherhood, Legal Dilemma" [1986] *SALJ* 381.

[180] Also see Lind, n. 1, 490–1. Cf. the report on potential difficulties faced by a Scottish male couple who paid £10,000 for an American baby carried by a surrogate mother. Although they are listed as the fathers on the Manhattan birth certificate, they will probably have to return the baby if the mother so requests, since gay couples cannot adopt legally in the UK: "Gay Male Couple Buy Baby", 13 Sept. 1996, 5 (http://www.geocities.com/WestHollywood/3181/ne_child.html; 11 June 1997).

paramount importance" in terms of section 28 of the Constitution. However, the contents of these "best interests" are often merely a reflection of societal prejudices and value-judgements. It remains to be proved that a loving homosexual home cannot provide the same stability and security as a heterosexual one.[181] In any event, we are often faced with a less "ideal" alternative that calls for a pragmatic solution. By at least considering gays and lesbians as prospective parents irrespective of their sexual orientation, many children could be afforded the opportunity of an otherwise unattainable stable and secure family life.

CONCLUSION

With the "sexual orientation" clause entrenched in its Constitution, South Africa is at the forefront of the international trend of developing a human rights culture for dealing with gays and lesbians.[182] Many legal anomalies remain and it is not yet certain how far the legislature and the courts will be prepared to go in the quest for equal treatment on the basis of sexual orientation. Certainly the gay family has a claim to legal recognition and protection rivalled by no other constitution in the world and family law is poised to take a prime position in the human rights arena. "Family", in the inflexible context known to us for so long, may well present the perfect vehicle for the ushering in of a new dispensation that treats an individual as a complete person rather than the embodiment of a societal prejudice. This is in accordance with the very spirit of the constitution-making process which aimed at unifying a nation torn apart on the basis of arbitrary distinctions.

---

[181] In *Re Adoption by K and B* (n. 175) the court found no evidence that heterosexual parents are better with the physical, psychological, emotional or intellectual needs of children than homosexual parents. The court also concluded that the parents' sexual orientation is not an indicator of the sexual orientation of children in their care. See Mosikatsana, n. 177, 585–6.

[182] Other important role-players include the European Parliament who, in 1994, adopted a resolution calling for all member states to abolish legal criminalisation and discrimination against gays and lesbians: "Resolution on Equal Rights for Homosexuals and Lesbians in the EC", A3-0028/94.

26

Parental Rights and Social Responsibility in American Child Protection Law

SANFORD N. KATZ

INTRODUCTION

Child abuse and neglect are not unknown in American social history as far back as the founding of the country.[1] Children have suffered at the hands of parents, teachers, social agencies and even the state, although the suffering has often been justified as in the child's best interests. A law in the Massachusetts Bay Colony during the seventeenth century and taken directly from the book of Deuteronomy provided that if a son did not "obey the his voice of his father", he could be stoned.[2] Children were as vulnerable in certain respects as enslaved people.

During the eighteenth and nineteenth centuries children were exploited in the workforce, and it took the child labour laws of the nineteenth century to free children from the control of their employers who took advantage of the children subjecting them to all sorts of dangers. During the nineteenth century American states enacted child neglect laws that provided them with the legal basis for intervening into the parent–child relation. Some of those laws are still on the books today.[3] During the nineteenth and early twentieth centuries, many children found on the streets in Boston, New York and Philadelphia, whether homeless or not, were subject to being rounded up and sent to the mid-west and west where they were sold to farmers to assist them in their work. These children who were later to be called "the children of the orphan trains" were basically kidnapped by social service agencies in the name of advancing children's welfare. The agencies said that the children would be freed from the foul air of the cities and experience the openness of the mid-west and west where the air was clean and the opportunities limitless. Such statements were, of course, nonsense.

---

[1] See Jeanne M. Giovannoni and Rosina M. Becerra, *Defining Child Abuse* (The Free Press, 1979); Shippen L. Page, "The Law, the Lawyer, and Medical Aspects of Child Abuse", in *Child Abuse* (Eli Newberger, (ed.,)) (Little, Brown and Company, 1982), 105–11.

[2] See Sanford N. Katz and William A. Schroeder, "Disobeying a Father's Voice: A Comment on *Commonwealth* v. *Brasher*", 57 *Mass LQ* 43 (1973).

[3] See Sanford N. Katz, Melba McGrath and Ruth-Arlene W. Howe, *Child Neglect Laws in America* (American Bar Association Press, 1976).

Children of the orphan trains were lied to and sold to farmers for farm hands or kitchen maids.[4]

Throughout the history of child protection, there has been a struggle between parental authority and state responsibility.[5] The rhetoric has been that parents have the basic right to raise their children as they see fit, subject to their not over-stepping the bounds of reasonableness in all aspects of child rearing. Parental rights are not unlimited. Historically the state, the ultimate parent who looks after all the children in society under the *parens patriae* concept, has a right to subject parents to public scrutiny and legal examination. In the United States, child protection is basically the responsibility of the states and state legislation in the form of the criminal law and child abuse and neglect laws that govern the parent–child relationship. The executive and legislative branches of the federal government also play a role in child protection. The executive branch through the US Department of Health and Human Services provides model laws for states to adopt if they wish and technical services in order for states to conform to federal legislation including social security. The legislative branch through the US Congress enacts laws that basically fund child welfare programmes but provide certain requirements for states to fulfill in order to meet federal mandates. State and federal courts hear cases involving child protection depending on the issues involved. Normally, a state court is the venue for a child protection case brought under a state statute, e.g. child neglect and abuse law, a domestic violence law, criminal law, but if a federal statute is involved then the federal courts have jurisdiction to hear the case.

In this chapter I shall explore the struggle that exists between parental rights to rear their children and the state's responsibility to look after the best interests of all children. I shall begin by examining the historical basis for the state's intervention into the parent–child relationship, then I shall briefly summarise the federal government's direct and indirect influence on the child protection systems in the states.

THE CONCEPT OF PUNISHMENT

In American law, parents have used "parental immunity" in criminal and civil actions brought by the state's (or county depending on the jurisdiction) attorney or a department of social services in actions against them for child abuse. The parents' argument usually is stated in terms of the their right to discipline their children according to their own religious beliefs or culture. Over the past

---

[4] For a full discussion of the orphan train children, see Marilyn Irvin Holt, *The Orphan Trains— Placing Out in America* (University of Nebraska Press, 1992).
[5] See Sanford N. Katz, *When Parents Fail* (1971); Michael S. Wald, "State Intervention on Behalf of 'Neglected' Children", 27 *Stan. L Rev.* 985 (1975).

century, parents have become less and less successful in justifying their abusive behavior on religious grounds.

The maxim "Spare the rod and spoil the child", thought to be based on the Old Testament, but actually from Samuel Butler's poem, "Hudibras", has been part of American child rearing for centuries.[6] It has even been incorporated into American law. The idea is that parents and those in authority over children have the right to punish a child in order to inculcate values of obedience and respect. In the nineteenth century North Carolina case of *State* v. *Jones*,[7] Mr Jones was tried for an assault and battery on 16-year-old Mary C. Jones. During the trial, the young woman testified that Mr Jones had a severe temper and when angry whipped her without any reason. She said that on one occasion he gave her:

"about twenty-five blows with a switch, or small limb, about the size of one's thumb or forefinger with such force as to raise whelks upon her back, and then going into the house, he soon returned and gave her five blows more with the same switch, choked her, and threw her violently to the ground, causing dislocation of her thumb joint."

Mr Jones' defence, substantiated by his wife, Mary's step-mother, was that Mary was:

"habitually disobedient, had several times stolen money, and was chastised at the time spoken of for stealing some cents from her father; that he never whipped her except for correction, and this he was often compelled to do for that purpose, and that had never administered punishment under the impulse of high temper or from malice."

The judge's instruction to the jury expressed the North Carolina law at the time:

"a parent had the right to inflict punishment on his child for the purpose of correction, but the punishment must not be 'excessive and cruel,' nor must it be 'to gratify malicious motives;' that if the whipping was such as described by the daughter, there would arise a question as to the severity and extent of the punishment; that if the jury was convinced that it was cruel and excessive, the defendant would be guilty; that it was not necessary that it should result in a permanent injury to her, and if it was *excessive and cruel* it would be sufficient to make the defendant guilty."

Mr Jones was found guilty.

In setting aside the trial court's verdict, Chief Justice Smith of the North Carolina Supreme Court stated the nineteenth century view of family privacy that would allow for parents to have enormous discretion in raising their children and at the same time minimise governmental supervision. He wrote:

" . . . It will be observed that the test of the defendant's criminal liability is the infliction of a punishment '*cruel and excessive*' and this it is left to the jury without the aid of any rule of law for their guidance to determining.

---

[6] Prof. Philip Greven discusses the religious roots of punishment in his excellent study, *Spare the Child* (Alfred A. Knopf, Inc., 1990). See particularly 48.

[7] 95 N.C. 588 (1886).

It is quite obvious that this would subject every exercise of parental authority in the correction and discipline of children—in other words, domestic government—to the supervision and control of jurors, who might, in a given case, deem the punishment disproportionate to the offence, and unreasonable and excessive. It seems to us, that such a rule would tend, if not to subvert family government, greatly to impair its efficiency, and remove restraints upon the conduct of children. If, whenever parental authority is used in chastising them, it could be a subject of judicial inquiry whether the punishment was cruel and excessive—that is, beyond the demerits of the disobedience or misconduct, and the father himself exposed to a criminal prosecution at the instance of the child, in defending himself from which he would be compelled to lift the curtain from the scenes of home life, and exhibit a long series of acts of insubordination, disobedience and ill-doing—it would open the door to a flood of irreparable evils far transcending that to be remedied by a public prosecution. Is it consistent with the best interests of society, that an appeal should thus lie to the Court from an act of parental discipline, severe though it may be, and unmerited by the particular offence itself, perhaps but one of a series of evincing stubbornness and incorrigibility in the child, and the father punished because the jurors think it cruel and immoderate?"

Although the opinion is short, it includes the assumption that physical punishment may reflect parental affection. The linkage of physical pain with affection may have been an acceptable proposition in the nineteenth century but it is clearly thought to be misguided today. For example, Chief Justice Smith stated that physical punishment as a manifestation of parental affection "must be tolerated as an incident to the relation, which human laws cannot wholly remove or redress". He adopted the position taken by another judge in another case who wrote that the relationships of master and apprentice, teacher and pupil, parent and child and husband and wife should not be interfered with by trivial complaints "not because these relations are not subject to law, but because the evils of publicity would be greater than the evil involved in the trifles complained of; and because they ought to be left to family government".

Following that policy, the North Carolina Supreme Court held that although "the punishment seems to have been needlessly severe", it refused to consider it a criminal act, believing that "it belongs to the domestic rather than legal power, to a domain into which the penal law is reluctant to enter, unless induced by an imperious necessity". It is this kind of attitude that has given currency to the statement that the family can be an enclosure for all kinds of violence between husband and wife and parent and child, and one in which the state (the police) is reluctant to enter.

In many of the cases dealing with punishment, defendants often invoke the Bible for support of the proposition that corporal punishment is justified by the Old and New Testament and thus proper parental conduct. As late as 1988 in a South Carolina case, the parents' lawyer quoted Proverbs: "Withhold not correction from the child; for if thou beatest him with the rod, he shall not die" to justify the father's beating of his 13-year-old daughter while her mother stood by because the daughter had lied about her whereabouts instead of telling her parents that she had been to a friend's party. Her punishment included the father's whipping her with his belt and beating her until she was black and blue. He also slapped her in the face resulting in his daughter's having ringing in her ears for a day.

The case arose because of the parents' having been reported to a social service agency for child abuse. The agency investigated the case and thought the allegations serious enough to bring an action under the South Carolina child protection law. The lower court found that there had been child abuse and ordered both parents to participate in an agency counseling programme.

To support the defendants' argument that the Old Testament justified punishment a clergyman acted as a witness, and testified that the Bible was the "ultimate binding authority". The defendants claimed that the free exercise of religion was constitutionally guaranteed to them. The South Carolina court addressed the argument with the following:

> "the First Amendment embraces two concepts: the freedom to believe and the freedom to act. The first is absolute, but the second is not. The law cannot regulate what people believe, but the law can regulate how people act, even if how they act is based on what they believe . . . Indeed if the law were otherwise, the father in this case could beat his daughter into submission."

In the concluding paragraph the court stated:

> "We believe the mother and father love their daughter and, despite what had happened, we believe she loves them. We also believe the mother and father can, if they will, learn to express their love in better ways, and the child can, if she will, learn to obey her parents—a requirement, coincidentally, of both the Bible and the law."

The court did not accept the parents' justification. However, equating affection with physical pain is a curious child-rearing principle. It suggests that children will learn positive behaviour through experiencing pain. There appears to be no contemporary research results that confirm this conclusion.[8]

To what extent has the Bible justified corporal punishment? Professor Greven argues that while the Old Testament is replete with references to physical violence and punishment against children, the New Testament generally speaks of love, emphasising paternal restrain and advocating the affectionate nurturing of children rather than punishing them. Nowhere does he find corporal punishment ascribed either to the teaching of Jesus or to Paul.[9]

Culture was used as a defence in the New York case of *Dumpson* v. *Daniel M.*[10] In that case the New York Commissioner of Social Services brought an action to remove three children from their mother's and father's home because of the father's use of excessive force in punishing one of them. The father had allegedly struck his 7-year old son "with his hands, a belt and his feet". The result was that the boy suffered a cut lip and bruises.

---

[8] See Greven, n. 6 above, at 155 and 174.
[9] *Id.* at 46–54.
[10] N.Y. Law J., at 17, c. 7 (16 Oct. 1974).

An interesting fact in the case (for cultural understanding) was that the father was a taxi driver and was taking courses at Brooklyn College in order to become an engineer. His wife was a high school teacher of chemistry and biology in the New York school system. Thus the parents were educated and upwardly mobile.

The father claimed that his actions were a response to his son's poor school behaviour, which he said brought shame on the family. The father said that according to his Nigerian culture, "if a child misbehaves in school and causes shame to the family, the parent has the duty to punish immediately and in any manner he sees fit". He further testified that in Nigeria if a "villager is summoned to court for any reason, he cannot return home until he has purified himself by way of a special cleansing ritual. No matter what the reason, it is a cause for embarrassment and shame if one has to appear in court."

The New York Family Court decided that the father's form of corporal punishment was "excessive" and as such would be considered "neglect" under New York law. The judge ordered that the father and mother should undergo counselling; that the father should not physically punish his children; and three of the four children who had been temporarily removed from the custody of their parents should be returned to their parents' home. Further the court ordered that the child who had been beaten should remain under the care of the Department for the present.

The case raises interesting questions about the role of custom and culture in defining child rearing and the extent to which American law will tolerate or even sanction customs that deviate from the dominant American methods of child-rearing if such methods can be defined. Eunice Uzokike states that "the Nigerian Criminal Code authorizes parents and school teachers to inflict a 'blow or other force' for the purpose of correcting children under the age of sixteen".[11] The author then states that Nigerian law does not authorize physical punishment that would "exceed reasonable physical chastisement".

According to Uzokike, children are considered the personal property of their parents in Nigerian culture and consequently incidents of physical force on children are ordinarily not of great concern to the police who would be the proper authority to intervene. As at 1990, Uzokike states that there have been no recorded cases of physical abuse in Nigeria.

If Uzokike is correct about Nigerian culture, the father in *Dumpson* v. *Daniel M.* was truthful about the treatment of children in Nigeria. Uzokike makes the point, however, that physical punishment is more prominent among the poor, uneducated, and illiterate in Nigeria. The father in the *Dumpson* v. *Daniel M.* case did not have any of those characteristics.

---

[11] Eunice Uzodike, "Child Abuse and Neglect in Nigeria—Socio-Legal Aspects", 4 *International JL & Family* 83, 86 (1990).

DEFINING CHILD ABUSE

Is there a dominant American practice of child rearing that could be used to define appropriate punishment and differentiate it from child abuse? The answer is probably no. The research that comes closest as to determining whether there is a consensus on what kind of parental misconduct should be reported to social service agencies for investigation to determine if there has been child abuse is that conducted by Giovannoni and Becerra in the late 1970s.[12] They reported that child maltreatment is "not an absolute entity but, rather, is socially defined and cannot be divorced from the social contexts in which it occurs".[13] In trying to discover whether there was a consensus on the definition of child maltreatment, the researchers developed vignettes and presented them to lay persons and professionals to determine how they would categorize the conduct of the parents in each vignette. Giovannoni and Becarra reported that:

"Although the respondents concurred on the boundaries of different kinds of mistreatment, there was not always agreement about the valuations placed on each. Community members saw most kinds of mistreatment as more serious than did professionals, and among professionals, lawyers especially dissented from the other groups, generally regarding mistreatment as less serious than the others did. However, there was amazing similarity in the judgments of the relative seriousness of different *kinds* of mistreatment.

There were some notable exceptions to this general pattern. Among the professionals, police and social workers saw most kinds of mistreatment as more serious than did lawyers or pediatricians. This difference in opinion was most clearly related to the roles they play in the protective network as gatekeepers who make the initial decision as to whether a situation will be defined as one of mistreatment at all. This role provided them with particular kinds of responsibilities and experiences. Among the community respondents, differences in opinions related to ethnicity and social class. Contrary to common speculation, Black and Hispanic respondents, and those of lower socioeconomic statuses exhibited greater concern about all kinds of mistreatment. Further, socioeconomic status to the he respondents, while shown to be related to their perceptions of mistreatment, was not a factor that operated independently of their ethnicity. Rather, the ways in which social class and cultural values affected opinions about mistreatment were demonstrated to be very complex and not uniform across all ethnic groups."[14]

The Giovannoni and Becerra study is almost 20 years old. Yet it confirms generally held beliefs about the lack of uniformity in defining child abuse. The debate over definitions and the question of state intervention in the parent–child relationship took place in the early 1970s and was prompted by the federal government's concern about violence in the home that occurred in the 1960s.

---

[12] Jeanne M. Giovannoni and Rosina M. Becerra, *Defining Child Abuse* (The Free Press, 1979).
[13] *Id.*, at 239.
[14] *Id.*, at 241.

Indeed, violence in the home was a phenomenon that was not widely studied or taken very seriously before about 1970 although reported divorce cases are filled with wife abuse that was not even discussed in terms of domestic violence, but whether the abuse justified a ground for divorce. Husbands could beat up their wives or subject them to sexual assaults with legal immunity for all practical purposes because of the old notion that wives were essentially the property of their husbands as well as the adage that a man is king in his household. Wives were supposed to serve their husbands and not question his authority.[15] Children were in a worse position than their mothers because children could be dominated by both parents and could be subjected to all sorts of abusive conduct in the name of parental rights. Domestic violence, whether between adults or adults and children, is really an expression of power and aggression over the dependent and vulnerable.

THE ROLE OF THE FEDERAL GOVERNMENT

Model Mandatory Child Abuse Reporting Statute

It is interesting to observe that child abuse and neglect became important in the public consciousness about 20 years before violence against women. In 1962 the research of Dr C. Henry Kempe's and his associates in Colorado was published and their article that coined the phrase "battered child syndrome" was widely read and recognised by both the medical, psychiatric and social work communities.[16] About the same time Children's Bureau of the then United States Department of Health, Education, and Welfare (now called the Department of Health and Human Services) held a conference to discuss what the legal response should be to the phenomenon that Dr Kempe and his associates described. In 1963 the Model Mandatory Child Abuse Reporting Law developed from the conference.

To develop a mandatory child abuse reporting law was not without problems. It affected not only family privacy but it also was at first seen as an intrusion into the confidential relationship between doctor and patient. Thus the first laws were limited in scope and in the number of professional persons who were required to report abuse. As the concept of reporting was accepted, the number of mandated reporters grew.[17] For example, initially only physicians and surgeons were mandated to report in California. Now it can be said that mandated reporters often

---

[15] These issues are discussed in Walter O. Weyrauch, Sanford N. Katz and Frances Olsen, *Cases and Materials on Family Law—Legal Concepts and Changing Human Relationships* (1994) 212, 348. For an illustration of wife battering that is not even discussed as such, see *Warner v. Warner*, 76 Idaho 399, 283 P.2d 931 (1955) reproduced and commented on in that book.

[16] C. Henry Kempe *et al.*, "The Battered Child Syndrome", 18 *Journal of the American Medical Association* 17 (1962).

[17] See Douglas J. Besharov, "Gaining Control Over Child Abuse Reports", 48 *Public Welfare* 34 (1990).

include all health care professionals, school personnel, day care operators and even film developers.[18] Some statutes include a catch-all category such as other persons who regularly come into contact with children in the scope of their employment[19] and at least one state includes anyone with reasonable cause to believe a child has been abused.[20]

One of the major issues that met with resistance in persuading states to enact mandatory reporting laws was the extent to which those mandated to report were protected from cases where initial observation or diagnosis of the child's injury later proved to be something other than abuse. The resolution of that issue was to give immunity to mandated reporters whose report to the appropriate agency was made in good faith. For those mandated reporters who failed to report criminal sanctions (usually the crime is a misdemeanor with a fine and/or jail sentence) were put in place.

The basic elements of mandatory reporting statutes include:

1. definition of reportable conditions;
2. persons required to report;
3. degree of certainty reporters must reach;
4. sanctions for failure to report;
5. immunity for good faith reports;
6. abrogation of certain communication privileges; and
7. delineation of reporting procedures.[21]

Although there is no absolute uniformity in all American reporting laws, their passage has, to some extent, accomplished one of its primary goals, which is to make child abuse a public concern. The studies about child abuse reporting laws were mostly completed in the 1980s. One study indicates that nearly ten times the number of cases reported in 1965 were reported in 1985, totalling 1.5 million.[22] According to a US Census Bureau abstract, reports of child abuse increased from 669,000 in 1976 to 2,086,000 in 1986.[23] More than 2.5 million reports are expected each year during this decade.[24] Yet, studies show that a majority of child abuse and neglect cases remain unreported. And there is the problem of unsubstantiated reports, which comprise about one half million each year.[25]

[18] See, e.g., Cal. Penal Code §§11165, 11166 (1990).
[19] *Ibid.*
[20] Alaska Stat. §47 17 020.
[21] Educational Commission of the States, Report No. 106. *Trends in Child Protection Laws—1977,* (1978) at 18–21 app.
[22] See generally Douglas J. Besharov, "Doing Something About Child Abuse: The Need to Narrow the Grounds for State Intervention", 8 *Harv. JL Pub. Pol'y* 540, 542–50 (1985).
[23] Bureau of the Census, US Depar't of Commerce, *Statistical Abstracts of the United States* (1992), 186.
[24] US Advisory Board on Child Abuse & Neglect, Office of Human Development Services, *Critical First Steps in a National Emergency* (1990), 2, 15.
[25] See Besharov, *supra* n. 27 at 556–7; US Dep't. of Health & Human Services, *Study Findings: National Study of Incidence and Severity of Child Abuse and Neglect* (DHHS 1981), 34; Amy Buchele-Ash *et al.*, "Forensic and Law Enforcement Issues in the Abuse and Neglect of Children with Disabilities", 19 *Mental & Physical Disability L Rep.* 115 (1995).

CHILD ABUSE PREVENTION AND TREATMENT ACT OF 1974

About a decade after the US Department of Health, Education, and Welfare proposed its Model Mandatory Child Abuse Reporting Law, the United States Congress took action in the field of child protection. Under the leadership of Minnesota Senator Walter Mondale who would later become the United States Vice President, Congress held hearings on the plight of abused children. After the hearings he later wrote that he found the evidence of child abuse at his hearings to be "horrifying".[26] Through his efforts, Congress passed the Child Abuse Prevention and Treatment Act of 1974. The Act had two central elements—the founding of a National Centre on Child Abuse and Neglect and the establishment of minimum standards for state child protection system. Basically the Act gave Congress the power to appropriate money to undertake research, training and technical assistance to states in order to raise the level of services to children. In order to receive money, states had to conform to federal mandates. These mandates included the requirement that states provide for the reporting of known and suspected instances of child abuse and neglect, and that states amend their existing reporting laws to expand the group of persons required to report and to the increased attention for specific types of abuse.[27]

As one studies the role that government now plays in the area of child protection, one comes away with the observation that punishing one's own children, once a private family matter, if interpreted as abuse by neighbours, school personnel or governmental officials can become a public matter. That is to say, when a parent strikes a child for being disobedient and the injury that the child sustains is seen by a third person (e.g., a school teacher or a school nurse) who thinks the injury requires medical attention, the result might be the reporting of the incident to a social service agency. In cases defined as serious by agency officials, the result may be for the parents and the child to become involved with child protection process. Such a process might conclude a court hearing and a disposition that may involve the child's removal from her home and her placement with foster parents.

THE ROLE OF GOVERNMENT

The role of government in child protection is enormous and the power of a judge who decides child protection cases is profound. Often, the concept of *parens patriae* is invoked not necessarily to justify the governmental role, but to explain it.[28] With

---

[26] Walter Mondale, Introductory Comments, 54 *Chi.-Kent L Rev.* 535, 536 (1978).

[27] See generally, Douglas J. Besharov, "The Legal Aspects of Reporting Known and Suspected Child Abuse and Neglect", 23 *Vill. L Rev.* 458 (1978).

[28] For a discussion of *parens patriae* and its origins, see Homer H. Clark, Jr., *The Law of Domestic Relations in the United States* (2nd edn., West Publishing Co., 1988), 335; Katz, n. 5 above, at 5 n. 17.

all that power, does the government have any responsibilities? To help answer that question, one should look to history.

In his study of wardship jurisdiction,[29] John Seymour explains the origins of the law of wardship and its relationship to the concept of *parens patriae*. He discusses the conflict in English cases between those judges who believed that the Chancery Court judge stood in the shoes of the parents and those who held to the idea that the jurisdiction of the Chancery Court was wider than parents and was not derivative from parents but from the Crown. Seymour quotes from Lord Donaldson's observation in *Re R*: the jurisdiction of the Chancery Court "is not derivative from the parents' rights and responsibilities, but derives from, or is, the delegated performance of the duties of the Crown to protect its subjects and particularly children".[30] In other words, with the invocation of *parens patriae* comes the duty to protect children. But what kind of duty did Lord Donaldson mean?

From the 1960s until the 1980s, child welfare specialists and American legislators interested in the plight of children struggled with the question of what can government do to prevent the break-up of families and if such a phenomenon occurs, how to reorganise them in such a way as to facilitate a child's entry into another family where the child can be safe and thrive. Leadership from the federal government took the form of the US Department of Health, Education, and Welfare providing a Model Mandatory Child Abuse and Neglect Reporting Law,[31] Model State Subsidised Adoption Act[32] and the Model Act to Free Children for Permanent Placement.[33] Congress enacted the Child Abuse Prevention and Treatment Act of 1974[34] and the Adoption Assistance Act of 1980.[35]

During the 1960s and 1970s, when government intervened in the parent–child relationship such intrusion was often the result of a report of child abuse. Once the child was removed from her parent's control, she was often placed in foster care. In many instances, public social service agencies saw their job as having been completed since the child was now safe. Little thought was given to the ultimate disposition of the case. The reason was that there were so many cases that agencies were just not able to process all of them or even to keep track of where the child had been placed and the duration of the placement.

---

[29] John Seymour, "Parens Patriae and Wardship Powers: Their Nature and Origins", 14 *Oxford J Legal Studies* 159 (1994).

[30] *Ibid.*

[31] Children's Bureau, US Department of Health, Education & Welfare, "The Abused Child-Principles and Suggested Language for the Reporting of the Physically Abused Child "(1963).

[32] Reproduced in Sanford N. Katz, and Ursula M. Gallagher, "Subsidized Adoption in America", 10 *Fam. LQ* 1, 11 (1976). The brief summary of the Act is based on that article.

[33] The Act is reproduced in Sanford N. Katz, "Freeing Children for Permanent Placement Through a Model Act", 12 *Fam. LQ* 203 (1978). The brief summary of the Act is based on that article.

[34] Pub. L. No. 96–272, 94 Stat. 500 (codified as 42 U.S.C. §§ 620–28 & 670–79).

[35] Pub. L. No. 96–272, 94 Stat. 500 (codified as amended in scattered sectiions of 42 U.S.C.). This paper will discuss aspects of §§ 620–28 & 670–79.

Out of the research that revealed the growing number of children in foster care and the lack of services provided for them came the Model Subsidized Adoption Act and the Model Act to Free Children for Permanent Placement.[36] To the question, why were so many children in foster care, one response that was often given was that the longer a child stayed in foster care, the more difficult it was to place her for adoption and those persons who might be willing to adopt the foster child were not financially able to do so. Another response was that the children who might be able to be adopted were not legally free.

The Model Subsidised Adoption Act was designed to provide a financial benefit for children who were candidates for adoption but for whom adoptive parents could not be easily found. Usually such children, labelled children with special needs, were in foster care and were medically handicapped, had been abused or neglected and were physically and emotionally scarred, were part of a sibling group, were older children, perhaps from ages 6 to 12, or from an ethnic group and difficult to place. The theory was that once these children were approved for a subsidy, they would become attractive candidates for adoptive parents. During the years that adoption subsidies have been made, there has been only marginal progress if any.

The Model Act to Free Children for Permanent Placement was meant to provide state legislatures with a model to replace their outdated termination of parental rights provisions. It had three goals: (1) to provide judicial procedures for freeing children for adoption or other placement by terminating parental rights; (2) to promote permanent placements of children freed from their parents; and (3) to insure that each party's constitutional rights and interests were protected.

Although state legislatures did not adopt the Model Act to Free Children for Permanent Placement as they did the Model Subsidised Adoption Act, the permanent placement model act along with social science research dealing with the idea of the need for permanency planning for children in foster care provoked the states and Congress to face the crisis in foster care. The Congress responded by enacting the Child Abuse Prevention and Treatment Act of 1974.

The federal government's role in child welfare is basically two fold: (1) to provide technical assistance to states by developing model legislation for states to use in their law reform; and (2) to provide financial assistance for federal or federal and state child welfare programmes, but with the requirement that the states fulfill certain requirements. It is because of the second role that the federal government can influence state legislation. To put it bluntly, if the states do not enact

---

[36] The number of children in foster care rose sharply after promulgation of the Model Child Abuse and Neglect Reporting Act, reaching 296,000 in 1966. By 1977 more than 500,000 children were living in foster care. The 1966 figures were found in David Fanshel and E. Shinn, *Children in Foster Care* (Columbia University Press, 1977), 29. The 1977 figures were found in Ruth-Arlene W. Howe, "Development of a Model Act to Free Children for Permanent Placement: A Case Study in Law and Social Planning", 13 *Fam. LQ* 257, 330 (1979).

certain laws or promulgate certain administrative regulations, they are not eligible to receive funds for a number of vital child welfare programmes.

The Child Abuse Prevention and Treatment Act of 1974 had two central elements (1) the establishment of a National Centre on Child Abuse and Neglect; and (2) the establishment of minimum standards for state child protective systems. The National Centre on Child Abuse and Neglect serves as a clearing house for information for developing and disseminating information about child protection research. In addition it provides funding for research, demonstration, training and technical assistance for funded projects.[37]

In order for states to acquire money for its child protection programmes, it had to comply with certain federal requirements. For example, the Act required states to "provide for the reporting of known and suspected instances of child abuse and neglect", broadening in some states the types of abuse reported to include all forms of child maltreatment. Through amendments of their reporting laws, states expanded the group of persons required to report abuse and added specific types of abuse that should be reported.[38] The Act also required states to streamline their child protection system to conform to the federal government's model of what a proper system should include.

Six years after the Child Abuse Prevention and Treatment Act of 1974 became a federal law, the US Congress passed another child protection law with far-reaching consequences: the Adoption Assistance and Child Welfare Act of 1980. This Act was directed to once again get control of the continuing crisis in foster care. With all the federal intervention in the child protection field, with all its financial incentives to states to manage the problem of child abuse and neglect, still there were far too many children in foster care. The challenge that had to be met was to resolve the conflict that can arise between parental rights to rear their children and society's responsibility to care for children. How can these rights and responsibilities be balanced?

Once again the Act was a funding vehicle for states to obtain money for the structuring and implementation of a foster care system according to the Act's requirements. The Act was concerned with family situations before a child enters the foster care system, the child's situation while in the foster care system, and the child's situation at the end of foster care. The Act attempted to improve these situations by providing for the following: (1) the provision of sufficient replacement services to families to prevent the need for children to enter the foster care system; (2) the protection and provision of services for children in the foster care system; and (3) the return of children to their homes or their placement in a permanent setting like adoption.

---

[37] The Act also required individual states seeking to qualify for a grant offered through the Act to provide for the dissemination of information to the public regarding child abuse and neglect and available services, essentially creating individual state Centers on Child Abuse and Neglect, Pub. L. 93–247, at §4(b)(2)(I).

[38] See Besharov, above n. 27.

The most important aspect of the Act for our purposes is that it introduced the concept of "reasonable efforts".[39] The Act required that social service agencies must make reasonable efforts to prevent a child from being removed from her parents, and if removed, the agency must make reasonable efforts to provide services to the parents and the child within a certain time frame in order to facilitate the child's return to her family.

The reasonable efforts concept was designed to place an affirmative duty on the part of the agencies to try to rehabilitate those parents whose children had been removed from their care. The hope was that by providing parents with services (e.g., referral to drug and alcohol addiction programmes) that the agency would pay for, and giving the parents a specific time (e.g. 18 months) to become able to provide proper care for their child, family reunions could occur. In order to protect parents, the Act required that states have in place a procedure by which cases could be reviewed, either administratively or judicially, each six months. In this way, it was thought that families would not be lost in the bureaucracy of an agency. If, within the time frame (e.g. 18 months), a parent did not rehabilitate herself, then termination of parental rights would be appropriate.

I have attempted to review federal legislation in child protection because the federal government has really been the impetus for states to reform its child protection laws and procedures. Now I wish to turn to a famous case, which tested the state's responsibility to children.

DESHANNEY V. WINNEBAGO COUNTY DEPARTMENT OF SOCIAL SERVICES

When Joshua DeShaney was one year old, his parents divorced in the State of Wyoming, and his father, Randy, was awarded custody of him. Shortly thereafter Randy Deshaney and his son moved to Winnebago County, Wisconsin. Randy remarried and soon after was divorced again. About two years after Randy had moved to Wisconsin, the Winnebago County Department of Social Services learned that Joshua might be experiencing abuse. Randy denied any abusive conduct and the Department did not pursue the matter.

About one year later, Joshua was admitted to a local hospital because of his having multiple bruises and abrasions. The examining physician suspected that Joshua had been abused and notified the Department. After investigating the matter, the Department sought legal action by placing the child in the temporary custody of the hospital. During this time the Department entered into a voluntary agreement with Randy to enrol Joshua in a pre-school programme, seek counselling and to have his girlfriend move out of his house. Randy agreed and the court dismissed the child protection case and returned Joshua to his father's custody.

---

[39] 42 USCA §671(a)(15).

One month later Randy was again was seen in the emergency room of a hospital, and again the medical personnel reported Randy's injuries to the Department. With this evidence, the caseworker decided that no action need be taken. However, for the next six months the caseworker visited Joshua in his home. Randy had not enrolled Joshua in the school programme and he had not asked his girlfriend to leave the house. In addition, the caseworker noticed bruises on Joshua. The caseworker recorded all this in Joshua's file and took no action. In the same year, Joshua was once again treated in the emergency room of the local hospital. The caseworker took no action. Nor did she take any action when she was not allowed to visit Joshua in his home because she was told that he was too ill.

Four months later, Joshua was admitted to the hospital because Randy had beaten him so badly that he suffered haemorrhages in his brain. Joshua survived brain surgery but suffered so much brain damage that he had to be confined to an institution for profoundly retarded children. Joshua's father was tried and convicted of child abuse.

The criminal action that the state brought against Randy DeShaney and that resulted in his conviction amounts to a certain kind of justice. Joshua's father was punished for the monstrous abusive acts he committed on his child. But the more important question concerns the liability of the state department of social services. Under the common law a parent has a positive duty to care for his child. If the state stands in the shoes of the parent, does the state have a positive duty to protect children?

In *DeShaney* v. *Winnebago County Department of Social Services*,[40] Rehnquist CJ, writing for the majority of the US Supreme Court held that it did not. The case arose when Joshua and his mother brought an action under the federal civil rights act against the Winnebago County Department of Social Services in which they claimed that the Department through its employees had deprived Joshua of his liberty without due process of law, in violation of his rights under the Fourteenth Amendment, by failing actively to prevent Joshua from harm from his father. Joshua and his mother claimed that the Department knew or should have known that while in his father's care, Joshua was at an enormous risk of being abused.

Specifically, Rehnquist CJ, writing for majority of the Court, held that the State of Wisconsin could not be liable under the Federal Civil Rights Act[41] because the conduct of the state social worker and any other state employees involved in making decisions about Joshua was not considered "state" action (the Fourteenth Amendment to the US Constitution covers state, not private,

---

[40] 489 US 189 (1989). A full discussion of *Deshaney* is beyond the scope of this ch. For such a discussion, see Aviam Soifer, "Moral Ambition, Formalism, and the 'Free World' of *DeShaney*", 57 *Geo. Wash. L Rev.* 1513 (1989). See the similar position reached in the United Kingdom: *X (Minors)* v. *Bedfordshire County Council* [1995] 2 AC 633, discussed by Jane Wright, "Local Authorities, the Duty of Care and the European Convention on Human Rights" (1998) 19 *Oxf. J Legal Studies* 1.

[41] 42 USCA §199983.

actions). Because Joshua was injured by his father (in whose custody he had been placed) a private actor, not by any state worker, Joshua's rights under the constitution or federal law had not been violated.

Brennan, Marshal and Blackmun JJ dissented in the case. Brennan J stated that the state agency's actions were not merely passive but active state intervention. He thought that with such active intervention came a duty to protect Joshua.

The case is important in that it is an example of the Court's unwillingness to constitutionalise a tort. One can see the economic consequences of the case if Joshua and his mother had won. If state social service agencies were to be held financially liable for the negligence of its caseworkers and supervisors, the federal courts would be inundated with cases and the federal courts would be placed in a position of trying to second guess decisions reached by social workers. And it is probably safe to say that the budgets for state social service agencies would have to take into account the contingencies of law suits. States could probably have to become self-insurers as they normally do when they have to pay victims of the brutality of the police, prison guards and state mental health caretakers— all state actors. Rehnquist J stated that if states do want to make themselves liable for the negligence of its state employees that is up to the states, not the US Supreme Court.

The Court was unwilling to find a violation of any of Joshua's constitutional rights. Indeed Rehnquist J noted that the state has no duty to provide protective services for its citizens, let alone Joshua.

CONCLUSION

In this chapter I have tried to show the role of state and federal government in child protection in the United States. While in the early part of our country's history, the father had unusally great power over his children, that power has slowly been lessened. Now it can be said that of all family relationships, the parent–child relationship is the most vulnerable. Unlike the husband–wife relationship or sibling–sibling relationship, the parent–child relationship is subject to involuntary state intervention with the possible result of terminating the relationship.

With the enormous power of government to reorganise family relationships, are there no responsibilities? Federal mandates have made state agencies more cognizant of the need to try to keep families together and if separated, the need to reunify them. The courts have underscored the need for social service agencies to provide services. But when the ultimate test came to decide the liability of a state social service agency that failed every test of good social work practice, the US Supreme Court got the state agency off the hook. The US Supreme Court decided *DeShaney* by interpreting the US Constitution narrowly and by distinguishing away cases that were relevant by their specific facts. The hairline distinction between a child's being in the custody of a his father and not the state, even though the state social worker intervened in the relationship by visiting the home, meant the difference between abdication of responsibility and responsibility itself.[42] One is left with the feeling that the historic concept of *parens patriae* in contemporary America family law may be pure rhetoric.

[42] Chief Justice Rehnquist wrote in a footnote:
"Had the State by the affirmative exercise of its power removed Joshua from free society and placed him in a foster home operated by its agents, we might have a situation sufficiently analogous to incarceration or institutionalization to give rise to an affirmative duty to protect. Indeed, several Court of Appeals have held, by analogy to *Estelle* [*v. Gamble*, 429 US 97 (1976)] and *Youngberg* [v. *Romero*, 457 US 307 (19820], that the State may be held liable under the Due Process Clause for failing to protect children in foster homes from mistreatment at the hands of their foster parents."
Despite this language, the Court denied certiorari in *Taylor* v. *Ledbetter*, which held that the state owed a special relationship duty under the Due Process Clause to a child abused in foster care. 791 F.2d 881 (11th Cir. 1986) aff'd in part, rev'd in part on reh'g, 818 F.2d 791 (11th Cir. 1987) (en banc), cert. denied, 109 S. Ct. 1337 (1989).

PART FOUR

Constitutionalising Family Law

This Part examines the implications of constitutional and human rights norms on family law. Kurczewski (Chapter 27) gives a detailed account of the process of constitutionalising family law norms in Poland which can stand as an example of the way in which conflicting perceptions of the relationship between the family and the state can be accommodated within some overarching human rights principles. Kurczewski sees the submission of the family to these norms as being tantamount to making the family a public institution. He also emphasises the importance of reading constitutions against the social background from which they emerged as well as the interpretation which follws its promulgation. Woodhouse (Chapter 28) makes the same point with respect to the US constitution in her account of its limited application of constitutional norms to family matters compared to that of the South African constitution. Robinson, Steyn and Sinclair (Chapters 29, 25 and 30) provide detailed illustrations of the reach of the latter into family relationships. This can be contrasted with Ncube's account (Chapter 31) of the limited effect of constitutional norms within Zimbabwe and Banda's reflections on the mixed impact of the Convention on the Elimination of All Forms of Discrimination against Women in various African countries (Chapter 32).

27

The Constitutionalisation of the Family in Poland

JACEK KURCZEWSKI

1. THE POLISH CONSTITUTION AND THE FAMILY

The 1997 Constitution of the Republic of Poland has the obvious traits of a document resulting from years of laborious negotiations and last minute amendments. It starts with a complex preamble, which was among the most hotly debated sections, and continues with 12 chapters and 243 articles. One of its clearest features is the frequent references to the family. Of these, Article 18 seems to be crucial, stating that "Marriage as the union between woman and man, family, maternity and parenthood are under the protection and care of the people of Poland". It is interesting to note, first, that in the previous (Communist) constitution, only "marriage, family and maternity" were mentioned, and that supplementing the list with "parenthood" gives room for recognition of both parents' rights and duties; and, secondly, that the definition of marriage as heterosexual monogamy was introduced as if to counterbalance the first by acknowledging the request made by the Catholic Church.

Article 4, which states that "Everyone has the right to legal protection of private life, family life, honour and good reputation and to decide their own personal life" makes an interesting distinction betwen private life and family life. From the context it seems to reinforce the second circle of personal privacy which extends to one's dealing with other family members independently of their wish to surrender it. At the same time it serves to defend the collective rights to privacy of all family members against external threat.

This privacy does not exclude regulation of the relationships between members of the family. First, the principle of gender equality is strongly stressed and enshrined as a positive entitlement by Article 33: "Women and men in the Republic of Poland have equal rights in family, political, social and economic life". It is interesting to note that for the long period of drafting and redrafting, "family" was not on the list of the areas of equal rights, and was introduced only at the last moment on the personal initiative of Senator Gawronik. The amendment made explicit the equivalence of family life to the other three areas conventionally considered to constitute the public sphere of life.

Gender equality is involved also in the phrase "woman and man". "Maternity" was not equated with "paternity" but with "parenthood", which involves gender neutral rights and duties of parents. The priority given to "maternity" is also acknowledged in Article 71.2: "The mother, before and after giving birth, is entitled to special assistance on the part of public authorities as determined by law". This is one of many social and economic rights and entitlements that abound in the new Polish constitution, though with the reservation that the specific law issued by Parliament will define the contents of the right in question.

In this context the general entitlement of the family to the State's assistance should be mentioned. Under Article 71.1 "In its social and economic policy the State takes into account the welfare of the family. Families under economic and social duress, especially those with many children and incomplete families have a right to special assistance from public authorities." Related to this is Article 23, introduced at the special demand of the Agrarian Party (a junior partner in the ruling coalition) which states that "[t]he family farm is at the foundation of the agrarian regime in the State". The exact meaning of this provision was not clear to the parliamentarians who voted in favour of the amended draft.

Parent–child relations are also regulated by the constitution in a complex way which will raise issues to be resolved by the Constitutional Court and by Parliament. During the constitutional debates, the Catholic Right was defending rights of parents, whilst the post-communist Left was stressing the rights of children. It is no accident that the leading Communist legal theoretrician, who at one time justified widespread violations of freedom of expression, was at the same time honoured in the world as the promoter of the UN Convention on the Rights of the Child. The concern about chidren's rights may be understood as an attempt to counterbalance the bourgeois concern with political and human freedoms by emphasising social and economic rights.

Paradoxically, the new Constitition, while introducing a complete system for protecting human and political rights and freedoms, is supplemented by a strong component of social and economic rights, including children's rights. This in general characterises the post-Communist state when run by post-Communists. Thus, the definition of the new regime as given in Article 1 declares that "[t]he Republic of Poland is a democratic legal State fulfilling principles of social justice." Despite stereotypes to the contrary, the transformation did not lead to the abolition of the social welfare state. In fact, social and economic rights, previously abundant, have now been limited to those which may be more realistically implemented within a market economy.

The new Constitution introduces a special Children's Ombudsperson notwithstanding the existence of a powerful Ombudsperson for everybody. Article 72 is even more specific:

(1) "The Republic of Poland guarantees the protection of the child's rights. Anyone has the right to request a public authority to protect the child from violence, cruelty, exploitation and demoralsation."

(2) "Children deprived of parental care are entitled to care and protection by public authorities."
(3) "When establishing the child's rights, public authorities and those responsible are obliged to listen to and, if possible, take into account, the child's opinion."
(4) "The Children's Ombudsperson's competence and nomination shall be determined by law".

Parental authority is thus limited. It is conditional and may be terminated, though this must be through due process of law, as Article 48.2 stipulates: "Parental authority can be restricted or terminated only according to the law and only according to a valid court judgment". Despite this, it seems that even if parental authority has not been restricted or terminated by the law, the public authority must protect the child from malicious acts of parents at the request of any concerned individual. The constitutional limitation of parental authority is even more obvious if one takes into account Article 40: "Corporal punishment is forbidden". This Article has evoked several controversies, and was deliberately left as quoted, with both sides convinced that in the future the Constitutional Court will interpret it acording to their viewpoint, that is, either as extending to parental discipline or as stopping at the doorway to the home, which is "inviolable (except in cases and as determined by the law)" as the new Constitution mysteriously states.

The idea that parental authority is subject to public monitoring and intervention follows clearly from these Articles. In this sense one may feel inclined to claim that parental authority is the same as that of a private employer over an employee. The very fact that rights of parents are also listed suggests the same. The Catholic emphasis on parental freedom with respect to the moral and religious upbringing of their children was finally acknowledged, although limited in a way which could lead to future controversy. Under Article 48.1 "Parents have the right to bring up their children according to their beliefs. Upbringing should take into account the degree of maturity of the child as well as its freedom of conscience, faith and beliefs." Article 53.3 provides that "Parents have the right to secure the moral and religious upbringing and education of their children according to their beliefs: Article 48.1 applies". However, Article 70.3 fails to make reference to Article 48.1. This states that "Parents may choose schools for their children which are not public schools". One wonders if this is a deliberate exception to taking into consideration the child's viewpoint.

This review of consitutional provisions must be concluded by reference to the explicitly vague Article 38: "The Republic of Poland guarantees legal protection to each human being". This formulation was meant as a compromise between pro-choice and pro-life attitudes to abortion, though pro-lifers and the Catholic Church in fact requested a much more specific protection of human life from conception.

2. THE HISTORY OF THE CONSTITUTIONAL TEXT

This takes us back to the history of the constitutional text. The text has no meaning without its history, and history here does not refer to the sequence of events but the full social context. Even giving an account of the Articles of the newly accepted Constitution would be meaningless unless reference is made to the previous Constitution, various drafts and dissenting opinions. Of course the position will change when the Constitutional Court and other authoritative sources interpret the constitution. But these will require further historical interpretation. This point is made to dispel the notion that the historical interpretation which is available on Day 0 loses its signficance as the web of interpretations thickens around the text during its life.

The debate concerning the final 1997 draft will illustrate this. From the many sessions, the first part of the third session of the National Assembly, held from 24–28 February 1997 has been selected. This was the second reading of the draft prepared by the Constitutional Committee of the National Assemlby 1993–7, after which the draft was sent back to the Committee together with the amendments proposed during the debate. After Marek Mazurkiewicz MP (SLD) had presented the draft on behalf of the Committee, there were 344 interventions by deputies and senators (some twice or thrice) and one by the specifically invited president of Solidarity, Marian Krzaklewski. Six parliamentarians gave written opinions. The second reading allowed each parliamentarian to express an opinion on the draft. It is interesing that 45 of the 344 interventions referred to the "family" in general or some of the above-mentioned aspects of family life.

But first, it is notable that the *rapporteur* of the Constitutional Committee, while presenting the draft, did not mention the family at all, focusing on three main principles of the proposed draft: the State as *bonum omnium* of all citizens; the legal state; and fulfilment of social justice. When presenting the minority proposals, the *rapporteur* remarked that: "Some proposals aim at reinforcing the position of the family as the foundation of the Republic and to introduce the Children's Rights Ombudsperson as a constitutional institution. Here also we found the proposals to regulate the protection of life and right to life wider than in the committee's draft." Another perspective was taken by his party colleague, Jerzy Szmajdziński MP (SLD) who listed four sets of values as being present in the draft: liberal-democratic, social-democratic, christian-democratic and nationalistic. The first included principles of the democratic legal state, political pluralism, freedom to create political parties, freedom of the press and other means of social communication, legalism, constitutionalism, respect for international law, economic freedom, protection of property and inheritance and personal freedoms. Under the second were fulfilment of social justice, foundations of civil society, protection of labour, freedom of trade unions, social rights and protection of tenants and consumers. As christian democratic values he listed awareness of the common good of all citizens, religious freedom, ecclesiastical autonomy for all denominations, *the protection of the family and marriage* and protection of human life. The nationalistic group of values included the unitary and indivisible character of the state, protecting the national heritage and protection of the *family farm*.

The evident satisfaction with the compromise worked out by the post-communist coalition was somewhat undermined by Waldemar Pawlak MP (PSL), leader of the Agrarian Party, ruling in coalition with the post-communist leftist group, who remarked that "the role of the family and its reinforcement should be more precisely regulated in the constitution", though he stressed that several formulations from Solidarity's draft had already been included in the draft prepared by the Committee of the National Assembly. Tadeusz Mazowiecki MP, of the Freedom Party (UW), made a speech full of references to God, but none to the family. The leader of the non-communist Left Labour Party (UP), Ryszard Bugaj MP, attacked the Agrarians on the abortion issue and the Catholic idea of natural law. Of the first four speakers of the Right, only the first (Adam Słomka MP (BBWR)) attacked the draft for not recognising the family as the basic social unit. The topic was, however, much developed by Senator Alicja Grześowiak (Solidarity). While she spoke it appeared that the plan to achieve compromise had failed. She attacked the draft on many counts; as not effectively safeguarding social rights; as being not only ultra-liberal but even morally nihilistic and antipatriotic. She urged the full constitutional protection of human life from conception and the protection of the family. As she is the strongest exponent of Catholic Solidarity, her views should be set out fully:

"The draft constitution, though containing two articles relating to the family, does not secure its proper protection nor a proper place for it in Polish society. Yet the family is the fundamental community among the communities that make up the state. It should be recognised as the foundation of society and the state. Unfortunately there is no such formulation in the draft and therefore the constitutional position of the family is weakened. Although the committee has accepted that the family, marriage and maternity are under the protection of the Republic of Poland, it is hard to know what this means since the constitution has not proclaimed the family as primordial community which existed prior to the state, having its own inalienable rights which precede positive legislation. It is therefore necessary to specify that marriage entails the union of man and woman, in order to exclude it from people who are naturally excluded, that is, unions of two women or two men. The draft does not recognise rights of the family as a unit; it atomises the family by safeguardng the rights of individual members. Even if it supports the right of parents to bring up their children according to their views, it also implies restriction of the family's educational function by taking into account the maturity of the child and its freedom of conscience, religion and belief. Similar limitations to parental rights are included in the article which guarantees the right of parents to secure the moral and religious upbringing of their children according to their beliefs. The clause requiring them to take into account the freedom of conscience, religion and beliefs of the child gives rise to conflict, especially when the state adopts such a liberal attitude towards sects which fraudulently alienate children from their parents. Article 68 of the draft, which declares that in its social and economic policy the state should consider the interests of the family, does not secure its protection either. The formulaton imposes no obligation to follow pro-family policies."

The most important political event of the debate was, however, the speech by the Chairman of Solidarity, Marian Krzaklewski, the only non-parliamentarian invited. He criticised the draft prepared by the National Assembly, supported the critique of Senator Grześkowiak and other Solidarity-related parliamentarians, and then moved to present the seven areas of the Solidarity draft (called the "civic" draft) which had not yet been absorbed into the draft prepared by the National Assembly. This included the family issue. The rejection of what was assumed by the ruling coalition and the leftist and liberal opposition as the constitutional compromise shaped the remaining course of the debate. The Agrarians were busy working out another compromise whereby they would honour their commitment to share power with the post-communists while at the same time supporting as many of Solidarity's proposals as possible. Mirosław Pawlak MP (PSL) urged that "the Constitution should leave no doubt that marriage can be constituted only between people of the opposite sex . . . and have all the relevant consequences as to parental rights, specifically the right to decide on the religious and moral upbringing of children". Solidarity's Senator Mieczysław Biliński reiterated that "the state is not permanent. Only the nation, the family and within it marriage as the union of man and woman is permanent." Finally, it is important to note that Deputy Stanisław Kowolik (BBWR) evoked the Vatican Charter of Family Rights as demonstrating the family as being prior to the constitution and the state.

In a sense the views of the Right on family, marriage and the protection of life have been counterbalanced by another set of constitutional amendments proposed by speakers from the liberal Left. Independent Senator Zdzisława Jankowska, speaking on behalf of the Parliamentary Women's Group, supported a gender equality clause. She referred to the Group's draft of the Law on equal Status of Women and Men and proposed an Ombudsperson and Commission on Equal status to combat gender discrimination. A deputy of the leftist opposition party, Izabela Jaruga-Nowacka (UP), while supporting the parliamentary draft on the family, was in favour of extending the protected institutions to include not only "maternity" but also "parenthood" as "we want to reinforce the father as subject in the family and to strengthen his tutelary role in bringing up children. This may give women better opportunities for active participation in social and professional life". She criticised the proposal to ascribe a fundamental role to the family, pointing to the possibility of resulting discrimination against those who were accidentally or deliberately living alone. Care for the family should be safeguarded "according to the Labour Union, at least within the areas of health and free education at all levels." She succesfully supported the idea of an Ombudsperson for Children's Rights. The real safeguards for the family lay in well guaranteed social rights.

"Here we also propose amendment to Article 69.2 which states that 'A child without proper parental care has a right to care and assistance from public authorities.' Often the child is formally under their care, but is not so in reality. We want it to be possible to help the child in such circumstances. Although Poland has ratified the Conventon on the Rights of the Child, we are aware of the fact that, despite this, children's rights are widely violated, most often at home, at school, within the caring institutions and by the health service. Despite these Conventions, the child in Poland is often treated more as an object than a subject. We want the effective protection of children's and youth's rights and we support the amendments that establish an Ombudsperson on Children's Rights."

This was elaborated by Zofia Wilczyńska MP (SLD) and Senator Maria Łopatkowa (PSL). The latter referred to another issue which had until then not been mentioned in the debate; that is, a ban on corporal punishment.

"Parents differ. Their beliefs vary from being fully humanistic to racialist. This is why, if parental patterns are negative, inculcating hatred, not love, then a child, especially if capable of critical thought, has the right to build up his own beliefs by drawing on external positive sources: from school, literature, art, science and religion. And parents must take this into account. A family which does not respect a child's rights is not a community of love but a community of egoistical adult interests, within which the child is unhappy. Article 19 of the Convention on the Rights of the Child, which prohibits any violence, is safeguarded by Article 38 of the constitutional draft which prohibits corporal punishment. Finally, it will be clear that nobody can be beaten, not even the child."

Joanna Starega-Piasek MP (UW) proposed an amendment to extend the constitutional guarantees of public assistance to families who are not only under "material" but also under "social" hardship. Equally succesful was the amendment by Jan Zaciura MP (SLD) to raise the compulsory school age to 18 years.

On 16 January 1997, M. Mazurkiewicz, President of the Constitutional Committee of the National Assembly, presented the report. In the introduction he mentioned seven drafts which were taken into account at the first reading by the National Assembly between 21 and 3 September 1994. After 82 meetings held between 8 November 1994 and 16 January 1997 the draft was prepared together with 47 minority motions, of which two entailed complete alternative drafts of the constitution. The majority draft as then presented referred to the family in a slightly different way from the final text stated at the beginning of this chapter. Thus Article 18 then stated that "[t]he family, marriage and maternity are under the care and protection of the Republic of Poland". There is no reference to parenthood, and the definition of marriage is left open, but whether it was truly open is doubtful because the issue had not then been raised. But possibilities of interpretation are infinite. For example, might it be argued that since it is not stated that the union must be established in due legal form, informal unions might also be protected? Although parliamentarians discussed the heterosexuality of unions, they evidentally overlooked this issue.

The parliamentary draft of 16 January already included protection of the family farm (Article 21) as well as the gender equality clause, though without reference to family life (Article 31). Corporal punishment was forbidden (Article 38).

The right to bring up one's child according to one's beliefs was also proclaimed (Articles 46 and 56.3). The family and child's rights chapters were shorter than in the final text.

We should consider the content of the minority motions. In the 1989–91 Senate, which was dominated by Solidarity, draft 4 guaranteed everybody the legal protection of private life, family life, honour and good reputation, as in Article 45 of the parliamentary draft and Article 47 of the final text. The old Senate's draft referred to the family in Article 14, which to a large degree has been superseded by the parliamentary draft of 1997.

> "1. The family and parenthood are protected by the state. 2. In its social and economic policy, including taxation, the state takes into account the interests of the family. Families under economic hardship have the right to special assistance from the state. 3. The Republic safeguards family rights, especially the rights of parents to bring up and educate their children according to their beliefs. Suppression or limitation of parental authority may only be made through a court judgment. 4. A mother, before and after giving birth, has the right to special assistance from the state as determined by law. 5. The state guarantees the protection of the child's rights, especially against cruelty, exploitation and demoralisation. Children without parental care have the right to special care and assistance from the state."

It is evident that the Left had no monopoly in advocating children's rights. The rightist Senate had formulated the children's rights clause, however, in such a way that legislation and judicial decisions were needed to specify the conditions, if any, for the state to intervene to protect a child against its parents. The draft is also silent on corporal punishment, which was later opened up by the Left and by liberals. The Solidarity Senate also promoted the protection of the family's economic interests, a formulation akin to the pre-1989 Communist formulation and which in turn became the basis for the post-1993 leftist constitutional formulation. It is also interesting to observe that the Right was inclined to use the gender-neutral concept of parenthood and that the definition of marriage was not an issue at the start of the debates. In this draft, gender is listed as one of several grounds of prohibited discrimination, while the parliamentary draft and final draft repeat the prohibition against gender discrimination. On the other hand, the notion of family corporate rights is explicitly introduced in the Solidarity Senate's draft as being based on Catholic social doctrine and the Vatican Charter of Family Rights. It is here where the Catholic concept of family rights was lost in the constitutional struggle.

The Solidarity Senate's draft was the first draft prepared after the change of regime in 1989, while the Solidarity "civic" draft was the last in the series, so it took into account the controversies that arose in the intervening period. The latter draft recognises the "special protection of human life from conception to natural death" (Article 9.1), while the Solidarity Senate's draft protected human life from conception and prohibited the death penalty. It is silent on the issue of corporal punishment, but this might be deliberate in view of the controversial issue of the limits of parental authority. The article on the family is exactly the same as

Article 14 of the Senate's draft. Controversies over children's rights are, however, reflected in Article 24.2: "Parents have the right to secure the religious education f their children". This is silent on the child's right to dissent.

3. CONCLUSION

The 1997 Constitution, interpreted through its political history, has established a distinct model of the family. This is a family in which relations beteen parents and children are subject to public intervention on the request of anyone concerned; a family in which parental authority is counterbalanced by the need to take into consideration the growing beliefs and decision-making capacity of the child; a family instituted by a procreative monogamous heterosexual union institionalised as marriage; a family in which gender relations are based upon equality as protected by law and the public authorities. So, however private family life may seem, it is clear that the family, as constitutionalised, has become a public institution.[1]

On 25 April 1997 the new Constitution of the Republic of Poland was accepted by the nation. The sociological truth is found in the figures. Only 42 per cent of the public voted, despite the declared conviction of the majority that the Constitution was a matter of major importance for the country. Of those who voted, only 53 per cent voted in favour of the Constitution; 46 per cent were against. Both sides declared their satisfaction with the public support for their position. Post-communists claimed that after four years of crisis (1990–3) their accession to power had brought stability and constitutional safeguards for democracy. Solidarity leaders confirmed their desire to change the Constitution once elected to Parliament. This is no utopian dream as any article may be changed by qualified majority. However Solidarity won the 1997 election but without achieving such a majority in Parliament.

Shortly after the promulgation of the Constitution, and a few days before the pilgrimage of the Pope to his native country, the Constitutional Court, by a majority, held that the 1996 law which liberalised abortion to the point of making it effectively available on request was unconstitutional. This makes it likely that Article 38 of the new Constitution, protecting human life, will be similarly interpreted.

This survey of the constitutionalisation of the family in Poland has focused on certain areas of controversy. As the life of the constitution unfolds, this choice of issues can be seen as a set of conjectures as to what will be the main areas of future controversy.

---

[1] See J. Kurczewski, "The Famly as an Institution of Civil Society in Poland", 4 *The Polish Sociological Review*, 1996.

28

Constitutional Interpretation and the Re-constitution of the Family in the United States and South Africa

BARBARA BENNETT WOODHOUSE

I. INTRODUCTION

The citizens of the Republic of South Africa recently completed the arduous process of drafting their 1996 Constitution (RSA Constitution), a document that not only redistributes political rights to people of all colours, but also redistributes power within the family by explicitly recognising the rights of women and children.

No two documents could be more different in style and form than the Constitution of the United States (US Constitution) and the RSA Constitution. While the RSA Constitution's text speaks boldly and in detail about the specifics of family rights, the US Constitution speaks in archaic language, and often indirectly, via judicial interpretation. The older document, now well into its third century, is short—only about 8,000 words—and often frustratingly vague or ambiguous. The RSA Constitution is ten times as long, with 243 detailed sections, followed by 40 pages of tables and schedules.[1] It addresses rights of bodily integrity, including reproductive freedom; protection against discrimination, including discrimination based on sex, marital status, pregnancy, sexual orientation and age; protections of religious, linguistic and cultural values; and protection of economic rights to housing, medical care and education central to family survival. Explicitly embracing the newest category of rights-bearers, the RSA Constitution provides a detailed listing of the rights of children.[2] By contrast, the US Constitution's text says nothing about gender or age discrimination, nothing

---

[1] See Frederick Schauer, "Constitutional Invocation", 65 *Fordham L. Rev.* 1295 (1997). *Id.* at 1297–8.

[2] Constitution of Republic of South Africa 1996, Ch. 2, ss. 9 (equality); 12(2) (bodily integrity and reproductive freedom); 15 (religious and customary family law); 16(2) (protection from race and gender based hate speech); 18 (freedom of association); 26 (right to housing and protection from eviction); 27 (health care, food and water, social security); 28 (children's rights); 29 (education); 30 (protection of language and culture).

about pregnancy or reproduction, and nothing about parents, families, or children.[3]

The RSA Constitution is explicit not only about the substance of rights but about procedural and jurisprudential issues. It makes various rights binding not only on public but on private actors, and establishes government structures for monitoring and enforcing these rights. By contrast, the US Constitution is silent, restrictive or ambiguous on the scope, application and enforcement of rights affecting the family. The South African document includes careful instructions on its interpretation, and many provisions which constitute "tests" to apply in situations where competing rights and interests clash. Here again, the US document provides only minimal guidance, leaving a vacuum that has been filled, over the years, by elaborate constructions of judicial interpretation.

Comparison of these two constitutions not only exposes to view the role of constitutional law in the reconstitution of the family, but allows us to examine legal change through the lens of two very different experiences: one, an incremental process of judicial interpretation and re-interpretation of a general text; the other, a transformational moment of explicit and specific textual enactment. How has each country's contrasting constitutional experience shaped the substance of family law in each of these settings?

Many modern scholars challenge the common wisdom that judges choose between two incompatible modes of analysis, either approaching texts from a position of rigid textualism or treating them as invitations to free-wheeling judicial policy-making.[4] In this chapter, I look especially closely at the role of judicial interpretation. While this process still lies ahead for South Africa's Constitution, and other new constitutions around the world, it provides the bulk of operative American constitutional law. After more than 200 years of judicial interpretation and elaboration, judicial opinions have displaced much of the text, providing new texts and outlining the methodology for discerning emerging rights. First, I will examine the gradual rejection of patriarchy and emergence of rights for women in the United States. I will look at avenues for constitutional growth in the American system and trace the erratic path which our constitutional law of the family has travelled to arrive at its present place.

Next I will contrast the American constitutional experience with the concentrated process of research, drafting, and public consultation that lead to the inclusion of rights for women and children in the text of the South African

---

[3] The only explicit prohibition on sex or age discrimination in the US Constitution is in the Nineteenth and Twenty-sixth Amendments which extended to women and youths 18 and over the right to vote.

[4] Prof. Mitchel Lasser employs the tools of literary theory to show how judges in both French and US systems combine textually oriented and policy oriented discourse to portray the law as both inherently stable and socially responsive. See Mitchel de S.-O.-l'E. Lasser, " 'Lit. Theory' Put to the Test: A Comparative Literary Analysis of American Judicial Tests and French Judicial Discourse", 111 *Harv. L. Rev.* 689 (1998). See Also Lourens du Plessis and Hugh Corder, *Understanding South Africa's Transitional Bill of Rights* (1994), 60–107 (describing nuances of interpretation in South African context).

Constitution's Bill of Rights. I will suggest, not surprisingly, that the South African process, which has been described as a "revolution negotiated between the oppressor and the oppressed", contributed to creation of a very explicit text in which women and children earned a special place because of their role in South Africa's struggle against apartheid. I will argue that Americans must learn from South Africa's experience if we are to re-invigorate the US Constitution and reshape our approach to constitutional interpretation to enhance rather than suppress the recognition of children's emerging claims of rights to dignity, protection and respect.

II. THE AMERICAN EXPERIENCE

A. Towards a More Perfect Union: Avenues for Constitutional Growth

All constitutions are born imperfect. To believe otherwise is to believe in human infallibility. It is also to believe, against all evidence, in the existence of a static, textual "plain meaning", rather than understanding meaning through contextualized trial and error.[5] The US Constitution is a compelling case in point. As originally drafted, it had at least two flaws so serious they might well have been fatal. First, in weighing property interests and the interest in social stability against principles of liberty and equality, our Constitution sacrificed justice in favour of order. Second, and less widely discussed, the US Constitution, as originally promulgated in 1789, lacked any explicit protection of what we now call fundamental or human rights. While the first ten amendments, known as the "Bill of Rights", were added in 1791, even this amended version remained imperfect as a guardian of rights due to a third fundamental flaw—the framers' casting of the new government in a purely passive role, as bound to respect pre-existing rights, but not as an active agent in promoting, enforcing and interpreting them.

From its inception, the US Constitution allowed two primary avenues for evolution.[6] One is explicitly set forth in the process for formal amendment, described in Article V. This process makes change extremely difficult, especially if the change is controversial—as is always the case with new claims of rights which threaten vested interests. Amendment V requires a supermajority both to initiate the amendment process and to ratify any new amendments. Like any authors, the framers must have wanted to minimise meddlesome editing. Their choice of

---

[5] Surely the most amusing illustration of this truth is Jordan Steiker, Sanford Levinson and J. M. Balkin, "Taking Text and Structure Really Seriously: Constitutional Interpretation and the Crisis of Presidential Eligibility", 74 *Tex. L Rev.* 237 (1995), a "parody" which employs a literal reading of the text of the US Constitution to disqualify all persons born after 1789 from election to the Presidency of the United States.

[6] Various students of constitutional evolution and constitutional history have defended the validity of additional unenumerated means of amending the Constitution. See e.g., Bruce Ackerman, *We the People* (1991), 34–57 (informal amendment through judicial re-interpretation) and Akhil Reed Amar, 94 *Colum. L. Rev.* 457, 487–94 (1992) (amendment by direct majority vote).

methods for formal amendment is consistent with the conservative thrust of the US constitutional scheme, which employed numerous checks and balances to minimise the dangers of radical or imprudent change.

Given the difficulty of formal amendment, Americans would have had to invent another avenue for protecting emerging rights had it not already existed. Fortunately, the common law tradition provided another avenue for informally "amending" the US Constitution—judicial re-interpretation of the constitutional text, in the course of judicial review of government laws and actions.[7] The power of judicial review, most famously articulated in the case of *Marbury* v. *Madison*, gives the judiciary authority to strike down laws and government actions if they violate the "supreme law" of the land, embodied in the Constitution. Since the US Supreme Court, sitting in Washington, DC, has final appellate jurisdiction of constitutional cases, its nine justices are the ultimate arbiters of "what the law is".[8]

B. The Interpretive Process: Discovering and Rediscovering Meaning Between the Lines

The common law tradition has always relied on a gradual accretion of precedent in successive cases, to flesh out the meaning of laws and legal principles. In contrast to many other constitutional schemes, under Article III, the US federal courts may not consider hypothetical questions, or pass on the constitutionality of a law before it is enacted.[9] Courts may consider only actual cases and controversies that have ripened into lawsuits. Thus the law is inevitably shaped as much by the litigants and by their times as by the courts. Presented with a concrete dispute in a specific factual context, judges must give meaning to the constitutional text, not in the abstract but as it applies to a particular party and set of current facts. Judges understand that each decision not only explains but potentially "makes" new law.[10]

[7] A massive literature has grown up around the methods judges use to interpret the meaning of the US Constitution. See, e.g., "Symposium, Fidelity in Constitutional Theory", 65 *Fordham L. Rev.* 1247 (1997); Antonin Scalia, *A Matter of Interpretation: Federal Courts and the Law* (1997); Dworkin, *Freedom's Law: The Moral Reading of the American Constitution* (1996); Robert H. Bork, "The Constitution, Original Intent, and Economic Rights", 23 *San Diego L Rev.* 823 (1986); Michael W. McConnell, "The Role of Democratic Politics in Transforming Moral Convictions into Law", 98 *Yale LJ* 1501 (1989).

[8] This phrase comes from John Marshall CJ's famous description of the "province of the judiciary" in *Marbury* v. *Madison*, 5 US (1 Cranch) 137 (1803).

[9] Art. III gives the federal courts jurisdiction of "cases and controversies" arising under the Constitution and has been interpreted as forbidding advisory opinions. *Muskrat* v. *United States*, 219 US 346 (1911).

[10] See Lasser, *supra* n. 5, at 702–35, showing how, in the American system, the original constitutional text is often displaced by a series of judicially created multi-pronged Tests. These Tests assume the role of authoritative texts to be applied in subsequent cases, creating the perception that law is inherently stable (because based on application of a specific text to the problem at hand) but also socially responsive (because the Test incorporates examination of an array of external purposes and effects relevant to the problem).

American scholars and jurists have long debated various theories to describe and justify the roles of judges in this process. Critics of "judicial activism" are made uneasy by charges that the process of interpretation poses risks of translations which slide into substitutions and ultimately repudiations of the text as originally written and intended. They wonder how to maintain fidelity to the words on the parchment without sacrificing its larger purposes. They worry about the "counter majoritarian difficulty"—the power of unelected judges to strike down popular laws.[11] On one extreme are critics who believe judges should be confined to applying the text according to its "original intent" or "original understanding" and can thus avoid changing or expanding the law at all.[12] On the other, are those who claim the text and its framers' and ratifiers' intentions are so inherently subjective, contingent, unknowable, diffuse and/or irrelevant that we should frankly admit that the judiciary is imposing value choices as a player in the game of politics.[13] A third approach would allow judges great authority to police the democratic process, stepping in to correct failures of representation, but would allow very little room to second guess bad substantive results if arrived at through good procedures.[14] Finally, many modern US scholars endorse an eclectic or pragmatic approach, often called "practical reason" or "pragmatism", which employs a variety of methods—including recourse to external social and moral values—to arrive at a functional and sensible reading of the text.[15]

Unfortunately, the framers gave us no Owner's Manual. Nor can recourse to "history" tell us precisely what they imagined we would do with their text. Debates about the respective importance of original intent, overarching purposes and principles, and political pragmatism began well before the Constitutional Convention convened in 1787 and opinion was as divided during the early years of the nation's history as it is today.[16] Examination of US Supreme Court

---

[11] See Alexander Bickel, *The Least Dangerous Branch* (1962).

[12] See Robert H. Bork, *The Tempting of America: The Political Seduction of the Law* (1989) (arguing that judges must give the constitutional text whatever would have been its generally accepted public meaning at the time of its adoption).

[13] This is a rather gross characterisation of the arguments made far more subtly by the Critical Legal Studies (CLS) movement. See, e.g., Mark Tushnet, *The Red, White, and Blue: A Critical Analysis of Constitutional Law* (1988) (critiquing interpretivist, representation-reinforcing and normativist theories); Derrick Bell, "*Brown* v. *Board of Education* and the Interest-Convergence Dilemma", 93 *Harv. L. Rev.* 518, 523 (1980) (describing the "subordination of law to interest group politics").

[14] See John Hart Ely's "Representation-Reinforcing" theory of review, expounded in his book, *Democracy and Distrust: A Theory of Judicial Review* (1980), 88–103; see also Gerard E. Lynch, "Review of John Hart Ely's *Democracy and Distrust*", 80 *Colum. L Rev.* 857 (1980) (critiquing Ely's approach).

[15] See Richard Posner, *The Problems of Jurisprudence* (1990), 302–9 (describing the Supreme Court's change of direction in interpreting the Fourteenth Amendment in *Brown* v. *Board of Education* to strike down American apartheid as justified not by technical legal materials but by ethical and political ends such as "promoting social peace through racial harmony, . . . finding a new institutional role for the Supreme Court to replace the discredited one of protecting economic liberty; [and] breathing new life into the equal protection clause"); Daniel Farber and Phillip Frickey, "Practical Reason and the First Amendment", 34 *UCLA L. Rev.* 1615, 1645–56 (1987).

[16] See Jack N. Rakove, *Original Meanings: Politics and Ideas in the Making of the Constitution* (1997). Rakove shows how different players held differing views of the interpretive process, and how

opinions provides convincing evidence that no one methodology has reigned supreme. The Court often relies on close textual reading but it has also played an active role in "apply[ing] values not articulated in the constitutional text"[17] to the resolution of constitutional questions. The results are sometimes plainly inconsistent with a strict interpretation of the text and hard to square with what we know of the drafters' and ratifiers' specific intentions. The Supreme Court often overtly draws upon what it conceives as shared contemporary (even cutting edge) ideals about fairness and justice. I am not suggesting that the justices create these ideals out of whole cloth—rather, the Court anchors its rulings in various broad concepts located within the document, as well as upon inferences drawn from the Constitution's structures and purposes. The Court attempts to articulate and apply these values, "even when the content of these ideals is not expressed as a matter of positive law in the written Constitution".[18]

Change through interpretation is an historical fact of American jurisprudence and one I believe the framers would accept as inevitable and even desirable. They generally understood that the interpretive process would continue to shape the law, long after they were gone. They also agreed on the strategy of keeping the text simple and focused on "essential principles only; lest the operations of government should be clogged by rendering those provisions permanent and unalterable, which ought to be accommodated to times and events; . . . "[19] Over the course of time, perhaps to an extent undreamed of by the framers, the judiciary has become the primary vehicle for "up-dating" textual meaning. Inevitably, judges bring modern knowledge and evolving social and moral sensibilities to defining and applying the document's terms in contemporary contexts. Judges, however, do not act in isolation. Their partners in this enterprise are ordinary people, from the voters whose choices influence judicial appointments and Senate confirmations, to the litigants and advocates who call upon the courts to confront emerging constitutional problems. Although this concept of judges as interpreters and translators gives the judiciary great power, that power is checked and balanced in ways, both practical and political. The most powerful check on judicial power is the fact that judges are embedded in a particular legal culture. It is the judge's commitment to and training in a craft of judging which obligates her to perform her task with circumspection, consistency, impartiality, and restraint, to truly hear and respond in good faith to reasoned argument, and to explain and justify her conclusions in written opinions.[20]

---

key players, such as Madison or Hamilton, changed their views and tactics according to the issue at hand or in response to pragmatic judgments: *id.*, 339–65.

[17] Thomas C. Grey, "Do We Have an Unwritten Constitution?", 27 *Stan. L Rev.* 703 (1975).

[18] *Id.*

[19] Rakove, at 342, quoting from advice of Randolph to the Committee of Detail at the Constitutional Convention in Philadelphia.

[20] See Robin West, "Integrity and Universality: A Comment on Ronald Dworkin's *Freedom's Law*", 65 *Fordham L. Rev.* 1313 (1997) (arguing that interpretation is constrained by principles of legal justice, including consistency).

The interpretive process I have described plays a significant role in every arena of American constitutional law, from separation of powers to federalism. Arguably, it makes its most dramatic and controversial appearances when dealing with new claims of liberty and equality. In American constitutional history, repeatedly we have seen subjugated members of society seek to "re-constitute" the legal principles governing the institutions which perpetuate their subjugation. Advocates for the rights of people of colour, women, sexual minorities, children, and others, have used the open ended phrases of the Constitution to reshape old institutions. These subjugated groups have challenged hierarchies of age, race and gender grounded in concepts of dominance and ownership and have argued for rules predicated on concepts like equality and dignity. Constitutional principles have been agents of change not only in institutions like governments and schools, which we all recognise as "public," but also in supposedly "private" institutions such as work places, social settings, homes and families.

Often, judicial interpretation has provided the vehicle for the vindication of rights that were too controversial to command the supermajorities required by the formal amendment process. Does this make them illegitimate? I think not, both as a matter of morality and of pragmatics. Even the harshest critics of "activist judges" have never seriously advocated a return to plain meaning and originalism because the consequences would be unthinkable in an age which has come to accept formerly controversial claims as self evident truths.[21] If we were to purge American constitutional law of every doctrine not grounded in original intent, we would have to kiss goodbye not only those controversial cases involving abortion and gay rights,[22] but also landmark cases on racial and gender justice, family privacy and fundamental liberty, which have become universally accepted icons.[23] If plain meaning were the test, we could no longer rely on a host of textually suspect but absolutely pivotal legal constructs, such as the "incorporation doctrine", which makes portions of the Bill of Rights binding on the states as well as on the federal government.[24] Consider the even more astonishing "reverse incorporation doctrine", which Thurgood Marshall and other civil rights activists persuaded the Court could be used to overcome the lack of

[21] Steven G. Calabresi, "The Tradition of the Written Constitution: A Comment on Larry Lessig's Theory of Translation", 65 *Fordham L Rev.* 1435, 1449 (1997) (observing that Justices Scalia and Rhenquist endorse many interpretations that conflict with the framers' original intent).

[22] *Roe* v. *Wade*, 410 US 113 (1973) (protecting abortion rights); *Romer* v. *Evans*, 116 SCt. 1620 (1996) (protecting gays and lesbians from invidious discrimination).

[23] *Brown* v. *Board of Education*, 347 US 483 (1954) (striking down American apartheid laws); *Loving* v. *Virginia*, 388 US 1 (1967) (forbidding race discrimination in marriage laws); *Skinner* v. *Oklahoma*, 316 US 535 (1942) (prohibiting forced sterilisation); *Griswold* v. *Connecticut*, 381 US 479 (1965) (declaring right of privacy protects married partners use of contraception); *Frontiero* v. *Richardson*, 411 US 677 (1973) (holding that sex discrimination violates the Equal Protection Clause of the US Constitution); *Mississippi University for Women* v. *Hogan*, 458 US 718 (1982) (subjecting segregation by sex to heightened constitutional scrutiny).

[24] *Palko* v. *Connecticut*, 302 US 319 (1937) (holding that certain rights protected in the federal Bill of Rights are so "implicit in the concept of ordered liberty" that they must be deemed to have been absorbed into the Fourteenth Amendment guarantee of due process and are thus binding on the states).

an equality principle explicitly binding the federal government. In *Bolling* v. *Sharpe*, the Court held that the principle of equal protection, announced in 1868 in the Fourteenth Amendment, was binding on the federal government by incorporation into the Fifth Amendment due process clause, ratified in 1791 in the time of legalised slavery.[25] Surely, this exercise of interpretive creativity defies linear logic. How terrifying for Americans, admiring the crisp clarity of South Africa's new Constitution, to realise that we owe so many of our own fundamental freedoms to this *ad hoc* process of missed moves, power plays, tricky strategies, and creative lawyering.

In fact, the process of judicial interpretation which I have depicted as necessary and proper, has its dark side. The very qualities that permitted the US Constitution to grow and survive—the open textured language, the openness of the process to political and historical influence, the *ad hoc* and context-specific nature of case-by-case adjudication—have often proved dangerous to human rights. In addition, the lack of specificity about the scope and application of rights and about methods of interpretation has allowed reactionary judges, arriving after a moment of constitutional transformation, to backslide and evade responsibility for maintaining advances in human rights. Judicial activists have played a role in reading new rights out of, as well as into, the Constitution.

Fortunately, a mistaken or outmoded interpretation remains more malleable than an explicit text. In *Brown* v. *Board of Education*,[26] for example, the Court overruled its earlier finding in *Plessy v, Ferguson*[27] that the Fourteenth Amendment's equality principle was satisfied by facilities that were "separate but equal". Women won a similar battle in *Frontiero* v. *Richardson*,[28] which rejected the reasoning of *Bradwell* v. *Illinois*[29] that women had no equal protection clause claims because they were suited only to domesticity. Often, these reconstructions of constitutional meaning responded to emergence of novel rights. The traditional rights of whites to choose with whom they associate and of the patriarch to control all family decision-making, generally accepted at one time, gave way to competing claims for equality and dignity from people of colour and from women. Currently, pressure is mounting both domestically and internationally to acknowledge that children have their own unique set of human rights deserving of constitutional protection.

III. THE FAMILY IN US CONSTITUTIONAL LAW

Over the past half century, the US Supreme Court's interpretations of the open-textured language of the Bill of Rights and of the Civil War Amendments have

[25] *Bolling* v. *Sharpe*, 347 US 497 (1954).
[26] 347 US 483 (1954).
[27] 163 US 537 (1896).
[28] 411 US 677 (1973) (rejectiing sex stereotypes)
[29] 83 US (16 Wall.) 130 (1873) (upholding Illinois' denial of a married female's application for a licence to practise law).

created a fragile edifice of family-related rights which has re-shaped our underlying conceptions of relations between family members and relations of the family to the state. Because of their reliance on implicit norms rather than explicit
language, these rights are controversial and their status is questioned even by
members of the US Supreme Court.[30] They are constantly subject to revocation
through outright overruling, or to piece-meal dismantling by re-interpretation.
They are protected only by the doctrine of *stare decisis*—a principle never mentioned in the US Constitution.[31]

While women's rights and family rights enjoy only implied protection, children's rights are largely unprotected. Contemporary American children generally
enjoy few independent constitutional rights other than attenuated forms of protection in criminal or administrative proceedings. Children's rights (generally
described as "interests" rather than as "rights") are treated as subsumed in the
rights of the parent. Children's interests are defined by parents, exercising the
parent's constitutionally protected right to physical custody and control of children's upbringing.[32] If children have few "first generation rights" (those individual liberties associated with our Bill of Rights) they have absolutely no
"second generation rights" (rights to public protection and support). American
children enjoy no federal constitutional rights to education, to programmes of
protection from abuse and exploitation, and no rights to the basic nutrition,
income supports, shelter, and health care on which the right to life obviously
depends.[33] Children's federal welfare entitlements, addressed only by statute,
have been increasingly "privatised" by Congress in keeping with contemporary
market theories. International pressure has done nothing to change this balance.
The US is a lone holdout among all the nations of the world in refusing to consider ratification of the 1989 UN Convention on the Rights of the Child, the most
rapidly and universally accepted human rights document in the history of international law, having been adopted before its tenth anniversary by every nation
save two: Somalia, which currently lacks a functioning government, and the
United States of America.[34] Conservatives and the Religious Right claim it would
undermine constitutional rights of parents to raise their children as they see fit,
and fear that recognition of children's socio-economic rights would deprive parents and local government of autonomy and drain state and private resources.[35]

---

[30] *Planned Parenthood* v. *Casey*, 505 US 833, 979–1002 (Scalia J dissenting).

[31] 505 US 833 (joint opinion).

[32] *Michael H.* v. *Gerald D.*, 491 US 110 (1989); *Parham* v. *J.R.*, 442 US 584 (1979).

[33] *DeShaney* v. *Winnebago County Social Services*, 489 US 189 (1989).

[34] Within four years of its adoption by the United Nations General Assembly, 136 nations had
ratified the Convention. See Treanor, at n. 146. At latest report, Senator Jesse Helms, powerful Chair
of the Senate Foreign Relations Committee, had notified Secretary of State Madeleine Albright that
he would veto any attempt to place the Children's Convention on the Senate's agenda. Barbara
Bennett Woodhouse, *The UN Convention on the Rights of the Child: Cultural and Political Barriers to
Ratification by the USA in Contemporary International Law Issues: New Forms, New Applications*
(T.M.C. Asser Instituut 1998), 420.

[35] *Id.*

What accounts for this striking judicial and political hostility to children's rights, so different from the discourse found in the new South African Constitution? In the following section, I will offer some historical and legal background on American constitutional law and the process of growth through judicial interpretation which may partially explain the differences.

A. The Conservative Force of Substantive Due Process "Tradition" and Equal Protection "Difference"

In the American system, liberty and equality are both measured with reference to socio-cultural as well as legal traditions. The role of "tradition" is most obvious in the context of substantive due process theory, one of the more bizarre creations of the interpretive process. Substantive due process theory locates "substantive" limits on law making within the due process clause of the Fourteenth Amendment.[36] The first sentence of the Fourteenth Amendment overrules the case of *Dred Scott* v. *Sandford*,[37] in which the pre-Civil War Court had held that African-Americans, although born in the US, could not be considered "citizens" within the meaning of the Constitution. It continues:

> "No State shall make or enforce any law which shall abridge the privileges or immunities if citizens of the United States; nor shall any State deprive any person of life, liberty, or property, without due process of law; nor deny to any person within its jurisdiction the equal protection of the laws."

On its face, the term "due process" means procedural protections such as notice and the opportunity to be heard. All persons, it suggests, must be treated equally and fairly. Within a few years of its ratification, however, the Fourteenth Amendment, designed to advance racial equality, had been derailed by a post-Civil War backlash. In a series of rulings including *Plessy* v. *Ferguson* and the *Slaughter House Cases* in 1873 and the *Civil Rights Cases* in 1883, the Court interpreted the Fourteenth Amendment's clauses on equality and on privileges and immunities so narrowly they were useless in combating invidious discrimination.[38]

Meanwhile, creative conservative advocates managed to build instead on the language which prohibited the state from depriving any person of life, liberty or property without "due process". They persuaded the Court to strike down all sorts of economic legislation, on the ground that such regulation amounted to a "deprivation of property" or of "liberty" in violation of vested common law

---

[36] Barbara Bennett Woodhouse, "'Who Owns the Child?': *Meyer* and *Pierce* and the Child as Property", 33 *Wm. & Mary L. Rev.* 995, 1068–80 (1992).

[37] 60 US (19 How.) 393 (1857).

[38] The *Slaughter House Cases*, 83 US (16 Wall.) 36 (1873) interpreted the privileges and immunities clause narrowly to apply only to certain political privileges. *The Civil Rights Cases*, 109 US 3 (1883) held that Congress lacked the power to ban the exclusion of African Americans from public accommodations.

rights. While refusing to interpret the Fourteenth Amendment to protect the powerless former slaves, the Court transformed it instead into a tool to protect already powerful business interests. Substantive due process illustrates how judges can sometimes take the interpretive process down dead ends and along dangerous detours, even going so far as to repudiate the principles which provided the textual point of departure.

Traditions have also frozen our notions of equality and inequality, of capacity and incapacity, by endowing stereotypes with the force of fact. One of the Revolutionary period's most influential figures, John Adams, imagined that the legislature would be "a miniature of society". How right he was. Each of society's traditional injustices, justified by stereotypes of race and gender difference, was reflected in the original constitutional scheme. When Adam's wife Abigail protested the exclusion of women, and asked that "the ladies" be remembered by those meeting in Philadelphia to draft the Declaration of Independence, her husband scoffed at the idea.[39] One hundred years later, the Supreme Court remained convinced of women's essential unfitness for public life. In *Bradwell* v. *Illinois*,[40] the Supreme Court upheld Illinois denial of a law licence to Myra Bradwell, noting that as a married woman she could not enter into contracts or manage her own property. Women and men naturally occupied different spheres—women caring for the private sphere of home and children while men went forth into the public world of commerce, the professions and politics. In barring women from the practice of law, the Supreme Court concluded, Illinois simply recognised the reality of difference. The Court in *Bradwell* attributed constitutional meaning to the Victorian model of family life, which concentrated authority and control over all family members and all family assets in the hands of the patriarch. This tradition of exalting gender difference is reflected in the Court's continuing reluctance to subject sex discrimination to the same strict scrutiny applied to other forms of discrimination.[41]

B. Substantive Due Process Roots of Parental Rights

The forces of "tradition" and "difference" have blocked the constitutional evolution of American children's law. I have described in other writings the legacy of two early twentieth century Supreme Court cases, *Meyer* v. *Nebraska*[42] and *Pierce* v. *Society of Sisters*,[43] both decided during the heyday of economic substantive due process.[44] I have traced the relationship between substantive due

[39] Letter from Abigail Adams to John Adams (31 Mar. 1776), reprinted in *Familiar Letters of John Adams and His Wife Abigail Adams During the Revolution* (1875), 149.

[40] 83 US (16 Wall.) 130 (1873) (upholding Illinois' denial of a married female's application for a licence to practice law).

[41] *Rostker* v. *Goldberg*, 453 US 57 (1981) (applying "intermediate scrutiny" to gender classifications).

[42] 262 US 390 (1923).

[43] 268 US 510 (1925).

[44] Woodhouse, *supra* n. 36.

process theory and family rights, examining these seminal cases in the larger historical context of opposition to turn of the century social and economic reforms. *Meyer* and *Pierce* are revealed as an integral part of resistance by conservative forces favouring privatisation of social welfare. They were linked to contemporary opposition to a large range of programmes such as mandatory free public schooling, restriction of child labour, and maternal and infant health initiatives supported by progressives advocating a public role in support of children.

During the late nineteenth and early twentieth centuries, American children were still widely perceived as quasi-property of the patriarch. The claims of their parents that mandatory schooling laws, health laws, and laws against child labour infringed their vested common law rights to custody and control of their offspring fell neatly into the substantive due process paradigm which made of the Constitution a bulwark against state regulation of private property, and against changes in the *status quo*. The cases, taken out of historic context, seem innocuous. In *Meyer*, the Court drew upon substantive due process theory to strike down laws requiring schools to teach in English, and in *Pierce* the Court used it to strike down a law requiring all elementary students to attend public schools.

The results of these cases may have been correct, but their reasoning was troubling. While *Meyer* v. *Nebraska* and *Pierce* v. *Society of Sisters* are now often described as cases about intellectual liberty and family integrity, their rhetorical focus and legal underpinnings were the rights of parents not of children. Family rights, many now argue, might have been articulated as belonging to all members of the family, either collectively or individually. They might have been conceptualised as shielding the family as an entity—a group of people linked by blood and social relationships—from unwarranted intrusions by the state. Or all individuals within a family—women, men, elders and children—might have been viewed as bearers of individual yet interlocking rights. Parents rights to custody and control might have been mirrored by children's rights to their parents' love and to be raised by their parents, or the right to parental custody might have been conceptualised as a fundamental right of the child, with the parent acting as trustee of the child's interests. Instead, writing in the 1920s, the Court took parents' rights as its central focus, a bias which continues to the present day in cases on custody, adoption and child protection.[45]

The Supreme Court soon repudiated its economic substantive due process cases, opening the way for New Deal economic reforms.[46] However, the line of personal substantive due process cases rooted in *Meyer* and *Pierce* remains alive and well. Even in contemporary American law, "tradition" too often translates into the powers traditionally enjoyed and acknowledged by free white men, imposing a backward looking methodology for deciding which claims will be priv-

---

[45] See Barbara Bennett Woodhouse, "Hatching the Egg: A Child-Centered Perspective on Parents' Rights", 14 *Cardozo L Rev.* 1746 (1993).

[46] *West Coast Hotel Co.* v. *Parrish*, 300 US 379 (1937) (signalling end of economic due process constraints).

ileged as "fundamental liberties".[47] Most deeply rooted among traditional family liberties is the father's possessory right to custody and control of his children, now rendered gender neutral as a "parental" right. Children caught in divorce are torn between warring parents, and children at risk of abuse are caught between parent and state, since the parent has a constitutionally protected right that must be vindicated, even at great cost to the mere "interests" of the child. Meanwhile, the Court ignores the child's claims of "rights" to functional nurturing relationships.[48] And the Court refuses to recognise children's rights to public support when their parents cannot provide for them, or to public protection when their parents or care givers abuse them.[49] American family law remains locked in a formalistic tradition of possessory, privatised rights, when other systems have moved towards a more functionally based emphasis on protection of family relationships and on social investment in the next generation.

In sum, the American focus on parents' rights has created barriers to a constitutional theory of childhood, a fact that is glaringly evident in Americans' reaction to international initiatives on children's rights.[50] The difficulty of constructing a theory of children's rights on the foundation of American constitutional doctrine arises in part from the fact that children are different from adults, and our constitution deals badly with difference. It is complicated by the fact that children are essentially dependent on adults, and our Constitution deals poorly with dependency. And, as illustrated, it is complicated by the fact that children figured in early constitutional cases on the family as a form of parental "property", and control of children appeared as an element of parental "liberty", both values which receive explicit recognition in the text of the US Constitution. In addition, children have suffered from being on the wrong side of the sharp line between public and private spheres drawn by a Constitution that requires "state action" to trigger constitutional protections.

IV. THE NEW SOUTH AFRICAN CONSTITUTION

In contrast to the élite group of white men working in secrecy at the Philadelphia Convention of 1787–9, the Constitutional Assembly (CA) sought, and indeed, was pushed to include the voices of politically disempowered groups like women and children. They intentionally borrowed from these "outsider" perspectives.[51] In addition, the drafters embodied in written text not only substantive constitutional

---

[47] See *Michael H.* v. *Gerald D.*, 491 US 110, 113–14 (1989) (claims of substantive due process right must fail absent evidence of a deeply rooted historical tradition).

[48] *Id.*

[49] 491 US at 131; *DeShaney* v. *Winnebago County*, 489 US 189 (1989) (holding state is not responsible for protecting children from abuse).

[50] See *supra* n. 35.

[51] See Wing, at n. 162 and n. 237 (describing the protests of the ANC Women's League demanding inclusion of women in CODESA negotiations and the creation of the Women's National Coalition (WNC) to lobby for changes during the drafting process).

principles, but also various canons of interpretation and principles of application, with an eye to entrenching not only the text itself but the transformational spirit behind it.

An Explanatory Memorandum which prefaces the text states, "the process of drafting this text involved many South Africans in the largest public participation programme ever carried out in South Africa. After nearly two years of intensive consultations, political parties represented in the Constitutional Assembly negotiated the formulations contained in this text which are an integration of ideas from ordinary citizens, civil society and political parties represented in and outside of the Constitutional Assembly. This text therefore represents the collective wisdom of the South African people and has been arrived at by general agreement."[52] Here is how the Constitutional Court, in its September 1996 decision, described the process:

"Numerous public and private sessions were held and a wide variety of experts on specific topics were consulted on an ongoing basis. In response to an intensive country-wide information campaign, including public meetings and open invitations to the general public, the CA also received numerous representations, both oral and written." When the new text of the Constitution was submitted for certification, "because of the importance and unique nature of the matter, the directions [issued by the Constitutional Court] also invited any other body or person [besides political parties] wishing to object to the certification to submit a written objection."[53] Examination of the documents in the CA's on-line archives illustrates the reach of this process. Individuals, as well as political parties and non governmental organisations (NGOs) contributed extensively. A telephone hot line was created allowing any person to submit oral comments, and information was disseminated in all eleven of South Africa's official languages.[54] As the Court explained, in order to achieve certification the document would have to entrench all "fundamental rights", and thus the CA and the Justices were obliged to consider the status of rights worldwide, to determine whether all those rights generally deemed "fundamental" had been properly entrenched in the new document.

A. Women's and Children's Inclusion in the Constitution of the Republic of South Africa

The record suggests, at least to this observer, that the consultative process contributed to greater specificity, both linguistic and analytical, in the text of the final document. Explicit protection of "decisions concerning reproduction", which in

---

[52] Constitutional Assembly, Constitution of the Republic of South Africa 1996, as adopted by the Constitutional Assembly on 8 May 1996 and as Amended on 11 Oct. 1996: *Law for One Nation* (1996).

[53] Case CCT 23/96 Certification of the Constitution of the Republic of South Africa, (decided 6 September 1996).

[54] Author's interview of Justice Yvonne Mokgoro, 13 August 1997; see also www.constitution.za/cgi (collecting citizens' letters and oral comments).

American doctrine wanders like a lost child between theories of liberty, due process, family privacy and individual autonomy, was clearly articulated as a form of "bodily integrity" in section 12 (Freedom and security of the person) of the RSA Constitution. The RSA Constitution not only recognised the importance of gender equality but it also provides the most explicit constitutionalisation to date of children's rights. It is no accident that the South African Constitution singles out women and children for special recognition. Modern scholars have suggested that "the conception of justice in periods of political change . . . is alternatively constituted by, and constitutive of, the transition. As a state undergoes political change, legacies of injustice have bearing on what is deemed transformative."[55] Families had borne the brunt of apartheid. Women suffered greatly, forced into separation from their mates and children. Women's claims for equality were a transformative part of reshaping South Africa into an anti-racialist society, pushing it to reject sexism and to advocate second generation rights for children.[56] In addition, the transitional moment in South Africa coincided with a transitional moment for children world wide and in Africa—the promulgation and virtually universal acceptance of the 1989 United Nations Convention on the Rights of the Child and the 1990 promulgation of the African Charter on the Rights and Welfare of Children.

Perhaps even more telling is the fact that children played a central and highly visible role in the South African struggle for dignity, freedom and equality. Participants in the national debate on rights emphasised the debt owed by the nation to its youth, the sacrifices of youth in the battle against apartheid and the destructive impact of the apartheid system across every aspect of the lives and prospects of the majority of the country's children.[57] Observers emphasised how apartheid laws such as the Group Areas Act and "influx control" laws forced parents to leave their children in order to find work, forced children to leave their homes and seek survival on the streets. Enforced separation and inequalities in safety, education, shelter and every other arena stunted the mental growth of children of all races and classes. The struggle against apartheid engaged a generation of children as active combatants.[58] For those seeking to articulate a scheme of children's rights, the brutality of children's experiences under apartheid and children's status as freedom fighters provided a powerful motivating context. Before the fall of apartheid Justice Albie Sachs observed "[t]he greatest abuse to which South African children are subject today comes from the organized might

[55] Ruti Teitel, "Transitional Jurisprudence: The Role of Law in Political Transformation", 106 *Yale L.J.* 2009 (1997).

[56] Lorens du Plessis and Hugh Corder, *Understanding South Africa's Transitional Bill of Rights* (1994), 186 (women pressed for inclusion of children's rights in the Interim Constitution).

[57] Timothy J. Treanor, "Relief for Mandela's Children: Street Children and the Law in the New South Africa", 63 *Fordham L. Rev.* 883, n. 67 (citing conclusions in 1994 of Goldstone Commission of Inquiry into the Effects of Public Violence on Children that apartheid had been "uniformly and profoundly destructive" of children). See duPlessis, at 186 (citing sentiment among female representatives favouring trenchant protections of children's rights).

[58] See *id.*; UNICEF and National Children's Rights Commission, *Children and Women in South Africa: A Situation Analysis* (1993).

of the state. Any charter of children's rights in a democratic South Africa has to take this fact as a starting point." In arguing for a right to play, he pointed to a history in which children's "school grounds are occupied by troops, when their courage is displayed not on the sports field but in the torture chambers of the police".[59] In addition to those children jailed for political activism, large numbers of street children who should have been served by a child protective system were instead swept into criminal systems and detained indefinitely for petty offences, often in the same facilities as adult offenders.[60] In his 1994 State of the Nation Address, President Mandela specifically highlighted the plight of children in detention and of street children and committed national resources to meeting their needs.[61]

Women and children also played a direct role in setting the nation's human rights agenda. Foremost in this struggle was the African National Congress Women's League, whose members demanded inclusion in the process. These protests lead to the creation of the Women's National Coalition (WNC) to lobby for changes during the drafting process, and to make women's concerns a key element of the constitutional agenda.[62] Children also participated. In May and June 1992, the International Summit on the Rights of Children in South Africa brought together over 200 children between 12 and 16, representing all races and classes and all regions of South Africa. They drew up a "Children's Charter of South Africa" and demanded the right to a children's council of representatives in any future governments. The Charter concludes: "Children will no longer remain silent about their rights, but will speak and even shout out about their needs and demands".[63] In response to pressures for representation, the perspectives of children and young persons are now included in policy-making.

Most crucial is the explicit constitutionalisation of children's rights in section 28 of the RSA Constitution. It draws upon a number of comparative and international law sources, including "pre-eminently, the United Nations Convention on the Rights of the Child (1989)".[64] The enumeration of rights to name and nationality, to parental care, to social rights, to representation of counsel, and to have decisions based on the child's best interest, all bear a strong resemblance to principles of the UN Convention. A striking feature of the RSA Constitution is the intentional casting of the right to parental care as a *child's* right, not a parental right.[65] Also striking are the detailed rights accorded to children in detention, the

---

[59] Albie Sachs, *Protecting Human Rights in a New South Africa* (1990), 79–81.

[60] Treanor, at n. 273.

[61] Nelson R. Mandela, State of the Nation Address (24 May 1994) (cited in Treanor, *supra*, at n. 273).

[62] See Adrien K. Wing and Eunice P. De Caravalho, *Black South African Women: Toward Equal Rights* (1995), at n. 162 and n. 237.

[63] See www.constitution.org.za/cgi. The Children's Charter includes all of the rights adults often include in their formulations, but the spirit and emphasis is different is many subtle ways, with a greater focus on children's direct participation in decision-making.

[64] See Chaskalson *et al.*, *The Constitution of the Republic of South Africa*, at 33.1; Albie Sachs, *Protecting Human Rights in a New South Africa* (1990), 87.

[65] See du Plessis, at 186.

specific provisions regarding "family care" for children separated from their parents, and the right to counsel at public expense for children not only in criminal but also in civil cases. The constitutional rhetoric of the new South Africa explicitly commits all South Africans to sustaining and protecting all children.

B. Jurisprudential Specificity: Textualising the Concepts of Horizontality and Interpretation

The South African experience also lead to textualising of jurisprudential concepts the US Constitution had left largely to judicial interpretation. The 1996 RSA Constitution makes explicit one crucial difference between US and RSA schemes. In American constitutional theory, rights generally are interpreted as restraints on government, but not on private action.[66] In order to sustain a constitutional claim, the individual must show a causal connection between "state action" and harm to the constitutionally protected right. South African scholars approach this issue with different terms: "the term 'horizontal application' . . . indicates that those rights also govern the relationships between individuals, and may be invoked by them in their private disputes" while "the term 'vertical application' is used to indicate that the rights conferred on persons by the Bill of Rights are intended only as protection against the legislative and executive power of the state in its various manifestations".[67] The 1996 RSA Constitution was re-drafted to authorise horizontal application in certain situations, stating in section 8(2) that "[a] provision of the Bill of Rights binds a natural or a juristic person if, and to the extent that, it is applicable, taking into account the nature of the right and the nature of any duty imposed by the right". This section also requires courts, in the absence of statutory law, to develop common law to give effect to fundamental rights. While the Court will certainly be called upon to "interpret" this language, and may yet interpret it narrowly, many observers see it as a significant strengthening of the Bill of Rights. Horizontality has major ramifications for developing emerging rights, because it erodes the wall of separation between "public" and "private", and prompts critical scrutiny of relationships rooted in common law and tradition.[68]

The 1996 Constitution also clarified provisions regarding interpretation. The new section on interpretation tells the Court, when interpreting rights, it "must promote the values that underlie an open and democratic society based on human dignity, equality and freedom. It must also consider international law, and "when interpreting any legislation, and when developing the common law or customary law, every court, tribunal or forum must promote the spirit, purport and objects

---

[66] E.g., *Shelley* v. *Kraemer*, 334 US 1 (1948) (requiring state action but finding that judicial enforcement of a private racially restricted covenant constitutes state action).

[67] Delisa Futch, "*Du Plessis* v. *De Klerk*: South Africa's Bill of Rights and the Issue of Horizontal Application", 22 *N.C.J. Int'l Law & Com.* Reg. 1009 (1997) (citing 1996 (5) BCLR).

[68] See Chaskalson, *et al.*, n. 64 above, at 10–34.

of the Bill of Rights". The RSA Constitution clearly elevates "dignity" to a par with the key principles of equality and freedom. The Constitutional Court will surely be called upon to further clarify the content of "dignity", which, at its broadest, could be interpreted to encompass the entire range of human rights, including the socio-economic rights essential to achieving human dignity. In this endeavour, children's rights, which incorporate every "generation" of rights, will be on the cutting edge in formulating a re-constitution of the relation between children, parents, families and society.[69]

V. CONCLUSION

The foregoing thumbnail sketch of the RSA Bill of Rights shows how emerging rights of women and children functioned at a transitional moment to re-constitute the notion of "family", reshaping it to reflect a troubled nation's hopes for a more democratic, egalitarian and open society across all realms, both "public" and "private." The RSA Constitution explicitly protects rights of gender equality, and adds the new category of children to the list of rights-bearers. In the South African scheme, children of both sexes are given a set of specially defined rights beyond those enjoyed by "everyone". It seems clear that children's rights are viewed as part of a transformative agenda, and potentially binding on public as well as private actors. Many aspects of children's rights in South Africa can be traced to the participation of women and children in the transitional struggle to defeat apartheid and in the process of constitution-building that followed. As a result, children's rights have been rendered explicit and justiciable, individual and social, and children are empowered by procedural protections of their rights and by their inclusion in detailed constitutional scheme which encourages purposive and holistic interpretations of those rights.

The clarity of the RSA Constitution, in recognising rights for women and children, and in assigning broad social responsibility for the welfare of dependent children, stands in sharp contrast to the convoluted and reactionary legacy of American constitutional law of the family. Substantive due process theory, long ago abandoned as a theory of economic organisation, lives on as the primary theory undergirding family rights. Entrenched traditional stereotypes mask the institutionalised inequalities of women and children from constitutional view. The US Supreme Court's emphasis on tradition as the touchstone for identifying those rights protected by the theory of substantive process tends to entrench outmoded beliefs about women's and children's "natural" inferiority and difference. Meanwhile, the state action requirement places abuses of power within the family circle beyond the reach of our Bill of Rights. These legacies of constitutional interpretation encourage entrenchment of subordination and inequality rather than challenging traditional divisions of power. Since property rights are

---

[69] Du Plessis, at 187.

often perceived as a zero sum game, each new class of rights-bearers that battles its way into the safe haven of substantive due process protections potentially becomes a gate-keeper, excluding those who wish to follow. This is especially evident in the arena of family rights, where women defined freedom from patriarchy by the yardstick of control not only of their own bodies but of the bodies of their children. In constitutionalising the powers of the patriarch in the form of "parental rights", American law has become trapped in the amber of a specific historical moment—the Lochner era—and is burdened by this conservative legacy. By conceptualising the child as a form of private property, and the parent–child relationship as a private liberty interest of the parent, the US Supreme Court gave constitutional force to traditional hierarchies of power and essentialist views of difference, erecting barriers to recognition of women's and especially children's rights that advocates are still struggling to dismantle.

29

The Child's Right to Parental and Family Care*

J. A. ROBINSON

1. INTRODUCTION

The entrenchment of fundamental rights for individuals in South African law is a development of recent origin. The Constitution of the Republic of South Africa 200 of 1993 (hereafter referred to as the Interim Constitution) and the Constitution of the Republic of South Africa Act 108 of 1996 (hereafter referred to as the Constitution) contain Bills of Rights which provide for the constitutional protection of individuals, including children. Section 28(1)(b) of the Constitution provides, *inter alia*, that every child has the right to family care or to parental care, or to appropriate care when removed from the family environment. Section 28(2) provides that a child's best interests are of paramount importance in every matter concerning the child.

This chapter aims at considering in rather brief fashion the concepts "parent", "family" and "care" in its specific South African context and to theoretically analyse these provisions.

2. EVALUATION OF SECTION 28(1)(B)

1 Who is a parent in South African law?

This question, which apparently has a simple answer, is in fact not so simple to answer in South African law. Two instances suffice to illustrate the point. In the

---

* The following sources have been used : De Villiers, B., "The Rights of Children in International Law: Guidelines for South Africa" [1993] *Stellenbosch Law Review* 289; Sloth-Nielsen, J., "Ratification of the United Nations Conventionon the Rights of the Child: Some Implications for South African Law" [1996] *South African Journal on Human Rights* 401; Doek, J. E., "Hoe ver kan de Appel van de Boom vallen? Enkele Beschouwingen over ons toekomstig Afstammingsrecht" [1996] *FJR* 70; Van Bueren, G., *The International Law on the Rights of the Child* (Martinus Nijhof, 1995), Kluver; Henegan, M. and Atkin, W., *Family Law Policy in New Zealand* (Oxford University Press, 1992 Auckland); Davel, C. J. and Jordaan, R. A., *Law of Persons Students' Textbook* (Juta, 1995) Kenwyn.

first place, South African common law does not acknowledge the natural father of an extra-marital child as a parent. It is in fact no exaggeration to say that he is in law a stranger to his child. The father does not even have an inherent right of access to the child and even though he is under the obligation to maintain his child, the obligation is not reciprocal in nature.

It goes without saying that this situation may negatively influence the right of the child to parental care. In particular this may be the case where the father and the mother have been involved in a stable relationship of long duration and the father is caring well for the child. This exposition of the legal position consequently has been under severe attack for some time now. However, two recent developments have brought relief in this regard.

In the first instance the Constitutional Court ruled in *Fraser* v. *Commissioner of Child Welfare, Pretoria North*[1] that section 18(4) of the Child Care Act 74 of 1983 is unconstitutional. This section provides as follows:

> "A children's court to which application for an order of adoption is made . . . shall not grant the application unless it is satisfied—
> (d) that consent to the adoption has been given by both parents of the child, or, if the child is illegitimate, by the mother of the child, . . . "

The basis for holding that this provision is unconstitutional is that it discriminates between different "classes" of fathers of extra-marital children and that such discrimination is constitutionally forbidden. Regrettably, one seeks in vain for any consideration of the best interests of the child as the determining factor. In view of the provisions of section 28(2) that the child's best interests are of paramount importance *in every matter concerning the child*, this omission by the Constitutional Court is inexplicable. The result, however, that this section discriminates against some natural fathers, is to be welcomed.

The Natural Fathers of Children Born out of Wedlock Bill which was published recently, aims at normalising the relationship of the natural father and his extra-marital child. Section 2(1) provides that a court may on application by the natural father of an extra-marital child make an order granting the natural father access rights to, or custody or guardianship of the child on conditions determined by the court. Subsection (2) determines that such an application shall not be granted unless the court is satisfied that it is in the best interests of the child, and until the court, if an enquiry is instituted by the Family Advocate, has considered its report and recommendations. Section 3 creates a discretion for the court to cause any investigation which it may deem necessary and section 4 sets out a list of factors which the court must take into account when considering the application. The court may, in terms of section 5, make any order which it may deem fit and may, if it considers it to be in the best interests of the child, grant either party sole guardianship or custody of the child.

---

[1] 1997 2 SA 261 (CC).

The real importance of this Bill, it is submitted, is that it considers the best interests of the child of paramount importance. The focal point is shifted away from the natural father to the interests of the child. It is evident that the Bill takes as its point of departure that there may be circumstances where it will be in the child's best interests that its natural father has guardianship over or custody of or access to it.

A second problem area which manifests itself relates to a lacuna which was left by the legislature in the Children's Status Act 82 of 1987. This Act deals, *inter alia*, with artificial insemination and defines it so comprehensively that surrogate motherhood can be included as well. In the definition of "artificial insemination" the legislature did not specify that the child conceived in this way comes into being through insemination with the female gamete or gametes of the particular woman concerned. It can consequently be argued that the child is the legitimate child of the surrogate mother and her spouse where they both consented to her to be inseminated in this way and not the child of the husband and wife whose gametes have been implanted in the surrogate mother. This result is directly opposed to the objective of surrogate motherhood, namely to give birth to a child for a couple in a case where the woman is unable to carry the foetus and/or to complete the birth process.

It is uncertain how the Constitutional Court will react to this situation. It appears, though, that the solution to the problem will revolve around the Court's interpretation of section 28(1)(a) which provides that every child has a right to a name. Even though there are many legal and ethical questions involved, it is submitted that the mother who gave birth to the child will in law be considered to be the mother of the child. The reason is twofold:

(i) Section 10 of the Constitution provides that everyone has the right to dignity and the right to have his or her dignity respected and protected. If a contract were to be the basis of the eventual relationship coming into existence after the birth of the child, such contract would be the basis of the parent–child relationship and the child can in such case be considered to be the object of the negotiations between the surrogate mother and the mother whose gametes have been used. Such result would be objectionable in terms of section 10.

(ii) There is an old rule *mater semper certa est* which should apply. The fact that the gametes of another woman have been implanted in the surrogate mother should not have any influence on this rule.

2 Who is the family of the child?

In terms of the South African common law, the term "family" is restricted to an institution which comprises a union between a husband and wife who are legally married and their offspring. This conclusion derives from the definition of a marriage which is still adhered to for purposes of the common law, and which has been defined in the following terms in the well-known case of *Seedat's Executors* v. *The Master (Natal)*:[2]

> "Polygamy vitally affects the nature of the most important relationship into which human beings can enter. It is reprobated by the majority of civilized peoples, on grounds of morality and religion and the Courts of a country which forbids it are not justified in recognizing a polygamous union as a valid marriage."

The submission is made that because of marriage being regarded as an exclusive union, the idea of exclusivity also relates to the family concept. Consequently, polygamous unions are considered to be void and children born from such unions have extra-marital status. The same rule applies to indigenous marriages.

The provisions of the Constitution may lead to a radically different approach to the interpretation of the family concept. There are clear *indiciae* that the intention pertaining to the child's right to family care is in fact aimed at the extended family. This deduction stems from, *inter alia*, the provisions of section 15(3) of the Constitution which reads as follows:

> "(3)(a) This section does not prevent legislation recognising—
> (i) marriages concluded under *any tradition*, or a system of religious, personal or family law; or
> (ii) systems of personal and family law under any tradition or adhered to by persons professing a particular religion" (italics added).

The tribal/clan system which prevails in South Africa among indigenous people, is well known. The emphasis in these social structures falls on the extended family as a means by which society is organised and one's status is determined within the framework of his or her family. There can be no doubt that the true meaning of the words '*any tradition*' in section 15(3) of the Constitution was to convey that the child's right to family care extends not only to the nuclear family (as it would in terms of the common law) but also to the extended family.

It would also appear that the family is to be regarded as the primary institution within which the child must grow up. By placing the right to family care before the right to parental care, and by linking the concepts of family and parental care with the word '*or*', the conclusion may be drawn that the Constitution attaches more weight to family care than to parental care when it comes to the care of children. The concept of parental care, which is typically reflected in terms of exclusivity as set out in sources relating to the common law, must be elaborated upon by a definition of *family* which lacks such exclusivity. This interpretation would also leave room for typical indigenous and religious views on the family to be considered as included in the meaning of *family* in the Constitution.

---

[2] 1917 AD 302.

3 What is meant by parental care?

By using the word '*care*', the Constitution radically deviates from the parental *authority* notion of the common law. There can be little doubt that the *authority* of the *pater* has lost much of its harshness in modern South African law, and the best interests of the child almost always serve as a qualification to the exercise of parental power. However, its origin as an institution favouring the interests of the parents, rather than those of the child, remains.

By stating that the child has a right to family *care* or parental *care*, a definite nuance is placed on the parent–child relationship. The use of the concept of care clearly denotes an acknowledgement that children are vulnerable and lack maturity of judgment and experience. The concept of care consequently has a radically different basis, namely that the parent–child relationship is to be defined in terms of the care that is owed to the child to assist him or her to overcome its own vulnerability and lack of maturity relating to judgment and experience.

It is not foreseen that the use of *care* in the Constitution will lead to major changes in South African law. The High Court as upperguardian of all children in its jurisdiction, has in any case always seen its function to protect and advance the best interests of children. Nuances that may be expected to result because of the emphasis on the child's right to care may, in conjunction with the rights of the child which are of paramount importance in every matter concerning the child, relate to the permission required by the child to marry. Presently section 25(1) of the Marriage Act 25 of 1961 provides that a court may interfere in the refusal of the parents to the marriage of their child on the grounds that the refusal was without sufficient reason *and* that the consent to such marriage would be in the interests of the child. It is submitted that in view of the fact that care aims only at serving the interests of the child, the provisions of section 25(1) will have to be reconsidered.

3. A BRIEF THEORETICAL ANALYSIS OF THE PROVISIONS OF SECTION 28

(a) The very wording of section 289(1)(b) makes it clear that no constitutional protection is afforded to the family as an institution. It is submitted that such protection should have been the focal point of the section in view of the socio-economic background to the Constitution which was characterised by the policy of *apartheid*. The implementation of this policy led to a severe destruction in family life, especially among Black families. In fact, the urge for rebuilding the family *qua* institution has in 1983 already been voiced as "probably the most fundamental problem which will face any democratic government coming to power in the future". Clearly, this challenge, and the wrongs done to families in the name of *apartheid*, are not met by this provision.

It is further submitted that the Constitution in general has a distinct individualistic character. Consequently, no room is left for the recognition of rights of a family. In fact, other provisions of the Constitution render it a definite possibility that the integrity and authority of the family may be negatively affected. Two examples to illustrate this point suffice.

— The omission to recognise any rights for the family as an institution, results in fewer obligations on the State to protect the family; and
— The individualistic nature of the rights to education and freedom of religion may deny the inherent competence of parents to educate their children within the family in matters of this nature.

In this regard reference should be made to section 5 of the Convention on the Rights of the Child (1989). This section provides that States Parties shall respect the responsibilities, rights and duties of parents or, where applicable, the members of the extended family, to provide in a manner consistent with the evolving capacities of the child, appropriate direction and guidance in the exercise by the child of the rights recognised in the Convention.

As such, it is clear that the omission in the Constitution to protect the family as an institution falls short of the prescriptions of this international document. In fact, other international documents may also be referred to in this regard. Article 16(3) of the Universal Declaration of Human Rights specifically provides that "[t]he family is the natural and fundamental group unit of society and is entitled to protection by society and the State". Article 10(1) of the International Covenant on Economic, Social and Cultural Rights requires "the widest possible protection and assistance" for the family, particularly while it is responsible for the care and education of dependent children. There can be very little doubt that these international documents convey a clear intention that the unity of the family as a basic unit must be ensured and that the most effective means to do just that is to offer it the necessary support. They are also unambiguous that it is the duty of the State to ensure the development of institutions, facilities and services for the care of children. In terms of the Convention on the Rights of the Child referred to above, there is also a duty on the State to provide appropriate assistance to parents and guardians in the performance of their child-rearing responsibilities. The Declaration on Social Progress and Development (1969) considers "appropriate assistance" as assistance at a level which enables the family to assume its responsibilities fully within the community.

(b) The right of children to family or parental care, however, does serve as an acknowledgement of the importance for a child to grow up within a family environment. As indicated above, it can be assumed that the term 'family' includes both the nuclear and the extended family. The recognition of the extended family by the Constitution is of particular significance in the South African context as this family form is commonly accepted and adhered to by indigenous people. It can also be expected that this change in attitude will lead to a major impact regarding a definition of family in our common law. One can expect, for instance, that the definition of an extra-marital child will have to be considered anew. Exclusivity is clearly no longer the qualifying consideration in the definition of a family.

It is submitted that the recognition of the extended family will definitely serve the best interests of children. For instance, child care within the extended family is very much considered as a communal activity, leading to a minimum of state intervention. Put briefly, the philosophy is that the family must take care of its own. An example may be used to illustrate this point. The clan system which prevails in South Africa resembles that of the Maori of New Zealand. The so-called Family Group Conference, which is a development of fairly recent origin in New Zealand, is based on the extended family as viewed by Maori custom. The basic principle underlying the Family Group Conference is that the family of the child (including the extended family) is primarily responsible for the well-being of the child and must consequently also be regarded as the first line of remedy to resort to if, for instance, the child is in need of care. This development has resulted in a situation whereby matters which can be resolved within the family environment, are not referred to State Departments as a first step, but instead the interests of the child are determined and protected by his or her family and within his or her family environment. It would certainly serve the best interests of children if a similar development could take place in South Africa. One could add, however, in a more cynical vein, that the added advantage from the State's point of view, would obviously be the fact that the burden on the coffers of the State would be substantially alleviated. The potential of extended family members as a resource which the State could utilise, particularly in situations where children's own parents are unable to care for them, or where they are ill-treating or abusing the child, is an advantage not to be overlooked.

(c) It appears that no clear distinction is drawn between the roles of the State and parents *vis-à-vis* the child. The right of the child to family or parental care is a typical social right which is enforceable against the State. As a so-called second generation right it places the State under an obligation to act positively towards the fulfilment of the particular right. Other examples of second generation rights in the Constitution are contained in sections 26 and 27. Section 26 provides that everyone has the right to have access to adequate housing and that the State must take reasonable legislative and other measures within its available resources to achieve the progressive realisation of this right. Section 27 provides that everyone has the right to have access to health care services, sufficient food and water and social security and that the State must also in this instance take reasonable steps, within its available resources to achieve the progressive realisation of these rights. The duty of the State in terms of sections 26 and 27 is clear to understand. However, the position is more ambiguous in the case of section 28(1)(b)—family care and parental care, it is submitted, cannot be treated on the same basis as the right to adequate housing. What needs to be established, consequently, is the true nature of the rights contained in section 28(1)(b).

If one were to argue that the right of children to family care or parental care *qua* second generation right is unambiguous in its wording and that the State is directly responsible to provide family or parental care, the implication would be that the common law right of parents, and customary law right of families as instances of first responsibility towards the child, would be disregarded. This could never have been the intention behind section 28(1)(b) as it would imply that parents and families would be delegates of the State in the caring for and upbringing of their children. As such it would bring the result about that the best interests of the child would be the determining factor in the parent–child relationship or family–child relationship. Such a consequence is simply not tenable, as parents and families are under a constant duty under a variety of circumstances to consider what would be best for the child. Except for the fact that from a legal–theoretical point of view, it would be wrong to burden parents and families with this criterion, it would also not be practical to apply it in the day-to-day life of children. Parents and families take decisions regarding their children in the light available at a certain point in time while subjectively involved in the care of their children. It would be wrong if the best interests of the child could be used as a yardstick to establish whether a decision of the parents or family should be upheld or not.

The correct approach towards this particular right of children, it is submitted, is also to be gleaned from international documents. The intention conveyed by such documents is that the right of children to family or parental care is that the position of the State towards the child and the family is defined both in negative and positive terms. Section 17(1) of the International Covenant on Civil and Political Rights couches the obligation of the State in negative terms. It reads as follows:

> "No one shall be subjected to arbitrary or unlawful interference with his privacy, family, home or correspondence, nor to unlawful attacks on his honour and reputation."

Article 8 of the European Convention for the Protection of Human Rights and Fundamental Freedoms conveys the intention in positive fashion. It reads as follows:

> "Everyone has the right to respect for his private and family life, his home and his correspondence."

The phrasing of the obligation in negative terms prohibits interference which is unlawful and arbitrary. The term "unlawful" implies that State-authorised interference can only take place on the basis of law, which itself must conform to the Covenant. The requirement of arbitrariness is aimed at guaranteeing that even where the interference is lawful, it is also reasonable in the particular circumstances. States are under a duty to adopt legislative and other measures to implement and protect against interferences with this right.

In terms of the positive approach which has been adopted in Article 8, the European Court on Human Rights has stated that Article 8:

> "does not merely compel the State to abstain from such interference: in addition to this primarily negative undertaking, there may be positive obligations inherent in an effective respect for private or family life . . . The obligations may involve the adoption of

measures designed to secure respect for private life even in the sphere of the relations of individuals between themselves."[3]

The positive obligation emanating from Article 8 entitles the child to expect a State to implement positive measures to ensure that his or her respect for family life is protected. The negative approach contained in section 17(1) merely protects the child from the State, but it is rather the positive approach of section 8 which results in the child achieving a more equal status.

Read in conjunction, the negative and positive approaches to this particular right of children are of particular importance, because if the family is unable to exercise its primary role in bringing up children, they become more vulnerable to violations of other fundamental rights. The Preamble to the Convention on the Rights of the Child bears this out by stating that for the full and harmonious development of the child, the family environment should be one of happiness, love and understanding. The right of children to family or parental care consequently results in principles that only "the most pressing grounds" can be sufficient to justify the disruption of family ties, even if the material conditions of the family are poor; that where a State determines that a child is at risk from its parents and seperates the child in its own best interests from its family, the child's right includes the right to maintain personal relations and direct contact with both parents on regular basis; that parents have a basic right to bring up their own children and that where there is a dispute between the parents and the State concerning the care of the children after which the State takes the child into care, two criteria have to be met, namely that such care must represent the minimum necessary measure and that the object of the care must be aimed at the reintegration of the child into the natural family.

4 CONCLUSION

There can be little doubt that South African jurisprudence still has a long way to go in the interpretation of Constitutional measures. In this regard section 39 of the Constitution is to be welcomed since it provides for a court, when interpreting the Bill of Rights, to

> "(a) promote the values that underlie an open and democratic society based on human dignity, equality and freedom; (b) must consider international law; and (c) may consider foreign law."

The Constitution has made serious inroads into fixed common law values. It has brought about fundamental changes in attitude towards the most basic of institutions. In incorporating the new values into our law, international and foreign law will have to be relied upon.

---

[3] *X & Y* v. *The Netherlands*, ECHR, 20 March 1985.

30

Ways of Seeing*—"Lawyering" for a New Society in South Africa

JUNE SINCLAIR

I INTRODUCTION

The jury will be out on South Africa's new constitutional dispensation until it becomes less contemporaneous and more historical. The questions that will inevitably be asked of us and what we made of our opportunity to abandon oppression in favour of democracy will be many, and varied. One kind of question that bears some consideration now, in the afterglow of our 1994 miracle, is: what sort of law and what sort of "lawyering" will conduce to the society we are striving to create? Are our efforts to procure democracy, justice, open government and individual freedom misguided, or well informed? Do we really know what we are doing? Are (family) lawyers that relevant to the exercise, anyway?

Freud (put as crudely as his lessons can be put) teaches that functioning, well adjusted individuals need two basic things in their lives: a loving relationship, and a fulfilling job. As lawyers who influence the regulation of the "private sphere of the family", we are intimately concerned with the first ingredient, and frequently insufficiently aware of the interrelationship of that ingredient with the second—the public world of work. Achieving an acceptable balance of power between men and women in the home and in the workplace remains elusive, despite nearly universal entrenchment of formal or institutional equality in most legal systems. The rich literature on this subject demonstrates that the reasons and the implications are neither arduous to articulate nor difficult to document. They derive in part from the law and in part from the preferences of society, including choices made by women themselves. They are profoundly influenced by the structure of the system of paid labour. The fact is that women still occupy inferior and precarious positions within and in the aftermath of intimate relationships, more especially when they head one-parent families. And the fact is that this reality falls within the province of both public and private law to resolve.

The way the state chooses to regulate intimate relationships brings a public-law

---

* This expression is taken from a television series directed by the art critic, John Berger, later reworked as a fascinating book entitled *Ways of Seeing*.

dimension to family law that does not receive sufficient attention.[1] There are no longer rigid boundaries behind which private lawyers can shelter, for the boundaries between public and private law have been blurred, the bright line between them fudged.[2] "Private law ceases to be regarded as some brooding Roman-Dutch omnipresence in the sky and is revealed to be a public mechanism sanctioned by the state for the regulating of social transactions."[3]

"Equality", that enigma, is not a concept deeply embedded in South African culture. Lawyers, judges the legislature and the public at large grope yet for direction as they travel down the narrow footpath of formal equality, towards the broad highway of a true democracy that will lead to the kind of society described in our new Constitution.

II THE NEW BILL OF RIGHTS AND ITS APPLICATION

The application of the Constitution is crucial to the creation of such a society. The precise reach of the Bill of Rights remains a vexed technical and ideological question, albeit not quite as vexed as it was during the operation of the interim Constitution,[4] which was worded differently, and less clearly.

Whether the Bill of Rights applied in disputes between private persons was a question that gave rise to substantial dissension under the interim Constitution, and remains an issue likely to excite controversy. It is, put (too) simply, whether the Bill of Rights binds private persons in a particular instance and, if it does, then how. Put another way, when does the Constitution apply vertically (between state and private persons) and when also horizontally (in dealings between private persons) and, if the latter, how.[5] The interpretation of clauses regulating application in the interim Constitution was the subject of the important decision of the Constitutional Court in *Du Plessis* v. *De Klerk*.[6] That case held (*inter alia*)

---

[1] See June Sinclair (assisted by Jacqueline Heaton) *The Law of Marriage, Vol. 1* (Jute & Co. 1996), ch. 1, esp. 3–5, 66–71.

[2] See Alfred Cockrell, "Can you Paradigm?—Another Perspective on the Public Law/Private Law Divide" [1993] *Acta Juridica* 227 at 234; P. J. Visser, "Enkele Beginsels en Gedagtes oor die Horisontale Werking van die Nuwe Grondwet" (1997) 60 *THRHR* 296 at 303.

[3] Cockrell, *ibid*. He observes that "the rules of 'private law' are doctrinal artefacts by means of which the state regulates and coerces all of civil society, and as such might qualify to be categorized as a matter of 'public' law" (*op. cit.*, 229).

[4] Act 200 of 1993.

[5] The formulation of questions about the meaning of "horizontality" has spawned its own debate. See, e.g., Alfred Cockrell, "Private Law and the Bill of Rights: A Threshold Issue of Horizontality" in *Bill of Rights Compendium* (1997) 3A–2, and Halton Cheadle and Dennis Davis, "The Application of the 1996 Constitution in the Private Sphere" (1997) 13 *SAJHR* 44 at 49, 51. Cheadle and Davis point out, importantly, that "there is a difference between a zone of privacy where individuals can behave as they wish, and a legal dispute in terms of which one party seeks to rely upon the law to enforce a claim . . . " (*op. cit.*, at 47).

[6] 1996 (3) SA 850 (CC). Important critiques of the *Du Plessis* case are provided in Stuart Woolman and Dennis Davis, "The Last Laugh: *Du Plessis* v. *De Klerk*, Classical Liberalism, Creole Liberalism and the Application of Fundamental Rights under the Interim and the Final Constitutions" (1996) 12 *SAJHR* 361, and by Halton Cheadle and Dennis Davis, above n. 5 at 51–4.

that the Bill of Rights did not have general horizontal application and could not be invoked between private individuals in a dispute over a rule of the common law, that is, where the state was not involved. The finding answers (at least part of) the enquiry about what is known as direct horizontality.

The alternative to direct horizontal application is known as "seepage" or indirect horizontal application, which would influence only the interpretation or development by the courts of the common law (in the elucidation of notions like "public policy", "good faith", *"boni mores"* and the like) in such a dispute.

Section 8 of the final Constitution makes it clear that the Bill of Rights applies to all law, that is, common law, legislation, judicial decisions and customary law. It declares unequivocally that the Bill of Rights binds the legislature, the executive, the judiciary and all organs of state. Not only natural, but also juristic persons can invoke the rights contained in the Bill of Rights. However, section 8(2) declares that a provision of the Bill of Rights binds natural or juristic persons, but only "if, and to the extent that, it is applicable, taking into account the nature of the right and the nature of any duty imposed by the right". This text means that some rights (such as the right to dignity, privacy, equality before the law and equal protection and benefit of the law) may be held to apply as between private persons while others (such as the right to citizenship and those pertaining to arrest and detention) will not, and that it will be up to the courts to elucidate the matter on a case-by-case basis. Their task will be a daunting but crucial one. It will be infused with the vision of each of the judges charged with the responsibility of giving meaning to our new dispensation, replete with political predeliction and constrained by the technical touchstones of statutory interpretation.

For family lawyers in South Africa, a country with a history of sexual inequality and racial discrimination, one of the most important enshrined rights is that to equality. Section 9 proclaims the right of everyone to be equal before the law and to have the right to equal protection and benefit of the law. It also expressly states that "[n]o person may unfairly discriminate . . . against anyone . . . ".[7] These words, internal to this right, as distinct from words governing the general application of the Bill of Rights, are notably different from the more conventional and widely used formulation "everyone has the right to . . . " employed elsewhere and suggestive of rights that an individual has against the state. The words make it clear that the proscription against unfair discrimination indeed binds private persons in their dealings with each other.

But, regrettably, the matter of interpretation is still not uncomplicated. The wording of several provisions in the Constitution reveals the persistent division of opinion between proponents of vertical operation of the Bill of Rights (coupled perhaps with indirect horizontal application) and those who favour, whenever it is not manifestly inappropriate, direct horizontal application.[8] The words

---

[7] S. 9(4).

[8] There are of course those holding positions between these two views. Cheadle and Davis, n. 5 above, at 50, speaking of the interim Constitution, point to the fact that it was a political compromise which left the language open to differing interpretations: "Once ambiguity was admitted, the

tacked onto the end of section 9(4), to the effect that national legislation must be enacted to prevent or prohibit unfair discrimination by one person against another[9] may be seen to dilute the effect of direct horizontal application of the equality provision.[10]

Further, section 8(3), part of the general application clause, enjoins a court, when applying a provision of the Bill of Rights to a natural or juristic person in terms of section 8(2), to apply "or if necessary develop the common law to the extent that legislation does not give effect to that right". It goes on to provide further that a court "may develop rules of the common law to limit the right". The direction to the court to "develop" the common law is repeated very specifically in section 173.[11]

Precisely what is meant by the word "develop" is not yet known. Does it encompass the right to strike down? Does it require the courts, in order to comply with the injunction in the Constitution, in each case where the common law is found to be inconsistent with the Constitution, not only to strike down, but also to rewrite what is bad? Does it require the courts to write new law where there is no common law (and no statute, or a defective statute) regulating an issue requiring adjudication? In disputes between private persons, must the court develop actions in delict and determine damages for violations of fundamental rights?[12]

verticalist argument found favour amongst many lawyers for it reflected a deep commitment to a rigid division between private and public law embedded in our legal system." Differences of approach among lawyers will persist, given the formulation of s. 8.

[9] S. 23 of Sched. 6 to the Constitution requires such legislation to be enacted within three years of the coming into operation of the Constitution, that is, by no later than 4 Feb. 2000. There are other sections instructing the legislature to enact statutes to give effect to protected rights: s. 25(6), read with s. 25(9) of the property clause, enjoins the legislature to enact legislation to guarantee either legally secure tenure or comparable redress to persons or communities whose tenure of land is insecure as a result of racially discriminatory laws; s. 26(2) requires the state to take reasonable legislative measures to achieve the right to housing; s. 27(2) makes the same demand in respect of health care, food, water and social security; ss. 32(2) and 33(3) require national legislation to give effect to the rights to acess to information and to just administrative action (and, as with the case of the equality provision, this legislation must be enacted within three years of the coming into operation of the Constitution—s. 23 of Sched. 6). As Cheadle and Davis point out (n. 5 above, at 59–60) these latter rights are not the kind of rights infringed by private persons, nor do they espouse the kind of obligations that should be imposed on private individuals. They flow from the duty of the state to provide basic equality to its citizens via the provision of appropriate facilities and services.

[10] Cheadle and Davis, n. 5 above, at 59 consider these words in s. 9(4) to provide a persuasive argument against horizontality. They point out that the words can be interpreted as a clear constitutional preference for legislation (rather than judicial intervention) as the appropriate means of implementing the right horizontally. They concede that the words provide to the "narrow constructionists" an argument that the provisions of s. 9(4) are not intended to apply or are not suitable for application to private persons (*ibid.*).

[11] Which sets out the inherent jurisdiction of various courts. It is elaborated upon in s. 39(2). "Develop" suggested to Kentridge AJ in his interpretation of the interim Bill of Rights in the *Du Plessis* case (n. 6 above) that a court could not declare a rule of the common law invalid in litigation between private individuals where the state was not involved (see his judgment at 885, with which the majority of the court concurred).

[12] M. M. Corbett, "Aspects of the Role of Policy in the Evolution of our Common Law" (1987) 104 *SALJ* 52 considered the judicial tasks of interpreting a statute and developing the common law to be similar. His explanation was offered at a stage when South African courts had no power to

Nowhere is it expressly stated in the Constitution that a court, in "developing" the common law, may or should declare a rule of it invalid. Nowhere is it clearly envisaged that a court issuing such a declaration might leave it at that, declining to enter a domain it considers to be that of the legislature.[13]

Another dimension to this possible problem arises from the fact that section 167(5), the provision describing the Constitutional Court, declares that the Constitutional Court "makes the final decision whether *an Act of Parliament, a provincial Act or conduct of the President* [emphasis added] is constitutional", and must confirm any order of invalidity made by another court before that order has any force. Its confirming counterpart is section 172(2)(a). Both of these provisions seem directed at the work-product of the legislature and the executive. Neither hints at a judicial declaration of invalidity of a rule of the common law, or the consequences of such a declaration. By contrast, section 172(1) (a), dealing with the powers of courts in constitutional matters, says that a court *must* declare invalid "*any law* [emphasis added] or conduct" inconsistent with the Constitution (regardless, it seems, of source). It goes on to empower the court to give equitable relief in its order and to suspend the declaration of invalidity to allow a competent authority to rectify the deficiency. Section 172(2)(b), however, again refers to a decision of the Constitutional Court on the *validity of an Act or conduct*—the work-product of the legislature and the executive.

Other than the injunction to "develop" the common law, neither instruction nor guidance is given to a court in the event of its making a finding that a rule of the common law violates the Constitution. Formulations of the kind described here, which spawned great controversy about the interim Bill of RIghts, and which persist in the final Constitution, are clearly reflective of a maintained mindset of vertical operation.[14] Taken together, the points outlined above seem

declare any law unconstitutional, and he provides examples of the courts making policy decisions in developing the law determining delictual and criminal liability and the validity or otherwise of contracts. The learned judge's exposition puts beyond doubt the proposition that the courts do function in a policymaking capacity. It also highlights the differing proclivities of judges for moving into the realm of policy and beyond the bare necessities of the case before them. While some consider it to be their proper function to "see the distant scene" (*op. cit.*, 57), others feel uncomfortable expounding generally the law on the topic before them. Now that our courts are charged with the responsibility of protecting enshrined rights, the question must be posed how they should do so in "developing" the common law. Has their task been changed and, if so, how? Cheadle and Davis, n. 5 above at 64–6, say that courts developing the common law give new content to existing concepts; they are mandated now to a similar approach in giving content to the commitments made in the Constitution. South African lawyers will have to analyse the common law, its scope and promise, and test it against the Constitutional commitments. With these statements no one can quarrel. But the unanswered question is how far the courts will be prepared to go in stepping into a domain that many will regard as the preserve of the legislature. It is the boundaries of the judicial function that remain to be determined: Dawid van der Merwe, "*Iudicis est Ius Dicere, non Dare*: Judicial Law-making by Institutional Development of the Common Law" in C. W. van Wyk and H. van Oosten, *Nihil Obstat: Essays in Honour of W. J. Hosten* (Butterworths, 1996), 225.

[13] The declaration of invalidity itself can, not without some strain, one might suppose, be construed as a "development" of the common law.

[14] They assisted Kentridge AJ in the *Du Plessis* case (n. 6 above) to reach the conclusion that declarations of invalidity of a rule of the common law in a dispute between private individuals was not permissible.

to represent an attempt to "put the brakes on the application of the Bill of Rights to private persons".[15] They create a zone of ambiguity about the proper role of the judiciary and the proper role of the legislature in our new constitutional dispensation, which remains committed to the principle of the separation of powers.

As it is not obvious what the "development" of the common law will entail or permit, one may be forgiven the thought that, if the separation of powers is to retain its (never precise) meaning, a court faced with common law that is unconstitutional may (indeed, should) strike it down, but may also wish to use its power under section 172 to refer the matter to the legislature. It may prefer this option over one requiring it to formulate an appropriate set of perhaps entirely new rules to govern the situation before it and, by implication in some cases, others that may be inextricably related.

It is beyond the scope of this chapter to traverse the complex arguments on either side of the horizontality debate. But some comment regarding concerns expressed about the courts having power to strike down rules of the common law may be apposite in a paper dealing with the role of lawyers and family law—a field notorious for outmoded common-law conceptions regarding fairness and equality of the sexes. Many of these concerns emerge from the judgments of the majority of the Constitutional Court in the *Du Plessis* case.[16] While it seems to be comfortably and universally accepted that in a dispute between private persons involving legislation the Bill of Rights can be invoked by a party if the legislation infringes a protected right, the same is not true about the common law. The common law, in private disputes, is accorded a sacrosanctity by some judges and commentators that is hard to explain.[17] It is worth observing here that any

---

[15] Cheadle and Davis, n. 5 above, at 55–6.

[16] N. 6 above.

[17] We know that the source of an offending rule can be fortuitous. A rule of the common law which discriminates unfairly on the ground of sex, say, may simultaneously find expression or modification or attenuation in a statute. Defining its source for the purpose of deciding whether it can be declared unconstitutional in a dispute between private individuals could be as difficult and unsatisfying an enterprise as deciding that issue in a dispute between the state and a private person (see Sinclair (assisted by Heaton), n. 1 above, at 73–4). Striking down the statute can of course also potentially produce worse hardship than the statute produced, because the striking down, it could be argued, have the effect of reinstating the common law, which may have been softened by the statute. The marital power of the common law and its substantial attenuation by the Matrimonial Affairs Act 37 of 1953 and prospective abolition by the Matrimonial Property Act 88 of 1984 is a fine example, and was referred to by Kentridge AJ in *Du Plessis* v. *De Klerk* (n. 6 above) at 881. Athough the Court's ruling in that case is an interpretation of the interim Constitution and of provisions that are now differently worded, it contains important broad, policy statements about vertical and horizontal application. One of the views expressed by Kentridge AJ was that in a case where striking down a statute would produce a harsher result by reason of the resurrection of the common law, the lesson is that the court should be particularly circumspect about striking down the statute (at 881). On this line of thinking, to use his example, if the marital power had been challenged on the basis of the insufficiency of the limitations placed upon it by the Matrimonial Affairs Act, say, the court, we are advised, should have been especially circumspect about declaring unconstitutional the statute, in order not to revive the harsher, untrammelled marital power of the common law. Can it seriously be contemplated that the court might have been persuaded *not* to strike down the Matrimonial Affairs Act 37 of 1953, which accepted and entrenched a manifestly unacceptable and discriminatory regime, on the ground that the common law was even worse?

rule that infringes fundamental rights remains a part of our law, whether of our common law or of our enacted law, only for as long as and to the extent that the legislature chooses not to change it. No court should hesitate to declare unconstitutional any rule that offends against the rights enshrined in the Constitution, regardless of its source.[18] The courts make law when they strike down the work-product of the legislature, thereby contradicting the will of the democratically elected representatives of the people, and they make law when they declare unconstitutional the lack of work-product of the legislature—a persisting infringement of the Bill of Rights left unaltered in the common law. It is quite possible that the legislature deliberately fails to alter a rule of the common law. Omitting to legislate can be as much a policy decision and as much of an infringement of human rights as legislating can be.[19] It is a form of state action. Classical liberal theory that demands a sphere of privacy into which the state should not intrude overlooks that the *status quo*, the failure to intrude, often perpetuates some of the worst injustices in society.

Our common law has afforded a number of examples of failure of the legislature to intrude. Several injustices were left intact for many years, in the face of vigorous campaigning for amelioration. The issues included the domicile of married women, the marital power, guardianship of children and marital rape. Remaining issues include several rules of customary law, the custody of children and the financial consequences of divorce, and parental rights in respect of extra-marital children. There has been a "quiet occupation of private space", an "unarmed occupation of individual lives" by a body of common law that restricts the life choices and governs private relationships of the majority of South Africans.[20] That occupation calls for judicial scrutiny.

It is not being suggested that the court should lightly usurp the function of the legislature in reformulating law it finds bad or in making entirely new law in areas not previously regulated. It should, in appropriate cases, especially where reformulation is not a simple matter of substituting one rule for another, exercise its power[21] to order the legislature to rectify the offending position whether the offense derives from a statute or from the common law. The court's crucial task is to determine whether the rule, statutory, common-law or customary violates the rights enshrined in the Constitution. The courts are the guardians of the values enshrined in the Constitution. They cannot fulfil that role if they do not ensure that the legislature *does not act* in ways inimical to the achievement of fundamental rights and freedoms and, equally, if they do not ensure that it *does*

---

[18] See Woolman and Davis, n. 6 above.

[19] The lesson of Kentridge AJ in relation to the marital power, to the effect that "the radical amelioration of the common law has hitherto been a function of Parliament; there is no reason to believe that Parliament will not continue to exercise that function" (at 881C), is not convincing. The marital power is a shining example of a denial of full legal status to women that persisted in our common law until 1993, despite tenacious and sustained campaigns over many years to have it removed (see Sinclair (assisted by Heaton), n. 1 above, at 126–31).

[20] Woolman and Davis, n. 6 above, at 385–6.

[21] Contained in s. 172(1).

act where necessary to prevent existing, outmoded rules from remaining part of the legal system and continuing to perpetrate infringements of protected rights. We cannot be satisfied to let the courts interfere with the positive output of the legislature but not with its omissions. We cannot permit it to ignore rules inherited from a bygone age, reflective of outmoded *mores*, discriminatory, yet left intact to reside in the treatises of the Roman-Dutch jurists or in customary law, which determine the outcome of crucially important disputes between private persons, often in the sphere of greatest concern to them—the private sphere of the family.

III THE SEPARATION OF POWERS AND THE ROLE OF SOUTH AFRICAN COURTS IN REWRITING THE LAW

The comments above, on the application of the Bill of Rights, suggest that it is not always proper, indeed, it is often undesirable, for the courts to reformulate ("develop") the common law. This is especially true in areas of major national importance where policy decisions should be taken by the elected representatives of the people after due and open debate.[22] It has been argued here that the Constitution should be interpreted to demand judicial scrutiny of all law, regardless of its source, for compliance with the Bill of Rights. However, in cases where the common law, and, *a fortiori*, a statute, falls foul of the Constitution, the courts should not, it is suggested, be reluctant to use their referral power to require the legislature to act within a given time to rectify the situation. Refusal by the legislature to comply would evidence constitutional collapse and the end of responsible government. The implications of such a catastrophic constitutional impasse are not explored in this chapter.

The legal profession, in its turn, and those charged with educating people about their rights, could do well not to create the impression that the judiciary should always be the first line of atttack/defence against injustice. Taking more seriously our civic responsibility to improve the quality of national and local government through full participation in the political process could in the end prove to be a better route than relentless litigation in fostering the democratic values we cherish and to which we aspire.

IV THE EXPECTATIONS EXCITED BY THE GENERATION OF A RIGHTS CULTURE—CAN WE MEET THEM?

One of the central tasks of the South African Human Rights Commission is to educate the population about its rights. Lawyers, too, see this as one of their pri-

---

[22] Like the question of abortion—regulated now by the Choice on Termination of Pregnancy Act 92 of 1996. It is interesting that this highly emotive issue was resolved by legislation, while that of the death penalty was left to be decided by the Constitutional Court.

mary roles. South Africa's billboards routinely proclaim: "Know your rights." The question is whether the rush to teach individuals that they have rights which they should enforce, undeniably necessary, could have any detrimental societal effects. The absoluteness of an attitude towards rights, and the relentless individualism with which they are pursued, foster a mentality of entitlement to the largesse of the state and to the profits of the organisations that wield enormous power within the society. They emphasise freedom, which becomes confused with licence, and exclude service, participation and good citizenship. The question is: will expectations of what the law, the Constitution, can deliver not become unrealistic? There is a risk entailed in our rights teaching. It is that, in our anxiety to propagate a healthy rights culture, we permit, even encourage, the confusion of needs/wants/desires with rights. The societal danger of doing so cannot be overstated. It will breed discontent and disillusionment; it will feed the demon that is destructive social behaviour. Are we not seeing some of the signs of this confusion in the appalling incidence of serious crime?

Mary Ann Glendon, in her book, *Rights Talk—The Impoverishment of Political Discourse*,[23] records very pertinently the response of people in the United States to questions about their Constitution. They say: "The Constitution guarantees me the freedom to do as I want". Glendon warns that the rights discourse, the rights talk, what she calls "the intemperate rhetoric of personal liberty", now so deeply embedded in the United States, has caused Americans to live and think as atomised, unconnected individuals—all rights and a diminished sense of duty and responsiblity.[24] Glendon singles out constitutional law, criminal law and family law as the most significant terrains within which lawyers can help to define for people what they are and what kind of society they wish to bring into being.[25]

---

[23] (New York: The Free Press, 1991), at x.

[24] See ch. 4. The sequel to *Rights Talk* is Glendon's book, *A Nation Under Lawyers* (New York: Farrar Straus and Giroux, 1994), in which the author documents, and laments, what has happened to the legal profession. Legal firms operate like other businesses, pursuing profit as a first if not only priority. Providing a service has been discounted. Winning for your client has replaced peacemaking. Contributing to social harmony is no longer regarded as a key role of the legal profession. In a (not uncritical) review of Glendon's two books, Robert E. Rodes, (1995) 40 *American Journal of Jurisprudence* 411 points to some additional features of the current state of the legal profession and its impact on society. He observes that Hohfeldian theory of the correlativity of rights and responsibilities tends to force rights into an adversarial framework. "If you have a right that is not being implemented, you are necessarily the victim of someone who is failing in a duty to implement it. Your perception that you are a victim will become more and more acute as you cast about . . . for someone to blame" (at 416). Rodes dubs this "the classic problem of assignability" (*ibid.*), and accuses liberals of ignoring it, thereby giving ammunition to their opponents by adopting a package of unenforceable rights. By contrast, the "hard-line conservatives", as he calls them, rigorously refuse to recognise any right that does not come with a clearly designated person under a duty to implement it. Thereby, the latter absolve the rich of any duty to the poor, since no one poor person has a claim against any one rich person. Rode proposes resolution of the problem via the invocation of the concept of "social justice", which imposes on all of us, not a duty to any specific person to share our wealth, for example, but a duty to use our best efforts to reform institutions that impoverish people. A rights doctrine that ignores the problems associated with assignability fails the society it seeks to enrich.

[25] Above, n. 23, at 3, 105.

A fundamental distinction between South Africa and the United States that may be being overlooked, and may be important, is the already deeply embedded notion of *group* identity, *group* responsibility, *group* dignity that underpins African culture—that is, the culture of the majority of South Africans. Human rights in African culture are more aptly expressed as human dignity. The dignity of the individual derives from his or her belonging to the group rather than from an assiduous insistence on individual rights and the inevitable litigation required to enforce these. It is far from clear that a radical shift away from this notion would be altogether a good thing. We may not want to turn the next generation into what Glendon calls "lone rights-bearers".[26]

It is significant that, after much debate about including the protection of the family in the Constitution, South Africans decided against doing so, largely on the ground that the protection of the rights of individuals would automatically protect families, at least from the state. Another reason advanced for singling out the individual for protection was the pluralistic nature of South African society and the resultant difficulty in defining "the family" that deserved protection. Criticism of this approach is becoming apparent in academic writing.[27]

V   CUSTOMARY AND RELIGIOUS LAW—SOUTH AFRICA IS A PLURALISTIC SOCIETY

Alongside any discussion of rules of the common law, legislation and judicial decisions, there resides the matter of African customary law and the consonance of its rules, particularly those governing the law of persons and family law, with the rights enshrined in the Constitution. (Similar questions arise in relation to Muslim family law.)

Customary law features prominently in the Constitution. Yet the application provision nowhere mentions it.[28] The equality provision[29] includes culture, social and ethnic origin, belief and religion among the express grounds upon which unfair discrimination is prohibited. Everyone is guaranteed the right to participate in the culture of his or her choice,[30] to enjoy and practise his or her culture or religion, and to form or join cultural religious organs/associations.[31] The rights guaranteed here must be exercised in a manner consistent with the Bill of Rights.

---

[26] Above, n. 23, at 109.

[27] See e.g. J. A. Robinson, "An Overview of the Problem of the South African Bill of Rights with Specific Reference to its Impact on Families and Children Affected by the Policy of Apartheid" (1995) 16 *Obiter* 99 at 106; P. J. Visser, "Die Moontlike Uitdruklike Erkenning van Fundamentele Regte ten aansien van die Huwelik en Gesin (Familie) in die Finale Grondwet van Suid-Afrika" (1996) *De Jure* 351 at 354.

[28] S. 8. S. 173 states that the Constitutional Court, the Supreme Court of Appeal and the High Court have inherent power to develop the common law, but customary law is not mentioned.

[29] S. 9.

[30] S. 30.

[31] S. 31.

When interpreting legislation and developing common or customary law, every court must promote the spirit, purport and objects of the Constitution.[32] The Constitution does not deny any rights of customary law if these are consistent with the Bill of Rights.[33] It provides for the establishment of a Commission for the promotion and protection of the rights of cultural and religious communities,[34] and the recognition and status of the institution of traditional leaders.[35]

Three issues are alluded to here to illustrate the difficulty of reconciling certain aspects of customary law with the rights enshrined in the Constitution. The first is the broad question of equality, the second the recognition of customary marriages, and the third the matter of intestate succession.[36]

We must be reminded that the status of an African woman married at customary law differs from that of one married at civil law; that the status of a woman married at customary law differs from that of a man similarly married.

---

[32] S. 39(2).

[33] S. 39 (3).

[34] S. 181, and see also s. 185.

[35] Ch. 12. Traditional authorities may function with regard to customary law. S. 211(3) dictates that the courts must apply customary law when that law is applicable, subject to the Constitution and subject to any legislation that specifically deals with customary law.

[36] The South African Law Commission's Project on the Harmonisation of the Common Law and the Indigenous Law (Project 90) is important. Discussion Paper 74, on *Customary Marriages*, published for comment in Aug. 1997, contains several recommendations and a draft bill. It is beyond the scope of this chapter to examine in any detail what is being proposed, but it must be said (not without a good deal of sympathy—the topic is fraught) that the document comes across as tentative, hesitating and too unclear. When the issues become truly difficult, the buck is simply passed to the courts to resolve them. See, for example, cl. 4. It prohibits a person already married at civil law from marrying the same or another person according to customary law, but refrains from prohibiting a person married at customary law from marrying the same person at civil law (currently permitted). Cl. 4(2) expressly envisages simultaneous marriage at civil and customary law, and it declares that the consequences of such a marriage will be determined by the law the spouses agreed would apply. To deal with the failure of such persons to declare their choice, the clause asks the court to consider the cultural orientation and rites and customs which predominate in the marriage, and make its choice. This is, it is sugggested, an unrealistic burden to place upon a court. It is nearly inevitable that in such situations there will be manifestations of commitment both to the tenets of customary law and to the content of the civil law. What is the court supposed to do about conflicts between the two? If customary law is to be accorded the same status in all respects as marriage at civil law, marriage according to one system should preclude the need to marry according to the other. The Discussion Document admits that "the law should discourage . . . any 'mixing' of the systems" (iv, para. 3.2.11). Polygyny is retained. Another example of buck-passing is clause 8(5)(a), which declares, almost nonchalantly, that a court ordering dissolution of a customary marriage shall have the same powers in terms of the Divorce Act that it would have in respect of a civil marriage. It overlooks that the existing powers are highly unsatisfactory, restricted and complex, with regard to the redistribution of property. The judicial discretion to distribute property depends, *inter alia*, on the race of the parties and the date of the civil marriage, and is temporary—it will disappear when the marriages to which it applies have been dissolved—see Sinclair (assisted by Heaton), n. 1 above, at 143–8, where it is suggested that a constitutional challenge to the limitations placed upon the judicial discretion could be mounted. It is most unfortunate, it is submitted, that the draft Bill (cl. 7(3)) envisages automatic separation of property within customary marriage, while community of property is the automatic consequence of civil marriage. Our law is so complex! Ordinary people are justifiably confused; and lawyers are unjustifiably occupied with interpreting unnecessarily intricate legislation. There is an unequivocal, commendable commitment to compliance with CEDAW, and to creating equality between men and women within customary marriage (cl. 7), and there is a clear indication that customary marriage should be fully recognised. Intestate succession, it seems, escapes the attention of the drafter.

In both cases it is inferior. These differences, the differences between the civil law and customary law and the way in which the two systems intersect, have hitherto been overlooked or underplayed. The notion of patriarchy, for example, fundamental to customary law, does not sit comfortably with constitutional guarantees of equality.[37]

The Constitution provides that legislation recognising marriages concluded under any tradition or a system of religious personal or family law is not prevented; that legislation recognising systems of personal and family law under any tradition or adhered to by persons professing a particular religion is not prevented; that the legislation referred to here must be consistent with the provisions of the Constitution.[38] Thus, when the legislature acts to recognise marriages that are not recognised at the moment because they are potentially polygynous,[39] the legislation will have to comply with the equality clause. This is an area of great difficulty and potential conflict. There are powerful arguments made by a variety of authors, which cannot be ignored, to the effect that concepts like polygyny and the system of bridewealth (*lobolo*) are discriminatory against women.[40]

Within the field of intestate succession, the rule of male primogemiture, central to African custom, provides another possibility for conflict between customary law and the equality provision. There is academic writing to the effect that the male primogentiture rule is discriminatory.[41] But there is also a recent case, decided under the interim Constitution, to the effect that the rule differentiates but does not unfairly discriminate.[42]

From the brief outline of the Constitutional provisions given here, there can be no doubt that the South African Constitution recognises the importance to the majority of South Africans of customary law. However, this recognition came only after lengthy and sometimes acrimonious debate.[43] The result has been an unequivocal commitment to rendering customary law consonant with human

---

[37] The Law Commission's draft Bill (n. 36 above) repeals the offensive s 11(3) of the Black Administration Act 38 of 1927. For an analysis of the intersection between customary and civil marriage and notice of the constitutional conundrums arising from patriarchy, polygyny, *lobolo* (bridewealth) and capacity see Sinclair (assisted by Heaton), n. 1 above, at 158–180 and ch. 3.

[38] S. 15(3). The interim Constitution did not have this proviso, so that legislation under this section would have trumped the equality clause. It cannot do so now—see Sinclair (assisted by Heaton), n 1 above, at 161.

[39] African customary and Muslim marriages have been denied full recognition by South African courts on this ground—see Sinclair (assisted by Heaton), n. 1 above, at 164–70 and *Ryland* v. *Edros*, 1997 (2) SA 690 (C). See also n. 36 above.

[40] The topic and the various views are discussed in Sinclair (assisted by Heaton), n. 1 above, at 158–80.

[41] See A. J. Kerr "Customary Law, Fundamental Rights and the Constitution" (1994) 111 *SALJ* 720 at 725–6.

[42] See *Mthembu* v. *Letsela*, 1997 (2) SA 936 (T). For a further and incisive list of the possible areas of conflict between the Bill of Rights and African custom, see Iain Currie, "The Future of Customary Law: Lessons from the Lobolo Debate" [1994] *Acta Juridica* 147 at 151.

[43] Referred to by Thandabantu Nhlapo, in his paper "Human Rights—The African Perspective" (1995) 6 *African Law Review* 38 about whether customary law should be subject to scrutiny for compliance with the rights enshrined in the Constitution, or whether it should be exempt from such scrutiny, a position for which many traditional leaders strenuously argued.

rights. But the problems that lie ahead are manifold. Changing the law does not change what people do and believe within their intimate relationships. There is a substantial dissonance between South Africa's newfound extolling of individual rights and the promotion of a rights culture, on one hand, and several deep-rooted notions of African custom, on the other. The point has already been made that African custom is based on the concept of human dignity, derived not necessarily through the relentless pursuit of individual liberty, but rather through membership of a group. It is stressed by several prominent writers in the field. They do not seek to devalue the protection of individual rights in national constitutions and international covenants, but they make us aware that the underlying notions of African custom do not fit altogether well with the rights culture that we are so avidly attempting to promote in our society. The courts, meanwhile, are left to interpret and "develop" customary law. They are left to determine the constitutional validity or otherwise of basic tenets of African customary (and Muslim religious laws). The question that must be posed is whether this process is optimal; whether there is not another way for lawyers to reconcile widely differing understandings of "the good society" that prevail in South Africa.

The courts may not be the best agents to bring about this reconciliation. Deciding on the validity of rules on a case-by-case basis will inevitably produce differences of opinion and a diverse range of outcomes on issues of general rather than merely individual importance. The judges will undoubtedly be influenced by the primacy of civil law, which has occupied a dominant position in South Africa, despite the fact that it was the law of the minority of the population. Not only has the civil law dominated, however. It has resulted in the stultification of customary law—by definition a living organism that would have grown over time to accommodate changes in African society. Statutes purporting to reflect customary law have been particularly problematic.[44] The transition from an agrarian economy to an industrial or mixed economy, and the participation of women in such economies, is just one of the multifarious factors that might have impacted upon the development of rules of customary law. Nevertheless, it must be doubtful whether the distortion of customary law brought about by the domination of the civil law could account for all the potential constitutional challenges. Can it be said, for example, that the institution of polygyny, fundamentally part of the patriarchal nature of customary law, would have evolved in a way that would now avoid a clash between it and the right to equality entrenched in the Constitution?

South Africa is obviously not the first or only country to grapple with this problem. The point is that it may well be more sensible to allow the legislature, after careful investigation, to attempt to resolve the conflicts that exist between the Constitution and customary law than to expect the courts to do so. The South

---

[44] The most crucial statute in this regard is the Black Administration Act. It cannot be said to reflect the state of customary law as it might have been had it been allowed to grow and develop with the evolving mores of African people. See also n. 36 and n. 37 above.

African Law Commission is currently charged with that daunting task.[45] Customary law has been used in this chapter to highlight the special nature of the challenge we face in building a society once founded on the denial of individual liberty, into a society based squarely on a constitutional dispensation that enshrines the rights of the individual. The arduousness of our task is no justification for ignoring the difficulty, or for proceeding without due deliberation and great caution.

VI   CONCLUSION

The interim Constitution of 1993 was a political compromise that contributed to the miracle of avoiding a bloody revolution. The Constitutional Assembly was then given two years to produce a carefully crafted final Constitution that would embody the principles to which the country had committed itself in the election of 1994. Unfortunately, the process became another bazaar in which strengths and weaknesses were traded off against each other and deals were struck at unearthly hours by exhausted politicians and their legal advisers. We expected an immaculate Constitution that would not generate a new industry of interpretive jurisprudence. What we got was another political compromise. Our expectations were too high in those wonderful years.

What should they be now? This chapter does not offer answers. Perhaps there is none. It laments the complexities surrounding the application of the Bill of Rights which might have been reduced, if not avoided, and it suggests a judicial practice that combines a commitment to striking down unjust laws with a determination not to intrude too readily upon the preserve of the legislature. It attempts to urge professionals involved in building a societal culture to be aware of the need for balance between insistence on individual rights and concomitant civic obligation. Until we inculcate in all citizens a clear understanding of the difference between needs and wants, on one hand, and rights, on the other, until we live out the notion that every right carries with it a corresponding responsibility, if not to an individual, then to the populace at large, we stand in danger of being judged as having participated in a failed experiment. Let us discharge our own responsibility in the way that we practise our profession. The role of lawyers in this enterprise is not a trivial one. The powerful language of rights that lawyers use and teach has a profound effect on the community they serve. Their role in the future could be pivotal. It could be at least part of the difference between the dream and the nightmare. Let us accept that role with great care and deeper insight, with dignity and courage, but not without humility. Learned Hand J's observation[46] that liberty lies in the hearts of men and women, and when it dies there, no law, no court, no constitution can save it, is undeni-

---

[45] See n. 36 above.
[46] Quoted by Glendon, n. 23 above, at 143.

able. The law itself, the practice of it, and the professing of it, cannot alone resolve this society's problems. But we, as lawyers, as family lawyers, operating in the public and private domain, should not stand accused of having failed to perceive what the problems are. And we should not stand accused of having contributed carelessly, without due caution, to the shaping of the society being born out there as we speak.

31

Defending and Protecting Gender Equality and the Family Under a Decidedly Undecided Constitution in Zimbabwe

WELSHMAN NCUBE

INTRODUCTION

Zimbabwe is party to virtually all international human rights instruments which oblige countries to, *inter alia*, protect and promote the family and family life for the benefit of its members; guarantee women equality with men during marriage and at its dissolution; guarantee women equal rights and responsibilities with men in marriage and family relations; and guarantee equal rights and responsibilities between men and women regarding entry into marriage, ownership, management and disposition of property within and without marriage. Since independence the state has sought to reform family laws with a view to granting women and children rights and protection, particularly against those traditional and customary practices which are perceived as unjustifiable. However, the approach to these issues has been uneven and sometimes inconsistent and muddled. On the other hand, social reaction, particularly from elders and traditionalists has often been sharp, aggressive and resistant.

The objectives of this chapter are to review, analyse and evaluate, within the framework of the country's obligations under international human rights treaties, Zimbabwe's legislative reforms which have been directed at achieving gender equality and the general protection of women and children within the family. Also evaluated are the social reactions to some of these changes which have struck at the core of traditional rights, norms and values. This chapter tells the story of how Zimbabwe has grappled, even though sometimes inconsistently and incoherently, with the complex issues relating to the co-existence of not only a formal plural system of laws but also a plural and highly contested system of norms and values. Modern and Western inspired values on equality between men and women, and on the rights of children have clashed with "traditional" and "customary" values on the same matters. The legislative reforms in the field of family law have thus resembled a Western dance to the sounds of traditional drums and music in what may be described as a dance trapped between the slippery slopes of modernity and quicksands of tradition and customary law.

Depending on which side of the debate commentators have found themselves, there have been two broad and opposed views on many of the family law reforms. One view encapsulated in the resistance of chiefs, traditional leaders and elders, has seen some of the reforms as a dangerous game sweeping Africans down the uncontrollable torrents of Western values which have poisoned African culture and torn asunder African traditional values which acted as a glue holding together not only the African family but also the African cultural way of life. The other view, has seen some of the changes as half-hearted, weak and too little often too late, by a state muddled and trapped in the quicksands of tradition. None of these extremes represent reality. They are, however, important ideological posturings by the activists on either side of the debate, one seeing the reforms as inadequate and too little and the other seeing them as simply too many too rapid. This chapter attempts to look at the reality from a less polarised perspective while capturing the essence of the social reactions to the reforms as represented by the disputants in the debate. That reality is essentially that the constitution of Zimbabwe, although amended recently to incorporate a prohibition of gender discrimination, remains decidedly undecided on whether or not the principle of gender equality should extend to all aspects of social life.

THE INTERNATIONAL HUMAN RIGHTS FRAMEWORK

Before discussing the constitutionalisation of gender equality and family law reform within the context of the protection of women and children's rights in family law it is instructive to give a general overview of those provisions of the various international human rights instruments which are relevant to gender equality and the reform of family laws in Zimbabwe. First, there is Article 23 of the International Covenant on Civil and Political rights which declares the family to be the "natural and fundamental group unit of society" which is entitled to protection by society and the state and also obliges States Parties to take all appropriate steps to ensure "equality of rights and responsibilities of spouses as to marriage, during marriage and at its dissolution".[1]

Secondly, the African Charter on Human and People's Rights ("the African Human Rights Charter") is more robust and emphatic about the importance of the family in its Article 18 which states that:

"1 The family shall be the natural unit and basis of society. It shall be protected by the State which shall take care of its physical and moral health.

[1] See also the Preamble to the Convention on the Rights of the Child and Art. 18 of the Charter on the Rights and Welfare of the African Child.

2 The State shall have the duty to assist the family which is the custodian of morals and traditional values recognised by the community.

3 The State shall ensure the elimination of every discrimination against women and children as stipulated in international declarations and conventions."

Article 29 places a duty on all individuals to preserve the harmonious development of the family and to work for its cohesion.[2]

Thirdly, there is Article 16 of the Convention on the Elimination of All Forms of Discrimination Against Women ("the Women's Convention") which mandates States Parties to take all appropriate measures to eliminate discrimination against women in all matters relating to marriage and family relations and in particular to ensure, on the basis of equality between men and women, *inter alia*:

i   the same rights and responsibilities during marriage and at its dissolution;
ii the same rights and responsibilities as parents, irrespective of their marital status, in matters relating to their children;
iii the same rights and responsibilities with regard to guardianship, wardship trusteeship and adoption of children;[3]
iv the same rights as husband and wife, including the right to choose a family name;
v   the same rights for both spouses in respect of the ownership, acquisition, management, administration, enjoyment and disposition of property and
vi all necessary action, including legislation, shall be taken to specify a minimum age for marriage and to make the registration of marriages in an official registry compulsory.

Fourthly, under Article 15 States Parties are required not only to ensure that women and men are equal before the laws but also to accord to women the same legal status or capacity as that applicable to men. Fifthly and finally Article 5 requires States Parties to take all appropriate measures to "modify the social and cultural patterns of men and women, with a view to achieving the elimination of prejudices and customary and all other practices which are based on the idea of the inferiority or the superiority of either of the sexes or on stereotyped roles for men and women".

When read together, all these provisions of international human rights instruments which have a bearing on the family and family law, mean no more than that the body of family law must recognise and implement the equality of men and women in family and matrimonial matters from the formation of marriage, through their personal and property rights during marriage and their rights and obligations in relation to their children to their rights and obligations upon dissolution of marriage by divorce or death. The question that then arises and which

---

[2] See also Art. 31 of the Charter on the Rights and Welfare of the African Child.
[3] See also Arts. 2 and 8(1) of the Convention on The Rights of The Child which when read together are to the same effect, namely that children should have the same rights *vis-à-vis* their parents regardless of their status. The equivalent provisions of the Charter on The Rights and Welfare of the African Child are Arts. 3 and 30.

is discussed and assessed throughout this chapter is the extent to which the body of Zimbabwe's family laws, both at customary law and general law, have been reformed to be in line with the country's obligations under the various international human rights treaties referred to above and to all of which Zimbabwe is a party.

THE CONSTITUTIONAL FRAMEWORK, THE FAMILY AND WOMEN'S RIGHTS

That national constitutions represent a powerful value framework which is used to link international human rights standards to national law is today well accepted,[4] even in Africa with its historical legacy of one party state constitutions which were described as constitutions without constitutionalism[5] and which at that time often bore a pale resemblance to the reality of political practice. Today, the importance of Constitutions in protecting fundamental rights in the new democratising Africa, particularly in East and Southern Africa, cannot be over-emphasised. Thus in presenting issues of gender equality, family rights and children's rights one has to begin by charting the Constitutional framework within which such rights are protected and are to be understood.

The Declaration of Rights in Zimbabwe's Lancaster House Constitution largely belongs to the old fashioned Westminster-given post-colonial type of declaration of rights and hence, like its Botswana counterpart, did not until 1996 specifically provide for gender equality. It did not even provide for the equality of all Zimbabweans before the law[6] and hence the clause dealing with the protection of the law did not and still does not embody the important value/principle of non-discrimination or (put positively) the notion of equality of all citizens before the law.[7] It is also old fashioned in that, unlike the new democratic con-

---

[4] See, e.g., S. Goonesekere, "The Best Interests of the Child: A South Asian Perspective" in P. Alston (ed.), *The Best Interests of The Child: Reconciling Culture and Human Rights* (Clarendon, Oxford, 1994), 117–49, at 145; B. Rwezaura, "Domestic Application of International Human Rights Norms To Protect The Rights of The Girl Child in East and Southern Africa", in W. Ncube (ed.), *Law, Culture, Tradition and Children's Rights in Eastern and Southern Africa* (Ashgate, London, 1998); and W. Ncube, "Recognition and Monitoring of Children's Rights in Africa: Challenges and Prospects", in Eugeen Verheuen (ed.), *Understanding Children's Rights* (University of Ghent, Ghent, 1997).

[5] Okoth-Ogendo, "Constitutions without Constitutionalism: Reflections on an African Political Paradox", in I. Shivji (ed.), *The State and Constitutionalism: An African Debate* (Sapes, Harare, 1991), 3.

[6] The relevant provision, departing from international trends, only provided that "Every person is entitled to the protection of the law" whereas equivalent provisions in international human rights treaties and comparative constitutions normally provide for the equal protection of all by the law or simply for the equality of all before the law.

[7] More modern Constitutions in the region unequivocally provide for equality of all before the law. For example, s. 9(1) of the South African Constitution states that "Everyone is equal before the law and has the right to equal protection and benefit of the law". See also Art. 10 of the Namibian Constitution which is to similar effect.

stitutions in the region such as those of South Africa and Namibia, it makes no provision for family and children's rights.[8]

In its original version the non-discrimination clause of the Zimbabwean Declaration of Rights, namely, section 23, simply outlawed discrimination based on race, tribe, place of origin, political opinions, colour and creed and conspicuously absent was any reference to sex or gender as a prohibited basis of discrimination.[9] This meant that it was possible to enact laws which discriminated against women without offending the Constitution. However, in other jurisdictions it has been held that the failure of a constitutional provision to specifically mention sex as a prohibited basis of discrimination was not to be read to mean that that form of discrimination was permissible. For example, in the case of *Dow* v. *Attorney-General of Botswana*,[10] it was held that even though the anti-discrimination provision did not specifically mention sex or gender, the Constitution of Botswana nonetheless prohibited sex-based discrimination since it had to be read and interpreted to be in line with the country's obligations under international human rights treaties such as the Women's Convention and the African Charter on Human Rights, both of which Botswana is a party to. Since these treaties prohibited all forms of discrimination including those based on sex or gender, the court reasoned that, while such treaties did not confer direct enforceable rights on individuals until national law has been enacted to localise them, nonetheless the courts were at liberty to use them as aids to the interpretation of ambiguous constitutional provisions. Whatever interpretation the courts chose had to be in compliance with the international obligations of the state.[11]Virtually the same approach was adopted by the Zambia High Court in *Sara Longwe* v. *International Hotels*.[12]

[8] E.g., ss. 28 and 23 and Art. 15 of the South African, Malawian and Namibian Constitutions respectively incorporate most of the essentials of children's rights found in the Convention on The Rights of the Child. S. 22 and Art. 14 of the Malawian and Namibian Constitutions respectively, and in line with international human rights treaties, recognise the family as the natural and fundamental group unit of society which is entitled to protection by society and the state. The Namibia provision goes even further to recognise the equal rights between men and women as to marriage, during marriage and at the dissolution of marriage.

[9] Similarly worded constitutions include those of Kenya and Botswana. As a result of this constitutional loophole it became necessary to enact various provisions in different statutes outlawing sex based discrimination. Such clauses were/are found in such statutes as, *inter alia*, the Labour Relations Act, the Education Act, the University of Zimbabwe Act and the Immovable Property (Prevention of Discrimination) Act. See also generally J. Stewart, W. Ncube, M. Maboreke and A. Armstrong, "The Legal Situation of Women in Zimbabwe" in J. Stewart (ed.), *The Legal Situation of Women in Southern Africa* (University of Zimbabwe, Harare, 1990), 167, at 169–70.

[10] [1992] LRC (Const.) 623 (CA).

[11] This approach to Constitutional construction was in line with the Bangalore principles and the Harare Declaration adopted by Commonwealth judges and Commonwealth African judges respectively as aids to the interpretation of human rights legislation. The Bangalore principles are to the effect that: (i) where a treaty has been ratified but not as yet incorporated into national/domestic law, its principles would nonetheless be used by the courts as aids to constitutional, statutory, and/or common law interpretation in the event of ambiguity; and (ii) when interpreting statutes, including Constitutions, judges should interpret them in such a way that they are consistent with the country's obligations under human rights treaties and Conventions.

[12] [1993] 4 LRC 221. For a fuller discussion of this technique in Constitutional interpretation see B. Rwezaura, n. 4 above and W. Ncube, n. 4 above.

The Zimbabwean Supreme Court had a golden opportunity to adopt and develop this technique in *Rattigan and Others* v. *Chief Immigration Officer and Others*[13] but the opportunity was lost because the court chose to decide the matter on other grounds. It had been argued in that case that, even though section 23 of the Constitution did not specifically mention sex as a prohibited basis of discrimination, section 11 of the Constitution did mention that all persons were entitled to the fundamental rights set out in the Constitution without regard to, *inter alia*, sex and therefore, section 23, being ambiguous, had to be interpreted so as to be consistent with the country's obligations under the Women's Convention which prohibited sex-based discrimination. The case of *Dow* was cited in support of this approach since Zimbabwe had not specifically incorporated the Women's Convention into domestic law as is required by section 111B(I)(b) of the Constitution before it could be applied directly in domestic courts. Unfortunately, in its judgment the Supreme Court did not even make reference to these arguments and made no pronouncements at all, even in *obiter dicta*, relating to these issues. It chose to decide the case solely on the ground that the exclusion of the foreign husbands of the applicant Zimbabwean women was unconstitutional on the basis that they offended the protection of freedom of movement in section 22 of the Constitution. Thus regrettably a golden opportunity to broaden our jurisprudence on the incorporation of international human rights standards on issues of gender equality was lost.[14]

In 1996 following several years of lobbying and activism by women's organisations, particularly during the run-up to the Beijing Women's Conference and thereafter, the government of Zimbabwe, through section 9 of the Constitution of Zimbabwe Amendment (No. 14) Act, finally amended section 23 of the Constitution to specifically include gender discrimination as a form of constitutionally prohibited discrimination. However, for reasons which will become apparent below, the prohibition is not as comprehensive as it could have been and does not go as far as do other constitutions in the region. All that the amendment did was to insert the word "gender" in the provisions which list the prohibited forms of discrimination so that section 23(1) and (2) now read:

"(1) Subject to the provisions of this section—
(a) No law[15] shall make any provision that is discriminatory either of itself or in its effect; and
(b) no person shall be treated in a discriminatory manner by any person acting by virtue of any written law or in the performance of any public office or any public authority.

---

[13] 1994 (2) ZLR 54 (SC).

[14] For a brutal and trenchant criticism of the *Rattigan* judgment see L. Madhuku, "Magic and Constitutional Interpretation: A Case Note on *Rattigan and Others* v. *Chief Immigration Officer and Others*" (1994) 6 *Legal Forum*, 9.

[15] Law is defined in s. 113 as including statutory enactments, the Roman-Dutch common law and customary law. However, as will be seen below, the potential of this provision being used to challenge discriminatory principles of law is greatly diminished by a later provision which places virtually the whole of family law outside the reach of the provision.

(2) For the purposes of subsection (1), a law shall be regarded as making a provision that is discriminatory and a person shall be regarded as having been treated in a discriminatory manner if, as a result of the law or treatment, persons of a particular description by race, tribe, place of origin, political opinions, colour, creed or gender are prejudiced—

(a) by being subjected to a condition, restriction or disability to which other persons of another such description are not made subject; or

(b) by the according to persons of another such description of a privilege or advantage which is not accorded to persons of the first-mentioned description; and the imposition of that condition, restriction or disability or the according of that privilege or advantage is wholly or mainly attributable to the description by race, tribe, place of origin, political opinions, colour, creed, or gender of the persons concerned."

Even though this formulation is relatively wide on the question of non-discrimination as a principle it is not as comprehensive and broad in its recognition of women's rights as comparable provisions of other constitutions in the region. The Constitution of Malawi for example has a two-pronged approach to the issues of gender equality which, when taken together, comprehensively lay down the principle of equality and non-discrimination. In the first place, section 20 provides that:

"(1) Discrimination of persons in any form is prohibited and all persons are, under any law, guaranteed equal and effective protection against discrimination on grounds of race, colour, sex, language, religion, political or other opinion, nationality, ethnic or social origin, disability, property, birth and other status."

Even though this provision can be said to comprehensively outlaw sex or gender based discrimination, section 24 goes further to provide specifically for women's rights and gender equality by providing that:

"(1) Women have the right to full and equal protection by the law, and have the right not to be discriminated against on the basis of their gender or marital status which includes the right—

(a) to be accorded the same rights as men in civil law, including equal capacity—

   (i)   to enter into contracts

  (ii) to acquire and maintain rights in property, independently or in association with other, regardless of their marital status;

 (iii) to acquire and retain custody, guardianship and care of children and to have an equal right in the making of decisions that affect upbringing; and

 (iv) to acquire and retain citizenship and nationality.

(b) on the dissolution of marriage—

   (i)   to a fair disposition of property that is held jointly with a husband; and

  (ii) to fair maintenance, taking into consideration all the circumstances and, in particular, the means of the former husband and the needs of any children.

(2) Any law that discriminates against women on the basis of tender or marital status shall be invalid and legislation shall be passed to eliminate customs and practices that discriminate against women, particularly practices such as—

(a) sexual abuse, harassment and violence;

(b) discrimination in work, business and public affairs; and

(c) deprivation of property, including property obtained by inheritance."

This constitutional formulation of women's rights and gender equality is so comprehensive that it would subject to the constitutionality test virtually the entire body of family law whether under the common law or customary law or statutory law. In Zimbabwe it would bring, for example, the marital power, customary inheritance laws, polygyny, custody, guardianship and matrimonial property rights laws, be they customary, common law or statutory law, under the constitutionality test. Unfortunately, Zimbabwe's constitution does not have any constitutional provision that approximates section 24 of the Malawi Constitution.

As if the failure of Zimbabwe's Constitution comprehensively to make provision for gender equality and women's rights in marriage and within the family were not enough, section 23 specifically provides for a host of exceptions which effectively place the whole area of family law and customary law outside the scope of the constitutionalisation of gender equality. First, subsection 5 states that a law may discriminate against women to the extent that it "takes due account of physiological differences between persons of different gender except as far as that law . . . is shown not to be reasonably justifiable in a democratic society". It remains to be seen how the courts will interpret this exception to the principle of gender equality. All that may be said at this stage is that historically many of the discriminatory practices against women have been justified and defended on the basis of physiological differences between women and men. Clearly, in the hands of a sexist government and a sexist judiciary this provision opens wide the possibilities of discriminating against women, particularly within the field of family law.

Secondly, and more ominously, are the exceptions to gender equality provided for in subsection (3) which reads in part:

"(3) Nothing contained in any law shall be held to be in contravention of subsection 1(a) to the extent that the law in question relates to any of the following matters—

(a) adoption, marriage, divorce, burial, devolution of property on death or other matters of personal law;

(b) the application of African customary law in any case involving Africans . . . "[16]

This provision effectively excludes the principle of gender equality from the whole area of family law and customary law and hence the various provisions of the Roman-Dutch common law, customary law and statutory law which discriminate against women in marriage and outside marriage cannot be constitutionally successfully challenged. Clearly, the Zimbabwean constitutional provisions on gender equality fall far short of the country's obligations under international human rights treaties, particularly Article 16 of the Women's Convention which, as we have seen, obliges States Parties to ensure that men and women have the same rights during marriage and at its dissolution and indeed

---

[16] See also Arts. 17 and 23 and ss. 82 and 15 of the Constitutions of Ghana, Zambia, Kenya and Botswana respectively which contain similar exceptions on adoption, marriage and other aspects of personal law as well as the application of customary law.

outside marriage in matters such as guardianship, custody and adoption of children. Also under Article 15 States Parties are obliged to ensure that women and men are equal before the law in all respects. Remember too that Article 23 of the Civil and Political Rights Covenant mandates States Parties to ensure equality of rights and responsibilities of spouses.

Notwithstanding the Constitution's failure comprehensively to protect women's rights the Supreme Court of Zimbabwe has, seemingly half-heartedly, attempted to read broadly some of the fundamental rights recognised and protected in the Constitution to advance women's rights and gender equality and to protect the integrity of the family. The leading cases in this regard are *Rattigan and Others* v. *Chief Immigration Officer and Others (supra)* and *Salem* v. *Chief Immigration Officer and Another.*[17] However, there have also been lost opportunities and failures to protect the integrity of the family and women's rights such as in the case of *Ruwodo N O* v. *Minister of Home Affairs and Others*[18] and *In re Wood and Another.*[19]

In the *Rattigan* case the Chief Immigration Officer had refused to grant the alien husbands of the three women applicants, who were all citizens of Zimbabwe, permanent residence in Zimbabwe. Following that refusal the applicants petitioned the Supreme Court for an order declaring that their rights as citizens under, *inter alia*, section 22 (which protects freedom of movement) of the Constitution were being breached by the refusal. In finding in favour of the applicants on this issue the Supreme Court relied on the marriage bond and the need to protect the family and hence its conclusion that to exclude the husbands from Zimbabwe had the effect of placing the applicants in the invidious position of having to choose either to leave Zimbabwe to reside with their husbands elsewhere or to effectively bring the matrimonial relationships to an end by remaining in Zimbabwe. In the course of the judgment the court observed that:

> "Marriage is a juristic act *sui generis*. It gives rise to a physical, moral and spiritual community of life—a *consortium omnis vitae*. It obliges the husband and wife to live together for life (more realistically for as long as the marriage endures) and to confer sexual privileges exclusively upon each other. Conjugal love embraces three components: (i) eros (passion); (ii) philia (companionship); and (iii) agape (self-giving brotherly love) . . . The duties of cohabitation, loyalty, fidelity, and mutual assistance and support, flow from the marital relationship. To live together as spouses in community of life, to afford each other marital privileges and to be ever faithful, are the inherent commands which lie at the very heart of marriage. . . . Marriage, . . . is one of the basic rights of man, fundamental to our very existence and survival."[20]

The Court went on to make reference to Article 17 of the International Covenant on Civil and Political Rights and Article 8(1) of the European Convention on Human Rights, both of which afford protection against interference

---

[17] 1994 (2) ZLR 287 (SC).
[18] 1995 (1) ZLR 227 (SC).
[19] 1994 (2) ZLR 155 (SC).
[20] At 61.

with family life and emphasise the importance of preserving and protecting established family ties. Cases decided by the UN Human Rights Committee[21] and the European Court of Human Rights[22] protecting the integrity of family life, including the preservation of and respect for the relationship of husband and wife, were cited with approval. The Supreme Court relied on provisions of international human rights treaties protecting the integrity of family life as aids to the interpretation of the right of freedom of movement protected in Zimbabwe's Constitution in spite of the fact that Zimbabwe's constitution does not have any provision protecting family life, family ties and marriage. Realising this, the court justified its approach as follows:

> "Although there is no provision in the Constitution of Zimbabwe which equates directly to Article 17 of the Covenant or Article 8(1) of the Convention, S 11 guarantees every person 'protection for the privacy of his home'. Taken in conjunction with S 22(1) and interpreting the whole generously and purposively so as to eschew the 'austerity of tabulated legalism', I reach the conclusion that to prohibit husbands from residing in Zimbabwe and so disable them from living with their wives in the country of which they are citizens and to which they owe allegiance, is in effect to undermine and devalue the protection of freedom of movement *accorded to each of the wives as a member of a family unit*[23] [my emphasis].

In *Salem* v. *Chief Immigration Officer and Another* (*supra*) the Supreme Court not only upheld its reasoning in *Rattigan* based on the protection of the family unit and marriage but went further to hold that since married parties have a reciprocal duty to support each other, an alien husband resident in Zimbabwe could not be prevented from taking up employment in Zimbabwe so as to support his family. To prevent him from working would have the effect of compelling him and his family to leave Zimbabwe and go elsewhere where both spouses could work to support each other and this would amount to a violation of the citizen wife's freedom of movement as she would effectively have been compelled to leave Zimbabwe so as to be in a country, with her husband, where he would be allowed to work. In the Court's own words:

> "It has long been recognised that there is a reciprocal duty of support as between husband and wife. . . . The duty, . . . endures *stante matrimonio*. It depends on the one spouse's need for support and the other's ability to provide it. In practice, however, the primary duty of maintaining the household rests upon the husband. . . . It is he who has to provide the matrimonial home as well as food, clothing, medical and dental care, and whatever else is reasonable required. . . .
>
> It follows, in my view, that unless the protection guaranteed under section 22(1) of the Constitution embraces the entitlement of a citizen wife, residing permanently with her alien husband in Zimbabwe, to look for partial or total support, depending on her

---

[21] See, e.g., *Aumeeruddy-Czifre and Others* v. *Mauritius* (1981) 66 International Law Reports 255.
[22] See *Abdulaziz Cabales and Balkandali* v. *UK* (1985) 7 EHRR 471; *Barrehab* v. *Netherlands* (1989) 11 EHRR 322; *Moustaquim* v. *Belgium* (1991) 13 EHRR 802; and *Beljoudi* v. *France* (1992) 14 EHRR 801.
[23] At 64–5.

circumstances, *the exercise or her unqualified right to remain residing in this country, as a member of a family unit, is put in jeopardy*[24] [my emphasis].

In *In Re Wood and Another* (*supra*) the Supreme Court refused to extend the protection of the integrity of the family and family life to two alien women, one married to but separated from a Zimbabwean citizen and the other formerly married to a Zimbabwean and residing with her Zimbabwean citizen child. In this case there were two women applicants. The first woman had been married to a Zimbabwean man but had been divorced. She had a son, Martin, who was a citizen of Zimbabwe by birth and whose custody she had been awarded at divorce. She sought to argue that she could not be excluded from Zimbabwe as that would force Martin, a Zimbabwean citizen, to accompany her to wherever she went or to remain alone in Zimbabwe without a home and a guardian and thereby infringing Martin's right to freedom of movement. Counsel for the first woman, Mrs Wood, had argued that "in order both to avoid impairing, if not destroying, the family unit and to preserve and not circumscribe the exercise by Martin of the freedom of movement accorded him under S 22(1) of the Declaration of Rights, it is essential that Mrs Wood live with her son in Zimbabwe; a situation that will persist until Martin attains majority".[25] The Court rejected this argument, essentially holding that only citizens and permanent residents had a constitutional right to reside permanently in Zimbabwe and hence Mrs Wood, as a non-citizen and non-permanent resident, had no right which could be infringed. Only her son, Martin, as a citizen "might claim that his right to reside in Zimbabwe was being infringed by the expulsion of his mother as he would be forced to accompany her in order to avoid separation from his mother and this would interfere with his freedom of movement". However, the application before the court had not been made by Martin or on his behalf.

For substantially the same reasons, the application of the second woman, Mrs Hansard, also failed, because she was an alien who was estranged from her Zimbabwean citizen husband. It was, the Court reasoned, only Mr Hansard, her husband, who might argue that the expulsion of his alien wife from Zimbabwe was infringing his freedom of movement as he would be obliged to accompany her to establish a matrimonial home outside Zimbabwe in order to maintain the marital relationship. But then Mr Hansard was not before the Court and he was not complaining. In the Court's own words:

> "It is not Mrs Hansard who has the requisite *locus standi* to complain of a threatened or actual contravention of S 22(1) of the Declaration of Rights. This protection relates to her husband and not to her."[26]

In *Ruwodo* v. *Minister of Home Affairs and Others* (*supra*) an application brought by a Zimbabwean citizen minor child represented by her alien mother to stop the expulsion of the mother from Zimbabwe also failed, even though it had been

---

[24] At 291–2.
[25] At 158.
[26] At 160.

brought by a Zimbabwean citizen child seeking to keep his family (i.e. his mother) in Zimbabwe. The Court, which had implied in *In re Woods* that if the son had been the Applicant he might have succeeded, apparently had no sympathy for the very argument it had appeared to support in *In re Woods*. It now reasoned that since the minor child, as an infant, was not *sui juris* and was devoid of understanding and therefore incapable of exercising volition, any decision by the parent that the child should live with her in another country effectively overrides that child's constitutional right to remain in Zimbabwe. While Mrs Ruwodo (the applicant's mother), as guardian of the applicant, had the right to assert Michael's right to reside in Zimbabwe, she had to do so in good faith as the right attached to the child and not to her. As such it had to be shown that it was in the child's interests to remain in Zimbabwe rather than go to another country with her mother. The Court concluded that there was no evidence that it was in the child's best interest to remain in Zimbabwe. What was clear was that Mrs Ruwodo, with whom the Court had no sympathy,[27] was making use of the child's "rights as a tool to achieve her own ends—to avoid her being returned to the United States".[28]

Surprisingly, in both *In Re Wood* and *Ruwodo* the Court did not seek guidance from international human rights treaties from which it would have found provisions in favour of the applicants.[29]

The decision in *Rattigan and Others* v. *Chief Immigration Officer and Others* (*supra*), in so far as it recognised the right of Zimbabwean women to reside with their alien spouses without being subject to the discretionary powers of the immigration authorities, was found unacceptable by the executive. It responded by causing Parliament to enact The Constitution of Zimbabwe Amendment (No. 14) Act 1996 which *inter alia* amended section 22 of the Constitution to state that the right to freedom of movement shall not exclude the power of the state to exclude from Zimbabwe any non–citizen whether or not he/she is married to a citizen or permanent resident of Zimbabwe.[30]

When the Constitution of Zimbabwe Amendment (No. 14) Bill was published it was widely criticised by women's organisations, human rights organisations and academics. The thrust of the women's organisations' criticism was that the attempt to reverse the ruling in *Rattigan* was discriminatory in that foreign

---

[27] Apparently the court took a dim view of the fact that Mrs Ruwodo had had 5 children from 4 different fathers, 4 of whom were born out of wedlock, and that she was destitute and dependant on the state and hence the unkind and perhaps unjudicious remark: "Mrs Ruwodo . . . is endeavouring to make use of Michael's rights to avoid being returned, with the children, to the United States of America. Not one word is spoken about why it is in Michael's best interests to remain living in Zimbabwe. He has no formative ties here, having been cast aside by the Wong family [the child's paternal family]. Moreover Mrs Ruwodo is an undesirable person in Zimbabwe. She has had five children from four different fathers, four of them born out of wedlock" (at 232–3). The Court went so far as to suggest that Mrs Ruwodo's marriage (which had since been dissolved) to Mr Ruwodo, a Zimbabwean citizen, may have been one of convenience.

[28] At 232.

[29] See, e.g., Arts. 8, 9 and 10 of the Convention on the Rights of the Child.

[30] See s. 8(1) of the Constitution of Zimbabwe Amendment (No. 14) Act.

women married to Zimbabwean men would continue to have a right, not only to enter Zimbabwe as of right, but to be entitled to citizenship by virtue of only the marriage. The government responded, not by withdrawing the offending provisions, but by arguing that if women wanted equal treatment with men the government would amend section 7 of the Constitution to also deprive male citizens of the right of their alien wives to automatic entry into Zimbabwe. Accordingly, by the time it was enacted, the Constitution of Zimbabwe Amendment (No. 14) Act had a provision amending section 7 in such a way as to prospectively take away the right of alien wives married to Zimbabwean men to be granted Zimbabwean citizenship upon application.[31] Somewhat surprisingly, some may say naively, some women's organisations and human rights organisations applauded this as a victory of their lobbying efforts and as one more nail in the coffin of gender discrimination. Any serious analysis would have disclosed that there was nothing to celebrate and every reason to mourn, for what had happened was that the government had somewhat arrogantly, and maliciously, refused to retain the rights which were being defended, but instead chose to take away more rights in the name of achieving non-discrimination. Men lost their rights in the struggle for equality with women. The idea that a much broader denial of rights could be applauded as a victory is, at the least, shortsighted and at worst naïve.

What will happen in practice is that the immigration authorities will continue to allow alien wives of Zimbabwean men virtual free entry into the country while alien husbands will be closely vetted, which is exactly what the immigration authorities always wanted and had been doing in the past. It is extremely improbable that the wife of any Zimbabwean citizen will ever be denied entry and residence in the country. So much then, for the celebrations of gender neutral constitutional provisions.

What remains is to make an overview analysis of the ordinary legislative interventions which had been introduced in the post-independence period to address some of the gender inequalities that exist in family law. In this respect I propose to look at legal pluralism and conflict of laws, capacity, marriage and property rights in marriage.

LEGAL PLURALISM AND MARRIAGE

Zimbabwe, like most former colonies in Africa, has a legal system characterised by legal pluralism in that customary laws, the Roman-Dutch common law and statutory law[32] are all recognised and enforceable within the judicial system. These systems of law intersect, interact and interface resulting in a multiplicity

---

[31] See s. 4 of the Constitution of Zimbabwe Amendment (No. 14) Act.
[32] The Roman-Dutch common law and statute law are collectively known as the general law.

of complications as individuals seek to maximise their rights by tracking from one system to the other in the regulation and organisation of their lives.

The post-independence state crafted a choice of law process designed to achieve the maximum degree of flexibility based on social criteria in the determination of which system of law to apply to a particular case.[33] The existence of customary law and general law means that the rights of Zimbabweans in family law matters will vary depending on whether the general law or customary law applies. Clearly, therefore, it is impossible in these circumstances to have equality of rights when different systems with different rules may be invoked to determine disputes in family law. The differences are well illustrated by the laws of marriage which recognise or partly recognise three different types of marriage, namely, the general law civil marriage contracted and registered under the provisions of the Marriage Act, Chapter 5:11[34] whose consequences are governed by the Roman-Dutch common law and statute law; the registered customary marriage contracted and solemnized under the provisions of the Customary Marriages Act, Chapter 5:07 whose consequences are governed by customary law except where customary law has been specifically ousted by statute;[35] and the unregistered customary union which is technically an invalid marriage and therefore without legal consequences except that for specific purposes it is recognised or treated as if it were a valid marriage.[36] Such purposes include the status of the children born out of such unions, their rights in respect of guardianship, custody and inheritance;[37] the reciprocal duty of the "spouses" to maintain each other;[38] the surviving spouse's claim for loss of support in the event of the unlawful killing of the other spouse;[39] the husband's claim for adultery damages[40] and the inheritance rights of each of the spouses from each other's estates.[41] The post-independence state has, through legislative amendments extended, greater recognition to customary law unions[42] and the Supreme Court has, by a

---

[33] See s. 3 of the Customary Law (Application) Act, Ch. 8:05, W. Ncube, *Family Law in Zimbabwe* (LRF, Harare, 1989), at 3–24; D. Galen, "Internal Conflicts Between Customary Law and General Law in Zimbabwe: Family Law as a Case Study", *ZL Rev.*, Vols. 1 and 2, 1983–4, 3; and B. Donwa, W. Ncube and J. Stewart, "Which Law? What Law? Playing with the Rules" in W. Ncube and J. Stewart (eds.), *Widowhood, Inheritance Laws, Customs and Practices in Southern Africa* (WLSA, Harare, 1995), 73–107.

[34] Every Zimbabwean regardless of race may contract this type of marriage which is monogamous.

[35] Only Africans are permitted to contract this type of marriage which is potentially polygynous.

[36] An unregistered customary marriage is invalidated by s. 3(1) of the Customary Marriages Act. See also W. Ncube, (1989), n. 33 above, at 134–7; *Choto* v. *Matiye* [1974] RLR 302 and *Kurambakuwa* v. *Mabaya*, SC 158/87.

[37] S. 3(5), Customary Marriages Act.

[38] S. 6(3), Maintenance Act, Ch. 5:09.

[39] *Zimnat Insurance* v. *Chawanda*, 1990 (2) ZLR 143 (SC).

[40] *Carmichael* v. *Moyo*, 1994 (2) ZLR 176 (SC).

[41] See s. 2 of the Administration of Estates Amendment Act, No. 6 of 1997.

[42] See, e.g., 6(3), Maintenance Act, Cap. 5:10; s. 2, Income Tax Act, Ch. 23:06; and s. 2, Administration of Estates Amendment Act, 1997.

process of interpretation which I have described elsewhere as magical and mystical[43] also extended the recognition even further.[44]

However, in spite of this extended recognition, a customary union still has no proprietary consequences at "divorce".[45] In any event, the parties cannot divorce each other as they are in law not validly married.[46] The continued extended recognition of unregistered customary marriages is contrary to the country's obligations under the Women's Convention, which as seen earlier, requires States Parties to ensure that all marriages are registered in an official registry.[47] Also problematic and inconsistent with principles of gender equality is the continued recognition of the polygynous nature of customary marriages and unions. What is even more disturbing are the new provisions of the Administrations of Estates Amendment Act, 1997 which seek to turn civil monogamous marriages into polygamous ones for the purposes of inheritance in all those circumstances where a civil marriage was preceded by a customary union with another woman. Thus where a man first "marries" one woman in a customary union and then marries another in terms of a registered civil marriage, for purposes of inheritance upon his death, the two women will both be treated as his widows, thereby effectively rendering the subsequent civil marriage a polygynous one. The creation of endless legal opportunities for the recognition of polygynous marriages is evidently contrary to the country's obligations under international human rights treaties already cited above.

CAPACITY, EQUALITY AND PROPERTY RIGHTS

The Women's Convention, as already seen, mandates States Parties, in Article 15 to accord to women, in civil matters, a legal capacity identical to that of men and the same opportunities to exercise that capacity.[48] In colonial Zimbabwe, the capacity of Africans was always determined by reference to customary law[49] which was held by the colonial courts to render African women perpetual minors, always under guardianship, either of their fathers, if unmarried, or that

---

[43] W. Ncube, "Magic and Mysticism as Aids to Statutory Interpretation: The Case of Judicial Recognition of Customary Unions in Zimbabwe" (1995) *ZL Rev.* 13.

[44] See judgments in *Zimnat Insurance* v. *Chawanda, (supra)* and *Carmichael* v. *Moyo (supra)*. For a fuller discussion of these cases and why they are technically indefensible see W. Ncube, n. 45 above.

[45] Thus the equitable redistributive powers of the courts under s. 7 of the Matrimonial Causes Act, Cap. 5:13 are inapplicable.

[46] *Joseph Tinga* v. *Joshua Shekede*, 1970 AAC 30.

[47] See Art. 16(2).

[48] The Art. goes further to require that women be given "equal rights to conclude contracts and to administer property" and shall be treated equally with men at all stages of procedure in courts and tribunals.

[49] The colonial Legal Age of Majority Act Ch. 46 did not apply to Africans as it was expressly excluded from so applying. See also s. 3 of the African Law and Tribal Courts Act, Cap. 237 which was repealed soon after independence by the Customary Law and Primary Courts Act, No. 6 of 1981.

of their husbands, if married.[50] Almost immediately after independence the new government rectified this by enacting the Legal Age of Majority Act,[51] No. 15 of 1982 which came into force on 10 June 1982. At the time of its enactment, few could have imagined not only the profound effects this simple five-section statute[52] would have on numerous areas of personal laws but also the widespread national controversy it would cause. As it has turned out, few statutes in the history of Zimbabwe have caused as much controversy as the Legal Age of Majority Act and fewer still have affected so many aspects of the law and people's lives. The courts have used the Act to decide a wide range of issues ranging from ordinary capacity to inheritance issues. In *Jena* v. *Nyemba*[53] it was held that the effect of the Act was to grant African women full legal capacity embracing contractual capacity, *locus standi in judicio*, and proprietary capacity.

In *Katekwe* v. *Muchabaiwa*[54] it was held that the full contractual capacity possessed by African women means they could, if above 18 years, now enter into marriage contracts without the assistance of their parents. This has profoundly affected the very nature of the customary/African marriage systems which are based on the authority of the family, particularly over women's marriage capacity.[55] In *Katekwe* v. *Muchabaiwa*, it was also held that, without guardianship over a woman above 18 years, an African father could no longer sue for and recover seduction damages upon the seduction of his major daughter. This ruling means that one of the principal legal leverages parents had over the sexuality of their daughters was being pulled from under their feet. The unclaimability of seduction damages upon the seduction of major daughters and the capacity of "children", particularly daughters, to marry without parental consent and therefore without *lobola* caused the most resistance to the Act from parents and the elders in general. The Act was widely condemned as unAfrican and uncultural. All sorts of social problems, ranging from teenage indiscipline and pregnancy through prostitution and the high rates of divorce to baby dumping were all conveniently blamed on the Legal Age of Majority Act.[56] Up to today parents throughout the country passionately blame the Act for practically every perceived social evil hav-

---

[50] For a fuller discussion see W. Ncube, "Released from Legal Minority: The Legal Age of Majority Act in Zimbabwe" in A. Armstrong and W. Ncube (eds.), *Women and Law in Southern Africa* (ZPH, Harare, 1987), 193, and A. Armstrong, "Zimbabwe: Away from Customary Law: (1987) 2 *Journal of Family Law* 194.

[51] Today the provisions of the Legal Age of Majority Act have been inconspicuously tucked away by the Law Revisor under the umbrella of an innocuous statute entitled the General Law Amendment Act, Cap. 8:07.

[52] The Act simply made provision that every person shall attain the age of majority on attaining 18 years of age and that this provision "shall apply for the purpose of any law, including customary laws". See also A. Armstrong, n. 52, at 345.

[53] 1986 (1) ZLR 138 (SC).

[54] 1984 (2) ZLR 112 (SC).

[55] See A. Armstrong *et al.*, "Uncovering Reality: Excavating Women's Rights in African Family Law" (1993) 7 *International Journal of Law and the Family* 314–69 at 316–17.

[56] For a fuller discussion see W. Ncube, "Dealing With Iniquities in Customary Law: Action, Reaction and Social Change in Zimbabwe" (1991) 5 *International Journal of Law and The Family* 58–79, at 66–70 and W. Ncube, (1987), above n. 50.

ing anything to do with youth and sometimes having nothing to do with them, such as the perceived disintegration of the traditional African family which was, in the past, supposedly stable and protective of its members.[57]

Also affected by the Legal Age of Majority Act was section 13 of the Customary Marriages Act which provided that the property rights of African spouses were always to be determined by reference to customary law regardless of whether they had a general law marriage. In *Mujawo* v. *Chogugudza*[58] the Supreme Court held that section 13 was inconsistent with the notion of the full capacity of women, particularly when read with the flexible choice of law criteria in section 3 of the Customary Law (Application) Act. This has meant that those Africans who have contracted non-customary marriages have the property consequences of their marriages governed by the general law which gives women better inheritance rights upon the death of their husbands as compared to customary law which completely excluded the surviving spouse from the inheritance process.[59]

In *Chihowa* v. *Mangwende*[60] the Legal Age of Majority Act was held to have removed the disability of daughters from inheriting from their fathers and hence where the daughter is the eldest surviving child she is the heir to her deceased father's estate.[61]

However, the widow in *Murisa* v. *Murisa*[62] could find no joy in the provisions of the Legal Age of Majority Act as it was held that a widow could never inherit from her deceased husband at customary law and this disentitlement had nothing to do with whether she was or was not capable of majority status.[63]

It is clear that in terms of capacity Zimbabwean law recognises that women and men have the same legal capacity, except for the woman married in community of property (which marriage regime is extremely rare in Zimbabwe) who still falls under the husband's Roman-Dutch common law marital power and is thereby disabled in respect of capacity to administer the joint matrimonial estate

---

[57] See generally W. Ncube *et al.*, *Continuity and Change: The Family in Zimbabwe* (WLSA, Harare, 1997).

[58] 1992 (2) ZLR 321 (SC).

[59] See generally K. Dengu-Zvobgo, *Inheritance in Zimbabwe: Law, Customs and Practices* (Sapes, Harare, 1994).

[60] 1987 (1) ZLR 228 (SC).

[61] See also J. Stewart, "The Legal Age of Majority Act Strikes Again: (1986) 4 *Zimbabwe Law Review* 168; W. Ncube, *Customary Law of Succession in Zimbabwe*, paper delivered at WLSA seminar, Kadoma, 1981; and K. Dengu-Zvobgo *et al.*, n. 12 above, ch. 2. Note also that subsequent cases (*Mwozozo* v. *Mwozozo* SC–121–94 and *Vareta* v. *Vareta*, 1992 (2) ZLR 1) have pushed back the frontiers drawn by the *Chihowa* judgment, by holding that the eldest daughter will inherit only in the absence of male issue. In fact, in *Mwozozo* the court expressed the view that minority and majority status have nothing to do with customary principles of inheritance which are determined by the patriarchal nature of Zimbabwean society and not women's legal capacity.

[62] 1992 (1) ZLR 167 (SC).

[63] See J. Stewart, "Untying the Gordian Knot: *Murisa* v. *Murisa* S–4–92; "A Little More than a Case Note" (1992) 4(3) *Legal Forum* 8 and L. Madhuku, "Is Custom Customary Law? The Case of *Murisa* v. *Murisa* S–41–92 and a Reply to Mrs Julie Stewart" (1993) 5(1) *Legal Forum* 32.

arising out of the community of property.[64] Another capacity related problem is that, under section 15 of the Deeds Registries Act, Cap. 20:05, a woman married in community of property is required to be assisted by her husband in dealing with the registration of any document relating to immovable property. Before this section was amended in 1989 it used to require all married women to prove their capacity before they could participate in any registration or conveyancing processes involving immovable property.

Article 16(h) of the Women's Convention requires that married women and men enjoy the same rights "in respect of ownership, acquisition, management, administration and enjoyment and disposition of property". In Zimbabwe, the bulk of women's lack of equal rights with men are to be found in the laws regulating access to and control of matrimonial property. First, in respect of freehold immovable property, even though women have the same capacity as men to acquire and own freehold tenure property, because of their unequal access to education, skills training, employment and credit, they often are unable to take benefit of their proprietary capacity as they have limited financial resources to purchase freehold tenure property either in the form of urban houses or commercial farms.[65] Secondly, in relation to communal land (where the great majority of African families live) landed property is formally allocated by District Councils in terms of customary principles[66] which provide that land will be allocated to married men and shall be held by them. Women have no independent access to this type of land and have access only derivately as wives and hence upon divorce they have to leave the land and settle elsewhere either in urban areas or return to their natal homes.[67] In respect of resettlement land, which is a new land tenure system invented after independence, the criteria for settlement favours men in that priority is given to married men in whose name the resettlement permits are issued and thus exposing wives to the same problems as faced by those in communal areas upon divorce. That is to say, they have to leave the resettlement land as the permit belongs to the husband. However, widowed women with dependents can be resettled as they also qualify. However, in practice very few women do get allocated resettlement land in their own right.[68] Clearly, Zimbabwean law regulating access to communal and resettlement land is discriminatory against married women both in its theory and application and therefore falls short of the country's obligations under international human rights treaties.

---

[64] For fuller details see W. Ncube, *The Matrimonial Property Rights of Women in Zimbabwe*, MPhil. Thesis, UZ, Harare, 1986, 3: W. Ncube, *Family Law in Zimbabwe* (LRF, Harare, 1989), ch. 10; W. Ncube, *Comparative Matrimonial Property Systems* (University of Oslo, Oslo, 1989) at 49–71; and W. Ncube, "Underprivilege and Inequality: The Matrimonial Property Rights of Women in Zimbabwe" in A. Armstrong and W. Ncube (eds.), *Women and Law in Southern Africa* (ZPH, Harare, 1987).

[65] See generally W. Ncube *et al.*, *Paradigms of Exclusion: Women's Access to Property in Zimbabwe* (WLSA, Harare, 1997).

[66] See s. 8 of the Communal Lands Act, Cap. 30:04.

[67] See generally W. Ncube *et al.* n. 65 above.

[68] *Ibid.*

As to the law regulating matrimonial property in general, section 7 of the Matrimonial Clauses Act, Cap 5:10 gives courts discretionary powers to order what they consider to be fair and equitable division of the matrimonial assets at divorce. In practice, the approach of the courts has been uneven and inconsistent in the application of these provisions mainly to the prejudice of women. In practice, rarely do the courts order equal division of matrimonial assets. More often than not the husband is given the greater proportion of the property.[69] What is important though, is that section 7 of the Matrimonial Causes Act has displaced both the inequitable customary law property regime which excluded women from having a share of matrimonial property at divorce and the general law out-of-community regime which also prejudiced women, the majority of whom either worked as housewives or, if employed, had their income utilised mainly for the subsistence needs of the family. However, what is still required is a more equitable matrimonial property regime which will ensure that the courts do not exercise their discretionary powers to the prejudice of women. In this respect, a presumption of equal sharing displaceable only in exceptional circumstances, needs to be established by statute.

CONCLUSION

This chapter has shown that the Constitution of Zimbabwe, unlike some of its counterparts in the region, fails to create a firm and solid base for gender equality in the field of family law and thereby fails to live up to the country's obligations under *inter alia* Article 2 of the Women's Convention which requires national constitutions to embody the principle of equality of men and women. This failure of the Constitution has meant that the array of discriminatory and inequitable laws in family law, both at general law and customary law, cannot be challenged as falling short of the standard of the constitution. Such laws exist in the regulation of access to communal and resettlement land which exclude women from having direct, independent and secure access to land in these tenure systems.

The courts have also not been consistent in upholding the rights of women where opportunities of creative and sensitive constitutional and statutory interpretation have presented themselves. Evidence of this is to be found in the immigration cases involving expulsion of women formerly married to Zimbabweans and in the allocation of property at divorce by the courts. However, in other instances the courts have upheld the principles of equality, such as when applying the provisions of the Legal Age of Majority Act.

---

[69] For some of the evidence in proof of this see W. Ncube (1986), n. 64 above; W. Ncube (1987), n. 64 above; W. Ncube, *Family Law in Zimbabwe* (1989), n. 64 above; W. Ncube (1991), n. 56 above; and W. Ncube, "Reallocation of Matrimonial Property at the Dissolution of Marriage in Zimbabwe", (1990) 34(1) *Journal of African Law* 1.

Reaction to some of the legislative changes, particularly those directed at protecting women and children from excessive control by male elders, has resulted in silent resistance whereby families have often sought to opt out of state regulation of their affairs, particularly in matters of marriage and inheritance. This has tended to blunt the effectiveness of some of the laws intended to benefit women and children within the family framework and environment.[70] However, notwithstanding this, the effects the laws have been profound for those prepared and able to assert and defend their new rights. Zimbabwe is still a long, long way from some form of gender equality within the family both in terms of the theory of law (i.e. principles of law in force) and social practice, but a few significant strides have been made in that direction and ultimately the family will be the better for it.

---

[72] See generally B. Rwezaura *et al.*, "Parting The Long Grass: Revealing and Reconceptualising The African Family" (1995) 35 *Journal of Legal Pluralism and Unofficial Law* 25 and A. Armstrong *et al.*, "Towards a Cultural Understanding of the Interplay Between Children's and Women's Rights: An Eastern and Southern African Perspective" (1995) 3 *The International Journal of Child Rights* 333–68.

32

Meaningless Gestures? African Nations and the Convention on the Elimination of All Forms of Discrimination Against Women

FAREDA BANDA

I

Given the proliferation of human rights conventions and the number of countries which are signatories thereto it seems surprising that the human rights situation in the world still seems so pitiful.[1] This may be because human rights norms incorporated into the conventions seldom find their way into the domestic sphere. The issue is particularly problematic in the family law field dealing as it does with issues usually outside of state control and also outside of areas traditionally regarded as being the concern of international law.[2] Van Bueren[3] has argued:

> "The private/public distinction possibly bears some responsibility for the inequality in the societal power distribution, but the private/public distinction does not bear full responsibility for the failure of international human rights legal system to protect women and children within the family. Rather, the failure to protect women and children results from the devaluation of the private sphere and the mistaken presumption of consent within the private realm. Women and children represent the majority of the world's population, but the international human rights legal system has failed to protect them; therefore, the boundaries of the private sphere must be reassessed. The historical origins of international human rights law should not predetermine its scope."

This chapter tries to ask why countries ratify treaties whose provisions they have little intention of implementing and whether international human rights

---

[1] Cf. Bayefsky, A. (1994), "General Approaches to Domestic Application of Women's International Human Rights Law" in Cook, R. (ed.), *Human Rights of Women* (University of Pennsylvania Press, Philadelphia) 351.

[2] Cf. Charlesworth, H., Chinkin, C., and Wright, S., "Feminist Approaches to International Law", 85 *AJIL* 613, Charlesworth, H., and Chinkin, C. (1993), "The Gender of Jus Cogens", 15 *HRQ* 62.

[3] Van Bueren, G. (1995) "The International Protection of Family Members' Rights as the 21st Century Approaches", 17 *HRQ* 732, 756.

norms have had any impact in the domestic sphere/family law. Given the large number of treaties, most of which contain provisions dealing with family issues,[4] this chapter will concentrate on the Convention on the Elimination of All forms of Discrimination Against Women (CEDAW).[5] Other instruments including the Universal Declaration of Human Rights, the International Covenant on Civil and Political Rights, the International Covenant on Economic Social and Cultural Rights all contain provisions calling for respect and protection of family life as do regional conventions such as the European Convention[6] and the African Charter[7] on Human and Peoples' Rights. The Women's Convention is unique in that it contains the most explicit provisions dealing with private law family issues and outlawing discrimination against women wherever it occurs.[8]

The chapter will focus on countries on the African continent and in particular Egypt, Namibia, South Africa and Zimbabwe.

Of the six parts, part two looks at methods of incorporation of human rights norms into domestic law before moving on to consider the efforts made by countries to change their laws to accord with international obligations undertaken in part 3. Part 4 considers domestic implementation whilst part 5 tries to answer the question why it is that countries sign on to human rights conventions. The conclusion is part 6.

II

International law provides for two modes of transferring international law obligations into the domestic sphere. They are known as the adoption or transference methods.[9] The constitutional provisions of the countries chosen for discussion will be examined to ascertain the model which operates in each country.

All three Southern African countries have only recently ratified, without entering any reservations, the Women's Convention with Namibia acceding to the Convention on 25 September 1992, Zimbabwe ratifying in 1991 while South Africa signed on 29 January 1993 and ratified it on 13 September 1995. The Namibian constitution[10] provides that:

---

[4] UN Declaration of Human Rights, UN Doc. A/810, Art. 16; International Covenant on Civil and Political Rights 1966, reprinted in 6 ILM 368, Art. 23; International Covenant on Economic, Social and Cultural Rights 1966, reprinted in 6 ILM 360, Art. 10.

[5] Convention for the Elimination of all Forms of Discrimination Against Women, reprinted in 19 ILM 33, hereafter referred to as the "Women's Convention".

[6] European Convention for the Protection of Human Rights and Fundamental Freedoms, 213 UNTS 221, Art. 8.

[7] African Charter on Human and People's Rights, 21 ILM 58, Art. 18.

[8] Art. 16. Other provisions such as Arts. 2(f), 9 and 15 also cover family associated rights or obligations.

[9] Bayefsky, A., n. 1 above, 351, 360, also called monist and dualist approaches.

[10] Mtopa, A. (1991), "The Namibian Constitution and the Application of International Law", *SAYIL* 104.

"Unless otherwise provided by this Constitution or Act of Parliament, the general rules of public international law and international agreements binding upon Namibia under this constitution shall form part of the law of Namibia."[11]

This must be read together with Article 63(2)(e) which provides that the National Assembly:

"is required to agree to the ratification of or accession to international agreements which have been negotiated and signed in terms of article 32(3)(e)."[12]

In contrast, the South African and Zimbabwean constitutions require parliamentary approval of international agreements and treaties before they can be incorporated into domestic law. The Zimbabwean constitution provides:

"Except as otherwise provided . . . any convention, treaty or agreement acceded to, concluded or executed by or under the authority of the President . . .
a) shall be subject to approval by Parliament and
b) shall not form part of the law of Zimbabwe unless it has been incorporated into the law by or under an Act of Parliament."[13]

The final constitution of South Africa is couched in similar terms to that of Zimbabwe providing as it does that Parliament must approve international agreements before they can become part of the domestic law.[14] According to Keightley,[15] this is supposed to have a "democratising effect" on the law. She also notes that the provision has:

"The practical effect of making it much easier and quicker to ensure that treaty obligations are translated into domestic law."[16]

However she does note that there are a number of treaties which have been signed by South Africa but which have not been ratified. Keightley suggests that this may be because state departments delay in presenting international agreements for ratification fearing that the domestic law does not accord with international agreements.[17]

Egypt was the first Muslim country to ratify[18] the Women's Convention which entered into force in Egypt on 17 December 1981. Article 151 of the Egyptian Constitution provides:

"The President of the Republic shall conclude treaties and communicate them to the People's Assembly, accompanied with a suitable clarification. They shall have the force

---

[11] Art. 144, Constitution of the Republic of Namibia—Government Notice No. 1 of 1990.
[12] Art. 32(3)(e) provides that the President "is empowered to 'negotiate and sign international agreements, and to delegate such power'".
[13] S. 111B, Constitution of Zimbabwe as amended.
[14] S. 231(3), Constitution of South Africa.
[15] Keightley, R. (1996) "Public International Law and the Final Constitution", 12 *SAJHR* 405, 410.
[16] *Ibid.*
[17] *Ibid.*, at 414.
[18] Tunisia was the first Muslim country to sign the Convention.

of law after their conclusion, ratification and publication according to the established procedure."

In common with other Muslim countries Egypt entered a reservation to, *inter alia*, Article 16,[19] which reservation will be considered in greater detail later.

III

Article 16 of the Women's Convention is the main provision dealing directly with the family. It calls for the elimination of discrimination against women in all matters relating to marriage and family relations. It is also the most reserved provision in the Women's Convention. This leads one to ask whether the signing of international conventions by countries is merely a meaningless gesture? It provides:

"16(1) States Parties shall take all appropriate measures to eliminate discrimination against women in all matters relating to marriage and family relations and in particular shall ensure, on a basis of equality of men and women:
a) The same right to enter into marriage;
b) The same right to freely choose a spouse and to enter into marriage only with their free will and consent;
c) The same rights and responsibilities during marriage and at its dissolution;
d) The same rights and responsibilities as parents, irrespective of their marital status, in matters relating to their children; in all cases the interests of the children shall be paramount;
e) The same rights to decide freely and responsibly on the number and spacing of their children and to have access to the information, education and means to enable them to exercise these rights;
f) The same rights and responsibilities with regard to guardianship, wardship, trustee-ship and adoption of children, or similar institutions where these concepts exist in national legislation; in all cases the interests of the children shall be paramount;
g) The same personal rights as husband and wife, including the right to choose a family name, a profession and an occupation;
h) The same rights for both spouses in respect of the ownership, acquisition, management, administration, enjoyment and disposition of property, whether free of charge or for a valuable consideration.
    2) The betrothal and the marriage of a child shall have no legal effect, and all necessary action, including legislation, shall be taken to specify a minimum age for marriage and to make the registration of marriages in an official registry compulsory."

The rights enumerated in Article 16 are comprehensive. However, for many countries in Africa, difficulties arise over the direction that men and women should be given the "same rights".[20] This is because of "traditional" or cultural

---

[19] Egypt's other reservations are to Arts. 2, 9(2) and 29(2).
[20] Cf. Diagne, S., "Defending Women's Rights—Facts and Challenges in Francophone Africa" in Kerr, J. (ed.), *Ours By Right—Women's Rights as Human Rights* 43, 45–7.

considerations which find expression in state sanctioned customary law. In most countries where customary law is found, the private domain of the family is heavily regulated by customs which disadvantage women.

Although states undertake to fight to eradicate all forms of discrimination, including that based on sex,[21] the issue of customary law or culture and tradition continues to be a politically sensitive one. This is because any attempt to remove gender discrimination and equalise the position of men and women is met with great resistance from reactionary forces who argue that it is against culture and tradition and who then go on to accuse such attempts of being no different from the actions of colonial governments which did not respect the "African way".[22] Women are generally the losers in this game. This is despite the entreaties of the Women's Convention which provide that the state is under an obligation:

> "To take all appropriate measures, including legislation, to modify or abolish existing laws, regulations, customs and practices which constitute discrimination against women."[23]

There is also Article 5(a) which requires the State "to take all appropriate measures"

> "To modify the social and cultural patterns of conduct of men and women, with a view to achieving the elimination of prejudices and customary and all other practices which are based on the idea of the inferiority or the superiority of either of the sexes or on stereotyped roles for men and women."

The difficulty, as An-Na'im has noted, is the perception that human rights on the African continent may not always have cultural legitimacy,[24] or indeed reflect cultural values.[25] He answers this point by suggesting that a mediated settlement be reached between domestic concerns and international human rights norms:[26]

> "the norms of the international system should be validated in terms of shared or similar values and institutions of all cultures. This can be achieved I suggest, through what I call 'internal discourse' within the framework of each culture, and 'cross-cultural dialogue' among the various cultural traditions of the world."

He argues that:

> "In this way, the combination of the processes of internal discourse and cross-cultural dialogue will, it is hoped, deepen and broaden universal cultural consensus on the concept and normative content of international human rights."

---

[21] Indeed the African Charter goes on to provide in Art. 18(3): "The State shall ensure the elimination of every discrimination against women and also ensure the protection of the rights of the woman and the child as stipulated in international declarations and conventions."

[22] Cf. Butegwa, F. (1993), "The Challenge of Promoting Women's Rights in African Countries" in Kerr, J. (ed.), *Ours By Right—Women's Rights as Human Rights*.

[23] Art. 2(f).

[24] An-Na'im, A. (1994), "State Responsibility Under International Human Rights Law to Change Religious and Customary Laws" in Cook, R. (ed.), *Human Rights of Women* 167, 170–5.

[25] Cf. Kaganas, F., and Murray, C. (1994), "The Contest Between Culture and Gender Equality Under South Africa's Interim Constitution", 21 *Journal of Law and Society* 409.

[26] An-Na'im, A., n. 24 above, at 174.

Although a potentially useful way of resolving a thorny problem, it still remains open to question whether women will be active participants in the process of cultural dialogue. The experience with the formulation of what is now known as customary law would seem to signal a need for caution.[27] When discourses meet, it is difficult to escape from or ameliorate pre-existing power imbalances. Article 29(7) of the African Charter provides that every individual has a duty:

> "To preserve and strengthen positive African cultural values in his relations with other members of the society, in the spirit of tolerance, dialogue and consultation and in general, to contribute to the promotion of the well being of society."

Armstrong *et al.* note that the process of deciding/negotiating values is not unproblematic:

> "The difficulty is that the outcome of this process may largely depend on power relations which disadvantage women. It is with respect to such relations that the principle of non discrimination against women should apply. There is no doubt that the area of the family ranks as a prime category for the positive reformulation of African cultural values."[28]

The existence within Africa of religious considerations in the form of Islamic law further complicates the position *vis-à-vis* women's rights within the family. Connors has noted that all of the Muslim countries in Africa which had ratified the Women's Convention as at 26 October 1993 had done so with reservations.[29]

Egypt seeks to explain the rationale behind its reservation to Article 16 by arguing:

> "This is out of respect for the sacrosanct nature of the firm religious beliefs which govern marital relations in Egypt and which may not be called into question and in view of the fact that one of the most important bases of these relations is an equivalency of rights and duties so as to ensure complementarity which guarantees true equality between the spouses. The provisions of the Shariah lay down that the husband shall pay bridal money to the wife and maintain her fully and shall also make payment to her upon divorce, whereas the wife retains full rights over her property and is not obliged to spend anything on her keep. The Shariah therefore restricts the wife's rights to divorce by making it contingent on a judge's ruling, whereas no such restriction is laid down in the case of the husband."[30]

This argument for complementarity fails to take into account the question of choice, or rather the absence of choice on the part of the women. They may

---

[27] Chanock, M. (1985), *Law, Custom and Social Order: The Colonial Experience in Malawi and Zambia* (Cambridge, Cambridge University Press); Ranger, T. (1983), "The Invention of Tradition in Colonial Africa" in Hobsbawm, E., and Ranger, T. (eds.), *The Invention of Tradition*, 211.

[28] Armstrong, A. *et al.* (1993) "Uncovering Reality: Excavating Women's Rights in African Family Law", 7 *IJLF* 314, 321.

[29] Connors, J. (1997), "The Women's Convention in the Muslim World" in Gardner, J. P. (ed.), *Human Rights and a State's Right to Opt Out* (British Institute of International and Comparative Law, London), 85, 89.

[30] Steiner, H. J., and Alston, P. (1996), *International Human Rights in Context*, 921.

appear to be advantaged by the operation of the Shariah law during marriage, but arguably they are disadvantaged and discriminated against by virtue of the fact that they do not have the same choices as men to end the marriage nor to acquire any property from the marriage. This last point can be said to apply to children as well. Egypt made a reservation to Article 9(2) of the Women's Convention which grants men and women equal rights with respect to the nationality of their children. Opting to retain the male preference, the Egyptian reservation to Article 9(2) provides:

> "It is clear that the child's acquisition of the father's nationality is the procedure most suitable for the child and that this does not infringe upon the principle of equality between men and women, since it is *customary* [my emphasis] for a woman to agree, upon marrying an alien, that her children shall be of the father's nationality."[31]

It is of note that the countries give different interpretations of the Shariah when justifying the reservations and this in itself raises questions about the malleability of religious and customary laws.[32] This raises the possibility of the exploitation of religious beliefs for political ends.[33] It could of course be argued that this "flexibility" can be used positively in making progressive interpretations of the Shariah.[34]

Addressing Egypt's reservations to the Convention, it has been argued:

> "Thus the justifications used by the Egyptian government for its reservations can be easily refuted on the basis of the experience of other Islamic countries. This shows the necessity of studying these experiences; examining the Islamic jurisprudential schools that support women's rights; and drawing upon them to improve women's conditions and to drop the larger part of Egypt's reservations."[35]

It is in the limiting of its obligations under international law that a state's commitment to the treaty is thrown into relief.[36] Article 28(2) of the Women's Convention provides:

> "A reservation incompatible with the object and purpose of the present Convention shall not be permitted."

Is Egypt's reservation incompatible with the object and purpose of the Women's Convention? *Prima facie* yes.[37] Whilst there is a general obligation not

---

[31] Steiner, H. J. and Alston, P., n. 30 above, 921.

[32] Connors, J., n. 29 above, 85, 101.

[33] However an attempt by the CEDAW committee to call for an investigation into the Shariah laws was vetoed by ECOSOC highlighting the contentiousness of challenging reservations based on religious beliefs and arguably highlighting the growing politicisation of Islam. Connors, J., n. 29 above, 85, 98.

[34] Helie-Lucas, M.-A. (1993), "Women Living Under Muslim Laws" in Kerr, J. (ed.), *Ours By Right*, 52, 58.

[35] Cairo Institute for Human Rights Studies (1996) "Reservation is not a Justification", 12 *Sawasiah* 8, 8–9.

[36] Cf. Cook, R. (1990), "Reservations to the Convention on the Elimination of All Forms of Discrimination Against Women", 30 *VJIL* 643.

[37] Cf. An-Na'im, n. 24 above, 167, 169.

to undermine a treaty as a treaty,[38] there is the further obligation not to undermine those provisions of the treaty which are said to encapsulate its object and purpose.[39] The Committee which oversees the Women's Convention has stated that it considers Articles 2, 9 and 16 as the objects and purpose of the Convention.[40] The Committee has also made two general recommendations requesting that states make efforts to withdraw reservations.[41] It is arguable therefore that any country which fails to grant women the rights found in these Articles by entering a reservation or by simply not acting because it decides that to remove discrimination against women would be contrary to culture or in contravention of any religious or customary law, is in breach of its international obligations. Unfortunately the Committee does not have any power to force a state to uplift its reservation and has therefore to rely on the goodwill of states parties.[42]

The Egyptian case has been easy to consider because Egypt has reserved parts of the Women's Convention. What of those countries which have not? Have the norms found within the Women's Convention found expression in the domestic sphere?[43] The answer would appear to be mixed. It is to the domestic implementation of the provisions in Namibia, South Africa and Zimbabwe that we now turn.

IV

The constitutions of the countries under discussion are all said to form the supreme law of the respective countries. All contain within them provisions outlawing discrimination on the basis of sex,[44] the Zimbabwean one being via a fairly recent amendment.[45] The question thus becomes—does the anti-sex discrimination provision in the respective constitutions mean that those customs which apply unequally between men and women have by implication been repealed?

---

[38] Linzaad, E. (1994), *Reservations to Human Rights Treaties: Ratify and Ruin* (Martinus Nijhoff, Dordrecht), 360.

[39] Vienna Convention on the Law of Treaties, 1969 UNTS 1155.331, Art. 19(c).

[40] Linzaad, E. n. 38 above, 303. See also Linzaad's comment at 303.

[41] General Recommendation No. 4 UN Doc CCPR/C/1/Rev.1 (1994), A/42/38; General Recommendation No. 20 UN Doc CCPR/C/1/Rev.1 (1994) A/47/38.

[42] Engle, K. (1992), "International Human Rights and Feminism: When Discourses Meet", 13 *Michigan Journal of International Law* 517, 560n. See also Stratton, L. (1992), "The Right to Have Rights: Gender Discrimination in Nationality Laws", 77 *Minnesota Law Review* 195, 216; and finally Galey, M. (1984), "International Enforcement of Women's Rights", 6 *Human Rights Quarterly* 463, 482.

[43] Welch, C. (1993), "Human Rights and African Women: A Comparison of Protection Under Two Major Treaties", 15 *HRQ* 549, 550–1.

[44] Constitution of the Republic of Namibia, Art. 10; Constitution of the Republic of South Africa Art. 9(1); Constitution of the Republic of Zimbabwe, Art. 23.

[45] S. 23 of the Constitution of Zimbabwe as amended by s. 9 of the Constitution of Zimbabwe Amendment Act (No. 14). For a fuller discussion of this provision see Ncube (chapter 31).

Given the contentiousness of what constitutes custom and "customary law" this is an issue which will remain controversial for some time to come.[46]

The Namibian constitution goes some way towards fulfilling the obligations contained within the Women's Convention. As already noted, Article 10 of the constitution outlaws discrimination on the basis of, *inter alia*, sex while Article 2 grants equal rights of citizenship to alien spouses of citizens of Namibia[47] whether male or female thus meeting the obligations imposed under Article 9 of the Convention. It is worth noting that under the Namibian constitution, the State is permitted to enact legislation or put forward policies which take into account that:

" . . . women in Namibia have traditionally suffered special discrimination and that they need to be encouraged and enabled to play a full, equal and effective role in the political, social, economic and cultural life of the nation."[48]

Additionally, the Principles of State Policy contained within Article 95 call upon the state to adopt policies aimed at:

"a) enactment of legislation to ensure equality of opportunity for women to enable them to participate fully in all spheres of Namibian society; in particular the Government shall ensure the implementation of the policy of non discrimination in remuneration of men and women; further, the Government shall seek, through appropriate legislation to provide maternity and related benefits for women."

Although not justiciable,[49] these two provisions go some way to meeting the requirements of Article 4 of the Women's Convention on special measures.

The Namibian constitution also makes specific provision for the family in Article 14 which mirrors the provisions of Article 16 providing as it does:

"14(1) Men and women of full age, without any limitation due to race, colour, ethnic origin, nationality, religion, creed or social or economic status have the right to marry and found a family. They are entitled to equal rights as to marriage, during marriage and at its dissolution.

(2) Marriage shall be entered into only with the free and full consent of the intending spouses.

(3) The family is the natural and fundamental group unit of society and is entitled to protection by society and the state."

Many issues are raised by this provision. Like many countries in Africa, Namibia has plural legal systems which co-exist. The general law is Roman-

---

[46] Cf. Munalula, M. (1995), "Law as an Instrument of Social Change: The Constitution and Sexual Discrimination in Zambia", 1 *International Journal of Discrimination and the Law* 131; Nhlapo, T. (1991), "The African Family and Women's Rights: Friends or Foes?", *Acta Juridica* 135.

[47] Compare the Zimbabwean position as considered in Ncube (chapter 31).

[48] Art. 23(3). Arguably this special treatment is to be seen in the context of the disadvantages suffered by women as a result of the policy of apartheid. This is because s. 23 addresses the issue of Apartheid and Affirmative Action.

[49] This is because of Art. 101 of the Constitution which provides: "The principles of state policy herein contained shall not of and by themselves be legally enforceable by any Court, but shall nevertheless guide the Government in making and applying laws to give effect to the fundamental objectives of the said principles. The Courts are entitled to have regard to the said principles in interpreting any laws based on them."

Dutch while the customary laws cover patrilineal, matrilineal and mixed matrilineal and patrilineal groups. The customary laws, particularly of the patrilineal
groups, do not grant men and women equal rights to property at the dissolution
of marriage.[50] Additionally, as has been noted by Armstrong *et al.*,[51] the issue of
consent to marriage often results in the interests of the individual being overrid-
den by the interests of the group. They go on to note:

> "In those countries where the father of the bride is able to use his giving or withhold-
> ing of consent to secure higher bridewealth payments, and even to pressure the woman
> into a particular marriage, the issue of consent is a very significant feature in the life of
> the woman."[52]

A final point worth noting concerns the issue of polygamy which is still practised in Namibia and indeed other African states. This raises issues of equality
within marriage because men have the right to marry additional spouses yet
women do not.

Despite these reservations, it can be said that the Namibian constitution goes
some way towards meeting its international pledges.

It has been said that the provision of local remedies is a key element in the
implementation of rights.[53] The existence of international conventions which the
state has ratified can be a good way of developing a positive human rights culture with domestic courts playing a vital role in the translation of international
human rights norms into the domestic sphere.

The creative use of international legal norms by the courts resulted in the landmark rulings in the cases of *Dow*[54] in Botswana and *Rattigan*[55] in Zimbabwe.[56]
In both cases the courts held it was discriminating to allow men to bring alien
wives into the country but not to allow the same for women. The Zimbabwean
government's response to the *Rattigan* case, namely "equalising" the position
between men and women by giving both fewer rights, raises the question of what
is to be done with a state which honours its international commitments by limiting or curtailing pre-existing rights.

Part of implementing human rights involves reporting to the supervisory body
set up under the treaty.[57] Zimbabwe has not always met her international report-

[50] Armstrong, A. n. 28 above, 314, 345.
[51] *Ibid.*, at 331.
[52] *Ibid.*, at 332.
[53] Judicial Colloquium in Bangalore, Developing Human Rights Jurisprudence: The Domestic
Application of Human Rights Norms and Judicial Colloquium in Harare, Developing Human Rights
Jurisprudence: A Second Judicial Colloquium on the Domestic Application of International Human
Rights Norms.
[54] *Dow* v. *The Attorney General* [1991] LRC (Const) 574.
[55] *Rattigan & Others* v. *Chief Immigration Officer* 1994 (2) ZLR 287 (SC).
[56] These are discussed by Ncube in some detail in chapter 31. The *Dow* case is also discussed in
Stratton, L. (1992) and Human Rights Watch Africa (1994), *Botswana Second Class Citizens
Discrimination Against Women Under Botswana's Citizenship Act* (Human Rights Watch Africa,
London).
[57] UN General Assembly, "Effective Implementation of International Instruments on Human
Rights, Including Reporting Obligations Under International Instruments on Human Rights",

ing obligations, sending in her first report under the United Nations Convention on the Rights of the Child more than four years after its 1992 due date.[58] The 1995 Zimbabwean report to the Women's Committee[59] has been criticised for not presenting a true picture of the difficulties faced by women in Zimbabwe.[60] Reporting under Article 9 and considering the question of the unequal operation of the nationality laws *vis-à-vis* Zimbabwean women married to foreign citizens, the Zimbabwean government report acknowledges the discrepancy and says:

> "The Government is currently considering amendments to the Constitution and the Citizenship Act and it is likely that foreign spouses will in future be treated equally thus removing the advantage that Zimbabwean men have hitherto enjoyed over their female counterparts in that regard."[61]

The government did indeed amend the constitution—but, as noted above, it did so in a way which removed the rights of Zimbabwean men married to alien wives, thus putting them in the same position as Zimbabwean women.[62]

The Zimbabwean government report acknowledges that many people, including civil servants, are unaware of the provisions of the Women's Convention which raises the question of how the convention's provisions can be adequately implemented if there is such an information vacuum.[63]

Given the recent adoption by South Africa of the Women's Convention, it may be too early to assess South Africa's commitment to human rights principles. However the strong human rights rhetoric which is such an inherent part of the South African legal and political landscape would suggest that South Africa is committed to upholding principles contained within the various international conventions, including the Women's Convention. Reconciling customary law with human rights norms will prove to be a challenge for South African courts.[64]

V

Given all the difficulties which obviously exist in meeting international obligations and the additional burdens put upon countries in the form of reporting

Resolution A/C.3.48.L.61, 3 Dec. 1993 as cited by Hatchard, J. (1994), "Reporting Under International Human Rights Instruments by African Countries" in 38 *JAL* 61.

[58] See Hatchard, *ibid.* and Banda, F. (1997), "Family Law Reform in Zimbabwe 1987 to the Present" in Bainham, A. (ed.), *The International Survey of Family Law 1995*, 543, 548.

[59] *Zimbabwe's First Report on CEDAW* (1995) Unicef. Updated and to be considered in New York in Jan. 1998 (personal correspondence from Ms A Tsanga of the Faculty of Law, University of Zimbabwe).

[60] Similar criticisms have also been made about Zimbabwe's 1992 report to the African Commission on Human and People's Rights. See Tigere, P. (1994), "State Reporting to the African Commission", *Journal of African Law* 66.

[61] Zimbabwe's First Report on CEDAW 1995.

[62] S. 8(1) Constitution of Zimbabwe Amendment Act (No. 14).

[63] Zimbabwe's First Report 57.

[64] Cf. Bennett, T. W., *Human Rights and African Customary Law* (1995).

requirements,[65] the question which remains to be considered is why do they sign international treaties?

Starting from a positive stance, countries sign and ratify international conventions because they believe in the norms contained therein and because they have a genuine commitment to seeing those norms reflected in the domestic sphere. Arguably, this is the starting point of countries such as South Africa whose unhappy history of institutionalised human rights violations makes it an imperative that citizens be protected from a recurrence of the apartheid years. Ratifying human rights conventions may also provide a "cover" for those countries which would like to improve the situation of disadvantaged groups such as women, but who fear domestic backlash if the proposals were seen to originate "at home".[66]

Becoming less positive and more cynical, countries sign because the prevailing or dominant ideology is that of countries committing themselves to uphold human rights standards.[67] Being seen to have ratified the major human rights conventions is used as evidence of a commitment to human rights norms. Ratifying human rights conventions is seen as positive proof of that commitment.

Linked to this is the adoption by international money lending institutions such as the International Monetary Fund and the World Bank of policies linking loans to a commitment to human rights.[68] Ratifying treaties is mutually beneficial for the lender is able to look principled and the recipient country is able to show apparent commitment. Commenting on this issue as it relates to women, Welch notes:

> "In the judgement of Fatma Alloo, women's issues in Africa have been raised not because of a belief that they are part of human rights, but rather to respond to global tendencies which demand certain criteria to fit into 'aid patterns' and to feminist struggles at the global level."[69]

VI

In conclusion, then, is the ratification of international conventions merely a meaningless gesture or is it based on genuine commitment to human rights? The

---

[65] Welch, C., n. 43 above, discusses some of the difficulties presented by the onerous reporting requirements of some of the treaty bodies, noting at 564 "[t]he demands for data may be too great, and the instructions too confusing. Some African countries confront reporting requirements that are difficult to meet, yet low in the scale of government priorities. The legal, statistical and diplomatic skills and time needed to draft an effective report, especially an initial report, must not be underestimated".

[66] Welch, C., n. 43 above, 549, 550.

[67] Indeed three years ago the Commonwealth group of nations meeting in New Zealand agreed in the Millbrook Programme of Action to lay down rules and prescribe punishment for member countries that do not come up to scratch on human rights, good governance and democracy. However discussing the general principle of linking aid to democracy, Helie-Lucas, n. 34 above, 52, 61, notes that "there is no sign that the fate of women will be seen as a valid indicator of democracy by the international community. What we see instead is a narrow interpretation of democracy in the sense of parliamentary democracy."

[68] Murphy, J. L. (1995), *Gender Issues in World Bank Lending, A World Bank Operations Evaluation Study* (World Bank, Washington).

[69] Welch, C., n. 43 above, 549, 572.

criterion for assessment must be by examining the extent to which international legal norms have been used in the domestic sphere. Using this yardstick, the answer to the question would appear to be that some progress has been made but not enough. The reasons for this are manifold. There is the question of ignorance of human rights norms highlighted in the Zimbabwean government report under the Women's Convention:

> "The Convention has not been translated into local languages and very few people are aware of the fact that Zimbabwe has ratified it. The media has not widely and adequately covered the Convention, its provisions and implications for the people of Zimbabwe in general and Zimbabwean women in particular."[70]

This raises the question—how central is law to the lives of most African citizens? Can people afford to access domestic justice or demand that their human rights be respected?[71] Given that most are unaware of the existence of these rights, finding themselves caught up in the daily struggle of survival, one has to ask—do these human rights have any resonance in people's lives?[72] How many of those rights are realisable? An important consideration when looking at the family from a human rights perspective is the fact that the problem in Africa is not with changing the law, but with challenging long held views based on "culture" and "custom". It is changing these attitudes which poses the greatest challenge to governments committed to meeting international obligations to ensure human rights within their countries.

Despite these constraints, I would still argue that governments *should* be encouraged to ratify international human rights conventions. At the very least, it brings them within the human rights fold and makes challenging human rights violations easier. Finally, like Welch, I am of the opinion that:

> "Human rights treaties serve as standards of achievement to be attained over time; the gap between long term goals and short term achievement is therefore not overly troubling."[73]

[70] Zimbabwe's First Report on CEDAW 1995, 57.
[71] Cf. Munalula, M., n. 46 above, 131.
[72] Welch, C., n. 43 above, 549, 551–3.
[73] Welch, C., n. 43 above, 549.

PART FIVE

Social and "Natural" Parenthood

This Part opens with a sharply focused description by Doek (Chapter 33) of the ways in which new forms of family living are separating biological from social parenthood. Eekelaar and Maclean (Chapter 34) describe the varying circumstances in which a child might find itself in a household apart from one natural parent, and suggest that the extent to which the "outside" parent plays a part in the child's life is related to the extent to which that parent had at some time lived with the child. It does not follow that "natural" parents who had never lived with the child should not be considered part of the child's family. Indeed, the European Court of Human Rights, in the *Keegan* case, implied that a father shared "family life" with a child with whom he had never lived, at least if he had lived with the mother before its birth and had intended its procreation. Nevertheless, an outside parent is unlikely to be under an enforceable duty to play a part in the child's life (other than by providing financial support), and if no such part is played it may be difficult to regard that parent as being a more important part of the child's family than its social parent. Doek gives a useful summary of the kinds of circumstances that may arise in modern conditions where "natural" and social parenthood may be separated. Such separation occurs of course also in adoption, and Kounegeri-Manodelaki (Chapter 35), Tokotani (Chapter 36) and Lowe (Chapter 37), in their respective accounts of the new Greek adoption law, special adoption in Japan and of developments in English adoption law, demonstrate contrasting attitudes to the weight that can be given to the position of natural parents who are not living with the child as against that of the child's social parents. Incorporation of an "outside" parent into the familial network raises novel problems of co-operation between the adults involved, which are explored by Davies (Chapter 38).

33

The Nuclear Family: Who are the Parents?

1. INTRODUCTION

The classic picture of the nuclear family in the western world is of two married adults—a man and a woman—with one or more children born to or adopted by them. This picture still exists but is no longer the only one. Others have developed over the past 25 years. This chapter refers to two of them.

1 The development of artificial reproduction technology

The new technologies offer methods of reproduction without sex including artificial insemination by donor (AID), *in vitro* fertilization (IVF), surrogate embryo transfer (SET) and surrogate motherhood.

They affect the traditional concept of the family and of parenthood. Who is the father of a child conceived via AID: the man who has donated his sperm, the biological father or the man who is married to or cohabits with the mother of that child as his "social" father?

And who, in cases of surrogacy, is the mother? The woman who donated her eggs for an embryo transfer to the wife of the man who is the sperm donor or the woman who carried the child for nine months, the gestational mother, because of her greater biological and psychological investment in the child? And what if the woman is not only the genetic but also the gestational mother, but was contracted by another woman (and her husband) to produce the child? Is this contracting woman the mother and why? Because her intention is to have that child and raise it as her own?

2 The increase of divorce and of informal family relationships (cohabitation, *union libres*, *Lebensgemeinschaft*, *samenleving*)

One of the results of the many divorces in the western world is not only that many children lose contact with one of their parents but also that in many instances they will acquire a new parent when the mother (or father) who cares for them remarries or cohabits with a new partner (not necessarily of the opposite sex). For example, in the Netherlands of the 82,982 marriages (1994) almost 20,000 were second (or third etc.) marriages. (It is not known how many minor children were involved.)

Furthermore—and regardless of a previous marriage—the percentage of men and women living together unmarried is increasing, at least in the Netherlands (in 1994 about 10 per cent of men 19 years and older were not married to the women they were living with). The number of children born out of wedlock is on the rise (in the Netherlands for example from 24,667 in 1992 to 28,115 in 1994; an increase of almost 15 per cent) where at the same time fewer children were born to a married couple (in the Netherlands for example down from 172,251 in 1992 to 167,712 in 1994; a decrease of about 3 per cent. Percentage of children born out-of wedlock in 1992: 12.5 per cent; in 1994: 14.5 per cent).

In many countries it is a rule of law that the mother of the child is considered to be the woman who gave birth to her/him. But is the man with whom she is cohabiting at birth the legal father of that child? And what when she is a single mother and starts living with another man (other than the biological father of the child)? Can he become a legal father? To what extent can a subjective intention determine parenthood? The picture of the nuclear family becomes even more complicated when we look at homosexual (gay and lesbian couples). Suppose a gay couple who have cemented their relationship by taking matrimonial vows apply to be foster parents of children with AIDS whose biological parents have died or abandoned them and the children are placed with them. Can these two men become legal parents of the two children e.g. via adoption? Suppose a lesbian couple have a long-term monogamous relationship and one of the women is inseminated via AID and gives birth to a child. What is the parental status of the partner of this woman?

The central question behind all these questions is the following: should the legal recognition of parenthood be based on a biological relationship or can it also be based on a psychological/social relationship? In connection with this question there is another one: should the concept of "parent" be the same in all circumstances?

This discussion will be based on recent and important changes in the Netherlands in the rules for affiliation and custody/responsibilities of individuals who are not the biological parents of the children they are caring for.

As a "Leitmotiv" to this discussion I want to refer to Article 7 of the Convention on the Rights of the Child. In paragraph (1) of that Article the child is accorded (among others) with the right to know and be cared for by his or her parents, as far as possible.[1] Secondly I refer to Goldstein's *Beyond the Best Interests of the Child*:

---

[1] This right was added during the discussion in the Open-ended Working Group Convention at its 1989 session. The exact reason for this addition is not clear but some delegates expressed as their view that e.g. not all adopted children should have the right to know their biological parents. See

"Unlike adults, children have no psychological conception of blood tie relationship until quite late in their development. For the biological parents, the experience of conceiving, carrying and giving birth prepares them to feel close to and responsible for their child. These considerations carry no weight with children who are emotionally unaware of the events leading to their existence. What matters to them is the pattern of day-to-day interchanges with adults who take care of them and who on the strength of such interactions, become the parent figures to who they are attached."[2]

2. PARENTHOOD AND REPRODUCTIVE TECHNOLOGY

1 The mother

Regardless of the medical technology applied to give birth to a child, the Netherlands and—as far as I know—all other countries, stick to the rule from the old Roman Law: *mater semper certa est*. This means that the woman who carries and gives birth to the child (the so-called gestational mother) is the legal mother of the child.

It is possible to consider the genetic contribution as being determinative for motherhood. But so far I have found few supporters for the view that egg donation in itself should be enough to constitute legal motherhood. There is a similarity with sperm donation. This donation does not make the donor the legal father of the child conceived with the donated sperm.

This principle (*mater semper certa est*) has consequences for surrogacy arrangements: the surrogate mother is the legal mother, even if the contracting man and woman who intend to be the parents of the child have contributed the genetic material (sperm + egg). As is stated in section 27 (1) of the UK Human Fertilisation and Embryology Act 1990: the woman who is carrying or has carried a child as a result of the placing in her of an embryo or of sperm and eggs, *and no other woman*, is to be treated as the mother of the child (for all legal purposes: section 29 (11)). If the surrogate mother, complying with contract, hands the child over to the other contracting parties, this does not make them legally the mother and the father. In order to obtain that position it is in the Netherlands necessary to adopt the child.

Some authors are in favour of facilitating this process, by making it easier to terminate the parental power of the surrogate mother.[3] But no one has suggested making it a rule of law that the contracting woman, if she is the genetic mother, should be considered and registered as the legal mother instead of the surrogate mother who gave birth to the child. In the light of the *Marckx* decision of the

Sharon Detrick, *The United Nations Convention on the Rights of the Child. A Guide to the "Travaux Préparatoires"* (Martinus Nijhoff Publishers, 1992), 123–31.

[2] Joseph Goldstein and others, *The Best Interests of the Child* (a revised and updated trilogy) (The Free Press, 1996), 9.

[3] See e.g. E. Ph. R. Sutorius and H. L. J. M. Kersten, "Het gezag van draagmoeders", (1997) 25 *Ned. Juristen Blad*, 1116–20.

European Court on Human Rights (ECHR) of 1979 it is not very likely that legislation in Europe will change this principle. The Court stated among others: "*le droit interne de la grande majorité des Etats membres du Conseil de l'Europe a évolué . . . vers la consecration juridique intégrale de l'adage 'mater semper certa est'*".[4]

The French Civil Code (Article 341, paragraph 1) makes it possible that the mother's identity at her request can be kept confidential. This may facilitate surrogacy arrangements. But it is not clear whether this implies that the contracting woman who wants to be the mother can simply register as such. Furthermore, there is increasing support for the right of the child to knowledge of her/his genetic/biological origin, which makes this rule questionable. I will return to this point later.

In conclusion, the position of the mother seems to be clear. The genetic background is not decisive: the gestational mother is considered to be the legal mother. George Annas gave as a justification for this rule the greater biological and psychological investment of the gestational mother in the child.[5]

2 The father

In cases of AID, Dutch Law, and the law of many other countries, applies the Roman Law rule: *pater is est quem nuptiae demonstrant*. This means that if a child is conceived via AID and is born to a married woman, the husband of that woman is considered to be the legal father. The condition is however that the AID treatment took place with the consent of the husband. In the UK this consent is assumed. This means that he will not be considered the legal father if he can prove that he has not consented to the treatment (Human Fertilisation and Embryology Act 1990, section 28 (2)) and also that the child is not in fact his. In other words: the parenthood of the father does not depend upon proof of his consent in a written and signed document.

Dutch Law is slightly different: the father cannot deny his paternity if he has consented to the AID treatment. In other words, he is the legal father and only if he can prove that he did not consent he can deny (in court) his fatherhood (Article 199 of the Civil Code).

Unmarried couples: if AID is used to conceive a child for a woman in cohabitation with a man the picture is different. The UK Act of 1990 mentioned earlier states (section 28 (3)) that if the AID treatment took place "in the course of treatment services provided for her and a man together" by a licensed facility then that man is considered to be the child's legal father. The fact that the couple is treated together and *not* the man's actual or presumed consent, is decisive. The Code of Practice (1990) therefore advises centres to record at each appoint-

---

[4] *Marckx* v. *Belgium*, 13 June 1979, Series A no. 31. See for the consequences of this decision particularly for Belgium: A. Heyvaert and H. Willekens, *Beginselen van het gezinsen familierecht na het Marckxarrest* (Kluwer, Antwerp, 1981).

[5] See George J. Annas, *Hastings Center Report* 18 no. 2 (1988), 21–4.

ment whether or not the man was present and to try and obtain his written statement that they are treated together and that donated sperm is used. Otherwise the rule may give rise to all kinds of difficulties when it comes to provide evidence. However this father does not have "parental responsibility" automatically but is able to acquire it at his request (this rule is not a violation of the right to respect for family life as guaranteed in Article 8 of the ECHR. See *McMichael*, ECHR, 24 February 1995, Series A, Vol. 307 B).

Dutch Law does not have a similar provision and Bill 24 649 concerning changes of the Civil Code dealing with affiliation does not contain proposals in that regard either. It means that the partner of an unmarried woman using AID can only become the father of the child if he recognises the child, for which he needs the consent of the mother. If the mother refuses the consent he can go to court and try to overrule the mother's refusal.

The chances that he will succeed may largely depend on what he and the mother have agreed upon. So far, the Dutch courts have not dealt with such a case. But if the couple have made a cohabitation contract containing the provision that the man will recognize the child born to the mother and that the mother in that case will give her consent, the court may decide in favour of the man and allow him to recognise the child and become his legal father.

3 The child's right to know his/her origin

A serious ethical and legal problem connected with artificial reproductive technology is how this affects the well-being of the (potential) child. A child who has donors intruded into its parentage will be cut off from its genetic heritage and part of its kinship.[6] Many countries have struggled or are struggling with the question: does the child have the right to know his biological origin? Or, more precisely, should he/she have the right to know the identity of the sperm donor and/or the egg donor? If so, should certain conditions/limits be set to that right? In 1979 Sweden adopted a law giving the child conceived via AID the right to know the identity of the donor. More recently other countries have adopted or are considering the adoption of similar legislation.

Austria: the Act of Procreative Medicine of 14 May 1992. Article I section 20 gives a child of 14 years or older, conceived via AID, the right of access to personal data of the sperm donor. For medical reasons the court can authorise access for parents or guardians.

Germany: in 1989 the German Constitutional Court confirmed the right of an individual, protected by the German Constitution, to ascertain his or her own parentage. Frank expressed concerns about this development resulting among others in a growing number of actions against fathers of legitimate children and raising questions regarding motives (genuine concern about genetic parentage?

---

[6] See Sidney Callahan in John E. Monagle and David C. Thomasma (eds.), *Medical Ethics: A Guide for Health Care Professionals* (Aspen Publish., 1987).

revenge?). He notes an over-emphasis upon blood relationship and opposes the introduction of an action solely designed for ascertaining true (= genetic) parentage without creating any legal relationship.[7]

Switzerland: in a referendum on 17 May 1992 a constitutional amendment was accepted allowing the Confederation to guarantee by law a person's access to data concerning her/his ancestry, including the identity of biological parents and applicable to AID and adopted children.

The Netherlands: a Bill has been submitted to Parliament in which the child conceived by AID is given the right to know the identity of his biological father (= the sperm donor). The child has to be at least 16 years of age and the donor will be asked for permission. If the donor refuses his permission, the Board of the Foundation in charge of keeping data on AID can nevertheless decide to provide the child with identifying data unless the interests of the donor in maintaining his anonymity clearly prevails over the interests of the child (Bill 23 207). The Bill has been criticised mainly because of the possible negative effects it may have on willingness to donate sperm for AID. The Bill furthermore grants the child of 12 years and older the right to receive nonidentifying data about the sperm donor e.g. for medical reasons.

Although sometimes reference has been made to Article 7 of the Convention on the Rights of the Child (the right to know his/her parents) the discussion in the working group on the drafting of the Convention (*travaux préparatoires*, see Detrick mentioned in note 1) does not contain indications that this right was given in order to reveal genetic origin to the child. Yet this Article in combination with Article 8 (the right to preserve her/his identity) may well be used to support the idea that the child is entitled to information about her/his genetic origin. One may also argue that the right to know his genetic origin should be subjected to certain conditions. In other words, the rights of donors should be taken into account as well as the practical implications such as the risk of fewer donors.

The first point can be dealt with e.g. by limiting the legal consequences of the fact that a child finds out that somebody other than the person who has been his legal father as long as he knows is his biological father. The second point can be dismissed as irrelevant to the child's rights.

There does not seem to be any decisive argument or interest for not granting a child the right to know his/her genetic origin (if he/she wishes to exercise it). Put another way, why should adults have a right to make this genetic origin a secret to which the child has no access?

In the area of new artificial reproductive technology we are struggling to find a balance between what I would call the biological and emotional reality. We like to acknowledge the genuine desire of couples who want to have and care for a child. The child is wanted and that is a good start in life. At the same time, we should not try to keep biological origin a secret. The child who wants to know,

---

[7] See Rainer Frank in (1990–1) 29 *J. Fam. L.* 371 and the *Annual Survey Family Law 1992*, 335–44.

should have a right to be provided with data about his genetic origin including, if requested by the child, identifying data.

3. SOCIAL PARENTHOOD

As described in the introduction, the increasing divorce rate and all kinds of informal cohabitation (opposite or same sex couples) mean that there are many individuals who take care of children in a family setting without having a biological relationship with those children, such as new partners of divorced parents of the opposite or same sex, unmarried mothers moving in with new partners (again opposite or same sex), partners of lesbian mothers or gay fathers etc.

The main question for all these cases in the present context is whether the social parent should have the right to be recognised as the legal parent and if so with what legal consequences (name, custody, financial obligations, succession etc.). A well established method of giving a social parent a legal status is adoption. In this regard a distinction can be made between *full adoption* which leads to a full legal integration of the child in the family of his social parent and to a total break in the legal ties with the original family and the *simple adoption* which makes the child a member of the family of the adopting (social) parent while he/she retains certain rights (e.g. inheritance, financial support) within the original family.

In his comparative study (France, Germany, the Netherlands) Guus E. Schmidt notes that the countries involved in his study increasingly favoured full adoption. He submits that the real reason for this development is not of a legal but of psychological nature: full adoption was not supported in order to create the best legal relationship (which could be attained by other means) but to support and even influence the development of emotional ties between the child and the adopters.[8]

He questions the need or usefulness of full adoption to provide social parents with a legal status. In the Netherlands a step-parent can adopt her/his step-child with the consent of the legal parents of the child i.e. the parent who has the custody and with whom the step-parent is living together (married or unmarried)[9] and the other parent. Adoption by the step-parent means however that all legal ties between the child and the non-custodial parent will be broken. For step-parents I would be in favour of a form of simple adoption as not only suggested by Schmidt but also by another Dutch author[10] as a way to give legal status to

---

[8] Guus E. Schmidt, *Sterke en zwakke adopties; een rechtsvergelijkend onderzoek* (IMC Asser Instituut, 's-Gravenhage, 1996).

[9] The adoption by an unmarried step-parent is not yet possible but will become so when Bill 24 649 (Revision of the Law on affiliation and adoption) is accepted by Parliament and enacted (foreseen for spring 1998).

[10] Marianne Meydam-Slappendel, *De adoptie in Nederland* (Leiden/Bussum, 1996). She makes a distinction between absolute and relative adoption. The latter should be possible at the request of unmarried cohabitating couples (opposite sex), single persons and step-parents. In these cases the legal family ties with the original family are not severed.

the step-parent. This form of adoption could have legal consequences for the name of the child, for alimony and parental authority but it would not sever the family ties with the other non-custodial parent. But should this form of simple adoption be available for same sex partners of custodial parents and more generally for lesbian/homosexual couples? This does not seem to be allowed in any country. The Dutch Bill 24 649 proposes for this kind of case the possibility of shared parental responsibility i.e. shared parental authority and child support obligations for the partner of a lesbian or homosexual parent of the child. In my view, ways should be found to give social parents a legal status which on the one hand is an adequate (legal) recognition of their defacto role and on the other hand does respect existing legal ties of biological parents.

CONCLUSION

As to the question "who are the parents?" I would submit that we should try to develop legislation that respects the genetic origins of the child but which at the same time does recognise the social reality of parenthood. We have to find a balance between the legal acknowledgement of the genetic origin of the child (and her/his need to be informed about it) and the fact that those who act as parents for the child are not always the biological parents and should be given a legal status adequate for the parental responsibilities they voluntary assume.

34

Families or Households? The Importance of Social Parenthood

JOHN EEKELAAR and MAVIS MACLEAN

One way of trying to understand the nature of the family is to examine the nature of familial obligations. These can be defined as those obligations which individuals perceive themselves to owe to others for no other reason than that they stand in a certain relationship one to the other. Obligations of this kind may be imposed by law, but they can also arise independently of the law: we call such legally-independent obligations *social* obligations. There appear to be three conditions under which familial obligations normally arise, at least in Britain, (either legally or socially): (1) where individuals are or have been married to one another; (2) where a blood relationship exists between individuals; and (3) where individuals are or have been sharing a common household.

A close examination of the modern law governing support obligations on divorce shows that, in many western countries, being or having been married *in itself* no longer, or only weakly, sets up either a legal or social obligation of support.[1] Usually, for a substantial obligation to arise, it will be necessary to show that the spouses lived together for many years, or that one of them was disadvantaged unduly (for example, by bringing up children). As far as blood relationships are concerned, in English law it is only the parental relationship which establishes an obligation to support, and this has only relatively recently been directly legally enforceable. Finally, while living (or having lived) together with someone in a common household does not (yet) *in itself* constitute the basis for directly imposing a legal obligation in English law, it may create a social obligation and, when accompanied by marriage or parenthood, this will form part of a legal obligation.

Our interest in the nature of these obligations led us to explore more fully the character of the *parental* obligation. Partly as a response to the effects of the Child Support Act 1991, we wished to discover how this obligation was perceived and acted on when one of a child's parents lived separately from the child and the other parent. We could do this by obtaining data about the contexts in which committed contact occurred between the "outside" parent and the child and the

---

[1] See the discussion in Mavis Maclean and John Eekelaar, *The Parental Obligation* (Hart Publishing, Oxford, 1997), ch. 3.

circumstances in which such parents supported their children financially. The results of our investigation throw light on the question whether in these circumstances the unit can still be called a "family". For is a father who hardly ever sees the child and its mother, and acknowledges little or no obligation to them, part of that family unit? The research[2] therefore raised questions about the very nature of family forms, and in particular, the extent to which these are grounded in biological connection and (or, perhaps, and/or) in social arrangements; in particular, household living.

1. THE NATURE OF THE SAMPLE

Our sample consisted of 249 parents, mothers and fathers, who were living apart from one another and where a child of theirs was living with one of them. The sample was obtained by screening out our eligible respondents from a national survey, and is therefore representative of the population at large. The demographic characteristics of our sample were strongly consistent with standard national data sets where we were able to make comparisons, so we can generalise from our data with considerable confidence within the constraints imposed by the small numbers in some categories.

How many children was our sample representative of? To answer this requires careful calculation because our research population did not correspond directly to those which are identified in standard demographic data. That is because the standard sets usually distinguish between one-parent and two-parent families. We have a good deal of information about children who are born into or live in one-parent families. It is well-known that the increase in one-parent families has been sharp (from 2 per cent of all households in 1961 to 10 per cent in 1994 in Great Britain). In 1961, 5 per cent of households with dependent children were headed by a single parent; in 1994 this had risen to 23 per cent, slightly more than one in five of such households.[3] The estimated number of dependent children living in one-parent households increased from about 1 million in 1971 to around 2.3 million in 1992.[4] These children will by definition always have one parent living in another household (if that parent is still alive). But so will stepchildren who are living in two-parent families, and our sample included these as well. It is estimated that in Great Britain in 1991 just under 7 per cent of all families with dependent children, including one-parent families, were stepfamilies. Just under 5 per cent were married-couple families and 2 per cent were cohabiting couples. This amounts to just over 1 million children in Great Britain.[5] So somewhere near three and a half million children under 16 in Britain do not live together

---

[2] Supported by the Nuffield Foundation and reported in *The Parental Obligation*, n. 1 above.

[3] *General Household Survey 1994*, Table 2.13.

[4] Utting, D., *Family and Parenthood: Supporting Families, Preventing Breakdown*, (Joseph Rowntree Foundation, London 1995) 22.

[5] Haskey, J., "Stepfamilies and stepchildren in Great Britain", *Population Trends*. No. 76, 17 (1994).

with both their parents, that is, about 3.5 per cent of all children under 16. This was the population from which our sample was drawn.

We divided our sample population into three groups.

1. Those children whose parents had *never lived together with the child*. This formed 18 per cent of our sample, a proportion close to the proportion of children born to unmarried mothers in England and Wales who do not share an address with the father (15 per cent). We call this the "never-together" group.
2. Those children who *had lived at some time with both their parents* in one household *but whose parents were not married to each other at the time*. This formed 20 per cent of the sample, a proportion almost identical to the 19 per cent of children born to apparently unmarried cohabiting couples in 1994. We call this the "former cohabiting parent" group.
3. Those children who *had lived at some time with both their parents* in one household and *whose parents were married to each other at the time*. This proportion (62 per cent) is comparable to the proportion of all children born to married couples in 1994 (68 per cent). We call this the "formerly married" group.

2 CHILDREN WHO HAD NEVER LIVED TOGETHER WITH BOTH PARENTS: THE HETEROGENEITY OF FAMILIAL LIVING

The family circumstances of the children whose parents had never lived with them at the same time were very diverse. The fathers of 13 per cent of them were either married to or living "as married" with a woman, *not the mother*, when the study child was born. Another 13 per cent of the fathers had been married to, or had been living with, *the mother* before the study child was born, but had left her by the time of the birth. Just over one-third of the fathers were known to be living at the home of their parents and 33 per cent were living independently of their parents when the children were born. Following the child's birth, three further groups had emerged by the time of interview. One comprised those where the father later formed a partnership with one or more women other than the mother; another comprised fathers who were known still to be living at their parents' home at the time of the interview and remainder those who were living alone, independently of their families.

We know that three of the fathers had children by other women prior to the birth of the child and seven had children by other women after its birth. There may therefore have beeen a small group of fathers who were procreating children by various mothers without forming steady relationships. But 13 per cent of the fathers had another child *by the child's mother* after the child's birth and while they were still not living with the mother. These were, therefore, clearly ongoing relationships, types of family-formation without a common household. However we found that the fact that the father had another child by the same mother did not seem to make him any more disposed to keep contact with the child. So, although the man continued to father children by the woman, could he really be said to be part of the family?

These descriptions show the heterogeneity of familial experiences of this group of children. But nearly half of the children were born into a household comprising the mother's family of origin. At the time of the birth, in nearly two out of three cases the mothers were in touch with the fathers. Since more than one-third of the fathers were known to be living at home with their parents, the possibility arises that in a number of cases the mother and the child may form a familial relationship *with the father's kin-group* which could survive eventual loss of contact with the father. Finally, there remains the possibility that a number of parents who were not living together when the child was born later do form a common household with the child. Since such households fell outside our sample population, we cannot tell how often this occurs.

These are very small subsets within our sample, and we cannot therefore generalise confidently about their behaviour. Nevertheless, their presence reveals that where someone (the father), who is normally considered to be a family member, does not share a household with the remainder of the family, the permutations of the kinds of relationships which might exist are many. Perhaps we should be cautious in considering him as part of the mother–child family at all, unless he maintains consistent contact with them and regards himself as being obligated towards them.

3. COMPARISONS BETWEEN THE GROUPS

1. The relevance of socio-economic factors

Clear socio-economic differences emerged between the three groups. The mothers in the never-together group were younger than the formerly cohabiting mothers, who, in turn, were younger than the formerly married mothers. They were also financially the worst off of all the groups when the child was born. 87 per cent of those living in independent households had annual incomes below £6,000. However, 46 per cent of the mothers were living with their own parents. But most of these moved out of their parental home, usually when the child was in its second year, and almost always into social housing in the rented sector.

As regards the formerly cohabiting parents, our findings are consistent with other evidence that parents who live together without marrying have a less successful socio-economic profile than married parents. However, we were also able to show that the relationships of the less economically successful *of the cohabitants* were more vulnerable to breakdown than the more economically successful cohabitants. It has been known that economically weaker married people are more prone to divorce than the better off married people. The same seems to apply to unmarried cohabitants.

There appears to be a clear correlation, therefore, in the United Kingdom at least, linking parental cohabitation and marriage with economic success and stability. That is to say: parents who never live together come at the bottom of the socio-economic scale; those who live together without marrying come next; and those who marry are at the top. However, it should be stressed that in this context we are effectively referring to the financial security provided by the *father*. There was little difference in our sample population in the employment patterns of formerly married and formerly cohabiting mothers in the period before the separation. Nor did these patterns differ from those of actually married and cohabiting mothers (that is, those whose marriages and cohabitations had not broken down). The difference in the socio-economic status between the formerly cohabiting and formerly married groups, and between those groups and actually married and cohabiting parents, appeared to be related to the employment patterns of the fathers, not the mothers. We may put this another way: the extent to which fathers become members of the households of their children and the likelihood that they will remain members of the household appears to be directly related to the fathers' economic security.

The evidence also showed that where unmarried parents separated, they did so when their children were younger than when married parents separated, indicating that *unmarried* cohabitations which produce children and which terminate do so more quickly than *married* cohabitations where there are children. The evidence also suggested that unmarried cohabitations which produce children may break up *more frequently* than married cohabitations which produce children. We should be quick to add that this does not *prove* that the fact of not having married results in a more fragile union. We must recall that parenthood in unmarried cohabitation is also associated with lower socio-economic status, so it may be that factor which leads to the greater vulnerability of these unions rather than the absence of the marital tie.

We are led to hypothesise that, for British parents, marriage operates largely as a *confirmation* of social and economic stability which they have already secured. This does not mean that British people do not become parents when they lack that security; but they are more likely to do so without marrying, sometimes without even living together. We do not discount the *possibility* that being married can *cause* (or contribute to) the social and economic stability of parents. However, we cannot demonstrate that from our evidence. The evidence is, however, consistent with the hypothesis as we have stated it: that marriage is a reflection of a stability already attained in the social and economic lives of the parents, and that the security of the marriage is put at risk if that stability is lost.

It will be seen that much turns on the relative stability which is associated with marriage when we consider the nature of the familial experiences of children when a parent leaves the home.

2. Circumstances immediately after the parents' separation

As the parents in the "never-together" group were not living together, we take the time of the child's birth as equivalent to the time of separation between parents in the other categories in making the comparisons which follow.

We found that in the never-together group, *in the period immediately following the child's birth*, the mothers were in contact with the fathers in nearly two-thirds of cases. Furthermore, their relationships with the fathers were the *least poor* of the whole sample (though often this meant that there was no real relationship at all). The formerly married parents experienced the highest level of conflict between each other. However, while there were no reports of any form of joint decision-making on matters concerning the child in the never-together group, a small proportion (12 per cent) of former cohabitants and 17 per cent of the formerly married parents claimed to have made joint decisions regarding the child during their cohabitation. No former cohabitants claimed that this continued after they had separated, but 10 per cent of the formerly married said it occurred on some issues after they had separated.

3. The significance of contact

However, by the time of interview, contact between the outside parent *and the child* was maintained most frequently by formerly married parents (69 per cent); next by formerly cohabiting parents (45 per cent) and then by fathers in the never-together group (35 per cent). We classified as being in contact only those cases where we adjudged that this was being maintained in a committed manner. When contact was exercised between the formerly married, the most common arrangements were for it to occur once (24 per cent) or twice (13 per cent) a week, without overnight stays. But overnight stays occurred in 25 per cent of cases, at frequencies varying between once and four times a week.

It turned out that the exercise of contact was powerfully associated with the provision of financial support for the child. Financial support was hardly ever paid in any of the groups where contact was not exercised. For the never-together and formerly cohabiting groups, its regular payment was almost confined to cases where contact was continuing, though it was not always paid in those circumstances. For the married parents, it was as likely to be paid if contact was continuing or if it was interrupted. But generally formerly married mothers were much more likely to receive some form of support from the father (64 per cent) than the others (27 per cent for former cohabitants and 37 per cent for the never-together group). Only 10 per cent of formerly married fathers were known to be in full-time work, living on their own and paying no financial support; the proportion was much higher for former cohabitants (29 per cent) and in the never-together group (30 per cent).

It thus appeared that the exercise of contact was a pivotal factor on which any form of familial relationship between the child and parent who was living outside the household depended. It seemed important therefore to understand why there were such strong differences between our groups in the extent to which contact was maintained. Could we identify factors which explained why contact was maintained in some cases but not in others?

The evidence indicated that the distance an "outside" parent lived from the child was not a significant factor in the exercise of contact where that was desired. In the never-together group, the fathers most likely to be in contact were those living with their own parents, and those least likely to were those in existing relationships. But where the fathers were living with their parents, the children were also younger, and contact rarely continued if either parent later acquired a partner. In the case of the former cohabitants, too, the continuation of contact seemed to be adversely affected by the subsequent acquisition of a partner by either parent.

So, was repartnering the crucial factor? No, because the formerly married parents acquired subsequent partners more quickly than parents in the other groups (the never-married parents did so the slowest), yet they kept the highest level of contact. Also, unlike the other groups, formerly married fathers who remained in contact continued to pay support whether or not they had repartnered. So it did not seem that subsequent partnering by the parents was the most significant determining factor in the continued exercise of contact.

It turned out the the most important factor associated with the continuation of contact was the age of the child at separation; the older the child, the more likely contact was to continue and support to be paid. The reason contact was most likely to continue in the case of the formerly married parents seems to have been that the formerly married parents *had lived in the same household as the child for longer than was the case for the former cohabitants; and, of course, the fathers in the never-together group had never lived with the child.*

The importance of this is particularly striking when one considers that the relationships between the formerly married parents were the worst of all the groups at the time of separation. *Despite this fact*, contact was exercised at higher levels in this group than in any of the others. *And not only that*, in all groups, the continuation of contact was associated *with an improvement in the relationships between the parents over time.* This was most noticeable in the case of the formerly married parents, despite the higher incidence of poor relationships at the time of separation. Thus the fact that the father maintained a relationship with the child over the long term seemed to help to improve his relationship with the mother. We found no evidence that this improvement was associated with the intervention of third parties, for example, through mediation or counselling. This must raise the possibility that improvements in inter-parental relationships which are frequently reported as following mediation may have occurred in any event without such interventions.

4. THE SIGNIFICANCE OF SOCIAL PARENTHOOD AND THE RESPONDENTS' ATTITUDES

The reason many more formerly married fathers kept in contact with their children after separation than did the formerly cohabiting fathers seemed to be that

Table 1. Ages of children at time of separation. Former cohabiting parents and formerly married parents

	Former cohabiting parents n = 51 %	Formerly married parents n = 152 %
Under 2	45	12
2–4	33	30
5–6	8	20
7–10	12	23
Over 10	2	11

they had developed stronger ties of social parenthood with their children. They had lived with them for longer in the same household (see Table 1).

This relationship, as we have said, was unaffected by subsequent repartnering by either parent. At the other end of the spectrum were those married (or already partnered) fathers who had a child outside the marriage, but who remained with their wives (or partners). None of these men formed any kind of relationship with the child. For them, their pre-existing relationship prevented the establishment of a familial bond with the child, and even with its mother. Then we had the fathers who did not live with the mother, but who nevertheless kept close contact with the mother and baby after its birth. Often they were living with their own parents. But these relationships were fragile. Should the mother or father later acquire a partner, the biological relationship could rarely be sustained in competition with the newly developing social relationships of the mother or the father with another person in their household. In between were the former cohabitants. Typically the fathers had lived with the child for under three years. They might maintain contact with the child when they left the home, but this relationship was also vulnerable and seemed less able to survive competition with new social/household relationships by either parent than in the case of the formerly married fathers who had lived with the child for longer periods.

We stated at the beginning of this chapter that familial relationships were important as being seen as being the basis for obligations between people. The association between the exercise of contact and the payment of financial support illustrated this relationship: fathers acted as though they were under a stronger obligation to support children they were seeing than those they were not seeing. This raises the question how far familial obligations are, or should be, related to social parenthood and how far to biological parenthood. The findings suggest that social parenthood is an important factor in people's *actual behaviour*; or, to be more precise, in the actual behaviour of *fathers*. But we broadened our study to discover our respondents' *views* of what people's obligations were. Their attitudes were elicited by presenting them with three scenarios in the following manner. Respondents were shown a card which stated:

"1. Take a married couple, who have two young children. The marriage breaks down, and the man later starts a relationship with a new partner who already has two children of her own.

(a) As far as financial support is concerned, who do you think should come highest in the man's priorities—his *own* biological children who are living apart from him, or the children of his new partner?

(b) Should the fact that the man is now living with a second family affect the amount of financial support he gives to hs first family?

2. Now imagine that the man has another child of his own with his new partner. Should this affect the financial support he is giving to his first family?

3. Now imagine that the man's *first* wife remarries. What do you think should happen now to the maintenance arrangements?

Analysis showed that the most significant variations in response were gender related. The answers are set out in Table 2.

Table 2.

Question 1 (a): priority between own children and stepchildren

	own	stepchildren	equal	depends
	%	%	%	%
Fathers (n = 62)	59	8	22	11
Mothers (n = 188)	73	9	10	8
Total (n = 250)	70	7	14	9

Question 1 (b): should stepchildren affect financial support of first family?

	yes	no	depends
Fathers (n = 62)	66	18	16
Mothers (n = 188) parents	37	46	17
Total (n = 250)	44	39	17

Question 2: should subsequent own child affect the support to the first family?

	yes	no	depends
Fathers (n = 62)	42	40	18
Mothers (n = 188)	28	58	14
Total (n = 250)	31	54	15

Question 3: what should happen if the first wife remarries?

	No change	Payments reduced	Stop paying for wife	Stop paying for child	Depends Other
	%	%	%	%	%
Fathers (n = 62)	26	11	7	29	27
Mothers (n = 188)	45	11	12	11	21
Total (n = 250)	40	11	11	16	22

The results show a strong attachment by *mothers* to a support obligation founded on natural parenthood, whereas *fathers* relate the obligation much more closely to social parenthood. To the opening, general, question of priority between the man's natural children and his stepchildren, the majority of both fathers and mothers (but more mothers) thought the man's own children should come highest in his priorities. However, without necessarily changng this order of priority, 66 per cent of men felt that the fact that a father is living with stepchildren should *affect* the amount he gives his first family, whereas only a minority of mothers felt the same. The mothers, in other words, held to their sense of priority without making allowances for the obligations which a father might feel towards his step-family. Indeed, despite their attachment to the father's obligation towards his natural children, most mothers were unwilling to alter this priority even in favour of a later *natural* child of the father. The fathers, however, were equally divided on whether a new child of their own should make any difference. About half of them, it seems, made no distinction between their own child and stepchildren in the father's new social family. The men were also equally divided on whether the father should continue to pay for his children if the mother remarried, but, consistently with their favouring of the social family, were more likely than the mothers to think that they should stop paying, transferring the burden to the new social father. The mothers, equally consistently, were much more likely to think that the remarriage should make no difference to the father's obligation, though only 45 per cent expressed this view positively. Others were prepared to accept reduced payments for the mother only. Our attitudinal data therefore reveal that men adjust the extent of the obligation which they feel they owe towards their natural children by reference to their subsequent social parenthood, but women generally do not think they should do so.

5. CONCLUSIONS

One conclusion to be drawn from the study is that the child support legislation is therefore aligned more closely to women's perceptions of familial obligations than those of men. The women in our sample, it will be recalled, placed greater emphasis on the natural fact of parenthood than men did. However, it must be observed that, for women, social parenthood and natural parenthood almost always coincide: a woman who bears her child almost always brings it up. Women seldom personally experience the conflict between obligations based on biological and social facts which many fathers face. Were they to experience this, it is not clear where their preferences would lie.

We do not wish to propose here how these conflicts should be resolved. We do, however, wish to draw attention to the significance which sharing a common household could have in determining the nature of certain affective relationships, in the present case, parenthood, and in affecting the perceptions which people have of the obligations adhering to that relationship. Although we were concerned with parenthood, household-sharing may have similar consequences when it supplements an affective relationship between adults only. For without household sharing those other relationships may count for little, at least when they come into competition with later relationships which do have a household base.[6] That at least was the experience of the parents and children of our sample. And the longer the parents and children remained in the common household, the more likely it was that the affective relationships would survive beyond the demise of the household. Any account of familial obligations which fails to take into account the role of household-sharing will therefore be very incomplete.

[6] This is not to argue that household-sharing alone, unaccompanied by some affective relationship, necessarily has such consequences; nor to argue that some affective relationships cannot exist without a household base (for example, aunts/uncles and nephews/nieces).

35

Child Welfare and Adoption
in Modern Greek Law

EFIE KOUNOUGERI-MANOLEDAKI

In Greece, owing to important social changes which have resulted from the economic development of the country, family law was amended in 1983 by Law 1329,[1] which took into account the principle of the equality of men and women and partially modernised family law in two other fields, i.e. in the law of divorce and the law of children born out of wedlock. The legislative changes in these fields were considered absolutely necessary because of changes in the structure, functions and social purpose of the Greek family, which nowadays is no longer primarily an economic unit nor a unit of production, but functions almost exclusively as a place where those feelings of companionship and love which are so necessary for survival can be developed.[2] This change in social conditions has influenced adoption too. That is to say, adoption also functions in a different way nowadays, owing to the changes that have taken place in society. More specifically, whereas in the past adoption was principally intended to secure hereditary succession, today, the first aim of adoption is not to keep the family property within the family, but to safeguard and promote the welfare of the adopted child.[3] Furthermore, the protection of the child's best interests assumes at the present time much greater importance than another old aim of adoption: that of the consolation of childless couples. The number of these couples has decreased because of the advances in medical science, especially the wide use of artificial fertilisation. In view of all these factors, we can say that in Greece today adoption must be seen as an institution of social welfare in favour of the child,[4] and this is why our old and anachronistic legislation on adoption—which did not change in 1983 because the amendment of family law was interrupted by an intervening political change—was replaced by Law 2447/1996 on the Reform of the Laws of Adoption and Guardianship.

---

[1] Law 1329/1983 on the application of the constitutional principle of the equality of men and women as well as on the partial modernisation of family law.

[2] Kounougeri-Manoledaki, *Family Law* (in Greek) Ia (1995), 9 f.

[3] Kounougeri-Manoledaki, *op. cit.*, IIb (1990), 103 f.

[4] Deliyannis, "Reforming the Law of Adoption", in *The International Survey of Family Law* (1995), 180.

This chapter seeks to provide a general overview of the new Greek family law, especially adoption, since I was one of the members of the Law Commission which prepared it. In general, Law 2447 is an attempt to reflect the new face of adoption and contains regulations which provide new protection for the adopted child. The new law contains rules governing the essential requirements for adoption, the adoption process, the legal consequences of adoption and its termination. Before referring to each of these, I would like to stress that the modern law also contains one very important *general* change: the abolition of the adoption of adults. The adoption of adults is considered to be inconsistent with the modern aim of adoption, which is the protection of the child's best interests, and to reflect only the old purpose of the devolution and acquisition of property. However, since this purpose had essentially ceased to exist, in reality the adoption of adults only remained to be inappropriately used as a means of evading the laws of succession or special rules about army and tax obligations, and that is the reason why it has been abolished.[5] To the abolition of the adoption of adults as a general rule there is, however, a notable exception: it is permitted for an adult to be adopted by the husband or the wife of her or his parent.[6] In this case it has been suggested that the aim of the adoption is the establishment of an artificial parent–child relationship, which deserves protection just as in the adoption of minors.

Now let us return to the adoption of minors and focus on the provisions of the new law that relate to the *essential requirements* for adoption. An innovative provision of Law 2447 establishes, for the first time, upper limits for the age of the prospective adopter. Since it is in the child's best interests to have young parents, who are physically strong and not old-fashioned, the new law contains two new rules: first, the adopter must not be over 60 years of age[7] and, secondly, the adoption is not permitted if there is a difference in age of more than 45 years between the adopter and the child.[8]

Formerly, a fundamental requirement for adoption was that the adopter must not have descendants of his or her own, i.e. children or grandchildren. This restriction is not repeated in the new law, which in addition provides that, when the adopter already has children of his or her own, the court which grants the adoption order is obliged to ascertain those children's views, if they are mature enough to express an opinion.[9] This provision was designed to ensure that adoption will not be harmful to the adopter's own children, and accordingly it can be used against all those who argue that adoption by a person who already has children of his own endangers the institution of the legal family. In any case, this argument cannot be accepted now that adoption has a predominantly social and moral meaning, with which the possibility of placing the adopted child among other natural children accords perfectly.

---

[5] Greek Civil Code, new Art. 1542 (as amended by Law 2447/1996).
[6] Greek Civil Code, new Art. 1579.
[7] Greek Civil Code, new Art. 1543.
[8] Greek Civil Code, new Art. 1544.
[9] Greek Civil Code, new Art. 1556.

As far as the adoption *process* is concerned, a crucial subject, which was thoroughly discussed by the members of the Law Commission, was whether the new law should authorise both private and public (state) adoptions (like the previous legislation) or whether it should permit state adoptions only. The argument against private adoptions was that private adoption encourages trafficking in babies, but an answer to this argument was that the abolition of private adoptions would simply lead to a worse situation, *viz.* simulated pregnancies and births. Thus the new law finally allows both possibilities: private adoptions and state adoptions (i.e. seeking the child to be adopted by appealing to a state social service with babies available for adoption). However, in both cases a compulsory preliminary social investigation by state adoption services as to the "circumstances of the prospective adoption" must take place prior to the hearing, and this investigation must be followed by a written report to the court, which will help it to determine whether the adoption order is for the child's benefit.[10] "Circumstances of the prospective adoption", which are investigated by the social service, include not only the special characteristics of the adopter and the child (such as health, family situation and financial position), but also the involvement of third parties and the payment to them of any illegal reward[11] (and this is considered to be a way of putting an end to trafficking in babies).

All the parties to the adoption must give their consent to the court which makes the adoption order. An innovation of the new law in this respect is that the child must consent to its adoption once he or she reaches the age of 12,[12] instead of 16 years as demanded by previous legislation. Furthermore, the new law also provides that the child, after coming of age, can appeal to the civil registry and require information about his or her birthparents.[13]

Another innovative procedural regulation lays down that all the parties to the adoption must consent in person, in private and without publicity, before a member of the court which is to order the adoption.[14] This rule aims, first, to ensure that the consenting parties truly support the petition for adoption and, secondly, to guarantee the secrecy of the adoption. The secrecy of the adoption is also enforced with a new rule stating that the court may order the main proceedings to be held in camera.[15]

Finally, the new law contains some rules relating to intercountry adoptions, the most important of which states that, when either the adopter or the child has their habitual residence outside Greece, a social investigation will always be required, even if it is not demanded by the foreign legal system in question.[16]

---

[10] Greek Civil Code, new Arts. 1557, 1558.

[11] Deliyannis, *op. cit.*, 185, 188.

[12] Greek Civil Code, new Art. 1555, para. 1.

[13] Greek Civil Code, new Art. 1559, para. 2. Under previous legislation the right of the adopted child to be informed about his or her natural parents was based only on the interpretation of Art. 5, para. 1 of the Greek Constitution which protects the free development of personality.

[14] Greek Code of Civil Procedure, new Art. 800, para. 2 (as amended by Law 2447/1996).

[15] Greek Code of Civil Procedure, new Art. 800, para. 6.

[16] Law 2447/1996, Art. 4.

The *legal consequences* of adoption have also been modified in the new legislation. Law 2447 has established the so-called "full adoption", which means the complete severance of the legal relationship between the child and his whole natural family[17] and the creation of a new legal relationship between the child and the whole family of the adoptive parent.[18] According to previous law, adoption created only a legal relationship of parent and child between the adopter and the adopted person, and this meant the cessation of the legal relationship only between the child and his natural parents. Consequently, according to previous legislation, the adopted child continued to have as brothers and sisters the children of his or her natural parents and not the children of the adoptive parents, with whom the child lived and grew up.

The new law fortunately put an end to that unreasonable situation by stating that the adopted child becomes legally related not only to the adoptive parents, but also to all their relatives, and accordingly acquires, for example, adoptive uncles, adoptive grandparents and adoptive siblings. This effect has so much to commend it—not only from the practical point of view (including that of hereditary rights), but also from the point of view of the desired psychological development of the child—that we must disregard the negative comment that the new law establishes legal relationships between the child and persons who have not given their consent to the adoption. This comment may be countered with the argument that, when a man and a woman decide to have natural children, they do not ask for the consent of their relatives, and in any case it is provided that, as far as the natural *children* of the adopter are concerned, the court is obliged to ascertain their views about the adoption. On the other hand, the new law contains the following exception to the rule that adoption severs the child from his natural family: namely, if the child is adopted by the spouse of his or her natural parent, the child continues to be legally related to the natural parent[19] and consequently has two legal parents and can live, like all other children, in a strongly united family.

A special subject relating to the legal effects of adoption is that of the right to access, i.e. the problem whether the natural parents can see or visit the child. This issue was hotly disputed during the discussions of the members of the Law Commission; finally the opinion prevailed that natural parents have no right to personal contact with the child. This opinion was based upon article 10, paragraph 2, of the European Convention "on the adoption of children", which provides that adoption severs the legal ties of the child with the natural parents. Needless to say, in most cases cutting the child out of the natural family is a desirable measure in order to prevent conflicts between natural and adoptive parents damaging to the child. Nevertheless, when the adopted child is not a baby and is able to remember his or her parents, the absolute prohibition of the right

---

[17] With the exception of the normal rules on impediments to marriage.
[18] Greek Civil Code, new Art. 1561.
[19] Greek Civil Code, new Art. 1562.

to access may act to the child's detriment,[20] and this is why I think that it would be better if an access condition could be added in exceptional circumstances by the court, giving weight to the child's welfare.

So far as *termination* of adoption is concerned, a new rule of Law 2447, which is of extraordinary significance, establishes the *consensual* termination of adoption through a provision which reminds us of the rule governing consensual divorce. In other words, it is provided that, if the adoption has lasted for at least one year and the adopted child has attained his majority, the parties to the adoption may present to the court a joint petition for the termination of adoption by consent. Apart from this petition, the parties must return to the court after a period of at least six months and again state that they consent to the termination of the adoption. It is obvious that this interim period should be used by the parties for reflection and reconsideration.[21]

The new institution of consensual termination of adoption is an innovation at a universal level, since it cannot be found in foreign laws, which are very conservative as regards termination of adoption in view of the argument that the artificial relationship of parent and child created by adoption must be as steady as the relevant blood relationship. However, since our law establishes the dissolubility of adoption, there is no reason why a contested termination of adoption should be preferable to a consensual termination, which reflects the will of the parties to maintain their dignity by ending their relationship in an amicable and civilised way. Moreover, since the new law provides for requirements which ensure that the parties—all adults—truly support their petition for the termination of adoption, consensual termination—apart from contributing to civilised family relations—must be approved also for another reason: because an unhealthy adoption, which is not acceptable to the parties concerned, cannot fulfil its social purpose and its maintenance cannot but harm the parties as well as the whole institution of adoption and society in general.

To conclude, let us now see what is the new form of the adoptive family introduced by the new Greek law on adoption. First, it may be noted that it is a family with relatively young parents, which is created while the child is still a minor, i.e. when the child is really in need of a family and, on the other hand, is able to build strong emotional ties with the adoptive parents as well as with the other—natural—children of these parents. The fact that natural and adoptive children coexist in the same family shows that the adoptive parents truly love children (being already experienced in that respect) and have not decided to adopt simply in order to cover their own personal needs—something that is also indicated by the fact that the parents adopt the child while they are young and able to help him by providing him with a secure and stable home.

---

[20] Kounougeri-Manoledaki, "Essential Requirements, Effects and Termination of Adoption According to the Draft Bill of the Law Commission of the Ministry of Justice" (in Greek), in *The Reform of the Law of Adoption*, 27 *Jurists Society of Northern Greece* (1996), 46.

[21] Greek Civil Code, new Art. 1573.

It is obvious that under such conditions it is probable that adoption will promote the welfare of the child, and not only of the adopted child—whose consent, if it is older than 12 years, is a requirement for the adoption—but also of the other, natural children of the adopter, who, too, are entitled to be heard by the court. As regards these children, the adoptive child becomes their brother or sister and, what is more, he becomes legally related to all the relatives of the adoptive parents, in whose environment he now lives. This situation fully corresponds to the ideal of the normal psychological development of the child, who wishes to live, like all other children, in *one* family and to be closely connected with *all* its members.

To be sure, if the child learns later that he or she is adopted and wishes to trace his or her roots, the new law provides that, as soon as the child reaches 18, he can apply to the civil registry and demand to be informed about his natural parents. Finally, if for some reasons the relationship between the child and the adoptive parent breaks down, there is the possibility of consensual termination of the adoption, which, however, presupposes that the child has already attained the age of 18.

In conclusion, the new Greek law on adoption reflects the contemporary socioeconomic situation and new ideas on the role and functions of the modern family. In this family the child takes a predominant position, and the full protection of the interests of the child is precisely the object of the modern Greek law on adoption.

36

Adoption and Child Welfare in Japanese Law: Has the Special Adoption Law Failed?

FUMIO TOKOTANI

I. INTRODUCTION

Older people consider that Japanese society has been thoroughly corrupted as Japan has become a rich country; younger people have abandoned traditional morals, and no longer respect elder people. Sometimes young girls are tempted into making money by exploiting their sexuality. If they become pregnant they have an abortion. From the point of view of older people even the provisions for special adoption of children (referred to as "Special Adoption" in this chapter) which were introduced in 1988 for children in need of protection reflect the immorality of modern Japanese society, because this law makes it legally possible to break the relationship between parents and their unwanted children. However, Special Adoption was in fact introduced to save children in a special category and to place them under strong judicial control. Immediately after the introduction of the law there were about 1,000 Special Adoptions in 1988 and 1989, but the number decreased to 479 in 1995. Has the reform of Japanese adoption law as a system for securing the welfare of children failed?

In Japan there has always been wide use of adoption of children. The institution has been one of the most important social parent and child relationships in the Japanese patriarchal family system. Traditional Japanese adoption law gave the interests of adoptive parents with no biological children the most important consideration. The adoptive parents wanted an adoptive child as a successor to their house, property and family name. So an adoptive child had to be a healthy boy from a good family. In those days children whose parents were unknown or children born out of wedlock were not candidates for adoption by people in the upper and middle classes. However many children born in poor families were adopted by farmers or fishermen and used to provide hard labour.

After World War II, in accordance with the completely reformed new Japanese Constitution, the part of the Civil Code concerning family and succession law was revised in 1947. Some elements of the patriarchal family system were eliminated[1] and permission of the Family Court for an adoption of minors was required as a safeguard for the welfare of children when the adoptive child was not a descendant of the adoptive parent or his or her spouse (Japanese Civil Code [hereinafter JCC], Article 798). The institution of adoption was used in those days to save many orphans or children born in poor families. In 1950 there were abut 40,000 adoptions carried out with the permission of a Family Court—40 per cent of all (100,000) adoptions, which included the adoption of adults.

Such adoption of children is now called "ordinary adoption"[2] because it is applicable to all people. It is contrasted to a second type of adoption, namely, "special adoption" of children in need of special protection, a system which was introduced in 1988 after long and controversial discussion.[3]

II. THE SPECIAL ADOPTION LAW AND THE WELFARE OF THE CHILD

In many respects the Japanese Special Adoption System was established under the strong influence of the adoption law reforms in many European countries, which were based on the European Convention on the Adoption of Children (Council of Europe, 24 April 1967),[4] that is, full adoption. However, unlike that in many Western countries, Japanese special adoption is designed to be an exceptional type of adoption especially for younger children in need of special protection and care.

1. Conditions and Effects of "Special Adoption"

(a) Requirements Concerning the Adoptive Parent and Child

The prospective adopter must have a spouse and neither husband nor wife may become an adopter unless the spouse also becomes an adopter. However, this does not apply when either husband or wife becomes the adopter of a legitimate child of his or her spouse (this excludes a child adopted as an ordinary adoptive relation) (JCC, Article 817–3). There are also age restrictions on adopter and adoptee. A person who has not attained the age of 25 may not become an adopter. However, this does not apply when one of the prospective adoptive spouses of a

---

[1] E.g. restrictions on the adoption of a man by a person with a male successor, posthumous adoption by testament, and the institution of the adoption of a daughter's husband were abolished.

[2] An ordinary adoptive relationship is established by a mutual agreement between the adopters and the adoptive child and its registration at a family register office. This is a simple adoption which does not terminate the legal relationship between the adopted child and his or her original parents. Any person who has attained majority in law (20 if not married) may adopt a younger person (JCC, Art. 792).

[3] In the 1950s there was discussion about the necessity of a new type of adoption of children as Special Adoption.

[4] European Treaties Series No. 58.

married couple has not attained the age of 25 providing he or she has attained the age of 20 (JCC, Article 817–4).

A child who has attained the age of 6 at the time of the application may not become an adopted child. However, this does not apply in cases where the child is under the age of 8 and was placed under the continuous care or custody of the prospective adopter before the age of 6,[5] for example in the case of a foster child or an "ordinary" adopted child of the adopters (JCC, Article 817–5). The reason for this age restriction is, according to the legislature's comment, to create the same situation as if there were a biological child-and-parent relationship between the adoptive child and adopters. Also, it is not good for a child of school age to have the relationship with the biological parent broken.

Other proposals concerning the age of adoptees were made at the time. These were based on the opinion, which I share, that from the viewpoint of the interests of children in need of protection, it should also be possible for older children of 12 or 15 years old to be adopted. However, this proposal was not accepted, because, since the special adoption was already going to make drastic changes in Japanese adoption law, it was felt this would be too extreme.

(b) Consent of Parents

In a special adoption, the consent of the legal father and mother of a child to be adopted must in principle be obtained. However, this does not apply in cases where the father or mother are unable to declare their intention or where there is cruel treatment, malicious desertion by father or mother, or any other cause seriously harmful to the interests of the child to be adopted (JCC, Article 817–6).[6]

The consent of the parent is revocable until the adoption decree comes into effect. In practice there have been some cases in which the adoption was ultimately rejected because of revocation of such parental consent.[7]

(c) Procedure

To protect and promote the best interests of the child, a special adoptive relationship is established by a declaratory decision of the Family Court after careful examination of the necessity of that adoption (JCC, Article 817–2). In establishing a special adoptive relationship, the attitudes and behaviour of the prospective parents towards the prospective adoptee over a period of six months or more are taken into account (JCC, Article 817–8). In many cases, caseworkers of the Child

---

[5] In one case where a child was already 8 years and 2 months old when the Special Adoption Law was enacted, an application for special adoption was rejected (decision of the Family Court, Hiroshima, 12 Mar. 1988, Kateisaibangeppou (FLR), vol. 40, 192). However, every year there are still 6 or 8 applications for special adoption which are rejected because of the age restrictions.

[6] See High Court of Fukuoka, Decision of 27 Dec. 1991, Hanreitaimuzu No. 786, 253.

[7] See High Court of Tokyo, Decision of 27 Mar. 1989, Kateisaibangeppou, vol. 41, 110 and High Court of Tokyo, Decision of 30 Jan. 1990, Kateisaibangeppou, vol. 42, 47.

Guidance Centre or licensed adoption agencies supervise and assess the relationship during that period.

(d) Effects

In case of a special adoption, the adoptive child obtains the status of legitimate child of the adoptive parents; and the legal relationship between the child and its original parents and their blood relatives is terminated (JCC, Article 817–9).

For Japanese people, who have a strong consciousness of blood relationships, to break the parent–child relationship is a drastic measure, and some people were against special adoption because they considered it to be unnatural.

(e) Registration of a Special Adoption

A child adopted under special adoption is registered in the family register of the adoptive parents almost as if he or she were a biological child of the adopters.[8] This is because the adoption must be protected against third parties by a special method of registration in the Japanese family register, with restrictions on access to the register of the adoptive child. In many cases, adopters make applications for a special adoption mainly to obtain this special kind of family registration, but such applications have to be rejected, because in such cases the child is not in need of special protective care.

2. Historical Background of Special Adoption

Besides the influence of the European law of adoption already mentioned, there are some other background aspects to the Japanese Special Adoption Law.

(a) Social Usage of False Birth Registration of the Child

In the past, there was a social usage in Japan that a new-born baby could be given away to a childless person and the baby treated as if he or she were a biological child of the recipient. The child thus had a parent–child relationship as a biological and legitimate child in spite of the lack of a real biological relationship with the formal parents. For adopters, such a child was their legal child and the child would obtain the family name and right of succession. A child born out of wedlock was also sometimes adopted in this manner. In this case, the most

---

[8] A child adopted by special adoption is registered as "first son" or "second daughter" of "father and mother", while a child adopted by ordinary adoption is registered as "adopted son" or "adopted daughter" of "adoptive father and/or mother". The Japanese Family Registry system is a complicated and characteristic system recording all Japanese people and is used to certify a person's capacity or civil status. Therefore anybody can in principle obtain a certified copy of the family register of anybody else, though there are now some restrictions on access made from the viewpoint of the right to privacy, introduced since 1976.

important thing was not the happiness of the child, but the interests of the adoptive parents, and in many cases, also the interests of the biological parents.

However, there were sometimes disputes between parents and the child or between relatives of parents and the child, and then the parents or their relatives might institute a suit to ascertain that the child was not their biological child and therefore had no succession rights. The child might assert that he or she had the status of an adoptive child at least, and that the parental attempts to disinherit were invalid because they themselves had registered him as their biological child following traditional Japanese social usage. The Supreme Court of Japan has decided in such cases in favour of parents, for there were no legal formalities, i.e. registration of the adoptive relationship. Many scholars criticise this Supreme Court precedent and would recognise the child as a legally adopted child.

In 1973 a gynæcologist caused a national sensation by revealing that he had arranged more than 100 adoptions of babies for over 15 years and made false registration of babies as biological children of adopters by using false birth certificates, because he wanted to stop illegal abortions and to make all parties happy, including both the birth mother and her legitimate family. He was very critical about the Japanese adoption law of those days. In his opinion, couples who had an earnest desire for a child could find a child to be adopted if they could register the child as their legitimate biological child ("illegal adoption" instead of "illegal abortion").

(b) Frequency of Adoption of Foster Children

Foster care[9] is an alternative method of child raising in addition to children's and infants' homes for children without family care.[10] However, in this case there is no legal parent–child relationship between foster parent and foster child. While foster parents can use routine factual custodial rights in connection with the foster child, the legal representation rights of the foster child, the right of consent to legal transactions of minors and the right of management of money remain with the biological and legal parents, even if the child was placed with the foster parent with the permission of a Family Court. As a result, many foster parents have a desire to adopt their foster children, to avoid intrusions by the original parent and to establish stronger relationships with their children. In 1985 there were 352 adoptions of foster children arranged by the Public Child Guidance Centre.[11]

---

[9] See Tokotani, "The Triangle of Biological, Social and Legal Parenthood in Japan" in Choo Soo Kim (ed.), *The Legal Relationship between Parents and Children* (Seoul, 1997), 178–82.

[10] In Japan 90% or more of children without biological family care live in homes for children or babies. In 1995, there were about 29,700 children in need of protective care placed in the 529 children's or 117 infants' homes, while only 2,029 foster parents had charge of 2,566 children. In the same year there were 479 special adoptions and 950 ordinary adoptions of minors.

[11] This was about 13.4% of 2,614 adoptions of children with permission of a Family Court in 1985. In 1984, 305 of 866 foster relations (35%) were dissolved because the foster parents adopted their foster children. On the other hand, there were 1,170 adoptions by uncles or aunts, and 386 by other relatives, in 1985.

In 1995, there were 409 applications for Special Adoptions of foster children, 67 per cent of all (607) applications, and of these, 392 were approved, 81.8 per cent of all (479) special adoptions. Foster care has now become a preliminary stage in a special adoption.

3. The Current Situation: Special Adoption Compared with Ordinary Adoption

(a) The Number of Adoptions of Children in Japan

In the 1950s there were about 100,000 adoptions a year. Though the number of adoptions is decreasing, there are still about 80,000 a year. However, two–thirds of them are adoptions of adults in order to obtain a family successor. On the other hand, the number of ordinary adoptions of minors with the permission of a Family Court has decreased strikingly. There were only 956 ordinary adoptions with permission of a Family Court in 1995 (1,074 adoptions in 1994), whereas there were 43,849 adoptions with permission of a Family Court in 1949, 29,619 adoptions in 1953 (about 30 per cent of all adoptions) and 2,614 adoptions in 1985 (only 3 per cent of all adoptions).

On the other hand, the number of intercountry adoption cases has increased to 273 in 1995 (28 per cent of ordinary adoptions). Before the adoption law reform there were 146 intercountry adoptions in 1982 (4.6 per cent of 3,150 adoptions with permission of a Family Court) and 301 intercountry adoptions in 1985 (11 per cent of 2,614 adoptions with permission).

The number of special adoptions is smaller because it is permitted only under much judicial restriction. There were about 1,000 special adoptions in 1988 and 1989, but after nine years the number decreased to 479 in 1995 (including 25 intercountry special adoptions).

(b) Personal Status of Children to be Adopted

It is estimated that three-quarters or more of adoptions of minors are now adoptions of stepchildren. A frequent motive for a stepchild adoption may be stabilisation of the custodial relationship of stepparent with stepchild by acquisition of parental authority and rights in maintenance and succession on the basis of legal parenthood. Also, it is sometimes used to change the family name of a stepchild[12] or to prevent access of another parent to the stepchild.[13]

---

[12] If a stepchild wants to take the family name of his or her mother, which is at the same time the name of his or her stepfather, he or she can change his or her name by registration at the family register office with permission of a Family Court (JCC, Art. 791). However, an easier and more usual way of changing his or her name is by ordinary adoption. In this case, there is no control by a Family Court.

[13] However, an adoptive relation with a stepchild can be easily dissolved, when the marriage of the stepparent (father) and biological parent (mother in most cases) is dissolved, because an ordinary

A special adoption of a stepchild is not prohibited (JCC, Article 817–3). However, in practice it is still rare,[14] because in formation of a special adoptive relationship, the consent of another parent of the child has to be obtained, and there must be special circumstances in which a special adoption of the stepchild seems to be particularly necessary, in the interests of stepchild (JCC, Article 817–7). For instance, when his or her biological father tends to make intolerably harmful intrusions upon the child and stepparent family, a special adoption of the stepchild can be established.

If a stepchild was born out of wedlock, special adoption is easier, because the consent of the biological father is not necessary if he has not acknowledged his paternity.[15] In practice, in 80 per cent (382 adoptions) of all special adoption cases in 1995, the adoptive children were born out of wedlock, and in most cases the father had not acknowledged his paternity (358 adoptions). On the other hand, with ordinary adoptions, only 30 per cent of the adoptive children were born out of wedlock (299 out of 956 cases).

(c) Ages of Adopted Children

In almost 80 per cent of special adoption cases, the children were under 4 years old (383 out of 479 adoptions) and only in 30 cases (6 per cent) were children 6 or 7 years old in 1995, whereas in 1989 in 26 per cent (316 out of 1,205 adoptions) of special adoptions children were 6 or 7 years old. On the other hand, in the case of ordinary adoptions with permission of a Family Court, 200 children (21 per cent) were under 4 years old, 81 children (8 per cent) were 4 or 5 years old, 102 children (10.6 per cent) were 6 or 7 years old and 265 children (27.7 per cent) were under 15 years old (and older than 8) and 302 children (31.6 per cent) were under 20 years old (and older than 15).

(d) Adoption via Adoption Agency

After the introduction of the special adoption law, the Public Child Guidance Centre could work more effectively in arranging the adoption of children in need of protective care, and in keeping contact with related public organisations and

adoptive relationship can be dissolved simply by registration of mutual agreement for its dissolution at the family register office, without permission of a Family Court (JCC, Art. 811, 812). It is said that about 43% of about 17,000 dissolved adoptions a year are those of adoptions of minors. This also emphasises the frequency of stepchild adoption.

[14] See Family Court Miyazaki, Decision of 30 Nov. 1990, Kateisaibangeppou, vol. 43, 35, and High Court of Tokyo, Decision of 20 Nov. 1996, Kateisaibangeppou, vol. 49, 78. There were only 3 special adoptions of children by biological parents or their spouses in 1995. Considering the fact that dissolution of special adoption is strictly restricted and not easily approved, even if the marriage of biological parent and stepparent breaks down, the necessity for stepchild special adoption has to be examined very carefully.

[15] However, if a biological father asserts his paternity in a civil suit, a Family Court is not permitted to establish a special adoption in spite of the possibility of his paternity: Supreme Court of Japan, Decision of 14 July 1995, Minshu, vol. 49, 2674.

private adoption agencies. Though in 381 special adoptions in 1995 (out of 479) there were arrangements of adoption by the Child Guidance Centres (322 cases) or other adoption agencies (59 cases), there were still 98 cases without any arrangement by an adoption agency, in other words independent adoptions or adoptions by other private arrangement. However, more than half of the applications for special adoption without public arrangement were not approved. Independent adoption or adoption by private arrangement was not prohibited, because it seemed that there would be many such adoptions. In fact, in 1989 there were still 823 adoptions without arrangement, while there were 382 adoptions by arrangement of an agency.

III. CONCLUSION

Japanese adoption law should be considered anew in order to make more use of special adoption of children. Though our dual system of ordinary adoption and special adoption has some problems, in principle I accept this system. However, in my opinion, special adoption would be more useful if the restrictions on the eligibility of children for adoption were to be abolished or reduced and official arrangements by adoption agency made compulsory. Therefore, the conditions for special adoption should be changed as follows:

(a) Age restrictions for special adoption should be raised to fifteen and consent of children aged 12 or over should be obtained.
(b) However, it should be possible for *de facto* adoptions to be acknowledged legally as special adoptions by order of a Family Court in spite of such age restrictions.
(c) With special adoptions the Child Guidance Centre and other certified adoption agencies should have exclusive authority to arrange adoptions and should be given the powers to do it more actively. It should be made easier for children in children's homes to be adopted by mitigating the requirement for consent of the biological parents.
(d) Special adoptions should be granted more generously even in the case of stepchildren or ordinarily adopted children when there is or would be maltreatment by the biological parents.
(e) In intercountry adoptions the child should automatically gain Japanese nationality, if the Child Guidance Centre has lawfully arranged the adoption.

Special adoption should no longer be considered exceptional and the mistaken belief that children adopted under special adoption are always illegitimate should be eliminated.

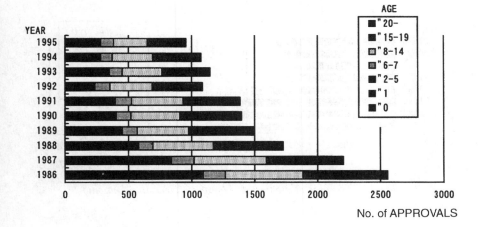

Figure 1 Number of Approved Adoptions (Ordinary Adoptions)

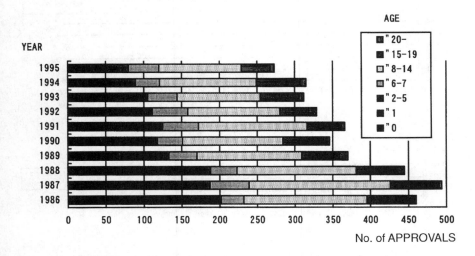

Figure 2 Number of Approved Adoptions (Ordinary Adoptions, Inter-country)

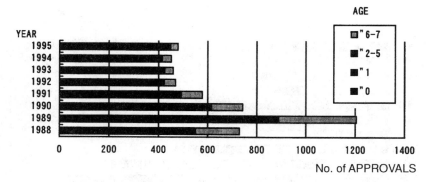

Figure 3 Number of Approved Adoptions (Special Adoptions)

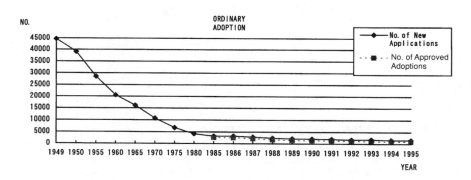

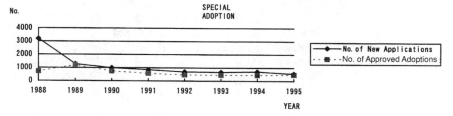

Figure 4 Number of New Applications and Approved Adoptions

37

The Gift/Donation Model Versus the Contract/Services Model—The Changing Face of Adoption in England and Wales

N. V. LOWE

I. INTRODUCTION

This chapter begins by explaining just how much adoption has altered during the 70 or so years of its existence under English law.[1] In particular it examines how the nature of the work has changed, how the organisation of adoption work has developed, how practice has altered, and finally how the law itself has been modified. These enquiries, however, are really a means to an end, which is to explore whether in the light of the changed nature of adoption, the current law and practice is adequate. It is the thesis of this chapter that the "mind set" which is, rightly or wrongly, associated with the adoption of babies still permeates thinking not only behind the law and, possibly to a lesser extent, practice, but also the attitudes of the adopters themselves. Under this "mind set", which in this chapter is labelled the "gift/donation model", adoption is seen very much as the last and irrevocable act in a process in which the birth parent (normally, of course, the mother) has "given away" her baby via the adoption agency to the adopters, who are then left to their own devices and resources to bring up the child as their own. Associated with this model is the "exclusive" view of adoption, that is, that the child is both *de jure* and *de facto* transplanted *exclusively* to the adoptive family with no further contact or relationship with the birth family. This model, however, sits uneasily with the adoption of older children and it is contended that in these instances, at least, a different model is needed in which it is recognised

---

* The author is indebted to his colleague, Prof. Mervyn Murch for his many helpful comments on earlier drafts.

[1] Adoption was first introduced into English law by the Adoption of Children Act 1926 (in Scotland it was introduced by the Adoption of Children (Scotland) Act 1930). Such legislation was necessary, because common law regarded parental rights and duties as being inalienable (see e.g. *Humphrys* v. *Polak* [1901] 2 KB 385 (CA) and *Brooks* v. *Brooks* [1923] 1 KB 257) and hence had no comprehension of adoption.

that adoption is not the end of the process but merely part of an ongoing and often complex process of family development.

By way of background information it should be noted that, unlike French law,[2] for example, where provision is made for two types of adoption, namely, "full" adoption which entails the transfer of parentage, and "simple" adoption which does not break all the links with the birth family, under English law there is but one form of adoption, namely, that which effects a complete and irrevocable transfer of parentage. Furthermore, English law differs sharply from civil law systems which inherited the Roman concepts of *adoptio* and *adrogatio* in that its *primary* goal is and always has been to provide a new permanent, secure and loving home for the child and not to govern succession rights.[3] In other systems[4] which, unlike English law, allows adoption of adults, adoption is sometimes used primarily to confer succession rights on the adopted person.[5]

It should also be explained also by way of introduction that the underlying thesis has been prompted by research funded by Department of Health, that my colleague Professor Mervyn Murch and I have been conducting into support services for families of older children adopted out of care.[6] In the course of this research, which was about support *during* the adoption process, that is, from the time adoption was proposed until one year after the order in relation to children aged 5 or over, we received detailed questionnaire returns from 115/160 adoption agencies (85 statutories and 30 voluntaries) followed up by an intensive study comprising 45 interviews with agency workers, and from 226 families with whom a child aged 5 or over had been placed between 1 January 1992 and 31 December 1994, followed up by 48 interviews.

---

[2] See respectively Arts. 343–62 and Arts. 363–71 of the French Civil Code. See the reference in Review of Adoption Law: Discussion Paper No 1, *The Nature and Effect of Adoption* (1990), at para. 116, and Pierre Verdier, " 'Limited Adoption' in France" (1988) 1 *Adoption and Fostering* 41–4.

[3] As was pointed out by Stephen Cretney, *Principles of Family Law* (4th edn.), 418. Note also the Roman concept of "*alumnus*" by which was meant abandoned children brought up by someone else, see the discussion by J. Boswell, *The Kindness of Strangers* (Allen Lane, The Penguin Press, 1988), 116 ff.

[4] See e.g. H. D. Krause, "Creation of Relations of Kinship" in *International Encyclopaedia of Comparative Law* (1974), vol. IV, ch. 6.

[5] See Japan, e.g., I. Shimazu "Japan: Trailing the West in Family Law" (1988–9) 27 *Journal of Family Law* 185, 188–93.

[6] This project was conducted at Cardiff Law School from Jan. 1993 until May 1998. The research team, apart from the Directors, comprised Margaret Borkowski, Verna Beckford, Caroline Thomas and Anna Weaver. The final report, *Support Services for Older Children Adopted out of Care* was presented to the Department of Health in June 1998. It will be published in due course. The final part of the project, Adopted Children Speaking, resulting from interviews of 41 children (aged 8 or over) who have recently been adopted was completed in June 1998.

II. THE CHANGING FACE OF ADOPTION

A. The Changing Nature of the Work

The changing face of adoption is in part well illustrated by the statistics.[7]

Two messages are clear. First, adoption in England and Wales is in decline, at the moment deep decline. Secondly, baby adoptions have virtually disappeared. Whereas from its creation by the Adoption of Children Act 1926 until the late 1960s the numbers steadily rose from 2,943 in 1927, 7,775 in 1940, 12,739 in 1950 (there had been a marked post-War surge 1944–8), 15,099 in 1960 to a peak of 24,831 in 1968 (the 1960s saw an explosion of adoptions)—since then it has declined—22,373 in 1970,[8] under 10,000 in 1980 (7,908 excluding magistrates);[9] 7,452 in 1992,[10] 5,962 in 1996[11]—which incidentally is comparable to the figures of the mid 1930s.

So far as baby adoptions are concerned (i.e. children under the age of 12 months), whereas in 1970 some 8,833 babies were adopted amounting to 39 per cent of the total number,[12] in 1977 there were but 3,000, amounting to 23 per cent of the then total of 13,000 adoptions[13] and in 1991 there were said to be 900 or 12 per cent of then total of at least 7,059 adopters.[14] At any rate according to the *Marriage and Divorce Statistics* in 1992 there were just 660 baby adoptions amounting to some 9 per cent while in 1995 that figure again dropped to 332 or 6 per cent of the total.[15]

The obvious corollary of the decline in baby adoption is the rising *proportion* of older child adoptions. In 1970, for example, 20 per cent of the children adopted were aged between 5 and 9 with a further 10 per cent aged 10 or over.[16] By 1995 these proportions had risen to 37 per cent and 31 per cent respectively.[17] These figures, however, mask another important change: in 1970, for instance, whereas most adoptions by non relatives were of babies or toddlers, most of the adoptions of older children—in fact 90 per cent of the 5 to 9 age group and 84 per cent of those aged 10 or over—were by step-parents.[18] Today the profile is different. About half of all adoptions are step-parent adoptions (in 1996, 55 per

[7] One has to be say that the official statistics have become less informative and even vary from one source, e.g. *Annual Judicial Statistics*, to another, e.g. the *Marriage and Divorce Statistics*.

[8] See the *Report of the Departmental Committee on the Adoption of Children* (the "Houghton Report") (1972) Cmnd 5107, Appendix B, Table 1 of which contains statistics from 1927 until 1971.

[9] *Judicial Statistics*, Annual Report 1980, Cmnd 8436, Table D3.

[10] *Judicial Statistics*, Annual Report 1992, Cmnd 2268, Table 5.11.

[11] *Marriage and Divorce Statistics*, ONS Series SM2, No. 22. Note that according to the *Judicial Statistics*, Annual Report 1996, Cmnd 3716, Table 5.4 only 4,936 orders were made.

[12] This statistic is based on the author's analysis of the figures produced in Table 2 of Appendix B to the Houghton Report.

[14] Query the accuracy of this figure?—it was quoted by the Government's White Paper, *Adoption the Future*.

[15] *Marriage and Divorce Statistics*, ONS, Series SM2, No 22.

[16] Based on the figures given in Table 2 of App. B to the *Houghton Report*.

[17] *Marriage and Divorce Statistics*, supra.

[18] Based on the figures given in Table 2 of App. B to the *Houghton Report*.

cent of adoption orders (2,737) were made in favour of step-parents[19]), and half by strangers. But in a recent study by the Social Services Inspectorate,[20] half the children referred to the adoption service of the agencies inspected were aged 6 or over. In our own study, out of a national sample of 1,525 children placed for adoption by adoption agencies (both statutory and voluntary) in 1993–4, 42 per cent were aged 5 or more. In other words, so far as adoptions by non relatives are concerned, baby adoptions have now become relatively unusual while the adoption of older children, those aged 5 or above, has become quite normal.

B. The Changing Organisation of Adoption Work

When adoption was first introduced into England and Wales by the Adoption of Children Act 1926 it was remarkably unregulated. The 1926 Act essentially provided, as Stephen Cretney has put it,[21] "a process whereby, under minimal safeguards supervised by the court, a civil contract was registered and recognised". There were no provisions regulating who could arrange adoptions. However, following the recommendations of the Horsburgh Committee[22] the Adoption of Children (Regulation) Act 1939, section 1, made it an offence for a body of persons other than a registered adoption society or a local authority to make any arrangements for the adoption of children. By section 2 a system of local registration of adoption societies was introduced. Under section 4 the Secretary of State was empowered to make regulations *inter alia* to: (a) ensure that parents wishing to place their children for adoption were given written explanation of their legal position; (b) prescribe the inquiries to be made and reports to be obtained to ensure the suitability of the child and adopter and (c) secure that no child would be delivered to an adopter until he had been interviewed by a Case Committee.

Although the 1939 Act made express provision for local authorities to arrange adoptions, the major work continued to be done by the voluntary societies. However the law was later clarified, by section 7(2) of the Adoption of Children Act 1949, to make it clear that the local authorities had power "under any enactment relating to children to make and participate in arrangements for the adoption of children". The Hurst Committee (which reported in 1954[23]) recommended that local authorities should be empowered to arrange for the adoption of any child without that child having to be in care. The Committee made that recommendation not because it wished to see local authorities usurp the function of voluntary adoption societies but because it had been "impressed

[19] *Judicial Statistics*, Annual Report, 1996, Table 5.4.
[20] *For Children's Sake* (1996).
[21] "From Status to Contract?" in *Consensus Ad Idem* (ed. F. P. Rose, 1996), 252.
[22] 1937 Cmd. 5499.
[23] 1954 Cmd 9248, para. 24. See also Iris Goodacre, *Adoption Policy and Practice* (Allen and Unwin, 1966), who advocated that all adoptions by strangers be handled by local authorities.

by the fact that it is clearly impossible for the small number of societies [then numbering 60–70] to cover the needs of the whole country".

The Hurst Committee was particularly concerned with the placement stage which it saw as the crucial stage since, as it put it: "Once the child is placed, much harm and unhappiness may result if a change has to be made". It was its view that adoptions arranged by persons of special experience and training stood a much better chance of success. However, while it recommended that social workers employed by societies be fully trained, it stopped short of recommending the prohibition of private or third party placements. That particular bullet was bitten by the Houghton Committee[24] and, following its recommendation, private placements of children for adoption by non-relatives became an offence with effect from 1982 (when section 28 of the Children Act 1975 was brought into force).

It was at that moment that one might say the process of the "professionalisation of adoption work" was completed. The Houghton Committee wanted to see the establishment of a *nationwide* comprehensive adoption service. As they noted, at the time of their Report (i.e. 1972) only 96 of the 172 local authorities in England and Wales acted as an adoption agency. What the Committee wished to see was a comprehensive service available to "all those needing it in any part of the country". It accordingly recommended that *all* local authorities should have a statutory duty to provide an adoption service as part of their general child care and family case work provision. Further, having acknowledged that voluntary adoption societies had been pioneers of adoption and that they had a valuable continuing role to play, *inter alia*, to provide a choice of service, Houghton recommended that local authorities should have a statutory duty "to ensure, in cooperation with voluntary societies, that a comprehensive adoption service is available throughout their area".[25] Registration of voluntary societies was recommended to be national rather than local.[26]

These recommendations were accepted and, so far as the Adoption Service was concerned, were implemented in 1988 under what became section 1 of the Adoption Act 1976. Although voluntary societies continued to deal with the majority of agency adoptions through to the 1970s (in 1966, for example, of adoptions arranged by agencies, 73 per cent were arranged by voluntaries as against 29 per cent by local authorities. By 1971 the gap was already closing with voluntaries dealing with 60 per cent of cases). Now with the demise of baby adoptions, the majority of agency work is done by the statutory agencies, though exact figures are not available. In our study, for example, out of a national sample of 1,557 children placed for adoption in 1993–4, 84 per cent were placed by statutory agencies compared with 16 per cent by voluntary agencies.

---

[24] (1972) Cmnd 5107, paras. 84–90 and Recommendation 13.
[25] *Ibid.*, para. 42 and Recommendation 3.
[26] *Ibid.*, paras. 51–5 and Recommendation 5. Registration was recommended to be renewable every 3 years.

So far as individuals seeking to adopt a non-relative is concerned, adoption is fully regulated. They must first be approved by an agency. That entails a thorough screening process conducted by what are now known as Adoption Panels[27] both of the applicants' commitment to and motive for seeking to adopt as well as of their life-style, stability of their relationships and of course their ability to provide a loving and permanent home for any child. Having been approved, applicants will then have to wait, often for several months, until the agency has found what it considers to be a suitable match. There are then various and sometimes elaborate and imaginative introduction processes before placement and then, if the placement is successful, after a minimum period of 13 weeks an application can be made to the court for an adoption order. Each of these stages is fraught with difficulty and anxiety and often requires considerable support. Our research certainly confirms what was recognised by the Horsburgh, Hurst and Houghton Committees, just what a crucial stage the matching and introduction process is. To back this up we obtained an interesting analysis by agencies replying to our questionnaire of the disruptions occurring in the last year of the agencies' records, as to the stage when those disruptions occurred, namely,

	Statutories	*Voluntaries*
During placements (pre order)	94%	80%
One year after order	3%	7%
More than one year	3%	13%

Overall sample size: 188 cases

C. Changing Practice

As already mentioned, a key change in adoption practice was that of placing older children out of care for adoption. That in turn sprung from the child care policy which in the 1970s began in the United Kingdom to be termed permanency planning.[28] It was undoubtedly stimulated by the seminal work of Goldstein, Freud and Solnit, *Beyond the Best Interests of the Child* published in 1973, in which they challenged the then-prevailing traditional mode of thought that biological and legal parenthood should take precedence over psychological parenthood. Their thesis was intended to reinforce the security of the adoptive,

---

[27] Panel membership comprises two social workers employed by the agency with at least one person who, in the case of a local authority, is a member of that authority's social services committee (in the case of a voluntary society that person should be a member of that agency's management committee); the medical adviser to the agency and three other "lay" members including "where reasonably practicable" an adoptive parent and an adopted person aged 18 or more. The Panel should be chaired by "a person who has such experience of adoption work as the agency considers appropriate": Adoption Agencies Regulations 1983, reg. 5 as substituted by SI 1997/649.

[28] See particularly R. A. Parker, *Planning for Deprived Children* (National Children's Home, 1971).

psychological parent/child relationship. Many of their, at the time, revolutionary notions subsequently came to be accepted by social work and legal practitioners working in the child care and adoption fields and although such ideas were later questioned and qualified a powerful residue has permeated professional thinking ever since. Certainly they strengthened the view that children from neglectful, disrupted and severely disordered families might often do much better if placed permanently with loving, secure and more stable families.

This change of attitude was accompanied by a much more determined effort to secure adoption placements for so called hard to place children. To agencies' initial surprise, they were able to find people willing to take on children with all sorts of disadvantages. Today, such willingness would no longer be commented upon, indeed it is now almost taken for granted.

Adoption of older children meant of course that the legal fiction of a family transplant was more difficult to sustain and it is no accident that adoption with some form of continuing contact began in the 1970s while at the same time there were stronger efforts and entreaties that children should be told of their adoption (though in this respect it might be noted that the Hurst Committee specifically recommended[29] that all adopters should be required to give a formal undertaking to tell the child about his/her adoption) and the eventual enactment of the "right" of adult adopted children to obtain their original birth certificate.[30]

Today the practice of so-called "open adoption" is very much a fact of adoption life.[31] Of the respondents to our family questionnaire we found that about half had met the birth mother and 21 per cent the father. There were also a substantial number who had had some form of contact with other birth relatives and nearly as many had ongoing contact after the adoption order. Indeed considerable post adoption work is involved with various forms of contact be it direct or indirect (e.g. through letter box and telephone schemes).[32] Reflecting this *de facto* growth in post-adoption contact and evident change of policy is the change of recruiting practice. As one social worker told us:

"The whole issue of contact, letter boxes, post adoption work and that sort of thing has just come into our practice. It is also a standard feature of our assessment. There is a line in our agreement with prospective adopters which says Mr and Mrs Smith would be very happy for you to exchange information [reference to letter box contact scheme]. That's just par for the course now. In fact if Mr and Mrs Smith weren't happy with that then we would wonder whether we should be approving them as adopters."

This last point was echoed by another comment:

"Our agency has a policy of only recruiting prospective adopters who understand what openness means and are prepared to actively work with it."

[29] Cmd. 9248, para. 150.
[30] Discussed further below.
[31] That is not, however, meant to imply that continued contact is *always* in the child's interests.
[32] A detailed discussion of contact will be included in our Full Report.

This is not to say that we did not find consumer resistance to this. Indeed one adoptive couple questioned the whole rationale for contact and whether it is really helpful to a child's development especially as the child has to hold in mind and understand so many relationships. When he sought to explain this to adoption agency staff he was told in no uncertain terms that his views were "old fashioned" and unacceptable in the light of the agency's policy on open adoption and supporting contact. He had therefore in his own words "to soft peddle" and keep his mouth shut.

D. Changing Legal Position

1. Introduction

Under the Adoption Act 1976, sections 12(1) and (3) and 39, an adoption order effects a complete and irrevocable transfer of legal parentage. In other words it is of the very essence of adoption that the prior legal relationship between the adults (usually the birth parents) or institution (i.e. local authorities) and the child is permanently extinguished and replaced by a new legal relationship between the adopters and the child. It is this permanence and totality of the transferred relationship that distinguishes adoption from fostering, residence orders under the Children Act 1989 and even guardianship. It is to be observed, however, that in the past the legal effects of adoption have not always been the same, while the central notions of permanence and legal severance, particularly the latter, have to some extent been softened or come under recent attack.

Although I would maintain that from the beginning adoption meant the irrevocable transfer of legal parentage, there are those[33] who maintain that because the Adoption of Children 1926 Act, section 5(2), expressly refrained from altering an adopted child's succession rights, in its early years adoption could best be described as creating a special kind of guardianship. Be that as it may, such arguments ended when sections 9 and 10 of the Adoption Act 1949 (a Private Member's Bill) provided that adopted persons should be treated for the purposes of the devolution or disposal of real or personal property as if they were children of adopters.[34]

Notwithstanding these foregoing statements—adoption has never been absolutely irrevocable nor has it ever provided for complete severance in the sense of totally ignoring the *de facto* origins of the child. This chapter will not explore those cases where an adoption has been set aside. Suffice it to say, that there have been some truly extraordinary cases where it has,[35] but there are lim-

---

[33] See e.g. the Hurst Committee, *op. cit.*, at para. 196.

[34] Although as Stephen Cretney has pointed out *(Consensus Ad Idem, op. cit.*, at 266), *total* integration of the child into the adoptive family for succession purposes was only finally achieved by the Children Act 1975.

[35] Not the least of which is the so-called "Bosnian child case", *Re K (Adoption and Wardship)* [1997] 2 FLR 221, [1997] Fam Law 316. Note also that former parents are not necessarily prevented

its to this power[36] in that it cannot be exercised many years after the order. However, it will explore in a little more detail what may be termed the *inroads to severance*. First, there are some long established incidences, *viz.* that the adopted child remains within the same prohibited degrees of his natural family, nor does the order affect the law relating to incest, nor does a child of British Citizenship lose it if adopted by a foreign national.[37] But aside from these rather specialised issues and more important from the point of view of this chapter are four areas, namely, post-adoption contact, tracing parents, adoption allowances and post adoption support, which do need to be explored further.

2. Inroads into Severance

(a) Post adoption contact

The first reported case in which it was held that continued contact was not fundamentally inconsistent with adoption was *Re J (A Minor) (Adoption Order: Conditions)*.[38] In that case Rees J said:[39]

> "the general rule which forbids contact between an adopted child and his natural parent may be disregarded in an exceptional case where a court is satisfied that by so doing the welfare of the child may be best promoted."

In that case the access order was made to avoid lengthy litigation which would have otherwise damaged the child.

This decision was authoritatively confirmed by the House of Lords in *Re C (A Minor) (Adoption Orders: Condition)*[40] in which Lord Ackner said:

> "The cases rightly stress that in normal circumstances it is desirable that there should be a complete break, but that each case has to be considered on its own particular facts. No doubt it will not, except in the most exceptional case, impose terms or conditions as to access to members of the child's natural family to which the adopting parents do not agree."

Before the Children Act 1989 any regime of contact had to be made under the power conferred by section 12(6) to attach conditions to an adoption order. Although this power still exists, the obvious and simpler method now is to couple an adoption order with a section 8 contact order.[41] Notwithstanding this power, the courts are generally reluctant to use it particularly if it means

from seeking a residence or contact order under s. 8—though like any other stranger they will require court leave

[36] As illustrated by *Re B (Adoption: Jurisdiction to Set Aside)* [1995] Fam. 239 (CA).
[37] See the Adoption Act 1976, s. 47(1) and (2) and the Sexual Offences Act 1956. For the effect on pensions and insurance see ss. 48 and 49 of the 1976 Act. For the background to some of these points see Stephen Cretney, *Consensus Ad Idem, op. cit.*, at 266–8.
[38] [1973] Fam. 106.
[39] *Ibid.*, at 115.
[40] [1989] 1 AC 1 at 17.
[41] In fact this is the only way contact can be provided for on a freeing order since the power under s. 12(6) to attach conditions only applies to full adoption orders.

imposing an order on unwilling adopters. Where they are agreed that contact should continue, it has been said[42] there is no need for an order. Although this approach seems eminently reasonable given the well known difficulty of enforcing contact orders, it is not clear that this is the sole reason behind the reluctance. Note, for example, the comment of Butler-Sloss LJ in *Re T*[43] that:

> "the finality of adoption and the importance of letting the new family find its own feet ought not to be threatened in any way by an order [for contact] in this case."

This comment is not exactly consistent with the *de facto* practice of open adoption.

In important contrast is *Re T (Adopted Children: Contact)*[44] in which Balcombe LJ held that adopters cannot agree to indirect contact and then simply resile from it without explanation. Where they do, then the court might well be disposed to grant the former parents leave to apply for a section 8 contact order. In *Re T*, leave was given, the court being satisfied that the proposed application would not disrupt the children's lives, though all that was in issue was the adopters' promise to provide the birth parents with annual reports.

(b) Tracing parents

An important inroad into severance is the provision under section 51 of the Adoption Act 1976 by which adult adopted children can obtain[45] a copy of their original birth certificate from which they may be able to trace their parents. Although this had been first recommended by the Hurst Committee—it was the Houghton Committee recommendation—based on John Triseliotis' work on the Scottish provisions which permitted it—that finally prompted reform. This provision came into force in 1975 and was controversially retrospective.

By 1990 it was estimated[46] that some 33,000 adopted children had taken advantage of this provision, while according to Stafford 3,500 people received birth records counselling in 1991.[47]

Although access to birth records enables some adopted persons to trace and make contact with their birth parents, until the creation of the Adoption Contact Register in 1991,[48] it was difficult to discover whether that contact would be welcome. The purpose of the Register is:

> "to put adopted people and their birth parents or other relatives in touch with each other where this is what they both want. The Register provides a safe and confidential

---

[42] *Re T (Adoption Contract)* [1995] 2 FLR 251.

[43] *Ibid.*, at 257.

[44] [1995] 2 FLR 792.

[45] Though not as an absolute right see *R. v. Registrar General, ex parte Smith* [1991] 2 QB 393—danger to birth mother.

[46] Adoption Law Review, Discussion Paper No 1 (*The Nature and Effect of Adoption*) (1990), n. 140.

[47] G. Stafford (1993) 1 *Adoption & Fostering* 5.

[48] Under the Adoption Act 1976, s. 51A (added by the Children Act 1989, Sched. 10, para. 21) the Registrar General is required to maintain such a Register. In fact the Register is operated on behalf of the Registrar General by the Office of Population Censuses and Surveys.

way for birth parents and other relatives to assure an adopted person that contact would be welcome and give a contact address."[49]

The Register comprises two parts:[50] Part I, upon which is maintained the name and address of any adopted person who is over 18 and has a copy of his birth certificate and who wishes to contact a relative and Part II upon which is entered, subject to certain prescribed conditions,[51] the current address and identifying details of a relative[52] who wishes to contact an adopted person.[53]

(c) Adoption Allowances

Consistent with the notion that adoption severs all previous legal relationships, including that with the local authority where the child was previously in care,[54] there was for a long time no provision for the payment of adoption allowances by an agency. The suggestion that some provision might be made was first floated in the Working Paper produced by the Houghton Committee[55] on the basis that more adoptive homes might be found for children in need. This suggestion was not well received,[56] the principal objection being that it would amount to discriminating against natural parents.[57] In any event it was argued that the subsidising of adoption went against the notion that the child should be put in precisely the same position as a child born to the adopters. Notwithstanding this opposition the Houghton Committee recommended that "the law should be amended to permit pilot schemes of payment of allowances to adopters under the general oversight of the Secretary of State".[58]

The issue proved equally controversial in Parliament and indeed in Standing Committee it was only the Chairman's casting vote that saved the provision.[59] Nevertheless a provision permitting an adoption agency to submit a scheme for the payment of an adoption allowances for approval by the Secretary of State was enacted under section 32 of the Children Act 1975. It was brought into force on 15 February 1982. This provision was later replaced by section 56(4)–(7) of the Adoption Act 1976.

[49] Department of Health's *Guidance and Regulations*, vol. 9, para. 3.2.
[50] Adoption Act 1976, s. 51A(2).
[51] *Viz.*, upon payment of a prescribed fee, that the applicant is aged 18 or over, that the Registrar General has either a record of the applicant's birth or sufficient information to obtain a certified copy of the record of the birth and that the applicant is a relative: s. 51A(3)–(6).
[52] I.e. "any person (other than an adoptive relative) who is related to the adopted person by blood (including half-blood) or marriage": s. 51A(13)(a).
[53] The proposed Adoption Bill contains in cl. 65(2) the provision that the Contact Register be extended to allow birth parents and relatives to register their wish *not* to be contacted.
[54] See the Adoption Act 1976, s. 12(3)(aa), added by the Children Act 1989, Sched. 10, para. 3(3).
[55] Houghton Working Paper on Adoption of Children (HMSO, 1970), paras. 119–22.
[56] In fact as the Committee acknowledged in its final report (Houghton, 1972, para. 94) most witnesses were opposed to the suggestion.
[57] As the British Association of Social Workers later put it: "It would be an intolerable situation if financial resources were made available to subsidise adoption when an allocation of similar resources to the natural parents may have prevented the break up of the family in the first place": *Analysis of the Children Bill*, at 22—cited by Bevan and Parry: *The Children Act 1975*, para. 121.
[58] Houghton, 1972, Recommendation 17.
[59] Standing Committee A (Ninth Sitting), cols. 447–80.

At the time of implementation the expectation was that there would be relatively few schemes, but it rapidly became apparent that most agencies would seek to have a scheme[60] and in fact by the 1990s virtually all statutory agencies and many voluntary ones as well had successfully applied for a scheme.[61] Reflecting this overall position, the law was changed by the Children Act 1989[62] so as to empower all agencies to pay an adoption allowance provided such payments conform to the requirements set out by the Adoption Allowance Regulations 1991.[63] In other words, instead of a series of individual schemes, there is now uniform provision covering all payments of adoption allowances. Now under the present law, all agencies have a discretion both whether to pay an allowance at all[64] and, if so, how much.[65] However, reflecting the original intention of the scheme, which was to target payments for a minority of children whose chances of being adopted needed special encouragement, the current guidance states: "Adoption allowances continue to be the exception rather than the norm". However, like the schemes they replace, the Regulations are intended to give agencies "sufficient flexibility to respond to individual needs and circumstances within this overall objective".[66]

Virtually nothing was said about adoption allowances in the Adoption Law Review Consultative Document other than it was a "valuable service" which should continue.[67] However, in clause 13 of the proposed Adoption Bill, the power to pay adoption allowances would be extended to enable allowances to continue to be paid to someone with parental responsibility for the child should the adopters die.[68]

(d) Post-adoption support

Mention has already been made of the Houghton Committee's vision of a nationwide *comprehensive* adoption service. What the Committee had in mind was that such a service:[69]

---

[60] Within two years 58 applications had been made of which 24 had been approved, see Lambert, "Adoption Allowances in England: An Interim Report" (1984) 8(3) *Adoption and Fostering* 12.

[61] For details of the early practice see Lambert and Seglow, "Adoption Allowances in England and Wales: The Early Years" (HMSO, 1988).

[62] Substituting s. 57A for s. 56(4)–(7) of the Adoption Act 1976.

[63] SI 1991/2030.

[64] However, as the Department of Health's *Guidance and Regulations*, vol. 9, *Adoption Issues*, at 2.3, point out, voluntary agencies which do not hold themselves out as normally paying allowances, unlike statutory agencies, are not even under an obligation to decide whether or not to pay an allowance, though they are not prevented from doing so in any particular exceptional case.

[65] In no event, however, can the allowance exceed the fostering allowance that would have been payable: reg. 3(4)(b) of the Adoption Allowance Regulations 1991.

[66] Guidance and Regulations, vol. 9, at para. 2.2.

[67] Consultative Document on Adoption Law (1992), para. 27.11.

[68] Adoption Bill: A Consultative Document, 1996. This proposal is apparently based on the lesson learned from the operation of the 1991 Regulations. An example might be where following the death of the adopters an older sibling decides to take care of the adopted child and applies for a residence order, see the notes to cl. 13 of the proposed Bill.

[69] *Ibid.*, at para. 38.

"should comprise a social work service to natural parents, whether married or unmarried, seeking placement for a child . . . , skills and facilities for the assessment of the parents' emotional resources, and their personal and social situation; short-term placement facilities for children pending adoption placement; assessment facilities; adoption placement services; aftercare for natural parents who need it; counselling for adoptive families. In addition, it should have access to a range of specialised services, such as medical services (including genetic, psychological assessment services, arrangements for the examination of children and adoptive applications, and medical adviser) and legal advisory services."

Wide though the Houghton Committee envisaged a comprehensive adoption service to be, they made no mention of *post*-adoption support at all. However, although based on the Houghton Committee's recommendations, the wording of section 1 of the 1976 Act is wide enough to impose a duty on local authorities to provide post-adoption support.

Under section 1(1) of the Adoption Act 1976

"It is the duty of *every* local authority to establish and maintain within their area a service designed to meet the needs in relation to adoption of

(a) children *who have been* or may be adopted

(b) parents and guardians of such children and

(c) persons *who have adopted* or may adopt a child and for that purpose to provide the requisite facilities, or secure that they are provided by approved adoption societies" [emphasis added].

It is now[70] accepted that by referring to children who "*have been adopted*" as well as those who may be adopted and to persons "*who have adopted*" as well as to "*persons who may*" adopt, section 1(1) imposes an obligation to provide a *post*-adoption service. These somewhat general provisions are supplemented to a certain extent by the Adoption Agencies Regulations 1983 and further guidance as to what an adoption service should comprise is to be found in the Local Authority Circular LAC (87) 8. However, notwithstanding the Regulations and Guidance, the fact remains that under the current law there is precious little detailed requirements or guidance as to what a *general* adoption service should comprise. There is, as the Adoption Law Review[71] pointed out, a lack of clarity about what post-adoption services adoption agencies are supposed to provide. This in turn has led to a variety of interpretations as to what is required and thus to a consequential patchy provision of services which are "more often likely to be available from voluntary sources".

The Consultative Document on Adoption Law made a number of detailed proposals in relation to the provision of an adoption service.[72] In particular it

---

[70] One of the first to mention this was Bevan and Parry: *Children Act 1975*, 15. Post-adoption support is specifically mentioned but only for adult adopted people in the list of services that must be provided in Local Authority Circular LAC (87) 8 and Welsh Office Circular 35(8).

[71] Inter-Departmental Review of Adoption Law, Discussion Paper Number 3, *The Adoption Process*, para. 88.

[72] 1992. See generally Recommendations 24–33, discussed in Part VII.

recommended that the legislative framework should underline an adopted child's right to know he or she is adopted and that the agency or guardian should provide a package of information to be given to the adoptive parents to make it available to the child about his or her background. It also recommended that agencies should have a duty to give birth parents the opportunity to have their own social worker so as to be able to participate in decisions about their child's future. It wanted a system whereby medical information may be passed to the child's doctor and to inform the adopter that this has been done. It also recommended that any legislation should make it clear that any user of a local authority adoption service should have access to the complaints procedure and that approved societies have a duty to operate a similar complaints procedure. It also recommended that inspection and approval of voluntary societies should revert to local authorities.

So far as post-adoption services are concerned the Consultative Document recommended that there be a general counselling service for birth parents, adopters and adopted children.

Notwithstanding the aforementioned recommendations, the Government White Paper on Adoption in fact said little about adoption services, save for the following:[73]

> "Adoptive parents have a right to as much information about their adopted child as is possible. Agencies will therefore be given a duty to prepare for the adopters a package of information including health and family history. The information will also be retained in court records to which the adopted child will have access as of right having reached the age of 18. *Agencies will be encouraged to offer post adoption support to new families.* This is particularly appreciated by adoptive parents of children with special needs" [emphasis added].

While most welcomed the idea of requiring agencies to provide adopters with a package of information, alarm was expressed at the phrase that agencies will be "*encouraged*" to provide post-adoption support, which seemed to imply that, unlike the current law, there would be no obligation to do so. In the event these fears seem unfounded since clause 2(1) of the proposed Adoption Bill provides, in similar terms to section 1(1) of the current law, that:

> "Each local authority must continue to maintain within their area a service designed to meet the needs, in relation to adoption, of
> (a) persons who have been or may be adopted[74]
> (b) parents or guardians of such persons and
> (c) persons who have adopted or may adopt a child."

Again the obligation to provide post-adoption support hangs on the phrases "*persons who have been adopted*" and "*persons who have adopted*". It would surely

---

[73] *Adoption: The Future* (1992), para. 4.25.

[74] The reference to "persons" rather than to "children" as in s. 1(1)(a) of the 1976 Act arguably extends the obligation to provide a general support service into adulthood, though whether this is intended, is unclear.

be better if the obligation to provide post-adoption support was expressly provided for in the statute. It might be noted that to allay any doubts whether there is an obligation to provide an adoption service in relation to intercountry adoption, clause 2(5) expressly so provides. A similar provision should surely be added to cover post-adoption support.

III. IS THE CURRENT LAW AND PRACTICE ADEQUATE?

A. The Need for a New Model

At the beginning of this chapter reference was made to the "mind set", which seems to stem from the practice of baby adoptions, that essentially adoption is a gift and is the final and irrevocable act in which the mother has given away her child. The mentality is perfectly captured in a work by Mary Ellison: "*The Deprived Child and Adoption*", who wrote in 1963:[75]

> "Once an adoption order is made . . . the infant passes irrevocably into the family of the adopter. After that neither the adopter nor the natural mother can revoke what has been done; that is the final step. The work of the adoption agency ends in every case with the granting of the order, although adopters sometimes wish to maintain a friendly contact with an agency, particularly when they intend to follow up a first adoption with a second or a sequence. Many people prefer to bring up a family together, rather than an only child who would lack the companionship of brothers and sisters. But once this process has been completed, most adoptive parents prefer to take the advice contained in Mrs Leah Manning's wise remark in the House of Commons—'the most important thing in regard to adoption is that the book should be closed and the curtain come down absolutely'."

It is the thesis of this chapter that this "mind set" is certainly inadequate for the adoption of older children and even possibly for all types of adoption, yet, notwithstanding the virtual ending of baby adoption, this type of thinking still permeates the law, and legal and social work practice.

So far as legal thinking is concerned this "gift mentality" is evident in the contact cases already cited but a further example is *Re S (A Minor) (Blood Transfusion: Adoption Order Condition)*,[76] which establishes that conditions should rarely be imposed under section 12(6), in which Staughton LJ commented:[77]

> "The best thing for the child in the ordinary way in that he or she should become as near as possible the lawful child of the adopting parents."

The "gift" mentality is also evident (a) in the State's thinking both in its ambivalence towards post adoption support in general and its reluctance to treat adoption allowances as being appropriate only in unusual circumstances; (b) in

---

[75] *The Deprived Child and Adoption* (Pan, 1963), 76.
[76] [1994] 2 FLR 416 (CA).
[77] *Ibid.*, at 421.

social work practice, in that it is essentially geared towards preparing the child and adopters for entry into the family—but not necessarily into the community nor in some ways for after life in the family, and (c) in some adopters who—perhaps naturally enough—consider the adopted child theirs—to the exclusion of all others.

The gift/donation model sits uneasily with the adoption of older children (which current adoption agency practice is increasingly all about) and it seems clear that a new model is needed. At the very least with regard to older children (if not for all children) it needs to be accepted that adoption is not the end of the process but only a stage (albeit an important stage) in an ongoing and often complex process of family development. It is further suggested that adoption of older children out of care is best understood as some kind of informal "contract" between the birth family, the child and the adoptive family—a "contract" which brings with it a pattern of reciprocal obligations between the "parties" and between the adoption agency which performs a brokering role, as well as providing continuing support, while the court holds the ring in this process and puts an important symbolic and official seal to the arrangements.

Under this "contract/services" model the state should expect to provide substantial support both before, during and after the adoption; the adopters should expect to be fully informed of all the circumstances of the child and to be properly warned of the risks of "failure" both for the child and for themselves. They should also expect that adoption will not necessarily mean the end of contact with members of the birth family and, though this proposition is made much more tentatively, they may also have to expect that the price of ongoing support is that they may not be in complete control of the child's upbringing. It remains now to examine some of the implications of this new model in more detail.

B. Some Implications of the Contract/Services Model

1. Legal Policy

Consistent with the general thesis that adoption should not be regarded as the end of the process the state cannot consider that its obligations towards such children are *ipso facto* discharged by the making of the order. In other words its duty to support these needy children and those who take on the task of looking after them must *prima facie* continue even after the adoption order has been made. Accordingly, it is submitted that it is simply not good enough for the legislation only to impose an *implicit* obligation upon local authorities to provide post adoption support as part of the general adoption service. The legislation should be changed so as to make provision of post-adoption support an *express* obligation. Furthermore it will be necessary to accompany this change by providing in subordinate legislation guidance as to precisely what is expected of a post-adoption service.

With regard to adoption allowances it is submitted that it is wrong that (a) they are regarded as the exception rather than the norm, (b) they are generally lower than fostering allowances, and (c) they should be dependent upon individual agency policy. There is surely a compelling case for society to continue to bear the costs of looking after these especially vulnerable and frequently highly damaged children, particularly those who have previously been removed from their birth family into local authority care on the basis of "significant harm"[78] and for whom therefore the state took on the responsibility looking after them into adulthood. At the very least these children should be entitled to the same level of support as if they were still fostered: the adoption process should surely not financially prejudice such children (or their adopters). Ideally a national standardised system of eligibility and level of support should be introduced.

2. Judicial approach

There remains a judicial assumption that adoption marks the end of the process which is evident in the approach to post adoption contact, the application of section 12(6) of the Adoption Act 1976 to impose conditions on adoption orders, and with regard to continued contact with the birth family when the long-term plan is for the local authority to place a child for adoption. Although it is submitted that such an assumption needs reassessing that does not necessarily mean that the judicial reluctance to *impose* contact orders on unwilling adopters, for instance, is wrong, for there is evident sense in being realistic about ensuing problems of enforcement. Nevertheless even in this regard care needs to be taken lest pragmatism effectively overrides the child's welfare. There will be cases where it is in the child's interests that he both be adopted and have continued contact with his birth family and sometimes resort might have to be had to the imposition of a contact order.

Difficulty of enforcement is also a legitimate concern with regard to the imposition of conditions under section 12(6) but it is noticeable that in this area a dominant concern has been neither to derogate from nor to enhance the parental responsibility conferred on the adopters by an adoption order. This has led the courts, it is submitted, to make some questionable decisions, such as the refusal to impose a condition to require adopters to provide an annual report[79] or a six-monthly photograph to the birth parents.[80] One might similarly question the Court of Appeal decision in *Re D (A Minor) (Adoption Order: Validity)*[81] that there was no power to grant an injunction under section 12(6) (to restrain

---

[78] I.e. under the criteria set out in s. 31 of the Children Act 1989 which is now the only route into care under English law.

[79] *Re C (A Minor) (Adoption Order: Condition)* [1986] 1 FLR 315 (CA).

[80] *Re D (A Minor) (Adoption Order: Condition)* [1992] 1 FCR 461.

[81] [1991] Fam. 137, [1991] 2 FLR 66. Though as Bromley and Lowe's *Family Law* (8th edn.), 450, point out, this ruling might be academic anyway since the court undoubtedly has a power to make a prohibited steps order under s. 8 of the Children Act 1989.

contact with the child by the natural grandparents) since that would give the adopters more extensive rights than those to which the natural parents of the child are entitled.[82] Of course in all these cases it is far better if the adopters are willing to accept contact or other conditions and where this is the case it equally seems right that no order is needed[83] especially in the light of the welcome ruling in *Re T (Adopted Children: Contact)*[84] that parties agreeing to such conditions cannot subsequently resile from them without explanation. Nevertheless there will remain cases where conditions will need to be imposed.

3. Agency practice

As part of this contract/services model it is vital that adopters are fully informed about the child's circumstances and about the risks that they are undoubtedly undertaking both to themselves and to other members of the family. They should also be able to expect to be told of all the support that is available from or through the agency. Although, and this needs to be stressed, we encountered during our research many examples of good and dedicated practice, it nevertheless has to be recorded that we also came across examples of bad practice. In particular we have been alarmed at what can only be described as the deliberate concealment of information from the prospective adopters. In its worst form we have come across cases in our study where information about child's development, for example of the child's violence or propensity for sexual abuse, has either been withheld or concealed from the prospective adopters. Quite apart from the question of whether this withholding of information is actionable,[85] it is clearly unacceptable practice. Also unacceptable is the apparent reluctance at least in some agencies to give information about what practical (including financial) support is available. Indeed it was our impression that this reluctance was at least in part motivated by a desire to reduce the level of demand upon the service.

In line with the contact/services model it is suggested that there should be some type of adoption agreement under which the placing agency should *inter alia* (a) give the adopters an "information pack" clearly explaining precisely what support is available, including information about adoption allowances and other financial support, and how and from where it can be claimed; (b) guarantee that the information about the child is complete and up to date (and that it will continue to be updated) and is clearly explained to the adopters; (c) respect the adop-

---

[82] *Per* Balcombe LJ, *ibid.*, at 150 and 76 respectively.

[83] As held by Butler-Sloss LJ in *Re T (Adoption: Contact)* [1995] 2 FLR 251, discussed above, at 590.

[84] [1995] 2 FLR 792 discussed above, at 590.

[85] Cf. *W* v. *Essex County Council The Times*, 9 April 1998, in which the Court of Appeal upheld Hooper J's ruling that a social worker had a duty of care to provide foster parents with "reasonable" information about the child and that a local authority could be vicariously liable for a breach of that duty. Accordingly, four children, who were sexually abused by a teenager fostered by the family, were given leave to sue the council.

tive applicants' own wishes (*viz.* as to the type of child they wish to adopt) and only to depart from them by agreement, and (d) to continue to offer support both after the adoption or, after the child has left, if the placement has "disrupted".[86]

4. The adopters

As has been mentioned many adopters still hold to the idea that upon adoption the child becomes "theirs" and that there should be no further contact with the birth family. This "exclusive" view of adoption, however, is not so easily sustainable in respect of older children, and most agencies make this clear both at the recruitment and placing stage. What cannot be denied however, is that as a matter of law an adoption order vests parental responsibility exclusively in the adopters. In other words they are legally in control of the child. Even so it has to be asked whether the price to be paid for continuing support after the order should be the surrender of some of that control. It has been suggested, for example, that the courts should perhaps be less reticent about imposing conditions, and it might be argued that provision of ongoing support carries with it a reciprocal obligation to use that support to benefit the child, as for example, continuing with therapeutic treatment.

IV. CONCLUSION

As this chapter has sought to demonstrate, modern adoption practice in the England and Wales is more about adopting older children than about adopting babies or toddlers, yet the "mind set" associated with the latter still permeates legal and social work thinking. The time has surely come for this thinking to take on board the reality of adopting older children. To do this it has been suggested that the "contract/services" model of adoption would more appropriately take account of modern practices. This model, however, poses awkward questions. For the state it means having to come to terms with the fact that adoption is not a cheap option for bringing up children currently languishing in care. For adoption agencies it may mean having to make agreements with the adopters, *inter alia*, undertaking to give full and up-to-date information both about the child's circumstances and about the risks to the adopters and their family about taking these children on, and having to come to terms with the fact that breach of that agreement might be actionable. For the adopters it may mean having to accept that they are not in complete control of their adopted child's upbringing. For the

---

[86] Some moves, it must be acknowledged, have already been made along these lines with the introduction in July 1997, under reg. 13A of the Adoption Agencies Regulations 1983, of the obligation on agencies to provide after the making of an adoption order, such information about the child as they consider appropriate. However, the proposals in this ch. go a lot further than those just introduced.

law it raises the question whether we should retain the concept of adoption for these older children and, if so, how can adoption then be sensibly distinguished from long-term fostering.

What, then, should the object of adoption be? Certainly its overall aim should be to continue to provide a legal mechanism by which a new and independent functional family without the need for public support can be created. At the same time, however, we should expect that for many of these very damaged children such a transition will not be straight forward and that therefore the state should expect, and the law and practice should ensure, that adoptive placements continue to receive full support even after the order.

38

The Effect of Social Change on Family Structure: Mobility Issues in the Canadian Context

CHRISTINE DAVIES

I. INTRODUCTION

"In our present society mobility is a reality which can have serious implications and importance on a parent's ability to achieve personal success or achievement in the broadest sense and to properly provide and care for her children to the best she is able."[1]

The guiding principle in matters of custody and access is indisputably the best interests of the child in question. Under the Divorce Act it is the sole consideration.[2] Where the custodial parent wanted to relocate the children at a distance from the other parent, there was, until recently, some uncertainty as to how the best interests test applied. Was choosing the place of residence of the children part and parcel of the custodian's rights and responsibilities, so that an access parent would have to prove the move was *not* in the children's best interests if he wished to thwart the move? Alternatively, once a material change of circumstances had been established, were the parents on a level playing field, with no presumptions going either way? The 1995 Ontario Court of Appeal decision in *MacGyver* v. *Richards*[3] sat uneasily with its earlier decision in *Carter* v. *Brooks*.[4] In 1996 the Supreme Court of Canada, in *Gordon* v. *Goertz*,[5] resolved this question. The purpose of this chapter is to examine *Gordon* v. *Goertz* and review the cases that have come after it.

---

[1] *Cote* v. *Cote* [1996] OJ No. 2552, *per* LaForme J.
[2] Divorce Act RSC 1985 (as amended), ss. 16(8) and 17(5).
[3] (1995) 11 RFL (4th) 432.
[4] (1990) 30 RFL (3d) 53.
[5] (1996) 19 RFL (4th) 177.

II. *GORDON* V. *GOERTZ*: THE FACTS

The parties divorced in February 1993 after an eight-day trial which dealt primarily with custody and the division of matrimonial assets.[6] The mother was granted custody of the child (a 7-year-old girl) and the father was granted generous access which he exercised to the full. The mother was a dentist in Saskatoon. In the fall of 1994 the father learned that the mother intended to move to Adelaide, Australia, in January 1995 to study orthodontics. He applied for custody of the child or, alternatively, an order restraining the mother from moving the child from Saskatoon. The mother cross-applied to vary the access provisions of the custody order to permit her to move the child's residence to Australia. The matter came before Gagne J in the Saskatchewan Court of Queen's Bench. He concluded that the mother should be permitted to take the child to Australia. The father could exercise access to the child, but only in Australia on one month's notice. The decision of Gagne J was upheld by the Saskatchewan Court of Appeal. The Supreme Court of Canada unanimously agreed that the child could go with the mother to Australia and she should retain custody. The Supreme Court of Canada varied the order, however, to the extent that the father's access could be exercised in Canada.

Albeit the disposition was unanimous, the reasoning was not. Both McLachlin J and L'Heureux Dubé J gave extensive reasons for their respective decisions. They differed on two significant issues.

III. *GORDON* V. *GOERTZ*: THE JUDGMENTS

McLachlin J wrote for the majority. She held that there are two stages in an application to vary a custody order under section 17 of the Divorce Act. First, the applicant must show a material change in the situation of the child. Secondly (and this stage is only reached if the first stage is met), the judge must enter into a consideration of the merits and make an order that best reflects the interests of the child in the new circumstances.[7]

In so far as the first stage is concerned (material change), this involves the judge being satisfied of a change in the condition, means, needs and circumstances of the child and/or the ability of the parents to meet those needs. This change must materially affect the child and not have been contemplated when the original order was made.[8] Thus, a move by the custodial parent will not in every case constitute a "material change". It will not do so if the move is not distant, if the access parent did not have meaningful access to the child or if the move was anticipated by the trial judge.[9]

---

[6] (1993) 111 Sask. R 1 (QB).
[7] *Gordon* v. *Goertz*, *supra* at 189.
[8] *Ibid.*, 190.
[9] *Ibid.*

In so far as the second stage (best interests) is concerned, it is an error on the part of the variation judge simply to defer to the decision of the judge who made the original decision. The inquiry cannot be confined to the change in circumstances alone. The variation judge must consider the matters of custody and access anew.[10]

The sole consideration in matters of custody and access is, of course, the child's best interests.[11] Two parts of the custody provisions are particularly pertinent to the issue of mobility. The first is the provision that stipulates that a parent's past conduct cannot be taken into account unless such is relevant to the person's ability to parent.[12] The second is the "maximum contact" principle.[13]

With respect to the first (past conduct), this means that the reasons or motives for the custodial parent's desire to move are generally irrelevant. Only where the reason or motive is connected to parenting ability should that reason or motive be considered by the court.[14]

With respect to the "maximum contact principle", it is not absolute. The judge must bear in mind, however, that Parliament has indicated that maximum contact with both parents is *generally* in the child's best interests.[15]

The mother in this case had argued that there was a presumption in favour of the decision of the custodial parent. This presumption was said to derive from a line of older cases[16] and, more recently, the Ontario Court of Appeal's decision in *MacGyver* v. *Richards*.[17]

The arguments in favour of such a presumption are as follows:

1. Determining the place of residence of the child is an incident of custodial responsibility. Thus, the decision of the custodial parent should be upheld unless demonstrated to be not in the child's best interests;
2. The personal freedom of the custodial parent requires that he or she be permitted to decide where to live ("the mobility right");
3. Such a presumption will make decision making more predictable and thus discourage litigation.[18]

---

[10] *Ibid.*, 192.

[11] Divorce Act, RSC 1985 (as amended), ss. 16(8) and 17(5).

[12] Divorce Act, RSC 1985 (as amended), s. 16(9):
"In making an order under this section, the Court shall not take into consideration the past conduct of any person unless the conduct is relevant to the ability of that person to act as a parent of a child".
This provision is carried into the variation provisions by s.17(6).

[13] Divorce Act, RSC 1985 (as amended), s. 16(10):
"In making an order under this section, the Court shall give effect to the principle that a child of the marriage should have as much contact with each spouse as is consistent with the best interests of the child and, for that purpose, shall take into consideration the willingness of the person for whom custody is sought to facilitate such contact."
This subsection is carried into the variation provisions by s. 17(9).

[14] *Gordon* v. *Goertz*, *supra*, 193.

[15] *Ibid.*

[16] Such as *Field* v. *Field* (1978) 6 RFL (2d) 278 (OHC).

[17] (1995) 11 RFL (4th) 432.

[18] *Gordon* v. *Goertz*, *supra*, at 196.

McLachlin J dismissed all three of these arguments. She rejected the notion of a presumption. She held that once the access parent[19] has satisfied the court that the proposed move constitutes a material change in circumstances then the judge must embark on a fresh enquiry on what is in the child's best interests unhampered by presumptions. The views of the custodial parent and her decision to live and work where she likes are, however, entitled to respect.

The reasons given for rejecting the presumption are, briefly, these:[20]

1. Such a presumption is not set out in the Divorce Act. Under the Divorce Act the burden is cast on the applicant to establish a material change. Once this is done, then the judge is charged with the fresh responsibility of determining the child's best interests "by reference to the change". To place a further onus on the access parent at this, the second stage, would detract from the finding that the child's interests may, by reason of a change, no longer be best protected by the earlier order.
2. If there was such a presumption, it must apply in all cases where variation of a custody order is sought, not just mobility cases.
3. Such a presumption would derogate from the Court's *parens patriae* jurisdiction. It is for the Court, not a parent, to decide what is in a child's best interests in an application under the Divorce Act.[21]
4. A technical presumption would deflect the enquiry away from the child's needs and focus on whether the access parent had met the burden of proof cast upon him.
5. Children are entitled to individual justice. A presumption would derogate from this and tend to predetermine the enquiry. Children's needs change over time. A presumption in favour of the existing custody arrangement would inhibit the Court's ability to review the situation afresh in light of the child's new needs.[22]

---

[19] In *Woodhouse* v. *Woodhouse* (1996) 136 DLR (4th) 577 at 582 (Ont. CA) (leave to appeal to SCC refused) Weiler J, in discussing *Gordon* v. *Goertz*, said: "The onus of meeting the threshold requirement is on the access parent". However, McLachlin J actually said at 201: "The parent applying for a change in the custody and access order must meet the threshold requirement of demonstrating a material change in the circumstances affecting the child" (emphasis added). She did, however, say that this parent will often be the access parent (*Gordon* v. *Goertz*, *supra*, at 198).

In most cases of this kind, there will be cross applications, one by the custodian seeking a variation of access to facilitate her move, one by the access parent seeking a change of custody or restriction on the children's moving. It would seem capricious at least to put the onus on who filed his or her Notice of Motion first! Thus, it is submitted, the onus should be placed on the access parent. To do otherwise would have the custodial parent emphasising the enormity of the move and the access parent downgrading its importance. This would be at odds with their respective positions when covering the second stage in the proceeding, that of best interests. See, however, the views of Hovius discussed later in this chapter at n. 63.

[20] *Gordon* v. *Goertz*, *supra*, at 198–201.

[21] This point responds to the argument that determining the child's place of residence is an aspect of custodial responsibility and thus should be left to her unless demonstrated to not be in the child's best interests.

[22] This point responds to the argument that a presumption would lead to predictability of results and therefore discourage litigation. Predictability would be bought at the expense of individual justice.

It has been suggested that a presumption in favour of the custodial parent increases litigation. This

6. A presumption in favour of the custodial parent shifts the focus from the best interests of the child to the interests of the parents. Underlying much of the argument for the presumption is the notion of the mobility right of the custodial parent. However, the Divorce Act does not speak in terms of parental "rights"; it talks in terms of a child's best interests.[23]

The judgment of McLachlin J was concurred with by six other members of the Supreme Court of Canada.[24] L'Heureux Dubé J wrote vigorous dissenting reasons which were concurred with only by La Forest J. The points of agreement between L'Heureux Dubé and McLachlin JJ were:

1. The sole consideration in custody matters under the Divorce Act is the best interests of the individual child.
2. The burden is on the applicant for a variation order under section 17 to establish a material change of circumstance.
3. The "maximum contact" principle is not absolute.
4. The reasons for the custodial parent's proposed move are irrelevant unless those reasons are relevant to that parent's ability to parent.

The chief points of difference were:

1. Once a material change of circumstance has been established by the applicant, what is the role of the variation judge? McLachlin J and the majority said he or she must consider the issues of custody and access anew. The enquiry cannot be confined to the change in circumstance. L'Heureux Dubé J disagreed. She said that once a material change of circumstance had been established, the Court should *not* normally re-appraise the whole situation of the parties and their children. Rather, it should assess the impact of the change on the custody of the child. Only where the change is of such nature or magnitude as to make the original order irrelevant or inappropriate, should an assessment of the whole situation anew be undertaken. In the instant case, the variation application should be restricted to an appraisal of the impact of the change in the child's place of residence.[25]
2. Once the non-custodial parent has established a material change of circumstance, must he then go on to establish that the proposed change of residence would be detrimental to the child's best interests? McLachlin J and the majority said "no". Once he has established a material change, the variation judge will look at the matter afresh. There is no presumption in favour of the custodial parent's decision. L'Heureux Dubé J disagreed. She wrote that a

is so because fathers would seek custody, which they would otherwise cede to their wives, for fear that they will otherwise lose access to their children, in light of their wives' unfettered decision to relocate. See Irving and Benjamin, "Mobility Rights and Children's Interests: Empirically-based First Principles as a Guide to Effective Parenting Plans" (1996) 13 *CFLQ* 249 at 255.

[23] This point responds to the argument that the personal freedom of the custodial parent requires that she be permitted to determine where she wants to live.

[24] Lamer CJC, Sopinka, Cory, Iaccobucci, Major and Gonthier JJ.

[25] *Gordon* v. *Goertz, supra*, 205, 206.

custody order must be assumed to have been made in the best interests of the child because the custodial parent was found to be the appropriate person to exercise custody. One of the incidents of custody is the right to determine where the child lives. Restrictions on the incidents of custody should not be made as a matter of routine. They are only justified if found to be required in the best interests of the child.[26] The non-custodial parent must bear the onus of showing that a proposed change of residence would be detrimental to the child's best interests. The onus is a heavy one, unless there is a contract or court order preventing a change of residence. In that case, the onus should shift to the custodial parent to establish that the decision to relocate is not made to undermine access and she is willing to restructure access.[27]

The views of L'Heureux Dubé J, in this regard, are consistent with those she expressed in *Droit de la Famille 1150*.[28] There she opined that decisions relating to a child's religion etc. fall within the mandate of the custodial parent. There is a presumption that when the custodian makes such a decision she is doing so in the child's best interest. Someone wishing to contest her decision making in this respect has the burden of proving that it is *not* in the child's best interests. In *Droit de la Famille 1150*, as in *Gordon* v. *Goertz*, the views of L'Heureux Dubé J, in this context, were in the minority and were opposed by McLachlin J.

IV. FACTORS TO BE CONSIDERED IN ASSESSING THE CHILD'S BEST INTERESTS

"What it boils down to is a balancing act between the benefits to the children of moving against the detriment to them that may result from the loss of contact with the non-custodial parent, the extended family and other things or people to whom or to which the children are attached."[29]

McLachlin J listed seven factors that she said should be considered in striking this balance:[30]

a. the existing custody arrangement and relationship between the child and the custodial parent;

b. the existing access arrangement and the relationship between the child and the access parent;[31]

---

[26] *Ibid.*, 217.

[27] *Supra*, at 218.

[28] (1993) 49 RFL (3d) 317 (SCC) discussed by this writer in "The Protection of Minority Cultures and Religions within State Boundaries" in Lowe and Douglas (eds.), *Families Across Frontiers* (Martinus Nijhoff Publishers, 1996), 407.

[29] *Brown* v. *Brown* [1997] MJ No. 53 (Man. QB) *per* Mullally J, paraphrasing McLachlin J in *Gordon* v. *Goertz, supra*, at 202.

[30] *Gordon* v. *Goertz, supra*, at 201, 202.

[31] These two first factors are seen as crucial by researchers in the field of social work: see Irving and Benjamin, "Mobility Rights and Children's Interests: Empirically-based First Principles as a Guide to Effective Parenting Plans" (1996) 13 *CLFQ* 249 at 255: "[In assessing the claims of either parent in relation to a mobility application, it is relationship quality that should be given the most weight, especially as that is perceived by the child in question".

c. the desirability of maximising contact between the child and both parents;
d. the views of the child;
e. the custodial parent's reason for moving *only* in the exceptional case where it is relevant to that parent's ability to meet the needs of the child;[32]
f. disruption to the child of a change in custody;
g. disruption to the child consequent on removal from family, schools, and the community he or she has come to know.

In cases decided subsequent to *Gordon* v. *Goertz* courts have considered the following factors relevant to the application of the above principles:

1. The support available to the children in the proposed environment—financial, familial and emotional;[33]
2. Facilities for the children in the proposed environment—schools, house, community etc.;[34]
3. What will be sacrificed by the children if the move is allowed? Are they living in a settled, close community replete with extended family, an established home, school and social life, or do they have a limited connection with their current environment?[35] Would the move involve separating the child or children from siblings or other family members with whom they are close?;[36]
4. The financial security of the children;[37]
5. The emotional and physical health of the custodial parent which will impact on the children;[38]
6. The benefit to the children of living in a two parent family;[39]
7. The distance away from the other parent of the proposed environment and the ability of the parents to maintain meaningful access at that distance given their strictures on time and money.[40] This access may include access to extended family;[41]

[32] E.g., where the custodial parent is moving in order to thwart access.

[33] *Brown* v. *Brown* (1997) MJ No. 53 (Man. QB); *Bruce* v. *Bruce* (1997) 26 RFL (4th) 219 (BCSC); *Chilton* v. *Chilton* [1996] BCJ 1757, affirmed (1996) 26 RFL (4th) 124 (leave to appeal to SCC refused).

[34] *Brown* v. *Brown, supra; Bruce* v. *Bruce, supra; Chilton* v. *Chilton, supra; Heydari* v. *Heydari* [1996] AJ No. 469 (Alta. QB).

[35] *Brown* v. *Brown, supra; Bruce* v. *Bruce, supra; Chilton* v. *Chilton, supra; Benson* v. *Benson* (1986) 140 Nfld. & PEIR 196 (Nfld. SC).

[36] *Heydari* v. *Heydari, supra.*

[37] *Woods* v. *Woods* (1996) 110 Man. R (2d) 290 (Man. CA); *Chilton* v. *Chilton, supra; Campbell* v. *Campbell* [1996] BCJ No.1 235 (BCSC); *Lundy* v. *Lundy* [1996] BCJ No. 1073 (BCSC); *Johnson* v. *Johnson* (1997) 28 RFL (4th) 25 (Alta. CA); *Schioler* v. *Schioler* (1997) RFL (4th) 31 (Man QB).
"One of the factors a Court should carefully assess before limiting a custodial parent's decision to move with the children is the economic effect of its decision on the children", *per* Weiler JA in *Woodhouse* v. *Woodhouse, supra,* at 592.
Economic considerations are, however, not overriding: *K(MM)* v. *K(U)*(1990) 28 RFL (3d) 189 (Alta. CA) (leave to appeal to SCC denied 31 RFL (3d) 366); *King* v. *Low* (1985) 44 RFL (2d) 113 (SCC).

[38] *Campbell* v. *Campbell, supra; Lundy* v. *Lundy, supra.*

[39] *Campbell* v. *Campbell, supra.*

[40] *Chilton* v. *Chilton, supra; Woodhouse* v. *Woodhouse* (1996) 136 DLR (4th) 577 (Ont. CA) (leave to appeal to SCC denied).

[41] *Campbell* v. *Campbell, supra.*

8. Would the child be moving to a totally alien culture?;[42]
9. The adaptability and stability of the child (which will often relate to the child's age);[43]
10. The likelihood of the custodial parent maintaining and fostering access with the other parent should the move be allowed;[44]
11. The terms of any agreement between the parties.[45]

The fact that the child is in the joint custody of both parents, rather than in the sole custody of one, is not determinative:

> "The legal status of the relationship between the child and the parent is not itself determinative of the best interests of the child. In this regard, it is the actual involvement of the parent, not the label attached to custody, which is important."[46]

Some of the above considerations warrant greater discussion. First, the limit the Supreme Court of Canada placed on examining the motive for the proposed move. Despite the Supreme Court's restriction in this regard, the custodial parent's reason for the proposed move will almost always be indirectly relevant.[47] For example, if the custodial parent is moving for a better job or educational opportunity, it will weigh in favour of the economic stability of the children. If she is moving to accompany a new husband or partner to his place of employment, the move may well mean economic stability for the children, a two-parent family and a relaxed and happy mother.[48] Where, however, the mother proposes to move for no good reason and has vague and ill thought out plans, the move could indicate poor prospects of stability for the children.[49]

The courts have emphasized that it is the quality of access that is important, rather than its frequency,[50] yet, as Weiler JA pointed out in *Woodhouse* v. *Woodhouse*:

---

[42] *Campbell* v. *Campbell, supra.*
[43] *Chilton* v. *Chilton, supra; Lundy* v. *Lundy, supra; Robinson* v. *Beertema* [1996] BCJ No. 1498 (BCSC).
[44] *Woodhouse* v. *Woodhouse, supra.*
[45] *Woodhouse* v. *Woodhouse, supra; Lougheed* v. *Lougheed* (1996) 185 AR 387 (Alta. QB); *Heydari* v. *Heydari supra; Cote* v. *Cote* [1996] OJ No. 2552.
[46] *Per* Weiler J. in *Woodhouse* v. *Woodhouse, supra,* 590. See also *Chilton* v. *Chilton, supra,* and *Levesque* v. *Lapointe* (1993) 44 RFL (3d) 316 (BCCA).
[47] See *Woodhouse* v. *Woodhouse, supra,* at 600 *per* Osborne JA:
"I think in most cases the reasons for the proposed move will surface because there is a manifest connection between the expected effects of the move and the custodial parent's reasons for proposing the move in the first place. The effect of the move . . . will be admissible and will generally be before the Court. Nonetheless, *Gordon* makes it clear that there is no burden, or onus, on a custodial parent who is proposing to move to justify the move against a standard of necessity, or any other less onerous standard."
See *Ligate* v. *Richardson* (1997) 34 OR (3d) 423 (OCA) for a case in which the custodian's lack of compelling reason for the move was deemed irrelevant.
[48] Of course, if the mother's new relationship is untried or unstable, the move could mean the converse of all these things.
[49] *Campbell* v. *Campbell, supra.*
[50] *Bruce* v. *Bruce, supra; Chilton* v. *Chilton, supra.*

"While it is the quality of the child's relationship and not simply the frequency of access which is the consideration, in general, the more frequently access has been, and can be exercised, the stronger the relationship will be."[51]

Whether quality of access will be adversely affected by a move will depend on many factors, such as the distance and the strictures on time and money to overcome that distance,[52] the age of the child (for younger children short frequent access is desirable to sustain a meaningful relationship with the access parent. For older children, the relationship may be properly maintained by longer, less frequent visits[53]).

Less frequent but more prolonged access visits might sometimes be advantageous to the child. This will be the case where the parents have an overly antagonistic attitude towards one another and distancing will bring a measure of serenity to the child.[54]

The terms of any agreement between the parties is a relevant consideration for the courts. In custody cases generally, courts have attached considerable significance to consensual agreements. The reasons for this are twofold:

a. When such an agreement is made it is presumed that the parties felt the terms to be in the best interest of the children:

"I do perceive that there must be, practically, a presumption that in all but exceptional cases, the parents themselves, as parents, must be presumed to be acting in the best interests of their children as they, the parents, perceive it. Accordingly, I would have to conclude that except in the clearest of cases, in considering this presumption in favour of the authority of the parents, that if a Court is not to enforce an agreement between spouses, then a Court must be clearly in possession of those relevant and pertinent and pressing facts which require the Court to intervene between the parties to preserve the children's welfare."[55]

b. Consensual orders and agreements pertaining to custody should be encouraged:

"[A]ny consent order must be encouraged, especially in conflicts over children, and especially on an interim basis where the feelings are still running very high, and the children are caught up in turmoil for which they are either ill prepared or totally unprepared to handle."[56]

It goes without saying that the agreement is not binding on the Court.[57]

Where the agreement contemplates a move by the custodial parent and that agreement is incorporated into the court order sought to be varied, then the

---

[51] *Supra* at 506.

[52] Compare *Gordon* v. *Goertz* on the one hand with *Campbell* v. *Campbell, supra* and *Woodhouse* v. *Woodhouse, supra*, on the other.

[53] *Lundy* v. *Lundy* [1996] BCJ No. 1073 (BCSC).

[54] *KJB* v. *BGB* [1996] OJ No. 3335 (OCJ–GD).

[55] *Colter* v. *Colter* (1982) 38 OR (2d) 221 at 224 (Ont. SC–MC), *per* Master Cork.

[56] *Ibid.*, at 225. See also *Sabbagh* v. *Sabbagh* (1994) 2 RFL (4th) 44 (Man. CA) and *Woodhouse* v. *Woodhouse, supra*, at 589.

[57] *Gordon* v. *Goertz, supra*, at 207.

proposed move may well not constitute a material change of circumstance. A material change of circumstance is a change that was not within the reasonable contemplation of the judge making the order.[58]

Again, if the agreement anticipates a move by the custodial parent, the move will likely be allowed on the basis that the parties believed such a move to be in the children's best interests when they signed the agreement.[59] Conversely, where the agreement prohibits the move, the inference is that the parties did *not* believe a move to be in the children's best interests when they signed it.[60]

The fact that the agreement provides that the custodian will give the access parent a period of notice prior to moving the child will not, without more, amount to an inference that the access parent sanctioned a move. Such a provision simply mirrors section 16(7) of the Divorce Act. Its purpose is to give the access parent an opportunity to object to the change and let the court decide what is in the best interests of the child.[61]

V. CHOICES FOR THE COURT

The matter usually comes before the court in one of two ways. First, there may be no custody order in place and both parents seek custody, either interim or permanent.[62] The one who choses *not* to move seeks, alternatively, a restriction on the children being taken from the jurisdiction. Secondly, there may be a custody order in place and the custodian wishes to move. She seeks a variation of the other's access. The access parent seeks, in the alternative, a restriction on the custodian moving the children out of the jurisdiction, or custody (or care and control) to him.[63]

In the first situation (where no order is in place) the court has two decisions to make:

a. To whom should custody be awarded?
b. If custody should go to the mover, should there be a restriction on the children being taken from the jurisdiction?

---

[58] *Gordon* v. *Goertz, supra*, at 190.

[59] *Lougheed* v. *Lougheed* (1996) 185 AR 387 (Alta. QB).

[60] *Cote* v. *Cote, supra*. See also *Gordon* v. *Goertz, supra*, at 218 *per* L'Heureux Dubé J: "Where, however, there is a covenant or Court order expressly restricting the child's change of residence, the onus should shift to the custodial parent to establish that the decision to relocate is not made in order to undermine the access rights of the non-custodial parent and that he or she is willing to make arrangements with the non-custodial parent to restructure access."

[61] *Woodhouse* v. *Woodhouse, supra*, at 589. See also *Ligate* v. *Richardson* (1997) 34 OR (3d) 423 (OCA).

[62] The same considerations apply in an interim application as in an application for permanent custody. However, maintenance of the *status quo* is more important in the former situation: *Cote* v. *Cote, supra*.

[63] In a case comment on *Woodhouse* v. *Woodhouse* and *Luckhurst* v. *Luckhurst* (1996) 20 RFL (4th) 376 at 384, Prof. Berend Hovius states that the method by which the matter comes before the court may be most important. If a custodial parent is seeking to vary access then she bears the burden of proving a material change of circumstances. If the access parent is seeking to change custody or restrict the children's move, then the onus is on him. For a contrary view, see above n. 19.

The decisions should be made in that order.[64]

In the second situation (variation application) the court must first determine if there has been a change of circumstances. If satisfied on that point, then the court has various options open to it:

1. To do nothing, leaving the current custody/access arrangement in place. This will generally have the effect of preventing the move.[65]
2. To change custody.
3. To prohibit removal of the children from the jurisdiction.

Since option 1 will nearly always have the same effect as option 3, I shall restrict my discussion to options 2 and 3, the options of changing custody and of prohibiting removal of the children from the jurisdiction.

The first question to address is this. Should the court work sequentially through the options? That is, after finding there to be a material change of circumstances, should the court *first* determine custody and *then* address the issue of restricting a move if the mover is to retain custody? Alternatively, should the court, having found there to be a change of circumstances, address the children's best interests in an omnibus fashion? Should the court consider all factors and make the decision that it considers to be in the child's best interests, that decision resulting in one of the options referred to above? This question was not addressed in *Gordon* v. *Goertz* nor in any case as yet decided since then.

In many cases, the realistic options of the court are limited to *either* ordering a change of custody *or* prohibiting removal. The full panoply of options do not have to be fully considered. For example, at the Court of Appeal level in *Woodhouse* v. *Woodhouse* there was no question of a change of custody. The sole question before the court was whether or not there should be a restriction on moving the children from Ontario. Osborne JA pointed out[66] that where the sole reason for an access parent bringing a variation application is the proposed move of the custodian, the claim for a change of custody is likely to be a tactical move. Normally, there is no question of the custodian going without the children. The real question then is: "Should there be a restriction on the removal of the children?" In such situations it does not make sense to embark on a full blown custody hearing.[67]

On the other hand, the true question before the court may be that of custody and a restriction on removal will not be a realistic option. This will be the case where the child has already moved with the custodian and is settled in the new

---

[64] See *Brown* v. *Brown, supra*; *Lundy* v. *Lundy* ([1996] BCJ No. 1073 (BCSC); *Woodhouse* v. *Woodhouse, supra*.

[65] In *Campbell* v. *Campbell, supra*, the court forbore to alter the regular and frequent access arrangement that the father enjoyed. This effectively prevented the mother from taking the children to Australia.

[66] *Woodhouse* v. *Woodhouse, supra*, at 602.

[67] In such a situation the proposed move will not constitute a material change with respect to custody. Rather, it will constitute a material change with respect to access. (*Woodhouse* v. *Woodhouse, supra*, at 602 *per* Osborne JA).

environment.[68] It will also be the case where the custodian says she will move regardless of whether the children can accompany her. In both situations, the court must determine whether the child should be in the custody of the access parent in the home jurisdiction or remain in the custody of the other parent situated in the new environment.

A custodial parent who wishes to move is surely in a better position if she limits the court's options so that the only true question is that of custody. A change of custody is a more draconian step than a restriction on removal from the jurisdiction. A change of custody is likely to be more traumatic to the child than a change of environment. If the custodial parent effectively illuminates the option of a restriction on moving the child, she is likely to get what she wants. Put another way, a court is more likely to restrict movement (the compromise solution) than it is to change custody. By eliminating the compromise solution, the custodian has a good chance of retaining the children *and* taking them away with her![69]

How does a custodial parent effectively remove the court's option of prohibiting removal of the children? Either by the custodian deposing she will go in any event regardless of whether the children can accompany her or by offering the court a *fait accompli*—the children already being settled in the new environment. The first possibility is unlikely. As Osborne JA said: "It is a rare case where the custodial parent's position will exclude the option of staying with the children rather than moving".[70] It is obviously a somewhat dangerous position to take, shedding a rather self- centered light on the person who takes it! An unsanctioned move with the children also has its risks. In *Woodhouse* v. *Woodhouse*, the mother took the children to Scotland for a holiday and remained with them there after the holiday in contravention of an order of the Ontario Court. This conduct did her no good at all. *Inter alia*, it reflected poorly on her attitude towards the promotion of access. Ultimately, she was denied permission to remove the children from Ontario. Yet in other cases the mother's move has not resulted in quick action by the father. In those cases the father allowed the grass to grow under his feet whilst the children were established in their new environment. Here the mother effectively reduced the court's option to that of changing custody which it declined to do.[71]

Let me briefly turn to the other scenario—that of the court-imposed restriction on moving the child. The Supreme Court of Canada in *Gordon* v. *Goertz* did not deal in any true sense with this option. In *Gordon* v. *Goertz* the child was already settled in Australia by the time of the Supreme Court of Canada hearing so that the court's options were limited to those of changing or reaffirming

[68] As in *Gordon* v. *Goertz* itself. See *Woodhouse* v. *Woodhouse, supra,* at 586, 601.
[69] See Hovius, "Mobility of the Custodial Parent: Guidance from the Supreme Court" (1996) 19 RFL (4th) 292. See also *Bruce* v. *Bruce, supra.*
[70] *Woodhouse* v. *Woodhouse, supra,* at 602. But see *Pisko* v. *Pisko* (1997) 151 DLR (4th) 189 (Alta CA). Hovius (1997) 32 RFL (4th) 9.
[71] See *Aldred* v. *Aldred* [1996] SJ No. 484 (Sask. QB); *Bruce* v. *Bruce* (1997) 26 RFL (4th) 219. (BCSC).

custody. However, McLachlin J indicated that this was indeed an option. In *Woodhouse* v. *Woodhouse* the court was directly concerned with the question whether a restriction on the children's movement should be imposed. Custody was not an issue before the court. Osborne JA in the Ontario Court of Appeal held that, in determining whether or not to impose the restriction, the court should not restrict itself to assessing the effect of the move on existing access arrangements. The effect of the move on existing access arrangements was merely one factor to be considered in balancing the benefits and detriments of the move to the children.[72] The other members of the Court of Appeal clearly agreed with this statement since they took into account all the factors mentioned in *Gordon* v. *Goertz* relating to a child's best interests. In other words, the factors relevant to a change of custody in the context of a move are equally relevant to the imposition (or otherwise) of a restriction against moving.

Finally, in this section we should ask whether or a joint custody order is consistent with parenting at a distance. The answer appears to be this. Distance itself does not dictate a sole custody order. As the British Columbia Court of Appeal said in *Levesque* v. *Lapointe*:[73]

> "Counsel for the respondent, as part of his argument, submitted that it was implicit in a joint custody order granted at the time of the divorce, that the parties would remain in the same locality, because otherwise 'co-parenting' was a practical impossibility. We seriously question the assumption that an order for joint custody, which contains no other term, condition or restriction, can be taken to impose a requirement that the parents live in close proximity to one another."

VI. IS A TRIAL NECESSARY?

One of the reasons given in favour of there being a presumption in favour of the custodial parent's decision regarding the child's residence was that such a presumption would lead to predictability of result and thus reduce the need for trials. McLachlin J in *Gordon* v. *Goertz* dismissed this argument for the following reason:[74]

> "The argument that a presumption would render the law more predictable in a way which would do justice in the majority of cases and reduce conflict damaging to the child between the former spouses . . . founders on the rock of the Divorce Act. The Act contemplated individual justice. The judge is obliged to consider the best interests of a particular child in the particular circumstances of the case . . . "

Interim custody and variation applications are generally dealt with in Chambers on Affidavit evidence. Do the demands of "individual justice" mean that the court is obliged to conduct a trial in each case when asked to do so?

---

[72] *Woodhouse* v. *Woodhouse, supra,* at 602.
[73] (1993) 44 RFL (3d) 316 at 325 (BCCA) cited with approval in *Chilton* v. *Chilton* (BCSC), *supra.*
[74] *Gordon* v. *Goertz, supra,* at 197.

This question was addressed by the Ontario Court of Appeal in its recent decision of *Luckhurst* v. *Luckhurst*.[75] There the Court said:

"We are of the opinion that the trial judge did not err in the manner in which he exercised his discretion in refusing to order the trial of an issue. The fact that the Affidavits contain conflicting statements is a factor to be considered very carefully but it is not itself determinative of the question of whether the trial of an issue ought to be directed. The main facts are not in dispute. Where, as here, the Affidavits contain sufficient information for the trial judge to weight the relevant factors and to come to a decision concerning the best interests of the children, it is not necessary to order the trial of an issue."

Thus the question is: do the materials before the court contain sufficient information for the judge to come to an informed decision concerning the best interests of the children? Conflicting statements in the Affidavits do not, in themselves, demand a trial. If, however, the conflict is such that the judge cannot determine what are the principle facts of the case, a trial should be directed.[76]

VII. CONCLUSION

In *Gordon* v. *Goertz* the Supreme Court of Canada set out clear principles that govern the question of mobility. One thing above all is clear; mobility rights do *not* mean that the custodial parent has the *right* to move the child. Rather, the child has the right to have his or her interests considered first and foremost.

In *Gordon* v. *Goertz* L'Heureux Dubé J gave a vigorous dissent. However, her views were concurred in by only one other Justice.[77] Recently, the Supreme Court of Canada has refused leave to appeal in two cases, those of *Woodhouse* v. *Woodhouse* and *Chilton* v. *Chilton*. It seems likely that it will now be left to the lower courts to flesh out the principles established in *Gordon* v. *Goertz*.

---

[75] (1996) 20 RFL (4th) 373 (OCA).

[76] *Heydari* v. *Heydari* [1996] AJ No. 469 (Alta. QB); *Strandlund* v. *Martin* [1996] S.J. No. 414 (Sask. QB).

[77] La Forest J.

PART SIX

Reconciling Changing Norms and Changing Forms

The volume closes with reflections by Nhlapo (Chapter 39), from the point of view of a South African Law Commissioner, on the tensions between traditional familial and normative structures and the modifications those structures are undergoing in contemporary South Africa. These tensions need to be accommodated and managed through law, and, in the case of South Africa, under the guidance of an "undecided constitution". While these issues appear with heightened intensity in the South African context as a result of its political and social history, they are found in varying degrees of strength throughout the world. Drawing on the contributions in this volume, and the experience of the conference which generated them, Nhlapo's conclusions will have a resonance well beyond South Africa.

39

African Family Law under an Undecided Constitution: the Challenge for Law Reform in South Africa

THANDABANTU NHLAPO*

I. INTRODUCTION

It is now almost three years since South Africans went to the polls in the country's first democratic election and, by that act, ushered in a period of great excitement, optimism and challenge in the field of law. It is generally acknowledged that reference to these beginnings of South Africa's transformation as a "miracle" essentially describes the fear in the minds of many at the time that a smooth transition from apartheid and entrenched race-based privilege to a non-racial democracy was not possible. Resistance, bloodshed or worse were routinely expected. This is a point worth remembering when one considers that, three years later, the process of transformation is far from complete: indeed the issues remain as complex as they ever were, some pockets of resistance are emerging daily, and the temptation to retreat to the comfort zone of previously entrenched positions is becoming a real threat. At one level this chapter is about sounding a warning on the dangers of careless law reform and law reform debates, with their potential for opening up old wounds which the country's experimentation with the fragile concept of national reconciliation can ill afford.

The reason for the "miracle", it is again generally accepted, lay in the nature of the settlement that was reached between the warring factions. That settlement was in the form of a negotiated constitution pervaded by the principle of compromise, rather than a political fight to the finish. This was felt to be the essential ingredient in ensuring a quick return to the peace and stability required for rapid transformation and economic development. In strictly legal terms, the main problem with our kind of negotiated settlement is that the resultant constitution "speaks with forked tongue" on a number of important issues including the central question of accommodating cultural diversity in an African country determined to develop a human rights culture backed by a strong bill of individual rights. Thus the constitution in attempting, for good reason, to be everything to everybody, gives full recognition to customary law and puts it on a par with the general law; it guarantees the right of every person to participate in the cultural life of his or her choice; and it makes all these grants subject to the bill of rights, which contains a strong equality and non-discrimination clause.

South African society today has to negotiate various categories and kinds of relationship. It sometimes seems as if nothing is destined to remain untouched. In the educational sphere, schools and universities are negotiating new relationships with staff and students, on the one hand, and with the government, on the other. In industry, employers and workers' unions are struggling to fashion mutually acceptable accommodations, again with government as a participant in the not-too-distant background. What seems clear is that of all these relationships that have to be negotiated, the ones that have ethnicity and/or culture at their centre are the ones which suffer most from the legacy of the past. The African customary law of marriage and the family is doubly vulnerable. The imperatives of transformation require that this law not only re-negotiate the primary relationship between spouses (and between spouses and their children), but also the "political" relationship between itself and the rest of the legal system. This has to be done against the background of a dominant legal system and a dominant culture whose relationship with African culture has not in the past been very positive.

In failing to clarify the issues the constitution lends itself not only to a range of interpretations but alto to correspondingly raised expectations from opposite sides of the cultural divide. The opponent of customary law looks to the bill of rights to feed the expectation that in the new South Africa there is no place for this legal system; the same document provides hope for the supporter of customary law who wishes to see an enhanced role for this legal system. Which way should the balance tilt? The subjection of customary law to the bill of rights might have been the result of a genuine desire to build a human rights culture in the country, but there are likely to be those who would use the situation to pursue an agenda against a value system considered "backward". In the same vein, are the recognition of customary law and the protection of culture intended to be taken seriously, or are they some form of appeasement?

II. AN UNDECIDED CONSTITUTION: THE POSITION OF CULTURE AND CUSTOMARY LAW

Much has been written[1] elsewhere about the political negotiations leading to the adoption of the interim constitution. That process is still important to an understanding of the various actors and their motivations. Two powerful lobbies were to play a crucial role in not only the final outcome but also in the tone of the

---

[1] See for instance Nhlapo, R. T., "Cultural Diversity, Human Rights and the Family in Contemporary Africa: Lessons from the South African Constitutional Debate" in *International Journal of Law and the Family* (1995) 9, 208–25; Corder, H. "Towards a South African Constitution" in *Modern Law Review* 57 (1994), 491.

debate preceding that outcome. On the one side were the human rights activists (notably, various women's groupings) who advocated the insertion of a strong equality clause in the constitution and, on the other were the traditional leaders, many of whom were organised under the banner of the Congress of Traditional Leaders of South Africa (CONTRALESA), who sought to have customary law exempted from the reach of any equality or non-discrimination provision of the constitution.

At the end of the negotiation process both sides could claim some victories. The women's lobbies claimed success when a strong equality provision was inserted into the 1993 constitution. This was section 8 in the Chapter on fundamental rights (Chapter 3) and it was framed as follows:

> "8(1) Every person shall have the right to equality before the law and to equal protection of the law.
>
> (2) No person shall be unfairly discriminated against, directly or indirectly, and, without derogating from the generality of this provision, on one or more of the following grounds in particular: race, gender, sex, ethnic or social origin, colour, sexual orientation, age, disability, religion, conscience, belief, culture or language."

The traditional leaders, too, won some significant concessions in the form of Constitutional Principles XI and XIII.[2] The former guaranteed cultural (and linguistic) diversity and the latter provided, in subsection (1):

> "The institution, status and role of traditional leadership, according to indigenous law, shall be recognised and protected in the Constitution. Indigenous law, like common law, shall be recognised and applied by the courts, subject to the fundamental rights contained in the Constitution and to legislation dealing specifically therewith."

Four further sections secured the position of traditional leaders and the customary law under which they enjoyed their status. Section 181 provided for the exercise by traditional leaders of their usual powers and functions; section 182 gave them a role in local government and sections 183 and 184 created Provincial Houses of Traditional Leaders and a national Council of Traditional Leaders, respectively.

As far as the development of a final constitution was concerned the 34 Constitutional Principles had to be read with section 71(1) and (2). Section 71 provided that the new text (i.e. in the final constitution) had to comply with the Constitutional Principles and that the Constitutional Court had to certify the new text as so complying for the constitution to come into effect.

The Constitutional Court sat to perform its task in accordance with section 71 from July to early September in 1996. There were in excess of 100 issues arising from objections to the new text. At the end of the process the court held that "in

---

[2] The 34 Constitutional Principles represented the political settlement reached by the multiparty negotiators. They were the guidelines within which the Constitutional Assembly (i.e. the two Houses of Parliament sitting jointly to work on a final constitution) had to operate. Failure to comply with the Principles would lead to the invalidity of any provision proposed for inclusion in the final constitution.

general and in respect of the overwhelming majority of its provisions, the new text was in compliance with the Constitutional Principles". The court struck down eight specific provisions on the ground that they did not comply with the Constitutional Principles.

Among the objections to the new text were a number dealing with the position of traditional leaders and of customary law, lodged by individuals and organisations. These included the Inkatha Freedom Party (IFP), the Congress of Traditional Leaders of South Africa (CONTRALESA), a group of academics from Potchefstroom University on behalf of the Traditional Authorities Research Group, and Professor A J Kerr of Rhodes University whose submission is discussed more fully below. What the objections had in common was the allegation that the subjection of customary law (section 211) or cultural rights (sections 30, 31) or the right to personal marriage laws (section 15(3)) to the Constitution or the bill of rights was a violation of Principles XI and XII. CONTRALESA argued further that the subjection of customary law to the equality provision (s8(2)) spelled the death of customary law and was a direct violation of Constitutional Principle XIII(1).

The Court dismissed the objections, holding that the recognition and protection granted to customary law complied with the relevant Constitutional Principles. The court then ordered the Constitutional Assembly to amend those provisions which were in violation of the Principles. The finalised text was assented to on 16 December 1996 and came into effect on 4 February 1997 as the Constitution of South Africa Act (108 of 1996). The provisions relevant to customary law and culture are the following: sections 15(3), 30, 31, 211(1) and (3). I reproduce the two most important ones below.

Section 15 (on freedom of conscience, religion, thought, belief and opinion) provides in subsection (3):

"(a) This section does not prevent legislation recognising—
    (i) marriages concluded under any tradition or a system of religious, personal or family law; or
    (ii) systems of personal and family law under any tradition or adhered to by persons professing a particular religion;
 (b) Recognition in terms of paragraph (a) must be consistent with this section and the other provisions of the Constitution."

"*Section 211 Recognition of customary law*
    (1) The institution, status and role of traditional leadership, according to customary law, are recognised, subject to the Constitution.
    (3) The courts must apply customary law when that law is applicable, subject to the Constitution and any legislation that specifically deals with customary law."

Noticeably, the rights guaranteed above and in the other provisions are to be enjoyed only when they are not in conflict with either the Constitution generally or the bill of rights. The language in which these qualifications are cast has yet to be interpreted by the Constitutional Court, of course, but there is a strong body of opinion within the country that matters of culture and customary law must give way in cases of conflict to the bill of rights, especially to the equality provision.[3] That provision is formulated as follows:

"*Section 9 Equality*
(1) Everyone is equal before the law and has the right to equal protection and benefit of the law.
(3) The state may not unfairly discriminate directly or indirectly against anyone on one or more grounds, including race, gender, sex, pregnancy, marital status, ethnic or social origin, colour, sexual orientation, age, disability, religion, conscience, belief, culture, language and birth.
(4) No person may unfairly discriminate directly or indirectly against anyone on one or more grounds in terms of subsection (3). National legislation must be enacted to prevent or prohibit unfair discrimination."

Briefly stated, the "indecision" referred to in the heading of this chapter has tended to produce several recognisable streams of opinion in the South African culture debate. While there is some consensus that in the constitutional era customary law cannot survive unscathed and that communities cannot be allowed to violate the human rights of their members in the name of culture, there seem to be some differences as to how this might be achieved. At the most worrying end of the scale, the claim is made that all of those aspects of customary law considered "problematic" are now unconstitutional and therefore *automatically abolished*.[4] Thus someone who dislikes polygyny might believe that, without any further action on anyone's part, polygyny is automatically no longer part of customary law and should the matter be litigated, the job of the court would be merely to declare this obvious fact. This is reminiscent of the old debates over the cut-off dates of colonial reception statutes. It is as if there are those who contemplate, not a "continuing reception" of customary law (as it is at present until challenged) but the application, as from midnight on 3/4 February 1996, of a drastically changed version throughout South Africa. Convincing authority for this proposition is very difficult to find.

A more reasoned opinion is that customary law and the culture it purports to underpin are (like the common law) subject to the constitution and that their scope is thus restricted in various ways. This point of view accepts that where legislation has not intervened the courts will have to rule on specific challenges to customary law. They will be aided in their task by a "purposive and

---

[3] Consider the Statement and Programme of Action adopted at the First National Conference on Human Rights by the Human Rights Commission on 20–23 May 1997. Para. 22.4 of the Statement (on Language, Culture and Religion) reads:
"Conference recommends that the South African Law Commission undertake research on potential conflict between rights especially as these relate to family law. Conference affirms that *culture, language and religion can most effectively contribute to nation-building to the extent that they operate in a manner consistent with the principles of the Bill Of Rights*" [emphasis added].
See also Kaganas, F. and Murray, C., "The Contest Between Culture and Equality under South Africa's Interim Constitution" (1994) 21(4) *Journal of Law and Society* 409–33.
[4] Of concern is the frequency of uninformed comments such as "Of course now that we have a constitution this *lobolo* thing of yours is no longer legal".

textual" interpretation of the Constitution which makes it clear that the right to participate in cultural life is subordinate "to the value of, and the right to, equality".[5] Veering slightly away from this view are those who believe that it is premature to talk of "subordination" before the whole notion of constitutional equality and what it entails in concrete terms are properly problematised.[6]

The path that will be taken by customary law in its development will depend on which of these approaches is adopted, especially by the courts. But before confronting that question, it is important to say a bit more about the customary law of the family and why it excites the interest of human rights activists.

III. AFRICAN CUSTOMARY LAW OF THE FAMILY

It is important to understand that the African customary law of the family is the outward sign of a deep and all-pervasive conception of the world and the meaning of life. Radcliffe-Brown's words are as true today as when he wrote them:

"For the understanding of any aspect of the social life of an African people—economic, political or religious—it is essential to have a thorough knowledge of their system of kinship and marriage."[7]

The family plays a role that is far wider than the immediate interests of the married couple and their children: it is a multi-purpose and multi-faceted corporate structure that is in many cases central to an individual's life. Because of its importance in the business of survival and security, its cherished values include procreation and group solidarity, deference to elders and selflessness.

"Family provides a sense of worth and a sense of pride; it is at once a social, emotional, moral, economic and political support system; it is as much a hedge against old-age poverty as it is a defiant stab at immortality."[8]

For a phenomenon that is considered so central in people's lives it is hardly surprising that the process by which the family is constituted—i.e. marriage—is pervaded by an elaborate network of principles, rules, rituals and ceremonies. The marriage negotiations themselves are characterised by play-acting and drama: the pretended hostility to the overtures of the groom's people, bringing into sharper focus the gradual bonding of the two families as the negotiations take

---

[5] Cathi Albertyn in the *Gender Research Project Bulletin* (Centre for Applied Legal Studies), vol. 2/97 Spring, commenting on the judgment in *Mthembu* v. *Letsela and Another*, 1997(2) SA 936 (TPD).

[6] See generally Kerr, A. J., "Customary Law, Fundamental Rights and the Constitution" in (1994) *South African Law Journal* 720–35.

[7] Radcliffe-Brown in Radcliffe-Brown, A. R., and Forde, D. (eds.), *African Systems of Kinship and Marriage* (London, 1950), 1.

[8] The quote is reproduced from a work by the present writer provisionally entitled "Case-study on Cultural Customary Law in Relation to the Establishment of Democratic Processes", commissioned by the United Nations Educational, Scientific and Cultural Organisation (UNESCO) for the first issue of the *World Culture Report*.

shape; the high drama of the discussions over the *lobolo* cattle; the mock "running away" of the bride; the spontaneous use of kinship terms between the two groups as soon as the betrothal is finalised.

This is all so starkly different from "western" marriage that misunderstandings are bound to occur. It has not dawned on many people that African marriage needs to be understood *on its own terms* and not in comparison with civil marriage. For anyone who cares to look, the ceremonies and rituals involved in the marriage process are riddled through with sex-based divisions. There are activities for boys only, and for girls only: there are men-only and women-only ceremonies. There is also plenty of inequality: indeed the whole marriage drama is premised on the notion that the man's family are the supplicants and the woman's people the holders of power.

The networks, structures and institutions of African family law include polygyny,[9] a classificatory system of kinship[10], and various kinds of social parenthood and pretend relationships.[11] It does not take much imagination to think of the myriad cultural practices surrounding marriage and family, and supported by customary law, which could face constitutional challenge. Among these one might include: courtship rituals (especially "mock abduction"); issues around age and consent; marriage consequences (especially institutionalised gender-inequality); divorce grounds and procedures; and the position of widows.

IV. CULTURE, CUSTOMARY LAW AND THE CONSTITUTION: RESOLVING THE TENSIONS

Resolution of these tensions requires in the first place that the tensions themselves be acknowledged as legitimate. That is to say that there should be more of a genuine understanding that diversity is normal and less of the often unarticulated assumption that some lifestyle choices are inherently backward and need to justify themselves. Secondly, resolution will require a realisation that the task is not an easy one and should not be undertaken lightly. Different factors, legal and non-legal, may be relevant in making the decision.

Often ignored in these debates is the "political" dimension, so called because it encompasses notions of democratisation, majority preferences and age-old inter-racial and intercultural suspicions. Whatever else it might mean, democratisation in the South African context is about bringing into the political equation those who were disadvantaged, disempowered and disenfranchised by apartheid

---

[9] Polygyny is that version of polygamy where a man may marry more than one woman: polyandry is the system allowing a woman to have more than one husband.

[10] A system in which relatives are reckoned according to the *level* that they occupy on the family tree, regardless of sex, thus allowing for usages such as "my female father" in reference to an aunt.

[11] See Nhlapo, R. T., "Biological and Social Parenthood in African Perspective: the Movement of Children in Swazi Family Law" in Eekelaar, J. and Sarcevic, P. (eds.), *Parenthood in Modern Society: Legal and Social Issues for the Twenty-first Century* (Martinus Nijhoff, London, 1993), for the creation of "artificial" relationships in African family law.

and its antecedents. In the main, these are people who expect that liberation will result in an enhanced, not diminished, profile for African culture. The more rural (or illiterate, or poor, etc.) they are, the more they believe that a democratic South Africa will be a place where they can at last be "themselves". And as mentioned earlier, for many people, to be themselves crucially involves their relationships of kinship and their ability to marry and found families in familiar and understood ways.

This factor alone is a significant signal to the law reformer to eschew reforms that will cause bewilderment, dislocation, resentment and lead—ultimately—to paper law. The expectations of the majority are not, however, the only consideration. Democratisation has also meant the creation of space for various groups within the majority Black population to break free from the mass. Women provide a good example and it is due to their efforts that the constitution makers produced a document which attempts to ensure "democratisation within democratisation".[12]

What is proposed below is a three-pronged approach to the problem of accommodating culture in an "open and democratic society based on human dignity, equality and freedom". The first prong refers to cultures themselves and their need to adapt to changed imperatives: the second suggests judicial, and the third, legislative, methods of realising the goals of a constitution that attempts to entrench cultural rights against the background of strong individual entitlements. There is obvious overlap between the methods. For instance, the way that cultural communities adjust and adapt their practices from within has important lessons for the research that must be done to inform effective law reform; at the same time courts engaged in developing customary law need an understanding of how social transformation takes place in real life.

(a) Internal adjustment

Ideally, the most desirable kind of change in customary law and in cultural practices is change that is generated by communities from within. Hinz[13] and Stewart[14] both give examples of autonomic legal and social change within the Southern African region: there is evidence of these movements in South Africa too. Here it must be realised that such adaptations are nothing new to customary law: invariably, when a rule no longer works to achieve a purpose originally set for it, it undergoes transformation or reinterpretation.[15]

---

[12] By this is meant the concern to secure within the broad, previously oppressed, Black majority the rights of groups whose interests might have been ignored after victory had been achieved over the main enemy, racism.

[13] Above, ch. 9.

[14] Above, ch. 13.

[15] See generally Wilson, M. *et al.*, *Keiskammahoek Rural Survey*, vol. 3 *Social Structure* (Shuter and Shooter, Pietermaritzburg, 1952).

In the constitutional era the focus should be on how communities may free themselves from rules which work to the benefit of some, but not all, the members. This may involve a head-on collision with patriarchy, but it is also true that a breakthrough here would do much to reclaim customary law from the scrapheap to which it is relegated by those who believe it has no capacity to accommodate modern rights and entitlements.

I have observed[16] elsewhere that an important aspect of the task is to make a clear distinction between the *substance* of a particular value considered important in African family law, and the *form* of its expression. On that occasion the value of the extended family was taken as an illustration, the point being made that as a value it was too entrenched in African thinking to be seriously challenged. Even so, creative ways of enabling this value to shed some of the discriminatory content of its expression have to be found. The conflicting interests of fathers and their lineages, on the one hand, and mothers and their children, on the other will have to be resolved and resolved against the background of constitutional entitlements.

To retain the positive values implicit in the institution of the extended family will thus require some re-adjustments to the ways in which these values have been expressed. For example, in matters of child custody and other rights over children the justification for preferring fathers (and grandfathers) has been rendered less compelling by changed economic and social conditions. "The pointed depersonalisation of mothers is not logically necessary to achieve the social ends of the extended family".[17]

This approach is rather akin to that adopted by Stewart in this volume. For Stewart an important starting point is to pursue the *principle* underlying a rule (or set of rules) of customary law because the enquiry might reveal that there is consensus amongst competing groups (for example, men and women or youngsters and elders) about its desirability, apparent disagreements being revealed to be merely about its application. She explains her thesis thus:

> "The underlying hypothesis in this chapter is that customary law as captured and applied in the formal legal system began as little more than a collection of end result determinations as pronounced by tribal authorities or as generalisations about outcomes at the level of rules recounted to early researchers. This hypothesis incorporates the notion that what may have been missed in these collection processes are the underlying social values that translate into general guiding principles that informed the decision making processes of traditional judicial authorities."[18]

The importance of understanding these approaches is two-fold. In the first place, searching for the underlying principle encourages communities to engage in a little introspection: they may discover that they disagree less than they thought they did. Secondly, whatever the outcome, the communities concerned

---

[16] "The African Family and Women's Rights: Friends or Foes?" in [1991] *Acta Juridica* 135–46.
[17] *Ibid.*, 143.
[18] At 221 above.

feel affirmed by taking charge of their own affairs and this undercuts any arguments about imposed changes in customary law.

(b) Judicial interpretation

The courts, more than any other actor in the legal arena, have the potential to exert the strongest influence on the direction taken by the development of customary law. They are the only ones who can really answer the question posed earlier as to whether the provisions protecting culture and customary law in the constitution amount to mere appeasement of certain groups, or were meant to be taken seriously.

A further look at the certification process provides some interesting hints of the direction that the courts might take in the future. As mentioned earlier, one of the objections to the new text of the final constitution came from Professor A. J. Kerr of Rhodes University. In an earlier article on "Customary Law, Fundamental Rights and the Constitution",[19] Kerr had argued that the subjection of customary law to the constitution in section 211(1) and (3) could not have been intended to enforce the application of a drastically changed customary law immediately upon the coming into force of the Constitution. In a meticulously crafted argument illustrated by the rules of succession, Kerr reviews the history of the multiparty negotiations and the measures adopted to secure the participation of the traditional leaders, especially the Zulu monarch. He concludes that the most likely understanding between the parties was that:

> "both the multiparty negotiators and the traditional leaders (in particular, the Zulu monarch) considered that the words 'customary law' meant customary law as it is at present, including, as is at present the case, the fact that it is subject to the normal processes of change."[20]

Kerr reiterates this point of view in his *Submission to the Constitutional Court on the Certification of the Constitution of the Republic of South Africa, 1996: the Provisions on Customary Law*. Referring to Constitutional Principle XIII Kerr argues:

> "What has to be 'recognised and protected' in terms of Constitutional Principle XIII is 'the institution, status and role of traditional leadership, according to indigenous law'. It is important to note that in this sentence in Constitutional Principle XIII there is no mention of indigenous law being subject to the Constitution. This means that the new Constitution's provisions on traditional leadership may not be made 'subject to the Constitution' unless that is what was meant by the phrase 'indigenous law' in Constitutional Principle XIII . . . in my view, the requirement of protection of the institution of traditional leadership 'according to indigenous law' in Constitutional Principle XIII means according to indigenous law as it was before the enactment of the interim

[19] N. 6 above.
[20] *Ibid.*, 728.

Constitution but subject, as it has always been . . . to the normal processes of change. . . . Further, if customary law in subsec 211(1) means customary law as it was before the enactment of the interim Constitution it must be the same in subsec 211(3)."[21]

The main thrust of these comments by Professor Kerr is that the history of the multiparty negotiations is relevant in understanding the new text; that a constitutional amendment[22] was passed specifically to woo the IFP and the Zulu monarch back to the negotiating table; that it is inconceivable that these parties (and traditional leaders in general) agreed to accept guarantees protecting a customary law that would be drastically emasculated and virtually unrecognisable on the dawn of the date of commencement of the Constitution; that if this result was not communicated to these parties during the talks then those talks were in bad faith; and that since those talks must be presumed to have been in good faith (as Kerr personally believes) then the inescapable conclusion is that at all material times the parties involved in the negotiations contemplated the protection of customary law as it is at present.

If these arguments are sound then there exist some plausible grounds for holding that those who looked to the words "subject to the Constitution" as automatically abolishing a rule of customary law which on the face of it appears to be in conflict with some constitutional language have got it wrong. It is to be remembered that the court decided to deal only with the issue of traditional leadership and not with that of customary law *per se*. Nevertheless in that judgment the Constitutional Court stopped short of lending its weight to the view favouring "automatic extinction" of an incompatible rule of custom: apparently, then, the issue of how to deal with incompatibility is still a live one. Indeed the court refers in congratulatory terms to the decision by the Constitutional Assembly to leave "the complicated, varied and ever-developing specifics of . . . how customary law should develop and be interpreted, to future social evolution, legislative deliberation and judicial interpretation".[23]

Although the court did not directly address Professor Kerr's objections, its conclusions tend to support his approach. The court acknowledges (at 195) that the Constitutional Principles taken as a whole expressly articulate the recognition of "a degree of cultural pluralism with legal and cultural . . . consequences". And again (at 197), the court approves the Constitution's new text, saying it complies with Constitutional Principle XIII by guaranteeing "the continued existence of traditional leadership and the survival of an *evolving* customary law" (emphasis added). This seems to suggest that as far as the courts are concerned a genuine attempt should be made to resolve the tensions between the cultural provisions and the bill of rights without assuming that any incompatibility automatically spells the death of the customary law principle in question.

[21] Para. 7.

[22] S. 2 of the Constitution of the Republic of South Africa Second Amendment Act No. 3 of 1994 amending Constitutional Principle XIII to provide for recognition by provincial constitutions of the position of traditional monarchs.

[23] *Ex p. Chairperson of the Constitutional Assembly: in re Certification of the Constitution of the Republic of South Africa* 1996 (4) SA 744 (CC) at 197.

Speaking in his personal capacity, Justice Albie Sachs also clearly shows a preference for a balancing of rights, as opposed to an either/or approach, which he finds unhelpful. In his keynote address at the Durban conference[24] he suggested a resolution of the problems of multiculturalism in a way that used two propositions as a starting point: that universalism is about "commonalities . . . certain shared experiences" in the lives of people wherever they are on the globe, and that the value of pluralism is itself a universally accepted value. He concludes that "there is a commonality in the acceptance of pluralism and if we can allow the pluralism then to seep into our concepts of the universal, the tensions remain but they are not inherently antagonistic or conflictual".

From that starting point Sachs J argues that a proper balancing exercise implies that "one should be looking at the intensity of the value in relation to the particular circumstance rather than whether that value trumps another value". He refers to this approach as one of "proportionality rather than choice". In an even more recent piece[25] Sachs J rejects any ranking of rights according to a categorical hierarchy and summarises his view in the words:

> "A peripheral transgression of a manifestly fundamental right might have less significance than a grievous violation of a right that might be regarded as less important. It all depends on the context, on the severity of the breach and on its impact on the dignity of the persons concerned, rather than on a formal classification of the right in question."

This seems to me to provide an important way of sidestepping the potentially pointless pursuit of an absolute ranking of rights which, it is believed, will produce clear answers in all cases of conflict. The balancing approach is particularly important in the South African debate where the view is widely held, for instance, that the right to equality trumps the right to culture.

But the right to equality itself is not adequately problematised in South African discourse. Does equality imply, for instance, a kind of artificial, tit-for-tat evenhandedness? If it does, would criticisms of polygyny be addressed for example by extending to women the right to marry more than one husband? And can the right to equality voluntarily be waived? And if so, can it be waived to such a level where the action/behaviour/situation consented to encroaches on the dignity of the consenter? One imagines a situation where the consenter has a right to tell society at large: "it is none of your business, it is my choice". One can also conceive of a situation where society might have a right to say, "you have gone too far, now you are demeaning the dignity of all of us by your actions".[26] Where is the line to be drawn?

---

[24] On Monday, 28 July 1997.

[25] Comment on *South African Law Commission Discussion Paper 74: Customary Marriages.* Quoted with permission.

[26] An example that comes to mind is that of the sport of midget-tossing where, for entertainment, normal sized people use short people like missiles in a contest to see which player can toss his the farthest. Members of society, offended by what they consider "undignified", may campaign to have the sport outlawed. The very same short people may argue that it is a job opportunity for them; if they are not worried, why should the rest of the world be? One can concoct even more bruising South

These questions are not merely academic. They have an obvious relevance to those aspects of customary family law that some might find unpalatable. If a woman tells us that she feels valued (and therefore dignified) by having *lobolo* paid in respect of her marriage, do we really have a right to overrule her on the basis of our own misgivings about the custom? Might it not be considered patronising for us to be totally comfortable with the right of an 18-year old who falls in love "at first sight" at a party to decide to marry her partner under the Act within a week, while we continue to doubt the decision of a mature African woman to become the second wife of someone she has known all her life? The "proportionality" approach advocated by Sachs J appears to be a useful tool in confronting these complex problems which lie at the intersection between the right to equality and non-discrimination, on the one hand, and the right to human dignity, on the other.

Recent decisions have given the first indications that the courts are not willing to employ a mechanistic approach to questions of the constitutionality of certain customary laws. This is to be welcomed. In *Mthembu* v. *Letsela and Another*, 1997(2) SA 936 (T), the court had to consider whether the customary law rule of succession which favours first-born males unfairly discriminated against women. The challenge was based on section 8 of the interim constitution, whose terms are broadly similar to the present section 9. The court took a broad view of the customary law principles of succession and found that an heir in these circumstances is under an obligation to support the widow and other dependants of the deceased. On the basis of this finding the court held that the rule of male primogeniture in succession does discriminate between persons on the ground of sex or gender but not *unfairly*. Le Roux J (at 945) said:

> "If one accepts the duty to provide sustenance, maintenance and shelter as a necessary corollary of the system of primogeniture, I find it difficult to equate this form of differentiation between men and women with the concept of 'unfair discrimination' as used in s 8 of the Constitution . . . In view of the manifest acknowledgement of customary law as a system existing parallel to the common law by the Constitution . . . and the freedom granted to persons to choose this system as governing their relationships. . . . I cannot accept the submission that the succession rule is necessarily in conflict with section 8."

The decision is not without its critics. Cathi Albertyn[27] expresses concern at the reasoning employed by the court and at the factual basis of some of the conclusions, calling them "doubtful". She refers to the judge's doubts about the application of the customary duty of support in urban areas which however did not seem to deter him from his conclusion that the discrimination was not unfair. Albertyn's major point is that the judgment was made in the absence of hard

African examples involving the emotive issue of race to underline the fact that matters of human dignity and equality, and the possible waiver of such rights, are not easy questions.

[27] Writing in the *GRP Bulletin*, n. 5 above, at 4. Dr Albertyn is the head of the Gender Research Project based at the Centre for Applied Legal Studies at the University of the Witwatersrand and a member of the Commission on Gender Equality.

research findings and without problematising key issues in the debate, such as the relationship between cultural rights and the right to equality.

It is easy to agree with the criticisms: the weaknesses in the judgment are obvious. Nonetheless, it is my contention that the *approach* is to be applauded. These are early days in constitutional litigation in South Africa, especially on issues of such sensitivity as those of culture and customary law. For the reasons set out in the body of this chapter, it is a welcome development when the courts are prepared to keep an open mind until a customary practice has been assessed on merit without resorting to any assumptions about the ranking of rights.

Ryland v. *Edros*, 1997(2) SA 690 (C), was a more policy-oriented decision in which Farlam J, in the Cape Provincial Division, held that a basic change in the values of South Africa had been ushered in by the constitution. Such was the change that a contract based on an unrecognised Islamic marriage could no longer be considered invalid solely for the reason that potentially polygynous marriages are not recognised by South African law. I quote from the judgment at page 708:

> "I agree with Mr Trengove's submission that it is quite inimical to all the values of the new South Africa for one group to impose its values on another and that the Courts should only brand a contract as offensive to public policy if it offensive to those values which are shared by the community at large, by all right-thinking people in the community and not only a section of it."

It is encouraging to note that the courts appear to be willing to acknowledge the existence of cultural practices that do not necessarily sit comfortably within a Western value system but which might nevertheless have to be accommodated according to the Constitution. It should also be noted that despite stricter subjection of customary law to the final Constitution (as opposed to the position under the interim Constitution), there might exist under the later document a fresh avenue for enforcing cultural rights. "Human dignity" makes a strong showing in the final Constitution. In the limitation clause (section 36(1)) a law can only limit a right guaranteed in the bill if it is reasonable and justifiable in an open and democratic society based on "human dignity, equality and freedom". (The corresponding formulation in the interim Constitution is " . . . based on freedom and equality"—section 33(1)(a).) And in addition to being guaranteed as a right in section 10, human dignity is emphasised as a founding value in section 1. With a broad concept such as that of human dignity the courts may be able to fashion a tool for assessing cultural practices and customary laws.[28]

---

[28] On some useful applications of human dignity in cultural matters see Nhlapo, R. T., "The African Customary Law of Marriage and the Rights Conundrum" a paper presented at a workshop on *Cultural Transformations in Africa* held at the Centre for African Studies, University of Cape Town, 11–13 Mar. 1977; and forthcoming in the *Emory Law Journal* in 1998.

(c) Law reform

Sensible and sensitive law reform can nudge the African customary law of the family into the constitutional era without alienating its adherents or forcing a confrontation between so-called Western values and African values. But it will not be easy: our history of racial division and confrontation will see to that. The South African Law Commission thus has to contend not only with the problems which it shares with other law reform agencies worldwide, but also with those of a purely South African hue.

To tackle the historical dilemmas first: one has to realise that South Africa's history is the raw material for her politics. There are few things that happen in the new South Africa which are not tainted by the old. And the "old" was basically about a lack of communication between the dominant culture (Western) and the subordinate (but majority-supported) indigenous culture. It was more than a lack of communication: it was a fight to the finish, either in the form of the actual abolition of particular indigenous practices or the assimilation of African people into Western culture (for reasons ranging from lack of choice, to perfectly voluntary attempts to distance themselves from their "backward" brethren). Both processes left their scars.

These scars are still visible and, taking a leaf out of Sachs J's book, I believe it is more useful to acknowledge their existence, to tackle them head on, than to pretend that they do not exist. The greatest tension of all, of course, is that between modern values and traditional values. (In the minds of many ordinary people "modern" translates to "Western" and "traditional" to "African"). This particular schism is of course not unique to South Africa[29] but in this country it is rendered deeper by the apartheid experience. As a result even where purely cultural matters are at issue, they quickly deteriorate into racial fingerpointing.

It is important to look this unpleasant fact squarely in the face. It explains more about black hostility to, say, feminism than any principled denial of the legitimacy of the women's case. What should be a straight contest of ideas between women's rights activists and their opponents of various persuasions invariably turns into an emotionally charged affair, with allegations of "cultural imperialism" and "cultural arrogance" being bandied about. Into this potent mixture is added a further complication: African resentment at what is perceived as the "evangelism" of anti-customary law activists, especially if they themselves do not live their lives according to that law. From the days of the multiparty negotiations at Kempton Park, through the two-year Constitutional Assembly process and the current campaigning for various reforms, few topics excite more anger in sections of the black community than what is seen as an unseemly obsession with customary law by non-participants, as if other cultures, religions and groups have already achieved a state of perfection in respect of their gender, and other, practices.

---

[29] See Hinz, ch. 13 above, on similar trends in the Namibian debate.

The Law Commission has to function against this background . Over the years it has developed a working methodology which includes the publication of a document series interspersed with public consultation. Since 1996 the reconstituted Commission has intensified the mechanism of public consultation and now routinely workshops the bulk of its proposals around the country. This has proved useful in certain types of investigation: experience shows that in those which involve ethnicity and/or culture, responses tend to fall into the categories described in the preceding paragraph.

In view of such enduring divisions the law reformer is faced with dilemmas every step of the way: divergent scholarly views on research methodology, usefulness of consultation where responses merely repeat entrenched positions, stimulating *real* public debate, balancing the need for deliberation against the impatience of the black majority to see change. To my mind, these resolve themselves into one momentous consideration, captured in two popular *caveats*: that law reform is not about changing law but about changing it for the better, and the need to avoid churning out "paper law". Allott[30] has noted on paper law that all over the world governments have frequently had ambitions "which outrun their capacity to implement them" and many radical reforms have therefore been doomed to failure. He writes:

> "Failure because of the basic impotence of power; governments propose but often their subjects dispose differently. The people—in whatever kind of society—have the capacity by deliberate or unintended non-compliance to bring all the efforts of law reformers and social transformers to naught . . . [G]overnmental lawmaking has most chance of success when it has the consensus of the people behind it, when it confirms attitudes and patterns which the people, by their behaviour, have demonstrated that they hold and value."[31]

Views such as these apply to all areas of lawmaking but obviously with much more force in the case of indigenous law. They do not necessarily imply approval of a do-nothing legislative conservatism: they are simply sensible words of warning in an endeavour that must constantly balance the ideal and the possible. In South Africa, where each reforming provision is likely to be scrutinised and adjudged to be a victory for one side or a defeat for another, such warnings cannot be taken lightly.

The South African Law Commission, in its Discussion Paper No. 74, attempts to rise to these challenges. Unveiled on 29 August 1997, it proposes the long-overdue legal recognition of customary marriages and seeks, simultaneously, to comply with many of the provisions of the Convention on the Elimination of All Forms of Discrimination Against Women, the International Convention on the Rights of the Child, and the South African Constitution. The Discussion Paper proposes minimum ages for customary marriages; it makes consent of the parties

---

[30] Allott, A. N., "Reforming the Law in Africa: Aims, Difficulties and Techniques" in Sanders, A. J. G. M. (ed.), *Southern Africa in Need of Law Reform* (Butterworths, Durban, 1981), 228–36.
[31] At 229.

a central requirement; it repeals laws enshrining inequality of the spouses; it introduces full property rights for wives and equalises the position of the spouses in respect of contractual capacity, *locus standi*, grounds for divorce and custody and guardianship of children. At the same time it attempts to retain the basic shape of the customary marriage by making allowance for *lobolo* and its return in the event of divorce, and by not recommending the abolition of polygyny. Time will tell whether South Africans are ready to make the compromises in marriage law that the framers of the constitution seem to have made in writing the founding document.

Since its release the Discussion Paper has attracted mixed reviews, basically of two types: that it is "too customary" and that it is "not customary enough". (There are other criticisms, of methodology, or questioning the role of customary law in the South African legal system). However, as the responses trickle in and the countrywide workshops gather momentum, it is clear that the people agree that customary marriages should be recognised. There are even indications that the issue of polygyny, originally expected to be controversial, is being met with indifference rather than hostility. These contradictory signs are considered by the project committee not to be a bad thing. They represent shades of genuine South African opinion and it is up to the Law Commission to produce a report to the Minister which includes a Bill that is capable of carrying the political representatives of the South African population, sitting in Parliament.

To that end, one may point out some of the concerns that will need to be confronted. The criticism that the proposals are too "Western" can be met if a clear distinction is drawn between those suggestions that have no merit other than the appeasement of sophisticated and westernised South Africans of all colours who are embarrassed by customary law, and those that can show independent merit regardless of their coincidental similarity to what is done elsewhere in the world. To my mind, the requirement that the parties should exchange rings or that the bride should wear white (or indeed—controversially—that she should cover her breasts) would be an unacceptable example of the former. On the other hand, registration of the marriage or the extension of proprietary capacity to a wife in a world where she is as likely as not to be matching or even surpassing her husband in earning capacity can be independently and objectively justified. These innovations are not "western": they are merely sensible and desirable arrangements in a situation that has changed drastically since the early days of customary law.

A final consideration is that of the Constitution itself. Despite mutterings to the contrary, it **is** the founding document of the new South Africa and does contain the negotiated framework for the new order. Difficult though it might be to do, some way must be found to make it work. Indigenous communities, like urban communities, must realise that the Constitution now forms the backdrop for all future legislation. What is being advocated in this chapter is not defiance of the Constitution but its creative and nuanced interpretation. The Law Commission, as advisor to the government of the day, would be failing in its duty if it did not signpost for indigenous communities the most constitutionally safe and trouble-free path for the future development of their laws. That would be to leave them in the lurch, and to the vagaries and costs of endless constitutional litigation.

V. CONCLUSION

In this chapter an attempt has been made to show that the South African constitution is a document that was developed through negotiation and therefore reflects diverse points of view. It clearly has a "modernising" mission in the sense that it seeks to turn its back on the apartheid era by laying the foundations for a strong human rights culture: at the same time it acknowledges the reality of cultural diversity in South Africa. The result is the existence, side by side, of provisions that do not sit comfortably one with the other. In the field of family law these are the equality provisions in the bill of rights, on the one hand, and the protection given to customary law and various cultural rights, on the other.

The point is made that, despite the varying expectations amongst scholars and commentators, creativity and finesse are required to make the constitution work. A major move in this direction, it is argued, will be to abandon any expectation that the battle against customary law was won when that law was recognised "subject to the constitution". Rather, an attempt should be made to balance the rights involved in a pragmatic fashion in each case, an approach which holds out the hope that some customary laws and practices will survive in recognisable form despite their unfamiliarity to the dominant western value system. This will serve to cement loyalty to the constitution and the new order on the part of those people who adhere to customary law: a not insubstantial consideration in a country that is emerging from a divided past and is desperately seeking to forge a single and united nationhood.